eBay® Business All-in-One For Dummies,® 2nd Edition

W9-CAX-262

Reader's Picks

I get many questions on my Web site (at www.coolebaytools.com) and at teaching seminars. I try to answer as many as I can, but here are the answers to the top queries, and where to find them in this book:

To Save Time or Money	Find More Info Here
Finding merchandise to sell on eBay	Book IV
Finding good auction-management vendors	Book VIII
Keeping professional accounting records	Book IX
Finding a hot item on eBay	Book VI
Setting reasonable shipping costs	Book III
Determining a starting bid amount	Book III
Understanding what your financial reports have to say	Book IX
Making your own auction templates	Book V
Finding out what licenses are required for your city and state	Book IX
Producing six-month merchandise plans	Book IV
Making a claim for a damaged shipment	Book VII
Using cost-per-click advertising to promote your listings	Book VI
Taking better pictures for your auctions	Book V
Figuring out who leaves feedback first	Book I

Typing Special Characters

Sometimes you may wonder why there isn't a certain key on your keyboard for a particular character. Windows has special (secret — **ssshh!**) codes for these characters. To get them to appear, hold down the Alt key on your keyboard while typing the numbers on the number pad. For your convenience, here are some important ones:

Cents	¢	Alt+0162	Copyright	©	Alt+0169
Euro	€	Alt+0128	Registered trademark	®	Alt+0174
Pound sterling	£	Alt+0163	Trademark	™	Alt+0153
Yen	¥	Alt+0165			

Apparel Sizes

When buying clothing to sell on eBay, realize that the average American woman's dress size is 14 (that's where plus-size clothing begins), not an 8. The average American man is a 40 regular. When buying clothes in lots for resale, ignore the standard "1 small, 3 medium, and 2 large" lot, and instead buy 1 small, 2 medium, 1 large, and 1 extra-large.

For Dummies: Bestselling Book Series for Beginners

eBay® Business All-in-One For Dummies, 2nd Edition

Cheat Sheet

United States Tax Deadlines

Note: Please check with your state government offices for due dates on sales taxes and license fees.

15th of every month: Prior month payroll-tax deposit date (if you're on the monthly deposit system)

January 15: Estimated taxes due

January 31: Last day to distribute 1099s and W2s to people you paid during the prior year

January 31: Payroll reports for quarterly period ending 12/31 due

February 28: Last day to send the government copies of your 1099s and W2s

March 15: Calendar year corporation tax due

April 15: Deadline for Individual or Partnership Annual Tax return, or deadline to file an extension

April 15: Estimated taxes due

April 30: Payroll reports for period ending 3/31 due

June 15: Estimated taxes due

July 31: Payroll reports for quarterly period ending 6/30 due

September 15: Estimated taxes due

October 31: Payroll reports for quarterly period ending 9/30 due

If the due date falls on a weekend or a federal holiday, the due date is the first business day after that date.

Auction Photo Tips

- ✔ Be sure that the item is clean, unwrinkled, and lint-free.
- ✔ Take the photo against a solid, undecorated background.
- ✔ Make sure that the picture is in focus.
- ✔ Be sure that you have enough lighting to show the details of your item.
- ✔ Take second and third images to show specific details, such as a signature or a detail that better identifies your item.
- ✔ Don't use more than 72 ppi for an online image.
- ✔ Try to keep the **total** size of **all** your pictures below 50K for a smooth and swift download.

General Tips for Sellers

- ✔ Answer all e-mail questions from prospective bidders and buyers within 24 hours and check your e-mail hourly before the close of your auctions: Good customer service goes a long way in promoting and building your eBay business.
- ✔ Research your new items and be sure that you know their current value and the going price on eBay.
- ✔ Before listing, weigh your item and estimate the shipping cost. Be sure to list shipping (and handling) costs in your ad whether you use a flat rate or the shipping calculator.
- ✔ See how many other sellers are selling your item and try not to have your auction close within a few hours of theirs.
- ✔ To encourage bidding, set the lowest possible starting bid for your item.
- ✔ Check the eBay guidelines to be sure that your item is permitted and that your listing doesn't violate any listing policies.

For Dummies: Bestselling Book Series for Beginners

eBay® Business
ALL-IN-ONE
FOR
DUMMIES®
2ND EDITION

by Marsha Collier

WILEY

Wiley Publishing, Inc.

eBay® Business All-in-One For Dummies® 2nd Edition

Published by
Wiley Publishing, Inc.
111 River Street
Hoboken, NJ 07030-5774

www.wiley.com

Copyright © 2009 by Wiley Publishing, Inc., Indianapolis, Indiana

Published by Wiley Publishing, Inc., Indianapolis, Indiana

Published simultaneously in Canada

For general information on our other products and services, please contact our Customer Care Department within the U.S. at 800-762-2974, outside the U.S. at 317-572-3993, or fax 317-572-4002.

For technical support, please visit www.wiley.com/techsupport.

Wiley also publishes its books in a variety of electronic formats. Some content that appears in print may not be available in electronic books.

Library of Congress Control Number: 2008943496

ISBN: 978-0-470-38536-4

Manufactured in the United States of America

10 9 8 7 6 5 4 3 2 1

WILEY

About the Author

Marsha Collier, one of the foremost eBay experts and educators in the world, is also a top-selling eBay author with over 1 million copies of her books in print. She is especially proud of two books: *eBay For Dummies,* the bestselling book for eBay beginners, and *eBay PowerSeller Business Practices For Dummies.* Marsha co-hosts the *Computer and Technology Show* on KTRB 860am in San Francisco and on www.wsradio.com along with Marc Cohen. She also shares her eBay business expertise through video training segments at Entrepreneur.com's *Entrepreneur's Coaches Corner* and on her blog.

Marsha intermixes her writing about eBay with her role as experienced spokesperson on the subject. She was one of the original eBay University instructors, as well as a regular presenter at eBay's annual convention, eBay Live. Marsha also hosted the highly acclaimed "Making Your Fortune Online," a PBS special highlighting online business. While traveling across the United States and around the world, she makes regular appearances on television, radio, and in print to discuss online commerce.

Marsha earned her eBay stripes as a longtime seller on the site. She began her eBay selling career in 1996 to earn extra money for her daughter's education (and eventually paid for university with her eBay earnings). She grew her business to a full-time venture and was one of the first eBay PowerSellers. Nowadays, you can find everything from autographed copies of her books to photo supplies, pet toys, and DVDs in her eBay store ("Marsha Collier's Fabulous Finds") and on her Web site.

Marsha currently resides in Los Angeles, CA. You can contact Marsha via her Web site, www.coolebaytools.com.

Dedication

This book is dedicated to all you prospective eBay sellers out there who have the dream and the drive to succeed. I wrote this book for you, and I share my expertise so you can skip the trial-and-error and go straight to work gaining the most profits. Those who succeed join me in knowing that hard work and loving what you do get the job done — and lead you to financial achievement and contentment.

Good luck in your endeavors. I know this book will help you get to the next level.

Acknowledgments

Writing a book is a monumental task. Lots of people have helped, but the lion's share of assistance comes from the encouragement that I receive from the eBay community and those I've met when "doing it eBay."

If it weren't for Patti "Louise" Ruby's friendship and support as the tech editor for this book, I think I might have lost my mind. She helped me keep on top of the many changes on the eBay site and never said no to my seemingly endless requests.

Once again, I was blessed with Leah Cameron and Barry Childs-Helton who were my editors on this book. Working with Leah is a dream. She's there to lend her unique style of smart savvyness to my words. She truly "gets it" like no one else. And Barry cleans up after us both. You'd almost think there's no one on earth with such vast experience with the English language — especially Victorian nouns. I'm honored to have them as my editors; they help create the very best in the For Dummies series. Thank you, Leah and Barry.

Then, of course, I thank the management at Wiley. My publisher, Andy Cummings, and my acquisitions editor, Steven Hayes, both work hard to fill the world with instructional and entertaining books.

Publisher's Acknowledgments

We're proud of this book; please send us your comments through our online registration form located at http://dummies.custhelp.com. For other comments, please contact our Customer Care Department within the U.S. at 877-762-2974, outside the U.S. at 317-572-3993, or fax 317-572-4002.

Some of the people who helped bring this book to market include the following:

Acquisitions, Editorial, and Media Development

Editors: Leah Cameron and Barry Childs-Helton

Executive Editor: Steven Hayes

Technical Editor: Patti Louise Ruby

Media Development Manager: Richard Graves

Editorial Assistant: Amanda Foxworth

Sr. Editorial Assistant: Cherie Case

Cartoons: Rich Tennant (www.the5thwave.com)

Composition Services

Project Coordinator: Lynsey Stanford

Layout and Graphics: Reuben W. Davis, Nikki Gately, Christin Swinford, Christine Williams

Proofreaders: Melissa Cossell, Christopher M. Jones

Indexer: Steve Rath

Publishing and Editorial for Technology Dummies

    Richard Swadley, Vice President and Executive Group Publisher

    Andy Cummings, Vice President and Publisher

    Mary Bednarek, Executive Acquisitions Director

    Mary C. Corder, Editorial Director

Publishing for Consumer Dummies

    Diane Graves Steele, Vice President and Publisher

Composition Services

    Gerry Fahey, Vice President of Production Services

    Debbie Stailey, Director of Composition Services

Contents at a Glance

Table of Contents

Book III: Selling Like a Pro 245

Chapter 1: Be Sure Your Listings Make Cents 247

Introduction

It seems I am always writing books about eBay. That's because eBay changes from year to year (as does the online market) and I am obsessive about keeping my books the most updated in the arena.

My books don't just give you the information you can find on eBay; I give you the ins and outs selling on eBay, based on my daily experience of the site. I also stay on top of the current trends in online and social marketing; test them out, and pass the results back to you. This book gives you more information than even many longtime sellers know. (Trust me — I consult with sellers, and the things I consider most basic are often new to old-timers on the site.)

I am lucky enough to have been selling on eBay since 1996 and am a charter member of the PowerSeller program. Running a business on eBay has given me the opportunity to spend more time with my loved ones and have better control of my life. I can make my own schedule and enjoy what I'm doing because my business is making a profit. Owning an online business can be empowering.

Those of us who run an eBay business always seem to be doing *something*. Buying, selling, even going on a vacation, our business keeps humming. There's no 9-to-5, no weekends or holidays. Our stores on eBay are always open for business — making sales and making us money.

Alas, all that success and freedom takes some work. That's why you have this book.

About This Book

This book will give you the basics, the hows and whys of setting up a home-based business on eBay. I've authored several best-selling books about running a business on eBay. This book gives you the information you need to get started in one nifty (albeit heavy) volume. You can get the info found in several books about eBay all in one place.

What You're Not to Read

There's a lot in this book that you'll find useful. If some of it seems too basic (say, if you're a more advanced seller), just skip right on by to the information that your business needs.

Sidebars are scattered through the book with additional information on a subject. If you want to know the subject in depth, read the sidebar. If it's not important to you right now, blow right past it.

There's no need to start at the beginning. Check out the Table of Contents and see whether something piques your interest. Have a question about eBay? Look it up in the index. This book is meant to be your useful desk reference on eBay.

Foolish Assumptions

While writing this book, I've made a few assumptions about you. Because you bought this book, naturally I assume you're an intelligent person with refined tastes. Okay, kidding aside, that may well be true — but the main assumption I've really made about you is that you want to find out more about eBay.

I assume also that you

✦ Have a computer and an Internet connection

✦ Are comfortable browsing the Internet

✦ Are familiar with e-mail

✦ Are looking for a way to make some extra money

✦ Have checked out eBay and perhaps bought a few items

You've probably sold a few items and made a couple of dollars. Perhaps you think eBay just might be a good place to earn a regular stream of extra income. It also helps if you've read my current edition of *eBay For Dummies* — where you get the basics of eBay.

If you can accept that nothing comes without a bit of effort, you might just be on the track of a new career.

How This Book Is Organized

Here, in one volume, are nine individual minibooks related to becoming an expert on eBay. Each book is broken down into individual chapters to give you more in-depth information on the subject at hand. Here's the lineup.

Book I: eBay Basics

Book I provides the beginning-level stuff you have to know to make your way on eBay. Sure, you can do business on eBay and *not* know all the small details, but knowledge is power; this book has the information that will give you the winning edge over other sellers. Even if you've been on eBay for a while, you might just discover a few things reading this book.

Book II: Essential Tools

Using eBay means using some of the basic tools that eBay has developed for buyers and sellers. In Book II, you research prices (for buying *or* selling), find an item (no matter how badly the seller mislisted it), and use PayPal with ease. You'll also find out how an Internet search can help you with your eBay business.

Also, there's a chapter on effective eBay communications. Sounds a bit stuffy, I know, but your e-mail communications are the cornerstone of your eBay business.

Book III: Selling Like a Pro

Anyone can list an item for sale on eBay, but after you read the information in Book III, you'll be among the elite who can squeeze extra profits from your sales. You also find out how to use advanced eBay tools that can cut your work time to a fraction of what other sellers spend.

Book IV: Sourcing Merchandise

The number one question that people ask me is "What should I sell on eBay?" To me, it's intuitive — but then again, I love to shop. Book IV gives you the tools for finding the right items to please your customers and make regular sales. The information in this book is not just someone's theory. Instead, it comes directly from professional retailers, people who are successes on eBay!

Book V: Presenting Your Items

All the salesmanship in the world won't sell your items if your pictures are fuzzy and your auctions look amateurish. Book V teaches you just a bit of HTML, so you can give your auctions some extra pizzazz. You'll also uncover the photography secrets of eBay pros.

Book VI: Promoting Your Goods

After you have some items selling well on eBay, it's time to expand your horizons. Find out how to use marketing tools to let the world know about your eBay sales and store. Start a Web site! A Web site can be a small investment that can up your monthly profits without increasing your workload. The Internet is open to the world — use it to bring more customers to your door.

Book VII: Storing and Shipping

Yawn. Storing and shipping may not be the sexiest topics in the world, but they are two places where many eBay businesses fall down. In Book VII, see how some of eBay's biggest PowerSellers organize their merchandise. Find out how you can turn your shipping area from a headache into a profit center. That turns shipping into a sexy topic, doesn't it?

Book VIII: Power Selling

Step up your sales to the next level. Become a PowerSeller, open an eBay store. Book VIII shows you how to grab information from your sales statistics and ramp up your profits.

Book IX: Office and Legal

The American dream (success) comes with some responsibilities (bookkeeping, licenses, taxes). And the more successful you become, the more you need to follow the rules. Read Book IX to understand the rules for your business in your own state. Successful is as successful does.

Icons Used in This Book

I've written quite a few books in the *For Dummies* series, and all the books have cute little icons to draw your attention to special comments. Following are the ones I use, along with what they mean.

This icon indicates a story about a real event. It may have been one of my auctions or one from a fellow user. I hope you find the story interesting and learn from another user's mistake (or dumb luck).

When you see this icon, it's a friendly reminder to keep in mind the short fact that follows. No doubt it will come up again, and you'll be ahead of the game if you remember it.

Here are a few words from me to you, to help you do things the easy way. I've made the mistakes, but you don't have to make them too.

This little bomb of a fact will keep you out of trouble. Often these facts are not generally known. Be sure to read them to avoid common pitfalls.

Where to Go from Here

It's time to open the book and dive in. Be sure to also visit my Web site, `www.coolebaytools.com`, for updates on this book. You'll also find articles about things going on at eBay. I also have a blog at

`http://mcollier.blogspot.com`

Often it provides a bit more fun posted on the Web.

If you'd like to ask me questions personally, you can call in to my radio show. It's live on the Internet on WsRadio; check out

`www.computerandtechnologyradio.com`

You can also e-mail me at `mcollier@coolebaytools.com`. I read all e-mails, and will try to answer as many as I can. But please remember that I'm just me. No giant staff, no big offices. I write books, research new products to help eBay sellers, consult with sellers just like you, run an eBay business, and try to have a home life.

Thank you for buying this book. Please e-mail me and let me know about your eBay successes.

Book I
eBay Basics

The 5th Wave   By Rich Tennant

"I got this on eBay from a power seller known as beer_n_browse."

Contents at a Glance

Chapter 1: Hooking Up with Online Technology

In This Chapter

- ✔ **Setting up your hardware**
- ✔ **Going online without your own computer**
- ✔ **Choosing your Internet service provider**
- ✔ **Getting e-mail**
- ✔ **Getting friendly with your browser**

1f the whole idea of *technology* gives you the creeps, don't back out now. I feel your pain. Every tech-oriented bit of knowledge that's entered my pea-sized brain has penetrated only after a great deal of mental whining. I suffered the pain so that you wouldn't have to.

Better yet, you don't need to know much technology (in the true sense of the word) to run a successful online business. Most online sellers have about as much knowledge as you will after you read this chapter.

Starting with the Right Computer

You don't have to know a lot of fancy computer mumbo-jumbo to do well on eBay, but you must *have* a computer. If you're in the market for a computer, you can buy or lease a new, used, or refurbished system, depending on your computing needs.

The absolute necessities

Although the following list is geared mainly toward the purchase of new PCs (which you can get for considerably under a thousand bucks), you should read this info even if you're thinking of buying a used computer:

- ✦ **Look for a computer with a good memory.** Remember that 1950s horror movie *The Blob?* The more time you spend using your computer, the more stuff you want to save on your hard drive. The more stuffed your hard drive, the more Blob-like it becomes. A hard drive with at least 60 gigabytes (GB) of storage space should keep your computer happy, but you can get hard drives as big as 300GB and more. I recommend you buy the biggest hard drive you can afford because no matter how large your hard drive is, you'll find a way to fill it up.

✦ **Make sure you have a top-quality modem if you have a dial-up connection.** Your modem connects your computer to the Internet using your telephone line. Even if you have a broadband connection (see later in this chapter), you should have a modem (usually built in to most computers) that can connect you on the off-chance that your high-speed service is down. (A modem transfers data over phone lines at a rate called *kilobytes per second,* or just plain *K*). A 56K modem is standard equipment, especially if you plan on using a lot of digital images (photographs) to help sell your items.

✦ **Get a big screen.** An LCD monitor that has at least a 17-inch screen can make a huge difference after several hours of rabid bidding or proof-reading your auction item descriptions. Anything smaller and you'll have a hard time actually seeing the listings and images.

✦ **Make sure the computer's central processing unit (CPU) is fast.** A CPU (also known as a "chip") is your computer's brain. It should be the fastest you can afford. You can always opt for the top-of-the-line, but even a slower 900 MHz (megahertz) processor could suffice. One of my computers is an antique slowpoke, but it's still fast enough that it won't choke when I ask it to do some minor multitasking. If you want lightning-fast speed (imagine a Daytona 500 race car with jet assist), you have to move up to at least 3 GHz (gigahertz).

✦ **Get a CD-R/DVD-R drive.** A disc burner is standard equipment. You use the drive to load new software programs into your computer from compact discs. You can also use the CDs or DVDs for your backups. Most models play and record DVD movies on your computer, but I think you'll be so entertained by eBay that you can skip the frills and save the bucks.

✦ **You must have a keyboard.** No keyboard, no typing. The basic key-board is fine. They do make funky ergonomic models that are split in the middle. But if the good old standard keyboard feels comfortable to you, stick with it.

Different keyboards have different feels. I like a keyboard with "clicky" keys because my fingers know that the letters I type actually appear. Test out several keyboards and see which one suits your typing style.

✦ **You need a pointing device, usually a mouse.** Some laptops come with touchpads or trackballs designed to do the same thing — give you a quick way to move the pointer around the screen so you can select options by clicking.

Buying a used computer

If you don't have a computer yet and don't have much money to spend, you might want to investigate the used market. Thousands of perfectly good used machines are floating around looking for a caring home. You can pick up a model that's a few years old for a few hundred dollars, and it will serve your budding eBay needs just fine. The same holds true for used Macs. Make sure a monitor is included in the purchase price. eBay's sellers sell their old computers when they upgrade. You can get some great deals.

Buying a refurbished computer

If you don't feel comfortable buying a used machine, you may want to consider a factory-refurbished model. These are new machines that were returned to the manufacturer for one reason or another. The factory fixes them so they're nice and spiffy, and then sweetens the deal with a terrific warranty. Some companies even offer optional, extended, on-site repairs. What you're getting is a new computer at a deep discount because the machine can't be resold legally as new.

For the most part, refurbished computers are defined as returns, units with blemishes (scratches, dents, and so on), or evaluation units. The factories rebuild them to the original working condition, using new parts (or sometimes used parts that meet or exceed performance specs for new parts). They come with 60- to 90-day warranties that cover repairs and returns. Warranty information is available on the manufacturers' Web sites. Be sure to read it before you purchase a refurbished computer.

Major computer manufacturers such as Dell, IBM, Sony, Hewlett-Packard, and Apple provide refurbished computers. Check whether their Web site has an outlet store. (Their outlet stores may reside in eBay Stores.) I visit `shopping.hp.com`, `www.sonystyle.com/outlet`, and `www.dell.com/outlet`, and check the sites for closeouts and refurbished goods all the time — and I've never been burned!

Because the inventory of refurbished computers changes daily (as do the prices), there's no way of telling exactly how much money you can save by buying refurbished instead of new. I suggest that you find a new computer system you like (and can afford) in a store or a catalog, and then compare it with refurbished systems. If you're thinking about buying from the Web or a catalog, don't forget to include the cost of shipping in the total price. Even with shipping costs, however, a refurbished computer may save you between 30 and 60 percent, depending on the deal you find.

Upgrading your system with the help of eBay

You may think I'm putting the cart before the horse with this suggestion, but you can get a new or used computer system at a great price by signing on to eBay *before* you buy your computer. You can get online at a local library or ask to borrow a friend's computer. I've seen eBay listings for workable, "vintage" PCs (a few years old), fully outfitted, for $400. Often such systems also come loaded with software. And when you have your new system in shape, why not auction off your old system on eBay?

You can also find on eBay all the bits and pieces you need to upgrade your computer. The items you may find most useful include

✦ Digital cameras and scanners

✦ Disk drives, including CD or DVD drives and memory cards

✦ Monitors

✦ Printers

Home wireless networks are becoming *de rigueur*; many people have them set up even if they don't have a business at home. You can now buy Wi-Fi printers that allow you to send print jobs through your network at a printer located elsewhere in your home.

You may have to keep checking in and monitoring the different auctions that eBay has going on; listings change daily. Go put in your best bid, and check back later to see whether you've won! (If you want to find out about the fine art of sniping — bidding at the last minute — skip to Chapter 6. I won't be insulted if you leave me for awhile now. Honest.)

Connecting to eBay without a Computer

Yes, sometimes life is a Catch-22 situation. Say your goal is to make some money on eBay so you can afford to buy a computer. Because you can't log on to eBay *without* a computer, you can't make money, right? Well, not exactly. Here's how you can start selling and bringing in some cold hard cash for that shiny new (or not-so-shiny used) hardware.

Libraries: From Dewey Decimal to eBay

If you haven't been to your local library lately, you may be surprised to find that most libraries are fully wired with computers that connect to the Internet. The card catalog has been replaced by computers that keep the Dewey Decimal System (DDS) alive and connected to libraries all over the world. For example, you'll find this book classified in 381.17, with the subject heading "Auctions — computer network resources."

Some libraries don't even require you to have a library card if you want to use a computer. Others limit the amount of time you can spend online and the sites you can log on to (often only adult sites are blocked). eBay is considered fair game, and exploring it is even considered research.

The upside of using the library's computer is that it's free. The downside is that you may have to wait for some kid to finish doing research for a term paper on the ceremonial use of yak milk.

Commercial cyber-outlets and cafés

If you strike out at the public library (or you're tired of the librarian shushing you as you cheer your winning bids), your friend throws you out of the house, and your boss watches you like a hawk, you can use a commercial outlet to kick off your eBay career. There's also the option of finding Internet cafés that have computers ready and waiting to use.

National chains such as FedEx Kinko's or your favorite local cybercafé offer computer usage at an hourly rate. FedEx Kinko's offers computers (both PCs and Macs loaded with all the software you need) that can get you online for around $15 per hour or $.25 per minute. No restrictions apply: You get full access to the Internet and can enjoy all the elements of eBay. You can conduct your auctions by posting them and checking back regularly. You can also watch for great computer deals that you may want to bid on.

Cybercafés can be another way to go. If you live near a college, you'll probably find some. Hourly rates are much cheaper because you end up ordering a cup of joe or a soda. I once checked on my auctions from a cybercafé in Peru; they charged only $1.50 an hour — what a deal!

Free Wi-Fi at Starbucks!

If you love Starbucks already, you're going to love it even more now that they're beginning to reward their most loyal customers with two consecutive hours of free Wi-Fi per day. To take advantage of the offer, all you have to do is register your Starbucks Card and join Starbucks Card Rewards. If you use your card at least once a month to buy your beverage of choice — voila — you're entitled to free AT&T Wi-Fi. Visit `www.starbucks.com/retail/wireless.asp` to sign up.

Hooking up from work

If you get a long lunch at work or have to kill time waiting for clients to call back, you may want to get started on eBay from your work computer. But give it a lot of thought before you do. Pink slips can come unbidden to those who run auctions on company time.

Choosing an ISP

Okay, so you bought (or found a way to access) a computer, and you're ready to surf eBay. Hold on a minute — before you start surfing, you need *access* to the Internet. (Details, details. . . .) The way to access the Internet is through an ISP, or *Internet service provider*, such as Earthlink, MSN (Microsoft Network), or RoadRunner. If you don't already belong to one of these, don't worry; joining is easy.

To join a telephone dial-up ISP (because dial-up requires no additional equipment or connections), just load the freebie software that comes with a computer (or free at the computer store) into your CD drive and follow the registration steps that appear on your computer screen. Have your credit card and lots of patience handy. With a little luck and no computer glitches, you'll have an active account and instant access to e-mail and the Internet in less than an hour.

When you go to a computer store or buy a computer, you're hit with all kinds of free trial offers that beg you to "Sign up now, first month free!" You can find free introductory deals everywhere! (They used to just come on CDs. I have a friend who painted all her free CDs and hung them on her Christmas tree. Another sawed them in half and made a very unattractive cyberbelt.) If you're new to the Internet and not sure which ISP to go with, your best bet may be to start with NetZero HiSpeed. NetZero has been around for years and offers accelerated speeds on its dial-up connections.

If you have a need for speed, and your time is worth a bit more than an increase in ISP cost, you may want to look into getting a broadband connection. The quality of the different types of broadband (DSL and cable) can vary greatly from area to area and even from street to street.

Before you decide what kind of broadband connection you want, go to the following:

www.broadbandreports.com

Type your ZIP code, and read the reports for other users in your area (see Figure 1-1). You can e-mail, post questions, and get all the information you need to decide what kind of high-speed connection will work best for you.

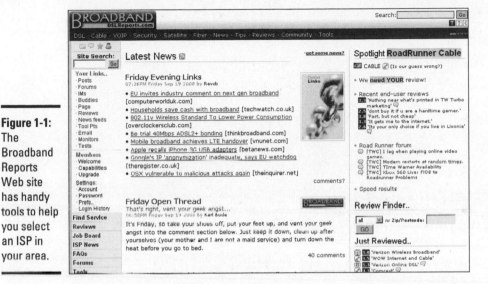

Figure 1-1:
The Broadband Reports Web site has handy tools to help you select an ISP in your area.

Broadband, or high-speed, connections can be a boon to your eBay business. Here's the skinny on the different types:

+ **DSL:** Short for *Digital Subscriber Line.* For as little as $19.95 a month, you can get rid of your pokey, analog dial-up connection and always be connected to the Internet. A DSL line can move data as fast as 6 MB per second — that's six *million* bits per second, or 140 times as fast as a 56K modem. At that speed, a DSL connection can greatly enhance your eBay and Internet experiences. For more information about what DSL is and how to get it, visit www.dslreports.com.

+ **Cable:** An Internet cable connection is a reliable method for Internet access if you have digital cable TV. Your Internet connection runs through your television cable and is regulated by your cable TV provider. With the advent of digital cable, this reliable and speedy Internet connection is an excellent alternative. (See my speed report from my wireless network in Figure 1-2.) Most cable accounts include several e-mail addresses and space to store your images.

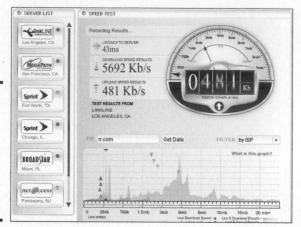

Figure 1-2:
Notice the
comparison
of
connection
speeds
on my test
results.

Accessing E-Mail

After you have access to the Internet, you need access to e-mail. If you have
your own computer and an ISP, you probably have e-mail access automatically. But if you're logging on to the Internet away from home, you might
want to look into setting up a free e-mail provider.

Most ISPs will allow you to check your e-mail from their Web sites, but
commonly, you'll be using Microsoft's Outlook Express to check your mail
on your home computer.

Google's Gmail, Yahoo!, and Hotmail are the most popular Web-based, free
e-mail providers. They are free and secure, and signing up is a snap. I like
them because all have a Mail Alert feature, which allows you to instruct Gmail,
Yahoo!, or MSN Mobile to contact you through your Web-enabled cell phone
when you have new e-mail. You can join Gmail at www.gmail.com, Yahoo!
e-mail at www.yahoo.com, and Hotmail by going to www.hotmail.com.

Some commonsense rules can help you protect your account:

✦ **Select a password that's difficult to guess.** Use letter-and-number
combinations or nonsensical words that nobody else knows. Don't use
common names or words relating to you (such as the name of your
street).

✦ **Keep passwords secret.** If someone asks for your password online, you
can bet it's a scam. *Never* give out your password.

✦ **Don't open an e-mail with an attachment from an unknown person.**
The attachment (another file attached to your e-mail message) could
contain a virus.

Book I
Chapter 1

Hooking Up with
Online Technology

✦ **Don't respond to spam e-mail.** *Spam* is online slang for harassing, offensive, or useless-but-widely-distributed messages or advertisements. If you ignore and delete such junk without even opening it, the senders will probably just go look for somebody else to bother.

Browsing for a Browser

When you get a computer, you get an Internet browser for free. A *browser* is the software program that lets your computer talk to the Internet. It's like having your own private cyberchauffeur. Type the address (also known as the *URL*, for *Uniform Resource Locator*) of the Web site you want to visit, and boom, you're there. For example, to get to eBay's home page, type www. ebay.com and press Enter. (It's sort of a low-tech version of "Beam me up, Scotty!" — and almost as fast.)

The two most popular browsers are Firefox (available both for MAC and the PC) and Microsoft Internet Explorer. (They are what Coca-Cola and Pepsi are to the cola wars.) Both programs are powerful and user-friendly. Figures 1-3 and 1-4 show you these browsers and how they show pages in the same way. (Sit, browser! Now shake! *Good* browser!) The one you choose is a matter of preference — I use them both!

Figure 1-3:
The eBay home page in Microsoft's Internet Explorer.

Figure 1-4:
Visiting
eBay in
the Firefox
browser.

You can get Microsoft Internet Explorer and Firefox for free. To find out more information (or to make sure you're using the most up-to-date version of the software):

✦ Go to www.microsoft.com for Microsoft Internet Explorer

✦ Go to www.mozilla.com/firefox for Firefox

Have you ever wondered what all those buttons and drop-down lists at the top of your browser do? In the following sections, I explain Explorer and Firefox in more depth. According to my recent eBay statistics (from Sellathon), 70 percent of the hits on my listings come from people using Internet Explorer, 23 percent are from people using Firefox, and the balance come from users of Safari, MSN, and AOL. Read on while we browse together.

Perusing the menus

At the top of almost all Microsoft-enabled programs are standard drop-down lists that invoke various programs. Who'd ever think you'd need to use menus, given all the colorful icons that Internet Explorer provides? Well, the drop-down lists give you more in-depth access to the program's capabilities. Tables 1-1 and 1-2 give you an overview of the various tasks you can perform from the menus.

Table 1-1	Internet Explorer Menus
Menu	*What You Can Do*
File	Open, print, save, and send HTML Web pages
Edit	Select, cut, copy, paste, and find text on the currently displayed page
View	Change the way Explorer displays Internet pages
Favorites	Save your favorite pages in the Favorites file
Tools	Enable pop-up blockers, add filters , and clear your history of Web sites visited
Help	Find help

Table 1-2	Firefox Menus
Menu	*What You Can Do*
File	Open, print, save, and send HTML Web pages
Edit	Select, cut, copy, paste, and find text on the currently displayed page
View	Change the way Firefox displays Internet pages
History	See and navigate back and forth in your current session sites visited
Bookmarks	Bookmark a page or access your saved bookmarks. (same as favorites)
Tools	Enable features, add add-ons, clear Private Data, and set browser options
Help	Find help

Dabbling with the toolbar

Being a graphical interface, Explorer presents you with lots of colorful icons that allow you to invoke programs or tasks with a click of the mouse. Table 1-3 gives you an introduction to these icons. You can customize which ones you view from the Tools menu, or you can choose just to see words (as I've done in Figure 1-3).

Table 1-3		**Internet Explorer Icons**
Button	*Name*	*What It Does*
Back	Back	Moves back to the previously viewed Web page
	Forward	Moves ahead to the page you moved back from
	Stop	Stops the Web-page loading process
	Refresh	Reloads the current Web page
	Home	Brings you to your preselected home page
	Search	Opens a box on the side of your browser to perform a specialized search on the Web
	Favorites	Opens a Favorites box that allows you to easily add to or organize your existing favorite Web pages
	Media	Opens a side box that allows you to view news, music videos, and movie trailers or listen to Web radio
	History	Opens a page with a list of all the Web pages you've visited in the past few days
	Mail	Opens your default e-mail program
	Print	Prints the page you're viewing
	Edit	Launches a text editor, such as WordPad or Notepad
	Discuss	Lets you join in the chat on certain MS-enabled Web sites
	AOL	Invokes the free Instant Messenger (IM) program, if you have an AOL IM nickname

Expert keyboard shortcuts

I'm all about using keystrokes instead of clicking! I also love the controls available on my mouse. Table 1-4 and 1-5 give you a list of all the shortcuts I could find. You'll see that Microsoft Internet Explorer and Firefox share many of the same shortcut keys. I hope they help cut down your desk time.

Table 1-4	Internet Explorer Shortcuts
Press This	*Explorer Will*
F1	Open a help window
F3	Open the Search box so you can perform search on the current page for a word
F4	Open your URL list so you can click back to a site that you just visited
F5	Refresh the current page
F11	Display full screen, reducing the number of icons and amount of stuff displayed
Esc	Stop loading the current page
Home	Go back to the top of the Web page
End	Jump to the bottom of the current page
Backspace	Go back to the last viewed Web page
Ctrl and mouse wheel	Enlarge or reduce the text on the screen
Ctrl+D	Add the current page to your favorites list (Don't forget to organize this list once in a while!)

Table 1-5	Firefox Shortcuts
Press This	*Firefox Will*
Backspace	Go to the previous page you've viewed
Ctrl+O	Open a window to open files from your computer
F5	Refresh current page
Ctrl+U	View Page source (to study HTML)
F11	Display full-screen, reducing the amount of icons and stuff displayed

(continued)

Table 1-5 (continued)

Press This	Firefox Will
Esc	Stop loading the current page
Ctrl+P	Print the page
Ctrl+S	Save the current page to a file on your computer
Backspace	Go back to the last viewed Web page
Ctrl++ or Ctrl+-	Enlarge or reduce the text on the screen
Ctrl+F	Find a word on the current Web page

Chapter 2: Navigating through eBay

In This Chapter

✔ **Homing in on the front page**

✔ **Going places lightning-fast with the navigation bar**

✔ **Browsing categories**

✔ **Using the home-page quick search**

As I've said before, the writer Thomas Wolfe was wrong: You *can* go home again — and again. At least with eBay you can! Day after day millions of people land at eBay's home page without wearing out the welcome mat. The eBay home page is the front door to the most popular e-tailing site on the Internet.

Everything you need to know about navigating eBay begins right here. In this chapter, I give you the grand tour of the areas you can reach right from the home page with the help of links.

Homing In on the Home Page

The eBay home page is shown in Figure 2-1. It includes several key areas:

✦ A navigation bar at the top of the page with five eBay links that can zip you straight to any of the many eBay areas, as well as a powerful link right below the navigation bar

✦ An important link to eBay's Live Help

✦ A list of links to auction categories

✦ Links to other eBay companies, and the 29 international eBay sites

At the top of almost every eBay page is a search box that helps you find items by title keywords.

Do not adjust your computer monitor. You're not going crazy. You may notice that a link was on the eBay home page one day but gone the next day. The links on the eBay home page change to reflect what's going on — not just on the site but also in the world.

Figure 2-1:
My very
favorite
home page
(other than
my own).

Home-page links, the next generation

If you look carefully on the home page, you can see several other links
that give you express service to several key parts of the site. Here are the
highlights:

✦ **From Our Sellers:** Click the link to visit the featured items near the
bottom of the page. Here at eBay, money talks pretty loudly, so a seller
can pay extra to feature his or her listing and *maybe* it will land on the
home page sometime during its run. eBay rotates six featured items
throughout the day so that as many sellers as possible get a shot at
being in the spotlight. When you click the From Our Sellers See All
Featured Items link, you're instantly beamed to eBay's Featured Items
section.

You can find everything from Las Vegas vacations to Model-T Fords
to diet products in the Home Page Featured Items section. Home Page
Featured Items are not for mere mortals with small wallets. They've

Book I
Chapter 2

Navigating
through eBay

been lifted to the exalted *featured* status because sellers shelled out lots of money to get them noticed. All you need to get your auction featured is $39.95 ($79.95 for Multiple Item listings), plus a second or two to click Home Page Featured Item on the Sell Your Item form.

Bidding on these items works the same way as bidding on regular items.

✦ **eBay Companies:** In the link area at the bottom of the page, you will find links to the ever growing family of eBay — other eBay-owned companies. Currently the list includes:

- **Half.com**. Half.com is a long standing Internet site where sellers offer items at fixed prices. These items have a UPC, ISBN, or SKU. They are not collectible items. The items sold on Half.com are books, textbooks, music, movies, video games, and video game consoles.

- **Kijiji**. Free Classifieds? How cool is that? *Kijiji* (the Swahili word for *village*) is a Web site for local classified ads. These are same kind of ads that appear in the newspapers, but in this case, they're online. Kijiji has sites for major cities in 29 countries, including the following: United States, Canada, Germany, Italy, France, Taiwan, China, India, Japan, as well as Intoko, Turkey. To visit the site, go to www. kijiji.com. See the Los Angeles area site in Figure 2-2.

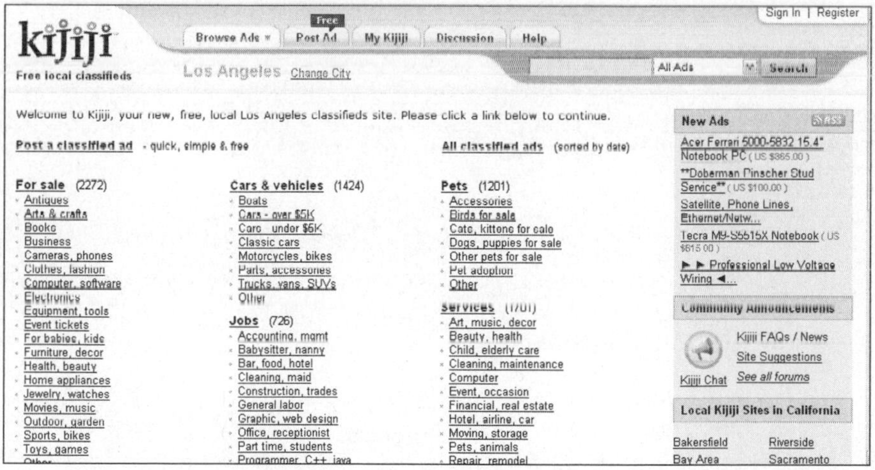

Figure 2-2: Los Angeles Kijiji — I've spent lots of time browsing this site!

- **MicroPlace**. "Invest wisely. End poverty." This is something unique, a Web site of "microfinance" where you can invest in very small businesses from every corner of the world. And you actually have the potential to earn interest.

- **PayPal**. PayPal's no secret. Visit Books II, III, and VI for the lowdown on the Internet's leading payment processor for small business.

- **ProStores**. An eBay company (at www.prostores.com) that will help you set up your own business on the Web. The stores are integrated with eBay — although you can also make a similar connection with a regular hosted e-store.

- **Rent.com**. Need to rent an apartment or home? Look no further than rent.com (www.rent.com). You'll be able to find large numbers of rental properties in most cities in the Unites States.

- **Shopping.com**. A Web-based price-comparison service. Shopping. com has features to help shoppers make informed shopping decisions. This site also has extensive product reviews and ratings from across the Web.

- **Skype.** A communication service where users download a software program that offers free calls over the Internet to other Skype users. In addition, they can make calls to landlines and mobile phones for a fee through SkypePro.

- **StubHub.** A service that acts as an online marketplace for buyers and sellers of tickets for sports, concerts, theater, and other live entertainment events. StubHub takes a 25 percent commission after the sale occurs (10 percent from the buyer and 15 percent from the seller).

- **StumbleUpon.** A Web browser plug-in that allows its users to discover and rate Web pages, photos, and videos. Web pages appear when the user clicks the "Stumble!" button on the browser's toolbar. StumbleUpon selects which new page to display based on the user's ratings of previous pages, ratings by their friends, and by the ratings of other users with similar interests.

✦ **Global sites:** Links you to eBay's international auction sites. From a drop down menu, you may enter eBay Argentina, Austria, Australia, Belgium, Brazil, Canada, China, France, Germany, Hong Kong, India, Ireland, Italy, Korea, Malaysia, Mexico, Netherlands, New Zealand, Philippines, Poland, Singapore, Spain, Sweden, Switzerland, Taiwan, Thailand, Turkey, and (whew) the United Kingdom. The international sites are in the country's native language. It might be a good place to practice your third-year French — or maybe not! Remember that after you leave eBay USA, you're subject to the contractual and privacy laws of the country you're visiting.

You may notice that the graphic links on the home page change from day to day — and even hour to hour. If you're interested in the featured areas of the site, visit this page several times a day to see the entire array of special happenings on eBay.

eBay's Center Square: The promotion du jour

The eBay community is constantly changing. To help you get into the swing of things right away, eBay provides a couple of special boxes, smack dab in the middle of the home page, packed with links that take you to the latest eBay special events.

Even if the main promotion box doesn't appeal to you, usually you can find some interesting links dotted around the home page without a headline. Also take a look at the small promotion boxes below the featured items.

You *can* get there from here — lots of places, in fact:

✔ A rotating list of special-interest links changes at least once a day. (Half the fun is getting a closer look at pages you haven't seen.)

✔ Special money-saving offers from third-party vendors can be a boon if you're on the lookout for a bargain.

Bottoming out

At the very bottom of the home page is an unassuming group of links providing more ways to get to some seriously handy pages. Here's a guide to some of the links you'll find:

✦ **Feedback Forum:** This link takes you to one of the most important spots on eBay. The Feedback Forum is where you can place feedback, respond to feedback left for you, and find out whether you've forgotten to place feedback on a transaction — all in one friendly location.

✦ **Downloads:** A link to eBay supplied software and toolbars. See Book II for more on these super tools.

✦ **Gift certificates & Gift Cards:** Send an eBay gift certificate for any special occasion. You can print it yourself, or eBay will send it to any e-mail address you provide. The gift certificate is good for any item on the site, as long as the seller accepts PayPal.

✦ **Jobs:** Click here if you want to work *for* eBay instead of *through* eBay.

✦ **Affiliates:** If you have your own Web site and want to make a few bucks, click this link. If you sign up for the program and put a link to eBay on your Web page, eBay pays you for new users who signs up directly from your Web site (plus other bonuses). Click the link for the current details.

✦ **Developers:** If you develop software and would like to design some to use with eBay, you can join the developers' network.

✦ **The eBay Shop:** This link enables you to browse and buy eBay merchandise from the eBay company store.

✦ **eBay Mobile:** eBay's mobile service for cell phones. eBay.com designed just for small screens. Stay connected to eBay from your mobile phone browser.

✦ **About eBay:** Click this link to find out about eBay the company and to get its press releases, company overview, and stock information. You can also find out about eBay community activities and charities — and even apply for a job with eBay.

✦ **Announcements:** Visit the General Announcements Board when you want to know about any late-breaking news.

✦ **Security Center:** This link takes you to a page where concerns about fraud and safety are addressed. Before buying or selling, it's a good idea to check out the Security Center in Chapter 3.

✦ **Policies:** This is a good place to visit to brush up on the site's policies and guidelines.

✦ **Government Relations:** Get active in the politics of online selling and buying. Join groups, send letters to congresspeople, make a difference!

✦ **Site map:** Here's a second link to the eBay site map (the other link is above the navigation bar).

✦ **Help:** For some reason, eBay felt the need to put another help link at the bottom of the home page. Save yourself some scrolling and use the link on the navigation bar!

On other eBay pages, the bottom navigation bar looks a little different. It often includes even more links so that you can cruise the site quickly without using the navigation bar.

Navigating eBay the Easy Way

The navigation bar is at the top of the eBay home page and lists five eBay links that take you directly to different eBay areas. Using the navigation bar is kind of like doing one-stop clicking. You can find this bar at the top of every page on eBay. Hovering over some of the links reveals a subnavigation list with links to other, related (and important) places.

Think of links as expressways to specific destinations. Click a link and, the next thing you know, you're right where you want to be. You don't even have to answer that annoying old question, "When are we gonna get there?" from the kids in the backseat.

Here, without further ado, are the five navigation bar links and where they take you:

✦ **Buy:** Takes you to the page that lists the top-level eBay categories and provides many buying-related links, links to the home page's Featured Items (see Book III), and a Search window, as shown in Figure 2-3. You'll find a mini-version of your My eBay page here, with drop-down links for your favorite searches, sellers, and categories. From this page, you have many ways of finding any one of the millions of items for sale on eBay.

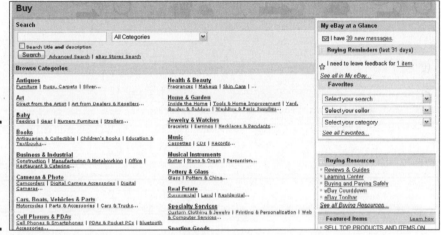

Figure 2-3:
The Buy page, linked from the navigation bar.

You'll find top-level categories on the Buy page. When you click to browse a category (for example, Books), you'll be brought to a category hub page that lists the subcategories of that category. Click your desired subcategory, and you arrive at the subcategory page, where you see three yellow tabs at the top of the listings. These tabs offer you different viewing options to browse:

• **All Items** is the default setting for the page. This option delivers on its promise — you see all items, including auctions and those items that can be purchased immediately using Buy It Now.

• Click the **Auctions** tab to see only the items that are up for auction.

• The **Buy It Now** tab isolates a view of all items listed with the Buy It Now feature.

Also, just below the tabs and above the listings is a Sort By drop-down box (see Figure 2-4) that allows you to sort your category results.

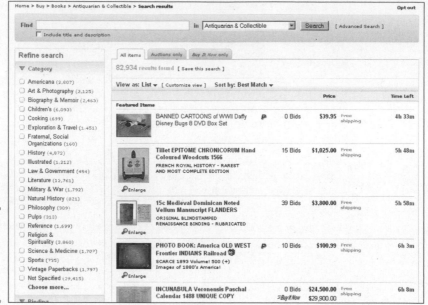

Figure 2-4:
Just
browsing a
category on
eBay.

You can sort in these ways:

- **Best Match** is the default search option; it sorts the listings you see by their relevance. A listing's relevance is based, in part, on past successful buyer behavior for similar items. The added reasoning behind this search is to identify sellers who provide great buying experiences and sellers who don't, all gauged by the use of Detailed Seller Ratings and feedback ratings.

- **Time: ending soonest** allows you to view the category listings in time order, with the soonest to end on top. (This is the way I always sort when I'm browsing.)

- **Time: newly listed** shows the items that have recently been listed in the category.

- **Time: ending today** displays items that end in the next 24 hours and are displayed with the item ending soonest listed first.

- **Time: new today** is where you can get the jump on other bargain hunters and see the full listing of items launched within the past 24 hours.

- **Price + Shipping: Lowest first** sorting can be deceiving. Many sellers list their items at an extremely low starting price to attract bidders. You may have to wade through twenty pages of ninety-nine cent items before you reach the dollar ones — a huge waste of time.

- **Price: Highest first and Price + Shipping: Highest first** are good choices if you're looking for high-ticket items in a category.

- **Distance: nearest first.** If you want to buy a large item (sofa? refrigerator? car?) and would rather save on shipping or want to drop by to inspect the item, this is the best search for you.

You can also search through the category. Type some keywords in the search box to find, for example, a particular book. Because more than 20 million items are up for auction at any given time, finding just one (say, a book on antique Vermont milk cans) is no easy task.

✦ **Sell:** Takes you to the first stop of the Sell Your Item form that you fill out to start your listings. (More on how to sell in Book III.) You also see a bunch of links that can take you to a zillion different places on eBay. Stop by someday when you have a lot of time on your hands.

✦ **My eBay:** Takes you to your personal My eBay page, where you keep track of your buying and selling activities, account information, and favorite categories (more about My eBay in Chapter 3).

✦ **Community:** Takes you to a page where you can find the latest news and announcements, chat with fellow traders in the eBay community, find charity auctions, and discover more about eBay. Several boxes in the subnavigation bar correspond to the links on the page (more on the eBay community in Chapter 8).

✦ **Help:** Opens the eBay Help Center overview page (which consists of a search box in which you can type your query) and links for help topics.

Below the eBay navigation bar (on most eBay pages) are powerful links that are just as important as the links on the navigation bar:

✦ **eBay Logo:** Takes you directly to the eBay home page. Use this link from any other page when you need to get back to the home page right away.

✦ **Categories:** When you click here, there's a drop-down menu for all eBay's top-level categories.

✦ **Motors:** Takes you to the eBay Motors site. Here, you can find links that connect you to the largest vehicle sales site on the Web.

✦ **Stores.** To view or browse eBay stores you click here.

✦ **Site map:** Provides you with a bird's-eye view of the eBay world. Every top-level (or main) link available on eBay is listed here. If you're ever confused about finding a specific area, try the site map first. If a top-level link isn't listed here, it's not on eBay — yet.

✦ **Sign In/Sign Out:** This link, which is below the navigation bar, toggles between Sign In and Sign Out depending on your sign-in status. This is an important link, and I remind you about it throughout the book. When you're signed in, it reads *Hello,* followed by your user ID.

Maneuvering the Categories

So how does eBay keep track of the millions of items up for sale at any given moment? The brilliant minds at eBay decided to group items into nice, neat little storage systems called *categories.* The home page lists most of the main categories, but eBay also lists tens of thousands of subcategories, ranging from Antiques to Weird Stuff. And don't ask how many sub-subcategories (categories within categories) eBay has — I can't count that high.

Well, okay, I *could* list all the categories and subcategories currently available on eBay — if you wouldn't mind squinting at a dozen pages of really small, eye-burning text. But a category browse is an adventure that's unique for each individual, and I wouldn't think of depriving you of it. Suffice it to say that if you like to hunt around for that perfect something, you're in browsing heaven now.

Here's how to navigate around the categories:

1. **From the drop-down menu, click the category that interests you, such as Books or DVDs & Movies.**

   You're transported to that category's page. You see categories and sub-categories listed next to each heading. Happy hunting.

   If you don't find a category that interests you among those on the home page, simply click the Buy button on the navigation bar, and you're off to the main Categories page. You get not only a pretty impressive page of main categories and subcategories, but also a short list of featured auctions — and links to them all.

   If you really and truly want to see a list of all categories and subcategories (see Figure 2-5), click See All Categories at the bottom of the category list on the main Buy page. Or, if you want to make it easy on yourself, go directly to the following:

   ```
   listings.ebay.com/ /ListingCategoryList
   ```

2. **After the category page appears, find a subcategory below the main category title that interests you. Click the subcategory, and keep digging through the sub-subcategories until you find what you want.**

   For example, if you're looking for items honoring your favorite television show, click the Entertainment Memorabilia category or the DVDs & Movies category. Note that the Entertainment Memorabilia category has many links, including the Television Memorabilia subcategory. Below the Television Memorabilia link, you'll see links to these subcategories: Ads, Flyers, Apparel, Clippings, Photos, Pins, Buttons, Posters, Press Kits, Props, Scripts, Wardrobe, and Other. Click the link that appeals to you and you're off on a shopping spree.

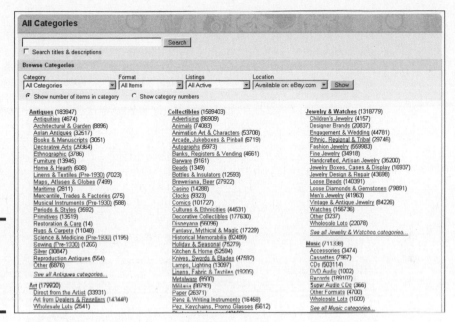

Figure 2-5:
Lots and
lots and
lots of sub-
categories.

3. **When you find an item that interests you, click the item and the full listing page pops up on your screen.**

   Congratulations — you've just navigated through several million items to find that *one* TV-collectible item that caught your attention. (Pardon me while I bid on that Lily Munster — Yvonne DeCarlo — signed picture.) You can instantly return to the home page by clicking its link at the top of the page (or return to the listings page by repeatedly clicking the Back button at the top of your browser).

Near the bottom of every subcategory or search-results page, you can see a list of numbers. The numbers are page numbers, and you can use them to fast-forward through all the items in that subcategory. So, if you feel like browsing around page 8 without going through 8 pages individually, just click number 8; you're presented with the items on that page (their listings, actually). Happy browsing.

If you're a bargain hunter by habit, you may find some pretty weird stuff while browsing the categories and subcategories of items at eBay — some of it super-cheap and some of it just cheap. There's even a Weird Stuff category — no kidding! Remember that (as with any marketplace) you're responsible for finding out as much as possible about an item before you buy — and definitely before you bid. So if you're the type who sometimes can't resist a good deal, ask yourself what you plan to *do* with the pile of stuff you can get for 15 cents — and ask yourself *now,* before it arrives on your doorstep. (Chapter 6 offers more information on savvy bidding techniques.)

Exploring Home Page Search Options

There's an old Chinese expression that says, "Every journey begins with the first eBay search." Okay, so I updated the quote. They're very wise words nonetheless. You can start a search from the home page in one of two ways:

✦ **Use the search box.** It's right there at the top of the home page (and most eBay pages), and it's a fast way of finding item listings.

✦ **Use the Advanced Search link (which is next to the search box).** This link will take you to the sophisticated Search area, where you can do all kinds of specialized searches.

To launch a title search from the home page, follow these steps:

1. **In the search box, type no more than a few keywords that describe the item you're looking for.**

   Refer to Figure 2-1 to see the search box.

2. **Click the Search button.**

   The results of your search appear in a matter of seconds.

You can type just about anything in the search box and get some information. Say you're looking for *Star Trek* memorabilia. If so, you're not alone. The original television show premiered on September 8, 1966, and even though it was canceled in 1969 because of low ratings, *Star Trek* has become one of the most successful science-fiction franchises in history. You can use the search box on the eBay home page to find all sorts of *Star Trek* stuff. I just ran a search and found around 13,762 items in numerous categories on eBay with *Star Trek* in their titles.

Try the Advanced Search link under the search box to narrow down your search. This link takes you to the basic search page, which has some powerful features (explained in Book II, Chapter 1).

When you search for popular items at eBay (a classic example is *Star Trek* memorabilia), you may get inundated with thousands of auctions that match your search criteria. Even if you're traveling at warp speed, you could spend hours checking each auction individually. ("Scotty, we need more power *now!*") If you're pressed for time like the rest of us, eBay has not-so-mysterious ways for you to narrow down your search to make finding a specific item much more manageable. Take a look at Figure 2-6 to see the way eBay helps break things down in that *Star Trek* search. Also, turn to Chapter 4 for insider techniques that can help you slim down those searches and beef up those results.

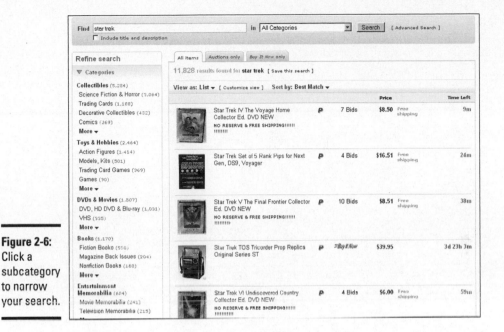

Figure 2-6:
Click a
subcategory
to narrow
your search.

Chapter 3: Signing Up and Getting Started

In This Chapter

- Registering with eBay
- Choosing a password
- Selecting a user ID
- Signing in
- Becoming ID verified
- Following eBay's rules

The prospect of getting started on eBay is exciting — and daunting. Perhaps you've visited the eBay Web site once or twice with the idea that you might buy something. Maybe you've heard your friends talk about the things they've bought. Did you look up something simple, such as a golf club? Did eBay come up with several thousand listings? Or maybe you figured you'd get smart and narrow the search down to a 3 iron, but you still got more than a thousand listings?

Did you consider buying something and then just left the site, for fear you'd get ripped off? eBay works much better for me than any quasi-convenient TV shopping channel because there's no overly made up huckster telling me how great I'd look in the outfit on the screen (displayed on a size-4 model). On eBay, you have the opportunity to give an item a leisurely once-over, read the description and terms, and click a link to ask the seller a question *before* you bid or buy. eBay's as simple as that. If you don't like the seller's response, you can just go on to the next seller. That's the great thing about eBay. There's always another seller — and always another item.

Registering on eBay

You can browse eBay all you want without registering, but before you transact any sort of business on eBay, you must register. I recommend registering while you're reading this book.

You don't have to be a rocket scientist to register at eBay. The only hard-and-fast rule is that you have to be 18 or older. Don't worry; the Age Police won't come to your house to card you — they have other ways to discreetly ensure that you're at least 18 years old. (Hint: Credit cards do more than satisfy account charges.)

If you're having a momentary brain cramp and you've forgotten your age, just think back to your childhood. If your first memory is watching *The Animaniacs* and *Chip 'n' Dale Rescue Rangers* on TV, you're in. Head to the eBay home page and register. The entire process takes only a few minutes.

During the early days of online trading, I was selling *Star Trek* memorabilia on Auction Web (the initial eBay site) and doing quite well. I ran into William Shatner (Captain Kirk of *Star Trek* fame) at a marketing meeting in mid-1997. Anxious to let him know how well I was doing with my merchandise online, I tried to explain Auction Web. Shatner scoffed, "No one will ever make any money on the Internet." (Really, I have witnesses — remember, this is the future Mr. Priceline.com.) Ah, well.

Before you can sign up, you have to be connected to the Web, so now's the time to fire up your computer. After you open your Internet browser, you're ready to sign up. In the address box of your browser, type **www.ebay.com** and press Enter.

Your next stop is the eBay home page. Right there, where you can't miss it, is the Register button — it's "fast and free!" Click this button and let the sign-up process begin. You can get to the Registration form also by clicking the register link next to the eBay logo at the top of the page.

When you're at the Registration form, you go through a four-step process. Here's an overview:

1. **Enter the basic required info.**
2. **Read and accept the User Agreement.**
3. **Confirm your e-mail address.**
4. **Breeze through the optional information.**

The following sections fill you in on all the details.

You register on eBay through an encrypted (supersecret) connection called SSL (Secure Sockets Layer). You can tell because the normal http at the beginning of the Web address is now https and a small closed padlock appears at the bottom-left (or bottom-right) corner of your screen.

The padlock icon means that eBay has moved you to a secure place on their site that is safe from unauthorized people seeing or receiving your information. Your information is treated with the highest security and you can fill out these forms with the utmost level of confidence. I could tell you how SSL works, but instead I'll just give you the bottom line: It *does* work, so trust me and use it. The more precautions eBay (and you) take, the harder it is for some hyper-caffeinated high-school kid to get into your data.

Filling in required information

After you click the Register button, you go to the first registration page. At the top of the page, eBay assures you that the registration process is easy and asks you to fill in some required information (see Figure 3-1).

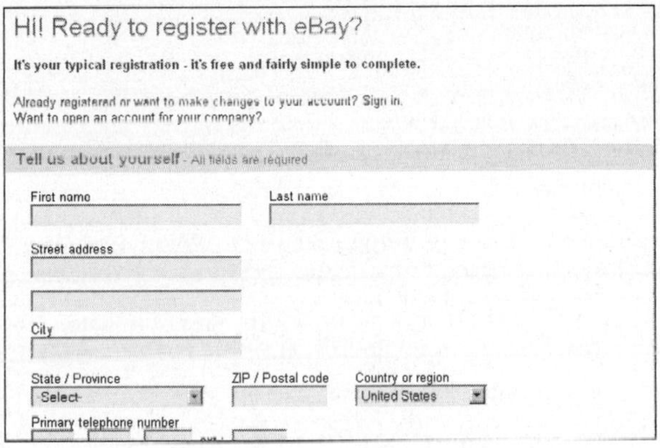

Figure 3-1:
Some of the required information for your eBay registration.

> Hi! Ready to register with eBay?
>
> It's your typical registration - it's free and fairly simple to complete.
>
> Already registered or want to make changes to your account? Sign in.
> Want to open an account for your company?
>
> **Tell us about yourself** - All fields are required
>
> First name   Last name
>
> Street address
>
> City
>
> State / Province   ZIP / Postal code   Country or region
> Select-   United States
>
> Primary telephone number

To get started, follow these steps:

1. **eBay needs to know stuff about you. Enter the following information:**

 • Your full name, address, and primary telephone number. eBay keeps this information on file in case the company (or a member who is a transaction partner) needs to contact you.

 • Your e-mail address (*yourname@myISP.com*).

If you register with an *anonymous e-mail service* such as Yahoo!, GMail, or Hotmail, you go to a page that requires additional information for authentication. You must provide valid credit-card information for identification purposes. Your information is protected by eBay's privacy policy, and your credit card won't be charged.

After you input your personal information, you're ready to create your eBay persona.

2. Scroll down the page to type your new eBay user ID.

Don't strain your brain too much right now over your choice of user ID. You can change your user ID once every 30 days. (See "Selecting Your User ID," later in this chapter, for some tips on selecting your user ID.) If your chosen ID is already taken, eBay has a handy tool to help you select another one, as shown in Figure 3-2.

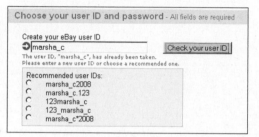

Figure 3-2: eBay's instant user ID suggestion form.

3. Choose a password, enter it in the Create Password box, and then type it a second time in the Re-enter Password box to confirm it.

The best passwords for eBay or any Web site are more than six characters long and include a combination of letters and numbers. Never use your user ID, name, pet's name, address, or anything that may be easily known by others. C'mon, get a little cagey. For more information on choosing your password, see "Picking a Pickproof Password," later in this chapter.

4. Create your secret question and input the answer.

eBay uses the secret question you select here as a security test should you need help to remember your password. There are six choices. I suggest you do not select the "What is your mother's maiden name?" question because banks and financial institutions often use this question for identification. Guard your mother's maiden name and don't give it out to anyone blithely. Select one of the other questions and fill in the answer. For more info on secret questions and their power, visit Book IX, Chapter 4.

5. Type your date of birth.

eBay needs to have your birth date. This is for two reasons. First, they want to be sure that you are of legal age to do business on eBay, and second, they may want to send you a nice birthday e-mail!

6. Make sure all the info you entered is correct, and then go to the not-so-fine print.

Think back to your second-grade teacher, who kept saying, "Class, check your work." Remember that? She's still right! Review your answers.

If eBay finds a glitch in your registration, such as an incorrect area code or ZIP code, you'll see a warning message on the next page. This is part of eBay's security system to ward off fraudulent registrations. Use the Back button to correct the information — if you put in a wrong e-mail address, for example, eBay has no way of contacting you. So you won't hear a peep from eBay regarding your registration until you go through the entire process all over again.

7. **Read the not-so-fine print and click Register.**

The section below will tip you in on what to expect in the "fine print."

It's safe to use your personal e-mail address for eBay registration. You will not be put on any spurious e-mail lists.

Sellers must register on eBay with a credit or debit card to pay for their eBay fees. *Buyers* do not register with a credit or debit card — unless they choose for their e-mail address one of the anonymous e-mail address services such as Hotmail or Yahoo! Mail, which do not verify users. Then they must register a credit card for identification. The credit card is not charged. If you'd rather not use a credit card, you may alternatively choose ID Verify. Read about ID Verify further on.

If you change your user ID, an icon of a little blue character changing into a gold one appears next to your user ID. This icon stays next to your user ID for 30 days. Double-check when you see others with this icon. The world being what it is, they may have just changed their user IDs to mask a bad reputation. They can't hide it completely, though. You can find the dirt on anyone on eBay by reading their feedback profile. (For more information on feedback, see Chapter 7 in this book.)

Don't tell anyone, but your info is safe on eBay

eBay keeps most personal information secret. The basics (your name, phone number, city, and state) go out only to answer the specific request of another registered eBay user (if you are involved in a transaction with that person), law enforcement, or members of the eBay Verified Rights Owner program (eBay's copyright-watchdog program). Other users may need your basic access info for several reasons — a seller may want to verify your location, get your phone number to call you regarding your auction, or double-check who you are. If somebody does request your info, you get an e-mail from eBay giving you the name, phone number, city, and state of the person making the request. Just one more reason you need to keep the information on your My eBay page up to date. If you don't, you risk being banished from the site.

Do you solemnly swear?

After you fill in your required information and scroll down, you should click the link to see the eBay User Agreement and Privacy Policy. At this page, you take an oath to keep eBay safe for democracy and commerce. You promise to play well with others, to not cheat, and to follow the golden rule. No, you're not auditioning for a superhero club, but don't ever forget that eBay takes this stuff seriously. You can be kicked off eBay or worse. (Can you say "Federal investigation"?)

Be sure to read the User Agreement thoroughly when you register. So that you don't have to put down this riveting book to read the legalese right this minute, I provide the nuts and bolts here:

✦ You understand that every transaction is a legally binding contract. (Click the User Agreement link at the bottom of any eBay page for the current eBay rules and regulations.)

✦ You agree that you can pay for the items you buy and the eBay fees that you incur.

✦ You understand that you're responsible for paying any taxes.

✦ You're aware that if you sell prohibited items, eBay can forward your personal information to law enforcement for further investigation.

✦ eBay makes clear that it is just a *venue,* which means it's a place where people with similar interests can meet, greet, and do business.

When everything goes well, the eBay Web site is like a school gym that opens for Saturday swap meets. At the gym, if you don't play by the rules, you can get tossed out. But if you don't play by the rules at eBay, the venue gets un-gymlike in a hurry. But fair's fair; eBay keeps you posted by e-mail of any updates in the User Agreement.

If you're a stickler for fine print, head to these Internet addresses for all the *Ps* and *Qs* of the latest policies:

pages.ebay.com/help/policies/overview.html

Before you can proceed, you have to click a check box that indicates you really, really understand what it means to be an eBay user — and agree to the terms. Then, because I know that you (as a law-abiding eBay member) will have no problem following the rules, go ahead and click the Continue button at the bottom of the page — which takes you to a screen stating that eBay is sending you an e-mail. You're almost finished.

It must be true if you have it in writing

After you accept the User Agreement, the screen notifies you that an e-mail has been sent to the e-mail address you supplied during your registration. It takes eBay less than a minute to e-mail you a confirmation notice. When you receive the confirmation e-mail, click the Complete eBay Registration link to continue your registration. If your e-mail doesn't support links, go to this address:

```
cgi4.ebay.com/ws/eBayISAPI.dll?RegisterConfirmCode
```

After you reconnect with eBay and it knows your e-mail address is active, you'll be heartily congratulated, as shown in Figure 3-3.

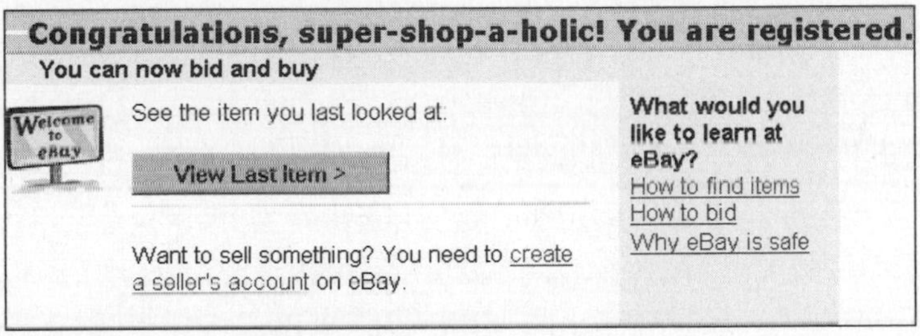

**Book I
Chapter 3**

**Signing Up and
Getting Started**

Congratulations, super-shop-a-holic! You are registered.
You can now bid and buy

Figure 3-3:
It's time
to start
dealing!

See the item you last looked at.

View Last Item >

Want to sell something? You need to create a seller's account on eBay.

What would you like to learn at eBay?
How to find items
How to bid
Why eBay is safe

In the unlikely event that you don't receive your eBay registration confirmation e-mail within 24 hours, your e-mail address most likely contains an error. At this point, the customer-support folks can help you complete the registration process. Go to the following address:

```
https://scgi.ebay.com/ws/eBayISAPI.dll?VAppEma&action=confirm
    code&resentemail=1
```

and enter your e-mail address. Click Submit. You will receive another e-mail with a special one-time confirmation password.

If, for some reason (brain cramp is a perfectly acceptable excuse), you incorrectly type in the wrong e-mail address, you have to start the registration process all over again with a different user ID (eBay holds the previous ID for 30 days). If you run into a snag, you can click the Live Help button that appears on the home page. See Figure 3-4 for my Live Help discussion.

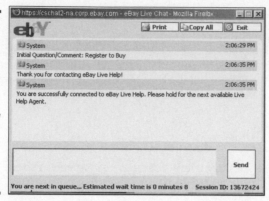

Figure 3-4:
I clicked
Live Help to
ask about a
registration
problem.
Within a few
minutes, I
was online
with a real
person.

Your license to deal (almost)

You are now officially a *newbie,* or eBay rookie. The only problem is that
you're still at the window-shopping level. If you're ready to go from window
shopper to item seller, just click the Sell button in the navigation bar. You'll
have to fill out a few more forms, and before you know it, you can start
running your own auctions at eBay.

Until you've been a member of eBay for 30 days, a picture of a beaming,
golden cartoonlike icon is next to your user ID wherever it appears on the
site. This doesn't mean you've been converted into a golden robot; the icon
merely indicates to other eBay users that you're new to eBay.

Now that you're a full-fledged, officially registered member of the eBay
community, you may see an eBay pop-up window, giving you the option to
provide more information about yourself. These optional questions allow
you to fill in your self-portrait for your new pals at eBay.

Although eBay doesn't share member information with anyone, you don't
have to answer the optional questions if you don't want to.

The following points show you the optional questions eBay asks. You decide
what you feel comfortable divulging and what you want to keep personal.
eBay asks for this information because the company wants a better picture
of who is using its Web site. In marketing mumbo-jumbo, this stuff is called
demographics — statistics that characterize a group of people who make up
a community. In this case, it's the eBay community.

Here is the optional information you can provide:

✦ **Sex:** Okay, it really asks you to indicate your *gender* by selecting a Male/
Female radio button set. (But starting the sentence off with *sex* really got
your attention, didn't it?)

+ **Annual household income:** eBay states that this info is kept anonymous, but I think it's too personal. If you're not comfortable with it, skip it.

+ **Your highest completed education level:** Again, if this is too personal, leave this area blank.

After selecting your responses from the drop-down box, you can click Submit. Or you can click Answer Later, and the pop-up box will reappear for your response later in your eBay dealings. If you don't want to answer any of the demographic queries, click Please Don't Ask Me Again, at the bottom of the pop-up window.

Picking a Pickproof Password

Choosing a good password is not as easy (but is twice as important) as it may seem. Whoever has your password can (in effect) "be you" at eBay — running auctions, bidding on auctions, and leaving possibly-litigious feedback for others. Basically, such an impostor can ruin your eBay career — and possibly cause you serious financial grief.

Many passwords can be cracked by the right person in a matter of seconds. Your goal is to set a password that takes too much of the hackers' time. With the number of available users on eBay or PayPal, odds are they'll go to the next potential victim's password rather than spend too many minutes (or even hours) trying to crack yours.

As with any online password, you should follow these commonsense rules to protect your privacy:

+ **Don't** choose anything too obvious, such as your birthday, your first name, or (*never* use this) your Social Security number. (*Hint:* If it's too easy to remember, it's probably too easy to crack.)

+ **Do** make things tough on the bad guys — combine numbers and letters (use uppercase and lowercase) or create nonsensical words.

+ **Don't** give out your password to anyone — it's like giving away the keys to the front door of your house.

+ **Do** change your password *immediately* if you ever suspect someone has it. You can change your password, by going to the Account Information area of your My eBay page or to the following address:

```
signin.ebay.com/ws/eBayISAPI.
    dll?ChangePasswordAndCreateHint
```

+ **Do** change your password every few months just to be on the safe side.

For more information on passwords and other security stuff, check out Book IX.

Selecting Your User ID

Making up a user ID is always a pleasant chore. If you've never liked your real name or never had a nickname, here's your chance to correct that situation. Choose an ID that tells a little about you. Of course, if your interests change, you may regret too narrow a user ID.

You can call yourself just about anything, but remember that this ID is how other eBay users will know you. Here are some guidelines:

+ Don't use a name that would embarrass your mother.

+ Don't use a name with a negative connotation, such as *scam-guy*. If people don't trust you, they won't buy from you.

+ Don't use a name that's too weird, you know, something like *baby-vampire-penguin*. People may chuckle, but they may also question your sanity.

+ eBay doesn't allow spaces in user IDs, so make sure that the ID makes sense when putting two or more words together. A friend of mine intended to register as "gang of one." She forgot the hyphens, so her ID reads *gangofone*.

If you're dying to have several short words as your user ID, you can use underscores or hyphens to separate them, as in *super-shop-a-holic*. And if you sign in to eBay for the whole day, you won't have to worry about repeatedly typing a complicated ID.

You can change your user ID once every 30 days if you want to, but I don't recommend it because people come to know you by your user ID. If you change your ID, your past does play tagalong and attaches itself to the new ID. But if you change your user ID too many times, people may think you're trying to hide something.

Nevertheless, to change your user ID, click the My eBay link, which appears at the top of most eBay pages. From your My eBay Summary page, click the My Account: Personal Information link, scroll to the User ID area, and click the Change link. Fill in the boxes, and then click the Change User ID button. You now have a new eBay identity.

eBay also has some user ID rules to live by:

+ No offensive names (such as &*#@guy).

✦ No names with *eBay* in them. (It makes you look like you work for eBay, and eBay takes a dim view of that.)

✦ No names with & (even if you *do* have both looks&brains).

✦ No names with @ (such as @Aboy).

✦ No symbols, such as the greater than or less than symbol (> <), and no consecutive underscores (__).

✦ No IDs that begin with an *e* followed by numbers, an underscore, a hyphen, a period, or *dot* (as in dot.com).

✦ No names of one letter (such as Q from *Star Trek*).

When you choose your user ID, make sure that it isn't a good clue for your password. For example, if you use *Natasha* as your user ID, don't choose *Boris* as your password. Even Bullwinkle could figure that one out.

Hey, AOL users, this one's for you. If you have Internet e-mail blocked, you need to update your AOL Mail Controls to receive e-mail from eBay. To do so, enter the AOL keyword **Mail Controls**.

Signing In to Deal

You don't have to wear one of those tacky "Hello, my name is" stickers on your shirt, but you and several million other folks will be roaming around eBay's online treasure trove. eBay needs to know who's who when we're browsing. So, keeping that in mind, sign in when you first go on to the eBay Web site, please!

By going to the Sign In page and signing in, you don't have to enter your user ID when you bid or post items for sale. The Sign In page also takes you to a link that allows you to change your sign in or My eBay preferences.

If you're the only one who uses your computer, be sure to select the box that says "Keep me signed in on this computer unless I sign out." This way, you're signed in to eBay every time you go to the site for an entire day. The sign-in process places a *cookie* (a techno-related piece-of-code thingy) on your computer that remains a part of your browser until you sign out. If you don't select the box, you will be signed in only while you're on the site. If there's no activity for 40 minutes or you close your browser, the cookie expires and you have to sign in again.

Here's how to get to the eBay Sign In page and sign in:

1. **Click the Sign In link next to the eBay logo on the eBay home page.**

2. **Enter your user ID and password.**

If you're on your home computer and want to make your eBay-ing easier, click the box next to "Keep me signed in for today." Your password will be saved in the browser until you sign out, even if you disconnect from the Internet, close your browser, or turn off your computer.

3. Click Sign In Securely.

You're now signed in to eBay and can travel the site with ease. You may go to your My eBay page's eBay Preferences to tell eBay where you want to land after you sign in.

Verifying Your ID

During the later years of the Cold War, the late President Ronald Reagan said, "Trust but verify." The President's advice made sense for dealing with the Soviet Union in those days, and it makes good sense with your dealings at eBay, too! (Even if you're not dealing in nuclear warheads.)

To show other eBay members that you're an honest type, you can buy a "trust but verify" option, known as *ID Verify,* from eBay for five bucks. The process is simple, and it allows new users of eBay to show other members that they are earnest in their desire to become responsible members of the community. A company called Equifax verifies your identity by asking for the following information:

✦ Name

✦ Address

✦ Phone number

✦ Social Security Number

✦ Driver's license information

✦ Date of birth

Equifax matches the info you give to what's in its humungous database — and presents you with a list of questions from your credit file that only you should know the answer to. Equifax may ask you about any loans you have, for example, or what kinds of credit cards you own (and how many).

Equifax sends only the results of its test (that is, whether you pass the test) to eBay — and *not* the answers to the private financial questions it asks you. Equifax doesn't modify or add information you provide to any of its databases.

Equifax' questions are meant to protect you against anyone else who may come along and try to steal this information from you and assume your identity. The questions aren't a credit check, and your creditworthiness is never called into question. This info simply verifies that you are who you say you are.

 If you pass the test and Equifax can verify that you are who you say you are and not your evil twin (can you say "Mini Me"?), you get a cool icon by your name. If any of your contact information changes, you have to reapply for a new ID Verify logo.

Although you can feel secure knowing that a user who's verified is indeed who he or she claims to be, you still have no guarantee that he or she is not going to turn out to be a no-goodnik (or, for that matter, a well-meaning financial airhead) during auction transactions.

Aside from the identification feature, ID Verify offers other benefits to buyers. ID Verify allows you to

✦ List with the Buy It Now or the Best Offer options.

✦ List using Fixed Price or Multiple Item formats.

✦ Bid above $15,000 (hey, Big Spender!)

✦ Become a seller (without putting a credit card on file).

✦ Access the Mature Audiences category.

 You should consider all of eBay's programs for protecting you from problematic transactions and people, but I think the undisputed heavyweight champ for finding out who someone *really is* and keeping you out of trouble is the first program eBay created. That's right, folks; *feedback* can show you other eBay members' track records and give you the best information on whether you want to do business with them or take a pass. Feedback is especially effective if you analyze it with eBay's other protection programs. I suggest taking the time to read all about feedback in Chapter 7 of this minibook.

eBay Is Watching Over You

The Security Center is where eBay's Trust and Safety gurus focus on protecting the Web site from members who aren't playing by the rules. Through this department, eBay issues warnings and policy changes — and in some cases, it gives eBay bad guys the old heave-ho.

You can find eBay's Security Center by clicking the Security Center link at the bottom of most eBay. Trust and Safety's Security Center page is more than just a link to policies and information. It also connects you with a group of eBay staffers who handle complaints, field incoming tips about possible infractions, investigate infractions, and dole out warnings and suspensions via e-mail in response to the tips.

eBay staffers look at complaints on a case-by-case basis, in the order they receive them. Most complaints they receive are about these problems:

✦ Shill bidders (see the section on "Selling abuses" in this chapter)

✦ Feedback issues and abuses (see the section on "Feedback abuses" in this chapter)

Keep in mind that eBay is a community of people, most of whom have never met each other. No matter what you buy or sell on eBay, don't expect eBay transactions to be any safer than buying or selling from a complete stranger. If you go in with this attitude and stay personable-but-vigilant, you won't be disappointed.

Staying notified about the rules

For an up-close online look at eBay's rules and regulations, click the Policies link (which is at the bottom of most eBay pages) and then read the User Agreement. (The agreement is revised regularly, so check it often.)

Another helpful link is the FAQ (frequently-asked questions) page for the User Agreement, which explains the legalese in clearer English. To visit the FAQ page, go to

```
pages.ebay.com/help/policies/everyone-ov.html
```

If you plan on being an active eBay member, it's probably worth your while to opt-in for eBay's User Agreement update e-mail. To do so, go to your My eBay page and click the eBay Preferences link in the My Account area. You'll see your Notification Preferences. To make a change, click View/Change. At this point, you're asked to type your password — this is to protect your security on eBay. Then you go to the magic page where you can change *all* your eBay notification preferences, including the User Agreement update.

Abuses you should report to Trust and Safety

Before you even consider blowing the whistle by reporting someone who (gasp!) gave you negative feedback to Trust and Safety, make sure that what you're encountering is *actually* a misuse of eBay. Some behavior isn't nice (no argument there), but it *also* isn't a violation of eBay rules — in which case, eBay can't do much about it. The following sections list the primary reasons you may start Trust and Safety investigations.

Selling abuses

If you're on eBay long enough, you're bound to find an abuse of the service. It may happen on an auction you're bidding on, or it may be one of the sellers who compete with your auctions. Be a good community member and be on the lookout for the following:

✦ **Shill bidding:** A seller uses multiple user IDs to bid, or has accomplices place bids to boost the price of his or her auction items. eBay investigators look for six telltale signs, including a single bidder putting in a really high bid, a bidder with really low feedback but a really high number of bids on items, a bidder with low feedback who has been an eBay member for a while but who's never won an auction, or excessive bids between two users.

✦ **Auction interception:** An unscrupulous user, pretending to be the actual seller, contacts the winner to set up terms of payment and shipping in an effort to make off with the buyer's payment. This violation can be easily avoided by paying with PayPal directly through the eBay site.

✦ **Fee avoidance:** A user reports a lower-than-actual final price or illegally submits a Final Value Fee credit. (Final Value Fee credits are explained in Book III.)

✦ **Bid manipulation:** A user, with the help of accomplices, enters dozens of phony bids to make the auction appear to have a lot of bidding action. Let the experts at eBay decide on this one; but you may wonder if loads of bids come in rapid succession but the price moves very little.

Bidding abuses

If you want to know more about bidding in general, see Chapter 6. Here's a list of bidding abuses that eBay wants to know about:

✦ **Bid shielding:** Two users work in tandem. User A, with the help of accomplices, intentionally bids an unreasonably high amount and then retracts the bid in the closing moments of the auction — leaving a lower bid (which the offender or an accomplice places) as the winning bid.

✦ **Bid siphoning:** Users send e-mail to bidders of a current auction to offer the same merchandise for a lower price elsewhere.

✦ **Auction interference:** Users warn other bidders through e-mail to stay clear of a seller *during a current auction*, presumably to decrease the number of bids and keep the prices low.

✦ **Bid manipulation (or invalid bid retraction):** A user bids a ridiculously high amount, raising the next highest bidder to the maximum bid. The manipulator then retracts the bid and rebids *slightly* over the previous high bidder's maximum.

+ **Unpaid item (nonpaying bidder):** No matter how eBay chooses to couch it by fancy verbiage, I call these bidders deadbeats. The bottom line is that these people win auctions but never pay.

+ **Unwelcome bidder:** A user bids on a specific seller's auction despite the seller's warning that he or she won't accept that user's bid (as in the case of not selling internationally and receiving international bids). This practice is impolite and obnoxious. If you want to ban specific bidders from your auctions, you can exclude them in your My eBay area links.

Feedback abuses

All you have at eBay is your reputation, and that reputation is made up of your feedback history. eBay takes any violation of its feedback system seriously. Because eBay's feedback is transaction related, unscrupulous eBay members find that manipulating the system is much harder. Here's a checklist of feedback abuses that you should report to Trust and Safety:

+ **Feedback extortion:** A member threatens to post negative feedback if another eBay member doesn't follow through on some unwarranted demand.

+ **Personal exposure:** A member leaves feedback for a user that exposes personal information that doesn't relate to transactions on eBay.

+ **–4.3 feedback:** Any user reaching a net feedback score of –4.3 is subject to suspension.

Identity abuses

Who you are on eBay is as important as what you sell (or buy). eBay monitors the identities of its members closely — and asks that you report any great pretenders in this area to Trust and Safety. Here's a checklist of identity abuses:

+ **Identity misrepresentation:** A user claims to be an eBay staff member or another eBay user, or registers under the name of another user.

+ **False or missing contact information:** A user deliberately registers with false contact information or an invalid e-mail address.

+ **Underage:** A user falsely claims to be 18 or older. (You must be at least 18 to enter into a legally binding contract.)

+ **Dead or invalid e-mail address:** When e-mails bounce repeatedly from a user's registered e-mail address, chances are good that the address is dead. Usually return e-mail indicates that the address is unknown.

+ **Contact information:** One user publishes another user's contact information on the eBay site.

Operational abuses

If you see someone trying to interfere with eBay's operation, eBay staffers want you to tell them about it. Here are two roguish operational abuses:

✦ **Hacking:** A user purposely interferes with eBay's computer operations (for example, by breaking into unauthorized files).

✦ **Spamming:** The user sends unsolicited commercial e-mail to eBay users.

Miscellaneous abuses

The following are additional problems that you should alert eBay about:

✦ A user is threatening physical harm to another eBay member.

✦ A person uses racist, obscene, or harassing language in a public area of eBay.

For a complete list of offenses and how eBay runs each investigation, go to the following address:

```
pages.ebay.com/help/buy/report-trading.html
```

See the next section for information on how to report violators to eBay.

Reporting abuses

If you suspect someone of abusing eBay's rules and regulations, go to the Security Center (the link is at the bottom of every eBay page) and click Report a Problem on the Security & Resolution Center main page. You are presented with the form shown in Figure 3-5. From this page, click the appropriate link for your issue.

Figure 3-5:
This handy-dandy, encompass-it-all form allows you to report violations.

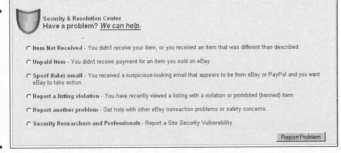

Giving eBay all the right information

If you have a troubled item and need to launch a report, follow these steps:

1. **Read all the information on the Security and Resolution Center page before filing a new complaint.**

2. **Click Report a Problem.**

You arrive at that handy form shown in Figure 3-5.

3. **Select the item that relate to your situation, and then click Report Problem.**

4. **If eBay presents you with a page full of links to teach you about their policies and some possible solutions to your issue, review them. Then scroll to the bottom of the page, and click the Start Here link.**

5. **You see a list of most requested FAQs (Frequently Asked Questions), but look at the tabs at the top and click Send Us an Email.**

6. **On the resulting page, use the drop-down menu to select your issue topic; then give a thorough description of what transpired. Sign the bottom of the form with your e-mail address and user ID, and type the item number (or numbers) if they're part of a related problem. Click Continue.**

Figure 3-6 shows you the form for one type of transgression. Be sure to review what you've written to confirm that your report is accurate.

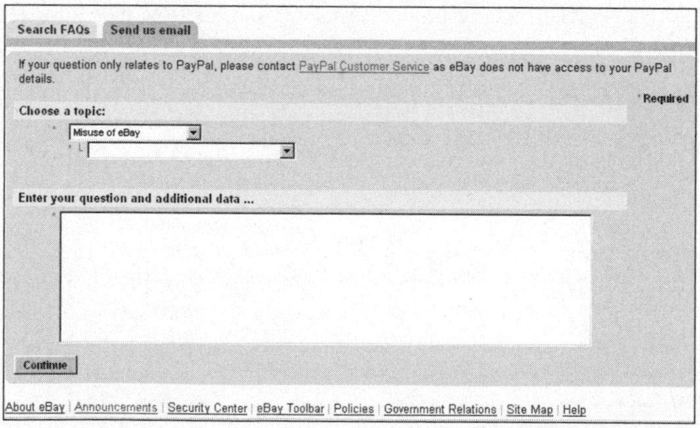

Figure 3-6: Here's where you spill the beans on policy violators.

7. **You'll be presented with a page of possible answers to your question. If the answer isn't there, send the report by clicking Send email.**

Be sure you send only one report per case — and one case per report.

If you file a report, make your message clear and concise by including everything that happened, but don't editorialize. (Calling someone a "lowdown mud-sucking cretin" doesn't provide any useful info to anyone who can help you and doesn't reflect well on you, either.) Keep your comments business-like — just the facts, ma'am. Be sure that the subject line of your report precisely names the violation and that you include all pertinent documentation.

Here's a checklist of backup documentation you may need for your Trust and Safety report:

+ **A copy of the facts you recorded on your report:** And remember to stick to *only* the facts as you know them.

+ **E-mail correspondence:** Attach any pertinent e-mails with complete headers. (*Headers* are all the information found at the top of an e-mail message.) Trust and Safety uses the headers to verify how the e-mail was sent and to follow the trail back to the author.

+ **Receipts and cancelled checks:** These help verify that a transaction took place, and when.

If the clock is running out on your case (for example, you suspect bidding offenses in a current auction), I suggest that you avail yourself of the Live Help link, which appears on the eBay home page. After eBay receives your report, you usually get an automatic response that your e-mail was received. Several days may go crawling by before eBay investigates your allegations. (They must look at a *lot* of transactions.)

eBay's response may vary

If your complaint doesn't warrant an investigation by the folks at Trust and Safety, they pass it along to someone from the overworked customer-support staff, who then contacts you. (Don't bawl out the person if the attention you get is tardy.)

Depending on the outcome of the probe, eBay may contact you with the results. If your problem becomes a legal matter, eBay may not let you know what's going on. The only indication you may get that some action was taken is that the eBay member you reported is suspended, or turns out to be NARU (Not A Registered User).

Unfortunately, NARU members can show up again on the eBay site. Typically, nefarious sorts such as these just use a different name. In fact, this practice is common, so beware! If you suspect that someone who broke the rules once is back under another user ID, alert Trust and Safety. If you're a seller, you can refuse to accept bids from that person. If the person persists, alert customer support by e-mail.

Make sure that you don't violate any eBay rules by sharing any member's contact information as you share your story in a chat room. In addition, make sure that you don't threaten or libel (that is, say untrue things or spread rumors about) the person in your posting.

Speeding up a response (or not)

As eBay has grown, so has the number of complaints about slow response from customer support. I don't doubt that eBay staffers are doing their best. Although slow response can get frustrating, *avoid* the temptation to initiate a reporting blitzkrieg by sending reports over and over until eBay can't ignore you. This practice is inconsiderate at best and risky at worst, and it just slows down the process for everyone — and won't endear the e-mail bombardier to the folks who could help.

If you're desperate for help and can't find a Live Help link, you can post a message with your problem in one of the eBay chat rooms. eBay members participating in chat rooms often share the names of helpful staffers. Often you can find some eBay members who faced the same problem (sometimes with the same member) and can offer advice — or at the very least, compassion and a virtual ear. (Jump to Chapter 8 for more info on discussion boards and chat rooms.)

If you're a PowerSeller, you can always contact PowerSeller support with your immediate problem. You can get to PowerSeller support by going to the site map and clicking the PowerSeller link in the middle of the page. You can also go directly to

pages.ebay.com/services/buyandsell/welcome.html

Don't get caught in a trading violation

Playing by eBay's rules keeps you off the Trust and Safety radar screen. If you start violating eBay policies, the company's going to keep a close eye on you. Depending on the infraction, eBay may be all over you like jelly on peanut butter. Or you may safely lurk in the fringes until your feedback rating is lower than the temperature in Nome in November.

Here's the docket of eBay no-no's that can get members flogged and keel-hauled — or at least suspended:

+ Feedback rating of –4.3

+ Three instances of deadbeat bidding

+ Repeated warning for the same infraction

+ Feedback extortion

+ Bid shielding

✦ Unwelcome bidding after a warning from the seller

✦ Shill bidding

✦ Auction interception

✦ Fee avoidance

✦ Fraudulent selling

✦ Identity misrepresentation

✦ Bidding when younger than age 18

✦ Hacking

✦ Physical threats

If you get a suspension but think you're innocent, respond directly to the person who suspended you to plead your case. Reversals do occur. But *don't* broadcast your suspicions on chat boards. If you're wrong, you may regret it. Even if you're right, it's oh-so-gauche.

Be careful about accusing members of cheating. Unless you're involved in a transaction, you don't know all the facts. Perry Mason moments are great on television, but they're fictional for a reason. In real life, drawing yourself into a possible confrontation is senseless. Start the complaint process, keep it businesslike, and let eBay's staff figure out what's going on.

Chapter 4: Understanding eBay Sales

In This Chapter

✔ **Checking out a listing page**

✔ **Bidding on an auction**

✔ **Buying something right now**

✔ **Visiting eBay's specialty sites**

Sometimes, when you know exactly what you want to buy, you find not one but many auctions and fixed-price listings with that same item for sale. In this situation, knowing the different eBay sales formats is important. In this chapter, I go over the various types of sales and show you the ways to use each type to your advantage.

Checking Out the Listing Page

All item pages on eBay — whether auctions, fixed-price items, or Buy It Now items — look about the same. Figure 4-1 shows a conventional auction-item page. If you were viewing this auction page on the screen, you could scroll down and see a complete description of the item, along with shipping information.

eBay auction listings have some subtle differences. (With a venue as big as eBay, you gotta have some flexibility.) Some auctions feature a picture at the top of the page and some don't, depending on how the seller sets up his or her sale page. You may also see the words *Financing Available* (more on that later). Some auctions also have preset item specifics that appear above the description written by the seller. If you're looking at an item in a fixed-price sale, you'll see the words *Buy It Now*, as shown in Figure 4-2.

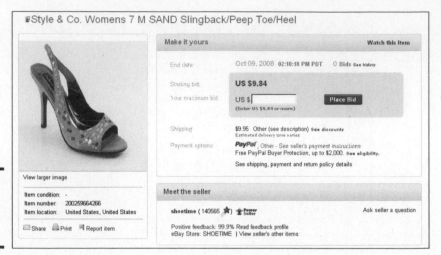

Figure 4-1:
Wow, if I
only wore a
size 7!

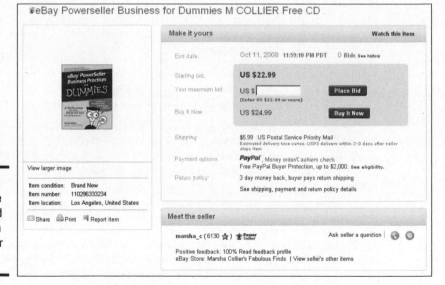

Figure 4-2:
Bypass the
starting bid
and buy on
the spot for
$24.99.

Here's a list of stuff you see as you scroll down a typical auction-item page:

✦ **Item category:** Located just above the item title and number bar, you can click the category listing and do some comparison shopping. (Book II, Chapter 1 offers some more searching strategies.)

✦ **Item title and number:** The title and number identify the item. Keep track of this info for inquiries later. Some sellers (refer to Figure 4-2) also use a subtitle to pass on more information about their items.

If you're interested in a particular type of item, take note of the keywords used in the title (you're likely to see them again in future titles). Doing so helps you narrow down your searches.

✦ **Watch this item:** Click this link, and the item is magically added to the Watching area of your My eBay All Buying page so you can keep an eye on the progress of the auction — without actually bidding. If you haven't signed in, you have to type your user ID and password before you can save the auction to your My eBay page.

✦ **Starting bid or Current bid:** This is the dollar amount that the bidding has reached. The amount changes throughout the auction as people place bids. If no bids have been placed on the item, it will read *Starting bid*.

Sometimes, next to the current dollar amount, you see *Reserve not met* or *Reserve met*. This means the seller has set a *reserve price* for the item — a secret price that must be reached before the seller will sell the item. Most auctions do not have reserve prices.

✦ **End Time:** Although the clock never stops ticking on eBay, you must continue to refresh your browser to see the time remaining on the *official* clock. When the item gets down to the last hour of the auction, you'll see the time expressed in minutes and seconds. You'll also see the date and time that the listing will close.

Timing is the key in an eBay bidding strategy (covered in Chapter 6), so don't forget that eBay uses Pacific Standard Time (PST) or Pacific Daylight Time (PDT) as the standard, depending on the season.

✦ **Shipping costs:** If the seller is willing to ship the item anywhere in the country for a flat rate, you'll see that here. This area may also link to eBay's shipping calculator if the seller customizes the shipping expense according to weight and distance.

✦ **Ships to:** If the seller ships to only the United States, it will state so here. If the seller ships to any other countries, this is where they will be listed.

✦ **Item location:** This field tells you at the very least the country where the seller is located. You may also see more specific info, such as the seller's city and geographic area. (What you see depends on how detailed the seller chooses to be.) The item location is handy if you'd like to go pick up the item — but e-mail the seller first to see whether he or she would be willing to meet you at (say) a local Starbucks to complete the transaction.

✦ **History:** This field tells you how many bids have been placed. The starting bid is listed in light gray next to the number of bids. When the listing is live, you can click the number of bids to find out who is bidding and when bids were placed. (In some circumstances, only the seller and buyer can access this data.)

You can click the number of bids to see how the bidding action is going, but you won't be able to see the high bidder's proxy bid (more about proxy bids later in this chapter).

✦ **High bidder:** This field shows you the user ID and feedback rating of the current high bidder. It could be you if you've placed a bid!

When you're bidding, eBay can hide your bidder ID by using anonymous names under certain circumstances. Your actual user ID is shown to the seller of this item only. Bidders are assigned anonymous names, such as a***k. Anonymous names are used for auctions that exceed a certain bidding level.

Sometimes an item has no bids because everyone is waiting until the last minute. Then you see a flurry of activity as bidders try to outbid each other (called *sniping,* which Chapter 6 explains). It's all part of the fun of eBay.

✦ **Buy It Now price:** If you want an item immediately and the price listed in this area is okay with you, click Buy It Now. You will be taken to a page where you can complete your purchase. Buy It Now is an option and does not appear in all listings.

✦ **Quantity:** This field appears only when multiple items are available. If you see a number other than 1 in this field and the item is open to bid, you're looking at a multiple-item auction (Dutch auction), which I describe later in this chapter. If it's a multiple-item, fixed-price sale, you have no opportunity to bid — you use Buy It Now to purchase whatever quantity of the item you want. You'll be prompted for a quantity when you buy.

✦ **Meet the Seller:** This area, on the right side of the page, gives you information about the seller. *Know thy seller* ranks right after *caveat emptor* as a phrase that pays at eBay. As I tell you nearly a million times in this book, *read the feedback rating!* (Okay, maybe not a million — it would drive the editors bonkers.) Like any community, eBay has its share of good folks and bad folks. Your best defense is to read the seller's feedback. You'll see several things in the Meet the Seller box (as shown in Figure 4-3):

Figure 4-3:
Lots of data
on the seller
here.

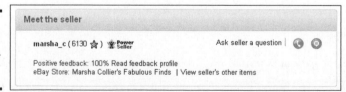

• **Seller icons:** Various icons that show the status of the seller. A varied color star reflects the feedback level of the seller. If the seller is a PowerSeller, you see the PowerSeller icon. To see if the seller has an About Me page, click on their feedback number and look for a blue-and-red *me* icon.

Book I
Chapter 4

Understanding
eBay Sales

- **Feedback score:** This number is also to the right of the seller's name in parentheses. Click the number next to the seller's ID to view his or her eBay ID card and entire feedback history. Read, read, and reread all the feedback to make sure you feel comfortable doing business with this person.

- **Positive feedback percentage:** The eBay computers calculate this figure. It's derived from all the positive and negative feedback that a user receives.

- **Member since:** You can find the date the seller joined eBay and the country in which he or she registered by clicking the Read Feedback Profile link.

- **Read Feedback Profile:** This link does the same thing as clicking the feedback score.

- **Ask Seller a Question:** Clicking this link hooks you up with eBay's e-mail system so you can ask the seller a question regarding the item. If the seller uses Skype (eBay's voice-over-Internet phone service), you may be able to click a nearby icon and chat live or call the seller with an immediate question.

- **View seller's other items:** This link takes you to a page that lists all the seller's current auctions and fixed-price sales. If the seller has an eBay store, a link to it appears here as well. I give you a step-by-step guide on how these links work later in this chapter.

✦ **Description bar:** In this section, you find the item description on the Description tab. It will state "revised" if the seller has made any revisions to the description during the run of the listing. There may also be a colorful header with links to the seller's eBay store. Also, if the seller is bonded through BuySAFE, that info will appear in the item description area. Read all this information carefully before bidding.

By clicking the Shipping and Payments tab, you'll find some other important data on the typical listing page, as shown in Figures 4-4 and 4-5.

Figure 4-4:
The shipping and handling details for the item listing.

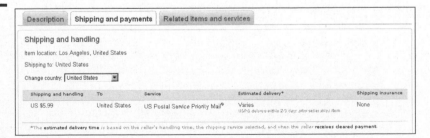

- Whether the seller is charging flat shipping or is offering more than one shipping option through a shipping calculator.

- Who pays (usually the buyer).

- Whether insurance is offered.

- Which states have to pay sales tax (if any) and the sales tax rate.

- Whether the seller is willing to ship to your area. (Sometimes sellers won't ship internationally, and they'll let you know here.)

Be sure to also check the item description for other shipping information and terms.

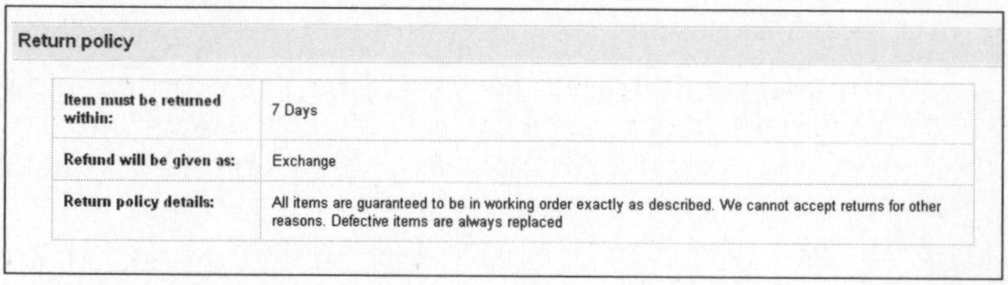

Figure 4-5:
The seller's return policy.

Return policy	
Item must be returned within:	7 Days
Refund will be given as:	Exchange
Return policy details:	All items are guaranteed to be in working order exactly as described. We cannot accept returns for other reasons. Defective items are always replaced

✦ **Item-related links:** From here you can e-mail the item to tip off a friend on a good find, get some advice from an antiques or collecting expert, or run the auction by someone who's been around the eBay block a few times and ask for strategy advice. You also have a link to a printer-friendly version of the page and an additional link you can use to ask the seller a question.

Be sure to use the Watch This Item feature when shopping around. Organization is the name of the game on eBay, especially if you plan to bid on multiple auctions while you're running auctions of your own. I figure you're in the bidding game to win, so start keeping track of items now.

Bidding on Auctions

To give you a sense of the auction process, here's a real-world example of my addictions put to the eBay test. I searched and found an item that I wanted, a "New York Pizza." After reading the seller's feedback (and skipping lunch), I wanted the item even more! None of this seller's previous buyers were unhappy with the product. As a matter of fact, no one seems able to say enough about the quality of their food. Yum! (If I buy the pizza for research for this book, it makes my pizza a tax write-off, no?)

The pizza's starting bid is $9.95, and the auction ends in over four days. So I need to observe several things about the auction. How many more are up for sale? A simple search shows that only one is up for auction. What did they sell for in the past? I run a completed auctions search, and see that they've sold for up to $20. (Shipping is free — this is as good as Domino's!)

You have to make some decisions. I have observed that these pizza auctions have an active bidding pattern, so at this early stage I bid the minimum amount just to get the item to show up as one of the items in the All Buying area of the My eBay page.

Bidding can be like games of poker. If you want to win a one-of-a-kind item, don't show your hand to other bidders. Simply mark the auction to watch. However, this strategy isn't necessary for an item that will be sure to be listed again, like the New York Pizza.

When it comes to auctions, the highest bid wins. *Remember this, please.* People are constantly boo-hooing because they've been outbid at the last minute (or *sniped,* as I explain in Chapter 6). You can't be outbid if you're the high bidder!

Automatic bidding

Bidding on eBay goes up by prescribed increments. But what if you're not able to sit in on an auction 24 hours a day, 7 days a week, upping your bid every time someone bids against you? (You mean you have a life?)

You do receive e-mail messages from eBay to let you know that you've been outbid, but eBay's computers are often busy doing other things and you might not get the notice in time to place a new competitive bid.

If you're interested in an item but you don't have the time to follow it closely from the beginning of the auction to its conclusion, you can place a *proxy bid* using eBay's automatic bidding system to place your bid for the highest amount you're willing to pay for an item — without spending your valuable time constantly following the auction.

Instead of waiting it out with eBay's automatic proxy bidding, you can also go to the seller's eBay store to see whether a duplicate item is for sale at a fixed price. Or, if the seller has set a Buy It Now price and (again) you're too impatient to wait until the end of the auction to win, click Buy It Now and go from there.

Placing a proxy bid

Before you place your proxy bid, you should give serious thought to how much you want to pay for the item. When you place an automatic bid (a proxy bid) on eBay, eBay's bidding engine places only enough of your bid to outbid the previous bidder. If there are no previous bidders and the seller has not entered a reserve price, your bid appears as the minimum auction bid until someone bids against you. Your bid increases incrementally in response to other bids against yours. Table 4-1 lists eBay's bidding increments.

Table 4-1	eBay's Bidding Increments
Current High Bid ($)	*Next Bid Increased By ($)*
0.01–0.99	0.05
1.00–4.99	0.25
5.00–24.99	0.50
25.00–99.99	1.00
100.00–249.99	2.50
250.00–499.99	5.00
500.00–999.99	10.00
1000.00–2499.99	25.00
2500.00–4999.99	50.00
5000.00 and up	100.00

No one will know how much your proxy bid is — unless someone outbids you and becomes the high bidder.

To place a proxy bid in an auction, follow these steps:

1. **Type your maximum bid in the appropriate box, or click the Place Bid button, as shown in Figure 4-6.**

   A confirmation page appears, and you have one last chance to back out.

2. **If everything is in order, click Confirm Bid. Or, if you get cold feet, click Back to Item.**

   After you've placed your bid, the next page lets you know whether you're the high bidder.

3. **If you're not the high bidder in an auction, just scroll down the acknowledgment page to the rebidding area and place another bid.**

Figure 4-6:
Enter your
maximum
bid.

Understanding reserve prices

You'll often come across auctions that have the words *Reserve not met* next to the bid amount. By placing a reserve on the auction, the seller ensures that the item will not sell until the bidding reaches the mysterious reserve figure.

If you're really interested in an item with a reserve price, e-mail the seller and politely ask how much the reserve is. Some sellers guard the reserve amount like the crown jewels; others graciously reveal the figure. The point of the reserve is to protect their investment and get qualified bidders, not waste your time.

Private auctions

Private auctions are handled the same way as plain vanilla auctions, except no one but the buyer and seller knows who the winner is. As a matter of fact, all bidders' names are hidden from investigation from anyone other than the seller.

After you've been on eBay a while, you might see the same group of names bidding on the same auctions as you. I like bidding in private auctions because they're handy for snaring items secretly, without my regular competitors knowing that I'm bidding on the item. (See Chapter 6 for bidding strategies.)

Multiple-item auctions

A multiple-item, or Dutch, auction allows a seller to auction multiple identical items. You can bid on one or as many of the item as you want. When the total number of items has been bid upon at the opening price, the next bids have to beat the previous bids by one bidding increment.

When the auction is over, all winning bidders (those with the highest bids) win their items at the lowest bid price. I know that sounds ridiculous, but that's the way it works. I'm only reporting this — it must have taken a creative mind to come up with this theory of auctions. If you want a more in-depth description of the Dutch process, go to eBay and read their description:

```
http://pages.ebay.com/help/buy/buyer-multiple.html
```

To place a bid in a Dutch auction, you must input the amount of items you want to bid on and the amount you want to bid per item.

Buying an Item Outright

Although eBay's success was built on auctions, eBay also allows sellers to handle outright sales. You can make a direct purchase

✦ By using the Buy It Now feature in an eBay auction

✦ In a fixed-price sale

✦ In one of eBay's stores

Buy It Now

You may have already looked at auctions and seen a Buy It Now price located below the minimum or starting bid amount. That little indicator means that if you want the item badly enough, and the Buy It Now price is within your budget, you can end the auction right then and there by buying the item for the stated amount.

Before using the Buy It Now option (because you think you've hit upon a bargain), be sure to check the seller's shipping charges. Many sellers set a low Buy It Now price but place a high shipping amount on the item to make up their missing profits. If the shipping amount isn't listed, be sure to e-mail the seller and ask for the shipping amount. A Buy It Now transaction is *final;* you can't withdraw your commitment to buy. It's best to know what you're getting into beforehand.

If you decide that you want to buy, scroll down to the bottom of the page and click the Buy It Now button. An eBay confirmation page appears. If you still want to make the purchase, you can click Confirm to tell eBay that you're willing to pay the purchase price. Then all you have to do is go through the checkout process and pay the seller.

You can still place a bid on an auction that has a Buy It Now option. When you do, the option to immediately buy disappears and the item goes into auction mode. If the item has a reserve, the Buy It Now option doesn't disappear until the bidding surpasses the reserve amount.

Fixed-price sales

eBay also offers items for sale without the option to bid. These fixed-price listings may be for a single item or for multiple items. When multiple items are offered (see Figure 4-7), you can buy as many as you like.

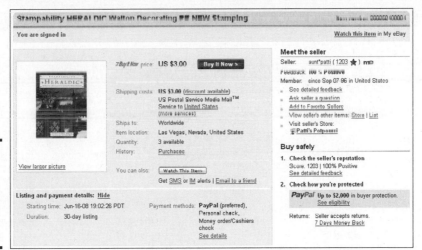

Figure 4-7: Buy one or up to three of this item in one transaction.

Shopping eBay stores

eBay stores are the secret weapon for knowledgeable eBay shoppers. First, of course, you can consistently find great deals. But you can also help small businesses make it against the behemoths. Sellers open eBay stores to make searching merchandise easier for buyers; stores also help save sellers money because sellers don't need to set up private e-commerce Web sites. Translation? Sellers can list items in their eBay stores for even lower fees, passing their savings on to you, the savvy bargain hunter.

TIP

Before you buy any item from a listing on eBay, check to see whether the seller has the small, red *stores* icon next to his or her user ID. If so, be sure to click the icon *before* you bid on the item. Most sellers run auctions for items to draw people into their eBay stores, where you may be able to find more interesting merchandise you can buy, have the seller put it in the same crate along with your auction item, and save on shipping.

You can get to the eBay Stores hub from the eBay home page by clicking the eBay Stores link under the search in the top bar or by typing the following Web address:

www.ebaystores.com

At the center of the eBay Stores hub page, as shown in Figure 4-8, you see a small group of store logos. These logos change every few minutes as eBay rotates its *anchor stores* through the area. Store owners pay a considerable amount to have their stores listed as anchor stores.

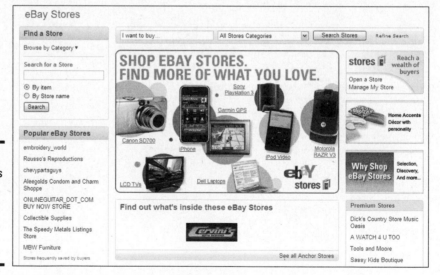

Figure 4-8: eBay Stores home page, the place to go to browse and buy.

Next to the store logos is a list of clickable links to stores. These are Popular eBay Stores. You can find more stores, including the smallest ones — the cottage-industry sellers — by browsing through the categories on the left side of the page.

Strolling through an eBay store

When you finally arrive at the eBay store of your choice, you see a page that looks similar to the one in Figure 4-9. An eBay store displays not only the items that the seller has listed in the store, but also every active auction or Buy It Now item the seller has placed on the eBay site.

Figure 4-9:
The home page for one of my favorite stores, Shoetime.

Most eBay stores have a column on the left side of the home page that displays the following:

✦ **Store search:** Below the store name banner is a column topped by a search box that allows you to search all the items this seller has for sale.

✦ **Store Categories:** eBay store owners may assign their own custom categories to the items they sell to better organize things within the store. You may click individual categories to see items in that classification from that seller.

✦ **Display:** You can decide how you'd like to view the items in the seller's store. Figure 4-10 shows you the store in gallery view and the remaining time before the auction ends.

✦ **Store policies:** This area shows the terms and conditions of the seller's auctions.

✦ **About the seller:** The last entry in this section is the seller's About Me page.

At the top and bottom of the store home page, you'll see a variety of things:

✦ **The store name:** This is the name the store owner has chosen for the store. Each eBay store has its own address that ends in the eBay store's name, like this: `www.stores.ebay.com/`*insertstorename*. For example, my store's URL is

> `www.stores.ebay.com/marshacolliersfabulousfinds.com`

Because `www.ebaystores.com` also gets you to the eBay Stores hub, an alternative URL for my store also works:

> `www.ebaystores.com/marshacolliersfabulousfinds`

✦ **Seller's user ID and feedback rating:** Some stores choose to put this on the home page; others replace it with graphics. Next to *Maintained by* are the seller's user ID and the ubiquitous feedback rating.

✦ **Add to My Favorite Stores:** If you click this link, the store is added to the favorites page in your My eBay area.

✦ **Sign up for Store newsletter.** If you'd like to receive promotional e-mail from your favorite stores, click here and e-mails can be sent to you from the seller through eBay's e-mail system. Your e-mail address will not be given to the seller, and you can discontinue the e-mails at any time.

✦ **Store logo and description:** In the middle of the page is the store's graphic logo, and to the right of that is the seller's description of the store. (This is the area that is searched when you search Stores by store name *and* description.)

Supercategories and Specialties

Aside from owning PayPal (the world's largest online payment service), eBay runs some special categories that make up a good deal of the business on eBay.

Real estate

Since the founding of our country, land has been valued as a great commodity; passed from generation to generation. As Gerald O'Hara so eloquently put it, "it's the only thing that lasts." (Remember that scene from *Gone with the Wind*?) People buy land for investment, vacations, or retirement. It's no longer common for a family to spend their entire life in one home. Real estate, although a major purchase, is becoming more and more an everyday transaction.

The smart people at eBay are sly trend-spotters, so they opened an official category for real estate transactions in the fall of 2000. You can access eBay's Real Estate category through the category link on the left side of the home page or by going directly to

`http://www.ebayrealestate.com`

Because substantial legal restrictions are involved in real estate transactions, sellers can choose to list their properties either as auctions or in the form of advertisements, depending on the laws in their areas.

When you participate in a listing that is in an ad format, you do not place bids. At the bottom of the item's description page is a form for you to fill out that's sent to the seller. After the seller receives this information, he or she can contact you, and the two of you may negotiate privately. When you browse the Residential Homes category, a small ad icon in the Bids column indicates items listed as advertisements. Most residential home sales are handled in this manner. Land and timeshares are typically sold in the auction format.

Because of a wide variety of laws governing the intricacies and legalities in real estate transactions, the auction format may be nonbinding. Before getting involved in any real estate transactions on eBay, I suggest you read the official rules, which you can find on the following page:

```
pages.ebay.com/help/policies/real-estate.html
```

Cruising eBay Motors

Buying a car — that's one purchase I don't enjoy making. Please don't misunderstand. I love cars and have a personal attachment to every car I've owned. It's just that each time I'm approached by a car salesperson, I get intimidated. The minute the salesperson says "I've got to check with my sales manager to see if I can do that," I know I'm a goner. And when I've finally decided on the car model I want, I still have to face *the deal*, when the finance manager tries to sell me warranties, alarms, and extras that I never wanted or needed. I feel the need to run out of the dealership — and I usually do.

If this feeling is familiar to you, I would like to introduce you to the sweetest deal of the 21st century, eBay Motors (see Figure 4-10). eBay Motors is the largest auto mall in the universe and is consistently ranked the No. 1 automotive site on the Web by Nielsen//NetRatings.

For some of us, eBay Motors is a magnificent fantasy site. I have a friend who browses the Volkswagen bus category; his eyes glaze over with hope and awe as he reads each listing. I'm sure he's reliving his hippie days of the late '60s. Another friend reads the Ferrari and Lamborghini listings; he pooh-poohs all the aftermarket changes to the classics. My best friend checks out the vintage Thunderbirds and pictures herself as Suzanne Somers flirting with the guys in *American Graffiti*. Then of course there's my fantasy car; the buttercup yellow Rolls-Royce Corniche convertible driven by Teensy in *Ya-Ya Sisterhood*. (I've yet to find one on eBay in that color — but then again, I couldn't afford one if I did find it!)

Figure 4-10:
eBay
Motors
home page.

Many of the cars on eBay Motors are private-party sales, bank cars (repossessions), and cars that have been cherry-picked by wholesalers and dealer overstocks. In addition, professional car dealers sell rare, hard-to-find cars to a marketplace that draws between 4 and 5 million visitors per month. You can't get that many people through the door at a local dealership! Dealers put up the rare colors and limited-edition vehicles because this *is* an auction site — the rarer an item, the more likely bidders are to get excited. The more excited bidders are, the more they lose their heads — and the higher the price goes.

With an average of seven to eight bids per sale, eBay Motors is a competitive environment for the most desirable cars. Dealers can sell cars for less on eBay because it costs them less to sell. (They don't have to pay the finance manager to twist your arm to buy the extras.)

You can enter the eBay Motors site in two ways. Click the eBay Motors link at the top left of any eBay page, or go to

www.ebaymotors.com

For more on eBay Motors bidding strategies, check out Chapter 6.

Finding more than cars

The truly amazing part about eBay Motors is that it has more than just the usual cars and vans. In fact, the rule seems to be that if it has an engine, you'll find it here. Here's a description of the Other Vehicles categories:

✔ **ATVs:** Within the ATV subcategory of Powersports, you'll find a wide selection of new and used 4x4s and 2x4s, three-wheelers and four-wheelers. I even found a few six-wheel amphibious vehicles! Bidding in this category is active and the items move quickly.

✔ **Aircraft:** Anything that flies can be found here, from hot-air balloons to military trainer jets. Browsing this category is amazing. Who could imagine that with a click of your mouse (and enough money) you could own your own Bell helicopter or Gulfstream jet? If you've ever dreamt of taking up flying, this might be the category to get your hobby started!

✔ **Boats:** This category was so full that I got seasick just browsing! It has its own subcategories of Fishing Boats, Personal Watercraft (Sea-Doo, Yamaha, Kawasaki, and so on), Powerboats, Sailboats, and Other (kayaks, canoes, pontoons, tenders, and dinghies). I know boats, and I saw some great deals in this category. There were some beautiful Bass boats and Boston Whalers at incredible prices. A dozen or so Bayliners caught my eye, especially the 47-foot Pilot House Motoryacht with a starting bid of $290,000.00 (sigh). It was also nice to see a wide selection of prices for sailboats. With some time spent shopping in this category, you can find just about anything you want within your price range.

✔ **Buses:** No kidding. You want to start your own bus line? Here's the place to find the buses — and it seems that plenty of people are interested in them! There's active bidding on old school buses in this category (and I thought the American family was getting smaller!).

✔ **Commercial trucks:** Since commercial trucks are something I know jack about, I went to some experts who browsed the site and examined the deals. Here's their review for those in the know. The items are good quality and of the type they'd like to find at commercial truck auctions. They tell me the prices are bargains and that they'll be visiting the site regularly from now on — sounds like a good recommendation to me!

✔ **Scooters and minibikes:** Aside from what you'd expect to find here, this is the home for beautiful vintage and new Vespa motor scooters.

✔ **Snowmobiles:** I've never lived in a snowy part of the country, so I can only imagine how much fun these bad boys are. You'll see everything from top-of-the-line new ones to gently used private sales.

✔ **Other:** How about a 1947 Coca-Cola vending truck — complete with fountain, cotton-candy machine, and propane-powered hot-dog cooker! Sounds like a carnival on wheels! Well, okay, it doesn't run, but hey — it's only $3000! There's also a Shelby Cobra kit, with no motor or tranny, but you need a hobby, don't you? I also found a Think Neighbor electric vehicle; a sandrail dune buggy four-seater; go-karts, and car haulers. There's nothing you can't find on eBay!

Supercategories

When it comes to unique shopping, the supercategories are the place to go. On the eBay home page, take a look at the long list of links on the left. Below the major category-listing links are a few links to even more eBay special areas.

These specialized categories have been put together by the eBay gurus to encompass areas of interest that cover more than one category. On the eBay home page, you'll currently find the following big three (eBay will no doubt add more in the future):

✦ Business & Industrial

✦ Collectibles

✦ Giving Works (Charity)

These supercategories come in handy when you're looking for cross-category merchandise.

Business & Industrial

If you're looking for anything to outfit a business, Business & Industrial category is the place to go. Shown in Figure 4-11, it covers everything from tractor parts to welding equipment to computers. You can browse the sub-category of your choice and see what's available.

Figure 4-11: The Business & Industrial category covers a varied group of items.

However, if you need a particular brand name or item, you may find it easier through eBay's search. For professional tips on eBay's search, check out Chapter 6.

Giving Works: Giving back to nonprofits

Many charitable organizations are selling their wares on eBay to raise money for their fine work (see Figure 4-12). You can get some rare and unusual items here, such as the annual NBC *Today Show* Green Room autograph book. This one-of-a-kind book has signatures and notes from the famous guests of the *Today Show*. One of these Green Room books sold for $87,500! The superhot auction was for lunch with Warren Buffet (the CEO of Berkshire Hathaway); it raised $250,000.

eBay has partnered with the leader in online charitable auctions, MissionFish, which has been helping organizations turn donations into cash through online auctions since 2000. MissionFish works with regular eBay sellers to raise money for nonprofit organizations.

Figure 4-12: Do a little shopping while doing some good.

When you list an item on eBay, you can choose a nonprofit from a certified list and designate a percentage of the proceeds (from 20 to 100%) to donate. The item appears in the search results with a Charity Auction icon. When you go to the item page, you'll see the name of the nonprofit, some information about it, and the percentage of the final bid that the seller is donating. You can search eBay for your favorite nonprofits by name.

Chapter 5: Checking Out the Seller and Leaving Feedback

In This Chapter

✔ **Giving feedback**

✔ **Reading eBay's DSR System**

✔ **Checking out the seller's reputation**

✔ **Comparing items**

✔ **Playing it safe with buyer protection programs**

*W*hen you're shopping on eBay, you're faced with hundreds of items, perhaps even hundreds of listings for the same item. How do you decide where to place your order or your bid? In this chapter, I show you the tools on eBay that guide you to a safe and positive transaction.

Understanding and Giving Feedback

One of eBay's strong suits has been the formation of a sense of community through its use of message boards, chats, and feedback. Many experts say the reason eBay has succeeded where dozens of other dot-com auction sites have failed is that eBay has always paid close attention to the needs of its users.

Even in the early days, the concept was clear. Pierre and his employees figured that if users complained openly (for all other members to see), feedback would be more genuine — not so much *flaming* as *constructive*. "Do unto others as you'd have them do" prevailed as a philosophy; above all else, Pierre encouraged buyers and sellers to give each other the benefit of the doubt and to conduct themselves professionally.

It soon became clear to eBay's three employees that they did not have time to adjudicate member disputes. Thus the feedback system was born. But the *pièce de résistance* of feedback policy, the part that makes eBay work, is the fact that Pierre and his staff encouraged users to give *positive* feedback as often as they give negative or neutral feedback.

The benefits of the feedback policy are immediately clear. Before even placing a bid with a seller, a buyer (you) can check the experience other eBay buyers have had doing business with this seller. You can see whether items in a seller's previous auctions shipped quickly, whether items were packed carefully, whether communication was clear and frequent, and so on. You now have more information about an eBay seller then you have when you walk into a new store in your neighborhood!

The types of feedback

Every eBay member has a feedback rating. Buyers rate sellers (more on that below), and sellers rate buyers — no one is immune. Although sellers can no longer leave negative or neutral feedback for a buyer, a seller still might comment on how quickly you paid for an item, how well you communicated, or how you reacted to a problem.

Leaving feedback for the seller comes in three exciting flavors:

✦ **Positive feedback:** Someone once said, "All you have is your reputation." Reputation is what makes eBay function. If the transaction works well, you get positive feedback — and whenever it's warranted, you should give it right back.

✦ **Negative feedback**: If there's a glitch (for instance, it takes six months to get your *Charlie's Angels* lunchbox, or the seller substitutes a rusty Thermos for the one you bid on, or you never get the item), you have the right — some would say *obligation* — to leave the seller negative feedback.

✦ **Neutral feedback:** You can leave neutral feedback if you feel so-so about a specific transaction. It's the middle-of-the-road comment that's useful when, for example, you bought an item that has a little more wear and tear on it than the seller indicated, but you still like it and want to keep it.

Keep in mind that a Neutral feedback will affect the seller's feedback percentage (and reputation). The feedback percentage (next to the feedback number) is calculated based on the total number of feedback ratings received in the last 12 months. This does *not* include repeat feedback from the same buyer in the same week.

Leaving feedback for a buyer isn't quite as colorful. A seller can leave only Positive feedback for a transaction — or none at all. If I've dealt with a particularly difficult buyer, there is a good chance that I won't leave any feedback at all.

You're not required to leave feedback, but because it's the benchmark by which all eBay users are judged, you should *always* leave feedback comments whether you're buying or selling. Every time you complete a transaction — the minute the package arrives safely and you've checked the contents, whether you're a seller or a buyer — you should go to eBay and post your feedback.

The magic feedback number

You know how they say you are what you eat? At eBay, you are only as good as your feedback says you are. Your feedback is made up of comments — good, bad, or neutral — that people leave about you (and you leave about others). In effect, people are commenting on your overall professionalism. (Even if you're an eBay hobbyist with no thought of using eBay professionally, a little business-like courtesy can ease your transactions with everyone.) These comments are the basis for your eBay reputation. You wouldn't be caught dead in a store that has a lousy reputation, so why on Earth would you want to do business on the Internet with someone who has a lousy reputation?

When you get your first feedback, the number that appears next to your user ID is your feedback rating, which follows you everywhere you go on eBay, even if you change your user ID or e-mail address. It sticks to you like glue.

Click the number next to any user ID and get a complete look at the user's feedback profile. When you do, here are some points to recognize about the user's magic feedback number:

✦ **This number is a *net figure*** of the positive and negative comments that were left for that eBay user. For example, if you get 50 positive comments and 49 negative comments, your feedback rating is 1.

For every positive comment you receive, you get a plus 1. For every negative comment, you get a minus 1. Negative comments deduct from your total of positive comments, thereby lowering the number beside your user ID. Theoretically, if you play nice, your feedback rating grows as you spend more time using eBay.

Anyone with a –4 rating has his or her eBay membership terminated. And don't make automatic assumptions just because someone has a high feedback rating. You should always click the number after the name to double-check the person's eBay ID card. Even if someone has a total of 1000 feedback messages, 250 of them *could* be negative.

✦ **This number shows more** than how good a customer or seller you are. As it grows, the feedback number also tells how experienced you are at doing business on the site.

✦ **This number ignores neutral comments.** A neutral comment is neither negative nor positive; it doesn't change the number that appears after your user ID. Neutral comments are used most often when someone is not completely happy with a transaction, but not so unhappy that they choose to destroy someone else's reputation over the situation.

eBay riddle: When is more than 1 still 1? Gotcha, huh? The answer is, when you get more than one feedback message from the same person in the same week. Confused? This example should help: You can sell one person 100 different items, but even if the buyer gives you a glowing review 100 times, your feedback rating doesn't increase by 100. In this case, the other 99 feedback comments appear in your feedback profile, but your rating increases by only 1. There's something else: Say you sell to the same eBay user twice. The user can give you positive feedback in one case and negative feedback in another case — neutralizing your feedback by netting you a 0 feedback rating from that person. eBay set up the system this way to keep things honest.

Members may affect your score by one point per week. If they leave you great feedback for multiple transactions spread from one week to another — you will get credit (hopefully) for two positives. To get credit for selling multiple items to one bidder, the bidder must leave feedback. For feedback purposes, eBay defines a week as Monday through Sunday, Pacific Time.

Giving Detailed Star Ratings Properly

In addition to a feedback comment and rating (positive, negative, or neutral), buyers can leave detailed seller ratings, too. After the buyer types a comment, he or she is prompted to rate the seller with one to five stars on four different factors of the transaction. Figure 5-1 shows the specific rating factors, and Table 5-1 outlines what the stars mean.

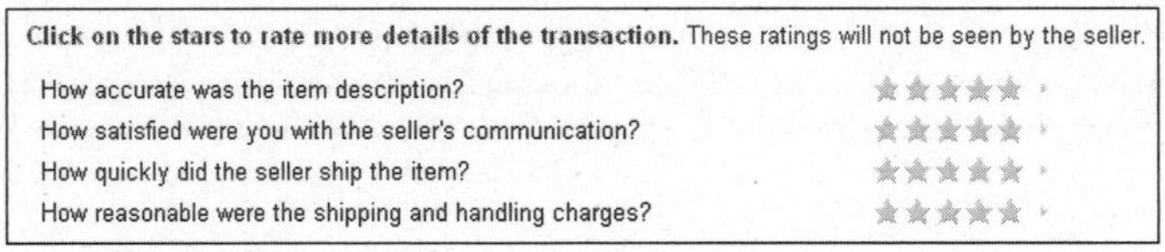

Figure 5-1: eBay Detailed Star Rating system.

> **Click on the stars to rate more details of the transaction.** These ratings will not be seen by the seller.
>
> How accurate was the item description?   ★★★★★
> How satisfied were you with the seller's communication?   ★★★★★
> How quickly did the seller ship the item?   ★★★★★
> How reasonable were the shipping and handling charges?   ★★★★★

Table 5-1	What the DSR Stars Mean	
Rating Question	*# of Stars = Meaning*	*In the Real World*
How accurate was the item's description?	1 = Very inaccurate 2 = Inaccurate 3 = Neither inaccurate or accurate 4 = Accurate 5 = Very accurate	In Marsha's world, the item was either described right or wrong — to me, there is no in-between. So when I rate a seller, the item is either is as advertised, or it isn't.

Rating Question	# of Stars = Meaning	In the Real World
How satisfied were you with the seller's communication?	1 = Very unsatisfied 2 = Unsatisfied 3 = Neither unsatisfied or satisfied 4 = Satisfied 5 = Very satisfied	As I buyer, I lean more with being very satisfied that I got enough communication from the seller, or not. If I get one e-mail, I'm usually satisfied. But if I haven't heard from a seller until the item reaches my door, I'm definitely rating in the 2-star range.
How quickly did the seller ship the item?	1 = Very slowly 2 = Slowly 3 = Neither slowly or quickly 4 = Quickly 5 = Very quickly	Now, here I have another issue: As a buyer, you need to check the postmark on the package you receive. If the seller ships the next day or the next — you've got to click 5 (Very Quickly), no matter how long the postal service took to get it there.
How reasonable were the shipping and handling charges?	1 = Very unreasonable 2 = Unreasonable 3 = Neither unreasonable or reasonable 4 = Reasonable 5 = Very reasonable	When I purchase an item, I know what the shipping cost will be. The only surprise here is when you get an item in a small envelope and you've paid $9.00 for shipping — or if you paid for Priority Mail and it comes in another class of service. This is, to me, pretty black-and-white. It's either going to be reasonable or not.

Here are some other items to keep in mind when you're deciding on the Detailed Star Ratings for sellers:

✦ **Shipping takes time:** As a buyer. you can choose Ground or Priority Mail (for the most part), and you've got to realize that Ground shipping can take up to 10 days. This isn't the seller's fault. So before leaving this rating, make sure to always check the postmark or the date on the shipping label.

✦ **Shipping costs money:** Sellers have to add a little charge to cover the costs of tape, boxes, and packing materials. As a buyer, you've got to keep that in mind. If you are unfamiliar with postage rates, you should also know that a package costs a lot more to ship across the country than to ship to the next state. So do a little homework and evaluate shipping costs before you buy. If the shipping is too high, go to another seller.

✦ **Ratings affect the seller's costs:** If your seller is a PowerSeller, you should also know that your star ratings affect the fees he or she pays to eBay. Being a good seller (with high DSRs) can save as much as 20% on Final Values Fees, so your rating is a very serious matter. Visit Book VIII, Chapter 5 for the lowdown on how these ratings affect the PowerSeller's pocketbook.

Becoming a Star

Yes, eBay *loves* the stars. When you first join eBay, it seems like everyone on eBay has a star next to the user ID except for you. It's so unfair isn't it? Well, not really. The stars of many colors are awarded based on the amount of your feedback rating. When you receive a feedback rating of 10, you get a bright new gold star (just like in school).

You may notice stars of other colors — even shooting stars; Table 5-2 gives you the lowdown on what each star color represents.

Table 5-2	Star Colors Reflect Feedback Rating
Star	*Feedback Rating*
Gold star	10 to 49
Blue star	50 to 99
Turquoise star	100 to 499
Purple star	500 to 999
Red star	1000 to 4999
Green star	5000 to 9999
Gold shooting star	10,000 to 24,999
Turquoise shooting star	25,000 to 49,999
Purple shooting star	50,000 to 99,999
Red shooting star	100,000 and higher

Once you have a star and you reach a higher level, I assure you that you will get a silly tingly feeling of accomplishment. Very silly, yes, but it's all part of being an active member of the eBay community.

Leaving Feedback with Finesse

Writing feedback well takes some practice. It isn't a matter of saying things; it's a matter of saying *only the appropriate things*. Think carefully about what you want to say — because once you submit feedback, it stays with the person for the duration of his or her eBay career. I think you should always leave feedback, especially at the end of a transaction, although doing so isn't mandatory. Think of leaving feedback as voting in an election: If you don't leave feedback, you can't complain about lousy service.

eBay says to make feedback "factual and emotionless." You won't go wrong if you comment on the details (either good or bad) of the transaction. If you have any questions about what eBay says about feedback, click the Community link in the navigation bar and on the resulting page click the Feedback Forum link at the top of the page.

In the Feedback Forum, you can perform the following feedback-related tasks:

✦ **Leave Feedback:** Here, you see all pending feedback for all transactions within the past 90 days — the ones for which you haven't left feedback. Fill them in, one at a time. Then, with one click, you can leave as many as 25 feedback comments at once.

✦ **View a Feedback profile:** Clicking here allows you to type any eBay member's ID to see that person's feedback profile (the same as if you clicked the number next to the member's name).

✦ **Reply to Feedback received:** If you've received feedback that you'd like to respond to, click this link.

✦ **Follow up to Feedback left:** Here, you may also leave follow-up feedback after the initial feedback should situations change.

✦ **Make Feedback Public or Private:** This is where you can decide to show your feedback profile to the public or keep it to yourself. Remember, if you make your feedback profile private, you will hinder your future business on eBay.

On this page, you also have more links that explain the ins and out of the eBay feedback system. Here are the details on a few:

✦ **Feedback Help:** A link that talks you to an exclusive help area for feedback questions.

✦ **Feedback Policies:** Learn about Feedback policies and the various forms of Feedback Abuse — and how eBay deals with them.

✦ **Feedback FAQs:** Answers to frequently asked questions about how to handle feedback — and how buyers can change their knee-jerk negative or neutral feedback entries to something more accurate after sober reflection.

Fetching feedback facts

How to get positive feedback

If you're selling, here's how to get a good reputation:

- ✔ Establish contact with the buyer (pronto!) after the auction ends.

- ✔ After you've received payment, send out the item quickly.

- ✔ Make sure that your item is exactly the way you described it.

- ✔ Package the item well and ship it with care.

- ✔ React quickly and appropriately to problems — for example, the item's lost or damaged in the mail or the buyer is slow in paying.

If you're buying, try these good-rep tips:

- ✔ Send your payment fast.

- ✔ Keep in touch via e-mail with the seller.

- ✔ Work with the seller to resolve any problems in a courteous manner.

How to get negative feedback:

If you're selling, here's what to do to tarnish your name big time:

- ✔ Tell a major fib in the item description. (Defend truth, justice, and legitimate creative writing — see Book III.)

- ✔ Take the money but "forget" to ship the item.

- ✔ Package the item poorly so that it ends up smashed, squashed, or vaporized during shipping. (To avoid this pathetic fate, see Book VII.)

If you're buying, here's how to make your status a serious mess:

- ✔ Bid on an item, win the auction, and never respond to the seller.

- ✔ String the seller out with constant claims of "the check is in the mail."

- ✔ Ask the seller for a refund because you just don't like the item.

In the real world (at least in the modern American version of it), anybody can sue anybody else for slander or libel; this fact holds true on the Internet, too. Be careful not to make any comments that could be libelous or slanderous. eBay is not responsible for your actions, so if you're sued because of negative feedback (or anything else you've written), you're on your own. The best way to keep yourself safe is to stick to the facts and don't get personal.

If you're angry, take a huge breather *before* you type your complaints and click the Leave Comment button. If you're convinced that negative feedback is necessary, try a cooling-off period before you send comments. Wait an hour or a day and then see whether you feel the same. Nasty feedback based on emotion can make you look vindictive, even if what you're saying is true.

Safety tips for giving feedback

And speaking of safety features you should know about feedback, you may want to study up on these:

✦ Remember that feedback, whether good or bad, is *sticky*. eBay won't remove your feedback comment if you change your mind later. Be sure of your facts and carefully consider what you want to say.

✦ Before you leave feedback, read what other people had to say about that person. See whether what you're thinking is in line with the comments others have left.

✦ Your feedback comment can be left as long as the transaction remains on the eBay server. This is usually within 60 days of the end of the auction. After 60 days have passed, you may still be able to leave feedback if you have the transaction number.

✦ Your comment can be a maximum of 80 letters, which is really short when you have a lot to say. Before you start typing, organize your thoughts and use common abbreviations to save precious space.

✦ Before posting negative feedback, try to resolve the problem by e-mail or telephone. You may discover that your reaction to the transaction is based on a misunderstanding that can be easily resolved.

✦ eBay users generally want to make each other happy, so use negative feedback *only as a last desperate resort.*

If, as a buyer, you leave a negative or neutral comment that you later regret, you can change it. You can go back to follow up and leave an explanation or a more positive comment and change the initial feedback. If you write a nice e-mail to the other person in the transaction and are able to solve a problem, make the change. See the "eBay will consider removing feedback if . . ." sidebar.

The ways to leave feedback

Several ways are available to leave feedback comments:

✦ If you're on the user's feedback page, click the Leave Feedback link; the Leave Feedback page appears.

✦ In the Buy — Won or the Sold area of your My eBay page, click the Leave Feedback link next to the transaction.

✦ Go to the listing and click the Leave Feedback link.

✦ In the Feedback Forum, click the Leave Feedback link to see a list of all your completed auctions from the last 60 days for which you haven't left feedback.

✦ On your My eBay page, scroll down and on the left side you will see the Shortcuts heading. This will take you to your pending Feedback list.

✦ Click the Community link, in the main navigation bar, and then click eBay Feedback Forum. On the next page that appears, click the Leave Feedback link.

TIP

Mincing words: The at-a-glance guide to keeping feedback short

eBay likes to keep things simple. If you want to compliment, complain, or take the middle road, you have to do it in 80 characters or less. That means your comment needs to be short and sweet (or short and sour if it's negative, or sweet and sour if you're mixing drinks or ordering Chinese food). If you have a lot to say but you're stumped about how to say it, here are a few examples for any occasion. String them together or mix and match!

Positive feedback:

✐ Very professional

✐ Quick e-mail response

✐ Fast service

✐ A+++

✐ Good communication

✐ Exactly as described

✐ Highly recommended

✐ Smooth transaction

✐ Would deal with again

✐ An asset to eBay

✐ I'll be back!

Negative feedback:

✐ Never responded

✐ Never paid for item

✐ Check bounced, never made good

✐ Beware track record

✐ Item not as described

Neutral feedback:

✐ Slow to ship but item as described

✐ Item not as described but seller made good

✐ Paid w/MO (money order) after check bounced

✐ Poor communication but item came OK

eBay will consider removing feedback if . . .

Only under certain, special circumstances will eBay remove feedback:

✔ eBay is served with a court order stating that the feedback in question is slanderous, libelous, defamatory, or otherwise illegal. eBay will also accept a settlement agreement from a resolved lawsuit submitted by both attorneys and signed by both parties.

✔ The feedback in question has no relation to eBay — such as comments about transactions outside eBay or personal comments about users.

✔ The feedback contains a link to another page, picture, or JavaScript.

✔ The feedback is comprised of profane or vulgar language.

✔ The feedback contains any personal identifying information about a user.

✔ The feedback refers to any investigation, whether by eBay or a law-enforcement organization.

✔ The feedback is left by a user who supplied fraudulent contact information when registering on eBay.

✔ The feedback is left by a person who can be identified as a minor.

✔ The feedback is left by a user as harassment.

✔ The feedback is intended for another user, when eBay has been informed of the situation and the same feedback has been left for the appropriate user.

eBay used to permit Buyers and Sellers to mutually withdraw feedback once they agreed the transaction went OK. This is no longer the policy. To check on the current feedback removal policies, go to

```
http://pages.ebay.com/help/
    feedback/remove-withdraw.
    html
http://pages.ebay.com/help/
    policies/feedback-abuse-
    withdrawal.html
```

To leave feedback for a seller, follow these steps:

1. **Enter the required information.**

   Note that your item number is usually filled in, but if you're placing feedback from the user's feedback page, you need to have the number at hand.

2. **Choose whether you want your feedback to be positive, negative, or neutral.**

3. **Type your feedback comment.**

4. **Fill in your star ratings by clicking the stars next to the questions (as I discuss in the earlier section, "Giving Properly Detailed Star Ratings").**

5. **Click the Leave Feedback button.**

You Have the Last Word — Responding to Feedback

After reading feedback you've received from others, you may feel compelled to respond. If the feedback is negative, you may want to defend yourself. If it's positive, you may want to say thank you.

Do not confuse *responding* to feedback with *leaving* feedback. Responding does not change the other user's feedback rating; it merely adds your response below the feedback comment in your own feedback profile.

To respond to feedback, follow these steps:

1. **Click the Leave Feedback link of your My eBay page, to the scroll to the bottom of the next page and click the Feedback Forum link.**

    You're transported to the Feedback Forum page.

2. **Click the Reply to Feedback Received link.**

3. **When you find the feedback you want to respond to, click the Reply link.**

4. **Type your response.**

You have another recourse if, as a seller, you receive negative or neutral feedback. eBay's Feedback Revision policy enables buyers to change feedback rating, comments, and DSRs under certain circumstances. First, the seller must address the cause for negative or neutral feedback to the buyer's satisfaction. Then, the seller can send a Feedback Revision request to the buyer (with a limit of 5 requests per 1000 feedback earned during a 12-month period), and the buyer has the option to accept or decline that request. For how-to information on feedback revision, go to

pages.ebay.com/help/feedback/revision-request.html

Scrutinizing a Seller's Reputation

You've finally found an item you'd like to buy. Don't place that bid just yet! Studying the seller's feedback will supply you with a good deal of information about the reputation of your potential trading partner.

The more expensive your transaction, the more intense your investigation may need to be. An unblemished feedback rating may not be as significant on a $9 purchase as it is for a $200 purchase.

I want you to be thoroughly educated in how the feedback system works. I'm not trying to be bossy. I'm just saying that buyers and sellers (especially those of us who have been using eBay for several years) take this stuff seriously. If you're just a dabbler, however, I can understand why you might want to opt for the "light" version of the eBay feedback system and save the high-octane rendition of a feedback investigation for when you decide to buy that yacht or the British crown jewels.

Conducting a "light" seller examination

As you look at the items for sale on eBay (both in auctions and in fixed-price sales), you'll notice that along with every auction listing you can find information about the seller in eBay's Seller Information box. Figure 5-2 shows you four Meet the Seller boxes; notice the differences in their reputations.

The Meet the Seller box gives you a very small picture of the seller's feedback reputation. It only shows the seller's ID and feedback rating, including his or her star award level. (Check out Chapter 4 to get the lowdown on the Meet the Seller box.)

Privacy in feedback may not be a good thing

I believe in the adage, "Keep your business private," except when it refers to feedback. In your eBay dealings, you may come upon a seller with private or hidden feedback. Most users show their comments, and eBay's default setting is for public viewing of feedback. This way, everyone at eBay can read all about you.

If you want to make your feedback a private matter, you need to go to the Feedback Forum (click the Feedback Forum link on the bottom of the eBay home page or from the Community link in the navigation bar). On the resulting page, click the Make Your Feedback Profile Public or Private link, and you'll see the page shown here.

> **Make Your Feedback Profile Public or Private**
>
> Your Feedback Profile is a valuable asset that helps you earn the trust of other eBay members
>
> ⦿ **Make your Feedback Profile public**
>   Keeping your Feedback Profile public increases the likelihood that members will trade with you.
>
> ◯ **Make your Feedback Profile private**
>   If you make your Feedback Profile private, your Feedback comments will be hidden from other users. This may decrease the chance that other members will want to do business with you.
>
>   **Note:** If you choose to make your Feedback Profile private, you will not be able to sell items.
>
> [Save] Cancel

Hiding your feedback comments is a bad idea. You want people to know that you're trustworthy; being honest and upfront is the way to go. If you hide your feedback, people may suspect that you're covering up bad things. It's in your best interest to let the spotlight shine on your feedback history.

Your feedback is your reputation, your money, and your experience as an eBay member. Keep in mind that all three are always linked.

Figure 5-2:
Meet the
seller boxes
from four
different
sellers,
including
me.

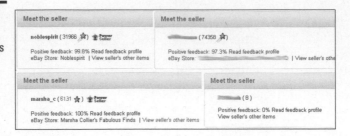

Consider a quick glance at the Meet the Seller box to be the lightweight version of a feedback investigation. A perfunctory glance at this box might be
okay if your purchase is for an item that's worth a few dollars to you — and
if the seller's information box shows you 99% to 100% positive feedback (as
in two of the four examples in Figure 5-1). However, if the Meet the Seller box
looks closer to the second or fourth example, and you're looking at a pricier
item, it's time for a more thorough analysis.

Even though the seller in the second example has a high overall feedback
rating, the percentage of positive comments is a little lower, and suggests
that further examination might be a good idea.

Making a full-scale seller investigation

When you consider buying a more expensive item, be sure to click the
seller's feedback number when you visit the auction-item page. Clicking the
number will show you the member profile: the Feedback Summary and the
DSR ratings, shown in Figure 5-3 and 5-4.

Figure 5-3:
A sample
member
profile.

After you click the feedback number, you should examine some important
details if you want to be a savvy, security-minded shopper.

Feedback summary

On the left side of the page you will see Recent Feedback Ratings and on the right, the seller's member profile. You will see the counts of feedback comments divided by time periods: 1 month, 6 months, and 12 months. Note the following significant entries:

✦ **Positive Feedback comments:** You may notice that the *actual* number of positive comments is higher than the positive figure. This is because every eBay community member can comment only once on another member and have it count in the feedback rating. (The net rating was previously based on comments from *unique* users.)

For example, when you buy an item from me and we leave each other feedback (glowingly positive, I'm sure), and then next month I buy something from you, the feedback we leave on the second transaction (again, glowingly positive) these days it not only feels good, it counts. In the old days, it didn't count toward our total feedback rating (though it did appear on the feedback summary page). Since then eBay has changed that policy; all feedback entries count as long as they're left in different weeks.

✦ **Neutral comments:** Neutral comments are usually left when a party wasn't thrilled with the transaction but nothing happened that was bad enough to leave a dreaded, reputation-ruining negative comment. You may also notice that some long-time eBay users have neutral comments that were previously converted from users no longer registered.

For a very short while, eBay had a policy that when a member was suspended (yes, members do get suspended) or the member chose to cancel his or her eBay membership, eBay turned all the feedback that member ever left or received (whether it was positive or negative) into neutral feedback.

This policy didn't last long because the eBay members put up such a fuss that eBay listened and stopped the practice. Unfortunately, eBay didn't rescind the neutrals that had been put in place.

✦ **Negative comments:** The number of negative comments may also vary, just as the positives do, for the same reason.

Detailed Seller Ratings

This is where all those little stars you place when leaving Feedback show up. You'll be able to see how many ratings have been left for each category and where the Average Rating lies, as in Figure 5-4.

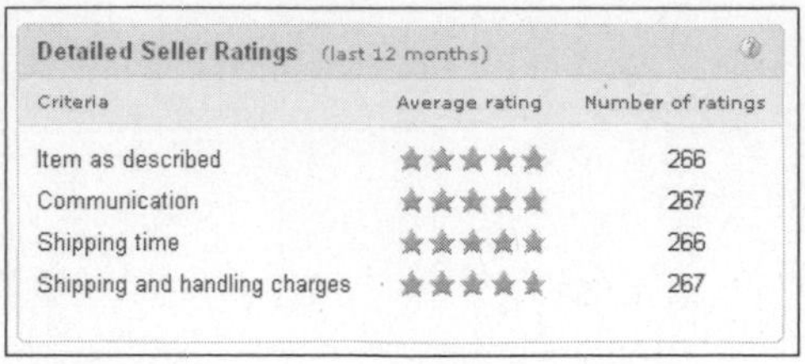

Figure 5-4:
The
Feedback
Profile
Detailed
Seller rating
stars.

Detailed Seller Ratings (last 12 months)		
Criteria	Average rating	Number of ratings
Item as described	★★★★★	266
Communication	★★★★★	267
Shipping time	★★★★★	266
Shipping and handling charges	★★★★★	267

Member profile

Also part of this comprehensive feedback page is the eBay member profile, which carries historic information about the member: Think of your feedback profile as an eBay report card. Your goal is to get straight As — in this case, all positive feedback. Unlike a real report card, you don't have to bring it home to be signed; here's what you find on it:

✦ **User ID:** The eBay member's nickname appears, followed by a number in parentheses — the net number of the positive feedback comments the person has received, minus any negative feedback comments.

✦ **Member links box:** This area contains data and links. The important piece of data is the date the person signed up as a member of the eBay community. Below that are the links: the country from which the seller is registered, links to the member's eBay store (if the seller has one, of course), his or her other auctions (where you can see whether the seller is experienced in selling the type of item you're looking to buy), his or her ID history (where you can view the seller's past user IDs, if any), and the seller's About Me page.

✦ **Contact member:** Click the Contact Member button to view an e-mail form allowing you to send an e-mail to the member through eBay's e-mail system.

✦ **Recent ratings:** In a snapshot, you can see the seller's recent eBay history for the past month, six months, and twelve months. This data is useful because often the last couple of months' transactions tell the tale. If a previously reliable eBay seller has decided to join the Dark Side, here is where the evidence will show up first. A number of new negative comments from different buyers constitute a definite danger sign (even if the seller has an overall high rating)!

If the last few transactions are negative in the recent reviews, think twice about doing further business with the seller, but that doesn't mean you should count the seller out completely. If the item is *really* a must-have, click the ID of the person (or persons) who left the negative feedback and ask politely for details so you can make your own decisions. Sadly, many buyers leave negative feedback for a seller before giving the seller an opportunity to make things right, so by getting the details, you can make your own decisions.

✦ **Bid retractions:** A history of bidding on items and then changing one's mind is a danger signal more for sellers than for buyers. As a buyer, you may, under certain circumstances, retract your bid (see Chapter 6). Just note that each time you retract your bid from an auction, the retraction shows up in this area. Sellers often check this area to determine a bidder's reliability.

Be careful when you retract a bid. All bids on eBay are binding, but under what eBay calls exceptional circumstances, you may retract bids — sparingly. Here are the circumstances in which it's okay to retract a bid:

✦ If you've mistakenly put in the wrong bid amount — say, $100 instead of $10

✦ If the seller adds to his or her description after you've placed your bid, and the change considerably affects the item

✦ If you can't authenticate the seller's identity by reaching him or her by phone or by e-mail

✦ If a bid has been placed in your name by someone other than you

You can't retract a bid just because you found the item elsewhere for less, or you changed your mind, or you decided that you can't afford the item.

Reading feedback reviews

Scrolling down the feedback history page, you'll be able to read the actual reviews left by other eBay members. In Figure 5-5, you'll see a sample of my current feedback. You see each the member's user ID, along with his or her feedback rating and comment.

Check the seller's About Me page

If you notice that the seller has a small Me icon next to his or her user ID, click the icon to learn more about the seller. Every eBay member may have his or her own home page on eBay called the About Me page (you can have one, too). The About Me page is where members talk about themselves, their businesses, and their collections. For example, you can find my About Me page at

http://members.ebay.com/
aboutme/marsha_c

I came across the About Me page in the figure when I was looking at an auction for a Limoges plate. This is a great example of how eBay members show their personalities and build trustworthy person-to-person (rather than computer-to-computer) relationships with other members of the eBay community.

Hello! Thanks for checking out...

specializing in new and gently-used quality children's clothing

Welcome! My name is Christine, and I'm mom to 3 great kids. I have a full-time job and ventured into selling on eBay part-time, where I specialize in quality, name-brand children's clothing, from gently-used to Brand New! I have to admit...I'm quite the "shop-a-holic", and having a 3-year-old little girl only justifies my condition! My older two are out of the stage where *I* can still dress them, so I'm having a blast with my youngest! I have so many clothes, it's like having my own little boutique! I have also come to admire the talent and uniqueness of the many great children's clothing designers right here on eBay!

My number one priority is making sure each transaction goes smoothly. If there are ever any questions or concerns, please e-mail me and I'll be happy to work with you. *I'll also have other great items to offer, so please check back often!*

Thanks for visiting!

If a new seller (without a lot of feedback) does the smart thing — puts up an About Me page and talks about his or her eBay goals and business — you may feel more comfortable about doing business with that person.

By default, you see the All Feedback Received tab. You may use the other tabs at the top of the page to sort the comments as follows:

✦ **Feedback as a Seller:** These are comments from people who bought something from this seller.

✦ **Feedback as a Buyer:** When you buy and play by the rules, you get some positive feedback.

✦ **All Feedback:** A conglomeration of all feedback left for the particular member, regardless of whether that person was a buyer or a seller in a transaction.

✦ **Feedback Left for Others:** Checking the type of feedback someone leaves about others can give you an insight into his or her personality. When considering making a big purchase, I always check this area; it helps me know the type of person I'm dealing with. When you read feedback that makes nasty slams at the other person, or if the person uses rude words or phrases when leaving feedback, it's a clue that you may be dealing with a loose cannon.

Figure 5-5:
Feedback
comment
page.

6,816 Feedback received (viewing 1-25)		
Feedback	**From / Price**	**Date / Time**
Good buyer, prompt payment, valued customer, highly recommended. ~ (#160264595963)	Seller: ▬▬▬ (10 ⭐)	Jul-31-08 20:33 View Item
Arrived as described....thanks.... Museum Putty QUAKE HOLD Wax Quakehold Earthquake LARGE (#110257294053)	Buyer: ▬▬▬ (850 ⭐) US $6.90	Jul-31-08 10:30 View Item
Item as described; fast delivery Museum Putty QUAKE HOLD Wax Quakehold Earthquake LARGE (#110257294053)	Buyer: ▬▬▬ (1010 ⭐) US $6.90	Jul-30-08 15:51 View Item
great book and very quick shipment eBay For Dummies 5 Book MARSHA COLLIER SIGND FREE Bonus (#110272136332)	Buyer: ▬▬▬ (99 ⭐) US $16.55	Jul-30-08 07:02 View Item
super fast shipment/ excellent product!! A+A+ seller Portable PHOTO WINGS Lighting Diffuse Soft Box Umbrella (#120148378419)	Buyer: ▬▬▬ (390 ⭐) US $28.99	Jul-29-08 00:20 View Item
best ebayer ever! easy to work with! great communication! love to do business w/ ~ (#2002(KX##H))	Seller: ▬▬▬ (8132 ⭐) ~	Jul-A9-09 00:06 View Item
AAAAA+++++ Excellent transaction! Fantastic seller, super fast shipping! Museum Putty QUAKE HOLD Wax Quakehold Earthquake LARGE (#110257294053)	Buyer: ▬▬▬ (3119 ⭐) US $6.90	Jul-28-08 18:57 View Item
great, thanks eBay For Canadians For Dummies CANADA Selling COLLIER (#350055229722)	Buyer: ▬▬▬ (15577 ⭐) US $21.99	Jul-28-08 10:54 View Item
As described. Arrived super quickly. Thanks. Museum Putty QUAKE HOLD Wax Quakehold Earthquake LARGE (#110257294053)	Buyer: ▬▬▬ (419 ⭐) US $6.90	Jul-26-08 07:01 View Item
Fantastic Kayak!! Very Smooth Transaction!! Love to Do Business With Again!!! OCEAN KAYAK MALIBU TWO with 2 paddles tandem FUCSHIA (#350081557090)	Buyer: ▬▬▬ (235 ⭐) US $300.00	Jul-25-08 17:09 View Item

Here's what else you see:

✦ The date the feedback was left, along with the transaction number. If the transaction is 90 days old or less, there is a clickable link to the transaction called View Item.

✦ Seller or Buyer on the right side of each comment. Seller means that the feedback was left by the seller in the transaction, and Buyer means it was left by a buyer.

Many independent eBay sellers are experienced buyers as well as sellers — they have an excellent grasp of how eBay feels from a customer's point of view, and know how to handle any of your concerns.

Here are some tips for assessing feedback, depending on the situation:

✦ When buying from a seller who sells the same item repeatedly, use the clickable links to past transactions to see whether *other* buyers of the same item were pleased with their purchases.

✦ When you come across neutral or negative feedback, look for the seller's response. A seller or a buyer may respond to the feedback by clicking the Reply to feedback received link at the bottom of the feedback page.

The feedback system relies on the expectation that members give each other the benefit of the doubt. When you come across negative (or neutral) feedback about a seller, look for the seller's response and see whether the problem was resolved before making your final judgment. You may even see a follow-up feedback comment from the buyer saying that everything has been settled.

Comparing Items Before Buying

By examining the results of your eBay search, you can get some useful information as to which item is the best deal.

In Figure 5-6, I performed a search for the *Poodle Hat* CD from Weird Al Yankovic. (This CD features his famous "eBay Song," a parody of the Backstreet Boy's version of "I Want It That Way." It's hysterical!).

By looking at the result I can identify certain facts about each listing:

✦ **Item title:** A clickable link to the listing and a link to watch this item.

✦ **Price:** The current bid or the Buy It Now price.

✦ **Shipping cost:** The seller's shipping cost to your ZIP code is posted for comparison, provided the seller input the flat shipping fee when the item was posted for auction or sale. If you don't see a shipping cost, you have to click the title to read the description.

✦ **Bid or Buy it Now:** See the number of bids that have been placed on an item or if the item is available for a flat sales price. This information gives you a quick snapshot of the costs for the item you're searching for.

✦ **Time Left:** The countdown to the end of the auction or fixed-price sale listing.

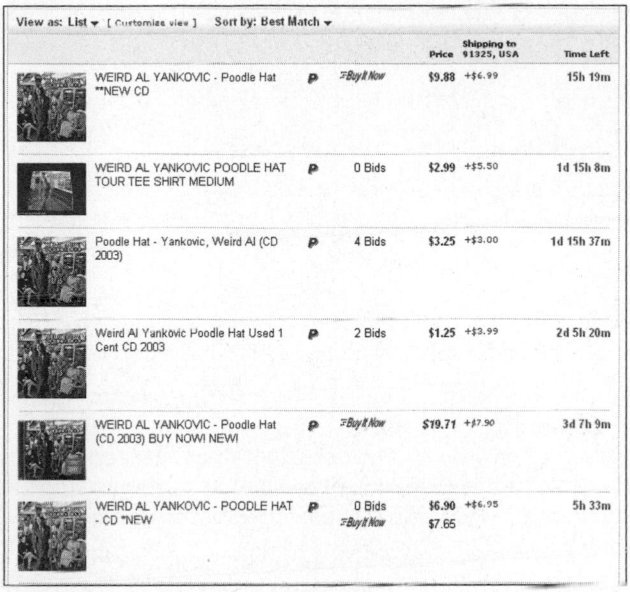

Figure 5-6:
Searching
for the
Poodle Hat
CD by
Weird Al.

Getting Protection on eBay

One thing's for sure in this world: Nothing is for sure. That's why insurance and bonding companies exist. Several forms of protection are available for eBay users:

✦ Insurance that buyers purchase to cover shipping (see Book VII, Chapter 3)

✦ eBay Motors Vehicle Purchase Protection

✦ PayPal buyer protection

✦ BuySAFE bond

✦ Verified Rights Owner program

For more information on how to acquire various protections for your buyers, see Book VIII, Chapter 2.

eBay Motors Vehicle Purchase Protection

A major benefit of buying a car on eBay is that you are covered against certain losses associated with some types of fraud. To qualify (this is the easy part), you simply need to purchase the car on eBay. (See? I told you it was simple.)

The Protection Plan gives you some pretty specific protections, such as these:

✦ You pay for a vehicle and never receive it.

✦ You send a refundable deposit for a vehicle and never receive it.

✦ You pay for a vehicle and receive it but suffer losses because

- The vehicle was determined by a law enforcement agency to have been stolen at the time of the end of the listing.

- The vehicle has an undisclosed or unknown lien against its title.

- The vehicle make, model or year is different than what was described in the seller's listing at the time you placed your bid or offer.

- A title is required for the vehicle by your state and the seller's state but you did not receive a title from the seller and it is not possible to obtain a title from the appropriate DMV.

- The vehicle has a title with an undisclosed salvage, rebuilt/rebuild-able, unrebuildable, reconstructed, scrapped/destroyed, junk, lemon, manufacturer-buyback, or water-damage brand at the time of the end of the listing. (This protection is not available for vehicles listed in the Dune Buggies, Race Cars, or Trailers categories.)

- The vehicle is less than 20 years old and has more than a 5,000-mile odometer discrepancy from the mileage as stated in the seller's list-ing. (This protection is only available for vehicles listed in the Cars & Trucks and RVs & Campers categories.)

- The vehicle had undisclosed engine, body, transmission, and/or frame damage at the time of purchase that will cost more than $1,000 to repair. The cost of repair to any one of those components must exceed $1,000. For vehicles in the Boats (engine and hull only), Buses, Commercial Trucks, and RVs & Campers categories, the cost of the undisclosed engine, body, transmission, or frame damage must exceed $1,500. Vehicles in the Race Cars category are not eli-gible for this protection (gee, I wonder why).

Learn more about this protection and any current updates at

`pages.motors.ebay.com/buy/purchase-protection/index.html`

PayPal buyer protection

Aside from safety, PayPal offers an even better reason to pay through their service. If you've purchased your item through a PayPal-verified seller, you may be covered for your purchase up to $2,000.

This protection covers you only for nondelivery of tangible items and tangible items that are received but are significantly not as described — it does not cover items that you are simply disappointed with.

If you've paid with a credit card through PayPal, be sure to make a claim with PayPal first. Do *not* make a claim with your credit card company. PayPal protection is for PayPal purchases and you are not covered if you've made a claim with your credit card company.

For the latest information on this program, go to

    www.paypal.com/cgi-bin/webscr?cmd=_pbp-info-outside

or

    www.paypal.com/cgi-bin/webscr?cmd=p/gen/protections-buyer-
        outside

Several types of protection are available to eBay buyers, as shown in Table 5-3.

Table 5-3		eBay Shopper's Assurance
Type	*Who Pays*	*Explanation*
Shipping insurance	Buyer	As the buyer, you must pay the seller the additional charge for package insurance. This will cover your purchase up to the insured amount while the item is in transit through the U. S. Post Office, UPS, or FedEx.
PayPal buyer protection	No charge	If you've paid for your purchase through PayPal to a PayPal-verified seller, you may be covered for up to $2000.
BuySAFE bond	Seller	BuySAFE bonds back a preferred seller's performance on the item, up to $25,000.
SquareTrade Seal	Seller	There is no warranty if you have been defrauded by a SquareTrade Seal member (more about that in an upcoming section). Note that the Seal only assures the buyer that the seller's positive feedback remains constant.

BuySAFE bond

BuySAFE helps make online auctions safer. The "BuySAFE with the Hartford" program offers one of the highest levels of protection available to online auction participants. It's the only program that enables sellers to present a credibility seal and financially protect their online auction transactions with surety bonds.

BuySAFE comprehensively qualifies sellers to display the BuySAFE seal. When a buyer sees the BuySAFE seal on an auction or fixed-price listing, the transaction is 100% guaranteed to be exactly as listed.

Verified Rights Owner program

eBay is a *venue* — a place where sellers sell their wares to smart shoppers like you. No one at eBay owns the items, and no one at eBay can guarantee that any item is as described in auction listings. That means you could, theoretically, buy a "genuine" Kate Spade purse on eBay for $24, and immediately realize when it arrives that the purse is counterfeit. That's *not* eBay's fault. (Shame on you for thinking you could get that kind of deal on a new Kate Spade purse — but if you can, for real, e-mail me and let me know where.)

Just because eBay doesn't take the blame for its fraudulent sellers' handiwork doesn't mean that eBay doesn't care if you get duped. Their VeRO (Verified Rights Owner) program connects eBay with companies or persons who care to protect their intellectual property rights (such as a copyright, trademark, or patent) against possible infringements in eBay listings. VeRO members send proof to eBay that they own the specified intellectual property. In return, they can report infringements to eBay — and eBay's listing police will end the counterfeit listings. This is not an automatic service, however, and the property owners are responsible for finding their own infringements on the site.

Many VeRO members have their own About Me pages. To see a list of links to these pages, go to

        http://pages.ebay.com/help/community/vero-aboutme.html

---

SquareTrade membership

Although the SquareTrade Seal used to be a way to assure the buyer that a seller maintained quality standards; these days it's more of a membership plan. The seller pays $9.50 a month to get a very official-looking seal that is updated daily.

The other benefit to sellers is that they can sell high-quality warranties from Square Trade to their buyers. The warranties are commission-able to the seller, and can easily outweigh the monthly membership fee.

It's unlikely that a SquareTrade seal holder is going to defraud you. SquareTrade checks sellers' feedback and reports on a daily basis to be sure they're playing within the eBay rules. SquareTrade yanks back its seal of approval if anything fishy is going on.

Chapter 6: Bidding to Win

A few years ago, on the day after Christmas, I was on *The Today Show* with Matt Lauer talking about after-holiday bargains on eBay. This wasn't the first time I'd been on the show with him; but this time Matt seemed very interested in getting a deal on a child's lamp that I happened to be selling. He and his wife had just had a baby, and everyone likes a bargain.

If everyone likes a bargain, then I'm not like everyone — because I *love* bargains! When I was teaching classes at eBay's own eBay University (yes, there really was one), my favorite class to teach was Buying and Browsing, because I love the thrill of the chase and the acquisition of a good deal without all the haggling.

Often, the first thing that people ask me is how they can stop getting outbid at the last minute of an auction. I always say the same thing — become an expert *sniper* and bid higher than the other guy!

Okay, but how? In this chapter I give you my tips and a few I picked up from other wise shoppers along the way.

eBay treats every bid — other than bids on some real estate sales or incorrectly placed bids — as binding. If you win an auction and do not go through with your commitment by purchasing the item, the seller will file an Unpaid Item (UPI) notice on you. If you establish a history as a nonpaying bidder with eBay (that is, you repeatedly back out of purchasing what you bid on), you have a strong chance of getting suspended from the community.

How much an item sells for depends on how many people see the item and how badly other bidders want it. You may think of the *retail price* or *book value* as a standard for pricing, but neither may be accurate when it comes to shopping on eBay. In fact, I say everything has three prices:

✦ The price a retailer *charges* for an item at the store

✦ The price *everyone* says something is worth

✦ The price an item *actually* sells for on eBay

Understanding the Bidding Action

Okay, you've found the perfect item to track (say, a really classy Elvis Presley wristwatch), and it's in your price range. You're more than interested — you're ready to bid. If this were a live auction, some stodgy-looking guy in a gray suit would see you nod your head and start the bidding at, say, $2. Then some woman with a severe hairdo would yank on her ear, and the Elvis watch would jump to $3.

eBay reality is more like this: You're sitting at home in your fuzzy slippers, sipping coffee in front of the computer. All the other bidders are cruising cyberspace in their pajamas, too, but you can't see 'em. (Be real thankful for little favors.)

When you're ready to jump into the eBay fray, find the bidding form (shown in Figure 6-1) at the bottom of the auction item page or click the Place Bid button at the top of the auction page. If the item includes a Buy It Now option, you see that next to the bid form.

Figure 6-1:
You can find the bidding form at the top of every auction page.

Placing your bid

To fill out the bidding form and place a bid, first make sure that you're registered. (For help in registering, see Chapter 3.) After you make your first bid on an item, you can instantly get to auctions you're bidding on from your My eBay page. Follow these steps to place a bid:

1. **Sign in to your eBay account.**

2. **Click the Buy It Now button on your selected item's page and enter your maximum bid in the appropriate box.**

The bid needs to be higher than the current minimum bid.

3. **If this is a multiple-item auction you will see a *Quantity* line and a number indicating that there is more than 1.pf the item Enter the quantity of items that you're bidding on.**

(If it's not a multiple-item auction, the quantity is always 1.) Figure 6-2 shows a multiple-item auction bidding form.

Figure 6-2:
The multiple-item auction bidding form requires you to enter the quantity of the items.

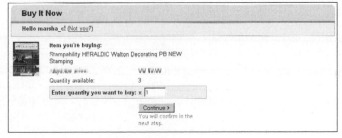

You don't need to put in the dollar sign, but you do need to use a decimal point — unless you really *want* to pay $1049.00 instead of $10.49. If you make a mistake with an incorrect decimal point, you can retract your bid (see "Retracting Your Bid in an Emergency," at the end of this chapter).

4. **Click Place Bid (or Buy It Now if you're making a direct purchase).**

The Review and Commit to Buy page, as shown in Figure 6-3, appears on your screen, filling it with all the costs involved in purchasing the item. This is your last chance to change your mind: Do you really want the item, and can you really buy it? To quote the form, "You are agreeing to a contract . . . You will enter into a legally binding contract to purchase the item from the seller." The bottom line is this: If you bid on it and you win, you buy it.

5. **If you agree to the terms, click Commit to Buy.**

After you agree, the Bid Confirmation screen appears.

Figure 6-3:
The serious
part —
Commit to
Buy.

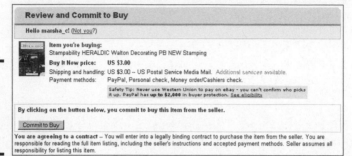

eBay's computer sends you an e-mail confirming your bid, if you've indicated that you want confirmation e-mails. However, eBay's mail server can be as slow as a tree-sloth marathon (yours would be, too, if you had a few million auctions to track), so don't rely on eBay to keep track of your auctions. After all, this is *your* money at stake.

eBay considers a bid on an item to be a binding contract. You can save your-self a lot of heartache if you promise *to never bid on an item you don't intend to buy.* Don't make spurious bids on the silly assumption that because you're new to eBay, you can't win; if you do that, you'll probably win simply because you've left yourself open to Murphy's Law. Therefore, before you go to the bidding form, be sure that you're in this auction for the long haul — and make yourself another promise *to figure out the maximum you're willing to spend* — and stick to it.

If you want to practice bidding, go to eBay's Test Bid page at

```
http://pages.ebay.com/education/tutorial/course1/bidding/
```

Bidding to the max with automatic (proxy) bidding

When you make a maximum bid on the bidding form, you actually make several small bids — again and again — until the bidding reaches where you told it to stop. For example, if the current bid is up to $19.99 and you put in a maximum of $45.02, your bid automatically increases incrementally so you're ahead of the competition — at least until someone else's maximum bid exceeds yours. Basically, you bid by *proxy,* which means the automatic-bid feature stands in for you so your bid rises incrementally in response to other bidders' bids.

No one else knows for sure whether you're bidding automatically, and no one knows how high your maximum bid is. And the best part is that you can be out having a life of your own while the proxy bidding happens automatically.

The *bid increment* is the amount of money by which a bid is raised, and eBay's system can work in mysterious ways. Buyers and sellers have no control over the bid increments that eBay sets. The current maximum bid can jump up a nickel or a quarter or even an Andrew Jackson, but there is a method to the madness, even though you may not think so. To determine how much to increase the bid increment, eBay uses a *bid-increment formula* that's based on the current high bid. Here's an example:

✦ A 5-quart bottle of cold cream has a current high bid of $14.95. The bid increment is $0.50 — meaning that if you bid by proxy, your automatic bid will be $15.45.

✦ A 5-ounce can of top-notch caviar has a high bid of $200. The bid increment is $2.50. If you choose to bid by proxy, your bid will be $202.50.

Table 6-1 shows you what kind of magic happens when you put the proxy system and a bid-increment formula together in the same cyber-room.

Table 6-1		eBay Auction Bid Increments		
Current	*Bid Increment ($)*	*Minimum Bid ($)*	*eBay Auctioneer*	*Bidders*
2.50	0.25	2.75	"Do I hear $2.75?"	Joe Bidder tells his proxy that his maximum bid is $8.00. He's the current high bidder at $2.75.
2.75	0.25	3.00	"Do I hear $3.00?"	You tell your proxy that your maximum bid is $25.00 and take a nice, relaxing bath while your proxy calls out your $3.00 bid, making you the current high bidder.

(continued)

Table 6-1 *(continued)*

Current	Bid Increment ($)	Minimum Bid ($)	eBay Auctioneer	Bidders
3.00	0.25	3.25	"I hear $3.00 from proxy. Do I hear $3.25?"	Joe Bidder's proxy bids $3.25, and while Joe Bidder is out walking his dog, he becomes the high bidder.
A heated bidding war ensues between Joe Bidder's proxy and your proxy while the two of you go on with your lives. The bid increment inches from $0.25 to $0.50 as the current high bid increases.				
7.50	0.50	8.00	"Do I hear $8.00?"	Joe Bidder's proxy calls out $8.00, his final offer.
8.00	0.50	8.50	"The bid is at $8.00.	Your proxy calls out $8.50 Do I hear $8.50?" on your behalf, and having outbid your opponent, you win the auction.

The Secret's in the Timing

A bricks-and-mortar auction, such as those held by Sotheby's or Christie's, ends when the bidding ends. No auctioneer is going to cut off the feverish bidding for that one-of-a-kind Van Gogh, right? As long as someone is bidding, all systems are go. The last bidder standing wins. Auctions on eBay, however, close at a prescribed time. Because of this fundamental difference in the way eBay runs its auctions, you need to do some special work to make sure that you can make the most strategically timed bid possible.

You can find out what time an auction ends by simply looking at the auction page. Note that eBay runs on Pacific Time and uses a 24-hour clock (00:00 to 24:00 versus the more familiar 1:00 to 12:00).

To get the serious deals, you need to synchronize your computer's clock with eBay's. To find out what eBay's official time is, go to

```
http://viv.ebay.com/ws/eBayISAPI.dll?EbayTime
```

Then compare eBay's time with your computer's clock. On most Windows-based computers, the time is in the lower-right corner of the screen on the taskbar.

To change the time on your computer's clock, follow these steps:

1. **Open your Internet browser and visit the following site:**

    ```
    http://viv.ebay.com/ws/eBayISAPI.dll?EbayTime
    ```

    The official clock at the eBay mothership appears, in the form of the Official Time page. Keep the browser open.

2. **Right-click your computer's taskbar and choose Adjust Date/Time.**

    The Date/Time Properties window appears.

3. **Click the Internet browser to activate it, and then click the browser's Refresh button.**

4. **After the page refreshes, immediately type the official eBay time into your computer's clock, and then click OK.**

If your computer is running the Windows XP or Vista operating systems, the box that appears when you right-click the taskbar has a third option: Internet Time. In this window (see Figure 6-4) you can synchronize your computer's clock to the Microsoft time server or the National Institute of Standards and Technology's atomic clock.

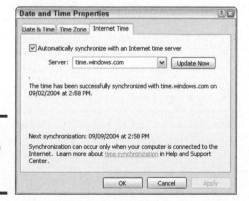

Figure 6-4:
Hooking up
to Internet
time.

Going, going, gone

Although many people list their auctions to end at all hours of the day and night, the amount of bidders in cyberspace is higher during certain hours. Between the hours of 23:00 (that's 11:00 p.m. Pacific Standard Time) and 03:00 (that's 3:00 a.m. Pacific Standard Time), things run a bit slowly on eBay. If you're online at that time, you may be able to take advantage of some very serious bargains. So swallow a shot of espresso and have fun if you're a night owl.

Going, going, gone is the name of the game my daughter and I used to play when we wanted to go shopping for fun on eBay. Visit your favorite eBay category and have fun.

You can choose to view the auctions that are going to end in the next few hours by using the Search Options on the left side of the page. Here you can cruise the auction closing while the world is asleep, and bid to your heart's content to get some great bargains.

Search Options

Location

☐ Worldwide ▾

☐ Items within 200 ▾

miles of 91325

Show only

☐ Items listed with PayPal

☐ Buying Options
Auctions ▾

☐ More Buying Options
Add Store Inventory ▾

☐ Free Shipping

☐ Completed listings

☑ Listings
Ending within ▾

1 hour ▾
| 1 hour
| 2 hours
| 3 hours
| 4 hours
| 5 hours
S | 12 hours
| 24 hours
| 2 days
Cust 3 days   displayed

Using the lounging-around strategy

Sometimes the best strategy at the beginning of an auction is to do nothing at all. That's right; relax, take off your shoes, and loaf. You may want to make a *token bid* (the very lowest you are allowed) or mark the page to watch in your My eBay area. I generally take this attitude through the first six days of a week-long auction I want to bid on, and it works pretty well. I do, however, check in every day to keep tabs on the items I'm watching on the My eBay page, and I revise my strategy as time goes by.

The seller has the right to up the minimum bid — if the auction has received no bids — up to 12 hours before the auction ends. If the seller has set a ridiculously low minimum bid and then sees that the auction is getting no action, the seller may choose to up the minimum bid to protect his or her sale. By placing the minimum token bid when you first see the auction, you can foil a Buy It Now from another bidder (because Buy It Now is disabled after a bid is in place) or prevent the seller from upping the minimum.

If you see an item that you absolutely must have, mark it to watch on your My eBay page (or make a token bid) and revise your maximum bid as the auction goes on. I can't stress enough how important this is.

As you check back each day, take a look at the other bids and the high bidder. Is someone starting a bidding war? Look at the time when the competition is bidding and note any patterns, such as lunchtime bidding. If you know what time your major competition is bidding, you can bid after he or she does (preferably when your foe is stuck in rush-hour traffic).

Using the beat-the-clock strategy

You should rev up your bidding strategy during the final 24 hours of an auction and decide, once and for all, whether you really *have* to have the item you've been eyeing. Maybe you put in a maximum bid of $45.02 earlier in the week. Now's the time to decide whether you're willing to go as high as $50.02. Maybe $56.03?

No one wants to spend the day in front of the computer (ask almost anyone who does). Just place a sticky note where you're likely to see it, reminding you of the exact time the auction ends. If you're not going to be near a computer when the auction closes, you can also use an automatic bidding software program to bid for you; see "Succeeding by Sniping," later in this chapter, for details.

In the last few minutes

With a half hour left before the auction becomes ancient history, head for the computer and dig in for the last battle of the bidding war. I recommend that you log on to eBay about 10 to 15 minutes before the auction ends. The last thing you want is to get caught in Internet gridlock and not get access to the eBay Web site. Go to the items you're watching and click the auction title.

With 10 minutes to go, if there's a lot of action on your auction, click reload or refresh every 30 seconds to get the most current info on how many people are bidding.

Shopping the Machiavellian Way

When you've shopped eBay for a while, you will know the user IDs of many of the people who win against you in auctions. Don't be surprised that other people in the eBay universe have the same quirky interests as you. Of course, even if that gives you something in common, you may come to dislike them if they outbid you often enough. It's a wretched feeling, being outbid, especially when it happens at the last minute.

The user ID of the person the item would belong to if the auction ended right now is listed on the auction-item page (assuming someone has bid on the item). Take a look at this name because you may see it again in auctions for similar items. If the high bidder has lots of feedback, he or she may know the ropes — and be back to fight if you up the ante.

eBay has made this tactic a bit more difficult by changing the Bidder's ID to a symbol (see Figure 6-5) that consists of numbers and asterisks. But once an auction is over, the winner's ID is revealed (note that in the figure I have smudged out this particular actual winner's ID, but you get the drift).

I remember once hearing a comedy routine about how much quicker it is to shop in a supermarket from other people's carts rather than running from aisle to aisle — and eBay is no different. When you get to know the IDs of your bidding competitors, you can run bidder searches on them.

Figure 6-5: Bidding History on a closed auction.

Bidders: 7   Bids: 21   Time Ended: **Jun-06-08 16:00:00 PDT**

This item has ended.

Only actual bids (not automatic bids generated up to a bidder's maximum) are shown. Automatic bids may be placed days or hours before a listing ends. Learn more about bidding.

Show automatic bids

Bidder	Bid Amount	Bid Time
(133302) me Top **10,000** Reviewer	US $610.00	Jun-06-08 08:02:09 PDT
o***o (21702)	US $600.00	Jun-03-08 21:06:24 PDT
(133302) me Top **10,000** Reviewer	US $690.00	Jun-06-08 07:55:50 PDT
(133302) me Top **10,000** Reviewer	US $570.00	Jun-05-08 12:32:57 PDT
(133302) me Top **10,000** Reviewer	US $550.00	Jun-05-08 12:32:24 PDT
(133302) me Top **10,000** Reviewer	US $525.00	Jun-05-08 12:31:59 PDT
d***a (188)	US $502.88	Jun-03-08 21:05:06 PDT
o***o (21702)	US $500.00	Jun-02-08 09:25:19 PDT
d***a (188)	US $488.00	Jun-03-08 21:04:38 PDT
w***o (195)	US $457.80	Jun-02-08 11:25:29 PDT
w***o (195)	US $440.67	Jun-02-08 11:25:13 PDT

Put in your two cents

Your two cents does matter — at least on eBay. Here's why: Many eBay members round off their bids to the nearest dollar figure or choose familiar coin increments such as 25, 50, or 75 cents. But the most successful eBay bidders have found that adding 2 or 3 cents to a routine bid can mean the difference between winning and losing. So I recommend that you make your bids in odd amounts, like $15.02 or $45.57, as an inexpensive way to edge out your competition. For the first time ever, your two cents may actually pay off!

For example, say meanguy123 outbids you in an auction for rare antique glockenspiels. You can run a bidder search on the old meany and find out what else he has been bidding on lately — and how much he bids.

You can find out the following information when you run a bidder search:

✦ **The items the bidder tends to be interested in:** Might as well let your competition do the legwork of finding good auctions for the items you like.

✦ **What time of day the bidder likes to make bids:** You can get a sense of whether the bidder is in another part of the country (or the world) and use the time difference to your advantage.

✦ **Other bidding habits:** Some bidders like to place an initial bid at the beginning of the auction and then swoop in at the end and snipe. Or they never bid until the end of the auction. Or they never snipe. No matter what strategy your competition chooses, you can come up with a counter-strategy to improve your likelihood of winning.

✦ **How high the bidder tends to like to bid:** This is a key to enable you to win the auction by as few pennies as possible. Does the bidder end with .27? End yours with .32. Also, if the bidder is accumulating items one at a time, you really have a good picture of *exactly* how much he or she will bid. Information is power!

Bidding in odd increments is just one of the many strategies to get you ahead of the rest of the bidding pack without paying more than you should.

Many of the strategies in this chapter are for bidders who are tracking an item over the course of a week or more, so be sure you have time to track the item and plan your next move. Also, get a few auctions under your belt before you throw yourself into the middle of a bidding war.

Investigating the opposing bidder is not snooping! It's totally legal and acceptable. (Okay, maybe it's a little sneaky.) When you've checked out your competition's shopping cart, you can swoop in and bid or snipe back if you like the other items this bidder is interested in. Isn't it easier to let someone else do the legwork and find the bargains for you?

You can run a bidder search by doing the following:

1. **Click the Advanced Search link, which appears next to the Search box that appears on almost every eBay page.**

2. **In the Search links area on the left, click the Items by Bidder link.**

3. **Enter the user ID of the bidder you want to check out.**

4. **To check the bidder's previous auction wins, click to add a check mark in the Completed Listings Only box (see Figure 6-6).**

Figure 6-6:
Running
a bidder
search to
uncover
bidding
patterns.

By studying the bidding history, you can see how high the bidder is willing to bid on certain items. This is invaluable information if you want to get a drift of how high *you* have to bid to win the next auction.

5. **Tell eBay whether you also want to see the person's bid even if he or she is not the high bidder.**

   Selecting the Even If Not the High Bidder option means that you want to see the bidder's activity in every auction, even if the person is not the *current* high bidder. I think you should check all the bidder's auctions to see how aggressively he or she bids on items. You can also see how badly a bidder wants specific items.

   If the bidder was bidding on an item in the past that you're both interested in now, you can get a fairly good idea of how high that person is willing to go for the item this time. Figure 6-7 shows you how this looks.

6. **Choose the number of items you want to see per page.**

7. **Click the Search button.**

Figure 6-7:
Bidder
Search
results for
me — note
that I have
not yet
won the
Nintendo
Wii Fit.

Current and recent auctions bid on by marsha_c (6027) me

To protect bidder privacy, not all items that this member has bid on may be displayed. When the price or highest bid on an item reaches or exceeds a certain level, User IDs will be displayed as anonymous names. For auction items, a bold price means at least one bid has been received.

Note: Anonymous names may appear more than once and may represent different bidders.

In some cases, marsha_c (6027) me may no longer be the high bidder.

1 - 4 of 4 total. Click on the column headers to sort

Item	Start	End	Price	Title	High Bidder	Seller
110255165900	May-21-08	Jun-02-08 16:08:49	US $22.95	St. Tropez Sunless Tan Whipped Bronze Mousse 8 OZ	Purchased on: Jun-02-08 16:08:49 See All Buyers	
330241264961	Jun-02-08	Jun-02-08 19:03:26	US $29.99	Sidekick II 2 Full Lcd Screen Flip with a screwdriver	marsha_c me (*)	
280241532251	Jun-30-08	Jul-01-08 13:31:00	US $0.99	1 NEW NINTENDO Wii Fit+WIIFIT BALANCE BOARD GAME SYSTEM	marsha_c me	
120214511781	Jan-23-08	Jul-21-08 13:16:17	US $3.25	SUPERSMILE-ALL NATURAL PROFESSIONAL WHITENING GUM (12PC	Purchased on: Jun-08-08 20:40:28 See All Buyers	

You may find that relying on the bidder search can give you a false sense of knowledge and confidence. Others may use the bidder search to become familiar with your habits, too. And many savvy buyers have *two* eBay user IDs and alternate between them to confuse those who try to follow their bidding patterns. Sniping can also help because no one will know you're interested in the auction until you win the item. Mix your bidding patterns up a bit to keep the competition wondering!

I keep links in my browser to bidder searches from some of my favorite bidders. When I'm in the mood to shop, I just look at what they're bidding on.

My Favorite Bidding Strategies

There used to be a time when I would tell beginning eBay members my favorite methods of bidding and winning, and if there was an eBay employee in earshot, you could see him or her wince. Things are considerably different these days. For example, eBay used to officially oppose the use of third-party payment options — until they purchased PayPal. And when sniping swept the online auction community and became *de riguer,* the eBay Powers That Be didn't endorse the practice. Finally, after some agonizing, the eBay insiders admitted that sniping *does* work in winning auctions.

As a matter of fact, eBay's instructors are now pitching many of the strategies that I've been talking about for years — because they work! While editing this book, my editor even reminisced about just how much the eBay "party line" has changed since I wrote my first book on eBay in 1999.

Hunting for errors

Some of my best buys on eBay were the result of searching for misspellings. Many sellers are in a hurry when they set up their auction listings, and to err is human (and to win, divine). I am more than willing to forgive sellers for their mistakes because the payoff for bargain hunters is, well, a bargain.

Think of alternate spellings when you search for an item. A favorite of mine is *Von Furstenburg* for *Von Furstenberg.* Usually, I search for the correct spelling and find a bunch of items where the bidding can get steep. But when I search for the misspelled version, I may find identical items that have no bids, because I'm the only one who has found the listing.

You can search for both the correct and incorrect spellings by using a search such as *(furstenberg,furstenburg).* Book II gives you lots more search tricks.

I was also successful during the holiday season of 2002, when those computer animated cats were popular (and going for extremely high prices on eBay, because they were sold out everywhere across the country). The brand name was FurReal. I searched for spellings like *fur real* and *furreal* and found many bargains.

eBay smartened up and now sometimes shows alternative spellings — but not always (what is the right way to spell L'Occitane?).

A couple of our favorite misspellings are *neckless* (instead of *necklace*) — currently 117 items up for sale and *vidio* (instead of *video*) — currently 14 on the site. I accidentally ran a search for a popular electronics game and noticed (as shown in Figure 6-8) that there were 2 items with the error. Note that eBay suggested the proper spelling of *Nintendo*, with 2,691 items.

Figure 6-8:
Look! A
"Nitendo"
Wii Fit!

Use asterisks as wildcards in your search, especially if you're not sure of the spelling of a word. You can also find some nuggets when searching for the plural of an item. (Check out Book II, Chapter 1.)

Researching your item

Sometimes we (that's me *and* you) find what we think is an incredible deal on eBay. It may well be, especially if we know that the retail price is, say, $80 and we're seeing a Buy It Now or an auction closing at $40. If a low, low price works for you, just go ahead and buy the item if you want it right away. To find the best price for any item on eBay, do your homework to find out what similar items on eBay tend to sell for.

When you conduct your eBay research, the best strategy is to look at the prices achieved in previous sales. Do a search for completed auctions. Then check an auction's bid history by clicking the Bid History link on the auction item page (the link appears next to the number of bids). You'll be presented with the screen like the one in Figure 6-9. This will at least give you an idea of how many people are duking it out for the item, if not their actual IDs.

Bidders: 4	Bids: 13	Time left: 2 hours 36 mins 51 secs

Only actual bids (not automatic bids generated up to a bidder's maximum) are shown. Automatic bids may be placed days or hours before a listing ends. Learn more about bidding.

Show automatic bids

Bidder ⑦	Bid Amount	Bid Time
l***r (204 ☆)	US $811.01	Jun-29-08 15:47:11 PDT
e***t (94 ★)	US $801.01	Jun-29-08 18:50:50 PDT
e***t (94 ★)	US $751.01	Jun-29-08 18:48:54 PDT
l***r (204 ☆)	US $666.69	Jun-29-08 14:51:18 PDT
e***t (94 ★)	US $351.01	Jun-29-08 14:47:12 PDT
l***r (204 ☆)	US $329.69	Jun-25-08 15:27:28 PDT
j***3 (16 ☆)	US $312.01	Jun-25-08 20:00:44 PDT
j***3 (16 ☆)	US $301.06	Jun-25-08 19:59:59 PDT
j***3 (16 ☆)	US $276.06	Jun-25-08 19:59:18 PDT
j***3 (16 ☆)	US $251.06	Jun-25-08 19:58:49 PDT
j***3 (16 ☆)	US $205.06	Jun-25-08 19:58:20 PDT
l***r (204 ☆)	US $151.69	Jun-24-08 18:40:30 PDT
o***a (38 ☆)	US $100.00	Jun-24-08 22:47:42 PDT
Starting Price	US $50.00	Jun-23-08 17:55:55 PDT

Figure 6-9:
I don't know who they are, but their bids sure seem persistent.

Pay attention to the times when bidders are placing their bids, and you may find that the people bidding in the auction are creatures of habit — making their bids about once a day and at a particular time of day. They may be logging on before work, during lunch, or after work. Whatever their schedules, you have great info at your disposal in the event that a bidding war breaks out: Just bid after your competition traditionally logs out, and you increase your odds of winning the auction.

Early in an auction, there may not be much of a bidding history for an item, but that doesn't mean you can't still check out the dates and times a bidder places bids. You can also tell whether a bidder practices *sniping* (discussed later in this chapter) if his or her bid is in the last few seconds of the auction. You may have a fight on your hands if the bidder uses sniping.

Multiple-item (Dutch) auction strategy

Multiple-item (Dutch) auctions are funky. (Yes, *funky* is a technical term.) Each winner pays the same amount for the item, and multiple-item auctions don't have a supersecret reserve price. But *winning* a multiple-item auction isn't all that different from winning other auctions. Therefore, wait until the closing minutes of the auction to bid and then follow my sage advice for optimum success.

Here are the key things to remember about a multiple-item auction:

✦ **The seller must sell all the items at the *lowest winning price* at the end of the auction, no matter what.**

✦ **Winners are based on the *highest* bids received.** If you up the ante, you could win the auction and pay only the lowest winning price, which may be lower than your bid. Confused yet? Say the minimum bid for each of ten Elvis watches is $10 and 20 people bid at $10, each person bidding for one watch. The first ten bidders win the watch. But suppose you come along at the end of the auction and bid $15 as the 21st bidder. You get a watch (as do the first nine people who bid $10), *and* you get the watch for the lowest successful bid — which is $10! Get it?

✦ **Know where you stand in the pecking order.** You can see a list of high bidders (and their bids) by clicking the Bidders List link on the auction page, so you always know where you stand in the pecking order.

✦ **Avoid being the lowest or the highest high bidder.** The highest bidder is sure to win, so the usual bidding strategy is to knock out the lowest high bidder. The *lowest* high bidder is said to be *on the bubble* — on the verge of losing the auction by a couple of pennies. To avoid being the bidder on the bubble, keep your bid just above the second-lowest winning bid.

✦ **If you want to buy more than one of an item up for auction, make sure you have that number of successful high bids as the auction draws to a close.** Huh? Remember, winners are based on the *highest* bids. If you're in a multiple-item auction for ten items and place five $15 bids, nothing guarantees that you'll win five of the item. Nine other people who want the item could bid $20 apiece. Then they each win one of the items at $15, and you end up with only one of the item. (At least you still pay only $15 for it.)

Quick Bidding Tips

When you get a tip, double-check who it's coming from. Visit eBay's community boards and chats, and listen to what the others have to say. Before taking anything to heart and changing the way you do things, check the tip-givers' experiences. Are they really experienced on eBay? Or are they just touting the current company line or passing on the latest misinformation? I love buying from eBay sellers who are also buyers, because they respect and understand what it's like to be a buyer on eBay!

Here are a few short tips that I know really work:

✦ **Shop eBay.ca, eh!** That's right. If you're in the U.S., why not bid on auctions on the eBay Canada Web site? In fact, if you're an international bidder and are willing to pay shipping from the U.S., you'll have no problem handling Canadian shipping charges.

If you're an American resident, all you have to do is think about the conversion between the U.S. and Canadian dollars — oh yes, there are bargains to be had. From the eBay home page, scroll down the left side of the page and click the Canada link. Or you can visit www.eBay.ca. Be sure the seller has reasonable shipping to the United States *before* you bid.

✦ **Place your bids in odd figures.** Many eBay bidders place their bids in the round numbers that match eBay's proxy system. You can win by a few cents if you place your bids in odd numbers like $10.97 or $103.01.

✦ **Don't get carried away in a bidding war.** Unless the item is rare, odds are that a similar item will show up on eBay again someday soon. Don't let your ego get in the way of smart bidding. Let your opposition pay too much!

✦ **Don't freak out if you find yourself in a bidding war.** Don't keel over if, at the split-second you're convinced that you're the high bidder with your $45.02, someone beats you out at $45.50.

✦ **Watch for item relistings.** If you see an item that you want but it has too high an opening bid (or too high a reserve), there's a good chance that no one else will bid on the item, either. Put that auction into your Watch area of My eBay. Then, after the auction ends, double-check the seller's auctions every so often to see whether the item has been relisted with a lower starting bid and a lower (or no) reserve.

✦ **Combine shipping when possible.** When you purchase an item, check the seller's other auctions and see whether you're interested in making a second purchase. If you see something else that appeals to you, e-mail the seller to see whether he or she will combine the items in shipping. That way, you can make two purchases for a smaller single shipping bill.

✦ **Never bid early, but if you do, bid high.** The only time this bidding early business works is if no one else is interested in the auction. Usually, though, the tactic will gear up another eBay user to outbid you because suddenly the item is valuable to at least one person. If you *must* bid before the auction's close, bid high. As a matter of fact, bid a couple of dollars more than you might want to pay. (I mean literally a couple, not a couple hundred.)

✦ **Try for a Second Chance offer:** If you get outbid and miss the chance to increase your bid on an auction item, you'd be smart to e-mail the seller and ask whether he or she has any more of the item. You may get lucky, and the seller can send you a Second Chance offer for your high bid.

A seller may send a Second Chance offer to underbidders in their auction under three circumstances: when the winner doesn't go through with the winning bid, when the reserve price wasn't met, or when the seller has more than one of the items that were sold. Any purchase you make in this manner will be covered under PayPal's Buyer Protection Program, and you will have the opportunity to leave feedback.

Succeeding by Sniping

Sniping is the fine art of outbidding your competition in the very last seconds of the auction — without leaving them enough time to place a defensive bid. Sniping is my number one favorite way to win an auction on eBay. When I first touted this method in 1999, it was a fairly new idea. Now everyone knows about sniping, and it's pretty much an accepted bidding method.

Bidders (that is, losing bidders) whine and moan when they lose to a sniper, but they should remember one thing: The high bidder always wins, whether you're sniping or using the automatic bid system. If you're going to snipe, assume that the current bidder has a *very* high-dollar proxy bid in the works.

Some eBay members consider the practice of sniping unseemly and uncivilized — like when dozens of parents used to mob the department-store clerks to get to the handful of Cabbage Patch dolls that were just delivered. (Come to think of it, whatever happened to *those* collectibles?) Of course, sometimes a little uncivilized behavior can be a hoot.

Sniping is an addictive, fun part of life on eBay. I recommend that you try it. You're likely to benefit from the results and enjoy your eBay experience even more — especially if you're an adrenaline junkie.

Sniping techniques for the beginner

Here's a list of things to keep in mind when you get ready to place your snipe bid:

✦ **Know how high you're willing to go.** If you know you're facing a lot of competition, figure out your highest bid to the penny. You should have already researched the item and figured out its value. Raise your bid only to the level where you're sure you're getting a good return on your investment; don't go overboard. Certainly, if the item has some emotional value and you just have to have it, bid as high as you want. But remember, you'll have to pay the piper later. You win it, you own it!

✦ **Know how fast (or slow) your Internet connection is.** Before you start sniping, figure out how long it takes to get your bid confirmed on eBay. Test it a few times until you know how many seconds you have to spare when placing a bid.

✦ **Don't lose heart if you lose the auction.** Remember, this is a game.

Although sellers love sniping because it drives up prices and bidders love it because it's fun, a sniper can ruin a week's careful work on an auction strategy. The most skillful snipers sneak in a bid so close to the end of the auction that you have no chance to counter-bid. Losing too often, especially to the same sniper, can be a drag.

If your Internet connection is slow and you want to do some sniping, make your final bid two minutes before the auction ends and adjust the amount of the bid as high as you feel comfortable so you can beat out the competition. If you *can* make the highest bid with just 10 seconds left, you most likely will win. With so many bids coming in the final seconds, your bid might be the last one eBay records.

This stuff is supposed to be fun, so don't lose perspective. If you can't afford an item, don't get caught up in a bidding war. Otherwise, the only person who wins is the seller. If you're losing sleep, barking at your cat, or biting your nails over an item, it's time to rethink what you're doing. If it's taking up too much of your life or an item costs too much, be willing to walk away — or log off — and live to bid another day.

To snipe a bid manually (without a sniping service), first make sure you're signed in. Then follow these steps to snipe at the end of the auction:

1. **In the last few minutes of the auction, locate the item you want to win and press Ctrl+N to open a second window on your Internet browser.**

Keep one window open for bidding, as shown in Figure 6-10.

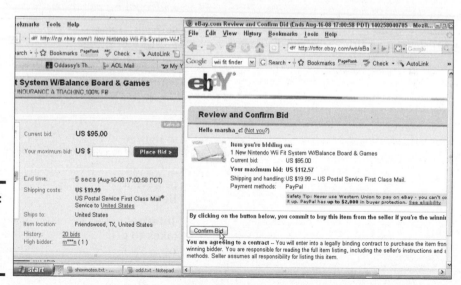

Figure 6-10:
My manual sniping system in action.

2. **Continuously click the reload or refresh button that appears in the last few minutes of an auction, just above the Place Bid button.**

By reloading the item continually, you'll be aware when you're in the last 60 seconds of bidding. You also can see instantly whether anyone else is doing any last-minute bidding.

3. **In the bid box of the second browser, type your maximum bid and then click the Place Bid button.**

    You then face a page that, when you press the button, finalizes and confirms your bid on the item. Do not click the Commit to Buy button yet.

4. **As the auction nears its end, confirm your final bid by clicking the Commit to Buy button.**

    You know when the auction is almost over because you're reloading your first browser continually. The longer you can hold off bidding before the auction ends, the better.

If you really want an item bad enough, you may want to set up a backup for your snipe. Try my three-screen system, in which you can place a backup high bid in case you catch another sniper swooping in on your item immediately after your first snipe.

Obviously, if you win with the first snipe, the second window is unnecessary. But if you lose the first one, that second window feels like a real lifesaver! If you're outbid after two snipes, don't cry. The winner paid way more than you were willing to pay. It's not *much* consolation, but rarely is an item so rare that you only see it come on the auction block once in a lifetime.

Auto-sniping your auctions

My daughter says that I can make almost anything high maintenance, and she may very well be right. When it comes to eBay bidding and winning, a bunch of software programs and Web sites can help automate your shopping and feedback process. I like that they will bid for me whether I'm near a computer or sleeping peacefully.

Here is one that I have used successfully: **BidRobot.** Shown in Figure 6-11, BidRobot deftly places sniping bids for you from its servers. It's won many an auction for me while I've been on the road or busy writing. The service is one of the least expensive out there, charging a low flat rate. Get a three-week free trial (all you can snipe for three weeks!) at

www.bidrobot.com/cool

They also have a BidGroup feature to use if you're bound and determined to get the lowest price for an item. This is accomplished by planning a bidding schedule at a set price. The bidding continues until you win your item (or not). Here's how it works.

1. **Search for your item.** Search for your specific item on eBay. You may find a large number of eBay auctions that offer your item.

2. **Select the auctions you'd like to bid on.** Review the listings (checking the seller's feedback, description and PayPal Buyer Protection availability) and select six different listings.

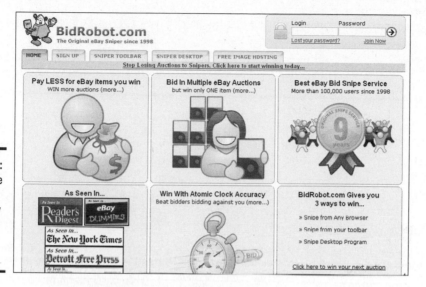

Figure 6-11:
Easily place
snipes in
advance by
using the
BidRobot
Web site.

3. **Create your first snipe.** Type your first snipe bid in the pale yellow Bid section at the very top of the BidRobot bid screen Click also to indicate that you want to create a group of bids with the other five auctions.

4. **Group the other auctions.** To bid on other seller's auctions, scroll down until you find the Pending Bid Group that contains your first item bid. Then use the form in that BidGroup area to add more snipe bids for other auctions in that specific BidGroup You may add bids for as many additional auctions to this group as you like

5. **Winning.** If you win any one of the auctions in your BidGroup, the remaining bids in that specific group will not be placed. This is automatic.

Knowing what you're buying

Before you place a bid, be sure that you know the item's *street price,* which is the price that people actually pay — not the MSRP (manufacturer's suggested retail price). You can use the Internet to check prices for many items. In fact, several consumer Web sites are dedicated to serving savvy consumers by offering this information. You can find prices for computer items at www.pricewatch.com. Prices for almost everything else can be found at this Google site: www.google.com/products. You may be comfortable paying slightly more than the street price because eBay is so easy to use — after all, the item is delivered to your door and you don't have to go to a bricks-and-mortar store to shop for the item.

Retracting Your Bid in an Emergency

We're all human and we all make mistakes. Luckily for everyone, eBay members are allowed to retract bids under certain circumstances. You may retract your bid if you meet one of the following criteria:

+ **You accidentally typed the wrong bid amount:** Say you typed $900 but you meant $9.00. Oops. In a case like this, you can retract the bid, but you'd better rebid the proper amount (that original $9.00) immediately, or you may be in violation of eBay's policies.

+ **The seller has added information to the item description that changes the value of the item considerably:** The bull that was let loose in the seller's shop has changed the mint condition of the Ming vase you just bid on? No problem.

+ **You can't reach the seller through eBay's e-mail or through the telephone number you got from eBay's find members area:** Seller gone AWOL and you have a question about an item you've bid on? You can use eBay's e-mail system by clicking Ask the Seller a Question in the Seller Information box on the auction page. Or to get the seller's telephone number, click the Advanced Search link (at the top-right corner of most eBay pages) and then click the Find a Member link (on the left side of the page). Next, input your transaction number and the seller's user ID. After checking to make sure that you've begun a transaction with this person, the good people at eBay will send the seller's telephone number in an e-mail message to your registered e-mail address. Your phone number will also be e-mailed to the seller.

Every time you retract a bid, it appears in the feedback area or your eBay feedback page.

Here are a couple of additional restrictions to retracting bids:

+ **You can retract a bid only if it was placed during the last 12 hours of an auction.** If you bid more than once in the last 12 hours of the same auction, you can retract it within one hour of placing it. In this case, only that bid will be retracted; any other bid placed before the last 12 hours of the listing remains valid.

+ **When you retract a bid because of a bidding error, you wipe out any of your previous bids in the auction.** To reinstate yourself as a bidder, you must bid again immediately.

If you want to retract your bid within the last 12 hours of the auction and you placed the bid before the last 12 hours, you must send an e-mail to the seller asking him or her to cancel your bid. It is up to the seller whether to cancel your bid. A bid retraction isn't a guarantee that you will get out of purchasing the item. Sometimes, sellers simply don't have the opportunity or time to cancel a bid. That means you have to buy the item.

You'll probably never need this link, but to retract your bid (or find more information), go to

```
http://offer.ebay.com/ws/eBayISAPI.dll?RetractBidShow
```

You can find your way to the Bid Retraction form also by clicking the Buying Related links on your My eBay All Buying page.

eBay vigorously investigates members who abuse bid retractions. Too many bid retractions and you may find yourself suspended from the system.

Chapter 7: Completing the Transaction

In This Chapter

✓ Buying an item and paying immediately

✓ Using plastic

✓ Paying through PayPal

✓ Sending a payment safely

✓ E-mailing the seller

✓ Leaving feedback

The thrill of the chase is over, and you've won your eBay item. Congratulations — now what do you do? You have to follow up on your victory and keep a sharp eye on what you're doing. The post-auction process can be loaded with pitfalls and headaches if you don't follow proper procedure. Money, like a full moon, does strange things to people sometimes.

In this chapter, you get a handle on what's in store for you after you win an auction. I clue you in on what the seller is supposed to do to make the transaction go smoothly and show you how to grab hold of your responsibilities as a buyer. You find out about proper post-auction etiquette, including the best ways to get organized, communicate with the seller professionally, and send your payment without hazards. I also brief you on how to handle an imperfect transaction.

Throughout the bidding process, the dollar amounts of items you're winning appear in green on your My eBay: All Buying page. If you've been outbid, they appear in red.

After the auction ends, there's no marching band, no visit from a camera crew, no armful of roses, and no oversized check to duck behind. In fact, you're more likely to find out that you've won the auction from the seller or the All Buying: Won section of your My eBay page than you are to hear it from eBay. eBay tries to get its end-of-auction e-mails (EOAs) out pronto, but sometimes there's a lag. After you win, you can go back to the item and see a checkout link on the item page. For a look at all the contact information in the end-of-auction e-mail, see Figure 7-1.

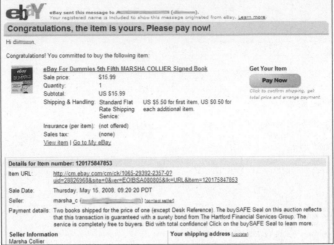

Figure 7-1:
Everything
you need to
know about
contacting
your buyer
or seller is
included in
eBay's end-
of-auction
e-mail.

If you can receive text messages on your cell phone, eBay will send EOA notices to your phone. Find out your wireless e-mail address from your cell-phone provider — it's usually available from the provider's home page (for example, www.sprint.com or www.t-mobile.com). Then go to your My eBay page, find the My Account: Personal Information area, and click the Change link. After you've entered your contact information there, click the Change My Notification Preferences link and select which notifications you want sent to your mobile phone. That way, no matter where you are, you'll know when you have won an auction (and need to get payment out ASAP)!

Checking Out

When you buy something in a store, you need to check out to pay. eBay isn't much different. eBay's checkout is a convenient way to pay for your completed auction or Buy it Now sale with a credit card or eCheck through PayPal. You may also use checkout to exchange information with the seller and pay for your item using a money order, a check, or another payment service that the seller accepts.

Checkout is integrated directly onto the item page so that you can win and pay for an item in less than a minute, as shown in Figure 7-2.

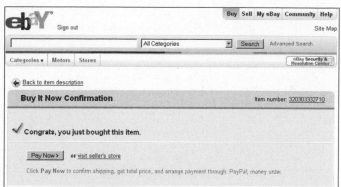

Figure 7-2:
You've won
the auction
and you
can check
out and pay
immediately.

When you click the Pay Now button, you are taken to the checkout page.
You can make an immediate payment only if the seller accepts PayPal. If
the seller accepts other types of payment, such as a personal check or a
money order, you can indicate which type of payment you want to use and
this page will send the seller your shipping information. If the shipping cost
is based on your ZIP code, or the seller offers discounts on buying multiple
items, you can make any such changes on the page and recalculate the total.
Then you can go ahead and send the payment.

When I talk to people about why they don't buy on eBay, the most frequent
answer is that they're afraid of giving out their credit-card information. The
second most common reason is that they don't want to send money to strangers. In addition to all the eBay safeguards that I mention in previous chapters,
the next section gives you the inside scoop on how to stay safe when sending
your payment to the sellers. You may be surprised to know that there are distinct levels of safety in how you can send a payment to a seller.

Using Your Credit Card Safely

The safest way to shop on eBay is to use a credit card. In most cases, your
credit-card company will stand behind you if you encounter problems using
your card online.

Knowing your credit-card company's policy

Before you start bidding, find out how your credit-card company handles
fraud claims. The major credit-card companies — American Express,
Discover, MasterCard, and Visa — have different policies regarding how
they stand behind your online purchases:

✦ **American Express:** American Express offers "ironclad protection" for online shoppers. The company claims that there's "no fine print and no deductible" if you need to rely on American Express to help you fight a fraudulent transaction.

> www.americanexpress.com/cards/online_guarantee

✦ **Discover:** Discover offers 100% fraud protection. The company offers a secure online account number, which generates a single-use card number each time you shop online so your account number is never transferred over the Internet.

> www.discovercard.com/customer-service/security/
> create-soan.html

✦ **MasterCard:** The program offered by MasterCard is called Zero Liability and is offered if MasterCard deems your account in good standing, you haven't broadcast personal account information online frivolously, and you haven't reported more than two "unauthorized events" in the past 12 months.

It appears that MasterCard's policy is conditional and that they (not you) are the final judge when it comes to determining fraud, so be careful.

> http://www.mastercard.com/us/personal/en/
> cardholderservices/zeroliability.html

✦ **Visa:** Visa seems to like the phrase *zero liability,* as well. Your liability for unauthorized transactions is $0. A new program, called Verified by Visa, lets you set up your own private password that you use with your Visa card anytime you use it online at participating merchants.

> http://usa.visa.com/personal/security/visa_security_
> program/zero_liability.html

Every once in a while, check your statement, visit your credit card company's Web site, or call the credit-card company's customer-service department to verify its current fraud-protection policy for online purchases.

Never — really, I mean *never ever* — send your credit-card information to anyone through e-mail. E-mail is the most insecure way to send information. As your e-mail makes its way from your computer to the recipient's desktop, it makes a whole lot of micro-stops along the way. These stops may take just nanoseconds, but your information is open for reading by outside parties (at least those who have the right expertise) at any stop along the journey.

Adding a layer of protection with an online checkout service

Many eBay sellers use an independent online checkout service that allows them to process shipping information, combine purchases, give an exact shipping total, and receive credit card payments. If the seller uses such a service, you probably see a clickable link in the e-mail that's sent to you at the end of the auction. The link leads you to an online checkout page.

When you come to the point in the checkout process where you must input your credit-card information (see Figure 7-3), look for the following:

✦ **Find the small closed padlock icon or the key icon:** These icons tell you that the site hosting the checkout is secure. You can find these icons in the lower-right corner of your browser window.

✦ **Check the URL for an** *s:* The URL (Web-site address) may change from a prefix of `http://` to `https://` (the s stands for secure).

✦ **Look for** *SSL:* You may also see the initials `SSL` in the Web site's address or somewhere on the page. SSL stands for Secure Socket Layer.

Any, some, or all of the preceding items indicate that the Web site uses *security encryption* methods. Translation? No one but you and the merchant can read or view your payment information.

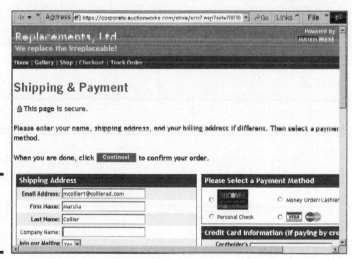

Figure 7-3:
A secure
credit-card
checkout.

Paying with PayPal

PayPal is my preferred method of payment on eBay. I've been happily using PayPal since the company was introduced to eBay, and I've always had positive results. Well, okay, not always. No service can make a slow or lazy seller into the picture of efficiency. The advantage of PayPal, though, is that you don't have to get your hands dirty.

For example, I once had a problem with a slow-shipping seller. Luckily, I had paid him using PayPal. I filed a complaint through PayPal and I got my merchandise shipped out within a day!

The folks at eBay know a good thing when they see it, so they acquired PayPal late in 2002. Now PayPal payments are integrated into eBay's checkout process.

Registering at PayPal

When you register to use PayPal, you have to give your name, address, phone number, and e-mail address. You also have to make up a password.

Make your password more than six characters, and use numbers *and* letters — revisit Chapter 3 for more information on registration security.

You have to select a security question. The safest is your pet's name, your city of birth, or the last four digits of your Social Security Number. You have to click to put a check mark next to the paragraph that says you have read and agree to PayPal's User Agreement and Privacy policy. (There are links so you can read them.) When you're convinced that you understand what PayPal's all about and what it expects of you, click Sign Up.

PayPal sends you an e-mail confirming your registration. The e-mail arrives almost instantaneously to the e-mail address you used at registration, and the message contains a link. When you receive the e-mail, click the link to visit the PayPal site. Enter the password that was used to create your account. Bingo — you're in.

Giving PayPal credit card or checking account information

Of course, you also have to add a credit card number to your PayPal account if you want to pay for anything with a credit card (or plan to sell on eBay). If you don't have a credit card — or would like to occasionally pay for things directly from your bank account — you have to register your checking account.

Your credit-card company and PayPal

To be a good consumer, you need to take responsibility for your transactions. Be sure you understand your credit-card terms and conditions when it comes to third-party payment services. Each credit-card company has its own agreement with PayPal — and each company has a different view of how to handle PayPal transactions. For example, Visa and MasterCard treat PayPal as the *merchant of record* in your transactions, meaning that PayPal ends up as the responsible party if you don't receive the merchandise or if you dispute the transaction. If you register a complaint about a charge made on your Visa or MasterCard, the credit-card company just

yanks the money from PayPal, and it's up to PayPal to settle things with the seller.

At the time of this writing, Discover and American Express treat PayPal transactions somewhat like a cash advance — a money transfer of sorts. I just checked a couple of my past Discover and American Express bills, and the PayPal charges look like any other charges. The only difference is how these credit-card companies handle their level of liability in third-party payment services. PayPal backs your purchases for $200 to $2000 – depending on the seller's experience.

I can see you beginning to squirm; you're not comfortable giving that type of information to anyone, much less putting it out on the Internet. Relax. PayPal uses military-strength encryption technology to keep your account information safe, so don't be afraid to give up your data.

To register your credit card, you'll have to input the name on the card (the last name is already filled in with the name you registered on the account), the expiration date, and the *card-verification number* — the three-digit number on the back of the card, imprinted next to the last few digits of the card number in the area where you sign. (American Express verification numbers are on the front of the card.) PayPal also asks you to supply a billing address.

On an American Express card, the card-verification number is the four-digit number on the right side of the face of the card.

When you enter all the information PayPal needs, click the Add button. PayPal submits your information to your credit card company for confirmation. This process may take a minute or so, but eventually your credit-card company says you are who you say you are, and the card is added to your PayPal account. You can register four active credit cards.

Registering your checking account is just as easy. You supply the information from the bottom of one of your checks, as shown in Figure 7-4.

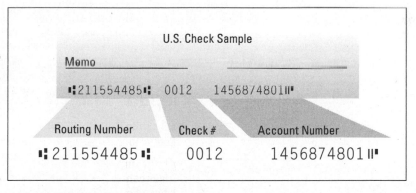

Figure 7-4:
Provide your bank routing number and your account number.

Getting PayPal-verified

When PayPal has the information it needs, it makes two small deposits into that account. (When I say *small*, I mean small!) After a week or so, call your bank or check your account online and find out the amount of these two deposits. When you have the amounts, sign on to the PayPal Web site with your password, and type the amounts in the appropriate place. Voilà! Your account is registered — and, not coincidentally, you're verified! PayPal has confirmed that you hold an active account with your bank. All banks are required to screen their account holders, and verification authenticates your identity to anyone who does business with you.

Here are some benefits of being PayPal-verified:

✦ No spending limit (Whoopie!).

✦ Higher level of account security.

✦ Better buyer and seller confidence. Verified status shows other PayPal members that you have passed PayPal's security checks.

If you don't want to give up your bank-account number, you can become verified by applying for and being accepted for a PayPal Plus credit card or PayPal Buyer Credit.

Ways to pay through PayPal

The easiest and most efficient way to pay for eBay purchases is by credit card. If you are not a PayPal-verified buyer, you still have your credit card's fraud-protection guarantee behind you.

eBay sees to it that PayPal is incredibly easy to use because PayPal is the official payment service at eBay. After the auction is over, a link to pay appears. If you prefer, wait until you hear from the seller.

You may also send money directly from your bank account (either savings or checking) through instant transfer or eCheck.

✦ **Instant transfer:** An instant transfer is *immediately* debited from your bank account and deposited into the seller's account — so you'd best be sure you have the funds in your account to back up the purchase *now* (not tomorrow, not next week). PayPal requires you to back up an instant transfer with a credit card, just in case you've miscalculated your account balance.

✦ **eCheck:** You may also write an eCheck, which is just like writing a check, only you don't write it with a pen. Like regular, plain-vanilla paper checks, eChecks take three to four days to clear, and do not post to the seller's account as paid until then. The seller won't ship your item until PayPal tells the seller that the check has cleared your bank.

✦ **Credit card:** You can use your American Express, Discover, Visa, or MasterCard to make your payment through PayPal. The cost of the item is charged to your card, and your statement reflects a PayPal payment with the seller's ID.

Sellers will not ship your item until the eCheck clears, so if you're in a hurry, don't use this option.

Making a PayPal payment

After you win an auction, buy an item in a Buy It Now transaction, or purchase an item from an eBay store, it's time to pay. You can pay immediately by clicking the Pay Now icon on the item page.

On the next screen, as shown in Figure 7-5, you see an invoice type page. Double-check that all the information is correct. If insurance is optional, and you don't want shipping insurance, just delete the amount. If you're entitled to a multiple-item discount, you can put that in too. If you are unclear about how much to pay, there's a link you can use to ask the seller for a total.

Figure 7-5: Reviewing your purchases before making your payment with PayPal.

Assuming that you've already become a registered (verified) PayPal user, you see a place at the very bottom of the page to input your e-mail address and password. Fill in this info, and click the button that says Continue.

A page appears and you must decide whether you want to pay by credit card or bank transfer. If you have a balance in your PayPal account, you must use that money to make your payment; so withdraw your PayPal balance first if you want to pay with a credit card. Finalize all the details of your transaction by filling in any open blanks and indicating your payment choice. You can even send a note to the seller along with your payment.

If you want some information to go to the seller regarding your transaction, send the information in a separate e-mail message. The *Note to seller* is buried in a much longer e-mail message that PayPal sends to the seller, and it's hard to find. (PayPal sends sellers an e-mail within a few hours saying that it has received your payment.) So any important messages should be sent separately. Put your transaction number or item name in the Subject line.

Sending Payment Promptly and Securely

How many times have you heard the saying "The check is in the mail"? Yeah, I've heard it about a thousand times, too. If you're on the selling end of a transaction, hearing this line from the buyer but not getting the money is frustrating. If you're on the buying end, it's bad form and may also lead to bad feedback for you.

Being the good buyer that you are, you'll get your payment out pronto. If you've purchased an item and intend to pay using PayPal, do it immediately — why wait? (The sooner you pay, the sooner you get that charming gold-trimmed Flying Monkey decanter you won!)

On October 20th, 2008 eBay changed their policies and checks or money orders will no longer be allowed on eBay

Most sellers expect to get paid within seven business days after the close of the auction. Although this timeline isn't mandatory, it makes good sense to let the seller know that payment is on the way.

Send your payment promptly. If you have to delay payment for any reason (you have to go out of town, you broke your leg), let the seller know as soon as possible. Most sellers understand if you send them a kind and honest e-mail. Let the seller know what's up; give him or her a date by which the money can be expected, and then meet that deadline. If the wait is unreasonably long, the seller may cancel the transaction. In that case, you can expect to get some bad feedback.

Here are some tips on how to make sure that your payment reaches the seller promptly and safely:

✦ If you're paying with a credit card without using a payment service and want to provide the number over the telephone, be sure to request the seller's phone number in your reply to the seller's initial e-mail and explain why you want it.

✦ You can safely e-mail your credit card information over the course of several e-mails, each containing four numbers from your credit card. Stagger your e-mails so that they're about 20 minutes apart and don't forget to let the seller know what kind of credit card you're using. Also, give the card's expiration date.

Buyers routinely send out payments with no name, no address, and no clue as to what they've purchased. No matter how you pay, be sure to include a copy of the eBay confirmation letter, a printout of the auction page, or a copy of the e-mail the seller sent you. If you pay with a credit card through e-mail or over the phone, you should still send this info through the mail just to be on the safe side.

Contacting the Seller

eBay rules and regulations state that buyers and sellers must contact each other by e-mail within three business days of the auction's end. For example, if an item closes on a Saturday, you need to make contact by Wednesday.

Most sellers contact auction winners promptly because they want to complete the transaction and get paid. Few buyers or sellers wait for the official eBay EOA e-mail to contact each other. If you've won an item and intend to pay through PayPal, it's *de rigueur* for you to use the Pay Now link on the item page as soon as possible after you've won.

If you need to contact the seller before sending payment, you have several ways to find contact information:

✦ **Click the Ask Seller a Question link** on the auction page, which takes you to the Ask Seller a Question form.

✦ **Click the Site Map link,** located above the navigation bar on every eBay page, and then click the Find a Member link. On the resulting page, click the link to find Contact Information.

✦ **Click the Advanced Search link** (at the top-right corner of all eBay pages), and then click the Find Contact Information link (on the left side of the page).

Getting the seller's phone number

If you don't hear from the seller after three business days and you've already tried sending an e-mail, you need to get more contact information. Remember back when you registered and eBay asked for a phone number? eBay keeps this information for times like this.

To get an eBay member's phone number on a transaction you're participating in, go back to the Advanced Search: Members: Find Contact Information link. Fill out the Contact Info form by entering the seller's user ID and the number of the item that you're buying, and then click the Search button. If all the information is correct, you automatically see a request-confirmation page and eBay generates an e-mail message to both you and the other user.

eBay's e-mail message includes the seller's user ID, name, company, city, state, and country of residence, as well as the seller's phone number and date of initial registration. eBay sends this same information about you to the user you want to get in touch with. Most sellers jump to attention when they receive this e-mail from eBay and get the ball rolling to complete the transaction.

Within the first three business days after an auction or a Buy it Now transaction, limit yourself to using the Ask Seller a Question form. The seller (if signed in) sees the buyer's e-mail address on the item page after the sale is closed.

eBay doesn't tolerate abuses of its contact system. Make sure that you use this resource to communicate with another user *only* about a specific transaction in which you are participating. To use contact information to complete a deal outside eBay is an infringement of the rules. If you abuse the contact system, eBay can investigate you and kick you off the site.

Leaving Responsible Feedback

Almost any eBay seller will tell you that one of his or her pet peeves about the eBay feedback system is that new community members tend to leave neutral or (even worse) *negative,* feedback the moment a shipment arrives and something is wrong. In this section, I tell you what you need to know to avoid getting a bad rap for being too hard on sellers.

Chapter 5 gives you the long version of leaving feedback on eBay; please read it for detailed information on the new seller ratings. These DSRs (detailed star ratings) allow buyers to get more specific with their transaction feedback.

The DSR part of the feedback system asks you to rate sellers by filling in one to five stars. Why be judgmental? If the transaction went through as promised, why not give the seller five stars? A 5-star rating doesn't cost you anything as the buyer, and if the seller is a PowerSeller, it can affect a discount they receive on their eBay fees.

Late Delivery

A late delivery is not always the seller's fault. Before dinging a seller's reputation for slow delivery, check the postmark on the package's label. You'll often find that the seller followed through with his or her shipping promise, but the package was held up in transit. The shipping services may deserve a 1-star rating, but if the seller shipped right away, why not give that person five stars for a good-faith effort?

Missing or damaged shipment

When a package leaves the seller's hands, it is *literally* (and completely) out of his or her hands. If UPS, Federal Express Ground, or Federal Express Air ships your package, the tracking number can track the item. Tracking offered by the U.S. Post Office can be casual (at best) and is often not scanned until the package is delivered to your door, thus negating the trackability (for lack of a better term) of the package. Here are a few things to remember:

✦ Be sure you know when the seller plans to ship the merchandise, so there's less question about when it will probably arrive. If this information isn't stated in the auction description, use the Ask Seller a Question link to find out — *before* you buy — determine whether the shipping schedule matches your needs.

✦ If you do not pay the seller extra money to purchase insurance before your item is shipped, it's unfair to hold the seller responsible for damaged or lost shipments. Period. End of story.

✦ Open your packages immediately upon receipt. A seller can't make a claim on an item that you report damaged in shipping a month after it arrives, so leaving negative feedback for the seller at that point is unfair. Most shippers insist that any and all damage be reported within five days of receipt. Also, if damage has occurred, keep all packing materials for inspection by the carrier. If you fail to save these materials, the carrier may not accept your claim and you will have no further recourse.

✦ A seller can't do much about a missing package. Sellers can't even make a claim on a postal shipment until 30 days have passed since mailing.

✦ If the item never arrives, only the sender can file a claim with the shipping company and must produce all shipping receipts. Notify the seller immediately by e-mail or telephone upon receiving a damaged shipment. Leaving negative feedback before contacting the seller is just plain unjust.

Item doesn't meet your expectations

If the item arrives and isn't as described in the item description, e-mail the seller. Communication is a good thing — and most sellers want to preserve their reputations. Give the seller the opportunity to work things out with you. Keep in mind these facts:

✦ If a new item in a manufacturer's sealed box arrives damaged, the damage could have happened at the manufacturer and the seller wouldn't even know about it.

✦ A seller may not be as experienced in a particular collectible as you are. If you didn't ask all the necessary questions before bidding, you may have received what the seller *assumed* was a collectible. It's up to the buyer to ask questions before placing a bid.

✦ If you receive the wrong item, the seller might have simply mixed up labels. Don't jump to leave negative feedback. Just notify the seller, who will no doubt work out the mistake with you.

Most important, sellers should be given the chance to prove they care. If you feel that you're a victim of fraud, you can apply for PayPal's Buyer Protection (see Chapter 5).

Choosing your words carefully

Good sellers should be rewarded, and potential buyers should be informed. That's why no eBay transaction is complete until the buyer fills out the feedback form. Before leaving any feedback, remember that sometimes no one's at fault when transactions get fouled up. Here are some handy hints on what kind of feedback to leave for a seller:

✦ **Give the seller the benefit of the doubt:** Selling on eBay is a source of income, and most are honest, hard working people. If the transaction could have been a nightmare, but the seller tried to make it right and meet you halfway, that's an easy call — leave positive feedback.

✦ **Whenever possible, reward someone who seems honest or tried to correct a bad situation.** For example, if the seller worked at a snail's pace but you eventually got your item and you're thrilled with it, you may want to leave positive feedback with a caveat. Something like "Item as described, good seller, but very slow to deliver" sends the right feedback message.

✦ **If the seller worked at a snail's pace but packaged the item adequately and the item was kinda-sorta what you expected, you may want to leave neutral feedback.** That is, the experience wasn't bad enough for negative feedback but didn't deserve praise. Here's an example: "Really slow to deliver, didn't say item condition was good not excellent, but did deliver." Wishy-washy is okay as a response to so-so performance; at least the next buyer will know to ask specific questions.

✦ **If the seller doesn't ship your item or the item doesn't match the description and the seller won't make things right, you need to leave negative feedback.** But never write negative feedback in the heat of the moment — and *never* make it personal. Life's interesting enough without taking on extra hassles.

Remember that you cannot retract feedback. You are responsible for your words, which will remain on the eBay site forever (with your user ID next to them for all to see). Be sure to leave a simple, factual, and *unemotional* statement. Important things to mention in your feedback are

✦ How satisfied you are with your purchase

✦ The quality of the packaging

✦ The promptness of shipping

✦ The seller's professionalism

✦ The level of communication

If you must leave a negative feedback comment, know that there is karma in this life. If you couldn't resolve things without a problem, chances are the seller wasn't happy with the trading experience either. Try to work things out first!

Chapter 8: Participating in the Community

In This Chapter

✔ Setting up your About Me and My World page

✔ Having fun in boards, chats, and discussions

✔ Joining an eBay group

*e*Bay is more than just an Internet location for buying and selling great stuff. Most of all, eBay is about people. Today, "social marketing" is the buzzword — and eBay wants the world to know that it has created (and works hard to maintain) a community. And prime real estate in *this* community costs nothing! As in real-life communities, you participate as much as works for you. You can get involved in all sorts of neighborhood activities, or you can just sit back, mind your own business, and watch the world go by.

As you've probably heard by now, one of the main ways to participate in the eBay community is through feedback (which I explain in detail in Chapters 5 and 7). In this chapter, I show you some other ways to become part of the community. You can socialize, get information from other members, leave messages, or just read what everybody's talking about on eBay's message boards, chat boards, and corporate announcement board. I include tips on how to use all these places to your benefit. The tools in this chapter help you solidify your place in the community that is eBay.

Your Home on eBay: About Me

Want to know more about the people behind those user IDs? Thousands of eBay members have created personal Web pages on eBay called About Me pages. eBay users with active About Me pages have a Me icon (with a blue lowercase *m* and a red lowercase *e*) next to their user IDs.

If you're on eBay, you *need* an About Me page. Checking out the About Me page of people you conduct business with gives you an opportunity to get to know them. Because eBay is a cyberspace market, you have no other way to let prospective bidders know that you're a real person. (Don't you shop at some stores because you like the owners or people who work there?) The About Me page takes a first step toward establishing a professional and trusted identity at eBay.

The About Me page enables you to personalize yourself as a bidder to sellers and as a business to prospective bidders. (See Figure 8-1 for an example.) Your About Me page also becomes your About the Seller page if you have an eBay store.

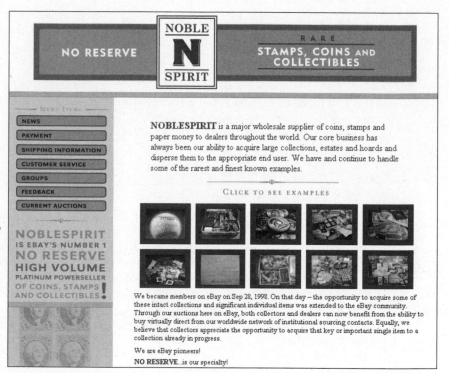

Figure 8-1: An excellent example of a business About Me page from member NobleSpirit.

An About Me page benefits you also when you buy. Sellers usually like to know about their bidders to build confidence in their trading partners. See an example of a personal My eBay page in Figure 8-2.

If you don't have an About Me page, put this book down and set one up immediately. It doesn't have to be a work of art; just get something up there to tell the rest of the community who you are. You can always go back later and add to (or redesign) it.

Figure 8-2:
Aunt Patti
tells us
about her
hobbies and
interests.

The About Me page can also be a deal-maker or a deal-breaker. Once I was looking around eBay for some extra-long printer cables, and I found several sellers selling just what I wanted. One of the lower-priced sellers had a low feedback rating because he was new on eBay. But he had an About Me page, so I clicked. I found out that the seller was a computer technician by trade and that he and his son made these computer cables together as a family business at home in the evenings. The money they made went to pay for their father-son trips to see their favorite baseball team play. What a great family enterprise! Better yet, he guaranteed the cables. As you might have guessed, I bought the cables, and we both got positive feedback.

Planning and Building an About Me Page

When you plan your About Me page, consider adding the following:

✦ Who you are and where you live.

✦ Your hobbies. If you collect things, here's where to let the world know.

✦ Whether you run your eBay business full-time or part-time, and whether you have another career. This is more integral information about you; let the world know.

✦ The type of merchandise that your business revolves around. Promote it here; tell the reader why your merchandise and service are the best!

✦ Your most recent feedback and a list of your current auctions.

To create your page, click the Me icon next to any user's name, scroll to the bottom of the About Me page that appears, find the line that reads "To create your own About Me page, click here," and click. You can also click the About Me link on the My Account: Personal Information page on My eBay. Or go to

```
pages.ebay.com/community/aboutme.html
```

Then follow the simple formatted template for your first page and work from there.

When you begin to sell on eBay, your About Me page is an important sales tool — so take your time when you create your page. A well-thought-out About Me page improves your sales because people who come across your auctions and check out your About Me page can get a sense of who you are and how serious you are about your eBay activities. They see instantly that you're no fly-by-night seller.

Before you create your About Me page, I suggest that you look at what other users have done. eBay members often include pictures, links to other Web sites (including their personal or business home pages), and links to just about any Web location that reflects their personalities. If your purpose is to generate more business, however, I recommend that you keep your About Me page focused on your auction listings, with a link to your Web site.

The page can be as simple or as complex as you want. You may use one of eBay's templates as presented or gussy up the page with lots of pictures and varied text using HTML.

Sellers with many auctions running at once often add a message to their About Me pages indicating that they're willing to reduce shipping charges if bidders bid on their other auctions as well. This direct tactic may lack nuance, but it increases the number of people who look at (and bid on) your auctions.

Gathering your thoughts

There are several things you must think about prior to setting up your page:

✦ **Title:** Come up with a title for your page. It should be as simple as a welcome greeting.

✦ **Subtitle:** This consists of a few words below your page title that elaborate on your page theme.

+ **Introductory paragraph:** This paragraph can tell a little about you and your hobbies or interests. You can also talk about the items you sell on eBay, but most of all it should reflect your personality.

  In the paragraphs of the About Me page, you can use HTML to add images or fancy text. The titles, however, are standard and won't permit HTML coding.

+ **Second subtitle and paragraph:** Here you can elaborate on your interests and business on eBay. Add more information. Pictures are good too!

+ **eBay activity:** Decide what you'd like to show on the page — how many of your most recent feedback comments and whether you'd like to show your current listings on the page.

  Don't get carried away by showing your last 100 feedback messages; doing so takes up too much space. Display either 10 or 25 and leave it at that. If visitors want to know more about your feedback rating, they can click your feedback number. (After all, they clicked your Me icon to get here, and that's next to your feedback number.)

+ **Links:** There are strict policies governing the use of links on eBay these days. You can link to your own Web site, but only from your About Me page. Visit Book III, Chapter 2 for all these details.

If you've been an advanced user on eBay for a while, consider adding the following to your existing My eBay page:

+ **Your logo:** If you've designed a logo for your eBay business, be sure to put it on the page.

+ **Returns policy:** Outline your standard returns policy for your customers.

+ **Shipping policy:** Explain how you ship and when you ship. Offer discounts on shipping for multiple purchases through your eBay store.

+ **Searchable index to your eBay store:** Let your customers search your store by apparel size, brand name, or item. You can accomplish this with HTML coding.

+ **Payment methods:** Let your customers know what payment methods you accept.

Setting up the page

To create your About Me page, do the following:

1. **Click the Site Map link at the upper right of every eBay page.**

   The Site Map page appears.

2. **In the Connect area, click the About Me link.**

Using little-known, eBay-unique HTML tags

It's not highly publicized, but you can use some unique-to-eBay HTML codes to give your My eBay page a custom look. Some of these codes can be combined with others (such as those for bold and color). Play around with them and see what you come up with! The following gives you the secret codes (sorry, no decoder ring) that you can type into the HTML portion of your text entry:

`<eBayUserID>`: Displays your user ID and real-time feedback rating

`<eBayUserID BOLD>`: Displays your user ID and feedback rating in boldface

`<eBayUserID NOLINK>`: Displays your user ID with no clickable link (useful if you plan to change your ID soon)

`<eBayUserID NOFEEDBACK>`: Displays your user ID with no feedback number after it

`<eBayUserID BOLD NOFEEDBACK>`: Combines two of the previous tags into one

`<eBayFeedback>`: Shows your up-to-the-minute feedback comments in real time

`<eBayFeedback COLOR="red">`: Changes the color of the second line on your feedback comment table to red

`<eBayFeedback TABLEWIDTH="75%">`: Changes the width of your feedback comment table as a percentage of the allowed space (the default value is 90%)

`<eBayItemList>`: Inserts a list of the items you currently have up for sale

`<eBayItemList BIDS>`: Displays everything you're currently bidding on

`<eBayTime>`: Inserts the official eBay time into your text

`<eBayMemberSince>`: Inputs the date and time of your initial eBay registration

---

3. **If you haven't signed in, type your user ID and password in the appropriate boxes.**

   You're taken to the About Me page, as shown in Figure 8-3.

4. **Click the Click Here button.**

5. **Decide whether you want to use eBay's easy step-by-step process or enter your own HTML code, and then click Continue.**

   Because entering HTML code assumes you really know what you're doing, I suggest that you choose the step-by-step process.

6. **Enter the following information:**

   - **Page title:** Type the title of your About Me page (for example, *Welcome to Larry Lunch's Lunchbox Place*).

   - **Welcome paragraph:** Type a personal, attention-grabbing bit of text that greets your visitors (something like *Hey, I like lunchboxes a lot* — only more exciting). You have the option of typing in your own

HTML coding or using the buttons at the top of the box to change the font, color, size, and attributes (see Figure 8-4). The HTML generator is similar to the Sell Your Item page — and similar to most word-processing programs.

You can preview your paragraph at any time by clicking Preview Paragraph at the bottom of the text-entry area. If you don't like what you see, close the Preview window and continue to edit your masterpiece.

Figure 8-3:
The About Me home page.

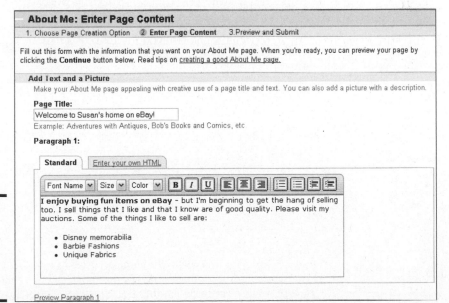

Figure 8-4:
Entering preliminary text and changing attributes.

- **Another paragraph:** Type text for the second paragraph of the page, such as *Vintage, Modern, Ancient*, or *I Collect All Kinds of Lunchboxes*. Then maybe talk about yourself or your collection (such as, *I used to stare at lunchboxes in the school cafeteria . . .* only more, you know, normal).

- **Picture:** If you're adding a picture, type a sentence describing it, for example: *This is my wife Loretta with our lunchbox collection.*

- **Picture URL:** Type the Web site address (URL) where people can find your picture. See Book V, Chapter 5 to find out how to upload digital images to your own (probably free) image area.

- **Feedback:** Select how many of your feedback postings you want to appear on your About Me page. (You can opt not to show any feedback, but I think you should put in a few comments, especially if they're complimentary, as in, "Larry sent my lunchbox promptly, and it makes lunchtime a blast! Everybody stares at it. . . .")

- **Items for Sale:** Select how many of your current auctions you want to appear on your About Me page. If you don't have any auctions running at the moment, you can select the Show No Items option.

- **Favorite Links:** Type the names and URLs of any Web links you want visitors to see, for example, a Web site that appraises lunchboxes. ("It's in excellent condition except for that petrified ham sandwich. . . .")

7. **After you've finished entering this information (and are happy with how it looks), click Continue at the bottom of the page.**

   Don't worry if you're not absolutely wild about your page on the first pass. The important part is to get it published. You can go back and make changes as often as you want.

8. **On the About Me Preview and Submit page, click the button that corresponds to the layout option you want.**

   You are presented with three layout options, as shown in Figure 8-5.

Figure 8-5:
Selecting your page layout style — purely a personal decision.

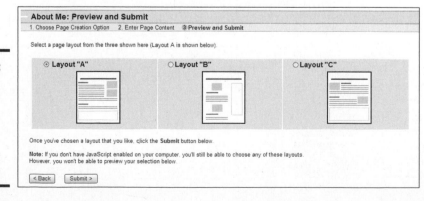

9. **Scroll down the page and check out what your About Me page will look like.**

   If you don't like your current layout, go back up the page and change the layout.

10. **If you don't like what you see, click the Back button and do some more editing.**

11. **When you're happy with your masterpiece, click the Submit button.**

    You did it. Now anyone in the world with access to the Internet can find your personal About Me page on eBay.

Don't forget to update your About Me page often. A good About Me page makes bidders eager to know more about your auctions. An out-of-date About Me page turns off potential bidders. If you choose to update, you need to edit it using HTML. If you don't use HTML, you have to create an entire new page.

You can link to your About Me page from your Web site or from your e-mail because all About Me pages have their own personal URLs. You can find your About Me page by typing members.ebay.com/aboutme/ followed by your user ID. Here's the URL for my page (shown in Figure 8-6):

members.eBay.com/aboutme/marsha_c

Figure 8-6: My About Me page on eBay.

Reaching the World through Your My World Page

If blogging is the key to the new Web, then your My World page is the hub of your eBay user interaction. Your About Me page is there for customers, and the My World page is mostly used by the eBay community. People like to know about other people, and the My World page shows your world, your way.

Although my editors would love for me to give you a long, drawn out, step-by-step list to show you how to get to your My World page – I won't. It's all too simple: Just click your user ID on your My eBay page (or any page for that matter) and you'll arrive at your own (ready-to-fill-out) My World page. To visit the hub (okay, here's the URL), just go to

```
http://myworld.ebay.com/
```

You'll arrive at the My World hub as shown in Figure 8-7.

Figure 8-7:
The My World Hub page.

If you go to the hub, click the *View My World* button. After you click through, you see a page ready to edit. Here's the lowdown on what you can do:

✦ **Edit Image.** By clicking here, you'll come to a page that allows you to automatically upload a picture from your computer, or use one of the handy (but unexciting) eBay-supplied avatars to appear on your My World page.

✦ **Items for Sale**. Here you can choose which and how many of the items you have for sale to show on your page.

✦ **Add Content**. Here you can add things about your eBay life that you'd like everyone to see.

- **Favorites**. Pick up your favorite searches, sellers, and stores, and show them here.

- **Bio.** This link takes you to a form where you can write up a quick and simple bio of yourself.

- **Neighborhoods.** Once you get going on eBay, if you have a little time, you might just want to joining these special interest groups. I am a member of Coffee Lovers (7,250 members), Photography (1,996 members), and Star Trek (256 members — hey, everybody needs to escape reality now and then).

- **Reviews and Guides.** If you've written reviews of items on the site, or written a guide on how to do something (anything), you can have these reviews show up on your My World page.

- **Guest Book**. Use this feature to enable people to leave you messages on your page. Visit my My World page at

      http://myworld.ebay.com/marsha_c

to view some of the comments left by other eBay users, as pictured in Figure 8-8.

Figure 8-8: marsha_c's (that's me) My World page.

✦ **Change Theme.** Don't like eBay's default peach color? Click here to select a color that's a little more you.

✦ **Change layout**. Once you've put in your content, this link allows you to move things around on the page, or even change the number of columns.

Playing Nice with Other eBay Members

The navigation bar has a handy Community link that connects you to the people and happenings on eBay. eBay has more than 100 million members — a bigger population than some countries — but it can still have that small-town feel through groups, chat rooms, and discussion boards. Start on the main page by clicking Community on the navigation bar. Now you can access more than three dozen category-specific chat and discussion boards, a bunch of general chat and discussion boards, and help discussion boards.

But there's a whole lot more to the eBay community, as you find out in this section. Take a little time to explore it for yourself.

News and chat, this and that

The Community Overview page is not quite like *The New York Times* ("All the News That's Fit to Print"), but it is the place to go to find all the news, Neighborhoods, chat rooms, and message board links. Figure 8-9 shows you what the page looks like.

Hear ye, hear ye! eBay's announcement boards

If you were living in the 1700s, you'd see a strangely dressed guy in a funny hat ringing a bell and yelling, "Hear ye, hear ye!" every time you opened eBay's announcement boards. (Then again, if you were living in the 1700s, you'd have no electricity, no computer, no fast food, or anything else you probably consider fun — like eBay!) In any case, eBay's announcement boards are the most important place to find out what's going on (directly from headquarters) on the Web site. And no one even needs to ring a bell.

You have your choice of two boards: the general announcement board and the system announcement board. The general announcement board is where eBay lists new features and policy changes. Visiting this page is like reading your morning eBay newspaper, because eBay adds comments to this page almost every day. You find out about upcoming changes in categories, new promotions, and eBay goings-on. Reach this page by clicking the link or going to the following

www2.ebay.com/aw/marketing.shtml

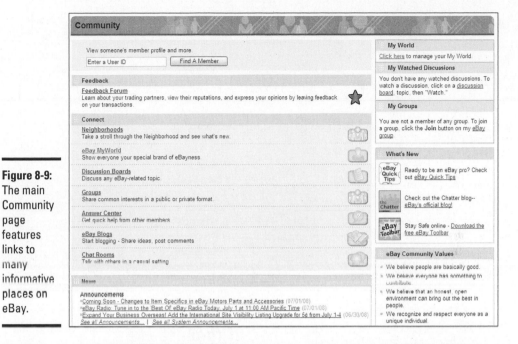

Figure 8-9:
The main
Community
page
features
links to
many
informative
places on
eBay.

Because the general announcement page carries announcements almost
back to the beginning of eBay time, let me give you a quick way to find what
you're looking for. Suppose you want to find out about any new Feedback
changes. Just use your browser's Find feature by pressing Ctrl+F. Type **feedback** in the box that appears, and you'll quickly find the announcements
you're looking for.

Figure 8-10 shows you eBay's general announcement board, complete with
information that could affect your listings.

When you look at some of eBay's URL addresses, you may notice a subfolder
named /*aw*/. The *aw* harkens back to the day when eBay wasn't eBay — but
was AuctionWeb instead (way back when I joined up).

eBay reports outages and system glitches on the system announcement
board, at the following address:

www2.ebay.com/aw/announce.shtml

eBay uses this board also to update users on glitches in the system and
when those may be rectified (should you wonder whether the problem is
lurking on your computer or on the eBay system).

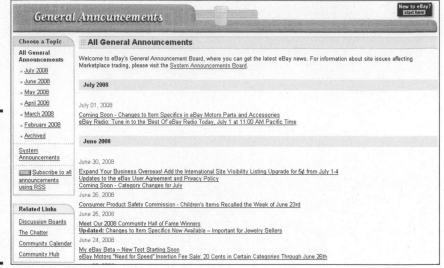

Figure 8-10:
Keep up to date on what's new at eBay by visiting the general announcement board.

Whenever eBay introduces new features, explanations, or links, they appear in the general announcement board, which is in the News area of the Community Overview page.

Help! I need somebody

If you ever have specific eBay questions, several eBay discussion help boards on the Community: Chat page can help you. You can also go directly to the chat rooms to pose your question to the eBay members currently in residence.

Boards work differently from chat rooms. Chat rooms are full of people who are hanging out talking to each other, all at the same time. Users of discussion boards, however, tend to go in, leave a message or ask a question, and pop out again. Also, to get an answer in a message board, you need to start a thread by asking a question. Title your thread with your question, and you'll no doubt get an answer to your query posted swiftly. Take a look at the technical issues discussion board in Figure 8-11.

You can get most eBay-related questions answered by going to eBay's Answer Center, which you get to by clicking the Answer Center link in the Connect area. You then see questions covering almost any topic you can think of regarding listings on eBay. Just post your question and some kindly eBay member will probably suggest an answer.

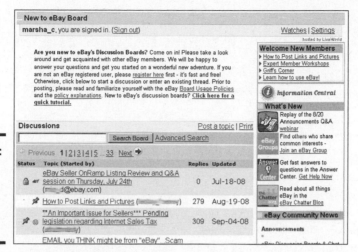

Figure 8-11:
One of
the handy
discussion
boards on
eBay.

eBay newbies often find that the boards are good places to add to their knowledge of eBay. As you scroll on by, read the Q & A postings from the past; your question may already be answered in an earlier posting. You can even ask someone on the board to look at your auction listing and provide an opinion on your descriptions or pictures.

Community chat rooms

Because sending e-mail to eBay's customer service people can be frustratingly slow if you need an answer right away (they get bombarded with a gazillion questions a day), you may want to try for a faster answer by posting your question on one of the community message boards.

You can always tell whether an eBay staff member is replying on a board because the top border line of his or her post is in pink (not gray, as with regular users). They've earned the nickname "Pinks" on the boards.

Knowledgeable veteran eBay members or customer-service "pinks" (if they're around) generally answer posted questions as best they can. The answers are the opinions of members and are certainly not eBay gospel. Most questions are answered in about 15 minutes. If not, repost your question — but make sure you do so on the appropriate board; each board has a specific topic of discussion.

Members who post on these boards often share helpful tips and Web sites and alert other members to scams. Newbies may find that *lurking* (reading without posting) on some of these boards helps them find out more about how eBay works. Occasionally, an eBay staffer shows up, which is kinda like inviting Bill Gates to a meeting of new Windows users. eBay staff members are usually hounded with questions.

Rating the member chat rooms and boards

You know you need help, but you don't know which area is best for you. Here's my take on which boards are most helpful:

✔ **Auction listings board:** This discussion board is a catch-all for many subjects. If you don't see a board specific to your question (or if you post to another board and get no reply), try this one — it's always hopping with lots of peeps (people).

✔ **Photos/HTML board and images/HTML board:** Good help from other eBay members for those with specific questions about using HTML and posting pictures in your auctions.

You can access a new board from any other board by scrolling the drop-down list at the top of each board page.

✔ **Discuss eBay's newest features chat:** This board (also known as DNF) is where you find many of the folks devoted to protesting eBay's policies and new features. Brace yourself — conversation on this board can become nasty. Keep in mind, however, that many of the regulars on this board are extremely knowledgeable about eBay.

If a new policy or some sort of big change occurs, the boards are most likely going to fill pretty quickly with discussion about it. On slow days, however, you may need to wade through personal messages and chatting with no connection to eBay. Many of the people who post on these boards are longtime members with histories (as well as feuds) that can rival any soap opera. On rare occasions, the postings can get abusive. Getting involved in personality clashes or verbal warfare gains you nothing. Duck the crossfire and look for the useful stuff.

No matter how peeved the users of a chat room or message board may get — and no matter how foul or raunchy the language — no one on eBay ever sees it. eBay uses a built-in vulgarity checker that deletes any (well, okay, *as many as possible*) words or phrases that eBay considers offensive or obscene.

The one cardinal rule for eBay chat boards and message boards is: *No doing business on the board.* No advertising items for sale! Not now. Not ever. eBay bans any repeat offenders who break this rule from participating on these boards.

User-to-user (General) discussion boards

In addition to chat boards, eBay also has *discussion* boards, in which the topics are deliberately open-ended — just as the topics of discussion in coffeehouses tend to vary depending on who happens to be in them at any given time. Check out these areas and read ongoing discussions about eBay's latest buzz. It's a lot of fun and good reading. Post your opinions to the category that suits you. Here are few of my favorites:

✦ **The eBay Town Square:** A potpourri of various subjects and topics.

✦ **The Soapbox:** The place to voice your views and suggestions to help build a better eBay.

✦ **Night Owls Nest:** A fun locale for creatures of the night and their unique postings. (As I'm writing this, for example, there's a thread with spirited advice to a community member who needs help with his "gassy" cat.)

✦ **The Park:** An interesting place where community members join in for fun ideas.

Checking Out Other Chat Rooms

About a dozen chat rooms on eBay specialize in everything from pure chat to charity work. In this section, I describe a few of these boards.

Café society

The eBay Café (eBay's first message board from back when eBay was mostly selling Pez candy dispensers) and AOL Café message boards attract mostly regulars chatting about eBay gossip. Frequent postings include the sharing of personal milestones and whatever else is on people's minds. You can also find useful information about eBay and warnings about potential scams.

Holiday board

Although eBay suggests that this is the place to share your favorite holiday memories and thoughts, it's really a friendly place where people meet and chat about home and family. Stop by for cybermilk and cookies next time you have a few minutes and want to visit with your fellow auction addicts.

Giving board

eBay isn't only about making money. On the Giving board, it's also about making a difference. Members in need post their stories and requests for assistance. Other members with items to donate post offers for everything from school supplies to clothing.

If you feel like doing a good deed, conduct a member-benefit auction or donate directly to those in need. For information on how to participate, visit the eBay's GivingWorks at

www.ebaygivingworks.com

Emoticons: Communicating graphically

When you visit the eBay boards, you may notice that many experienced posters to the board have cute little smiley icons, called emoticons, next to their posts to show emotion. The following table shows how you too can doll up your posts with a little emotion.

You can type the keyboard shortcuts or use the HTML image links to display your chosen

icon. Be sure not to put spaces between the characters in the key combinations. Using HTML is pretty easy; for example, `<img src="http://groups.ebay.com/images/emoticons/blush.gif">` gets you the blushing smiley.

Emoticon	Key Combinations	HTML
	X - (	http://groups.ebay.com/images/emoticons/angry.gif
	B -)	http://groups.ebay.com/images/emoticons/cool.gif
	] :)	http://groups.ebay.com/images/emoticons/devil.gif
	: D	http://groups.ebay.com/images/emoticons/grin.gif
	:)	http://groups.ebay.com/images/emoticons/happy.gif
	: x	http://groups.ebay.com/images/emoticons/love.gif
	:		http://groups.ebay.com/images/emoticons/plain.gif
	: (	http://groups.ebay.com/images/emoticons/sad.g6if
	: 0	http://groups.ebay.com/images/emoticons/shocked.gif

Emoticon	Key Combinations	HTML
☺	: p	http://groups.ebay.com/images/emoticons/silly.gif
☺	;)	http://groups.ebay.com/images/emoticons/wink.gif
☺	? : |	http://groups.ebay.com/images/emoticons/confused.gif
☺	: 8 }	http://groups.ebay.com/images/emoticons/blush.gif
☹	: _ |	http://groups.ebay.com/images/emoticons/cry.gif
☺	: ^ 0	http://groups.ebay.com/images/emoticons/laugh.gif
☺	; \	http://groups.ebay.com/images/emoticons/mischief.gif

Emergency contact board

The Emergency contact board is no *Rescue 911,* but if your computer crashes and you lose all your info, this board is the place to put out an all-points bulletin for help. If your ISP goes on vacation, your phone line is on the fritz, or you're abducted by aliens and can't connect to your buyers or sellers, use a friend's computer to post a message on the emergency contact board. A dedicated group of eBay users frequent this board, and they will try to help you by passing on your e-mails to the intended parties. Talk about a bunch of *givers!*

Recently a bidder posted to say that her computer had crashed *and* that she was in the process of moving. She asked her sellers to be patient and she would get to them as soon as possible. The friendly regulars of the emergency contact board looked up her bidding history and e-mailed the sellers whose auctions she'd won in the last week. Then they forwarded her the e-mails they'd sent on her behalf. The sellers understood the situation and did not leave negative feedback for the lack of communication.

If you're having trouble contacting other eBay members, posting for help from other members to track 'em down often gets the job done.

If you think you may be the victim of a rip-off, check the emergency contact board. The buyer or seller may have left word about an e-mail problem. On the flip side, you may find out that you're not alone in trying to track down an eBay delinquent who seems to have skipped town. Posting information about a *potentially* bad eBay guy is (at the least) bad manners on most boards. If you wrap it in the guise of an emergency contact, however, you can clue in other members about a potential problem. Stick to the facts and make the post as honest and useful (and non-inflammatory) as you can.

To access the emergency contact board, follow these steps:

1. **From the eBay navigation bar, click the Community link.**

   You are brought to the Community hub page.

2. **In the Connect area, click the Chat Rooms link.**

   You are now on the main Chat page.

3. **Scroll down the Chat page and click Emergency Contact.**

   You see a board full of messages from all the desperate sellers and buyers trying to locate each other.

eBay international chat boards

People from all around the world enjoy eBay. If you're considering buying or selling globally, visit the international boards. They're a great place to post questions about shipping and payments for overseas transactions. Along with eBay chat, the international boards have discussions about current events and international politics.

Got a seller or bidder in Italy? Spain? France? Translate your English messages into the appropriate language through the following Web site:

```
babelfish.yahoo.com
```

If you venture into unfamiliar foreign tongues, I suggest you keep things simple. Don't try to get fancy with your verbiage — stick to standard phrases that can translate literally with minimum hassle.

Sharing Knowledge in Category-Specific Chat Rooms

Want to talk about Elvis, Louis XV, Sammy Sosa, or Howard the Duck? More than twenty category-specific chat boards enable you to tell eBay members what's on your mind about merchandise and auctions. You reach these boards by clicking Community on the main navigation bar and then clicking Chat Rooms in the Connect area.

Discussions mainly focus on merchandise and the nuts and bolts of transactions. Category-specific chat boards are great for posting questions on items that you don't know much about.

You'll get all kinds of responses from all kinds of people. Take some of the help you get with a grain of salt, because some of the folks who help you may be buyers or competitors.

These boards are also great for finding out where to go for more information and to conduct research on specific items. You can also find helpful sources for shipping information about items in that category (such as large furniture in the Antiques section or breakable items on the Glass chat board).

Don't be shy. As your second-grade teacher said, "No questions are dumb." Most eBay members love to share their knowledge.

Joining eBay Groups

If you're the friendly type and would like an instant group of new friends, I suggest you click the Groups link in the Connect area. Here you can find thousands of user groups hosted on eBay but run by eBay community members. They may be groups consisting of people from the same geographic area, folks with similar hobbies, or those interested in buying or selling in particular categories.

eBay groups may be public clubs (open to all) or private clubs (invited memberships only) with their own private boards, accessible only by members of the group.

Joining a group is easy: Just click any of the links on the main Groups page, and you're presented with a dizzying array of groups to join. Your best bet is to participate in chats or discussions and find other members that you'd like to join up with.

Book II
Essential Tools

Contents at a Glance

Chapter 1: Researching on eBay

In This Chapter

✔ Using the search engine

✔ Figuring out what's your "Best Match"

✔ Working with search results

✔ Finding eBay members

✔ Figuring out the category structure!

Think of walking into a store and seeing thousands of aisles of shelves containing millions of Items. Browsing the categories of auctions at eBay can be just as pleasantly boggling, without the prospect of sore feet. Start surfing around the site, and you instantly understand the size and scope of what's for sale. You may feel overwhelmed at first, but the clever eBay folks have come up with lots of ways to help you find exactly what you're looking for.

Working eBay's Search Engine

Anyone can find an auction on eBay. Finding bargains or researching selling prices accurately, on the other hand, requires some finesse. The key is understanding how to search the site for hidden treasures. Just as knowing how to browse the categories is important, knowing how to work the search engine expertly will help you find your item for the lowest price.

The best part about shopping on eBay is that you can find just about everything, from that esoteric lithium battery to new designer dresses (with matching shoes) to pneumatic jackhammers. New or used, it's all here — lurking in the millions of daily listings. But finding the nuggets (deals) can be like searching for the proverbial needle in the haystack. The search secrets in this chapter will put you head and shoulders above your competition for the deals.

Going where the Search button takes you

The single most important button on any eBay page is the Search button. When you type some keywords and click this button, you'll be presented with a list of items matching your keywords on eBay.

TIP

Tips to keep in mind before you search

When searching on eBay, don't forget the following:

✔ **Ignore capitalization of proper names:** eBay doesn't care whether you capitalize. In other words, the search engine doesn't distinguish between caps and noncaps.

✔ **Don't use noise words:** *and, a, an, or,* or *the* are called *noise words.* In searches, these words are interpreted as part of your search unless you enclose them in quotes. Let's say we want to find items from the 1939 classic film, *Gone with the Wind.* I got 1,401 hits from *Gone with the Wind* and 1,486 hits with a search for *gone wind.* Many sellers drop the noise words from their titles, so use as few keywords as you can to expand your search.

✔ **Don't search just within specific categories:** Although a category-specific search narrows your results, you also might miss a great deal of items. Take a look at "Understanding eBay's Category Hierarchy," later in this chapter.

✔ **Think of possible synonyms:** For example, while searching for a ladies watch, I found the following synonyms and abbreviations for *ladies: lady's, ladys, lds,* and *femmes.*

✔ **Use the asterisk symbol to locate misspellings:** I've often found some great deals by finding items incorrectly posted by the sellers. Here are a few examples:

Rodri*. In this search I look for items by the famous Cajun artist *George Rodrigue.* His Blue Dog paintings are world renowned and valuable. By using this search, I managed to purchase a signed Blue Dog lithograph for under $200. (I resold it on eBay later that year for $900!)

Alumi* tree. Remember the old aluminum Christmas trees from the '60s? They've had quite a resurgence in popularity. You can buy these "antiques" in stores for hundreds of dollars, or you can buy one on eBay for half the price. You can find them even cheaper if the seller can't spell *aluminum.*

Cemet* plot. If you're looking for that final place to retire, eBay has some great deals. Unfortunately, sellers haven't narrowed down whether they want to spell it *cemetery* or *cemetary.* This search will find both.

Should you want a more advanced type of search, click the Advanced Search link next to the Search button. You're whisked to the Advanced Search: Find Items page, which will have your search options in a box on the left side of the page, as shown in Figure 1-1. Three categories of searches are available, and each enables you to search for information in a different way.

TIP

To enhance your search, ask the search engine to check both item titles and item descriptions. Select the check box next to Search Title and Description to open up your search. You'll get more hits if you select the Search Title and Description check box, but you may also get too many items that are out of your search range.

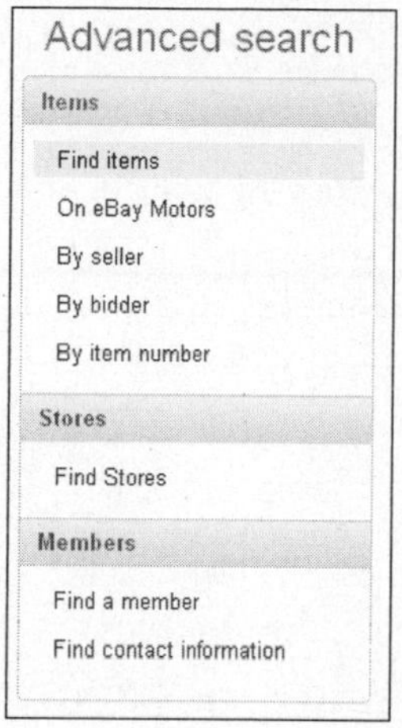

Figure 1-1:
The various
searches
available
in the
Advanced
Search
area.

Advanced search

Items

Find items
On eBay Motors
By seller
By bidder
By item number

Stores

Find Stores

Members

Find a member
Find contact information

Under the Items field, you can choose the following types of searches:

✦ **Find Items:** Search by keywords or item number. Type the keywords that describe an item (for example, *Superman lunchbox* or *antique pocket watch*) and click Search, and you can see how many are available on eBay.

✦ **On eBay Motors.** Looking for something related to wheels or an engine? Click here to see the form specifically designed for eBay Motors searches.

✦ **By Seller:** Every person on eBay has a personal user ID (the name you use to conduct transactions). Use the Items by Seller search if you liked the merchandise from a seller's auction and want to see what else the seller has for sale. Type the seller's user ID, and you get a list of every item that person is selling.

✦ **By Bidder:** User IDs help eBay keep track of every move a user makes at eBay. If you want to see what a particular user (say, a fellow *Star Trek* fan) is bidding on, use the Items by Bidder search. Type a user ID in the By Bidder search box, and you get a list of everything the user has won.

✦ **By Item Number:** Every item that's up for auction on eBay is assigned an item number, which is displayed next to the item name on its page. To find an item by number, just type the number and click Search.

The second search field is Stores. Once you click the link to search in Stores, you can search by two options:

✦ **Stores with matching items:** eBay stores have their own search engine. Listings of items in eBay stores will appear on a regular search for items only under select circumstances.

✦ **Store name only:** If you know an eBay store name or description, you can type a store name — or portion of a store name — and find the store you're looking for.

The final search area is Members:

✦ **Find a Member:** Here you can type the user ID of any eBay member to view his or her feedback profile, About Me page, or user ID history.

✦ **Find Contact Information:** When you are in a transaction with someone, you can type the person's user ID and the number of the transaction to receive an e-mail containing the phone number of your trading partner. This works only if you have a current bid or have bought an item.

Performing a basic search in Advanced

It's your choice — you can make your search as complex (or confusing) as you wish by using the gazillions of options on the Advanced Search page. You can also choose to keep it somewhat basic. I know, it sounds a tad bizarre, but the basic Find Items search is a bit more advanced than typing a few keywords into a box. You do have more options.

When you click Advanced Search on any eBay page, you are brought to the Advanced Search page. On this search form you'll see innumerable boxes. You can fill out some or all of them. The more information you type into this form, the more concise your search can be.

To illustrate this, let's do a basic search as you might do from the Search box. It's a lot easier to find your items in the simple method. Stumped on what words to use in your search? Consider the item you're trying to find. Look at it and determine which words best describe it. Suppose that your favorite china pattern has been discontinued and you want to search eBay for some missing pieces. To quickly find the pieces, follow this process:

1. **Determine the manufacturer's name.**

Since I'm looking for a plate, I turn over the plate I have to look on the back for the manufacturer's name — it's Dansk!

If you don't have all the information you need, check out the manufacturer's Web site or a Web site that specializes in the item you're looking for.

2. **Determine the name for the series, collection, pattern, or design.**

Sometimes an item has more than one name. For example, I'm searching for Bistro (the name of the collection) and Maribo (the pattern name).

3. **Narrow your search even further, if possible or necessary.**

For example, I need to replace a salad plate.

4. **Enter the words for your search.**

I typed *Dansk Bistro Maribo salad* into the keyword box. If someone has listed an item with all those words in the title, I'll be lucky and pull up some winners. However, it's more likely that the words in your initial search are buried in the description.

5. **After you get your search results, you can narrow your search by searching in a category.**

Use the drop-down list at the top of the results to limit your search to a particular main (or *top-level*) category, for example, instead of searching all eBay categories. This might be a good idea if you know for sure where the item is listed.

But items often cross over different categories. When they do, eBay lists (on the left side of the page) the actual categories where the search items were found. From my search results (pictured in Figure 1-2), I can see that my salad plates are listed in the sub-category of Pottery & China. In this instance, I'm lucky that they are listed in only one area, so it's clear that I've found exactly what I'm searching for.

Because my search turned up fewer than 20 items, eBay displays — below the core eBay Buy-it-Nows and Auction listings — the items that both match my search and can be found in eBay Stores.

I often leave this option alone so that my search encompasses all categories. Sometimes sellers (when listing many items at once) make mistakes and list in the wrong category. That's when you can find a real deal.

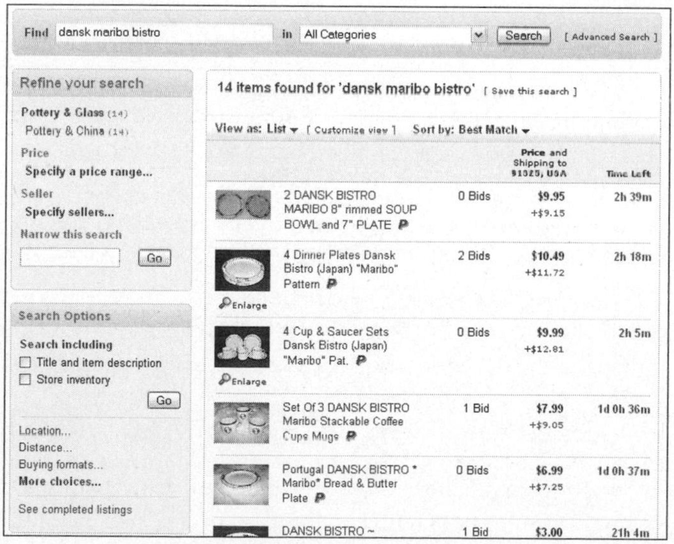

Book II Chapter 1

Researching on eBay

Figure 1-2:
Search results for my salad plates.

| Find | dansk maribo bistro | in | All Categories | Search | [Advanced Search] |

Refine your search

Pottery & Glass (14)
Pottery & China (14)

Price
Specify a price range...

Seller
Specify sellers...

Narrow this search

[Go]

Search Options

Search including
☐ Title and item description
☐ Store inventory

[Go]

Location...
Distance...
Buying formats...
More choices...

See completed listings

14 items found for 'dansk maribo bistro' [Save this search]

View as: List ▾ [Customize view]   Sort by: Best Match ▾

		Price and Shipping to 91525, USA	Time Left
2 DANSK BISTRO MARIBO 8" rimmed SOUP BOWL and 7" PLATE	0 Bids	$9.95 +$9.15	2h 39m
4 Dinner Plates Dansk Bistro (Japan) "Maribo" Pattern 🔍Enlarge	2 Bids	$10.49 +$11.72	2h 18m
4 Cup & Saucer Sets Dansk Bistro (Japan) "Maribo" Pat. 🔍Enlarge	0 Bids	$9.99 +$12.81	2h 5m
Set Of 3 DANSK BISTRO Maribo Stackable Coffee Cups Mugs	1 Bid	$7.99 +$9.05	1d 0h 36m
Portugal DANSK BISTRO * Maribo* Bread & Butter Plate	0 Bids	$6.99 +$7.25	1d 0h 37m
DANSK BISTRO ~	1 Bid	$3.00	21h 4m

6. Tell eBay how you want the results arranged by using the drop-down list.

For example, if you want to check out auctions in order of how soon they're closing, choose Items Ending Soonest. (This is my favorite option — you might miss the deal of the century while you're sifting through hundreds of listings in another order.) In the Sort By area, choose one of the following options:

- **Best Match:** This is eBay's default when you search for an item. It's the latest invention on searching. No one really knows exactly what this means. eBay describes it this way:

  Along with the listing keywords and other information, one of the most important elements in this calculation is the historical buyer behavior on the site for similar searches.

  Er, I always prefer my searches as Ending Soonest, but "Best Match" in my searches doesn't work that way.

  I can tell you that sellers, according to their information on the "seller dashboard," are raised and lowered in search according to buyer satisfaction and detailed seller ratings (DSRs). Also, offering *free shipping* (as long as you're in good standing) will bring your items higher up in Best Match searches.

  Here's another reason, that, as a buyer, you might not want to penalize a seller just because *"I don't give anyone five stars."* Those Star ratings mean a whole lot to sellers; please be generous when you've had a good transaction. (Rant over).

- **Time: Ending Soonest:** Auctions closing first appear at the top of the results.

- **Time: Newly Listed:** The most recently posted auctions are listed first.

- **Price + Shipping: Lowest First:** Auctions are listed based on the combined cost of shipping to your ZIP code and the price of the item. They are listed as lowest priced to the highest priced.

- **Price + Shipping: Highest First:** This search, too, is based on the combined cost of shipping and the current cost (or high bid) on the item. Items are listed from highest- to lowest-priced.

- **Price: Highest First:** This sort of ignores the shipping costs and goes right to the heart of the search; the price of the item. This is useful when you're searching for, say, a 1967 Corvette and you want to buy a car, not a Hot Wheels toy.

- **Distance: Nearest First:** If you're looking for a bunny-style, wrought-iron boot scraper or something as huge as a stove, you might want to buy from a seller who is close by to save shipping costs (you may even be able to pick up the item).

- **Category:** This groups the items in your results by category.

7. Use the next drop-down list to select how you want to view the results.

You've got three choices:

- **List View:** The standard eBay format of the gallery picture on the left and the listing information to the right.

- **Gallery View:** Here (as shown in Figure 1-3) you see the search results in little boxes. I don't find this method as efficient because each listing takes up more space on my viewable page — and I have to scroll more to view all the results. I also find it more difficult to compare listings at a glance, because so few show up on each screen.

- **Snapshot View.** I dunno, call me crazy, but looking at a bunch of pictures without pricing (as in Figure 1-4) seems pretty useless.

8. Select how many items you want to see on a page.

eBay searches default to 50 items per page. You may want to see more or less depending on the speed of your connection. In list view the options are 25, 50, 100, and 200.

9. After you've filled in all your search parameters, click the Search button.

A list of auctions appears, in the order you selected in the Sort By area.

Book II
Chapter 1

Researching
on eBay

The eBay search engine is more sophisticated than ever. If you want to perform a super-quick search by keyword or item number, just type it in any of eBay's search boxes throughout the site.

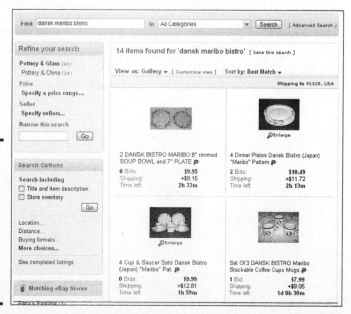

Figure 1-3: In the Gallery view, each listing takes up a large amount of your screen's real estate.

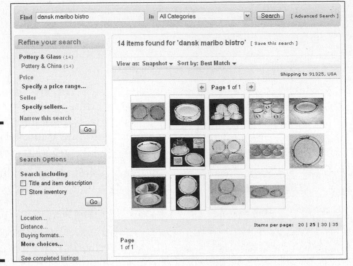

Figure 1-4:
You get to
see nice
pictures
and little
else in the
Snapshot
View.

If you want to search completed items to get an idea of what the salad plate has sold for before, select the check box next to Completed Listings Only. This search returns results of items that have already ended. This is my favorite search option on eBay; I use it as a strategic bidding and pricing tool. How? If you're bidding on an item and want to know whether the prices are likely to go too high for your pocketbook, you can use this search option to compare the current price of the item to the selling price of similar items from auctions that have already ended. You can go back about two weeks.

Refining even the most basic search

You can refine your search even further by clicking the Advanced Search link next to the Search box at the top of your search results page. This link throws quite a few more options into the package. Don't be intimidated; you need to understand just a few more bells and whistles.

All the options from the basic search are available on the Advanced Search page, plus a few more:

✦ **Words:** You can choose to search

    All of these words

    Any of these words

    Exact Phrase

    Exact Match only

To save yourself a lot of grief, photocopy Table 1-1. It features shortcuts you can use in the basic Search box to get the same results as the above options — and more.

✦ **Exclude words from your search:** If you're looking for some silver flat-ware, and you want it to be solid, not plated, you could type *plated*. That search would exclude any item listings that contain the word *plated*.

✦ **Items Priced:** Here's where you can narrow your search to a specific price range. I don't recommend using this option because you never know what you might miss.

✦ **From Specific Sellers:** If you want to locate an item being sold by up to ten sellers, you can type their user IDs here, separating each user ID by a comma or a space. If you want to find items excluding certain sellers, click the drop-down list and list the offending sellers in the text box.

✦ **Location:** You can elect to see your results from all items on eBay or you can search by country.

  • **All Items Listed on eBay.com:** Search all of eBay, no matter which country.

  • **Items Available To:** Select a country from the drop-down list and the search engine looks for items from sellers willing to ship to that country.

  • **Items Located In:** Use the drop-down box to find items from the country you specified.

✦ **Currency:** If you have a yen to pay for your item with a foreign currency (so to speak), you can search for sellers who accept the following:

  • Any currency

  • U. S. dollar

  • Australian dollar

  • Canadian dollar

  • Euro

  • Indian rupee

  • New Taiwan dollar

  • Pounds sterling

  • Swiss franc

✦ **Multiple Item Listings:** If you're looking for a gaggle of stuffed geese, you can input a number and indicate whether you want At Least, Exactly, or At Most that many. You may alternatively indicate that you're looking for any listing listed as a lot.

Next, you can select to display only particular items:

✦ **Auctions only:** If you love the thrill of bidding, you can limit your search to auctions only. (But why? There may be a better deal in Buy It Now.)

✦ **Buy It Now items only:** This option comes in handy when you simply must purchase something immediately. This would work well for the pair of tickets you've found to *The Producers* or when you're about to run out of your favorite moisturizer and don't have time to make it to the store within the next week to pick some up.

You can isolate Buy It Now items also by clicking the Buy It Now tab, which appears at the top of the search results.

✦ **Locate Items Near You:** If you're selling or buying something big that you can't (or don't want to) ship or pick up, this option allows you to select a mileage range of 10 to 2000 miles. You may also type in a ZIP code or select a popular city.

✦ **Items being sold for charitable organizations:** If you're looking for items being sold only to benefit nonprofits, you may indicate that here.

Should you not want to go through this tedious, step-by-step check-mark thing every time you want to make a thorough search, you might want to memorize the shortcuts in Table 1-1. These shortcuts can be typed in any simple search box on any eBay page to get a specialized search.

Table 1-1   Shortcut Symbols for Conducting Speedy Searches

Symbol	*Effect on Search*	*Example*
No symbol, multiple words	Returns auctions with all included words in the title.	*olympus mount* might return an item for an Olympus camera or an item from Greece.
"Term in quotes"	Searches items with the exact phrase within the quotes.	*"stuart little"* is more likely than *stuart little* to return items about the mouse because the former returns the words in the exact order you request.
Asterisk	Serves as a wild-card, good to use to include singular *and* plural of an item.	*budd** returns items that start with *budd*, such as Beanie Buddy, Beanie Buddies, or Buddy Holly.
Words enclosed in parentheses, separated by a comma and with no space	Finds items related to either item before or after the comma.	*(signed,autographed)* returns items with titles that have been listed as either signed or auto-graphed.
Minus sign	Excludes results with the word after the minus sign.	*signed −numbered* finds items that are signed but not numbered.

Symbol	Effect on Search	Example
Minus symbol and parentheses	Finds items with words before the parentheses but excludes those within the parentheses.	*Packard –(hewlett,bell)* finds those rare Packard auto collectibles.
Parentheses	Searches the main word plus both versions of the word in parentheses.	*political (pin,pins)* searches for political pin or political pins. *Be sure not to put a space in this search.*
At-sign (@) and number 1	Searches two out of three words.	*@1 new purse shoes dress* gets you a nice new outfit.

Searching for items by seller

The next search option in the Items search area is to find items by seller. After spending time on eBay, you'll find that you have favorite sellers. You can always access a seller's other items for sale by clicking the View Seller's Other Items link on the listing page.

If you intend to follow the auctions of certain sellers, it's a good idea to store their links in your My eBay page. (For more on that, see Chapter 5.)

Here's a way to see whether one of your competing sellers has an item like yours up for sale:

1. **Click the Items by Seller link.**

2. **On the resulting page, type the eBay user ID of the person you want to find out about.**

If you're a buyer looking for items from a seller you're doing business with and you only have the seller's e-mail address, you can just type that in.

3. **If you want to see auctions that this specific seller has conducted in the past, select the Include Completed Listings option.**

You can choose to see all current and previous auctions, as well as auctions that have ended in the last day, last week, or past 15 days, as shown in Figure 1-5.

If you want to see the auctions that are closing right away, select Time Ending Soonest.

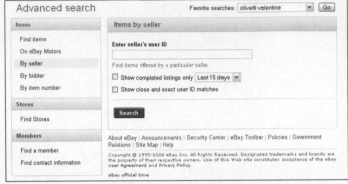

Figure 1-5:
You can search for all open or completed listings by an individual seller.

4. **Show close and exact User ID matches.**

   Sometimes you may not remember the exact User ID of someone. For example, I am *marsha_c*. You might not remember the underscore between the *a* and the *c*. When you click this option, you see all IDs that are similar to mine (although without the underscore, my ID doesn't show up at all).

5. **Click the Search button.**

Searching for items by bidder

Also on the main search page is the Items by Bidder option. Sellers and buyers alike use it when an auction is going on to figure out their strategies. You may be wondering why you'd ever want to run a bidder search. Well, when you've been outbid by the same person several times, you might not need to ask that question. If you want an item badly enough, you'll become interested in the bidding patterns of others. (See Book I, Chapter 6 for more bargain-shopping secrets.)

When researching your competition, always check out other bidders' completed auctions as well as the times they've been outbid. This will give you a good grasp of their bidding *modus operandi*.

A bidder search is similar to a seller search, except you can add a few bidding filters. You can select to see every item the bidder has won.

Understanding the icons

When you are presented with your search results, you may notice tiny icons next to some of the items. Here's a key to what those little pictures mean.

Icon	*What It Means*
	The listing is new. The icon stays the first 24 hours an item is listed.
	The seller has included a picture along with the item description, and you must open the item listing to see the picture.
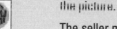	The seller may perform gift services for that item, such as wrapping and shipping to another address.

 The item is listed with a gallery photo (may show up in a category search). Gallery photos are the small pictures of the item that you see next to a listing when you run a search.

 You may purchase the listing for a set price without having it go into an auction.

 The item is being sold through a live auction. Click the item for more details.

 The vehicle for sale has been inspected. This icon appears on the eBay Motors site.

Searching stores

The next search link area allows you to search eBay Stores. If you look back at Figure 1-3, you'll see a Stores section on the left side of the page. You have a couple of options when you search from this area:

✦ **Items in Stores:** The search engine goes through all items listed in all eBay stores to find your selected keywords in the item title. (Searching eBay stores from the eBay search page allows you to search item titles and item descriptions as well as completed items.)

✦ **Find Stores:** The search engine searches only the store names and the brief store descriptions posted by the sellers.

When you run a search for an item on eBay, you'll see a column of yellow boxes on the left side of the results page. If you scroll down to the bottom, you'll see the heading Matching eBay Stores. This area offers links to eBay stores that also carry the item you're looking for.

Working with Search Results

With the growth of eBay, search results have become more and more complex. The results page will give you lots of extra clues for narrowing your quest and homing in on exactly what you want. This is especially handy when you've performed your search through the small search boxes on most eBay pages, rather than initiating your search from the "official" Search page hub. Take a look at Figure 1-6, and note some of the important links.

At the top of the search results are tabs that can narrow your search in a way that may better suit your shopping plans. You can use the tabs to sort your results in three ways:

✦ **All Items:** This is the default view of the results page and the best way to see every item that matches your search.

✦ **Auctions:** Click this tab if you want to see only items up for auction.

✦ **Buy It Now:** If you've placed a search for an item that you want to buy now, this is for you. Click this tab and you'll see the items that match your query that can be bought immediately.

You can also sort your results by listings ending soonest, newly listed items, the lowest or highest price plus shipping, the nearest location, and PayPal items first, Best Match or Category. All these options are available on the main search page, but you can sort on the results page as well.

Matching eBay Stores

When your search nets only a few items (for example, my search in Figure 1-3), eBay will give you some help by adding some store results under "Some of the matching items found in other eBay areas." Below this headline, you'll see stores listed, along with the price they charge for items that match the search.

Also, all eBay searches include links to stores that carry your item. These links are in the Matching eBay Stores area (on the bottom left). You'll also see a link to all stores that match your search.

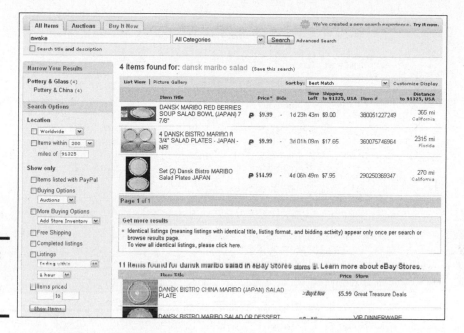

Figure 1-6:
A search
results
page.

Matching categories

On the left side of the page, the top links are matching categories, which can
be very helpful. In the search in Figure 1-7, I'm looking for a brand of cosmet-
ics called Awake. Reviewing those 434 results would be time-consuming.

Figure 1-7:
Search
results for
awake.

Rather than going through the pages of all results, I look at the category list on the left, and see a category that looks promising: Health & Beauty.

If I click the Health and Beauty category, I'll have only 20 results. My search results can be refined even further by choosing one of the subcategories within Health and Beauty.

Search options

Below the Matching Categories area are check boxes that allow you to further refine your search. Here are some of the handy options:

✦ **Buying Options:** Accomplishes the same thing as clicking the Buy It Now or Auction tab at the top of the results page.

✦ **Gift items:** Click here to see items with little blue box icons, which indicate that the seller thinks this a good gift item and has paid eBay extra to let you know that.

✦ **Completed Listings:** The perfect search to do your research on how an item will sell for — or how much you should expect to pay.

✦ **Free Shipping:** You can isolate your search to only those sellers who offer free shipping. But why? They may have hiked their pricing to include shipping.

✦ **Listings:** Use the drop-down list to select the number of hours or days you want reflected in your search:

   • **Started Within:** Items that are newly listed on the site (catch the Buy It Now deals before someone else does).

   • **Ending in More Than:** If you want to participate in an auction that closes in the future, make a selection here.

   • **Ending Within:** Select the number of hours within which you'd like to see item's auction ending. It's a turn on the old "going, going, gone" game that I used to play with my daughter when we'd check out auctions about to close and bid as they were closing.

✦ **Items priced:** Narrow your search within a specific price range.

✦ **Items within miles of a certain ZIP code:** When you're signed in, your ZIP code is filled in by default, but you can type in any ZIP code. You also select the mileage from a drop-down list.

In the quest for even more minutiae, a link at the bottom of this box allows you to customize the search queries even further. You can definitely take a good thing too far, and this is getting pretty close.

Finding eBay Members

With millions of eBay users on the loose, you may think it's hard to track folks down. Nope. eBay's powerful search engine kicks into high gear to help you find other eBay members in seconds.

The search page also has links to find people or get info about them from eBay:

✦ **Find a member:** This link takes you to the main Find Members page, where you can search for specific About Me pages. You can also look at the feedback profile of a user and view user ID histories of fellow eBay members.

✦ **Find contact information:** If you're involved in a transaction with someone, you can click this link to have the person's phone number e-mailed to you. Because this information is confidential, you must be involved in a transaction with the person. You'll be asked to type the other member's user ID and the transaction number you're dealing with before this information is sent out.

✦ **Find user ID:** If you know a friend's e-mail address, you can input it on this page to find out whether he or she is registered on eBay.

To protect privacy and prevent possible harassment, you'll have to be in a transaction with your friend before you get any information.

The first nine of your favorite searches appear in a drop-down list on every page in the search-hub area.

Understanding eBay's Category Hierarchy

Understanding eBay's categories was a lot easier when there were just a few. I remember thinking that the quantity of categories was daunting when the site boosted the number up to the unthinkable 4000. Now that the total number of categories is approaching the 20,000 mark, the time has come to either abandon all hope of understanding them or to take things in hand and appreciate the elegance and organization of a system that's just beyond the realm of comprehension. You may never totally understand the category structure, but that's okay — what's important is knowing which categories the sellers use most frequently.

As I write this book, eBay is adding, combining, and subtracting categories every two weeks to simplify the category structure. eBay works hard to keep the site in an organized fashion, but the constant reorganizing that's necessary can be a little daunting for new users.

Book II
Chapter 1

Researching
on eBay

How the structure works

Go ahead, ask me what I'm interested in. Let's see, I like art, golf, photography, fashion — I won't bore you with the rest, but it sounds like a fairly benign list, doesn't it? I'm sure your list of interests is straightforward too. Right?

Well, not quite. Say you like golf as much as I do. You might just click the Sporting Goods category link on the home page, figuring you'll find Golf on the next page as a link.

Surprise! The Sporting Goods category is made up of approximately 1200 sub-, sub-sub-, and sub-sub-subcategories of everything from golf balls to Pittsburgh Penguins jerseys. (Golf alone has 87 subcategories.) This hasn't been done to confuse you. It's just that there are so many areas that your sports interest might take you. To accommodate the countless auctions that sports aficionados, collectors, and participants list, eBay had to create a lot of small areas.

Drilling down to your item

Depending on what you're looking for, things can get confusing. For example, suppose I want to find a category with items relating to my dog, a somewhat obscure breed called schipperke. You might think I have it made. I mean, how could a category for such an esoteric breed of dog be anything but very simple?

Schipperkes have their own category in the main category of Collectibles on eBay. (eBay has categories in Collectibles for more than 120 breeds of dogs. Know anybody who collects dogs? See what I mean about mystifying?) Currently, 104 schipperke items are listed in the category.

But there are more auctions. When I ran a title search on *Schipperke,* I came up with 91 items, as shown in Figure 1-8. When I selected the check box to include descriptions, I got 124 listings. When I followed my own advice (earlier in this chapter) and entered a search for *schipperk*,* I found 129 items. When I searched for *shipperke* (misspelled), I found 2 more.

Items for schipperke (and its misspellings) were listed in all these categories:

Collectibles: Animals: Dog: Schipperke

Collectibles: Animals: Dog: Other

Collectibles: Animals: Dog: Schnauzer

Collectibles: Animals: Dog: Basset Hound

Collectibles: Animals: Dog: Rottweiler

Collectibles: Housewares & Kitchenware

Book II
Chapter 1

Figure 1-8:
Looking for
Schipperke
in any
category.

Researching
on eBay

Collectibles: Transportation: Automobilia: Decals & Stickers

Jewelry & Watches: Watches: Charm

Jewelry & Watches: Watches: Fashion

Jewelry & Watches: Watches: Sport

Jewelry & Watches: Fashion Jewelry: Charm Bracelets

Jewelry & Watches: Fashion Jewelry: Necklaces & Pendants

Jewelry & Watches: Handcrafted, Artisan Jewelry

Art: Direct from the Artist

Art: Art from Dealers & Resellers

Home & Garden: Pet Supplies: Dog Supplies: Other

Home & Garden: Pet Supplies: Dog Supplies: Signs & Plaques

Home & Garden: Pet Supplies: Dog Supplies: Dog Lover Products

Home & Garden: Inside the Home: Home Décor & Accents: Clocks: Wall Clocks

Clothing, Shoes & Accessories: Men: Casual Shirts

Clothing, Shoes & Accessories: Women: Misses

Antiques: Other

Books: Nonfiction Books: Hardcover/Softcover

Books: Children's Books

Everything Else

Business & Industrial: Office: Office Supplies: Mousepads

I hope you realize where I'm going with all this. Even though I chose an arcane item, searching only through the specific category designated for it would have affected my search significantly. I would have missed some of the more interesting items.

Chapter 2: Researching on the Web

In This Chapter

✔ Researching collectible auctions and values

✔ Common-sense buying guidelines

✔ Using online information in your research

If you don't know what your item is worth, then as a seller you may not get the highest price. If you don't know how to make your item easy to find, it may not be noticed by even the hardiest of collectors. If you don't know the facts or what to say, your well-written title and detailed description (combined with a fabulous picture) may still not be enough to get the highest price for your item.

Knowing your item is a crucial part of successful selling on eBay. An item may be appraised or listed in a book for a high value, but what you care about is the price at which the item will actually sell. Imagine someone uncovering a hoard of your item and, not knowing the value of it, dumping it on eBay with low Buy It Now prices. This scenario would drive down the value of the item within a couple of weeks. Great for buyers — but not so great for sellers.

The best advice you can follow as you explore any free-market system is *caveat emptor* — let the buyer beware. Although you can't guarantee that every one of your transactions will be perfect, if you research items thoroughly before you bid, you won't lose too much of your hard-earned money — or too much sleep.

Researching Collectible Auctions

If you're just starting out on eBay, chances are you like to shop and you also collect items that interest you. You'll find out early in your eBay adventures that a lot of people online know as much about collecting as they do about bidding — and some are serious contenders.

Understanding grading terms

Welcome to my version of grade school, without the bad lunch. One of the keys to establishing value is knowing an item's condition, typically referred to as an item's *grade*. The following table lists the most common grading categories that collectors use. The information in this table is used with permission from (and appreciation to) Lee Bernstein.

Category (Also Known As)	What It Means	Example
Mint (M, Fine, Mint-In-Box [MIB], 10)	A never-used collectible in perfect condition with complete packaging (including instructions, original attachments, tags, and so on) identical to how it appeared on the shelf in the original box.	Grandma got a soup tureen as a wedding present, never opened it, and stuck it in her closet for the next 50 years.
Near Mint (NM, Near Fine, Like-New, 9)	The collectible is perfect but no longer has the original packaging or the original packaging is less than perfect. Possibly used but must appear to be new.	Grandma used the soup tureen on her 25th anniversary, washed it gently, and then put it back in the closet.
Excellent (EX, 8)	Used, but barely. Excellent is just a small step under Near Mint, and many sellers mistakenly interchange the two, but Excellent can have very minor signs of wear. The wear must be a normal, desirable part of aging or so minor that it's barely noticeable and visible only upon close inspection. Damage of any sort is not "very minor." Wear or minor, normal factory flaws should be noted. (Factory flaws are small blemishes common at the time of manufacture — a tiny air bubble under paint, for example.)	Grandma liked to ring in the New Year with a cup of soup for everyone.

Category (Also Known As)	What It Means	Example
Very Good (VG, 7)	Looks very good but has defects, such as a minor chip or light color fading.	If you weren't looking for it, you might miss that Grandma's tureen survived the '64 earthquake, as well as Uncle Bob's infamous ladle episode.
Good (G, 6)	Used with defects. More than a small amount of color loss, chips, cracks, tears, dents, abrasions, missing parts, and so on.	Grandma had the ladies in the neighborhood over for soup and bingo every month.
Poor (P or G-, 5)	Barely collectible, if at all. Severe damage or heavy use. Beyond repair.	Grandma ran a soup kitchen.

Grading is subjective. Mint to one person may be Very Good to another. Always ask a seller to define the meaning of the terms used. Also, be aware that many amateur sellers may not really know the different definitions of grading and may arbitrarily add Mint or Excellent to their item descriptions.

How can you compete? Well, in addition to having a well-planned bidding strategy (covered in Book I, Chapter 6), knowing your stuff gives you a winning edge. I've gathered the opinions of two collecting experts to get the info you need about online collecting basics. I also show you how one of those experts puts the information into practice, and I give you a crash course on how items for sale are (or should be) graded.

The values of collectibles go up and down. *Star Wars* items are a perfect example. Values skyrocketed during the release of the latest movie, but then settled to a considerably lower level. A published book of value listings is valid only for the *moment* the book is written. If you stay on top of your market in a few specialties, you'll be aware of these market fluctuations. If you're looking for the highest price for *Star Wars* items, for example, instead of looking to liquidate excess inventory, I'd hold those items until the next film is released.

Following Collectible-Buying Guidelines

Buying collectibles on eBay can be a unique market unto itself. But still, certain rules apply. Here are a few things to keep in mind when buying collectibles on eBay:

✦ **Get all the facts before you put your money down.** Study the description carefully and make your bidding decisions accordingly. Find out whether all original parts are included and whether the item has any flaws. If the description says that the Fred Flintstone figurine has a cracked back, e-mail the seller for more information.

✦ **Don't get caught up in the emotional thrill of bidding.** First-time buyers (known as *Under-10s* or newbies because they have fewer than ten transactions under their belts) tend to bid wildly, using emotions instead of brains. If you're new to eBay, you can get burned if you just bid for the thrill of victory without thinking about what you're doing.

I can't stress how important it is to determine an item's value before you bid. But because value is such a flighty thing (depending on supply and demand, market trends, and all sorts of other cool stuff), I recommend that you get a general idea of the item's value and use this ballpark figure to set a maximum amount of money you're willing to bid for that item. Then *stick* to your maximum and don't even think about bidding past it. If the bidding gets too hot, there's always another auction. To find out more about bidding strategies, Book I, Chapter 6 is just the ticket.

✦ **Know what the item should cost.** Buyers used to depend on *price guides* — books on collectibles and their values — to help them bid. But price guides are becoming a thing of the past. Sure, you can find a guide that says a *Lion King* Broadway poster in excellent condition has a book price of $75, but if you do a search on eBay, you'll see that they're actually selling for $20 to $30.

When your search on eBay turns up what you're looking for, average the completed prices that you find. Doing so gives you a much better idea than any price guide of what you need to spend.

✦ **Timing is everything, and being first costs.** In the movie-poster business, if you can wait three to six months after a movie is released, you get the poster for 40 to 50 percent less. The same goes for many new releases of collectibles. Sometimes you're wiser to wait and save money.

✦ **Be careful of presale items.** You may run across vendors selling items that they don't have in stock at the moment but that they'll ship to you later. For example, before the second *Harry Potter* film came out, some vendors ran auctions on movie posters they didn't have yet. If you had bid and won, and for some reason the vendor had a problem getting the poster, you'd have been out of luck. Don't bid on anything that can't be delivered as soon as your payment clears.

✦ **Being too late can also cost.** Many collectibles become more difficult to find as time goes by. Generally, as scarcity increases, so does desirability and value. Common sense tells you that if two original and identical collectibles are offered side by side, with one in like-new condition and the other in used condition, the like-new item will have the higher value.

✦ **Check out the seller.** Check the seller's feedback rating (the number in parentheses next to the person's user ID) before you buy. If the seller has many comments with very few negative ones, chances are good that this is a reputable seller.

If you miss winning an auction and are offered a side deal, beware! Side deals off the eBay site are strictly prohibited. If you conduct a side deal and are reported to eBay, you can be suspended. Not only that, but buyers who are ripped off by sellers in away-from-eBay transactions shouldn't look to eBay to bail them out. They're on their own. Second-chance offers, on the other hand, are eBay-legal — and safer.

Quizzing the seller

You should ask the seller certain questions when making a collectible purchase. Assume that the object of your desire is a collectible GI Joe action figure from 1964 to 1969. In this section, I list some questions you should ask. The information here can give you an idea of what to ask when determining your maximum bid on other collectibles as well (or whether an item is even *worth* bidding on). As you imagine, the more you know before you place a bid, the happier you're likely to be when you win.

This checklist can save you considerable hassle:

✦ **Find out the item's overall condition.** For GI Joe, look at the painted hair and eyebrows. Expect some wear, but overall, a collectible worth bidding on should look good.

✦ **Be sure the item's working parts are indeed working.** Most GI Joe action figures from this period have cracks on the legs and arms, but the joints should move and any cracks should not be so deep that the legs and arms fall apart easily.

✦ **Ask whether the item has its original parts.** Because you can't really examine actual items in detail before buying, e-mail the seller with specific questions relating to original or replacement parts. Many GI Joe action figures are rebuilt from parts that are not from 1964 to 1969. Sometimes the figures even have two left or right hands or feet! If you make it clear to the seller before you buy that you want a toy with only original parts, you'll be able to make a good case for a refund if the item arrives as rebuilt as the Six Million Dollar Man.

**Book II
Chapter 2**

Researching
on the Web

✦ **Ask whether the item has original accessories.** A GI Joe from 1964 to 1969 should have his original dog tags, boots, and uniform. If any of these items are missing, you will have to pay around $25 to replace each missing item. If you're looking to bid on any other collectible, know what accessories came as standard equipment with the item.

✦ **Know an item's value before you bid.** A 1964 to 1969 vintage GI Joe in decent shape, with all its parts, sells for around $400 without its original box. If you are bidding on a GI Joe action figure and are in this price range, you're okay. If you get the item for less than $350, congratulations — you've nabbed a bargain.

✦ **If you have any questions, ask them** *before* **you bid.** Check collectors' guides, research similar auctions on eBay, and visit one of eBay's category chat rooms.

Hey, experts have been buying, selling, and trading collectible items for years. But just because you're new to eBay doesn't mean you have to be a newbie for decades before you can start bartering with the collecting gods. I wouldn't leave you in the cold like that — and neither would eBay. You can get information on items you're interested in, as well as good collecting tips, right on the eBay Web site. Visit the category-specific discussion boards in the Community area. You can also search the rest of the Web or go the old-fashioned route and check the library.

Keep in mind that there truly are several prices for an item. The retail (or manufacturer's suggested retail price — MSRP) price, the book value, the secondary market price (the price charged by resellers when an item is unavailable on the primary retail market), and the eBay selling price. The only way to ascertain the price an item will go for on eBay is to research completed auctions.

Useful publications

So what if your item isn't for sale on eBay and hasn't been for 14 days? What's the first thing to do? Check out your local newsstand for one of the many publications devoted to collecting. Go over to Yahoo! Yellow Pages at yp.yahoo.com. Type your ZIP code to limit the search to your part of the country and type a search for *newsstand* and *news stand.* You can also search for *Magazines — Dealers* in your area. Let your fingers do the walking and call the newsstands in your area and ask whether they have publications in your area of interest. If no newsstands are listed in your area, visit the local bookstore.

You might also want to check out some of the following specialty publications:

✦ *Action Figure Digest:* Find out who's hot in the action figure biz in this monthly magazine. Its Web site sells back issues; go to www.tomart.com.

✦ **Antique Trader:** This magazine has been the bible of the antiques collecting industry for more than 40 years. Visit its online home on the Collect.com Web site at www.antiquetrader.com for more articles and subscription information.

✦ **Autograph Collector:** This magazine gives the lowdown on the autograph business as well as samples of many autographs for identification. Its Web site, www.autographmagazine.com, features links to price guides it publishes.

✦ **Barbie Bazaar:** Once the official Mattel magazine was packed with everything Barbie! It seems the magazine couldn't find enough to say about Barbie, or they just didn't have enough readers — whatever. Now the Web site is Haute Doll. The new site covers everything in trendy dolls — even Barbie. Visit the site at www.barbiebazaar.com for subscriptions and news.

✦ **Coin World:** This respected magazine has many online services for their subscribers as well. Their Web site, at www.coinworld.com, is featured in Figure 2-1

✦ **Collector Editions:** You'll find information on plates, figurines, glass, prints, cottages, ornaments, and dozens of other contemporary decorative collectibles in this monthly magazine.

Figure 2-1:
The Coin
World
Web site.

✦ *Doll Reader*: www.dollreader.com. The ultimate authority, *Doll Reader* has been dishing out the scoop on collectible dolls of all sorts for more than 25 years. It's the place to go to catch the trends on the latest in doll collecting.

✦ *Goldmine*: www.goldminemag.com. This is the magazine for CD and record collecting. The Web site has many sample articles and information from its issues.

✦ *Numismatic News*: www.numismaticnews.net. Another standard, *Numismatic News* has been around for more than 50 years. The first issue each month includes a pull-out guide to retail U.S. coin prices. Every three months, it also includes a U.S.-paper-money price guide.

✦ *Sports Collectors Digest*: www.sportscollectorsdigest.com. Takes sports collectibles to the highest level. Visit their Web site and sign up for a free e-mail newsletter.

✦ *Linn's Stamp News*: www.linns.com. I subscribed to this magazine when I was in grade school, and it's still around. Actually it's been around a lot longer — since 1931. (Hey, I'm not that old!)

✦ *Teddy Bear Review*: www.teddybearreview.com. Since 1986, this review has offered pages of information on collecting teddy bears. For a free sample issue, go to their Web site.

It seems that every leading magazine has its own Web site. In the next section, I mention some useful Web sites for pricing references.

Online Sources of Information

Because you're all so Internet-savvy (what's better than getting the information you want at a millisecond's notice?), I assume you plan to visit the magazine Web sites that I mention in the preceding section. In this section, I give you a few more fun online sources where you might be able to get more insight about your items.

Web sites

Many Web sites devoted to different collectible areas list prices at recently completed auctions. These auctions are the best evaluation of an item's value because they're usually directed toward specialists in the collectible category. Most of the participants in these auctions *really* know their stuff.

You may have to poke around the following Web sites to find the prices realized at auction, but once you do, you'll have the Holy Grail of estimated values. Look for links that point to auction archives. Many of these sites will consign an item from you as well, and sell it to their audience:

- ✦ Antiques, art, all kinds of rare stuff: www.sothebys.com

- ✦ Art auctions: www.artprice.com (charges for its searches by artist, but has an immense database)

- ✦ Autographs, movie posters, and comic books: www.autographs.com

- ✦ Sports memorabilia: www.collectors.com

- ✦ Collectible advertising glasses: www.pgcaglassclub.com (you've got to see this stuff!)

- ✦ United States coin price guide: www.pcgs.com/prices/

- ✦ Currency auctions: www.lynknight.com

If you're researching prices to buy a car on eBay, look in your local newspaper to get a good idea of prices in your community. You should also check out sites on the Internet. I've had many of my friends (and editors) visit the various sites, and we've settled on www.nadaguides.com because it seems to give the most accurate and unbiased information.

Online search engines

If you don't find the information you need on eBay, don't go ballistic — just go elsewhere. Even a site as vast as eBay doesn't have a monopoly on information. The Internet is filled with Web sites and Internet auction sites that can give you price comparisons and information about cyberclubs.

Your home computer can connect to powerful outside servers (really big computers on the Internet) that have their own fast-searching systems called *search engines*. Remember, if something is out there and you need it, you can find it right from your home PC in just a matter of seconds. Here are the addresses of some of the Web's most highly regarded search engines or multi-search-engine sites:

- ✦ Google (www.google.com)

- ✦ MSN (www.msn.com)

- ✦ Yahoo! (www.yahoo.com)

The basic process of getting information from an Internet search engine is pretty simple:

1. **Type the address of the search-engine site in the Address box of your Web browser.**

   You're taken to the Web site's home page.

2. **Find the text box next to the button labeled Search or something similar.**

3. **In the text box, type a few words indicating what interests you.**

   Be specific when typing search text. The more precise your entry, the better your chances of finding what you want. Look for tips, an advanced search option, or help pages on your search engine of choice for more information about how to narrow your search.

4. **Click the Search (or similar) button or press Enter on your keyboard.**

   The search engine presents you with a list of how many Internet pages have the requested information. The list includes brief descriptions and links to the first group of pages. You'll find links to additional listings at the bottom if your search finds more listings than can fit on one page (and if you ask for something popular, like *Harry Potter,* don't be surprised to get millions of hits).

Always approach information on the Web with caution. Not everyone is the expert he or she would like to be. Your best bet is to get lots of different opinions and then boil 'em down to what makes sense to you. And remember — *caveat emptor.* (Is there an echo in here?)

Online appraisals

I've had a bit of experience with online appraisals, which seem tempting at first glance. At second glance, though, I realized that unless the person doing the appraisal could actually *see* and *feel* the item, an accurate appraisal couldn't be performed. Also, you have no guarantee that the person at the other end is really an expert in the field that relates to your item.

I had a few items *e-appraised* by a prestigious (and now defunct) online appraisal company, and the appraisals seemed a bit off. Then I took one item, a painting, to Butterfields (now Bonhams) in Los Angeles — and found that the value of the painting was ten times what my e-appraisal had said.

The bottom line here is that if you have an item of real value that's worth appraising, it's worth getting appraised *in person*. Most large cities have auction houses, and many of those auction houses have monthly *consignment clinics* (a way for auction houses to get merchandise for their future auctions). If you bring an item to the auction house, you aren't legally bound to have the auction house sell your item for you (but it may not be a bad idea). All you'll get is a free verbal appraisal; the auction house won't fill out any official paperwork or anything, but at least you'll get an idea of what your item is worth. Real appraisals are expensive, performed by licensed professionals, and accompanied by a formal appraisal document.

Authentication services

Some companies provide the service of *authenticating* (verifying that it's the real deal) or authenticating and *grading* (determining a value based on the item's condition and legitimacy). To have these services performed on your items, you'll have to send them to the service and pay a fee.

Following are a few excellent sites for grading coins:

✦ **Professional Coin Grading Service (PCGS):** www.pcgs.com. PCGS is considered to be the top of the line in coin grading. This company's standards are strict, but coins graded by PCGS usually sell for higher prices.

✦ **American Numismatic Association Certification Service (AMNACS)** — sold to Amos Press in 1990: www.anacs.com.

✦ **Numismatic Guaranty Corporation of America (NGCA):** www.ngccoin.com/ebay_ngcvalue.cfm. The site offers eBay users a discount and features a mail-in grading and certification service for your coins.

✦ **PCI Coin Grading Service (PCI):** www.dominiongrading.com. PCI, the longstanding coin-grading service, was sold in early 2008. The new name is DGS, or Dominion Grading Service.

To catch up on the latest pricing on American coins, go to www.pcgs.com (Figure 2-2). This site has an elaborate online price guide for all coin grades.

Book II
Chapter 2

Researching on the Web

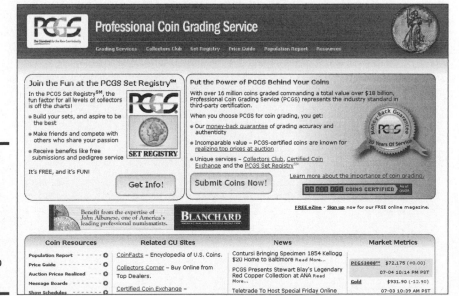

Figure 2-2:
The PCGS Web site has many links and an up-to-date price guide at no charge.

Stamp collectors (or those who have just inherited a collection from Uncle Steve) can get their stamps "expertized" (authenticated) by the American Philatelic Society. Visit this site for more information:

`www.stamps.org/services/ser_aboutexpertizing.htm`

For comic books, Comics Guaranty, LLC (CGC) at

`https://www.cgccomics.com/ebay_comic_book_grading.cfm`

will seal (enclose in plastic to preserve the quality) and grade at a discount for eBay users.

Sports cards and sports memorabilia have a bunch of authentication services. If you got your autograph or memorabilia direct from the player or team, you can ensure its authenticity. Having the item authenticated may or may not get you a higher price at eBay. Try these sites:

✦ **Professional Sports Authenticator (PSA):** `www.psacard.com`.

✦ **Online Authentics:** `www.onlineauthentics.com`. Reviews autographs by scans online or by physical review.

The best way to find a good authenticator in your field is to search the items on eBay and see who is the most prominent authenticator listed in the descriptions. For example, in the coins area, coins from certain grading services get higher bids than those from other services. You can also go to an Internet search engine (such as Google or Yahoo!) and type the keywords *coin grading* (for coins). You'll come up with a host of choices; use your good sense to see which one suits your needs.

Remember that not all items need to be officially authenticated. Official authentication does add value to the item, but if you're an expert, you can comfortably rate an item on your own in your auctions. People will know from your description whether you're a specialist. Your feedback will also work for you by letting the prospective bidder or buyer know that your merchandise from past sales has been top-drawer.

Chapter 3: Efficient Communications for Better Sales

In This Chapter
- Brushing up on your writing skills
- Writing perfect e-mail messages
- Writing to the seller

Business, bah! eBay's supposed to be fun! But business is business and if you're in business, you must remember that your customers are number one and customers deserve "five-star service." Businesses become successful by providing fantastic customer service and selling quality merchandise. You have to move in the same direction. The image that you project through your e-mails and listings identifies you to bidders as a good guy or a bad guy. No kidding. Your e-mails should be polite and professional. Your listings shouldn't make prospective buyers feel like you're hustling them, sneaking in hidden fees, or being pushy with severe rules for bidding.

You don't have to have the most beautiful auctions on eBay to succeed. Instead, you need products that sell — and you need to take the time to build good customer relations! This is what gives the little guy the advantage over the mega-company that branches onto eBay. In this chapter, I cover some ways — from writing effective auction descriptions to sending cordial e-mails — to let your customers know that they're number one in your book.

Communicating in Writing Takes a Little Effort

Perhaps English class wasn't your favorite, but good grammar, proper spelling, and punctuation in your communications portray you as a pro. Before writing this book, even I hooked up with some grammar and punctuation sites to brush up on my writing skills. (Okay, I also have brilliant editors covering up my transgressions. . . .)

Throughout the rest of this section, I provide some examples of effective e-mails. Study these and also check out a few business letter books, such as *Writing Business Letters For Dummies* by Sheryl Lindsell-Roberts (published by Wiley). And don't forget good manners. You don't want to be too formal, but you do want to be personable and polite.

Responding Appropriately to Initial Buyer Inquiries

The first written communication you might have with a prospective buyer is an inquiry e-mail. A bidder can ask you a question about your item by clicking the Ask the seller a question link on the auction or sale page, which generates an e-mail addressed to you, as shown in Figure 3-1. Often these questions are brief.

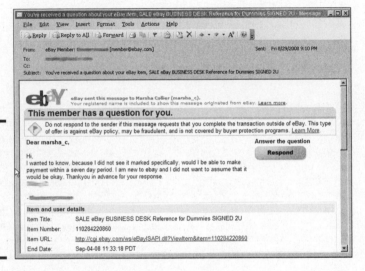

Figure 3-1:
A question from an eBay member regarding one of my listings.

At least 20% of the time that I send an inquiry to a seller, I don't get a response — guaranteeing that I won't be buying that product. I refuse to buy from someone who doesn't even care to respond to a question. When I do get responses, more often than not it's a terse, brusquely written note. Many people choose not to use punctuation or capitalization in their e-mails. How professional-looking is that? Not very. Sellers who take the time to write a short, considerate reply that includes a greeting and a thank you for writing get my money.

You should respond quickly, clearly, and politely — and with a sales pitch whenever possible. Remind the soon-to-be bidder that you can combine several wins to save on shipping costs. And by all means, use this opportunity to point out other auctions you have that may also interest the writer. (Now *that's* customer service.)

Replying online or personally

When a prospective buyer or bidder has a question, you will know about it in two ways: through e-mail and as a clickable link on your My eBay page. You'll get the e-mail from eBay alerting you that a question has been asked. Using this service goes a long way to protect your privacy. In the past, your only option was to respond through your regular e-mail, thereby revealing your e-mail address to a stranger.

Now you can click the Respond Now button in the e-mail and go directly to the online question to post your response, as shown in Figure 3-2.

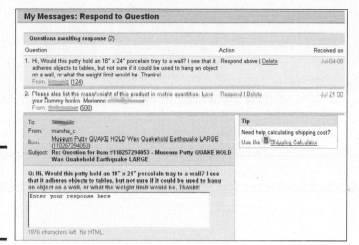

Figure 3-2:
Answering a question through eBay.

Type your answer and indicate whether you want the reply posted on the page for other prospective customers to see. You can also indicate that your personal e-mail address should be withheld from your reply mailed to the questioner from eBay's mail server. If you're in a hurry and need to make a short, factual reply, this is an excellent option — but it doesn't give you the punch that a personal e-mail can.

You can also go directly to the item page, where you'll see the notice that you have a question to answer (see Figure 3-3). Click the link and you'll be brought to the page where you can respond to the question (the same page the e-mail links to).

Figure 3-3:
The listing page will also let you know that there is a question to answer.

If you've responded to a question and indicated that you want it posted on the item page, the response to your question will appear at the bottom of your description, as shown in Figure 3-4.

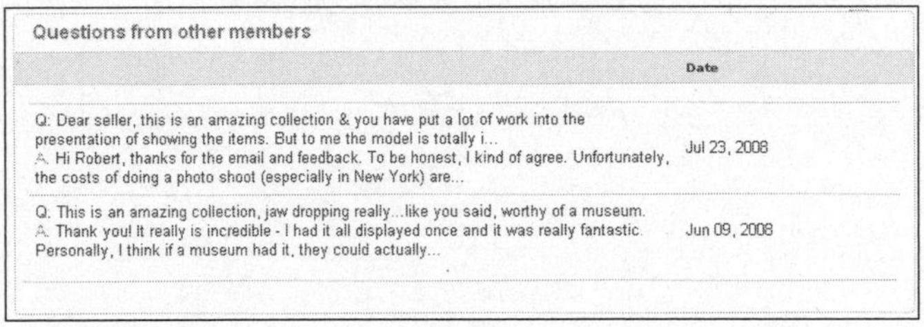

Figure 3-4:
Questions answered on the item page.

Making your response friendly, helpful, and productive

When answering a question, a brief and straightforward response is good. For example, I wrote the following note in response to a question regarding the condition of the Christmas tree in one of my auctions:

Hello,

Yes, the aluminum Christmas tree in my auction is in excellent condition. The 58 branches are full and lush and will look great for the holidays. Please write again if you have any more questions or concerns.

Don't forget to check my other auctions for a color wheel and a revolving tree turner. They would look great with this tree, and I can combine them for shipping.

Thank you for writing,

Marsha
`http://stores.ebay.com/Marsha-Colliers-Fabulous-Finds`

Isn't that nice? The note addresses the question in a respectful and personable manner. Writing a note like this doesn't take long. You should be doing it.

Putting your eBay store URL in your signature is a great way to get new customers to view your other merchandise.

Personalizing the Buyer's Notification

Have you ever received a bulk-generated, boilerplate buyer's confirmation letter? The seller hasn't bothered to fill in half the blanks, and you're almost insulted just by having to read it? Receiving a note like this after you've requested that the seller combine purchases (and the letter pays no attention to your request) is especially annoying. E-mails can cross, but a personal approach goes a long way with customers.

I'm not saying you shouldn't automate your eBay business. I'm merely suggesting — strongly recommending — that you take the time to personalize even your canned e-mail responses. If you decide to send automated responses, choose a program (such as eBay's Selling Manager, described in Chapter 5) that allows you to customize your e-mail, combine multiple wins, and apply the correct shipping costs the first time.

When you sell an item, you receive a notification from eBay, as shown in Figure 3-5. When you get this e-mail, simply click on the yellow, Send an Invoice button to send an invoice to your buyer. Here are some ideas to keep your communications safe, efficient, and professional:

✦ **Send the invoice from your My eBay page:** For security's sake, go directly to your My eBay page, find the sale, and send the invoice from there. That way, you won't accidently be fooled into clicking a link in a phishing e-mail (a message that's not from eBay and is designed merely to steal your user ID).

✦ **Combine purchases when you can:** If the buyer has purchased more than one item from you, you'll see a note from eBay indicating such. Be sure to click to combine purchases so you can combine shipping and get your payment quickly.

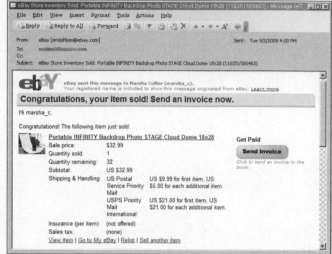

Figure 3-5:
eBay's
e-mail to the
seller upon
a completed
sale.

✦ **Include special offers:** At the end of a buyer's notice letter, offer your
buyer some special discounts or other offers from your eBay Store.
Include a few items this particular winner may be interested in (based
on the current win) and include a link to your site. Also include the
reminder that you can combine postage — and that you look forward to
a response.

If you want to send the invoice from your My eBay page, just click the Send
Invoice option from the drop-down menu in the Items I've Sold area, verify
all the information, and click Send Invoice. If you select the Copy Me check
box on this invoice, you receive a copy. The buyer's copy has a link,
enabling the buyer to pay directly through PayPal. Figure 3-6 shows what the
invoice e-mail looks like.

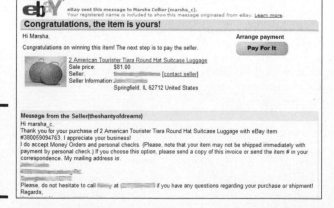

Figure 3-6:
An eBay
invoice, as
sent to a
buyer.

Keeping the Good E-Mails Going

If you've got a good transaction going (and the majority of them are good), the buyer will either pay immediately through PayPal or reply to your e-mail within three business days. (Most replies come the next day.) If your buyer has questions regarding anything in your invoice, you'll get those inquiries now. Most of the time, all you get back is, "Thanks. I'll pay as soon as I can." Hey, that's good enough for me.

If any last-minute details need to be worked out, usually the buyer asks to set up a time to call or requests further instructions about the transaction. Respond to this communication as soon as possible. If you can't deal with it at the moment, let the buyer know you're working on it and will shoot those answers back ASAP. *Never* let an e-mail go unanswered.

When you list an item on eBay, you have the option of indicating that you will accept Skype Chat or IM. So be sure you set up a free Skype account at www.skype.com. You can use this account as a free way to contact your buyer through the Skype system — using your computer's speakers and microphone.

As soon as you get the hang of sending e-mail, you can add an eBay link that takes the buyer right to the Feedback Forum with just a click of the mouse. Buyers and sellers can also get to the Feedback Forum from the final listing page by clicking the Leave Feedback link.

The payment reminder

Writing a payment reminder can get sticky. You don't want to aggravate the buyer, but time is wasting and you could spend this time reposting your item. When writing a payment reminder, you need to be firm but pleasant. Real things can happen in people's lives. Family members get sick, people just plain forget, or your buyer has suffered a computer problem. (That sort of thing happens. Okay, it was also my excuse when I forgot to send a payment — feel free to use it.)

When you honestly forget to send a payment, nothing is more humiliating than someone debasing you through e-mail. So remember that people do make mistakes, and check the winner's feedback before you send the letter. If you can garner from the feedback that this winner has a habit of not following through on bids, you can definitely be a bit firmer in your wording.

Always set a clear deadline for receiving payment, as shown in the following letter:

Hello,

You won an auction of mine on eBay last week for the Emilio Pucci book. Your payment still has not shown up in my PayPal account. Perhaps sending payment has slipped your mind considering your busy schedule. I know it can easily happen.

Please e-mail back within 48 hours and let me know whether you want to go through with our transaction. I'd like to put the item back up for sale if you don't want it.

Thank you for your bid,

Marsha Collier

How firm you choose to get with a nonpaying bidder is up to you. I've dealt with a few nonpaying bidders on eBay. Some people who tend to overbid are indeed violating the contract to buy, but legitimate reasons might explain why someone hasn't followed through on an auction. You must decide which method to take — and how far you want to stretch your karma (what goes around comes around). Assess each case individually, and don't go postal until you know the whole story.

The payment received and shipping notice

I know that you probably aren't going to send out a payment received letter for every transaction, especially when they're paid through PayPal. But it would surely be nice if you did. Staying in constant communication with your buyers will make them feel more secure with you and with buying on eBay. You want them to come back, don't you?

When you receive payment and are ready to ship, sending a short note like the following (again — eBay makes this easy with Selling Manager Pro) helps to instill loyalty in your customer:

Hi there, (insert name of winner),

Your payment was received and your item will ship tomorrow. Please e-mail me when it arrives so that I can hear how pleased you are with your purchase.

When the transaction is over, I hope you will leave five-star, positive feedback for me because building a good reputation on eBay is very important. I'd really appreciate it, and I'll be glad to do the same for you.

Thank you for bidding & winning,

Marsha Collier
marsha_c

Say thank you — I mean it! What do all the successful big-name department stores have in common? Yes, great prices, good merchandise, and nice displays. But with all things being equal, customer service always wins, hands down. One department store in the United States, Nordstrom, has such a great reputation that the store happily took back a set of snow tires because a customer wasn't happy with them. No big deal, maybe — until you notice that Nordstrom doesn't even *sell* snow tires!

The "Your item is on the way" e-mail

You can always send the automatic e-mail from your shipper announcing the shipment tracking number. I prefer sending the e-mail from PayPal (see Chapter 4) by inserting the tracking number into the PayPal payment record. This way you cover two bases: Your buyer is notified of shipping, and PayPal has the record that you've shipped an item.

These e-mails aren't very personalized (although you can personalize them somewhat), so I follow up through eBay's Selling Manager Pro program, with another, more personal note:

Subject: Your book is on the way!

Hi, (insert buyer's name)!

You will be receiving another e-mail from PayPal with the package's delivery confirmation number and information on the mode of shipment.

Thank you for buying my item. If there is any question when the package arrives, PLEASE e-mail me immediately. Your satisfaction is my goal, and I'm sure any problem can be easily taken care of. Please let me know when the package arrives so that we can exchange some very positive feedback!

Marsha Collier
http://stores.ebay.com/Marsha-Colliers-Fabulous-Finds

Communicating from the Buyer's Perspective

Top-notch sellers know that communication is the key to a successful transaction, and they do everything they can to set a positive tone for the entire process with speedy and courteous e-mails.

A good e-mail (or invoice) from a professional eBay seller should include the following information:

✦ Confirmation of the winning price

✦ The address for sending payment or a phone number for credit card processing

✦ A review of the shipping options and price

✦ Confirmation of escrow (if offered in the auction)

✦ The timeframe in which the item will be shipped

When you read the seller's invoice, be sure to compare the terms the seller laid out in his or her e-mail with those on the auction page. If you see significant differences, address them immediately with the seller — before you proceed with the transaction. Unless you're paying immediately through PayPal, when you e-mail the seller a reply, you should do the following:

✦ Let the seller know when you intend to make your payment.

✦ Include your address, name, and user ID.

✦ Include the item's title and number so the seller knows what you're referring to and can get your item ready to ship as soon as the payment arrives.

✦ Include your phone number if you plan to pay with a credit card on a secure Web page. If there's a problem with the credit-card number you've given, the seller can contact you promptly to let you know.

✦ Request that the seller e-mail you any shipping information, such as tracking numbers and an approximate arrival date.

Chapter 4: Simplifying Payment with PayPal

In This Chapter

🖙 **Understanding the PayPal system**

🖙 **Determining how you're protected**

🖙 **Deciding which account is best for you**

🖙 **Uncovering your payment history**

In the early days of eBay, online auctions were a scary place. You could send a check to your trading partner, but the wait for the product could be interminable. There was little feedback in the beginning, so you couldn't separate the good sellers from the bad. The most widely accepted form of payment was the money order. Somehow, in our small (but growing) community, we weren't afraid to send money orders to strangers. Heck, some sellers even shipped merchandise *before* they received payment! Things were a lot simpler, if riskier, in the old days.

Then, rising like a beacon on the horizon, came x.com. A bright man named Elon came up with the concept of e-mailing money; you could even beam cash to someone's Palm Pilot! There was no charge for using this service, which was even more amazing! The best part about signing up for the program was that they gave you a $10 credit just to join. You also received a $10 bonus for each friend you got to join. (The maximum any user could get in bonuses was $1000, but hey, that's no small change!)

With numbers like that, the early eBay (née AuctionWeb) crowd signed up quickly. x.com quickly became the most widely used service on the Internet, the first mover-and-shaker in online, person-to-person payments.

eBay countered, acquiring Billpoint in the spring of 1999 in the hopes of launching their own payment service in a partnership with Wells Fargo. In a disaster of bad timing, the service was not available to eBay members until the second quarter of 2000. Meanwhile, x.com — now reborn as PayPal — was growing by leaps and bounds and quietly taking over the market.

PayPal went public in February of 2002 to an encouraging Wall Street. The feud between PayPal and Billpoint heated up. The number of customers who signed up with Billpoint couldn't keep pace with the numbers joining PayPal. PayPal posted a profit, while Billpoint was losing millions per year. In October 2002, eBay bit the bullet and acquired PayPal in a deal valued at $1.5 billion. Billpoint was then simply phased out of the site.

If you've read any of my other books, you know that I've been a huge fan of PayPal from the beginning. PayPal is one of the safest and least expensive ways for a vendor to accept money over the Internet. For a small retailer, PayPal fees can be much more cost-effective than a credit-card merchant account (as I explain in the next section).

Understanding How PayPal Works

Joining PayPal is just the beginning. No, they don't give $10 bonuses for signups anymore, but the benefits far outweigh any fees they charge to sellers. Also, there's no charge to send money to anyone. As of this writing, small sellers can still accept money from eBay sales and not incur any fees.

Before planning on a free ride from PayPal, double-check the PayPal Web site, www.PayPal.com, for any changes in fees and policies.

You may register up to eight e-mail addresses with a PayPal account. However, you may not register an e-mail address that is already registered with another PayPal account.

Sending money through PayPal

You have several ways to fund the money you send to another party through PayPal:

✦ **Instant transfer:** Sending money this way means the money is immediately credited to the recipient's account. That person can then transfer the money to his or her personal bank account without delay. If you want to send a transfer, you must have a credit or debit card registered with PayPal as a backup for your funds — just in case your bank denies the transfer. It's just like writing a secure check — without exposing any of your personal information (such as your checking-account number) to another party.

✦ **eCheck:** Sending an eCheck isn't as "instant" as an instant transfer. Just like writing a check from your checking account, it can take up to four days for the eCheck to clear. You do not need a backup source of funds when you use eCheck.

+ **PayPal balance:** If someone sent you money through PayPal or you've sold something on eBay (and your buyer has paid you through PayPal), you have a balance in your PayPal account. This balance is first applied to any purchases you've made. Then when your account has no balance, you can choose to pay by credit card. It's simplest to keep your books balanced if you withdraw any PayPal balance to your business checking account before you make a purchase.

+ **Credit card:** Charge it! Putting your PayPal purchases on a credit card is a good idea. Not only are you protected by PayPal, but your credit-card company also backs you up in case of fraud.

You can register multiple credit cards on your PayPal account and select a different one for different types of purchases. That way, you can place personal purchases on one account and business purchases on another. It makes end-of-year bookkeeping a lot easier!

**Book II
Chapter 4**

Simplifying Payment with PayPal

Figuring out payment types

PayPal breaks types of payments into categories based on what you're paying for. You can pay for *almost* anything in the world on the PayPal system (as long as the recipient has an e-mail address). A few things that you *can't* pay for with PayPal include anything related to gambling, adult content or services, multi-level marketing, and buying, or selling prescription drugs from noncertified sellers. I recommend if you're planning to accept payments for something that may be a tad questionable, visit the PayPal help area to be sure your item is currently in the clear.

After you sign into your PayPal account, you can send money through PayPal in the following ways:

+ **Paying for eBay items:** When you pay for an eBay item, you're taken to a page where you can input the item number and your eBay user ID, so the payment will integrate directly with eBay's user records.

+ **Goods (other):** From this area, you can send money to anyone in the world for goods purchased anywhere other than in an online auction.

+ **Service/Other:** You can send payment for a service performed for you or your business, such as Web design, bookkeeping, psychic readings, or whatever.

+ **Cash Advance:** Use this when you need to send money to your kid in college or pay back your roommate for saving you from great embarrassment when you left your wallet at home on a double date.

When you're using the cash-advance feature, consider using a payment method other than credit card to avoid possible credit-card fees for a cash advance.

PayPal's Protection Plans

Safety: Isn't that what paying for things online is all about? Safety for the buyer and safety for the seller are primary concerns in the minds of those dealing on eBay. PayPal has created protection policies for both parties.

PayPal buyer protection

As a buyer who pays for eBay items through PayPal, you can be covered against fraud for up to at least $200. Many sellers (check the seller's information on the item page) qualify by PayPal to give up to $2,000 worth of buyer protection. You have to be sure that the seller's item has the correct standing with PayPal (as shown in Figure 4-1) in the Buy Safely box to get this buyer protection.

Figure 4-1:
The amount of PayPal Buyer Protection can vary from seller to seller.

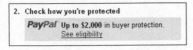

In this protection program, *fraud* is loosely defined as nondelivery of items or when you receive an item that's *significantly* different from the way it was described. Sorry — this doesn't cover you when you're merely disappointed with an item when you open the box. Oh yes, remember that it also won't cover downloadable software or digital items — even if you buy them on eBay.

When you're browsing eBay, notice that some listings have the PayPal icon, and some have no icon. When a listing has a PayPal icon, the seller accepts PayPal as payment, and you're covered under PayPal buyer protection.

Figure 4-2 shows a detail of eBay listings with the PayPal icon displayed.

Even if PayPal's buyer protection doesn't cover your item, PayPal still has basic coverage for all transactions if you've been defrauded. The PayPal protection shield in the Seller's information box (or in the listing) merely tells you that the seller maintains a level of professionalism and safety in his or her sales.

vintage SAMSONITE 50's AQUA GREEN Marbled suitcase 2of2	ℙ	3 Bids	$10.49 +$17.99	1d 23h 51m
Vintage Tan Full Size Samsonite Leather Suit Case	ℙ	0 Bids	$24.99 +$27.74	2d 0h 9m
Vintage Samsonite Swayger Bros. suitcase		0 Bids	$13.99 Not specified	2d 0h 36m
VINTAGE SAMSONITE TRAVEL CASE/MAKE UP MAUVE/MARBLED	ℙ	0 Bids	$12.00 +$22.60	2d 1h 24m
Vintage Samsonite Train Makeup Hard Case with Key VGC	ℙ	0 Bids	$9.99 +$20.15	2d 2h 31m

Figure 4-2:
Some eBay listings with PayPal icons.

Following are a few rules for using the buyer-protection system and making claims:

✦ **Number of claims:** You may make only one claim per PayPal payment.

✦ **Timing:** Your claim must be made within 45 days of your PayPal payment.

✦ **Participation:** You must be ready and willing to provide information and documentation to PayPal's buyer-protection team during the claims process.

When you provide protection for your buyers, you show that you're a professional — and you make it more comfortable for them to purchase from you. For sellers to qualify to offer buyer protection in their listings, they must

✦ Have a minimum of 50 or more eBay feedback comments

✦ Have at least 98% positive eBay feedback

✦ Use a Verified Premier or Verified Business Account PayPal account to accept payments

✦ Have a U.S. or Canadian PayPal account

✦ Select PayPal as a payment option when listing an item on eBay

✦ Have a PayPal account in good standing

For eBay's International sites, PayPal has different limits. See the Table 4-1 for more information.

Table 4-1	PayPal eBay International Buyer Protection		
Country	eBay URL	Basic Tier	Top Tier
United States	www.ebay.com	$200.00 USD	$2,000.00 USD
Australia	www.ebay.com.au	$400.00 AUD	$3,000.00 AUD
Austria	www.ebay.at	€1,000.00 EUR	n/a
Belgium	www.ebay.be	€200.00 EUR	€1,000.00 EUR
Canada	www.ebay.ca	$315.00 CAD	$2,000.00 CAD
France	www.ebay.fr	€200.00 EUR	€1,000.00 EUR
Germany	www.ebay.de	€1,000.00 EUR	n/a
Ireland	www.ebay.ie	€200.00 EUR	€1,000.00 EUR
Italy	www.ebay.it	€200.00 EUR	€1,000.00 EUR
Netherlands	www.ebay.nl	€200.00 EUR	€1,000.00 EUR
Spain	www.ebay.es	€200.00 EUR	€1,000.00 EUR
Switzerland	www.ebay.ch	1,500.00 CHF	n/a
United Kingdom	www.ebay.co.uk	£150.00 GBP	£500.00 GBP

PayPal seller protection

Don't think that sellers get left out of this protection thing. You do have some protection against unwarranted claims made on your eBay sales; it's called (logically enough) *seller protection*.

To see whether your transaction is covered under seller protection, follow these steps:

1. **In your payment received e-mail from PayPal, click the View the Details of the Transaction link.**

2. **Sign into your PayPal account.**

3. **Scroll down the Transaction Details page to the buyer's shipping address.**

   You'll see whether the shipping address is confirmed. (PayPal confirms the address by making sure that the credit card billing address matches the shipping address.) If it is, you must ship to that address to be protected.

When your transaction is protected, should any fraud be involved (a stolen credit card or identity hoax), you will not lose the money. PayPal guarantees the transaction.

What's this PayPal-verified business all about?

Being *PayPal-verified* is an important rating for both seller and buyer. It means that someone has checked and you really are who you say you are. Becoming verified isn't a big deal. All you have to do is register your checking account with PayPal. (Remember when you opened an account at the bank? They got information about you to be sure you were *you*, didn't they?)

PayPal will make two teeny (less than $1) deposits into your checking account. After

these have been transferred to your account, you can log back in to your PayPal account and confirm the two amounts. That's it — and you get free pennies too!

If you live outside the United States, you become verified by adding a credit card to your account and enrolling in the Expanded Use program, which is a similar confirmation scheme.

PowerSeller benefit! As an eBay seller, you are eligible for *expanded* seller protection. Items sold by PowerSellers on eBay and paid for with PayPal will be covered against claims, charge backs, reversals for unauthorized payments, and merchandise not received. Expanded Protection is free to sellers and *eliminates the need for confirmed addresses*.

If you receive a PayPal payment that ships to an unconfirmed address, drop the buyer a note and ask about the address. Usually you'll get a reply that makes you feel comfortable, and you'll ship. Remember that you will not be covered under seller protection if you ship to an unconfirmed address.

Surprise! There are a few other rules and restrictions. For sellers to be protected, they must

+ **Have a verified Business or Premier account:** You must have an upper-level PayPal account to be covered.

+ **Ship to a confirmed address:** You must ship to the buyer's address exactly as displayed on the transaction details page.

+ **Ship within seven days:** The item must leave your place of business within seven days of receiving payment. In the case of a pre-sale or customized item, you must post delivery time in your listing.

+ **Accept single payment from a single account:** You must have accepted one payment from one PayPal account to pay for the purchase. (No multiple-account payments for an item.)

+ **Ship tangible goods:** Seller protection is not available for services, digital goods, and other electronically delivered items.

✦ **Provide proof of shipping:** You need to provide reasonable proof-of-shipment that can be tracked online. The transaction details page must show that you shipped to the buyer's address. A delivery confirmation suffices for items valued up to $250.

If you use an automated shipping solution such as endicia.com, you also just copy and paste the delivery confirmation numbers onto the PayPal page. PayPal will send an e-mail to the buyer with the information for their records.

For items worth $250.00 or more (£150.00 or more for the U.K.), you must have a signature from the recipient as proof of receipt.

✦ **Not impose surcharges:** Imposing a surcharge on the buyer is against eBay policy anyway.

✦ **Cooperate with the complaint investigation:** If a complaint is filed, you must provide complete information about the transaction within seven days of a request from PayPal.

If PayPal is required by the buyer's issuing credit-card company to respond immediately to resolve a chargeback situation, you must provide all information within three days.

At this writing, seller protection is available only for U.S. and Canadian sellers transacting with U.S. buyers, and for U.K. sellers transacting with U.K. or U.S. buyers. Check back with the PayPal site for any changes in this policy.

Sorting Out PayPal's Accounts

PayPal has three types of accounts to accommodate everyone from the casual seller to the professional business: Personal, Business, and Premier accounts.

PayPal Personal account

When you begin your career with PayPal, you may want to sign up for a Personal account. With this basic account from PayPal, you can send and receive money (non-credit-card payments) for free. PayPal Personal accounts are for only one person and not for a business. (You can't have a joint Personal account, either.)

Business and Premier accounts

The PayPal professional seller (business and premier) accounts allow you to accept credit card payments, get a debit card, and participate in PayPal's high-yield money market fund. A premier account is held in an individual's name (although it may still be for a business); a business account can be held in a business name and allows multiple login names. At these account levels, you have access to a customer service phone number.

A fee is levied on all money you receive through PayPal at this level, but the costs are reasonable. (Just ask anyone with a brick-and-mortar business that accepts credit cards.) PayPal has a standard rate and a merchant rate, as shown in Table 4-2. The merchant rate has three tiers, based on your monthly sales volume. When you open your account, you're charged the standard rate. After your sales grow and you've been receiving more than $3000 per month through PayPal for three consecutive months, you can apply for a merchant account.

Table 4-2	PayPal Seller Transaction Fees			
Payment Currency	*Standard Rate — Monthly Sales up to $3000.00*	*Merchant Rate — Monthly Sales from $3000.01 to $10,000.00*	*Merchant Rate — Monthly Sales from $10,000.01 to $100,000.00*	*Merchant Rate — Monthly Sales Greater than $100,000.00*
U. S. dollars	2.9% + $.30 US	2.5% + $.30 US	2.2% + $.30 US	1.9% + $.30 US
Canadian seller dollars	.9% + $.55 CA	3.5% + $.55 CA	3.2% + $.55 CA	2.9 + $.55 CA
Euros	.9% + □.35 EUR	3.5% + □.35 EUR	3.2% + □.35 EUR	2.9% + □.35 EUR
Pounds sterling	.9% + £.20 GBP	3.5% + £.20 GBP	3.2% + £.20 GBP	2.9% + £.20 GBP
Yen	.9% + ¥40 JPY	3.5% + ¥40 JPY	3.2% + ¥40 JPY	2.9% + ¥40 JPY

Note: If you receive payment from a buyer in another country, there is an additional 1% fee for U.S. dollar payments and 0.5% for Canadian dollars, euros, pounds sterling, and yen. This fee is currently waived for Canadian sellers receiving payments from U.S. buyers.

If your transaction requires a currency conversion, you are charged an exchange rate. This includes an additional 2.5% above the current exchange rate.

Extracting Your Payment History from PayPal

I've been running a home-based business since the mid-1980s. Because I came from a corporate background working in the newspaper business, I've always known that recordkeeping is important. But recordkeeping has always been the bane of my existence. When I began my home-based business, the first thing I did was to hire a lawyer and a CPA to teach me what I had to do.

Recordkeeping means keeping track of everything: Every penny, sou, farthing, or ruble that you spend or take in. In the United States (and in most other countries), we have a little thing called taxes. We all have to turn in tax returns of several sorts when we run a business — and they'd better be correct. There may come a day when you receive a letter from a State or Federal tax agency asking to take a look at your books. This is simply a nice way of saying the dreaded word, *audit*.

The best defense against an audit is to have backup records. The more records you have proving your business income and expenses, the less painful your audit will be. One excellent piece of information to have at your fingertips is your PayPal history.

Besides meeting tax-reporting requirements, keeping good records keeps you on top of your business dealings. (See Book IX for more about how good recordkeeping helps your business succeed.) PayPal helps you with this all-important recordkeeping by providing reports on your buying and selling activity with these features:

✦ **24/7 availability:** PayPal allows you to customize and download your transaction reports at any time. You might want to consider downloading your reports on a monthly or quarterly basis — as well as generating one big report at the end of the year.

Or you may want to download the reports to coincide with your state sales-tax payments (for backup documentation) or to keep a record of your monthly totals.

✦ **Various formats:** You can download reports in several formats. The most flexible is a comma-delimited file that you can open and edit in a spreadsheet program, such as Excel or Microsoft Works.

Deciding What Info You Need from PayPal

PayPal is great when it comes to giving you control over your reports. You can narrow your downloads to incoming transactions for a one-day period or see all transactions for the year or more!

You may need all the information that PayPal gives you. If that's what you want, great. But PayPal can give you information overkill. I go over some of the options here so you can decide which types of information are important to keep in your permanent record.

All your downloadable PayPal reports can contain the following information by default. When you actually go to download, you can pick and choose what data you really need to have on hand:

✦ **Date:** The date each PayPal transaction occurred.

✦ **Time:** The time the payment was made.

✦ **Time zone:** The time zone used for recording transactions in your PayPal account.

✦ **Name:** The name of the person to whom you sent money or from whom you received money.

✦ **Type:** The type of transaction that occurred: deposit, withdrawal, ATM withdrawal, payment sent, payment received, and so on.

✦ **Status:** The status of the transaction (cleared, completed, denied, and so on) at the time you download the file.

✦ **Gross:** The gross amount involved in the transaction (before any fees are deducted).

✦ **Fee:** Any PayPal fees charged to the transaction.

✦ **Net:** The net dollar amount of the transaction. This is the total received, less any PayPal fees.

✦ **From e-mail:** The e-mail address of the sender.

✦ **To e-mail:** The e-mail address of the recipient.

If you use different e-mail addresses to classify different types of sales, this can be a good sorting point for your reports. For example, I receive payments for my personal auctions to one e-mail address, and payments for my business to another.

✦ **Item ID:** That strange combination of letters and numbers that PayPal assigns to each transaction. Decide whether this is important for your records. (I don't use it.)

✦ **Item title:** The title of the auction related to the transaction.

✦ **Shipping amount:** The amount the buyer paid for shipping. It's a good idea to use this field because it helps you separate merchandise revenue from shipping revenue.

✦ **Auction site:** If you're collecting money from other auction sites through PayPal, you might want to include this link so that you can sort your sales by auction site.

✦ **Item URL:** The Internet address of the auction or transaction. (For eBay, the URLs are on the site for up to 90 days — here you can go back a year.)

✦ **Closing date:** The date the transaction closed. The record will always contain the date the payment posted to your PayPal account, whether you indicate a closing date here or not.

✦ **Shipping address:** The address to which the item was shipped.

✦ **Counter party status (verified versus unverified):** A record of whether your buyer was PayPal verified.

✦ **Address status (confirmed versus unconfirmed):** Shows whether the address you shipped to was confirmed.

✦ **Sales tax:** Information about sales tax you collected.

Customizing and Downloading Your Reports

To get your reports from PayPal, follow these steps:

1. **Go to** www.PayPal.com **and log in to your account with your e-mail address and password.**

After you're logged in, the top of your page displays various tabs, as shown in Figure 4-3.

Figure 4-3:
The PayPal navigation bar.

2. **Click the My Account tab.**

3. **Mouse over the History item on the navigation bar and click Download History on the resulting drop-down menu.**

You land on the Download History page. Before you start clicking anything, consider customizing your reports.

4. **Scroll down the page to indicate your level of customization.**

You can customize the fields you require in your download through the links at the right.

5. **Select the fields you want to include by putting a check mark in the box next to the desired data.**

For details on the different options, see the list before this set of steps.

6. **Click Save.**

You're returned to the Download History page, as shown in Figure 4-4. Your customization is saved for future report downloads.

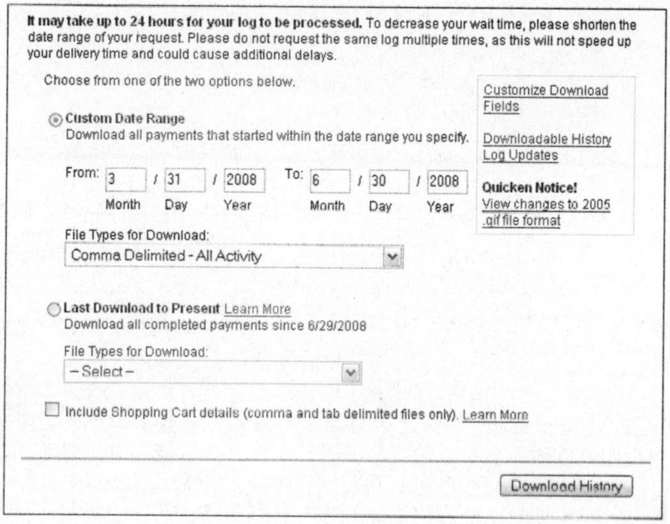

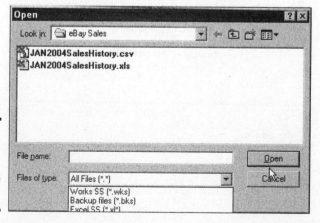

Figure 4-4:
Down-
loading my
second-
quarter 2008
transactions
for my state
sales-tax
filing.

**Book II
Chapter 4**

Simplifying Payment
with PayPal

If you're a seller in the U.K., your page will look slightly different than
the one pictured. Your dates will be in the format of DD/MM/YY.

7. **Type the dates that you want to span in the downloaded report.**

8. **Select a format for your download from the following:**

   • **Comma-delimited file:** This type of file downloads with the .csv
     extension. You can open a comma-delimited file easily in Microsoft
     Excel or Microsoft Works, using the All Files option, as shown in
     Figure 4-5. (Microsoft Works doesn't have a direct .csv importer,
     but the file will open with the All Files *.* command.)

Figure 4-5:
Opening
a comma-
delimited file
in Works.

- **Tab-delimited file:** This file downloads with the .txt extension. It can be opened not only in a spreadsheet program but also as a text file in Windows Notepad or a word processing program such as Microsoft Word for Windows.

- **Quicken or QuickBooks file:** These files download in the native format, ready to import into these Intuit bookkeeping programs. Just remember: After these files are imported, they're in there for good.

Saving these files for spreadsheet use does not limit you in the future as to what version of which program will open what. The .txt and .csv files are universal files that can be opened on any PC with basic spreadsheet capabilities.

By opting for a spreadsheet file as your record of customers, you're not bogging down a bookkeeping program with hundreds and eventually thousands of records of one-time buyers. Even a robust program like QuickBooks will max out at around 14,000 customers!

9. **Click the Download History button.**

If you've asked for a long timeframe (such as a year), go make yourself a cup of joe. When you come back, your file will be ready to download.

Saving and Editing Your Reports

When your computer is ready to receive the downloaded file (which may take a while — especially if you have a dial-up connection), a window like the one shown in Figure 4-6 pops up.

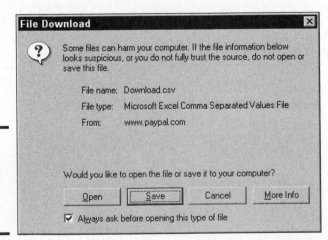

Figure 4-6: The Windows File Download window.

Click the Save button to save the file to a folder on your computer. In the next screen, select the folder where you want to save the file.

I recommend setting up a folder that contains only Internet and eBay sales files.

After the file is saved, you can open it. Figure 4-7 shows a downloaded history file opened in Microsoft Works. In this format, you can re-sort the columns, total the sales, and delete unnecessary columns.

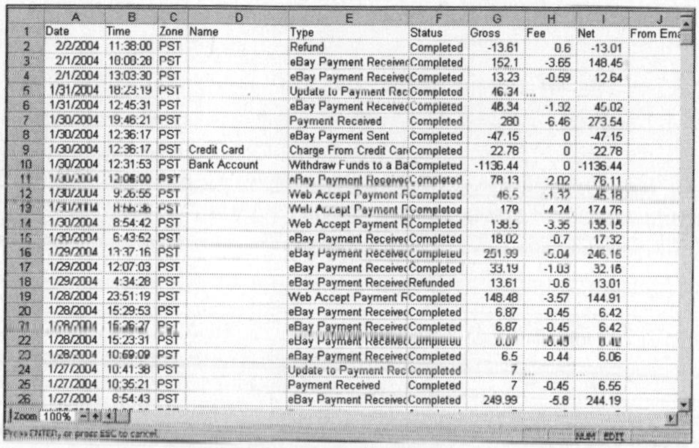

Figure 4-7:
The downloaded file, open in a spreadsheet program.

	A	B	C	D	E	F	G	H	I	J
1	Date	Time	Zone	Name	Type	Status	Gross	Fee	Net	From Ema
2	2/2/2004	11:38:00	PST		Refund	Completed	-13.61	0.6	-13.01	
3	2/1/2004	10:00:20	PST		eBay Payment Receive	Completed	152.1	-3.65	148.45	
4	2/1/2004	13:03:30	PST		eBay Payment Receive	Completed	13.23	-0.59	12.64	
5	1/31/2004	18:23:19	PST		Update to Payment Rec	Completed	46.34	...		
6	1/31/2004	12:45:31	PST		eBay Payment Receive	Completed	46.34	-1.32	45.02	
7	1/30/2004	19:46:21	PST		Payment Received	Completed	280	-6.46	273.54	
8	1/30/2004	12:36:17	PST		eBay Payment Sent	Completed	-47.15	0	-47.15	
9	1/30/2004	12:36:17	PST	Credit Card	Charge From Credit Can	Completed	22.78	0	22.78	
10	1/30/2004	12:31:53	PST	Bank Account	Withdraw Funds to a Ba	Completed	-1136.44	0	-1136.44	
11	1/30/2004	12:06:00	PST		eBay Payment Received	Completed	78.13	-2.02	76.11	
12	1/30/2004	9:26:55	PST		Web Accept Payment F	Completed	46.5	-1.32	45.18	
13	1/30/2004	8:56:36	PST		Web Accept Payment F	Completed	179	-4.24	174.76	
14	1/30/2004	8:54:42	PST		Web Accept Payment F	Completed	138.5	-3.35	135.15	
15	1/30/2004	6:43:52	PST		eBay Payment Receive	Completed	18.02	-0.7	17.32	
16	1/29/2004	13:37:16	PST		eBay Payment Received	Completed	251.99	-5.04	246.16	
17	1/29/2004	12:07:03	PST		eBay Payment Receive	Completed	33.19	-1.03	32.16	
18	1/29/2004	4:34:28	PST		eBay Payment Receive	Refunded	13.61	-0.6	13.01	
19	1/28/2004	23:51:19	PST		Web Accept Payment F	Completed	148.48	-3.57	144.91	
20	1/28/2004	15:29:53	PST		eBay Payment Receive	Completed	6.87	-0.45	6.42	
21	1/28/2004	15:26:27	PST		eBay Payment Receive	Completed	6.87	-0.45	6.42	
22	1/28/2004	15:23:31	PST		eBay Payment Receive	Completed	6.07	-0.45	8.42	
23	1/28/2004	10:59:09	PST		eBay Payment Receive	Completed	6.5	-0.44	6.06	
24	1/27/2004	10:41:36	PST		Update to Payment Rec	Completed	7			
25	1/27/2004	10:35:21	PST		Payment Received	Completed	7	-0.45	6.55	
26	1/27/2004	8:54:43	PST		eBay Payment Receive	Completed	249.99	-5.8	244.19	

Zoom 100%

Press ENTER, or press ESC to cancel.

This file is now part of your eBay business archive, should the day come that you need to produce it. Be sure to back it up, just in case.

Some CPAs recommend that you keep these files for up to seven years. To be safe, check with your own tax professional, who understands the needs of your particular tax situation.

Chapter 5: Using eBay's Management Tools

In This Chapter

✔ Signing in

✔ Understanding the parts of the My eBay page

✔ Checking out the My Summary area

✔ Touring the All Buying area

✔ Hanging out in the All Favorites area

✔ Working on the My Account page

✔ Ramping up with Selling Manager

*e*Bay offers you an amazing variety of tools. Because the site is constantly changing, few of us know where all these tools are and how to use them. It's always an eye-opener when I poke around the site and find a new cool tool or neat shortcut.

Aside from the tools I tell you about in this chapter, the most important shortcut I can give you is to remind you to sign in and select the box that says "Keep me signed in on this computer unless I sign out" before you attempt to do anything on eBay. This will permit you to do all your business on eBay without being bugged for your password at every turn.

Your computer holds your sign-in information for an entire day (unless you sign out). If you have more than one user ID or share a computer with other people, be sure to sign out when you're finished. For your protection, you still have to type your password for actions involving financial or personal information. To specify the tasks for which you want eBay to remember your sign-in information, go to the eBay Preferences area of the My eBay page.

Although I love (and use) eBay's management tools, many solid third-party services and tools are available. Book VIII clues you in on some of my favorites.

Signing In to Get Going

Before you do almost anything on eBay, it's best to sign in. What would be more of a disaster than to find an item you want, at the price you'd love to pay, with only two minutes to go — and not be signed in? You must be signed in to bid, sell, or buy, so do it!

1. **Click the Sign In link at the top of any eBay page.**

   (If you're already signed in, the link will read Sign Out.) You're sent to the Sign In page.

2. **Type your user ID and password, as shown in Figure 5-1.**

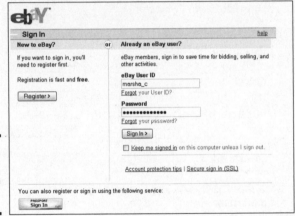

Figure 5-1:
Signed in
and ready to
deal!

Type your registered eBay user ID, not your e-mail address. Your user ID and e-mail address are no longer interchangeable on the site.

If you ever forget your eBay password, you can click the Having problems with signing in? Link or go to the following:

```
http://cgi4.ebay.com/ws1/eBayISAPI.
    dll?ForgotYourPasswordShow
```

If you remember the answer to the question you were asked during the eBay registration process, you can create a new password immediately.

3. **Click the Sign In button.**

   You're now signed in and ready to do almost anything on eBay! You are brought to your My eBay Summary page.

Taking Advantage of My eBay

The number one tool available at no cost to every eBay user is the My eBay page. This area of the site is unmatched for its organizational ability in helping you with your buying and selling activities. After you've registered on the site, you have a My eBay page automatically, so let's delve into exactly what it can do for you.

I call My eBay a page, but it's really an *area* — a group of several pages held together with links. The My eBay area gives you complete control of everything you are doing (or would like to do) on eBay.

You have to sign in to the site before you can use the My eBay area. To get to your My eBay page, click the My eBay link on the eBay navigation bar, which is at the top of every eBay page.

My eBay is divided into six areas: My Summary, All Buying, All Selling, My Messages, All Favorites, and My Account, as described in Table 5-1. You can visit each area by clicking links in the My eBay Views box, on the left side of the page. The top link of each My eBay area presents you with a summary of the activity in that area. The links below the top link take you to specific data, without having to scroll through a long page.

Book II
Chapter 5

Using eBay's
Management Tools

Table 5-1	In a Snapshot: Views of the My eBay Area
Click Here	*To See This on Your My eBay Page*
Summary	A page summarizing your My eBay area, with notifications of actions that need follow-up on the balance of the My eBay pages.
Buy	Every item for sale that you're watching or bidding on, and all items you've won and lost.
All Selling	All the information about any items you're selling on eBay.
My Messages	A separate tab to a direct and secure place to view the latest information about eBay. No more worry about phishing spam that pretends to be from eBay. When eBay has something to tell you, it appears here.
All Favorites	A collection of links to your favorite categories, searches, sellers, and stores.
Seller Dashboard Summary	How you've been rated by your buyers. If you are a PowerSeller, you'll be able to see the calculations regarding your Final Value Fee discounts.

(continued)

Table 5-1 *(continued)*

Click Here	*To See This on Your My eBay Page*
Account	A tab that contains links to several important areas: your eBay account information, such as seller's fees and invoices; the most recent feedback comments about you, links that send you to all the feedback you've left and received, and an area where you can respond to feedback; and finally, preferences you can specify so that eBay performs just as you want it to.

On the left side of the My eBay Activity All Selling is a box with convenient links to services and to answers you may need while doing business on eBay (see Figure 5-2). You can choose to specify which links appear here by clicking the *Edit Shortcuts* link. Clicking this link presents you with a box of options to select for showing on your page (Figure 5-3).

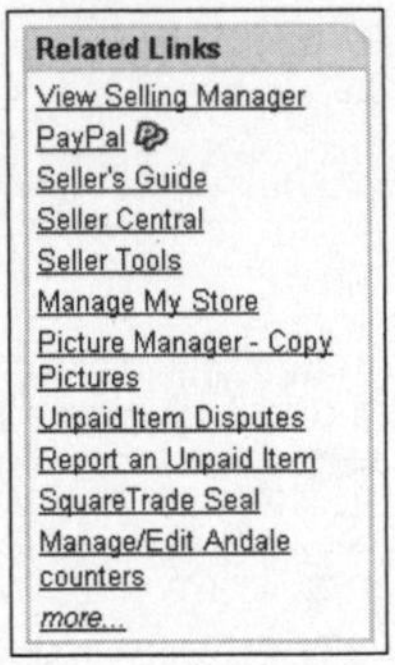

Figure 5-2:
The shortcuts link box on the My eBay All Selling page.

> **Related Links**
> View Selling Manager
> PayPal
> Seller's Guide
> Seller Central
> Seller Tools
> Manage My Store
> Picture Manager - Copy Pictures
> Unpaid Item Disputes
> Report an Unpaid Item
> SquareTrade Seal
> Manage/Edit Andale counters
> *more...*

The links you see repeat on the different pages of your My eBay area.

Before you freak out because you have a question about something on eBay that you can't remember the answer to, double-check the eBay Help area. You can always find help when you click the Help link on the navigation bar.

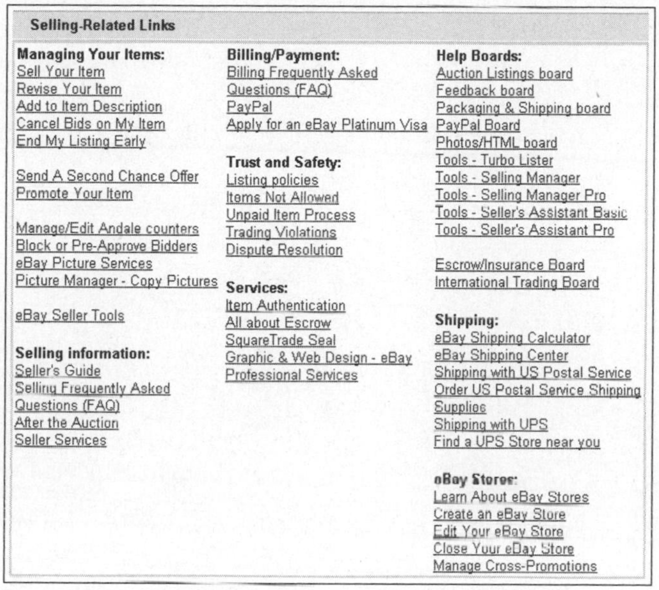

Figure 5-3:
Editing your
shortcuts
for the My
eBay All
Selling
page.

> **Selling-Related Links**
>
> **Managing Your Items:**
> Sell Your Item
> Revise Your Item
> Add to Item Description
> Cancel Bids on My Item
> End My Listing Early
>
> Send A Second Chance Offer
> Promote Your Item
>
> Manage/Edit Andale counters
> Block or Pre-Approve Bidders
> eBay Picture Services
> Picture Manager - Copy Pictures
>
> eBay Seller Tools
>
> **Selling information:**
> Seller's Guide
> Selling Frequently Asked
> Questions (FAQ)
> After the Auction
> Seller Services
>
> **Billing/Payment:**
> Billing Frequently Asked
> Questions (FAQ)
> PayPal
> Apply for an eBay Platinum Visa
>
> **Trust and Safety:**
> Listing policies
> Items Not Allowed
> Unpaid Item Process
> Trading Violations
> Dispute Resolution
>
> **Services:**
> Item Authentication
> All about Escrow
> SquareTrade Seal
> Graphic & Web Design - eBay
> Professional Services
>
> **Help Boards:**
> Auction Listings board
> Feedback board
> Packaging & Shipping board
> PayPal Board
> Photos/HTML board
> Tools - Turbo Lister
> Tools - Selling Manager
> Tools - Selling Manager Pro
> Tools - Seller's Assistant Basic
> Tools - Seller's Assistant Pro
>
> Escrow/Insurance Board
> International Trading Board
>
> **Shipping:**
> eBay Shipping Calculator
> eBay Shipping Center
> Shipping with US Postal Service
> Order US Postal Service Shipping
> Supplies
> Shipping with UPS
> Find a UPS Store near you
>
> **eBay Stores:**
> Learn About eBay Stores
> Create an eBay Store
> Edit Your eBay Store
> Close Your eBay Store
> Manage Cross-Promotions

My eBay: Summary Page

Until you set your preferences (as to which page you want to automatically
open your My eBay area to — see further on), you land on the My Summary
page. Mine is shown in Figure 5-4 (note that when you subscribe to Selling
Manager (which I do and you should too) it will replace the All Selling box.

The My Summary page gives you a snapshot of your current eBay business.
It provides data about your buying and selling business, and supplies links
to the items.

The Buying Reminders area tells you about

+ Items you're watching that close today

+ Items you're bidding on that close today

+ Items you've been outbid on (for which you may need to up your bid)

+ Feedback that you need to leave for items you've won

In the Selling Reminders area, you find info on

+ Questions pending on items from prospective customers

+ Buyers who have requested totals for their purchases

+ How many items you are awaiting payment on

✦ How many items you need to ship

✦ Cross-promotions that need to be revised due to items' auctions ending (if you have an eBay store)

✦ The number of items you're selling that are closing today

✦ How many items you've sold that need feedback

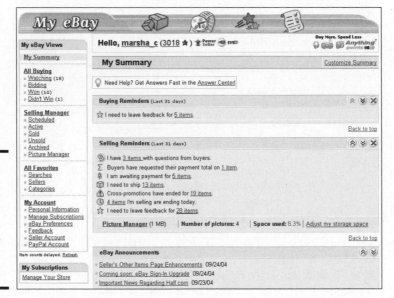

Figure 5-4:
My eBay
Summary
page (my
oh my!) —
the hub for
my eBay
activities.

You can customize what you'd like to appear on most of the My eBay pages by clicking the Customize Summary link in the upper-right corner. Figure 5-5 shows you the customizing options for the My Summary page.

Figure 5-5:
Customizing
the My eBay
Summary
page.

Should you subscribe to any of eBay's paid services such as Picture Manager or eBay Stores, there will also be a link to your subscription area. In addition, a link is provided to any important notices from eBay regarding changes in its policies or services.

My eBay: All Buying Page

The All Buying page is the hub for keeping track of your bids, your wins, items you're watching, and any items you didn't win. This area of My eBay helps you control everything you're currently shopping for on the site. I check this page several times a day to see the progress of items I'm interested in.

Watching link

Have you ever seen an auction that made you think, "I don't want to bid on this just now, but I'd like to buy it if it's a bargain"? Clicking the Watching link from the My eBay Views box will bring you to the Watching page (see Figure 5-6), one of the most powerful features of the My eBay area. This page lists each auction with a countdown (time left) timer, so you know exactly when the auction will close. When a listing on your watch list gets close to ending, you can swoop down and make the kill — if the price is right.

Figure 5-6:
Sit back and observe at My eBay.

Are you interested in an item? You can observe the bidding action — the number of bids and how fast the price is rising (or not) — without showing your hand to the competition.

Also a handy marketing tool, the Watching page allows you to store listings from competitive sellers. That way you can monitor the status of items similar to ones you plan to sell later — and see whether the items are selling high or low, helping you to decide whether it's a good time to sell.

You've probably seen the Watch this item link at the top of each listing page. If you're watching items (eBay allows you to monitor 200 listings at a time), you'll see a notation on the page, indicating how many auctions you're currently watching.

The watch-list function helps me keep my bargain-hunting quiet. Everybody knows when you're bidding on an item; nobody knows when you're watching the deals like a hawk. When you're looking for bargains to buy and resell, you may not want to tip off the competition by letting them know you're bidding.

Active Buying link

When you place a bid, eBay registers it in the Active Buying area, as shown in Figure 5-7, and displays a clickable link to the item.

Figure 5-7: Keeping track of your bidding.

Make the bidding page a daily stop on eBay, so you can see the status of your bids:

✦ Bid amounts in green indicate that you're the high bidder in the auction.

✦ Bid amounts in red indicate that your bid is losing. If you want to increase your bid, simply click the auction title to go to the auction.

✦ Dutch auctions appear in black. To determine whether you retain high-bidder status in a Dutch auction, you have to go to the actual auction.

✦ The My Max Bid area reminds you of the amount of your highest bid; if you see a bid that surpasses your own, you'll know it's time to throw in another bid to stay in the game.

✦ As auctions on which you've bid end, they are transferred to the Won or Didn't Win page, based on your success or failure in the bidding process.

You can make notations on your bidding or item-watching. Just click the drop-down menu next to the item you want to annotate, click the Add Note button, and then add the information.

Won link

Clicking the Won link in the Buy area in the My eBay Views box displays all the items you've won as far back as the last 60 days, as shown in Figure 5-8. The default is 31 days, which should suffice for most transactions. The Won page is a great place to keep track of items that you're waiting to receive from the seller. It's also a convenient way to keep track of your expenditures, should you be buying for resale.

If you do not see pictures next to your items, just click Customize at the upper right and make them appear.

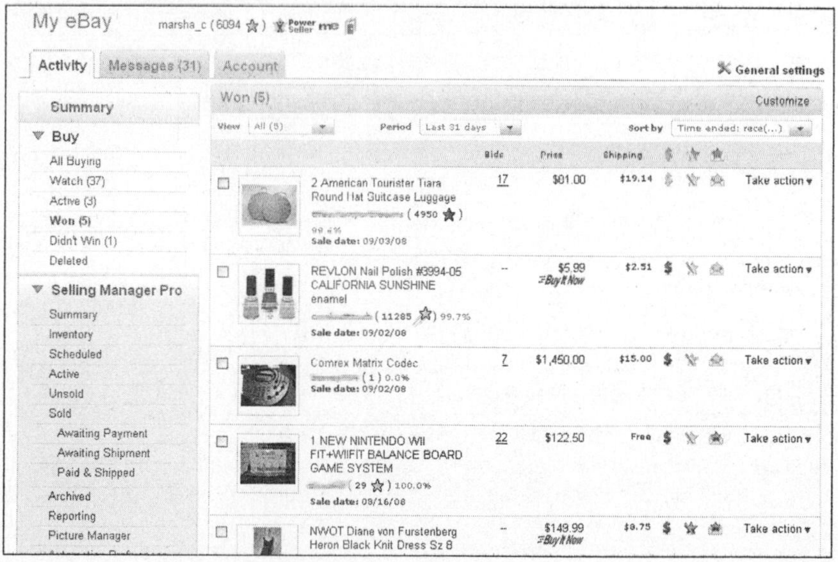

Book II
Chapter 5

Using eBay's
Management Tools

Figure 5-8:
What I won
on eBay (in
this case,
I got quite
a deal on
a $3,750
piece of
equipment
for my radio
show).

Helpful features on the Won page include the following:

✦ **Drop-down menu:** Click the drop-down menu next to any item you've won, and you'll be able to perform a plethora of tasks.

✦ **Seller's user ID:** This link sends you to the seller's Member Profile (feedback) page, where you can send an e-mail to the seller.

✦ **Listing title:** A link to the listing. I always use this when an item arrives so I can be sure that the item I received is exactly as advertised.

✦ **Item number:** The item number for your records.

✦ **Item sale date:** A convenient way to see whether your item is slow in shipping. After a week, it doesn't hurt to drop the seller an e-mail to check on the shipping status.

Using My eBay to manage your sales

For the newbie seller, the tools on the Selling pages are great. They're simple and get right to the point. To run their auction business, small sellers can use the All Selling page with the Sell an Item form for individual listings and everything should be sufficient.

On the Selling page, you can view details for your active listings, including:

✔ **Links for listings:** Each listing has clickable links you can use to go instantly to an item page.

✔ **Item number:** In case you need an item number to contact a bidder or send auction information to a friend, you'll find the item number here.

✔ **Current price:** This is the starting price of your item (if you have no bids) or the current price based on bids received.

✔ **Reserve price:** This handy feature reminds you of the reserve price that you've set on an item. There's nowhere else to check this.

✔ **Quantity available:** Here's where you can see how many of the item are still available for purchase on the site. When an eBay store item is listed, this feature shows you how many are left, as well as the original quantity you listed.

✔ **# of bids:** When you see that the price is rising on an item, check out this column to see how many bids have been placed to date.

✔ **Start date:** This is the date the listing was posted on eBay.

✔ **End date:** This is the date the listing will end.

✔ **Time left:** In this column, you can check how much time is left (to the minute) in your listing.

✔ **Action:** This is the handiest column of all. Here you have a link that lets you list a similar item. This is particularly handy if you want to use a template again for another item. It also allows you to revise a listing, add to the description, end a listing, or edit promotions if you have a store.

Visit Book III, Chapter 5 for an in-depth look at how the My eBay: All Selling area can help you manage your eBay business.

- ✦ **Sale price and quantity:** Helps you keep track of the money you've spent.

- ✦ **Drop-down menu:** This area displays a drop-down list where you can pick different commands based on the status of your transaction. You can choose to pay for the item through PayPal, view the payment status on paid items, mark the item paid if you paid through other payment methods, or leave feedback after you've received the item and are satisfied that it's what you ordered.

- ✦ **Icons:** Each item's listing has three icons that appear dimmed until the selected action is taken. A dollar sign indicates whether you've paid for the item, a star indicates that you've left feedback, and an envelope indicates whether feedback has been left for you.

After you receive an item and leave feedback, click the box to the left of the item listing, and then click the Delete button to remove the selected completed transactions from view.

Didn't win link

Sniff . . . the Didn't Win area is a very sad place. This My eBay section lets you know when you've been outbid and lost an item. This option isn't there to rub your nose in all the auctions you've lost — it's a handy tool that lets you search the seller's *other* items for something similar, or search the category for a similar item.

My eBay: Organize Links

If you sell and have an interest in a few categories, look no further than the My eBay Organize zone, which gives you some links for checking out what's hot and what's not. Saved searches helps you track trends and find some bargains to resell on eBay.

Saved Searches link

A tool that comes in handy for sellers as well as buyers is the Searches link (in the Organize area of the My eBay Views box). You can list as many as 100 saved searches. When you want to check one out, simply click the search name. If there are items matching your search, they will appear as icons in the search list. If not, the search box will appear empty (see Figure 5-9).

Are you always looking for certain things on eBay? For example, maybe you plan to search frequently for a Callaway Seven Heaven Wood — whatever. Add it to your list of saved searches and you won't have to retype *Callaway Seven Heaven Wood* more than once. (Now there's a blessing!) By organizing your saved searches, you can search for your favorite items with a click of your mouse on the title links.

Saved Searches

	Searches Shown 20 ▾	Sort by Title: A to Z ▾

▷ **altair 880*** Email: Last sent: - | Not subscribed — Go to search results ▾

▷ **baccarat nautilus** Email: Last sent: Oct-24-08 | Not subscribed — Go to search results ▾

▷ **diane von BRIDGET** Email: Last sent: Oct-24-08 — Go to search results ▾

▷ **diane von dion** Email: Last sent: Oct-22-08 — Go to search results ▾

▷ **diane von domino** Email: Last sent: Oct-27-08 — Go to search results ▾

▷ **ebay varsity jacket** Email: Last sent: Sep-17-08 — Go to search results ▾

▷ **express ce* jeans** Email: Last sent: - | Not subscribed — Go to search results ▾

▷ **for dummies ebook ebay, Search title and description** Email: Last sent: - — Go to search results ▾

Figure 5-9:
Some of
my favorite
searches
(this month).

You can view saved searches, change them, delete them, or indicate that you'd like to receive e-mail notification when a new item is listed. To add an item to the list, run a search from the search box on any eBay page and click the Save This Search link that appears at the top of the search results. The next time you reload your My eBay Saved Searches page, your new favorite will be listed.

Be sure to use all the search tricks and shortcuts I show you in the table in Chapter 1, because these searches are not performed in the search box. These are single-line searches that you normally would perform from the small search boxes on the eBay pages.

To set up a favorite search, click the Add new Search link on the results page of any eBay search. You're forwarded to eBay's Search page. Type your keywords and perform your search. When the results appear, click the Add to Favorites link at the top of the page, and your search will be saved to your My eBay All Favorites page.

If you choose to receive e-mail when your search locates a new listing, you can request that you receive notification over periods that range from seven days to a year. You're allowed to receive new listing e-mails on 30 of your 100 searches. Just click the drop down menu in the far-right of the row (refer to Figure 5-9). eBay sends its robot to check listings each night, so you'll get a notification of new listings the next morning.

Keeping track of favorite searches is a valuable tool when you're looking for particular items to resell and want to find them at bargain-basement prices. Be sure to take advantage of asterisks (wildcard characters) and alternate spellings so you can catch items with misspellings in the title. These are your best bets for low prices.

Saved Sellers link

When you've been on eBay for awhile, you will find that certain sellers carry a type of merchandise that interests you. By saving their user IDs in the Saved Sellers area, you'll be able to revisit their current auctions without having to run a seller search from the search area. Remember that the purpose of the My eBay page is to have all your controls in one area.

From a seller's point of view, Saved Sellers is where you can keep a list of people who sell items similar to what you sell. You can check up on them and see what they're selling, when they're selling it, and for how much. It's a helpful tool that can prevent you from listing an item right next to one of their auctions.

Saved Sellers is handy also when your competition is selling an item that you plan to sell, but at a deeply discounted price. When that happens, don't offer yours until they sell out of the item, at which time the price will most likely go back up — supply and demand, remember? I have a few quality wholesalers and liquidators under Saved Sellers, too, and search for lots that I can resell at a profit.

To add a seller to your Saved Sellers list, (if they have a store), you can click the link in the store header). When you search for a seller in the Advanced Search, you see a Seller Information box at the bottom of the left side page links. In that box, just click Add to Saved sellers, and they will appear on your list. You may add a maximum of 100 sellers to your list.

My eBay: Account tab

The Account tab lets you know how much you owe eBay and how much they'll charge your credit card that month. This is a quick and easy way to check your most recent invoice, payments and credits, and your account; all these links are located in one area. You can also access your PayPal account to see, for example, when deposits were sent to your checking account.

Book II
Chapter 5

Using eBay's
Management Tools

It's also a place where you can find a drop-down menu that links to the many areas that affect your selling and account (you can see mine in Figure 5-10). Below, I'll show you some of the important links you'll find on this page.

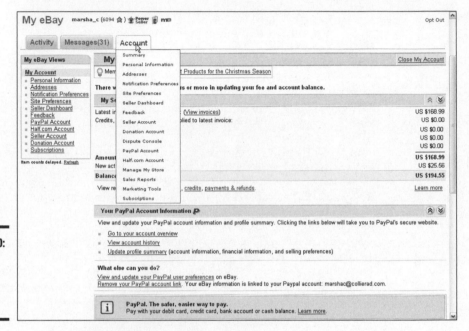

Figure 5-10:
The Account summary page.

Personal information link

Click the Personal Information link (below My Account in the My eBay Views box) to get to the Personal Information page. This page holds all the links to your personal information on eBay. This is where you can change your e-mail address, user ID (without losing your feedback), password, and credit-card information — and edit or create your About Me page. You can also change or access any registration or credit-card information that you have on file at eBay. There's even a link you can use to change your home address on record.

Keeping all your contact information up-to-date on eBay is important. If they should ever find that any of the contact information is wrong, they may suspend your membership.

Another link, *Change my notification preferences*, allows you to input your text-messaging number for your cellular phone, for example:

`areacodeandnumber@messaging.nextel.com`

That way eBay can notify you on your cell phone when you get outbid or when you win an item.

Adding a wireless e-mail address for your cell phone may seem like a great idea: eBay can send end-of-auction notices right to your WAP-enabled cell phone. The trouble is, sometimes these messages are sent hours after the listing ends. So don't count on receiving timely updates.

Manage subscriptions link

Click the Manage subscriptions link (below My Account in the My eBay Views box), and you'll be able to see just which additional selling tools you're paying for. From here, you can upgrade, downgrade, or unsubscribe.

eBay Preferences link

You'll find two links below My Account, Notification and Site preferences. A nifty feature of the eBay Site Preferences area (see Figure 5-11) is the opportunity to customize (under General Preferences by clicking the Show then Edit link) how you see your My eBay pages. If you run many listings, you can show as many as 200 items on these pages.

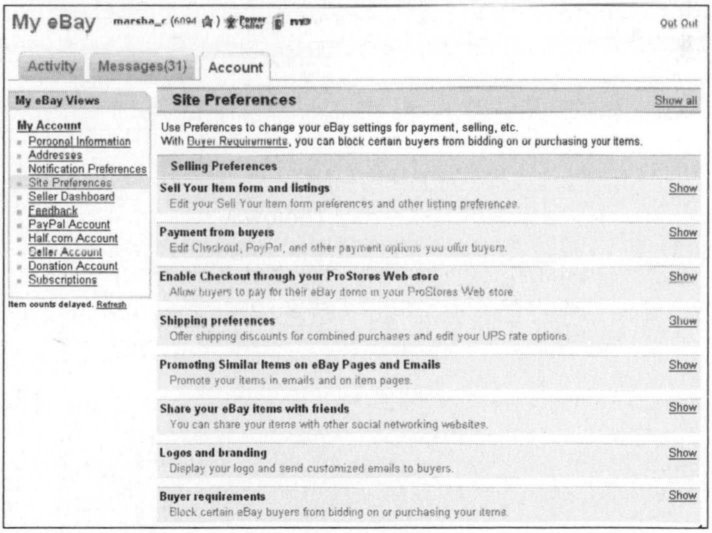

Figure 5-11:
My eBay
Site
Preferences
page.

> **My eBay** marsha_r (6094 ⭐) ⭐ Power Seller 🔲 me   Opt Out
>
> Activity | Messages(31) | **Account**
>
> **My eBay Views** | **Site Preferences** | Show all
>
> **My Account**
> • Personal Information
> • Addresses
> • Notification Preferences
> • Site Preferences
> • Seller Dashboard
> • Feedback
> • PayPal Account
> • Half.com Account
> • Seller Account
> • Donation Account
> • Subscriptions
>
> Item counts delayed. Refresh
>
> Use Preferences to change your eBay settings for payment, selling, etc.
> With Buyer Requirements, you can block certain buyers from bidding on or purchasing your items.
>
> **Selling Preferences**
>
> **Sell Your Item form and listings** | Show
> Edit your Sell Your Item form preferences and other listing preferences.
>
> **Payment from buyers** | Show
> Edit Checkout, PayPal, and other payment options you offer buyers.
>
> **Enable Checkout through your ProStores Web store** | Show
> Allow buyers to pay for their eBay items in your ProStores Web store.
>
> **Shipping preferences** | Show
> Offer shipping discounts for combined purchases and edit your UPS rate options.
>
> **Promoting Similar Items on eBay Pages and Emails** | Show
> Promote your items in emails and on item pages.
>
> **Share your eBay items with friends** | Show
> You can share your items with other social networking websites.
>
> **Logos and branding** | Show
> Display your logo and send customized emails to buyers.
>
> **Buyer requirements** | Show
> Block certain eBay buyers from bidding on or purchasing your items.

You may as well select everything and go through each option every once in a while. This way you'll have things set up just the way you want them while conducting business at eBay.

Seller Dashboard

Since customer service is what it's all about when building and maintaining a business on eBay, this space should be a regular stop for you. It'll keep you apprised of how you're doing with your customer service. Your average DSR (Detailed Seller Ratings) will appear in a box at the top of the page.

If you're a PowerSeller, the Seller Dashboard is a very important place — because this is where you can keep track of your Final Value fee discount (which is based on your ratings). Take a look at my page in Figure 5-12 for an example. Rolling over the lines on the chart will give you even more info on how you compare to other sellers on eBay.

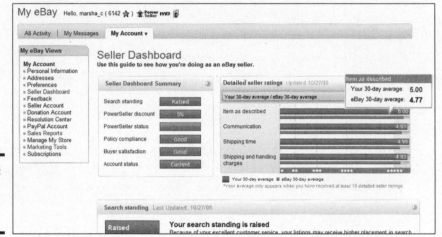

Figure 5-12:
My Seller
Dashboard
page.

Feedback link

In Book I, I talk all about the importance of feedback to the eBay community. In the Feedback area of the My eBay; My Account page, you can keep track of all your feedback duties.

When you click the Feedback link, you can see your items awaiting Feedback, and a link on the right will take you to the Feedback Forum, where you can perform many feedback-related functions:

✦ Find all item listings from the last 90 days that you haven't left feedback for. (For shame!)

✦ Review and respond to feedback left for you. Responding to feedback is especially important, especially if the feedback is less than stellar. Every story has two sides.

✦ See all feedback you have left for others. If you want to re-examine feedback that you've left, this is the place.

Below these boxes is a listing of all your feedback dating back to your first transaction on eBay.

Ramping Up with Selling Manager

When you've been bitten by the selling bug, it's a natural transition to go from a monthly listing of a few items to 50 or more. That means, dear reader, that you are officially running an eBay business. Congratulations!

This has a good and a bad side. The good is that you're making considerably more cash than you did before hooking up with eBay. The bad? It's time to start investing in tools to keep your business professional.

The first tool that can help smooth your transition makes the process of running eBay auctions and sales consistent — Selling Manager. This section tells you what Selling Manager does, but Book VIII goes into more of the program's intricacies.

Book III, Chapter 4 gets into eBay's free Turbo Lister program (it gets your items on the site without having to go through the slow, sometimes torturous Sell Your Item form). As with Turbo Lister, Selling Manager is a suite of tools for managing your selling business from any computer (as long as it has an Internet connection). eBay gives you 30 days to try out the service for free, and thereafter charges $4.99 per month. (Believe me, the time that Selling Manager saves you is well worth the fee.)

I've run well over 100 auctions in a single month, successfully managing them with Selling Manager. I use it along with PayPal's tools and QuickBooks. This approach provides a professional solution for my medium-sized eBay business.

First glimpse of Selling Manager

To subscribe to your free Selling Manager trial program, follow these steps:

1. **Below the eBay navigation bar, which is at the top of every eBay page, click the Site Map link.**

2. **In the second column of the Site Map, under the Selling Tools heading, click the eBay Selling Manager (or Selling Manager Pro) link.**

3. **Read the information on the Selling Manager hub page, and then click the Subscribe Now link.**

You're now subscribed to Selling Manager. If you have an eBay store, it's free; if not, eBay adds a $4.99 fee to your monthly bill. eBay automatically populates Selling Manager with your information from the My eBay: All Selling page. The All Selling link will change to Selling Manager when it's all set up.

With Selling Manager, you can click the link to view a summary of all your auction activities.

The Summary page lists at-a-glance statistics so you can quickly see what's going on with your sales, at any time — from any computer. Links to other pages in the Selling Manager tool also appear on the Summary page.

If you plan to exceed 100 transactions a month, consider using Selling Manager Pro, which costs $15.99 per month. The Pro version has bulk feedback and bulk invoice-printing features and incorporates inventory management.

Scheduled listings link

The Scheduled Listings link on the Summary page takes you to any auction, fixed-price listing, or store listing you've sent to eBay through Turbo Lister (or listed on the Sell an Item page) and scheduled as pending for a later starting date or time. You can view these pending listings also through links on the Summary page that narrow the listings down to Starting Within the Next Hour and Starting Today.

When you enter the Scheduled Listings area by clicking the Scheduled Listings link on the Summary page, you can go directly to the listing. If you want to promote your listing-to-be in a banner ad (or create a link to it from elsewhere on the Internet), you can do so using the URL of the pending listing.

From the Pending Listing page, you can confirm all information about the sale, as well as make any changes to the listing or to the scheduling time.

Active listings link

Click the Active Listings link on the Summary page, and you can observe the bidding action just as you can from the My eBay All Selling page. The color-coding that indicates bidding activity is the same as that on the My eBay All Selling page, and your listings are accessible with a click of your mouse.

You have the option to show only auctions, only store listings, or only fixed-price items on the Active Listings page. You can also search your own listings by keyword or item number.

For more about active listings, visit the Summary page, which includes links to items ending within the hour and those ending within the next 24 hours.

eBay's Selling Manager

Selling Manager replaces the All Selling area of your My eBay page with its own summary of your current transactions (see the figure). Many sellers (even PowerSellers) rely on Selling Manager to handle their eBay management chores. I subscribe to Selling Manager Pro, so you'll see some additional options on the screenshot below. Visit Book VIII, Chapter 1 to decide which version is right for you).

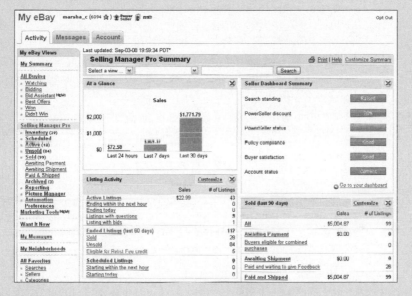

Book II
Chapter 5

Using eBay's
Management Tools

From Selling Manager, you can

- ✔ **View listing status:** You can see which sales activities you've completed and what you still have to do.

- ✔ **Send custom e-mail and post feedback:** Customize your e-mail templates and set up stored feedback comments to help you run through the post-sales process quickly.

- ✔ **Relist in bulk:** Relist multiple sold and unsold listings at once.

- ✔ **Maintain sales records:** See individual sales records for every transaction, including a history of the transaction status.

- ✔ **Print invoices and shipping labels:** Print labels and invoices directly from sales records.

- ✔ **Download sales history:** Export your sales records to keep files on your computer.

- ✔ **Keep track of items that qualify for relisting:** Relisting an item that hasn't sold may qualify for a listing fee refund when the item sells upon the second listing. There's a link in Selling Manager that will show you what qualifies.

Sold listings link

The Sold Listings feature (which you get to by clicking the link on the Summary page), is where Selling Manager really shines. You'll find quite a few links here, including these:

✦ **Awaiting payment:** This is where items that have been won or bought are listed before a payment is made.

✦ **Awaiting payment, buyers eligible for combined purchases:** When a customer buys more than one item from you, the transactions will show up here. By clicking this area you can easily combine the items into a single invoice, to give the buyer the benefit of a reduced shipping cost.

✦ **Awaiting Shipment:** If you input the fact that a buyer has sent payment, or if the buyer pays using PayPal, the transaction automatically moves to this category.

✦ **Paid and waiting to give feedback:** Once an item is paid for, a reference to it appears here so you can keep track of the feedback you need to leave.

✦ **Paid and shipped:** These are (you guessed it) items that the buyer has paid for and that you've indicated as shipped on the transaction record.

✦ **Dispute Console:** This is the sad category where buyers who don't pay go if, after all your attempts to get action, they have not responded and sent payment. (If they don't cough up within ten days after you file a Nonpaying Bidder Alert, the listing moves to this category automatically.)

Archived Listings link

From the Archived Listings link, you can access completed items that closed within the last four months. You can also download this information to your computer. These are good records, so download them and keep them.

Seller tools

The Seller Tools box on the left side of the Summary page contains a powerful group of links that allow you to download and export your sales history to your computer. You also have links to PayPal, the Selling Manager Discussion Board, My eBay Store, and the good old My eBay All Selling page — in case you get nostalgic for the old, pre-Selling Manager days.

Tracking payments from eBay's Selling Manager

Selling Manager makes many selling processes considerably easier. The number to the right of the Paid and ready to ship link on the Summary page indicates that you have items ready to ship. To see the details on these items, just click this link. You see each transaction; a bold dollar-sign icon to the right of a listing confirms that a payment has been made.

To indicate that you've shipped an item, click the record number next to the item and scroll down to the Sales Status & Memo area. Click Save, and the record moves from the Paid and Ready to Ship page (under Sold Listings) to the Paid and Shipped page.

Book II
Chapter 5

**Using eBay's
Management Tools**

Book III
Selling Like a Pro

The 5th Wave   By Rich Tennant

"For 30 years I've put a hat and coat on to make sales calls and I'm not changing now just because I'm doing it on the Web in my living room."

Contents at a Glance

Chapter 1: Be Sure Your Listings Make Cents

In This Chapter

✔ Knowing the costs of listing an item

✔ Getting more punch with options

✔ Figuring Final Value Fees

✔ Understanding the different types of auctions

✔ Including PayPal costs

✔ Letting our Fee Calculator do the math

✔ Establishing reasonable shipping and handling costs

Selling on eBay is a grand idea. You clean out your garage, sell things you would have thrown away anyway, and make a profit. What a wonderful marketplace! You can make money in your spare time and enhance your lifestyle with just a few clicks on your keyboard and mouse.

When you decide to sell on eBay in earnest, however, you can run into problems. Few eBay sellers have a background in retailing or marketing, and eBay is all about retailing and marketing. In this chapter, I give you tips on pricing strategies. The first item on the agenda is to understand all the fees involved with running an e-business on eBay.

Keeping an Eye on Where the Pennies Go

It doesn't seem so much: $.25 to list an item, plus a small Final Value Fee. Of course, a few cents (maybe dollars) go to PayPal. One by one, these minute amounts tend to breeze by even the most experienced seller. You don't really see your eBay fees, because they're not directly deducted from your sales. eBay bills you at the end of the month. It's easy to lose track of your costs unless you are keeping *very* good books (more on that in Book IX).

All those nickels, dimes, and quarters add up. The hundreds (thousands?) of people who are selling items on the site for $1 can't be making much of a profit — not even enough for a pack of gum! To avoid this low-profit trap, you must be keenly aware of every penny you spend of eBay listing fees, eBay Final Value fees, listing options, and PayPal fees.

Becoming complacent and blithely ignoring your eBay costs as you list items for sale is easy to do. As a person in business for yourself, you must always take into account outgoing costs as well as incoming profits. The cost of your initial listing is just the beginning of your advertising budget for that item. You have to factor in the cost of all the options and features you use as well. After all that, a Final Value Fee is paid to eBay after the item sells. (For fees regarding your eBay Store, check out Book VIII, Chapter 6.)

In this section, I review the costs for listing an auction on eBay. But if you use a credit-card payment service, they also charge a fee. Later in this chapter, I examine the costs of the most popular credit-card payment services.

Insertion (listing) fees

Your *insertion fee* (that is, fee for listing an item) is based on the highest dollar amount of two things: your minimum opening bid or the dollar amount of your reserve price. If you start your auction at $.99 and have no reserve, the listing fee is $.15 ($.10 if you're selling media: books, DVDs, CDs, or video games). But if you start your auction at $.99 and set an undisclosed reserve price of $50.00, your auction costs $2.15 to post. When you place a reserve on your item, you're charged an insertion fee based on the *amount* of the reserve price — plus the charge for the reserve option.

For a summary of eBay insertion fees, see Table 1-1. (I talk about the fees for eBay Motors later in this chapter and in Chapter 2.)

Table 1-1   eBay Listing Fees (Fixed-Price Single Item or Auction)

Opening Bid or Reserve Price ($)	Insertion Fee ($)	Media Insertion Fee ($) Books, Music, DVDs & Movies, Video Games
0.01–0.99	0.15	0.10
1.00–9.99	0.35	0.25
10.00–24.99	0..55	0.35
25.00–49.99	1.00	1.00
50.00–199.99	2.00	2.00
200.00–499.00	3.00	3.00
500.00 and up	4.00	4.00

If your item doesn't sell, don't think you can get your insertion fee back. It is nonrefundable. You do have the option of relisting your unsuccessful auction item and if your item sells with the second listing, your initial listing fee will be refunded. If it doesn't sell the second time, you will be charged again. Writing a better title, starting with a lower opening bid, or adding a snappier description and better pictures will help in selling the item. Maybe you should think about changing the category as well.

Whether you're listing one item with a starting bid of $1000.00 or 100 items for $5.00 each in a Dutch auction, your insertion cost per auction is never more than $4.00.

Reserve-price auctions

In a *reserve-price auction,* you're able to set an undisclosed minimum price for which your item will sell, thereby giving yourself a safety net. Figure 1-1 shows an auction in which the reserve has not yet been met. Using a reserve-price auction protects the investment you have in an item. If, at the end of the auction, no bidder has met your undisclosed reserve price, you aren't obligated to sell the item and the high bidder isn't required to purchase the item.

Figure 1-1: Wow! I bet this auction has a hefty reserve!

For example, if you have a rare coin to sell, you can start the bidding at a low price to attract bidders to click your auction and read your infomercial-like description. If you start your bidding at too high a price, you might dissuade prospective bidders from even looking at your auction, and you won't tempt them to even bid. They may feel that the final selling price will be too high for their budgets.

Everyone on eBay is looking for a bargain or a truly rare item. If you can combine the mystical force of both of these needs in one auction, you have something special. The reserve-price auction enables you to attempt — and perhaps achieve — this feat.

The reserve-price auction is a safety net for the seller but often an uncomfortable guessing game for the prospective bidder. To alleviate buyer anxiety, many sellers put reserve prices in the item description, allowing bidders to decide whether the item will fit into their bidding budgets.

You can't use the reserve-price option in a Dutch (multiple-item) auction.

Placing a reserve price on one of your auctions means that the item will not sell until the bidding reaches the reserve price. When your reserve-price item does sell you've sold your item at a profit (let's hear it for optimism!) The reserve fee is based on the reserve price you set, as outlined in Table 1-2, so be sure to set the reserve high enough to cover the fee and *still* give you a profit.

Put your reserve price at the top of your listing description. That way, there's a good chance the buyers will know what they're in for. You could also offer free shipping in a reserve auction to take the edge off.

Second chance to sell!

If your auction goes above the target sales price and you have more of the item in stock, you can offer items in stock to your underbidders. The figure shows you where you can click the Make Second Chance Offer button to offer the item to underbidders for their most recent high bids.

You will be charged only Final Value Fees — not a second relisting (insertion) fee — if the person purchases the item.

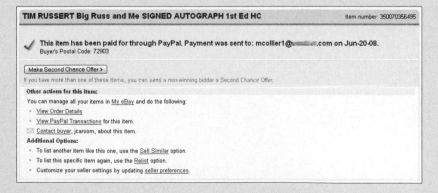

Table 1-2	eBay Reserve Auction Fees*
Reserve Amount ($)	*Fee*
0.01–199.99	$2.00
200.00 and up	1% of reserve price (maximum of $50.00)

Reserve fees for eBay Motors start at a flat $7.00 — and are refundable when the item sells.

If your item doesn't sell the first time with a low starting price and a reserve, you can always relist it at a slightly higher starting price without a reserve. If it sells, the initial listing fees are credited and you won't have to pay a reserve fee the second time you list.

eBay's Optional Listing Features

eBay listings have many options and upgrades. Figure 1-2 shows how even a random search on eBay listings can yield examples of some very popular listing options.

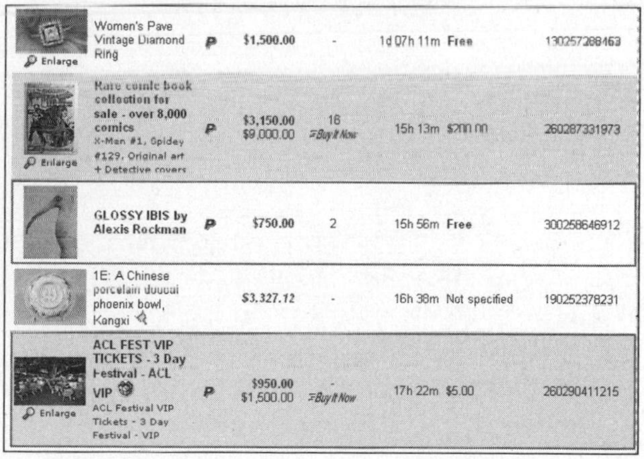

Figure 1-2: A category search showing various eBay option upgrades.

When you come to the point in listing your item that brings you to eBay's optional listing features, you see the headline, "Get more bids with these optional features! Make your item stand out from the crowd!" Sounds pretty good, doesn't it? But getting carried away by these options is easy — and can lead to spending all your expected profits before you earn them.

In eBay University's Advanced Selling) class, I quote auction success rates for the different features, but in the real life of your business, success varies from auction to auction and category to category. If you take the boldface

Book III Chapter 1

Be Sure Your Listings Make Cents

option and then your auction appears in a category full of boldface auction titles, the bold just doesn't have the punch you paid for. Your auction would stand out more without the bold option. It's the same with highlighting. Certain categories are loaded with sellers who go overboard in the use of the highlighting feature — all the auction titles appear in a big lavender blur.

I recap the cost of the various eBay listing options in Table 1-3. Weigh the pros and cons in terms of how these options affect your eBay business. Will spending a little extra money enhance your item enough to justify the extra cost? Will you be able to make the money back in auction profits? You must have a good understanding of what the options are — and when and how you can use them to fullest advantage.

Table 1-3	eBay Listing Upgrade Fees
Option	*Listing Fee*
Home page featured	$39.95 (single item); $79.95 (multiple items)
Subtitle	$0.50
Bold	$1.00
Border	$3.00
Highlight	$5.00
Listing Designer	$0.10
Gallery Plus	$0.35
Featured First	$24.95 for up to 10 days, and $74.95 for up to 30 days*
Gift services	$0.25
Buy It Now	$0.01–$9.99: $0.05; $10.00–$24.99: $0.10; $25.00–$49.99: $0.20; $50.00 and up: $0.25
Scheduled listing	$0.10
List in two categories	Double insertion fee
Value Pack	$0.65
Ten-day auction	$0.40

* Available to only those sellers who have not been demoted in Best Match search results.

In every listing you run, you have to pay an insertion fee for listing your auction and a Final Value Fee. If you accept credit-card payments, you must pay an additional fee to the payment service. Estimate your expenses from these basics before you consider spending money for advertising. (See "Totaling Fees with our Fee Calculator," later in this chapter, for fee-calculator software that can help you make up your auction budgets.)

Home-page featured auctions

A user who goes to www.eBay.com first arrives at the eBay home page. A Featured Items area appears in the middle of the home page; below this area are links to six home-page featured auctions, as shown in Figure 1-3. When you click the *See all featured items* link, the home page's featured-items page appears, as shown in Figure 1-4. Most of these items are fixed-price listings that feature hundreds of items at a time. Many also feature items that list for more than $1000.

Figure 1-3:
The See All Featured Items link on the eBay home page.

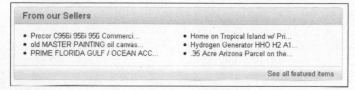

Figure 1-4:
The home-page featured-items page.

Book III
Chapter 1

Be Sure Your
Listings Make Cents

The home-page featured-auction option will set you back $59.95 for a single item. For big-ticket items, you've found the perfect location to draw an audience that may easily earn you back your $59.95. People who are new to eBay come in through the front page; this is prime real estate. The six auctions featured on the home page rotate at random throughout the day, but there's no guarantee that your listing will be among them.

If someone searches your keywords or browses through your category, auctions featured on the front page appear at the top of the page (along with Featured Plus auctions, which I describe next). But you must keep in mind how much you're paying for this option. Unless your auction will bring you more than a few hundred dollars, this feature probably isn't worth the additional cost.

Featured First

Featured Plus is an option that can be used with much success. When you choose the Featured First option, your item may be listed at the top of the page when a shopper searches for keywords or browses category listings. Although your listing doesn't appear on the eBay home page (see the preceding section), it may rotate at the top of your selected *category's* home page or item search (see Figure 1-5).

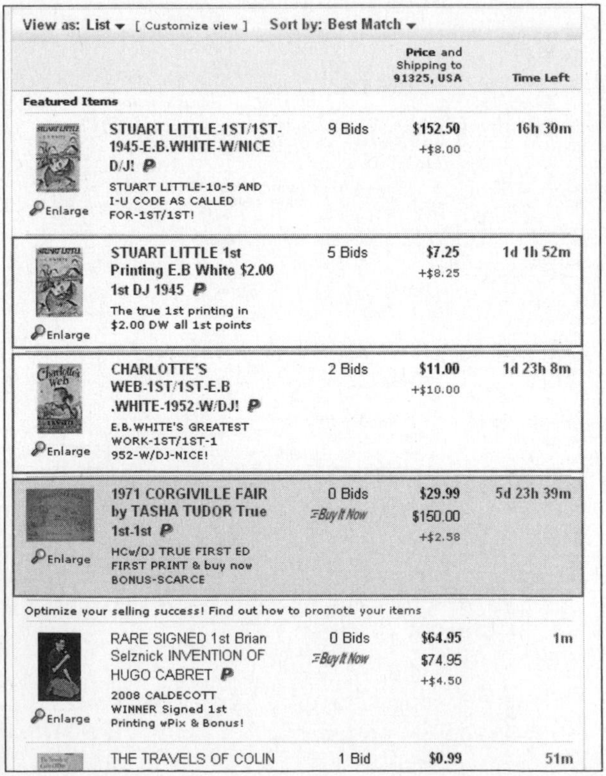

Figure 1-5: A category page, showing the premier position for Featured First listings.

You get extra exposure for $24.95 for up to 10 days and $74.95 for up to 30 days, but you must still consider your listing's budget. How much do you expect your item to sell for? Will the $24.95 cost benefit your listing's exposure enough to justify the expenditure? Be sure that your item will bring you more than a few hundred dollars before choosing this option.

Subtitle

You may use 55 characters for your item's title. Title search is the de facto search standard on eBay. From the statistics I've seen on my own auctions, more than 90% of searches were made for title only, versus title and description. But how can you make your item stand out when it shows up with hundreds of other items that look the same? Use the subtitle option!

Notice the subtitle under one of the listings in Figure 1-6. This is your opportunity to add additional text to your listing, readable by prospective buyers as they scan a search or browse a category. It works very well if you are one of several sellers selling the same item at a similar price — it sets your listing apart from the others. A caveat: This additional text will be picked up in a search only if the person chooses to search both titles *and* descriptions. The additional text does not get pulled up in a title-only search. The fee for this is $.50.

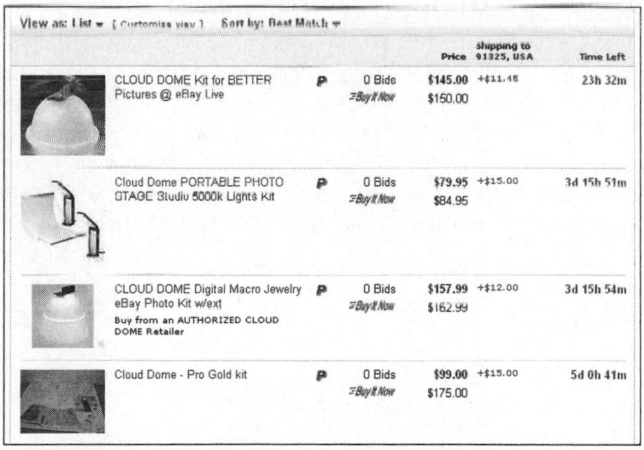

Book III
Chapter 1

Be Sure Your
Listings Make Cents

Figure 1-6: I try to set my more expensive items apart from the competition by using subtitles.

When your item has something special about it or could use some extra description, the subtitle option allows you more space to give the browsing shopper vital information.

Highlight

I was excited when eBay announced the highlighting option. Ever since college, I can't read a book without my trusty neon-yellow highlighter. Highlighting makes anything stand out on a white page of text. This works just as well on eBay as it does on paper — except eBay uses a lavender-colored highlighter — ick!

Unfortunately, as with anything in life, less is more. If you choose to list your item in a category in which all the sellers decide to use the highlighting option, the only listings that will stand out will be the ones *without* highlighting.

The highlight feature will set you back $5. Does your budget allow for that? To give your listing title a punch for a smaller amount of money, consider the Bold option or, even better, the Border option.

Border

Using a border around your listing immediately draws attention to it when someone is doing a search or browsing a category. At $4, it's a deal compared to the highlight, which costs $5. However, use this option only when your expected final price warrants such expenditure.

Listing Designer

eBay comes up with options to fill the needs (or wants in this case) of users. Some sellers enjoy putting colorful graphics around their descriptions. Listing Designer will include pretty graphics and help you design your description, placing pictures in different places on the page. But if you have a good description (creatively done with HTML color and emphasis) plus a good picture (inserted creatively with the HTML code I give you in Book V), your item will draw bids just the same as if you spent $.10 extra (per listing) for the Listing Designer option.

If you want your descriptions surrounded by graphics, make sure they aren't too intensive. Otherwise, the pages will load too slowly for dial-up users. Also, you can develop your own template or buy one from savvy eBay graphics gurus who sell their services on the site.

You can use a graphics template to brand your listings on eBay, giving them a uniform look. If you want to use a template, decide on one and make it your trademark.

Boldface

The Boldface option is one of my favorites and probably the most-used option in the eBay stable. A listing title in boldface type stands out in a crowd, unless . . . you got it, unless it's in a category loaded with boldface titles. If the $2 that eBay charges for this benefit is in your auction budget, odds are it will get you a good deal more views than if you didn't use it.

Applying boldface to your item title spices it up and pulls it off the page right into the reader's eye. Unfortunately, bold adds an additional $2 to your listing cost, so you better be in a position to make a good profit from the item. Also make sure your research shows that it can sell for your target price.

View counter

Counters have become a popular free option in the online world. Placed on your auction by an outside service at your request, the counter ticks up each time someone loads your page from eBay. A counter can impress bidders and convince them they're viewing a hot deal. It can also impress other sellers to run out and sell the identical item.

A counter is a terrific tool for marketing your auctions — sometimes. If you have an auction with no bids and a counter that reads a high number, newbie bidders may be dissuaded from taking a flyer and bidding on your auction. Their thinking goes something like this: If that many people looked at this auction and didn't bid, something must be wrong with the item. They'll tend to doubt their own instincts as to what is and isn't a good deal. In a situation such as this, however, what might be going on is that savvy bidders are just watching your auction, waiting to bid at the last minute.

A *private counter* shields the numbers from the eyes of casual lookie-loos. The figures are available only to you through a password-protected login page. Private counters come in different flavors. Some of the most helpful private counters offer a breakdown of visitors hour-by-hour. This type of smart counter is available from several online services. eBay offers you a free counter, but it's not a smart counter.

Gallery Plus

eBay bills the gallery as its miniature picture showcase, and indeed it is. By adding a gallery photo, a thumbnail image (96 x 96 pixels) of your item appears next to your listing when the user browses the category view or search results, which can reap you many benefits. If you'd like your picture to pop up to a humongous 400x400 when a prospective buyer mouses over your Gallery picture in a search, you'll have to pay an extra $.35.

Figure 1-7 shows how a Gallery Plus item looks in a search result. Gallery Plus pictures are not necessary if you're selling a stock item that looks the same in anyone's listing, such as a CD, a book, or an electronic product. But if it's in your budget, and you have a good picture of a unique item, see if it works for you.

**Book III
Chapter 1**

Be Sure Your
Listings Make Cents

Figure 1-7:
Note how giant gallery plus photos can draw your attention to unique items.

When you take advantage of the Gallery Plus, be sure to crop your photo tight to the subject. For more help with your images, see Book V.

Buy It Now

The Buy It Now feature, shown in Figure 1-8, has a few significant benefits. If you have a target price for the item you're listing, make that your Buy It Now price. You can also use this option during frenzied holiday shopping times or with hot items. Try posting a slightly higher-than-normal price and perhaps you'll get a bite, er, sale.

The Buy It Now feature disappears when someone bids on the item or, if you've placed a reserve on the auction, when a bidder meets your reserve price. You can't use Buy It Now with a Dutch (multiple-item) auction.

To use this feature, you must have a feedback rating of at least 10, have a PayPal account in good standing, or be ID-Verified. (ID Verify is eBay's secondary form of identification, permitting you to participate on the site without submitting a credit card.)

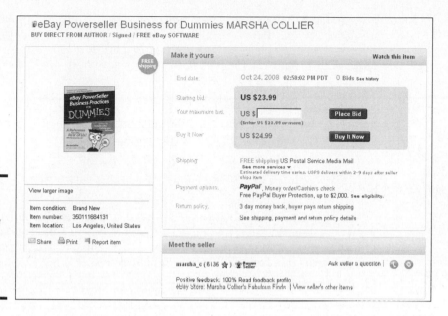

eBay Powerseller Business for Dummies MARSHA COLLIER
BUY DIRECT FROM AUTHOR / Signed / FREE eBay SOFTWARE

Make it yours	Watch this item
End date:	Oct 24, 2008 02:58:02 PM PDT 0 Bids See history
Starting bid:	**US $23.99**
Your maximum bid:	US $ [ ] [Place Bid] (Enter US $23.99 or more)
Buy It Now	US $24.99 [Buy It Now]
Shipping:	FREE shipping US Postal Service Media Mail See more services ▾ Estimated delivery time varies. USPS delivers within 2–9 days after seller ships item
Payment options:	**PayPal**, Money order/Cashiers check Free PayPal Buyer Protection, up to $2,000. See eligibility.
Return policy:	3 day money back, buyer pays return shipping See shipping, payment and return policy details

View larger image

Item condition: Brand New
Item number: 350111684131
Item location: Los Angeles, United States

Share   Print   Report item

Meet the seller

marsha_c (6136 ☆) Powerseller   Ask seller a question

Positive feedback: 100% Read feedback profile
eBay Store: Marsha Collier's Fabulous Finds | View seller's other items

Figure 1-8:
See the Buy It Now button just below the Place Bid button.

Buy It Now adds additional fees (below) to a regular eBay auction and $1.00 to an eBay Motors auction:

Buy It Now Price	Fee
$0.01–$9.99	$0.05
$10.00–$24.99	$0.10
$25.00 $49.99	$0.20
$50.00 and up	$0.25

If your item will sell for a low price, remember my golden rule: Before paying for a feature, ask yourself whether it's in your listing budget.

eBay Picture Hosting

If you are shopping the site or even researching your competitor's auctions, you'll notice that some sellers put small pictures of the items they're selling at the top of their auction page. That picture is called the *preview picture*. What a great selling point this is. The prospective buyers can see your item the second they click the page! Best of all, there's no additional cost to the seller.

Book III
Chapter 1

Be Sure Your
Listings Make Cents

You should definitely take advantage of this offer. Additional pictures (easily uploaded to your item page) cost $.15 each. If you want to add a group of photos (1 to 6), you can purchase a picture pack for $.75. If you have even more photos (7 to 12), the deluxe picture pack will set you back $1.00.

Always use the free Gallery picture — after all, it's free! But why not save extra fees by uploading your own additional pictures for your auction at *no extra cost*? See Book V, Chapter 5 for full instructions on how to do this on your own without incurring *any* extra charges.

Adding the Final Value Fees

eBay's version of the Hollywood back-end deal is the Final Value Fee. Big stars get a bonus when their movies do well at the box office; eBay gets a cut when your auction sells. After your auction ends, eBay charges the Final Value Fee to your account in a matter of minutes.

This chapter gives you the lowdown on Final Value Fees for auction type listings. If you're thinking of listing a Fixed Price item, the closing costs are entirely different. Check Book III, Chapter 3 for the breakdown of Fixed Price Final Value fees.

An ad in the Real Estate category is *not* charged a Final Value Fee. Successful auctions in the eBay Motors category are charged a flat Final Value Fee. (See Chapter 2 for information on fees in both categories.)

Even a rocket scientist would have trouble figuring out exactly how much eBay receives at the end of your auction. To help you calculate how much you'll owe eBay, see Table 1-4.

Table 1-4	Final Value Fees For Auction Type Listings
Final Item Price	*Final Value Fee*
$.01–$25.00	8.75% of the selling price
$25.01–$1000.00	8.75% on the first $25, plus 3.5% on selling prices of $25.01 to $1000.00
$1000.01 and up	8.75% on the first $25, plus 3.5% on selling prices of $25.01 to $1000.00, plus another 1.5% on selling prices over $1000.00

Final Value Fees (FVFs) are charges on the sale price for your item and do not include whatever you charge for shipping. Thank goodness eBay hasn't raised the FVF fees lately — they're hard enough to calculate as it is! So how do all these percentages translate to actual dollar amounts? Take a look at Table 1-5, where I calculated the Final Value Fees on some sample selling prices.

If you try to work out your own Final Value Fees, you may get an extreme headache — and come up with fractional cents. Know that eBay rounds up fees of $0.005 and more and rounds down below $0.005. These roundings are performed on a per-transaction basis, and generally even out over time. For more details, check out eBay's account-rounding explanation (perhaps a strong cocktail would help while reading it) at

```
http://pages.ebay.com/help/account/rounding-account-
    balance.html
```

Table 1-5	Sample Final Value Fees for Auction Listings
Closing Bid	*To Find Your Final Value Fee*
$0.01–$25.00	Multiply the final sale price by 8.75%. If the final sale price is $25.00, you owe eBay $2.19 ($25 × 0.0875).
$25.01–$1000.00	You pay $2.19 for the first $25.00 of the final sale price. Subtract $25.00 from your final closing bid and then multiply this amount by 3.5%. Add this total to the $2.19. The sum is what you owe eBay. If the final sale price is $1000.00, you owe $34.12 ($975 × 0.035) plus $2.19, or $36.31.
$1000.01 and over	You owe $2.19 for the first $25.00 of the sale price and $34.12 for the price between $25.01 and $1000.00. This amount is $36.31. Now, subtract $1000.00 from the final sale price (you've already calculated those fees) and multiply that amount by 1.5%. Add this amount to $36.31. The sum is the amount you owe eBay. If the final sales price is $3000.00, you owe $30.00 ($2000 × 0.015) plus $36.31, or $66.31.

If you're starting to get dizzy just reading these examples, perhaps doing your own calculations isn't for you. It's certainly not for me — this stuff makes my eyes glaze over! Later in this chapter (see the section "Totaling Fees with our eBay Fee Calculator"), I describe a cool spreadsheet devised by Patti Louise Ruby (my Tech Editor and co-author on *eBay Listings That Sell For Dummies*). This spreadsheet is downloadable, works with Microsoft Office Excel, and can handle all these calculations for you.

Because of the sliding percentages, the higher the final selling price, the lower the commission eBay charges. Math can be a beautiful thing, when applied for your benefit.

eBay doesn't charge a percentage Final Value Fee on an auction in the Real Estate category as in other categories. You pay a flat FVF of $35 for Timeshares and Land and no FVF for Commercial or Residential. But in the Automotive category, you pay a flat Successful Transaction Services Fee of $125 for vehicles and $100 for motorcycles if your auction ends with a winning bidder (and the reserve has been met).

When selling a vehicle (car, truck, or RV) through eBay Motors, you're getting a great deal. You pay $0 to list your item, and the transaction services fee is only $125 when the item sells.

Selling Variations in Auctions

An auction is an auction is an auction, right? Wrong! eBay has four types of auctions for your selling pleasure. Most of the time you'll run traditional auctions, but other auctions have their place, too. After you've been selling on eBay for a while, you may find that one of the other types of auctions better suits your needs. In this section, I review these auctions so you fully understand what they are and when to use them.

Traditional auctions

Traditional auctions are the bread and butter of eBay. You can run a traditional auction for 1, 3, 5, 7, or 10 days, and when the auction closes, the highest bidder wins. I'm sure you've bid on several and won at least a few. I bet you've also made money running some of your own.

You begin the auction with an opening bid, and bidders will bid up your opening price into a healthy profit for you (I hope).

Best Offer

If you've got a fixed-price listing, you can opt to insert a button under your sales price that will encourage buyers to *Make an Offer* on your item. This is probably one of the oldest sales methods around. (In some countries, it's an insult to buy something at the posted price; haggling is part of their retail culture.)

So, if you love the thrill of haggling (I don't, really), you can insert the Make an Offer button in your listings at no extra charge. See Figure 1-9 for an example. When someone makes an offer on one of your items, eBay sends you an e-mail asking that you reply regarding whether the proposed price is acceptable to you.

Multiple-item (Dutch) auctions

When you've purchased an odd lot of 500 kitchen-knife sets or managed (legally, of course) to get your hands on a truckload of televisions that you want to sell as expeditiously as possible, the multiple-item auction is what you'll want to use. In the *multiple-item (Dutch) auction,* which can run for 1, 3, 5, 7, or 10 days, you list as many items as you'd like and bidders can bid on as many items as they'd like. The final item price is set by the lowest successful bid at the time the auction closes.

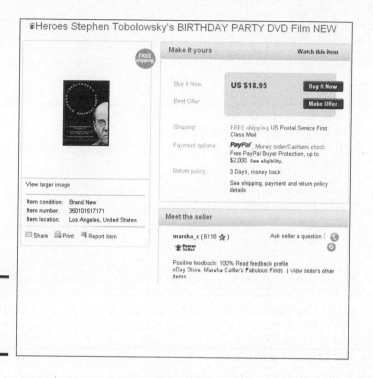

Figure 1-9:
Maybe I'll
get a bite
on this.

For example, suppose you want to sell five dolls on eBay in a multiple-item auction. Your starting bid is $5 each. If five bidders each bid $5 for one doll, they each get a doll for $5. But, if the final bidding reveals that two people bid $5, one person bid $8, and another bid $9, all bidders win the doll for the lowest final bid of $5.

The following list highlights the details of the multiple-item auction:

✦ The listing fee is based on your opening bid price (just like in a traditional auction), but the fee is multiplied by the number of items in your auction, to a maximum listing fee of $4.00.

✦ The auction's Final Value Fees use the same scale as in a traditional auction, but they're based on the total dollar amount of your completed auctions.

✦ When bidders bid on your Dutch auction, they can bid on one or more items at one bid price. (The bid is multiplied by the number of items.)

✦ If the bidding gets hot and heavy, rebids must be in a higher total dollar amount than the total of that bidder's past bids.

✦ Bidders may reduce the quantity of the items for which they're bidding in your auction, *but* the dollar amount of the total bid price must be higher.

✦ All winning bidders pay the same price for their items, no matter how much they bid.

✦ The lowest successful bid when the auction closes is the price for which your items in that auction will be sold.

✦ If your item gets more bids than you have items, the lowest bidders are knocked out one by one, with the earliest bidders remaining on board the longest in the case of tie bids.

✦ The earliest (by date and time) successful high bidders when the auction closes win their items.

✦ Higher bidders get the quantities they've asked for, and bidders can refuse partial quantities of the number of items in their bids.

Restricted access auctions

eBay won't allow certain items to be sold in nonrestricted categories, so you must list them in the adult only area of eBay. eBay makes it easy for the user to find or avoid these types of auctions by making this area accessible only after the user enters a password and agrees to the terms and conditions of the area, as shown in Figure 1-10.

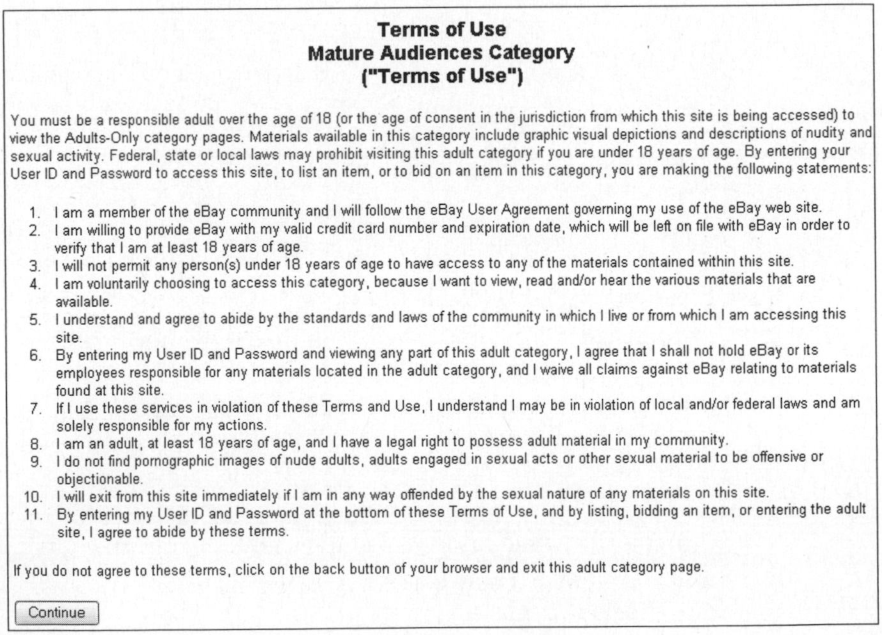

Figure 1-10:
You must
agree to the
legalities
to enter
the Mature
Audiences
category.

Terms of Use
Mature Audiences Category
("Terms of Use")

You must be a responsible adult over the age of 18 (or the age of consent in the jurisdiction from which this site is being accessed) to view the Adults-Only category pages. Materials available in this category include graphic visual depictions and descriptions of nudity and sexual activity. Federal, state or local laws may prohibit visiting this adult category if you are under 18 years of age. By entering your User ID and Password to access this site, to list an item, or to bid on an item in this category, you are making the following statements:

1. I am a member of the eBay community and I will follow the eBay User Agreement governing my use of the eBay web site.
2. I am willing to provide eBay with my valid credit card number and expiration date, which will be left on file with eBay in order to verify that I am at least 18 years of age.
3. I will not permit any person(s) under 18 years of age to have access to any of the materials contained within this site.
4. I am voluntarily choosing to access this category, because I want to view, read and/or hear the various materials that are available.
5. I understand and agree to abide by the standards and laws of the community in which I live or from which I am accessing this site.
6. By entering my User ID and Password and viewing any part of this adult category, I agree that I shall not hold eBay or its employees responsible for any materials located in the adult category, and I waive all claims against eBay relating to materials found at this site.
7. If I use these services in violation of these Terms and Use, I understand I may be in violation of local and/or federal laws and am solely responsible for my actions.
8. I am an adult, at least 18 years of age, and I have a legal right to possess adult material in my community.
9. I do not find pornographic images of nude adults, adults engaged in sexual acts or other sexual material to be offensive or objectionable.
10. I will exit from this site immediately if I am in any way offended by the sexual nature of any materials on this site.
11. By entering my User ID and Password at the bottom of these Terms of Use, and by listing, bidding an item, or entering the adult site, I agree to abide by these terms.

If you do not agree to these terms, click on the back button of your browser and exit this adult category page.

Continue

Items in the adults-only area are not openly accessible through the regular eBay title search, nor are they listed in Newly Listed Items. Anyone who participates in adults-only auctions on eBay, whether as a bidder or a seller, must have a credit card on file on eBay for verification.

Do not attempt to slip an adults-only auction into a nonrestricted category. eBay doesn't have a sense of humor when it comes to this violation of policy, and may relocate or end your auction. eBay might even suspend you from its site.

Private auctions

The eBay search page features an area where you can conduct a bidder search. You can find a list of the items that you've bid on in the past 30 days. Anyone not signing in on your eBay account sees a list of only the items you've won — but that's no real help. One December, my daughter told me that she didn't want a particular item — something that I had just bid on — for Christmas. My creative daughter had been regularly perusing my bidding action on eBay to see what I was buying for the holidays! A private auction would have kept my shopping secret.

Private auctions also work well for the buyers who avail themselves of the psychics, card readers, and fortune teller's listings on eBay and don't want their friends to think they are . . . well, you know. Sometimes it's just best to keep things quiet.

eBay *private auctions* don't place bidders' names on the auction listing. No one needs to know just how much you choose to pay for something. As a seller, you have the option (at no extra charge) of listing your auction as a private auction.

The private auction is a useful tool for sellers who are selling bulk lots to other sellers. It maintains the privacy of the bidders, and customers can't do a bidder search to find out what sellers are paying for the loot they plan to resell on eBay.

The private auction can save you the potential embarrassment associated with buying a girdle or the tie that flips over to reveal a racy half-nude female on the back.

Although the private auction is a useful tool, it may intimidate the novice user. If your customer base comes from experienced eBay users and you're selling an item that may benefit by being auctioned in secret, you might want to try this option.

Not quite adult enough. . . .

I was surprised to see a private auction listed on one of my favorite eBay seller's list. She usually doesn't sell items like "Fringe Black BRA 36B SEXY SEXY SEXY," so I looked through this seller's past auctions. I saw that she didn't get any bids when she listed the bra in the restricted (adults-only) area of eBay in the category Everything Else: Mature Audiences: Clothing, Accessory. When she put the bra up for private auction in the category Clothing & Accessories: Women's Clothing: Lingerie: Bras: General, she got five bidders and sold the item. I guess it wasn't sexy enough for the "adult" crowd!

PayPal Gets Its Cut

When you've sold your item, do you think that's the end of the fees? Nope! If your customer pays using PayPal, you're faced with additional fees. However, having a PayPal premier or business account is important for building your commerce for these reasons:

✦ eBay buyers look for the PayPal option because it offers them a high level of protection against fraud.

✦ Most customers prefer to pay with a credit card, either to delay the expense or to have complete records of their purchases.

✦ From a seller's point of view, using PayPal can be cheaper than having a direct-merchant credit-card account.

✦ PayPal helps with your paperwork by offering downloadable logs of your sales that include all PayPal fees. eBay fees are not included; you're on your own for those.

A business account requires the account to be registered in a business name. A premier account allows you to do business under your own name.

Check out Book II, Chapter 4, which covers the PayPal services and fees in depth.

Totaling Fees with our eBay Fee Calculator

I don't have the time (or the inclination) to total the applicable fees and expenses for every item I put up on eBay. But I do not recommend such laziness to anyone trying to earn a *living* on eBay.

To combat the laziness that I fear will drastically affect my bottom line, my dear friend Patti Louise Ruby designed a fee calculator that helps me make better business decisions on pricing my items — and it can do the same for you! You can download the program from my Web site www.coolebay-tools.com/eBayFeeCalculator. Here's how it works:

Here are the steps for using the spreadsheet:

1. **Download the eBay Fee Calculator spreadsheet and open it in Microsoft Excel.**

2. **At the bottom of the spreadsheet, click the appropriate tab to select the type of listing and/or category of the item you want to calculate fees for.**

You'll see a worksheet similar to the one shown in Figure 1-11.

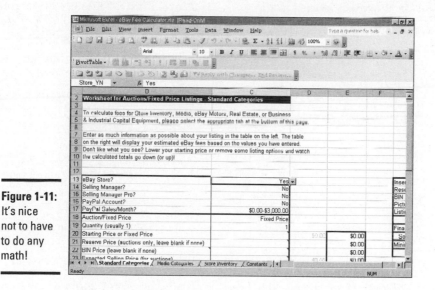

Figure 1-11: It's nice not to have to do any math!

3. **Fill in the business information as prompted in the first section on the left of the tab. For each prompt, click the box in the second column to display a drop-down list with a choice of acceptable answers.**

Info to enter includes:

• Whether you have an eBay Store

• Whether you subscribe to either Selling Manager or Selling Manager Pro

• Whether you have a PayPal account, and what level of payments you process per month through PayPal.

Forewarned is smart

After you know all the eBay fees involved in selling your item, you can play around with the pricing and figure out how much your Buy It Now (or target selling) price should be. Remember to include the following costs when pricing your items:

✓ How much you paid for the item you want to resell

✓ The Freight In amount (the cost of shipping the item to you)

✓ The cost of shipping the item to your buyer

This information shouldn't change very often, but it has an effect on the fees you're charged.

4. **In the table on the left, fill as much information as possible about your listing. As in Step 3, click a box in the second column to display a drop-down list with a choice of acceptable answers (when applicable).**

The table on the right will display your estimated eBay fees based on the values you enter on the left, as shown in Figure 1-12.

Insertion Fee		$0.00
Reserve Fee		$0.00
BIN Fee		$0.00
Picture Fees		$0.00
Listing Option Fees		$0.00
	Subtotal:	*$0.00*
Final Value Fee		$0.00
Sold: No PayPal Fees	Total:	*$0.00*
Minimum PayPal Fees*		$0.00
Final	Total:	***$0.00***
*PayPal Fees based on Final Selling		
Price (does not include shipping)		

Figure 1-12: This is so much easier.

Don't like the fees you see? Lower your starting price or remove some listing options and watch the calculated totals go down (or up)!

Setting Sensible Shipping Costs

Buyers who visit the eBay site are bargain shoppers. They want to get their items at the lowest possible prices. They're also more cognizant about the "hidden" expense buried in the item's shipping and handling fees. When you set these fees, you must take into account every expense involved in your packing and shipping. You can't make your shipping area a losing proposition.

However, too many eBay sellers have increased their shipping prices to outrageous amounts. I'll bet those sellers think they've found a cute way to save a couple of cents off their Final Value Fees (after all, Final Value Fees aren't charged on shipping costs). But when the shipping fee equals a third of the item's cost, a prospective bidder may think twice about placing a bid. Of course, if the item is big or the buyer wants it fast, he or she may feel better about paying higher shipping costs.

eBay penalizes sellers who charge high shipping fees and rewards sellers who offer Free Shipping by giving them better visibility in the Best Match search results. Try listing your item with the minimum shipping amount included in your selling price. Then offer buyers a second shipping option for Priority Mail (faster shipping) at a charge. Your item will still get the benefit of eBay's Free Shipping search preference.

Business is business, and when you're on eBay to make a profit, every penny counts. In this section, I tell you how to evaluate all the costs involved with packing and shipping the items you sell. I also show you how to use the tools at your disposal — such as eBay's shipping calculator — to make the best decisions about how much to charge your buyers for shipping costs.

For information on organizing your shipping area, be sure to read Book VII.

When calculating shipping costs, don't assume that all you have to worry about is just the cost of your postage. You also have per-item costs for boxes, padded mailers, shipping tape, labels, and pickup or service fees from your carriers. Now and again, you may even pay the college kid across the street five bucks to schlep your boxes for you. Expenses show up in the strangest places.

In addition to adding up the packing and shipping supplies, you need to amortize the monthly fees from any online postage shipping services. When you occasionally pay for a pickup from the carrier, you need to add that expense to the shipping charges, too. The following list runs down some of the expenses involved:

✦ **Padded mailers:** Select an average-size padded mailer that works for several types of items you sell. Selecting an average size for all your products works well because it's cheaper to buy in quantity. Even if a few of your items could fit in the next-size-down mailers, buying the bigger size by the case gives you a considerable discount. Why keep five sizes of mailers in stock in quantities of 100 if you don't have to? If you don't use all the bigger ones, you can always sell them. And besides, padded envelopes don't go bad.

Don't be misled by packaging suppliers' claims of low-cost mailers. They *usually* don't include the shipping costs in these price estimates.

When you price your cost-per-piece, be sure to include (as part of your cost) what you have to pay to get the item shipped to you. For example, if you purchase your mailers — say #4s (9½ x 14½) — by the hundred, they may cost you $.40 each. If you buy a case of 500, they may cost only $.28 each. By buying in quantity, you save $.12 per mailing envelope! The more business you do, the more significant the savings.

One of my favorite sources (with really reasonable prices and free shipping) is RoyalMailers.com. They carry every size imaginable, and if you use my Web site's name as your discount code, you *get an additional 10% off your order.* Just go to

www.royalmailers.com/coolebaytools.

+ **Packing peanuts:** I must admit that storing all those packing peanuts is a real drag. But here is where buying in bulk equates to huge cost savings. I just checked one of my favorite vendors, www.bubblefast.com, and found a *free-shipping* offer. From Bubblefast, you can purchase

> 3.5 cubic feet for $9.98 = $2.85 per cubic foot
>
> 7 cubic feet for $19.10 = $2.73 per cubic foot
>
> 14 cubic feet for $36.40 = $2.60 per cubic foot

As you can see, 14 cubic feet turns out to be the most economical deal. eBay sellers like Bubblefast, sell packing peanuts for *half* what they cost when you purchase them from a brick-and-mortar retailer. (That's because a store you can walk into has to use up square footage to store these babies, which means a higher cost.)

Here, in a nutshell (sorry, I couldn't resist), is my solution to peanut storage. Fill a drawstring-type trash bag with peanuts, and then tie the drawstring. Screw cup hooks into the rafters of your garage and hang the bags from the rafters. You can store a bunch of peanuts there! *Be sure to recycle!*

+ **Packing tape:** You need a stock of clear packing tape. The common size for a roll is 2 inches wide by 110 feet long. I searched eBay and found these deals, the following prices *include* shipping:

> 6 rolls = $17.07 = $2.85 per roll
>
> 12 rolls = $26.94 = $2.25 per roll
>
> 18 rolls = $29.94 = $1.66 per roll

Again, compare prices before buying.

+ **Boxes:** I won't take you through the various costs of boxes because *hundreds* of sizes are available. Shop eBay (but often the shipping prices are too high), and also check out www.uline.com for boxes at reasonable prices. For the example, let's just say a typical box will cost $.55 each.

♦ **G&A (general and administrative) costs:** For the uninitiated (translation: you never had to do budgets at a large corporation), G&A represents the costs incurred in running a company. But the principle is familiar: Time is money. For example, the time it takes you to research the costs of mailers, tapes, and boxes on eBay is costing you money. The time it takes you to drive to the post office costs you money. You won't actually put a figure on this just now, but it's something you need to think about — especially if you spend half an hour at the post office every other day. In effect, that's time wasted. You could be finding new sources of merchandise instead.

♦ **Online postage service:** If you're paying around $10 a month for the convenience of buying and printing online postage, that's an expense too. If you ship 100 packages a month, that amortizes to $.10 per package.

If you're questioning whether you need an online postage service, here's my two cents: Being able to hand your packages to the postal carrier beats standing in line at the post office.

Table 1-6 shows you the cost for mailing a tiny padded envelope cushioned with packing peanuts.

Table 1-6	Sample Shipping Costs
Item	*Estimated Cost per Shipment ($)*
Padded mailer	0.28
Peanuts	0.07
Tape	0.02
Mailing label	0.04
Postage service	0.10
Total	0.51

Book III
Chapter 1

Be Sure Your
Listings Make Cents

Before you even put postage on the package, you could possibly be spending $.51 — not including your time. (Excuse me while I go to eBay and raise my shipping charges!)

If you're shipping many packages a month, read Book IX, which tells you how to use QuickBooks to easily and simply track your shipping costs.

Chapter 2: Understanding the Finer Points of Selling

In This Chapter

✔ Discovering successful selling strategies

✔ Selling in other areas of eBay

✔ Following the rules

You can buy the "inside secrets" of eBay from lots of places. Some e-book sellers try to convince you that only *they* have the surreptitious bits of knowledge — gleaned from years (months?) of experience on the site — that reveal what's Really Going On. Truth be told, the online retail market changes so quickly that eBay can barely keep up with it — the profile of the online shopper changes constantly. How likely is it that anybody has the ultimate answer? Sure, you hear mysterious rumors of the way to sure-fire profits (cue up the *X-Files* theme in the background). Start an auction at a certain day and time, and you'll automatically make more money? Puh-leez! The only one who rakes in profits with that information is the guy who's selling it to you!

I've interviewed many eBay high-volume sellers (called *PowerSellers*) and almost all agree that popular eBay theories are bunk. However, the sellers do have some practical preferences for when and how they conduct their eBay transactions. This chapter gets to the gist of these preferences and the corresponding best practices.

Selling Strategies

The basic plan for running an auction is the same for everyone, except for decisions regarding the timing of the auction and the starting price. If you speak to 20 eBay sellers, you'll probably get 20 different answers about effective starting bids and when to end your auction. Until you develop your own philosophy, I'd like to give you the tools to make a sound decision. What works for one seller may not work for another.

You can also successfully promote your auctions online and offline, and you can legally offer your item to the next highest bidder if the auction winner doesn't come through with payment. I discuss a few of these ideas in this section.

The ideas in this technique come from my own experience and discussions with current eBay PowerSellers. These ideas are merely suggestions of methods and starting points that work for others. You definitely need to test them out to find out which practices work — for you and for the types of items you sell.

Starting the bidding

The most generally accepted theory about starting bids is that setting the bidding too high scares away new bids.

Some sellers begin the bidding at the price they paid for the item, including expected eBay and PayPal fees, thereby protecting their investment. This is a good tactic, especially if you bought the item at a price far below the current going rate on eBay.

To determine the current going value for your item, I recommend using the completed auctions search, which I explain in Book II, Chapter 1. If you know that the item is selling on eBay for a certain price and that there is a demand for it, starting the bidding at a reasonably low level can be a great way to increase bidding and attract prospective bidders to view your auction.

Years of advertising experience can't be wrong. If your item is in demand and people are actively buying, start the bidding low. Retail stores have done this for years with ads that feature prices starting at $9.99 or $14.98. Note that WalMart ends prices in $.97 or $.54 when they're on sale in a store, but on its Web site, the items' prices end evenly at $.00. Even television commercials advertising automobiles quote a low starting price. (To get the car as shown in the ad, of course, you may end up paying twice the quoted price.)

When sellers know that they have an item that will sell, they begin their bidding as low as a dollar or even a penny. Because of the eBay *proxy bidding system* (which maintains your highest bid as a secret, increasing it incrementally when you're bid against), it takes more bids (due to the smaller bidding increments) to bring the item up to the final selling price.

The downside is that new bidders who aren't familiar with the system may bid only the minimum required increment each time they bid. This can be frustrating, and they may quit bidding because it might take them several bids to top the current bid placed by someone who is familiar with the proxy bid system. Very few of us know the proxy increments by heart, so as a refresher, I give you the goods in Table 2-1.

Table 2-1	Proxy Bidding Increments
Current High Bid ($)	*Bid Increment ($)*
0.01–0.99	0.05
1.00–4.99	0.25
5.00–24.99	0.50
25.00–99.99	1.00
100.00–249.99	2.50
250.00–499.99	5.00
500.00–999.99	10.00
1000.00–2499.99	25.00
2500.00–4999.99	50.00
5000.00 and up	100.00

Auction length

Another debatable philosophy is auction timing. People are always asking me how long to run auctions and what's the best day to end an auction. You have to evaluate your item and decide which of the following is the best plan:

✦ **One-day auction:** Did you just get a load of an item that sells as fast as you post it on the site? Although a Buy It Now feature on any auction can bring great results, that works only if the item is *hot! hot! hot!* If people are bidding the item up — and they really gotta have it — you may do best by starting the bidding really low and listing the item with a one-day format.

When you list in a one-day format, your listing goes right to the top of the listings *Ending Soonest* list. Most savvy shoppers view their searches by listings ending first (rather than the eBay default of Best Match). With a one-day format, you can pretty much choose the time of day your item will be at the top.

This format can be very successful if you have an item that's the hot ticket for the moment on eBay. I used this format when I sold some *Friends* TV-show memorabilia. The 24-hour auction opened midday before the final show and ended the next day — at a healthy profit!

If the competition starts their auctions at \$.99 with a reasonable Buy It Now price, you'll find that bidders foil many of their Buy It Now offers. Retaliate by listing the item with a starting bid just a dollar or so below your Buy It Now price (and make that price at least \$.50 below the competition's), and you'll find your items will be snapped up quickly.

✦ **Three-day auction:** If, the item's price will shoot up right after you post it, a three-day auction works just fine. And it's great for those last-minute holiday shoppers looking for hard-to-find items.

A three-day auction is good, for the same reasons that a one-day auction is good — only it's better for the faint of heart and nervous Nellies (like me) because it gives your item more time to sell.

Another good use of a three-day auction is when you already have a seven-day auction up on the site and the bidding is going crazy. You've reached your sales goal by the middle of a seven-day cycle. Once the seven-day auction is in the last couple of days of the listing, put up a three-day auction.

With the Buy It Now feature, you can pretty much accomplish the same thing as a short-term auction. When you list your item for sale, set a price at which you are willing to sell the item immediately; this is your Buy It Now price.

✦ **Five-day auction:** A five-day auction gives you two days more than a three-day auction and two days less than a seven-day auction. That's about the size of it. If you just want an extended weekend auction or your item is a hot one, use it. Five-day auctions are useful during holiday rushes, when gift buying is the main reason for bidding.

✦ **Seven-day auction:** Tried-and-true advertising theory says that the longer you advertise your item, the more people will see it. On eBay, this means that you have more opportunities for people to bid on it. The seven-day auction is a staple for the bulk of eBay vendors. Seven days is long enough to cover weekend browsers and short enough to keep the auction interesting.

✦ **Ten-day auction:** Many veteran eBay sellers swear by the ten-day auction. Sure, eBay charges you an extra \$.40 for the privilege, but the extra three days of exposure (it can encompass two weekends) can easily net you more than your extra cost in profits.

A ten-day auction is good for special collectibles or an expensive item that normally doesn't get listed on the site by the hundred. Putting up a ten-day auction (start Friday night so you get exposure over two weekends) is a near-perfect way to attract bidders.

Your auction closes exactly one, three, five, seven, or ten days — *to the minute* — after you start the auction. Try not to begin your auctions when you're up late at night and can't sleep: You don't want your auction to end at two in the morning when no one else is awake to bid on it. If you can't sleep, prepare your listings ahead of time with the Turbo Lister program (which I discuss in Chapter 3) and upload them for future launching when the world is ready to shop.

The specific day you close your auction can also be important. eBay is full of weekend browsers, so including a weekend of browsing in your auction time is a definite plus. Often, auctions that end late Sunday afternoon through Monday close with high bids.

You'll need to do some research to determine the best times to run your auctions and for how long. In Book VIII, Chapter 3, I show you how to combine your search-engine research with a special kind of statistical counter to help you identify the best closing time for your items. (See Chapters 1 and 2 in Book II for the details about using the search engine as a valuable research tool.) The best person to figure out the closing information for your auctions is you. Use the tools and over time you'll work out a pattern that works best for you.

Knowing What Day to End an Auction

Back when eBay counted its listings by the hundreds (and then low thousands), it clearly made a difference what day of the week you chose to end an auction. That is, when the number of buyers and sellers on eBay was relatively small, matching your auction time with the bidders' online habits was important. Now that eBay spawns as many as 18 million listings a day with countless buyers and lookie-loos visiting the site, you find the eBay netizens looking for bargains at virtually all hours of the day and night. So for a traditional auction, you can choose almost any ending time and know that you'll still have some healthy bidding action.

The wildcards in the mix are the Buy It Now and fixed-price transactions, which have become wildly popular — and successful. Although they don't always follow a daily pattern of sales, they can still follow the preferred auction-ending days you find in this section.

To figure out when to end an auction, you need to know when to start it. Figures 2-1, 2-2, and 2-3 are the top preferred timelines for running a sale on eBay.

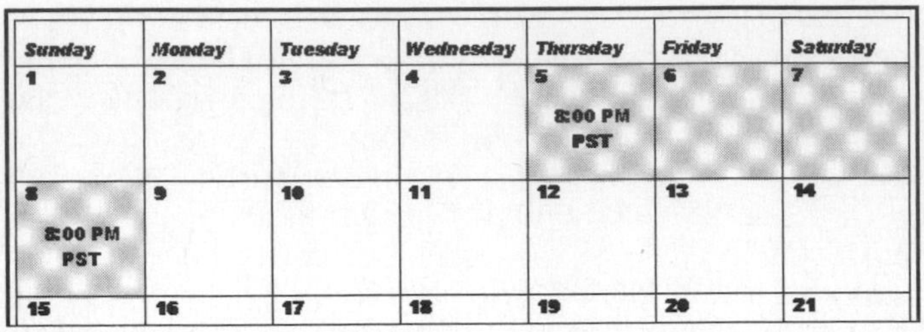

Sunday	Monday	Tuesday	Wednesday	Thursday	Friday	Saturday
1	2	3	4	5 8:00 PM PST	6	7
8 8:00 PM PST	9	10	11	12	13	14
15	16	17	18	19	20	21

Figure 2-1: A timeline for a 3-day auction.

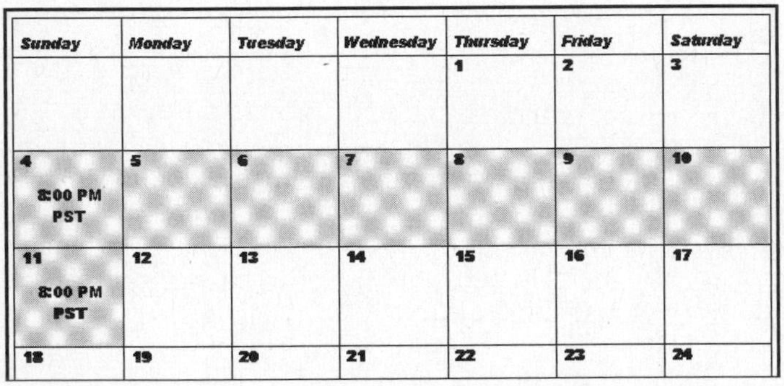

Sunday	Monday	Tuesday	Wednesday	Thursday	Friday	Saturday
				1	2	3
4 8:00 PM PST	5	6	7	8	9	10
11 8:00 PM PST	12	13	14	15	16	17
18	19	20	21	22	23	24

Figure 2-2: This is 7 days of auction action.

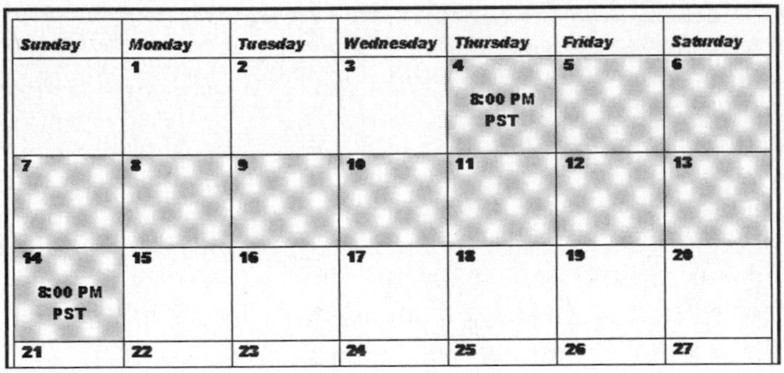

Sunday	Monday	Tuesday	Wednesday	Thursday	Friday	Saturday
	1	2	3	4 8:00 PM PST	5	6
7	8	9	10	11	12	13
14 8:00 PM PST	15	16	17	18	19	20
21	22	23	24	25	26	27

Figure 2-3: A full 10 days of bidding frenzy (if you're lucky).

You may notice that all these preferred datelines end on a Sunday. Sunday is the top-ranked ending day for auctions by eBay sellers.

Pirates of the Caribbean, er, "Carribean"?

Just before the *Pirates of the Caribbean* movie premiered, Disneyland gave out exclusive movie posters to their visitors. My daughter, savvy eBayer that she is, snagged several copies to sell on the site. She listed them (one at a time) when the movie opened and couldn't get more than the starting bid, $9.99, for each of them.

When we searched eBay for *pirates poster*, we found that the very same posters with a misspelled title, Pirates of the Carribean, were selling for as high as $30 each. We immediately changed her auctions to have the more popular (misspelling) *Carribean* in the title and quickly saw those dollar signs! After selling out her initial stock, she found another seller who had ten for sale — in one auction — with the proper spelling in the title. She bought those as well (for $5 each) and sold them with misspelled titles in the listing for between $15 and $27!

I can't list everyone's opinions on the subject — that would probably confuse you anyway — so here are the item-ending days ranked in order from most to least popular:

1. Sunday
2. Monday
3. Thursday
4. Tuesday
5. Wednesday
6. Saturday
7. Friday

Be sure to coordinate these dates with what you sell. Some buyers (say, men who buy golf goods during lunch hour and women who buy collectibles while their husbands are out golfing on weekends) can throw these days a curve.

A definite time not to close your auctions? Experience has taught many sellers never to close an auction on a national holiday. Memorial Day, the Fourth of July, and Veteran's Day may be bonanza sales days for retail shops, but eBay auction items closing on these days go at bargain prices.

Book III Chapter 2

Understanding the Finer Points of Selling

Knowing What Time to Start Your Auction

The only way to figure out when to end your auction is by planning when to start it. An auction beginning at 12:00 will end at that same time on the ending day.

eBay time is military time in the Pacific time zone. Table 2-2 converts the eBay clock to real time for your time zone. Make a photocopy of this table and keep it by your computer. (Even after all these years, it still takes too much time to decipher eBay time without a printed chart.)

If you ever need to check your time zone or want to know exactly what time it is in eBay-land, point your browser to

```
/viv.ebay.com/ws/eBayISAPI.dll?EbayTime
```

and you'll see the map pictured in Figure 2-4.

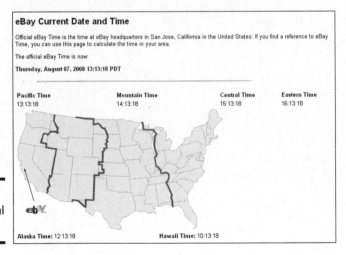

Figure 2-4: eBay official time.

Table 2-2	eBay Time versus Continental U.S. Time			
eBay Time	*Pacific*	*Mountain*	*Central*	*Eastern*
0:00	12:00 a.m.	1:00 a.m.	2:00 a.m.	3:00 a.m.
1:00	1:00 a.m.	2:00 a.m.	3:00 a.m.	4:00 a.m.
2:00	2:00 a.m.	3:00 a.m.	4:00 a.m.	5:00 a.m.
3:00	3:00 a.m.	4:00 a.m.	5:00 a.m.	6:00 a.m.
4:00	4:00 a.m.	5:00 a.m.	6:00 a.m.	7:00 a.m.

eBay Time	Pacific	Mountain	Central	Eastern
5:00	5:00 a.m.	6:00 a.m.	7:00 a.m.	8:00 a.m.
6:00	6:00 a.m.	7:00 a.m.	8:00 a.m.	9:00 a.m.
7:00	7:00 a.m.	8:00 a.m.	9:00 a.m.	10:00 a.m.
8:00	8:00 a.m.	9:00 a.m.	10:00 a.m.	11:00 a.m.
9:00	9:00 a.m.	10:00 a.m.	11:00 a.m.	12:00 p.m.
10:00	10:00 a.m.	11:00 a.m.	12:00 p.m.	1:00 p.m.
11:00	11:00 a.m.	12:00 p.m.	1:00 p.m.	2:00 p.m.
12:00	12:00 p.m.	1:00 p.m.	2:00 p.m.	3:00 p.m.
13:00	1:00 p.m.	2:00 p.m.	3:00 p.m.	4:00 p.m.
14:00	2:00 p.m.	3:00 p.m.	4:00 p.m.	5:00 p.m.
15:00	3:00 p.m.	4:00 p.m.	5:00 p.m.	6:00 p.m.
16:00	4:00 p.m.	5:00 p.m.	6:00 p.m.	7:00 p.m.
17:00	5:00 p.m.	6:00 p.m.	7:00 p.m.	8:00 p.m.
18:00	6:00 p.m.	7:00 p.m.	8:00 p.m.	9:00 p.m.
19:00	7:00 p.m.	8:00 p.m.	9:00 p.m.	10:00 p.m.
20:00	8:00 p.m.	9:00 p.m.	10:00 p.m.	11:00 p.m.
21:00	9:00 p.m.	10:00 p.m.	11:00 p.m.	12:00 a.m.
22:00	10:00 p.m.	11:00 p.m.	12:00 a.m.	1:00 a.m.
23:00	11:00 p.m.	12:00 a.m.	1:00 a.m.	2:00 a.m.

Book III
Chapter 2

Understanding
the Finer Points of
Selling

Here's the consensus of some experts in order of ending-time preference (in eBay time; check the table for a translation):

1. 18:00 to 22:00

2. 21:00 to 0:00

3. 15:00 to 18:00

4. 13:00 to 16:00

Here are the worst eBay times to end an auction:

1. 2:00 to 6:00

2. 0:00 to 3:00

This information should give you some good ideas for your own auction sales.

Selling Even More with Fixed-Price Sales

Recently eBay has put a lot behind new item and fixed-price sales. In the new era of e-commerce, many people like to come to a site to buy items outright at a given price as well as participate in auctions.

eBay Stores are a great way to have fixed-price items, but to get a better placement in eBay's search engine, you can list fixed-price items on the regular eBay site.

Fixed-price listings have a different pricing structure on the site. Any fixed-price listing — regardless of starting price or number of items for sale — costs 35 cents for a 3-, 5-, 7-, 10-, or 30-day listing, or a Good Till Cancelled listing. Great news, eh? If you're selling media, the cost is even lower. Any items in the categories of Books, Music, DVDs & Movies and Video Games are charged only 15 cents per listing for the same durations!

Sounds great, huh? Well, there's a catch (you knew there'd be a catch, didn't you?). Final Value Fees for these items are higher, and the fees vary by category. Table 2-3 gives you the details.

Table 2-3   Final Value Fees for Fixed-Price Listings by Category

Closing Price	How FVF Is Calculated	Computers & Networking	Cameras & Photo	Electronics & Video Game Systems	Books, Music, DVDs & Movies, and Video Games
$1.00 – $50.00	X% of the closing value	X=6.00	X=8.00	X=8.00	X=15.00
$50.01 – $1000.00	X% of the first $50.00, plus Y% of the remaining closing value balance	X=6.00 Y=3.75	X=8.00 Y=4.50	X=8.00 Y=4.50	X=15.00 Y=4.50

Closing Price	How FVF Is Calculated	Computers & Networking	Cameras & Photo	Electronics & Video Game Systems	Books, Music, DVDs & Movies, and Video Games
Equal to or over $1000.01	X% of the first $50.00, plus Y% of the initial $50.01 – $1000.00 plus Z% of the remaining closing value balance	X=6.00 Y=3.75 Z=1.00	X=8.00 Y=4.50 Z=1.00	X=8.00 Y=4.50 Z=1.00	X=15.00 Y=5.00 Z=2.00

Closing Price	How FVF Is Calculated	Parts & Accessories	Clothing, Shoes & Accessories	All Other Categories
$1.00 – $50.00	X% of the closing value	X=12.00	X=12.00	X=12.00
$50.01 – $1000.00	X% of the first $50.00, plus Y% of the remaining closing value balance	X=12.00 Y=9.00	X=12.00 Y=9.00	X=12.00 Y=6.00
Equal to or over $1000.01	X% of the first $50.00, plus Y% of the initial $50.01 – $1000.00 plus Z% of the remaining closing value balance	X=6.00 Y=9.00 Z=2.00	X=8.00 Y=9.00 Z=2.00	X=8.00 Y=6.00 Z=2.00

Making Money in Other eBay Zones

There's more to eBay than just the auction site. Don't lose a selling opportunity by not checking into the other viable areas described in this section.

eBay's half brother: Half.com

Half.com, founded in July of 1999, was the brainchild of Joshua Kopelman. He observed the insufficiencies of retailing in the area of used mass-market merchandise and went to work on developing a new outlet for secondhand merchandise. Kopelman's site was so successful that eBay bought out Half. com after its first year of business. Half.com ranks as one of the Internet's most visited sites.

Selling at Half.com is different from selling at your eBay (or other online) personal store because you're selling in a fixed-price marketplace. Your item is listed head-to-head against more of the same item from other sellers. Half. com isn't a home for your store; you might say that each item has its own store, complete with competing sellers.

The Half.com home page is shown in Figure 2-5. Half.com currently lists more than 15 million items, including books, CDs, DVDs, video games, and game systems. Because Half.com is part of eBay, your feedback follows you to the site.

Figure 2-5: The Half.com home page.

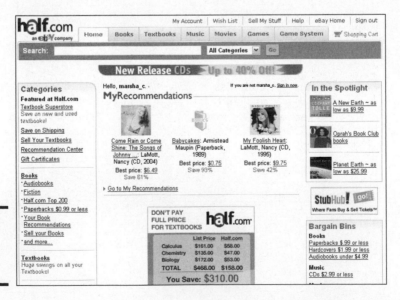

From a seller's point of view, the best features of Half.com are these:

✦ The item listing is free.

✦ The item stays on the site until the item is sold or until you take it down.

Just like your My eBay Page, half.com has a very user-friendly area where you can control your selling. You'll find it under *My account: Inventory*. Take a look at how clear cut it is in Figure 2-6. You can change the prices for your books right there — no need to access individual listings!

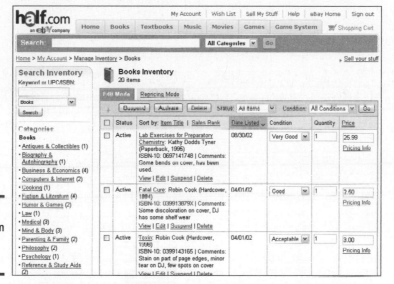

Figure 2-6: My Half.com Inventory page.

Half.com charges a commission after your item sells, as shown in Table 2-4. Commissions for items sold in the Books, Music, Movies, Games, and Game System categories are a percentage of the selling price of the item. The shipping cost is not added to the selling price.

Table 2-4	Half.com Sales Commissions
Selling Price Plus Shipping ($)	*Half.com Commission (%)*
0–50.00	15.0
50.01–100.00	12.5
100.01–250.00	10.0
250.01–500.00	7.5
500.01 and up	5.0

To list an item for sale at Half.com, you first need to locate the item's Universal Product Code (UPC) or, if you're selling a book, the International Standard Book Number (ISBN). In case you're wondering what an ISBN is, turn this book over and find the bar code on the back. The number written above it is this book's ISBN.

If you don't want to bring all your books, CDs, movies, or games to your computer, scan your items using an inexpensive handheld scanner (make sure it's a model that holds memory).

When someone searches on Half.com for an item, such as a book, a listing of all sellers who are selling that book appears. The listings are classified by the book's condition — categorized as Like New or Very Good — depending on what the seller entered. The list price of the book is included, as well as a comparison of selling prices on the eBay site.

If you don't have an item's outer box with the UPC, search Half.com from any of its pages for your particular item (including its brand name). When your search comes up with the exact item, copy down the code number and use it with your listing, or click the Sell Your Stuff link on the item page.

You'll find that by using the UPC or ISBN in your listing, Half.com comes up with an image of your item, so you don't even have to take a picture for your sale. When an item is out of print, Half.com may not have an image to upload with the listing. In this case, the text *Image not available* appears in the area where the picture would appear. (Half.com allows you to upload your own picture.) If your item doesn't have a code, you can upload your own photo and even add a 1000-word description. Half.com has an amazing database of items in the books, music, movie, and video game categories to help you find the specs of whatever item you want to list.

When a prospective buyer searches and finds an item for books or coded items, a box appears in the corner of the listing with a price comparison of the item from various other online sales sites.

For example, if you're selling a paperback book for $37.00, here's what happens:

1. Buyer buys your paperback, which is priced at $37.00.

2. Half.com charges the buyer $3.49 for Media Mail shipping and handling costs.

3. You pay Half.com a 15% commission, which is $5.55 on a $37.00 item.

4. You get a shipping reimbursement of $2.64.

    See Table 2-5 for Half.com shipping reimbursements.

5. Half.com sends you a net payment of $34.09.

Table 2-5	Half.com Shipping Reimbursements	
Item	*Media Mail*	*Expedited (Usually Priority Mail)*
Hardcover book	$3.07 for the first item $1.40 for each additional item	$5.24 for the first item $3.49 for each additional item
Paperback book	$2.64 for the first item $1.19 for each additional item	$5.20 for the first item $2.24 for each additional item
Music and DVDs	$2.39 for the first item $1.03 for each additional item	$5.20 for the first item $1.99 for each additional item
VHS movies	$2.14 for the first item $1.19 for each additional item	$5.20 for the first item $1.99 for each additional item
Audio books	$2.64 for the first item $1.15 for each additional item	$5.20 for the first item $1.94 for each additional item
Games	$2.89 for the first item $1.15 for each additional item	$5.20 for the first item $1.99 for each additional item

Automotive? Go eBay Motors

Anything and everything automotive can go in the eBay Motors category (see Figure 2-7), and it will sell like giant tires at a monster truck rally. Following are just a few of the car-related items that fit in this category.

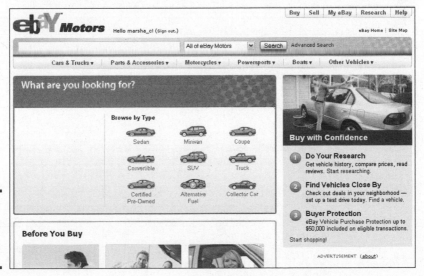

Figure 2-7:
The eBay
Motors
home page.

Car parts

Got used car parts? eBay has an enormous market in used car parts. One seller I know goes to police impound sales and buys wrecks — just to get some valuable parts that he can resell on eBay.

New car parts are in demand, too. If your local auto-parts store is blasting out door handles for a 1967 Corvette (a vehicle for which it's hard to find parts), it wouldn't hurt to pick up a few. Sooner or later, someone's bound to search eBay looking for them. If you're lucky enough to catch the trend, you'll make a healthy profit.

Cars

Yes, you can sell cars on eBay. In fact, used-car sales have skyrocketed online thanks to all the people who find eBay to be a trusted place to buy and sell used vehicles. Selling vehicles on eBay is a natural business for you if you have access to good used cars, work as a mechanic, or have a contact at a dealership who lets you sell cars on eBay for a commission or on a consignment basis. (For the ins and outs of consignment selling, check out Book IV, Chapter 3.)

To complete your sale, eBay Motors features a free passenger-vehicle purchase protection that covers up to $20,000 (with a $100 buyer co-pay should you have a claim), one-click access to Carfax reports, vehicle inspection and escrow services, and vehicle shipping quotes from Dependable Auto Shippers. Access eBay Motors and its services from the eBay home page or by going directly to www.ebaymotors.com.

Selling a car on eBay Motors is a bit different from selling on regular eBay, mainly in the area of fees. To encourage sellers to list and sell vehicles on the site, eBay has set up a tiered system of fees. The first four vehicles you list in a 12-month period are charged no listing fees, but have a slightly higher transaction fee when the sale is successful. Take a look at Tables 2-6 and 2-7 for significant differences.

Table 2-6	Vehicle-Specific Fees for the First Four Listings in a 12-Month Period
Type of Fee	*Fee Amount ($)*
Vehicle insertion (listing) fee	0.00
Vehicle Successful listing fee	125.00
Motorcycle insertion (listing) fee	0.00
Motorcycle Successful listing fee	100.00*
Reserve price in listing (refundable if the vehicle sells)	7.00

Table 2-7	Vehicle-Specific Fees Starting with the Fifth Listing in a 12-Month Period
Type of Fee	*Fee Amount ($)*
Vehicle insertion (listing) fee	20.00
Vehicle Successful listing fee	100.00*
Motorcycle insertion (listing) fee	15.00
Motorcycle Successful listing fee	80.00*
Reserve price in listing (refundable if the vehicle sells)	7.00

There is no final value fee for selling on eBay Motors. Instead, you pay the transaction service fee when your item gets a bid (or if you've used a reserve, when bidding meets your reserve price).

Although many people who have found the vehicle of their dreams on eBay are more than happy to take a one-way flight to the vehicle location and drive it home, shipping a vehicle is a reasonably-priced alternative. You can make arrangements to ship a car quickly and simply.

Here are just a few things to keep in mind if you plan to sell cars on eBay:

✦ To sell a vehicle on eBay Motors, you must enter the Vehicle Identification Number (VIN) on the Sell Your Item page. This way, prospective buyers can access a Carfax report to get an idea of the history of the car.

✦ An item that you've listed on eBay Motors will appear in any search, whether a potential buyer conducts a regular eBay search or a search in eBay Motors.

✦ If your reserve isn't met in an eBay Motors auction, you may still offer the vehicle to the high bidder through the Second Chance option. (More information on that later in this chapter.) You may also reduce your reserve during the auction if you feel you've set your target price too high.

Real estate: Not quite an auction

eBay Real Estate at `pages.ebay.com/realestate` isn't quite an auction. Because of the wide variety of laws governing the sale of real estate, eBay auctions of real property are *not* legally binding offers to buy and sell. However, putting your real estate on eBay (see Figure 2-8) is an excellent way to advertise and attract potential buyers. When the auction ends, neither party is obligated (as they are in other eBay auctions) to complete the real estate transaction. The buyer and seller must get together to consummate the deal.

Figure 2-8:
Grab your
piece of
America
here on
eBay's
Real Estate
section.

Nonetheless, eBay real estate sales are popular and the gross sales are growing by leaps and bounds. You don't have to be a professional real estate agent to use this category, although it may help when it comes to closing the deal. If you know land and your local real estate laws, eBay gives you the perfect venue to subdivide those 160 acres in Wyoming that Uncle Regis left you in his will.

For less than the cost of a newspaper ad, you can sell your home, condo, land, or even timeshare on eBay Real Estate in the auction format. You can also choose to list your property in an ad format, accepting not bids but *inquiries* from prospective buyers from around the world. On the Sell Your Item form, you must specify special information about your piece of real estate.

In Tables 2-8 and 2-9, I provide a listing of fees that you can expect to encounter on eBay Real Estate.

Table 2-8	eBay Real Estate Timeshare and Land Fees
Type of Fee	*Fee Amount*
Auction/Fixed Price listing for 1-, 3-, 5-, 7-, or 10-day	$35.00
Auction/Fixed Price 30-day	$50.00

Type of Fee	Fee Amount
Classified Ad 30 days	$150.00
Classified Ad 90 days	$300.00
Final value (Notice) fee	$35.00
Reserve fee (refunded when property sells)	$0.01 to $199.99: $2.00; $200.00 and up: 1% of reserve price (up to $50)

Table 2-9   eBay Real Estate Residential and Commercial Fees

Type of Fee	Fee Amount ($)
Auction/Fixed Price listing for 1-, 3-, 5-, 7-, or 10-day	$100.00
Auction/Fixed Price 30-day	$150.00
Classified Ad 30 days	$150.00
Classified Ad 90 days	$300.00
Final Value Fee	$0.00

Selling by the Rules

There are a lot of *shoulds* in this world. You *should* do this and you *should* do that. I don't know who is in charge of the *shoulds,* but certain things just make life work better. If you follow the advice on these pages, your eBay business will thrive with a minimum of anguish. If you've ever had a listing pulled by eBay, you know that anguish firsthand and don't want to have it again.

In the real world, we have to take responsibility for our own actions. If we buy a television set for $25 from some guy selling them out of the back of a truck, who do we have to blame when we take it home and it doesn't work? You get what you pay for, and you have no consumer protection from a seller of possibly "hot" TVs. Responsible consumerism is every buyer's job. Lawsuit upon lawsuit gets filed — and some are won — when someone feels they've been ripped off, but my best advice is that if you stay clean in your online business, you'll keep clean.

eBay is a community, and the community thrives on the five basic values below:

✦ We believe people are basically good.

✦ We believe everyone has something to contribute.

✦ We believe that an honest, open environment can bring out the best in people.

✦ We recognize and respect everyone as a unique individual.

✦ We encourage you to treat others the way that you want to be treated.

eBay is committed to these values, and it says so right on its Web site. eBay believes that community members should "honor these values — whether buying, selling, or chatting." So *should* we all.

Is what you want to sell legal?

Although eBay is based in California and therefore must abide by California law, sellers do business all over the United States. Therefore, items sold at eBay must be governed by the laws of every other state as well. As a seller, you're ultimately responsible for both the legality of the items you sell *and* the way that you transact business on eBay. Yes, you're able to sell thousands of different items on eBay. But do you know what you *aren't* allowed to sell?

The eBay User Agreement outlines the rules and regulations regarding what you can and can't sell, as well as all aspects of doing business on eBay. If you haven't read it in a while, do so. You can find it at the following address:

`http://pages.ebay.com/help/policies/user-agreement.html`

These policies can change from time to time. As an active seller, you should make sure that you're notified of any changes. You'll be notified when eBay makes changes to the User Agreement, through your eBay Message Center.

By now, you should have a firm grasp of the rules and regulations for listing auctions. But in addition to knowing the rules for listing items, you must consider the items themselves. In this section, I detail the three categories of items to be wary of: prohibited, questionable, and potentially infringing. Some are banned, period. Others fall in a gray area. You're responsible for what you sell, so you'd better know what's legal and what's not.

If you're found in violation of eBay's listing restrictions, you may be penalized in a variety of ways, including

✦ Listing cancellation.

✦ Limits on account privileges.

✦ Account suspension.

✦ Forfeit of eBay fees on cancelled listings.

✦ Loss of PowerSeller status.

You may think it's okay to give away a regulated or banned item as a bonus item with your auction. Think again. Even giving away such items for free doesn't save you from potential legal responsibility.

Prohibited and Restricted items

A prohibited item is banned from sale at eBay. You can't sell a prohibited item under any circumstance. Take a look at the following list. A little common sense tells you there's good reason for not selling these items, including liability issues for the seller. (For example, what if you sold alcohol to a minor? That's against the law!)

Restricted items involve more shades of gray. They may involve the sale of dangerous or sensitive items that may not be prohibited by law. EBay sets these limitations as a result of input by members of the eBay Community and others. eBay has a strong Offensive Material Policy which covers merchandise that "promote or glorify hatred, violence, racial or religious intolerance, or items that promote organizations with such views." As you can imagine, this is a slippery slope for some sellers.

Below is just a partial list; the current complete list can be found at
`http://pages.ebay.com/help/policies/items-ov.html`

Adult Material

Alcohol*

Animals and wildlife products

Art

Catalogs (current issues) and Web sales

Counterfeit currency or stamps

Counterfeit items

Credit cards

Drugs and drug paraphernalia

Embargoed goods from prohibited countries

Firearms, ammunition, replicas, and militaria

Fireworks

Government IDs and licenses

Human parts and remains**

Lockpicking devices

Lottery tickets

Mailing lists and personal information

Matrix programs

Multilevel marketing

Postage meters

Prescription drugs and devices

Pyramid programs

Recalled items

Satellite and cable TV descramblers

Stocks and other securities***

Stolen property

Surveillance equipment

Tobacco

Travel****

USDA-prohibited plants and seeds

*Alcohol may be allowed if the value of the item lies in the collectible container (bottle) exceeding the alcohol's retail price. The item should not be currently available at a retail outlet. The auction should state that the container has not been opened, and the seller should be sure that the buyer is over 21.

**Skulls, skeletons, and items that may contain human hair are permissible as long as they're used for educational purposes.

***Old or collectible stock certificates may be sold provided that they're canceled or are from a company that no longer exists.

****All sellers listing airline tickets, cruises, vacation packages, or lodging must be verified by SquareTrade.

Check the following address for updates:

```
http://pages.ebay.com/help/sell/questions/
    prohibited-items.html
```

Questionable items

Determining whether or not you can sell a *questionable item* is tricky. Under certain circumstances, you may be able to list the item for sale at eBay. To fully understand when and if you can list a questionable item, visit the links that I highlight in Table 2-10.

Table 2-10	Partial List of Questionable Items and Where to Find the Rules Regulating Them
Can I Sell This?	*Go Here to Find Out**
Alcohol	/alcohol.html
Art	/selling-art.html
Artifacts	/artifacts.html
Autographed Items	/autographs.html
Batteries	/hazardous-materials.html
Contracts and tickets	/contracts.html
Electronics equipment	/electronics.html
Event tickets	/event-tickets.html
Food	/food.html
Freon and other refrigerants	/hazardous-materials.html
Hazardous materials	/hazardous-materials.html
Human parts and remains	/remains.html
International trading — sellers	/international-trading.html
Mature audiences	/mature-audiences.html
Offensive material	/offensive.html
Pesticides	/pesticides.html
Police-related items	/police.html
Presale listings	/pre-sale.html
Recalled Items	/recalled.html
Stamps	/selling-stamps.html
Stocks and other securities	/stocks.html
Slot machines	/slot-machines.html
Used clothing	/used-clothing.html
Used medical devices	/medical-devices.html
Weapons and knives	/firearms-weapons-knives.html

* All URLs begin with http://pages.ebay.com/help/policies

Potentially infringing items

Potentially infringing items follow a slippery slope. If you list a *potentially infringing item,* you may infringe on existing copyrights, trademarks, registrations, or the like. Get the idea? These items are prohibited for your own protection.

Items falling under the "potentially infringing" category are generally copyrighted or trademarked items, such as software, promotional items, and games. Even using a brand name in your auction as part of a description (known as *keyword spamming*) may get you into trouble.

Repeating various un-trademarked keywords can get you in trouble as well. eBay permits the use of as many as five synonyms when listing an item for sale. A permissible example of this might be: purse, handbag, pocketbook, satchel, and bag. Adding many un-trademarked keywords would cause the auction to come up in more searches.

Knowing eBay's Listing Policies

eBay does not sell merchandise. eBay is merely a venue that provides the location where others can put on a giant e-commerce party (in other words, sell stuff). To provide a safe and profitable venue for its sellers, eBay must govern auctions that take place on its site. eBay makes the rules; you and I follow the rules. I like to think of eBay as the place that lets you hold your senior prom in its gym. When I was in school, my classmates and I had to follow the rules or see our prom canceled. If we don't agree to follow eBay's rules, a safe and trusted eBay community can't exist.

When alcohol becomes collectible

Many people collect rare and antique bottles of liquor or wine. I even sold a bottle of Korbel champagne whose bottle artwork was designed by Frank Sinatra on eBay in 1998. Korbel bottles have featured artwork by designer Nicole Miller and comedienne Whoopi Goldberg as well as designs by Tony Bennett, Frank Sinatra, and Jane Seymour.

People also collect Jim Beam bottles, Dug decanters, and miniatures that are even more valuable when they're full. You *can* sell these on eBay as long as you fulfill the following requirements:

✔ The value of the item is in the collectible container, not its contents.

✔ The auction description should state that the container has not been opened but any incidental contents are not intended for consumption.

✔ The item must not be available at any retail outlet, and the container must have a value that substantially exceeds the current retail price of the alcohol in the container.

✔ Sellers should take steps to ensure that the buyer of these collectibles is of lawful age in the buyer's and seller's jurisdiction (generally 21 years old).

eBay has some hard-and-fast rules about listing your items. One rule is that you must list your item in the appropriate category (that only makes sense). In this section, I highlight a few other rules that you should keep in mind when listing. What I discuss isn't a definitive list of eBay listing policies and rules. Take time to familiarize yourself with the User Agreement (which details all eBay policies and rules) at the following address:

```
pages.ebay.com/help/policies/user-agreement.html
```

I recommend that you check the eBay User Agreement regularly for any policy changes.

Offer limited choices in your auctions

Your auction must be for one item only: the item that you specifically list in your auction. It's against the rules to give the bidder a choice of completely different items in the same listing, but you can offer sizes, colors, or configurations of the same item. eBay protects you with its purchase-protection program, which covers all online eBay transactions. When you give your bidders a choice, it's an illegal sale on eBay and therefore not covered. Anything that's negotiated outside the eBay system can lead to either misrepresentation or fraud. You don't want to be caught up in that sort of grief and misery.

If eBay catches you offering a choice, they will end the auction and credit the insertion fee to your account.

No limit on duplicate listings

Remember the old supply-and-demand theory from your economics class? When people list the same items repeatedly, they drive down the item's going price while ruining all the other sellers' opportunities to sell the item during that time frame.

eBay allows you to list as many identical listings as you want... and why not? You pay a separate listing fee for every item. The powers that be at eBay aren't daft; they know that buyers using Search would be deluged with these identical item listings from the same seller. But sellers who want to "game" the system in this way, by listing a huge number of the same item, need to think twice. eBay policy states that the display of multiple identical items from the same seller will be *limited to one* in Search results. So what's the point?

If you're going to list an item that many times, at the very least be sure to list it in different categories. That's a rule, but it also makes sense. Nothing drives down the price of an item faster than closing identical auctions, one after another, in the same category. eBay also requires that you list your item in a category that's relevant to it.

The Chanel-style purse

I once listed a quilted leather women's purse that had a gold chain strap, which I described as a Chanel-style purse. Within two hours, I received an informational alert from the eBay listing police. I described the item to the best of my ability, but found that it became a potentially infringing item.

My use of the brand name *Chanel* caused my auction to come under the violation of keyword spamming (more on that in the section "Potentially infringing items").

In its informational alert, eBay described my violation:

"Keyword spamming is the practice of adding words, including brand names, which do not directly describe the item you are selling. The addition of these words may not have been intentional, but including them in this manner diverts members to your listing inappropriately."

Ooops! You can see how my ingenuous listing was actually a violation of policy. Think twice before you add brand names to your auction description. Thankfully, the eBay police judge each violation on a case-by-case basis. Because my record is clear, I merely got a reprimand. Had my violation been more deliberate, I might have been suspended.

If you have multiple copies of something, a better solution is to run a multiple-item (Dutch) auction for the total number of items you have for sale. Or perhaps run two multiple-item auctions in different (but appropriate) categories.

If you list many identical auctions, eBay will show only one at a time in search.

State it up front: Presale and drop-shipping listings

eBay doesn't like it when you try to sell something that's not in your hands (known as a *presale listing* — whether or not it's a drop-ship item). In many situations, being the first seller to put a popular item up for sale can get you some high bids. And if you can guarantee in your auction description that the item will be available to ship within 30 days of the purchase or the auction closing, you can run a presale. However, if you're not completely sure that you'll have the item in time, I don't recommend that you even attempt a presale listing.

If you know that you'll have the item to ship — and it won't be lost on its way to you — you may list the item with the following requirement: You must state in your auction description that the item is a presale. You'll also have to use a little HTML here because the text must be coded with an HTML font no smaller than font size 3. The presale policy also applies to drop-shipping.

Before you set up such an auction, check out the Federal Trade Commission 30-day rule covering these matters, which you can find at the following address:

`www.ftc.gov/bcp/conline/pubs/buspubs/mailorder.htm`

Ix-nay on the bonuses, giveaways, raffles, or prizes

Because eBay sells to every state in the United States, it must follow explicit laws governing giveaways and prizes. Each state has its own set of rules and regulations, so eBay doesn't allow individual sellers to come up with their own promotions.

If your auction violates this rule, eBay might end it and refund your listing fee.

The eBay Verified Rights Owner program

eBay can't possibly check every auction for authenticity. But to help protect trademarked items, it formed the Verified Rights Owner (VeRO) program.

Trademark and copyright owners expend large amounts of energy to develop and maintain control over the quality of their products. If you buy a "designer" purse from a guy on the street for $20, it's probably counterfeit, so don't go selling it on eBay.

eBay works with VeRO program participants to educate the community about such items. They work also with verified owners of trademarks and copyrights to remove auctions that infringe on their products. If eBay doesn't close a suspicious or blatantly infringing auction, then both you and eBay are liable for the violation.

To participate in the VeRO program, the owners of copyrights and trademarks must supply eBay with proof of ownership. To view the VeRO program information, go to

`http://pages.ebay.com/help/tp/`
`vero-rights-owner.html`

To report a violation of something, you have legal rights to download this form on eBay:

`http:// pages.ebay.com/help/`
`community/NOCI1.pdf`

Note: eBay cooperates with law enforcement and may give your name and street address to a VeRO program member.

To view a list of other VeRO members' About Me pages, go to

`http://pages.ebay.com/help/`
`community/vero-aboutme.html`

Preselling: Not worth the hassle

A seller I once knew presold Beanie Babies on eBay. She had a regular source that supplied her when the new toys came out, so she fell into a complacent attitude about listing presales. Then her supplier didn't get the shipment. Motivated by the need to protect her feedback rating (and by the fear that she'd be accused of fraud), she ran all over town desperately trying to get the Beanies she needed to fill her orders. The Beanies were so rare that she ended up spending several hundred dollars more than what she had originally sold the toys for, just to keep her customers happy.

Search and browse manipulation by keyword spamming

Keyword spamming happens when you add words, usually brand names, to your auction description that don't describe what you're selling (for example, describing that little black dress as Givenchy-style when Givenchy has nothing to do with it). Keyword spamming manipulates the eBay search engine by including an unrelated item in the listing for a copyrighted or trademarked item, and then diverting bidders to an auction of other merchandise. Sellers use keyword spamming to pull viewers to their auctions after viewers have searched for the brand name. To attract attention to their listings, some sellers use *not* or *like* along with the brand name, such as *like Givenchy*.

Here are the problems with keyword spamming:

✦ It's a listing violation and causes your auction to fall under potentially infringing items for sale on eBay. The wording you choose when you run this kind of auction manipulates the eBay search engine and prospective bidders.

✦ It's frustrating to the potential buyers trying to use the search engine to find a particular item, and unfair to other eBay sellers who've properly listed their items.

Keyword spamming can take many forms. Some merely mislead the prospective bidder while others are legal infringements. A few of the most common are

✦ Superfluous brand names in the title or item description.

✦ Using something like "not brand X" in the title or item description.

✦ Improper trademark usage.

✦ Lists of keywords.

✦ Hidden text — white text on a white background or hidden text in HTML code. The white text resides in the auction HTML, so it shows up in the search but is not visible to the naked eye. Sneaky, eh?

✦ Drop-down lists.

To get the latest on eBay's keyword spamming policy, go to

`http:// pages.ebay.com/help/policies/search-manipulation.html`

Limited linking from your auctions

Few issues set sellers to arguing more than eBay's rules on linking. In your auction item description, you *can* use the following links:

✦ One link to an additional page that gives further information about the item you're selling

✦ A link that opens an e-mail window on the prospective buyer's browser so that the buyer can send you an e-mail

✦ Links to more photo images of the item you're selling

✦ Links to your other auctions on eBay and your eBay store listings

✦ One link to your About Me page, besides the link next to your user ID that eBay provides

TIP

Now here's the "big secret" from one of those get-rich-quick, high-dollar eBay seminars. You *can* link to your own, personal e-commerce Web site from eBay. But *only* from your About Me page!

Chapter 3: Listing Your Items for Sale

In This Chapter

✔ **Getting ready to set up your auction**

✔ **Filling in the Sell an Item form**

✔ **Starting your auction**

✔ **Making changes after your auction has started**

Are you ready to make some money? Yes? (Call it an inspired guess.) Are you on the threshold of adding your items to the hundreds of thousands that go up for auction at eBay every day? Some auctions are so hot that the sellers can quadruple their investments. Other items, unfortunately, are so stone-cold that they may not even register a single bid.

In this chapter, I explain all the facets of the Sell an Item page — the page you fill out to get your auction going on eBay. You get some advice that can increase your odds of making money, and you find out the best way to position your item so buyers can see it and bid on it. I also show you how to modify, relist, and end your auction.

Getting Ready to List Your Item

After you decide what you want to sell, find out as much as you can about it and conduct a little market research. Then you should have a good idea of the item's popularity and value.

Before you list your item, make sure that you have the following bases covered:

✦ **The specific category under which you want the item listed:** Ask your friends or family where they'd look for such an item — and remember the categories you saw most frequently when you conducted your market research with the eBay search function.

To find out which category will pay off best for your item, run a search and then select the Completed listings option. See how many fixed-price listings and auctions of that item are running (and whether people are bidding on it). Then scroll down to the left of the page and, under Seach options, click the box next to Completed listings and perform your search. Sort your results by Price: highest first, and then look over the transactions to see which categories they're listed in. For more information on how to get ahead of the crowd through eBay's search, visit Book I.

✦ **What you want to say in your auction item description:** Jot down your ideas. Take a good look at your item and make a list of keywords that describe your item. *Keywords* are single descriptive words that can include

- • Brand names
- • Size of the item (citing measurements if appropriate)
- • Age or date of manufacture
- • Condition
- • Rarity
- • Color
- • Size
- • Material (fabric)
- • . . . and more

✦ **Get an idea of what picture (or pictures) of your item you want to put inside your description:** Pictures help sell items, but you don't have to use them if you're selling media items (eBay will supply them for you). (If you want to know more about using pictures in your auctions, see Book V.)

✦ **The price at which you think you can sell the item:** Be as realistic as you can. (That's where the market research comes in.)

The Sell an Item form is where your auction is born. Filling out *your* auction paperwork requires a couple of minutes of clicking, *ty*ping, and answering all kinds of questions. The good news is that *w*hen you're finished, your auction is up and running.

Before you begin, you have to be registered with eBay as a seller. If you still need to do so, go to Book I and fill out the preliminary cyber-paperwork. If you've registered but haven't provided eBay with your financial information (credit card or checking account), you'll be asked for this information before you proceed to sell. Fill in the data on the secure form. Then you're ready to set up your listing.

Deciding on a Sales Format

Just like the dizzying menu in a Chinese restaurant, you have four ways to sell an item on eBay. Four ways may not seem to be very dizzying, unless you're trying to decide just which format is the best for you.

Here's what you need to know about each type:

✦ **Online auction:** This is the tried-and-true traditional sale format on eBay. You can combine this auction with the Buy It Now feature, for those who want the item immediately. Often, if you're selling a collectible item, letting it go to auction may net you a much higher profit — remember to do your research before listing.

✦ **Fixed-price listing:** A fixed-price sale is easy for the buyer to complete; it's just like shopping at the corner store. The only problem is that many potential buyers may lean toward an auction because of the perception that they *may* get a better deal.

✦ **Sell in your eBay store:** Book VIII, Chapter 6 covers eBay stores — a convenient place to sell items related to your auctions or fixed-price items.

✦ **Advertise real estate:** If you don't want to put your property up for auction and you'd like to correspond with the prospective buyers, this is the option for you.

Say, for example, that you want to list a good old-fashioned eBay auction. You want to sell your item for a fixed price but are also willing to let it go to auction.

To find eBay's Sell an Item page from the eBay home page, you can use either of these methods:

✦ Click the Sell link on the navigation bar at the top of the page, and you're whisked to the Sell an Item page. eBay allows you to input keywords which help you select your category and download the Sell an Item page in seconds.

✦ You can also start your listing from your My eBay page. Just look under the Favorite Links and scroll down the page to the Sell My Item link.

Getting Your Sales Specifics In Order

Yes, the Sell an Item form looks daunting, but filling out its many sections doesn't take as long as you may think. Some of the questions you're asked aren't things you even have to think about; just click an answer and off you go. Other questions ask you to type information. Don't sweat a thing; all the answers you need are right here.

When listing your item, here's the info you're asked to fill out (each of these items is discussed in detail later in this chapter):

✦ **User ID and password:** If you're not signed in, you need to do so before you list an item for sale.

✦ **Category:** The category where you've decided to list your item (required).

✦ **Title:** The name of your item (required).

✦ **Description:** What you want to tell eBay buyers about your item (required). After you've written a brilliant title for your listing, prospective buyers click and scroll down to your description. Do they have to dodge through pointless verbiage, losing interest along the way? Or do you get right down to business and state the facts about your item?

✦ **eBay Picture Services or image URL:** The Web address of any pictures you want to add (optional). Note that you get a free preview picture at the top of your auction. Book V has more information on using images in your auction.

✦ **The Gallery:** You can add your item's picture to eBay's photo gallery. eBay charges nothing for this service, so why not do it?. (You can find more on the other Gallery options later in this chapter.)

✦ **Gallery image URL:** The Web address of the JPG image you want to place in the gallery (optional). If you're using eBay Picture Services, the first photo you upload is resized for the Gallery.

✦ **Item location:** The region, city, and country from which the item will be shipped (required).

✦ **Quantity:** The number of items you're offering in this auction is always one, unless you plan to run a multiple-item, or Dutch, auction (required).

✦ **Minimum bid:** The starting price you set (required).

✦ **Duration:** The number of days you want the listing to run (required).

✦ **Reserve price:** The hidden target price you set. This is the price that must be met before this item can be sold (optional). eBay charges you a fee for this feature.

✦ **Private auction:** You can keep the identity of all bidders secret with this option (optional). This type of auction is used only in rare circumstances (such as when you're selling psychic readings and your customers might not want their proclivities made public).

✦ **Buy It Now:** You can sell your item directly to the first buyer who meets this price (optional).

✦ **List item in two categories:** If you want to double your exposure, you can list your item in two categories. Note that double exposure equals double your listing fees (optional).

✦ **Home page featured:** You can place your auction in a premium viewing section, with the possibility that your listing will cycle through the direct links on the front page (optional). eBay charges from $39.95 for this feature.

✦ **Featured Plus!:** You can have your auction appear at the top of the category in which you list it (optional). eBay charges $19.95 for this feature.

✦ **Highlight:** Your item title is highlighted in the auction listings and search listings with a lilac-colored band, which may draw eBay members' eyes right to your auction (optional). eBay charges $5 for this feature.

✦ **Border:** Within the listings, your item will be surrounded by a bordered box. Not a bad option for $3.

✦ **Boldface title:** A selling option to make your item listing stand out. eBay charges $1 for this feature (optional).

✦ **Free counter:** If you want to avail yourself of view counters, indicate so here (optional).

✦ **Ship-to locations:** Here's where you can indicate where you're willing to ship an item. If you don't want the hassle of shipping out of the United States, check only that option. You can select individual countries as well (optional).

You may want to consider whether you *really* want to be in the international shipping business. Buyers pick up the tab, but you have to deal with customs forms and post office paperwork. Depending on what you're selling, shipping internationally just may not be worth the investment in extra time. But remember that if you don't ship internationally, you're blocking a bunch of possible high bidders. Give it a try and see how it works for you.

✦ **How you will ship:** Select the options that apply as to how you plan to ship the item.

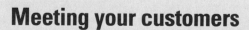

Meeting your customers

eBay is a person-to-person marketplace. Although many sellers are businesses (like you), the perception is that sellers on eBay are individuals (versus businesses) earning a living. The homespun personal approach goes a long way to being successful when you're selling on eBay. One of the reasons many buyers come to eBay is that they want to support the individuals who have the gumption to start their own small enterprise on the site.

✦ **Shipping and handling charges:** When prospective buyers know the shipping cost in advance (assuming it's a realistic price), they're more likely to bid right then and there. If they have to e-mail you with questions, they may find another auction for the same item — with reasonable shipping — and bid on that one. Winning bidders can pay you instantly through PayPal when they have all the costs. See information on eBay's handy shipping calculator, later in this chapter.

✦ **Payment instructions:** Here's the place you optionally put any after-sale information. If you want them to pay in a different manner, mention that as well. This information appears at the top of your sale when the sale is completed, at the bottom of the auction while it's active, and in the end-of-auction e-mail.

✦ **PayPal and immediate payment:** Fill out this area if you want to require the high bidder to pay through PayPal immediately when using Buy It Now. Add the Immediate Payment option if you know the shipping amount and would like the winner to pay with a click of the mouse (optional).

Since I'm talking here about listing an item for sale, I briefly go over some high points on strategies — but be sure you also check out Chapter 1 to get some serious insight on listing strategies.

Selecting a Category: The How and Why

Many eBay sellers will tell you that selecting the exact category isn't crucial to achieving the highest price for your item — and they're right. The bulk of buyers (who know what they're looking for) just input search keywords into eBay's search box and look for their items. Potential buyers, though, will select a category and — just as if they were going to the mall — peruse the items and see whether one strikes their fancy.

On the first page of the Sell an Item form, you need to select the main category for your item. After you select your main category, you land on the official working portion of the Sell an Item page.

With tens of thousands of categories, finding the right place for your item can be daunting. You need to apply some marketing techniques when deciding where to place your auctions. You can list an item in two categories, but you have to pay double for that. Does your budget allow for it?

Consider these ideas and techniques for finding the right category for your item:

✦ **Check out other sellers' successes:** To find where other sellers have successfully sold items that are similar to yours and see the prices the items sold for, you can perform a completed item search from the More Search Options page. In the Search box, type your item keywords, select the box to search Completed and then indicate to have your results sorted by highest prices first. After you have your results, select the completed listings with the highest priced bids. At the top of the auction page, you'll see the listed category. You may find that your item is listed successfully in more than one category.

✦ **Find out who's currently selling your item (and where):** Check the active listings; are lots of people selling your item? If you see that you're one of forty or fifty selling the item, you need to get creative as to where to list yours. Evaluate the item and its potential buyers. In what categories would someone shopping for your item search?

Here's where your creativity can come into play. Who says that a box of Blue Dog (the famous doggie icon painted by Cajun artist George Rodrigue) notecards belongs *only* in Everything Else: Gifts & Occasions: Greeting Cards: Other Cards? If you use the Find Suggested Categories tool (in a yellow shaded box) in the upper-right corner of the Select Category area, you may find some other creative places to list your item.

✦ **Use subcategories to catch in-the-know buyers:** Most bidders scan for specific items in subcategories. For example, if you're selling a Bakelite fruit pin, don't just list it under Jewelry; keep narrowing your choices. In this case, you can put it in a costume jewelry category that's especially for Bakelite. I guarantee that the real Bakelite jewelry collectors out there know where to look to find the jewelry they love.

As part of the Sell an Item form, eBay gives you a tool to find where the bulk of sellers are selling your item. The first thing you can do is to put your keywords (three or four) in the List Your Item for Sale intro box and click Start Selling. Figure 3-1 shows you how easy it is to see where your item is being sold.

Figure 3-1:
Let eBay
do some of
the work
in finding
the proper
category for
your item.

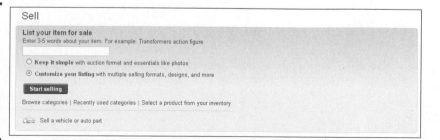

The next page will show you categories that may possibly match your item, as shown in Figure 3-2.

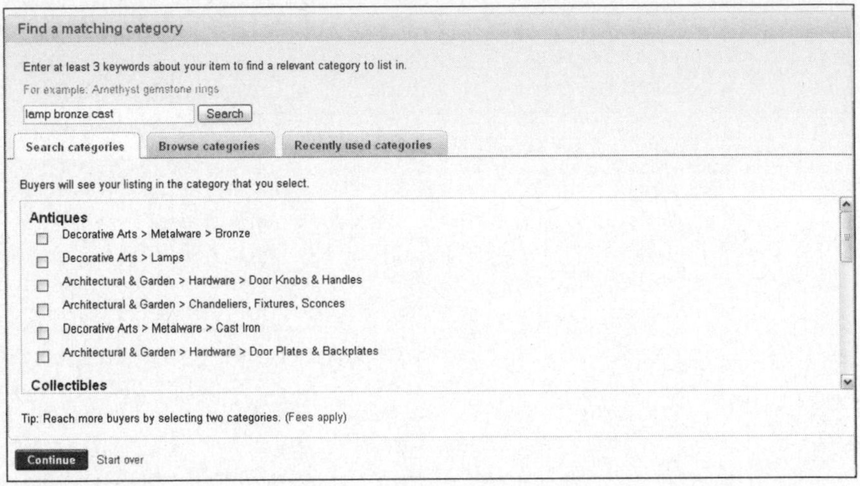

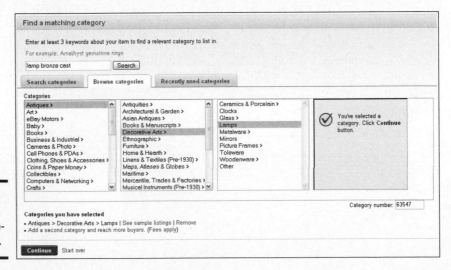

Figure 3-2: Scroll the resulting categories and see if one seems to fit.

You can also select your own category by using the standard category selection tool, just click the Browse Categories tab. eBay offers you a wealth of choices in a handy point-and-click way. If you're unfamiliar with the types of items you can actually find in those categories, you may want to check out the category before you choose one to describe your item. Figure 3-3 shows you how to narrow down the subcategory listings on the Sell an Item page.

Figure 3-3: Narrowing to your sub-categories.

Finding where to sell your stuff

The Internet is crowded with items for sale. Many major portals seem to now include auctions as part of their site. You wonder, should you sell there? The bottom line is that most bidders go to eBay. Why? Because more computers and electronics are sold on eBay than at Buy.com; more used cars are sold on eBay than at Autotrader; and more toys are probably sold at eBay than at KBKids. Even the United States post office has found a niche on eBay, selling the contents of undeliverable packages in odd lots.

Whether you're selling auto parts, toys, fine art, or land, you too must find your niche on eBay. Sounds easy enough. After all, deciding where to put your stuff for sale is straightforward, right? Not necessarily. After taking a look at the eBay Category Overview page, you can see that the inclusion of more than 8000 subcategories complicates this task.

Consider the example of a *Star Trek* toy. *Star Trek* toys are becoming increasingly popular with the continuing saga in the new series and movies. The easy choice is to list the item under Toys: Bean Bag Plush: Action Figures: Star Trek. But what about the category Collectibles: Pop Culture: Science Fiction: Star Trek? This is the when you must decide whether you want to list in two categories (and pay more) or count on the fact that your beautifully written listing title will drive those using the search engine directly to your item.

So you aren't into selling *Star Trek* toys? Suppose you're selling a VHS of the movie *The Red Violin*. Would listing it in Movies: Videos: General be the right choice? Or would you hit the proper audience of category browsers in Music: Musical Instruments: String: Violin, Viola? A book on 1960s fashion? Better in Books: Antiquarian, Rare: General or in Books: Nonfiction: Collectibles? Actually I have my best luck going directly to the fans of '60s fashion in the category Collectibles: Vintage Clothing, Accessories: Clothing: Women: Other Women's Clothing.

Believe it or not, popularity of categories varies from time to time. Potential buyers may search one category more than others, and their preferences depend on which way the wind blows. News stories, the time of year, hot trends, or whether Katie Couric makes a comment about something can change a particular category's popularity. Keeping up on these trends is sometimes tough, so you must do some research.

So how can you possibly know the best category for your item? Research your items on a regular basis by using my favorite tool: the awesome eBay search engine. After you've found the right category for the item you're listing, give it a try. But be sure to occasionally try alternatives as well because the popularity of different areas of the site can come and go with time.

**Book III
Chapter 3**

Listing Your Items for Sale

To select a category, here's the drill:

1. **Click one of the main categories.**

   On the next pane, you see a list of subcategories.

2. **Select the most appropriate subcategory.**

   eBay makes it easy to narrow the category of your item: Just keep clicking until you hit the end of the line.

3. **Continue selecting subcategories until you've narrowed your item listing as much as possible.**

   You know you've come to the last subcategory when you don't see any more right-pointing arrows in the category list.

If you've chosen to list an item, bid on an item, or even just browse in the Everything Else: Mature Audiences category, you need to follow separate, specific guidelines because that category contains graphic nudity or sexual content that may offend some community members. You must

+ Be at least 18 years of age (but you already know that all eBay customers must be 18 or older)

+ Have a valid credit card

+ Complete a waiver stating that you're voluntarily choosing to access adults-only materials

If you have adult or erotica items that you'd like to sell in a private auction, see the "I Want to Be Alone: The Private Auction" section, later in this chapter.

Listing Your Items in Two Categories

Suppose you've found two perfect categories in which to list your item. eBay allows you to list an item in two categories, but does that mean it's the best marketing decision for your auction? That depends. When you list an item in two categories, you must pay two listing fees. Depending on the time, the season, the availability of your item, and how much you paid for it, you may or may not have the budget for listing an item twice. In addition, many eBay buyers are savvy in their use of the search engine. If they search for your item by using the search engine rather than by browsing the categories, listing the item in two categories might be a needless expense.

You can change your category mid-listing, starting it in one category and ending it in another. And at the end of an auction in which your item doesn't sell, you can use the relisting feature to run the auction again in another category.

Even when you've been selling a particular item for a while — and doing well with it — you might be surprised to hear that changing to another related category can boost your sales. A little research now and then can go a long way to increasing your eBay sales.

Creating the Perfect Item Title

After you figure out what category you want to list in, eBay wants to get down to the nitty-gritty — what the heck to call that thing you're trying to sell.

Think of your item title as a great newspaper headline. The most valuable real estate on eBay is the 55-character title of your item. The majority of buyers do title searches (in my research, around 98% of searches are performed by *title* only), and that's where your item must come up to be sold! So the onus is on you to give the most essential information right away to grab the eye of the reader who's just browsing. Be clear and informative enough to get noticed by eBay's search engine. Figure 3-4 shows examples of good titles. Note how some sellers beefed up the titles by using the Subtitle option.

Figure 3-4: These item titles are effective because they're clear, concise, and easy on the eyes.

VHS Complete Set 60 Videos PERRY MASON CE TV Series Lot   Columbia House - Collector's Edition - 120 Episodes
BALLET DANCE ART Signed Print - Celebrating Romance
NEW Wonder Woman Halloween Costume Girls 4 6 $30 NR
$139 Zoece DVD / MP3 Progressive Scan Player DP-303 NR
VHS Baryshnikov The Dancer and the Dance Ballet Video
EBAY TIMESAVING TECHNIQUES For Dummies SIGNED by Author   Advanced PowerSeller Reference direct from the writer!
GOEBEL HUMMEL From This Day Forward BH 6 1996 Thailand
New Cloud Dome Background Backdrop PORTABLE Photo STAGE   Take Perfect eBay pictures anywhere in your home!

Here are some ideas to help you write your item title:

✦ Use the most common name for the item.

✦ If the item is rare or hard to find, mention that.

✦ Mention the item's condition and whether it's new or old.

✦ Mention the item's special qualities, such as its style, model, or edition.

✦ Avoid fancy punctuation or unusual characters, such as $, hyphens, and L@@K (or WOW), because they just clutter up the title — buyers rarely search for them.

Don't put any HTML tags in your title. (*HTML* stands for HyperText Markup Language, which in plain English means that it's the special code you use to create Web pages.) As a matter of fact, despite what you may have been told, you don't need an extensive knowledge of HTML to have successful, good-looking auctions on eBay. Later in the chapter, I list a few HTML codes to use in your description. And in Book V, I give you some serious HTML tutoring and tips on where you can find some easy programs that produce the minor HTML coding that you may want to use to dress up your auctions.

Ordinarily, I don't throw out French phrases just for the fun of it. But when making a profit is an issue, I definitely have to agree with the French that choosing or not choosing *le mot juste* can mean the difference between having potential bidders merely see your auction and having an all-out bidding war on your hands. Read on for tips about picking *the best words* to let your auction item shine.

Look for a phrase that pays

Here's a crash course in eBay lingo that can help bring you up to speed on attracting buyers to your auction. The following words are used frequently in eBay auctions and can do wonders to jump-start your title:

✦ Mint

✦ One of a kind (OOAK)

✦ Vintage

✦ Collectible

✦ Rare

✦ Unique

✦ Primitive

✦ Well-loved

There's a science to figuring out the value of a collectible (called *grading*). Do your homework before you assign a grade to your item. If you need more information on what these grades actually mean, Book II, Chapter 2 provides a translation.

eBay lingo at a glance

The common terms and the phrases just mentioned aren't the only marketing standards you have at your eBay disposal. As eBay has grown, so has the lingo that members use as shortcuts to describe their merchandise. Table 3-1 gives you a handy list of common abbreviations and phrases used to describe items. (**Hint:** "Mint" means "may as well be brand new," not "cool chocolate treat attached.")

Using titles to get eyes on your listing

Keywords! Keywords! Keywords! I can't stress enough that keywords are essential in your title. *Keywords* are single words that people would naturally use to search for an item. For example, if you're selling a shirt, common keywords for your title might include

✔ Color

✔ Size

✔ Fabric

✔ Men's, women's, or child's

✔ Manufacturer's name

✔ Is the item NWT (New With Tags)?

Another great place to find common keywords searched for on eBay is in eBay's fairly hidden directory of keywords, which is shown in the figure. You can find this page at `http://keyword-index.ebay.com/a-1.html`. In addition, some super programs will check your auctions to see which keywords are doing the best job for you. Check out Book VIII for the skinny.

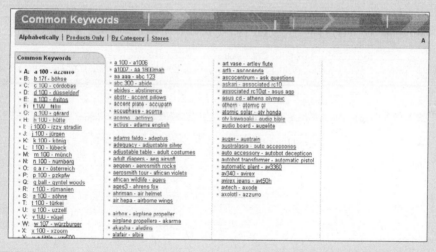

Table 3-1	A Quick List of eBay Abbreviations	
eBay Code	*What It Abbreviates*	*What It Means*
MIB	Mint in Box	The item is in the original box, in great shape, and just the way you'd expect to find it in a store.
MIMB	Mint in Mint Box	The box has never been opened and looks like it just left the factory.

(continued)

Table 3-1 *(continued)*

eBay Code	What It Abbreviates	What It MeansCode
MOC	Mint on Card	The item is mounted on its original display card, attached with the original fastenings, in store-new condition.
NRFB	Never Removed from Box	The item has never been opened.
COA	Certificate of Authenticity	Documentation that vouches for the genuineness of an item, such as an autograph or painting.
MWBMT	Mint with Both Mint Tags	Refers to stuffed animals, which have a hang tag (usually paper or card) and a tush tag (that's what they call the sewn-on tag — really) in perfect condition with no bends or tears.
OEM	Original Equipment Manufacture	You're selling the item and all the equipment that originally came with it, but you don't have the original box, owner's manual, or instructions.
OOAK	One of a Kind	You are selling the only one in existence!
NR	No Reserve Price	A reserve price is the price you can set when you begin your auction. If bids don't meet the reserve, you don't have to sell. Many buyers don't like reserve prices because they don't think that they can get a bargain. (For tips on how to allay these fears and get bids in reserve price auctions, see the "Writing your description" section.) If you're *not* listing a reserve for your item, be sure to let bidders know.
NWT	New with Tags	An item, possibly apparel, is in new condition with the tags from the manufacturer still affixed.
NWOT	New, but without store tags	Generally a new article of apparel that is missing the store tags, but is unused.
HTF, OOP	Hard to Find, Out of Print	Out of print, only a few ever made, or people grabbed up all there were. (HTF doesn't mean you spent a week looking for it in the attic.)

Normally, you can rely on eBay abbreviations to get your point across, but make sure that you mean it and that you're using it accurately. Don't label something MIB (Mint in Box) when it looks like it's been Mashed in Box. You'll find more eBay abbreviations on my Web site, www.coolebaytools. com. (Click the Tools tab, and then click the FWIW: eBay Terms link.)

Don't let your title ruin your listing

Imagine going to a supermarket and asking where you can find the *stringy stuff that you boil* instead of asking where the spaghetti is. You might end up with mung bean sprouts — delicious to some, but hardly what you had in mind. That's why you should check and recheck your spelling. Savvy buyers use the eBay search engine to find merchandise; if the name of your item is spelled wrong, the search engine can't find it. Poor spelling and incomprehensible grammar also reflect badly on you. If you're in competition with another seller, the buyer is likelier to trust the seller *hoo nose gud speling*.

In my travels, I meet so many interesting people with lots of great stories about their forays on eBay. One of my favorites is the story told to me by a lovely lady in Salt Lake City. She brought to my class her biggest eBay bargain. She won a Shaquille O'Neill signed basketball on eBay for 1 cent! Yep, one red cent (plus shipping). I'll bet that seller had a rude surprise when his listing closed! Oh, you want to know why such a valuable collectible sold for so little? The seller couldn't spell Shaquille and listed the item as *Schackeel*.

If you've finished writing your item title and you have spaces left over, *please* fight the urge to dress the title up with lots of exclamation points and asterisks. No matter how gung-ho you are about your item, the eBay search engine may overlook your item if the title is encrusted with meaningless **** and !!!! symbols. If bidders do see your title, they may become annoyed by the virtual shrillness and ignore it anyway!!!!!!!! (See what I mean?)

Another distracting habit is overdoing capital letters. To buyers, seeing everything in caps is LIKE SEEING A HYSTERICAL SALESPERSON SCREAMING AT THEM TO BUY NOW! All that is considered *shouting,* which is rude and tough on the eyes. Use capitalization SPARINGLY, and only to finesse a particular point or feature.

Giving the title punch with a subtitle

A new feature on eBay is the availability of subtitles. eBay allows you to buy an additional 55 characters, which will appear under your item title in a search. The fee for this extra promotion is $0.50, and in a few circumstances, it is definitely worth your while. Any text that you input will really make your item stand out in the crowd — but (you knew there would be a *but,* didn't you?) these additional 55 characters won't come up in a title search. So if you have all those words in your description, the words will be found either way with a title and description search. Keep in mind that a subtitle essentially *doubles* your listing fee.

Creating Your Item Description

After you hook potential bidders with your title, reel 'em in with a fabulous description. Don't think Hemingway here; think infomercial (the classier the better). Figure 3-5 shows a concise description of a silver dollar for sale. You can write a magnificent description, as well — all you have to do is click the box and start typing.

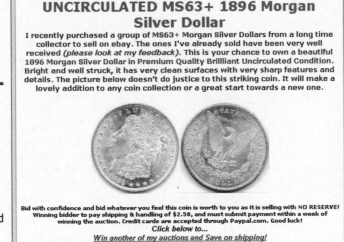

Figure 3-5: Writing a good description can mean the difference between success and failure.

Composing the description

Here's a list of suggestions for writing an item description:

✦ **Write a factual description.** Do you carefully describe the item, stating every fact you know about it? Do you avoid the use of jargon? Does the description answer almost any question a potential buyer might ask? If not, do some revising.

✦ **Accentuate the positive.** Be enthusiastic when you list all the reasons everyone should bid on the item. Unlike the title, the description can take up as much space as you want. Even if you use a photo, be precise in your description — tell the reader, for example, the item's size, color, and fabric. Refer to "Creating the perfect item title," earlier in this chapter, for ideas on what to emphasize.

✦ **Include the negative.** Don't hide the truth of your item's condition. Trying to conceal flaws costs you in the long run: You'll get tagged with bad feedback. If the item has a scratch, a nick, a dent, a crack, a ding, a tear, a rip, missing pieces, replacement parts, faded color, dirty smudges, or a bad smell (especially if cleaning might damage the item), mention it in the description. If your item has been overhauled, rebuilt, repainted, or hot-rodded (say, a "Pentium computer" that was a 386 till you put in the new motherboard), say so. You don't want the buyer to send back your merchandise because you weren't truthful about imperfections or modifications. This type of omission can lead to a fraud investigation.

✦ **Include some friendly banter.** You want to make the customer feel comfortable shopping with you. Don't be afraid to let your personality show!

✦ **Update your My eBay page.** Let people know a little about you and who they're dealing with. When customers have to decide between two people selling the same item and all else is equal, they'll place their bids with the seller who makes them feel secure.

✦ **Limit the number of auction rules (or terms of sale).** Some sellers include a list of rules that's longer than the item's description. Nothing turns off a prospective buyer like paragraph after paragraph of rules and regulations. If you really *must* put in a litany of rules, use the following bit of HTML to make the size of the text smaller: `<font size=-1>`.

✦ **Choose a reasonable typeface size.** Many users are still looking at eBay on an 800 x 600 display. If you design your auctions at 1024 x 768, your typefaces may be way too large for the average user. Forcing a user to scroll leads to frustrated customers.

✦ **Quote a shipping amount.** Many bidders pass up auctions that don't disclose the shipping charges. Make use of eBay's shipping calculator to give your customers a fair shake at the shipping costs. If many others are selling the same item you're selling, quoting reasonable shipping costs will help you reel in a buyer.

✦ **Keep photos a practical size.** Many users still connect with a dial-up Internet connection, and if they have to wait more than a few seconds for your large pictures to load, they may go elsewhere for the item.

✦ **Be precise about all the logistical details of the post-auction transaction.** Even though you're not required to list any special S&H (shipping and handling) or payment requirements in your item description, the majority of eBay users do. Try to figure out the cost of shipping the item in the United States and add that to your description. If you offer shipping insurance, add it to your item description.

✦ **Promote yourself, too.** As you accumulate positive feedback, tell potential bidders about your terrific track record. Add statements like "I'm great to deal with. Check out my feedback section." You can even take it a step further by inviting prospective bidders to your About Me page (where you may also include a link to your personal Web site — if you have one).

✦ **Be concise and to the point — don't ramble!** As my sixth-grade English teacher user to say, "Make it like a woman's skirt: long enough to cover the subject, yet short enough to keep it interesting." Too many sellers these days drone on and on, causing bidders to have to scroll down the page several times. You can quickly lose your audience this way. They'll look for a listing with a less complicated look.

✦ **Wish your potential bidders well.** Communication is the key to a good transaction; you can set the tone for your auction (and your post-auction exchanges) by including some simple phrases that show your friendly side. Always end your description by wishing bidders good luck, inviting potential bidders to e-mail you with questions, and offering the option of providing additional photos of the item if you have them.

Jazzing it up with HTML

When you input your description, you have the option of jazzing things up with a bit of HTML coding, or you can use eBay's HTML text editor, described in Book V, Chapter 3. If you know how to use a word processor, you'll have no trouble touching up your text with this tool. Table 3-2 shows you a few HTML codes that you can insert into your text to help you pretty things up.

Table 3-2	A Short List of HTML Codes	
HTML Code	*How to Use It*	*What It Does*
`<b></b>`	`<b>cool collecible </b>`	**cool collectible** (bold type)
`<i></i>`	`<I>cool collectible </i>`	*cool collectible* (italic type)
`<b><i></b></i>`	`<b><i>cool collectible </i></b>`	***cool collectible*** (bold and italic type)

HTML Code	How to Use It	What It Does
`<font color=red> </font>`	`<font color=red>cool collectible</font>`	Selected text appears in red
`<font size=+1></font>`	`<font size=+3>cool </font> collectible`	**cool** collectible (font size normal+1 through 4, increases size *x* times)
` `	`cool collectible`	cool collectible (inserts line break)
`<p>`	`cool<p>collectible`	cool collectible (inserts paragraph space)
`<hr>`	`cool collectible <hr>cheap`	cool collectible ——— cheap (inserts horizontal rule)
`<h1><h1>`	`<h1>cool collectible </h1>`	**cool collectible** (converts text to headline size)

You can go back and forth from the HTML text editor to regular input and add additional codes here and there by selecting the View/Edit HTML check box (when you're in the HTML text editor). I prepare all my auctions ahead of time in an HTML composer in the Mozilla SeaMonkey suite (see Book V, Chapter 3 for more details) and save them in my computer as plain TXT files. That way, my auctions are always retrievable for use (I just copy and paste) no matter what program or form I'm using to list them.

Occasionally, sellers offer an item as a *presell*. These sellers are either drop-shipping an item or don't yet have the item in stock but expect to have it. If you're offering this kind of item, make sure that you spell out the details in the description. eBay policy states that you must ship a presell item within 30 days of the auction's end, so be sure you'll have the item within that time span. Don't forget to include the actual shipping date. I have found that putting an item up for sale without having it in hand is a practice fraught with risk. The item you're expecting may not arrive in time or may arrive damaged. I've heard of one too many sellers who have had to go out and purchase an item at retail for a buyer to preserve their reputation when caught in this situation. By the way, this is not only eBay's regulation. The Federal Trade Commission (FTC) calls this the 30-day rule, and they are serious about enforcing it. (For more about presells, check out Book III, Chapter 2.)

Listing the Number of Items for Sale

Unless you're planning on holding a multiple-item (Dutch) auction, the number of items is always 1, which means you're holding a traditional auction. If you need to change the quantity from 1, just type the number in the box.

A matching set of cuff links is considered one item, as is the complete 37-volume set of *The Smith Family Ancestry and Genealogical History since 1270.* If you have more than one of the same item, I suggest that you sell the items one at a time, because you will more than likely get higher final bids for your items when you sell them individually.

Whether you list your items individually in auctions, fixed price listings or together in a multiple-item auction, eBay won't show more than ten auctions from a single seller at one time in search results.

Setting Bids, Prices, and Reserves

What do a baseball autographed by JFK, a used walkie-talkie, and a Jaguar sports car have in common? They all started with a $.99 minimum bid. eBay requires you to set a *minimum bid,* the lowest bid allowed in an auction. You may be surprised to see stuff worth tens of thousands of dollars starting at just a buck. These sellers haven't lost their minds. Neither are they worried someone could end up tooling down the highway in a $100,000 sports car for the price of a burger.

Starting with a low minimum is also good for your pocketbook. eBay charges the seller an insertion, or placement, fee based on your opening bid. If you keep your opening bid low and set no reserve, you get to keep more of your money. (See Chapter 1 for more about eBay fees.)

Before you set a minimum bid, do your homework and make some savvy marketing decisions. If your auction isn't going as you hoped, you *could* end up selling Grandma Ethel's Ming vase for a dollar. See "Making Midcourse Corrections," later in this chapter, on how you can make changes in your listing if you've made some egregious error.

Setting a minimum bid — how low can you go?

Setting an incredibly low minimum is a subtle strategy that gives you more bang for your buck. You can use a low minimum bid to attract more bidders who will, in turn, drive up the price to the item's real value — especially if, after doing your research, you know that the item is particularly hot.

The more bids you get, the more people will want to bid on your item because they perceive it as hot. A hot item *with lots of bids* draws even more bidders the way a magnet attracts paper clips.

When putting in your minimum bid, type only the numbers and a decimal point. Don't use a dollar sign ($) or a cent sign (¢).

If you're worried about the outcome of the final bid, you can protect your item by using a reserve price (the price the bidding needs to reach before the item can be sold). Then you won't have to sell your item for a bargain-basement price because your reserve price protects your investment. The best advice is to set a reserve price that is the lowest amount you'll take for your item, and then set a minimum bid that is ridiculously low. However, use a reserve only when absolutely necessary because some bidders pass up reserve auctions. (For more info about setting a reserve price, see "Using your secret safety net — reserve price," later in this section.)

Going with a Buy It Now price

eBay's Buy It Now (*BIN* in eBay-speak) is available for single-item auctions. This feature allows buyers to purchase an item *now.* Have you ever wanted an item really badly and you didn't want to wait until the end of an auction? If the seller offers Buy It Now, you can purchase that item immediately. Just specify the amount the item can sell for in the Buy It Now price area — the amount can be whatever you want. If you choose to sell a hot item during the holiday rush, for example, you can make the BIN price as high as you think it can go. If you just want the item to move, make your BIN price the average price you see the item go for on eBay.

In most categories, when your item receives a bid, the BIN option disappears and the item goes through the normal auction process. If you have a reserve price on your item, the BIN feature doesn't disappear until a bidder meets your reserve price through the normal bidding process. To list an item with Buy It Now, you must have a feedback of 10 or be ID verified.

The Buy It Now price will remain, if there is a bid that doesn't reach 50% of your BIN price in certain categories:

1. Parts & Accessories (eBay Motors)
2. Tickets
3. Clothing, Shoes & Accessories
4. Cell Phones & PDAs

Using your secret safety net — reserve price

Here's a little secret: The reason sellers list big-ticket items such as Ferraris, grand pianos, and high-tech computer equipment with a starting bid of $1 is because they're protected from losing money with a reserve price. The *reserve price* is the lowest price that must be met before the item can be sold. It is not required by eBay but can protect you. For this feature, eBay charges an additional fee that varies depending on how high your reserve is.

For example, say you list a first-edition book — John Steinbeck's *The Grapes of Wrath.* You set the starting price at $.99 and the reserve price at $80. That means people can start bidding at $.99, and if at the end of the auction the book hasn't reached the $80 reserve, you don't have to sell the book.

As with everything in life, using a reserve price for your auctions has an upside and a downside. Many choosy bidders and bargain hunters blast past reserve-price auctions because they see a reserve price as a sign that proclaims "No bargains here!" Many bidders figure they can get a better deal on the same item with an auction that proudly declares *NR* (for *no reserve*) in its description. As an enticement to those bidders, you see lots of NR listings in auction titles.

If you need to set a reserve on your item, help the bidder out. Many bidders shy away from an auction that has a reserve, but if they're really interested, they will read the item description. To dispel their fears that the item is way too expensive or out of their price range, add a line in your description that states the amount of your reserve price. "I have put a reserve of $75 on this item to protect my investment; the highest bid over $75 will win the item." A phrase such as this takes away the vagueness of the reserve auction and allows you to place a reserve with a low opening bid. (You want to reel 'em in, remember?)

On lower-priced items, I suggest that you set a higher minimum bid and set no reserve.

If bids don't reach a set reserve price, some sellers e-mail the highest bidder and offer the item at what the seller thinks is a fair price. Two caveats:

✦ eBay can suspend the seller *and* the buyer if the side deal is reported to Trust and Safety. This activity is strictly prohibited.

✦ eBay won't protect buyers or sellers if a side deal goes bad.

You can, however, offer an underbidder a second chance offer or relist the item for another whack at the buying public.

You can't use a reserve price in a multiple-item (Dutch) auction.

Timing Your Auction: Is It Everything?

Although I discuss auction length in depth in Chapter 2, it's important to mention a bit more here. eBay gives you a choice of auction length: 1, 3, 5, 7, or 10 days. Just click the number you want in the box. If you choose a 10-day auction, you add $0.40 to your listing fee.

My auction-length strategy depends on the time of year and the item I'm selling, and I generally have great success. If you have an item that you think will sell pretty well, run a 7-day auction (be sure to cover a full weekend) so bidders have time to check it out before they decide to bid. However, if you know that you have a red-hot item that's going to fly off the shelves — such as a rare toy or a hard-to-get video game — choose a 3-day auction. Eager bidders tend to bid higher and more often to beat out their competition if the item's hot and going fast. A 3-day auction is long enough to give trendy items exposure and ring up bids.

No matter how many days you choose to run your auction, it ends at exactly the same time of day as it starts. A 7-day auction that starts on Thursday at 9:03:02 a.m. ends the following Thursday at 9:03:02 a.m.

Although I know the folks at eBay are pretty laid-back, they do run on military time. That means they use a 24-hour clock set to Pacific time. So 3:30 in the afternoon is 15:30, and one minute after midnight is 00:01. Questions about time conversions? Check out www.timezoneconverter.com or look at the table in Chapter 2. And so you don't have to keep flipping back to that page, I also include a printable conversion chart of eBay times on my Web site (www.coolebaytools.com).

Going Dutch

If you have five Dennis Rodman Wedding Dolls, 37 Breathalyzers, or 2000 commemorative pins, and you want to sell them all at once to as many bidders as quickly as possible, sell them as multiple quantities in a fixed-price sale. (You can also sell the whole shebang in one lot in the Wholesale Lot category.) If you're not sure how much you can get for the items, you can always try a multiple-item (Dutch) auction.

eBay has requirements for starting a Dutch auction. You have to be an eBay member for at least 14 days with a feedback rating of 30 (if you have a PayPal account your feedback can be as low as 15) or higher or go through ID Verify. Visit eBay's help area for more information on how to conduct this type of auction, and check out Chapter 1 for more info on how a multiple-item auction works. You can also go directly to http://pages.ebay.com/help/sell/multiple.html.

Occasionally, eBay conducts a mandatory outage for database maintenance, which means that it closes up shop on a Friday from 1 a.m. to 3 a.m. Pacific time (that's 4:00 a.m. to 6:00 a.m. Eastern Time). Never post an auction right after this outage. eBay regulars won't be around to bid on it. Also, search updates often run 12 to 15 hours behind on Friday and Saturday, following scheduled maintenance.

With listings running 24 hours a day, 7 days a week, you should know when the most bidders are around to take a gander at your wares. Here are some times to think about:

✦ **Saturday and Sunday:** Always run an auction over a weekend. People log on and off eBay all day to look for desired items.

✦ **Holiday weekends:** If a holiday weekend's coming up around the time you're setting up your auction, run your auction through the weekend and end it a day after the "holiday" Monday. This gives prospective bidders a chance to catch up with the items they perused over the weekend and plan their bidding strategies.

Don't end an auction on the last day of a three-day holiday. People in the mood to shop are generally at department stores collecting bargains. If eBay members aren't shopping, they're out enjoying an extra day off.

✦ **Time of day:** The best times of day to start and end your auction are during eBay's peak hours of operation, which are 5:00 p.m. to 9:00 p.m. Pacific Time, right after work on the West Coast. Perform your completed auction research, however, to be sure that this strategy applies to your item, because this timing depends on the item you're auctioning.

Unless you're an insomniac or a vampire who wants to sell to werewolves, don't let your auctions close in the middle of the night. Not enough bidders are around to cause last-minute bidding that would bump up the price.

I Want to Be Alone: The Private Auction

In a *private* auction, bidders' user IDs are kept under wraps. Sellers typically use this option to protect the identities of bidders during auctions for high-priced big-ticket items (say, that restored World War II fighter). Wealthy eBay users may not want the world to know that they have the resources to buy expensive items. Private auctions are also held for items from the Adult/Erotica category. (Gee, there's a shocker.)

The famous sign that was pictured in almost every piece of Disney promotion (for the first 40 or so years of Disneyland's existence) was put up for sale on eBay in 2000. Rumor has it that the sign was purchased by actor John Stamos for a high bid of $30,700. Unfortunately for John, the Disney auctions did not use the private auction feature. After news of the winner's name hit the tabloids, the entire world knew John's eBay user ID! He had to change his ID in a hurry to end the throngs of lovey-dovey e-mail messages headed to his computer!

Adding Visuals to Highlight Your Item

With so many listings posted daily on eBay, you need some way to get your listing noticed. Adding visual interest to catch a potential buyer's eye is one way. As you fill out the Sell an Item page, take advantage of the visual elements that eBay offers.

Put me in the gallery

The gallery is an auction area where you can post pictures that are accessible from the listings. When you use the gallery, a postage-stamp-size version of your image appears next to your listing in the category or search. Many buyers enjoy browsing the gallery catalog-style, and it's open to all categories. If you choose to go this route, your item is listed in both the gallery and in the regular text listings. (I explain how to post your pictures in Book V.)

The best thing about using a gallery picture in your listings is that it increases the space your listing takes up on a search or category page — plus it's free! If you don't use a gallery picture and have just an image in your auction, all that will be next to your listing is a teeny, tiny camera icon.

A picture is worth a thousand words

Clichés again? Perhaps. But an item on eBay without a picture is almost a waste of time. If you haven't set up photo-hosting elsewhere, you can list one picture with eBay's Pictures Service for free, as shown in Figure 3-6. Additional pictures will cost you $.15 each.

Avail yourself of eBay's one free picture; when you do, eBay will give you a free top-of-the-listing-page picture. I use it and recommend it! Also, you can put all the additional pictures you want in your auction description for free. See Book V for the necessary coding and instructions.

**Book III
Chapter 3**

Listing Your Items
for Sale

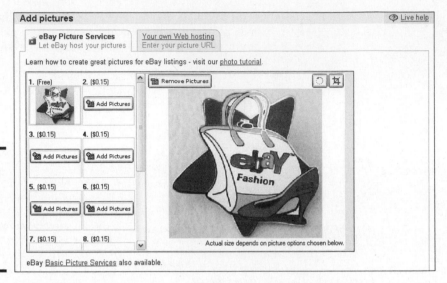

Figure 3-6:
Upload an
image to
eBay with
a couple
of mouse
clicks!

Listing Designer

How many times have you seen an item on eBay laid out on the page all pretty-like with a fancy colorful border around the description? If that sort of thing appeals to you, eBay's Listing Designer can supply you with borders for almost any type of item for $0.10. Will the pretty borders increase the amount of bids your auction will get? It's extremely doubtful. A clean item description with a couple of good, clear pictures of your item is all you need.

Listing the Payment Methods You'll Accept

Yeah, sure, eBay is loads of fun, but the bottom line to selling is the phrase "Show me the money!" You make the call on what you're willing to take as money from your auction's high bidder. eBay offers the following payment options — just select the ones that you like:

✦ **Money order or cashier's check (acceptable as payment only for Vehicles and some categories in Real Estate, Mature Audiences, and Business & Industrial):** From a seller's point of view, this is the safest method of payment. It's the closest thing you can get to cash. As a seller, you want to get paid with as little risk as possible. The only drawback? You have to wait for the buyer to mail the money.

✦ **Credit cards:** If you accept credit cards, using PayPal is the cheapest and most convenient way to go. If you have a merchant account through a retail store, be sure to select the little check boxes next to the credit cards you accept.

Offering a credit card payment option often attracts higher bids to your auctions. These higher bids usually more than cover the small percentage that credit card payment services charge you to use their services.

Some sellers who use credit-card services try attaching an additional fee (to cover their credit-card processing fees) to the final payment. However, that's against the law in California, home of eBay, and there-fore against eBay's rules. So forget about it. eBay can end your auction if it catches you.

✦ **Personal check (acceptable as payment only for Vehicles and some categories in Real Estate, Mature Audiences, and Business & Industrial):** This is an extremely popular option, but it comes with a risk. The check could bounce higher than a lob at Wimbledon. If you accept personal checks, explain in your item description how long you plan to wait for the check to clear before sending the merchandise. The average hold is about ten business days. Some sellers wait as long as two weeks. Accepting eChecks through PayPal leaves all the bookkeeping and waiting to PayPal; you don't have to call the bank for confirmation.

Cut down on the risk of bad checks by reading the bidder's feedback when the auction is underway. Be wary of accepting checks from people with negative comments. (I explain all about feedback in Book I.) Never ship an item until you're certain the check has cleared the buyer's bank.

✦ **Online escrow:** An escrow service acts as a referee, a neutral third party. Escrow companies typically charge 5% of the sale price, and the buyer usually pays for this service. Unless you're selling an expensive item, offering escrow is overkill. On big-ticket items, however, escrow may make the difference between a sale and a pass. If you do offer escrow, the winning bidder should inform you right after the auction if he or she intends to use it.

Most sellers offer buyers several ways to pay. You can choose as many as you want. When the auction page appears, your choices are noted at the top of the listing. Listing several payment options makes you look like a flexible, easygoing professional.

Where You Are and Where You'll Ship To

When listing an item for sale on eBay, you come to the area where you need to input your payment and shipping information. You have the option of using a flat rate, where you simply input your flat shipping charges. The charges appear in a box at the top and the bottom of your item description.

But how you handle shipping — and its associated cost for your buyers — depends on what you're shipping (how big it is), where you're shipping it, and the carrier you decide to use. So take a bit of time to consider your location and your shipping options before you fill out this section.

eBay has some new rules about how much you can charge for shipping in certain categories. Some greedy sellers would charge egregious amounts for shipping their items to avoid paying Final Value Fees on their extra profits, so eBay cracked down and made maximum shipping limits. Table 3-3 gives you the current shipping charge limits as of October 31, 2008.

Table 3-3	Shipping Charge Limits by Category	
Category: Books		
Subcategory	*Type of Merchandise*	*Maximum Shipping Charge*
Accessories	Address Books	$4.00
	Blank Diaries & Journals	$5.00
	Book Covers	$5.00
	Book Plates	$3.00
	Bookmarks	$3.00
	Other	$3.00
Antiquarian & Collectible	Antiquarian & Collectible	$4.00
Audiobooks	Audiobooks	$4.00
Catalogs	Catalogs	$4.00
Children's Books	Children's Books	$4.00
Cookbooks	Cookbooks	$4.00
Fiction Books	Fiction Books	$4.00
Magazine Back Issues	Magazine Back Issues	$5.00
Nonfiction Books	Nonfiction Books	$4.00
Other	Other	$4.00
Textbooks, Education	Textbooks, Education	$4.00
Wholesale & Bulk Lots	Audiobooks	$10.00
	Books > 101-500	$20.00
	Books > 11-50 Items	$8.00
	Books > 51-100 Items	$15.00

Category: Books

Subcategory	Type of Merchandise	Maximum Shipping Charge
	Books > 6-10 Items	$6.00
	Books > More than 500	$30.00
	Magazines	$8.00
	Other	$6.00

Category: DVDs & Movies

Subcategory	Type of Merchandise	Maximum Shipping Charge
DVD, HD DVD & Blu-ray	DVD, HD DVD & Blu-ray	$3.00
Film	Film	$6.00
Laserdisc	Laserdisc	$6.00
Other Formats	Other Formats	$3.00
UMD	UMD	$5.00
VHS	VHS	$3.00
VHS Non-US (PAL)	VHS Non-US (PAL)	$5.00
Wholesale Lots	DVDs > 101-250 Items	$30.00
	DVDs > 11-50 Items	$15.00
	DVDs > 251-500 Items	$60.00
	DVDs > 501-1000 Items	$120.00
	DVDs > 51-100 Items	$25.00
	DVDs > Up to 10 Items	$10.00
	Mixed Lots	$10.00
	Movies Accessories	$17.00
	Other	$10.00
	VHS > 101-500 Items	$30.00
	VHS > 11-50 Items	$15.00
	VHS > 51-100 Items	$25.00
	VHS > More than 500 Items	$120.00
	VHS > Up to 10 Items	$10.00

(continued)

Book III
Chapter 3

Listing Your Items for Sale

Table 3-3 *(continued)*

Category: Music

Subcategory	Type of Merchandise	Maximum Shipping Charge
Accessories	Accessories	$5.00
Cassettes	Cassettes	$3.00
CDs	CDs	$3.00
DVD Audio	DVD Audio	$3.00
Other Formats	Other Formats	$3.00
Records	Records	$4.00
Super Audio CDs	Super Audio CDs	$3.00
Wholesale Lots	Cassettes	$10.00
	CDs > 101-500 Items	$30.00
	CDs > 11-100 Items	$20.00
	CDs > More than 500 Items	$60.00
	CDs > Up to 10 Items	$10.00
	Other Formats	$10.00
	Records > 11-50 Items	$15.00
	Records > More than 50 Items	$25.00
	Records > Up to 10 Items	$10.00

Category: Video Games

Subcategory	Type of Merchandise	Maximum Shipping Charge
Accessories	Accessories	$6.00
Games	Games	$4.00
Internet Games	Games > Guild Wars	$6.00
	Games > World of Warcraft	$3.00
	Software & PC Versions	$6.00
Other	Other	$4.00
Systems	Systems	$15.00
Vintage Games	Vintage Games	$6.00

Category: Video Games		
Subcategory	Type of Merchandise	Maximum Shipping Charge
Wholesale Lots	Accessories	$10.00
	Console Systems	$50.00
	Games	$9.00
	Other	$9.00

Filling out the item location

eBay wants you to list the general area and the country in which you live. That way, you give the bidder a heads-up on what kind of shipping charges to expect. Don't be esoteric (listing where you live as *The Here and Now* isn't a whole lot of help), but don't go crazy with cross-streets, landmarks, or degrees of latitude. Listing the city and state you live in is enough.

If you live in a big area — say, suburban Los Angeles (who, me?), which sprawls on for miles — you may want to think about narrowing your region a little. You may find a bidder who lives close to you, which could swing your auction. If you do a face-to-face transaction, choosing a public place is a good idea. (I like doing my trades at Starbucks.)

Setting shipping terms

Ahoy, matey! Hoist the bid! Okay, not quite. Before you run it up the mast, select your shipping options. Here are your choices:

✦ **Ship to the United States only:** This option is selected by default; it means you ship only domestically.

✦ **Will ship worldwide:** The world is your oyster. But make sure that you can afford it.

✦ **Will ship to United States and the following countries:** If you're comfortable shipping to certain countries but not to others, make your selections here. Your choices appear on your auction page.

When you indicate that you will ship internationally, your auction shows up on the international eBay sites, which is a fantastic way to attract new buyers! eBay has lots of good international users, so you may want to consider selling your items around the world. If you do, be sure to clearly state in the description all extra shipping costs and customs charges.

Traditionally, the buyer pays for shipping, and this is the point at which you must decide how much to charge. You also have to calculate how much this item will cost you to ship. If the item weighs under a pound, you may decide to charge a flat rate to all buyers. To charge a flat rate, click the Flat Shipping Rates tab on the Sell an Item form and fill in the shipping amount. Before you fill in the amount, be sure to include your charges for packing (see Book VII for more info on how much to add for this task) and how much the insurance charges will be.

Offering a flat shipping fee for international shipping can be dangerous, unless you offer shipping to only one foreign country. That's because the rates to each country are different. You might prefer to put shipping-fee information in your description. (See the Cheat Sheet at the front of the book for instructions on how to type foreign currency symbols.)

eBay buyers love seeing a flat shipping fee. If you can find it in yourself to find a reasonable midway point, a fixed shipping price may just beat your competition. Figure 3-7 shows you the Sell an Item form's area to fill in for a flat shipping rate.

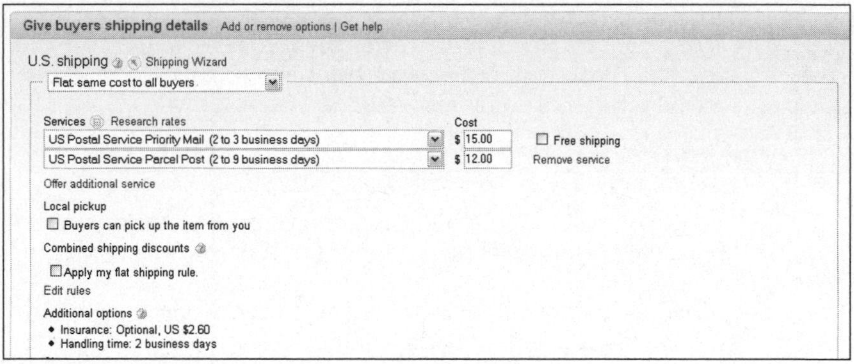

Give buyers shipping details Add or remove options | Get help

U.S. shipping · Shipping Wizard

Flat: same cost to all buyers

Services   Research rates   Cost
US Postal Service Priority Mail (2 to 3 business days) $ 15.00   ☐ Free shipping
US Postal Service Parcel Post (2 to 9 business days) $ 12.00   Remove service

Offer additional service

Local pickup
☐ Buyers can pick up the item from you

Combined shipping discounts
☐ Apply my flat shipping rule.
Edit rules

Additional options
• Insurance: Optional, US $2.60
• Handling time: 2 business days

Figure 3-7: The Flat Shipping Rates form.

Using eBay's shipping calculator

When your item weighs two pounds or more, you may want to use eBay's versatile shipping calculator to determine your flat shipping-and-handling cost or to quote a calculated shipping cost. Using the shipping calculator has these advantages:

✦ **It accounts for variable rates:** Because UPS and the U.S. Postal Service now charge variable rates for packages of the same weight, based on distance, using the calculator simplifies things for your customers (and you). Be sure you've weighed the item.

✦ **It includes your handling amount:** The calculator allows you to input a handling amount and adds it to the overall shipping total — but does not break out these amounts separately for the customer.

✦ **It calculates the cost of insurance:** The calculator also conveniently calculates the proper insurance amount for the item.

Figure 3-8 shows how simple the calculator is. You may select up to three levels of shipping per item.

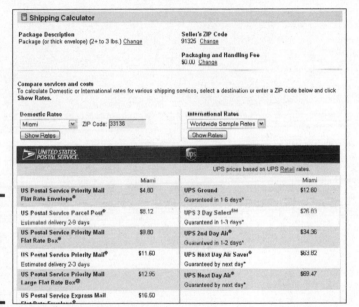

Figure 3-8: The results of checking out the shipping costs.

Book III
Chapter 3

Listing Your Items for Sale

You can check out the associated costs by clicking the Show Rates button, which shows you all shipping costs, so you can decide to ship with either the U.S. Postal Service or UPS. I always test my packages from a California ZIP code (because that's where I live) to a New York ZIP code. Doing this gives me an estimate for Zone 8, which is the most expensive option (coast-to-coast by distance) when shipping in the U.S.

You can check out the fees for different shipping services also by using the full eBay shipping calculator located at

```
http://cgi3.ebay.com/aw-cgi/eBayISAPI.dll?emitsellershipping
    calculator
```

The calculator appears on the item page so that prospective buyers can type their ZIP codes and immediately know how much shipping will be to their locations. Follow these steps to have eBay calculate the charges for you when your buyer supplies his or her ZIP code:

1. **In the Shipping Wizard, choose Calculated: Cost Varies by Buyer Location from the drop-down menu, as shown in Figure 3-9.**

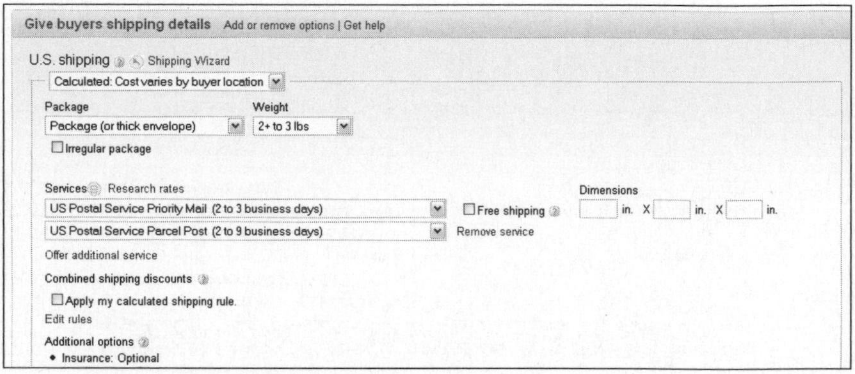

Figure 3-9: The Calculated shipping-rates form.

2. **Select your package's weight and size from the drop-down lists, as shown in Figure 3-10.**

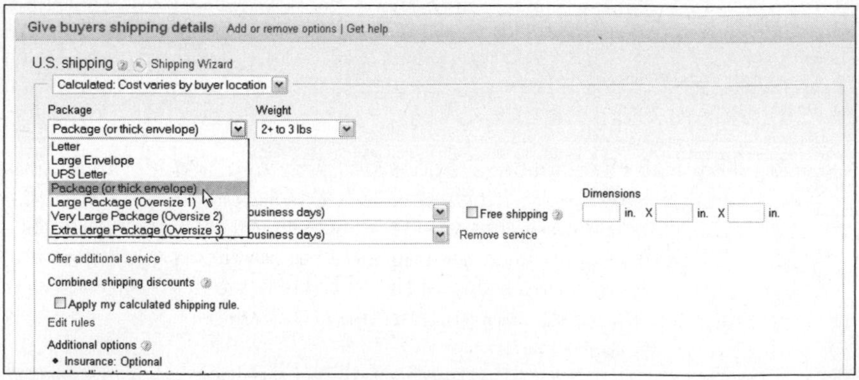

Figure 3-10: The Package Size drop-down list.

3. **Select a carrier from the drop-down lists.**

4. **In the Seller Zip Code box, type your ZIP code.**

5. **In the Packaging & Handling Fee box, type your packaging fees.**

    • When adding your packaging and handling charges, don't worry that the buyers will see these individual fees. eBay combines this amount with the shipping cost and shows the total as one shipping price.

    • If you selected the U.S. Postal Service as your carrier, be sure to add the cost of a delivery confirmation (if you use one) when you figure your packaging and handling fee.

6. **Select the appropriate options in the Shipping Insurance and Sales Tax drop-down lists.**

    If you require the buyer to pay for insurance, or even if insurance is optional, be sure to indicate it. eBay's calculator will give the buyer the actual insurance cost, based on the final bid.

After you've input all your information, you can forget about it because eBay takes over. Check out Book VII for more information on shipping options and how to mechanize the process.

Checking Your Work and Starting the Sale

After you've filled in all the blanks on the Sell an Item page and you think you're ready to join the world of e-commerce, follow these steps:

Book III
Chapter 3

Listing Your Items for Sale

1. **Click the Review button at the bottom of the Sell an Item page.**

    You waft to the Verification page, the place where you can catch mistakes before your item is listed. The Verification page shows you a condensed version of all your information and tallies how much eBay is charging you in fees and options to run this auction. You also see a preview of how your auction description and pictures will look on the site.

    You also may find the Verification page helpful as a last-minute chance to get your bearings. If you've chosen a general category, eBay asks you whether you're certain there isn't a more appropriate category. You can go back to any of the pages that need correcting by clicking the appropriate tab at the top of the Verification page. Make category changes or any other changes and additions, and then head for the Verification page again.

2. **Check for mistakes.**

    Nitpick for common, careless errors; you won't be sorry. I've seen eBay members make goofs such as the wrong category listing, spelling and grammatical errors, and missing information about shipping, handling, insurance, and payment methods.

3. **When you're sure everything is accurate and you're happy with your item listing, click the Submit My Listing button.**

    A Listing Confirmation page pops up. At that precise moment, your sale begins, even though it *may* be a couple of hours before it appears in eBay's search and listings updates. If you want to see your auction right away and check for bids, your Auction Confirmation page provides a link for that purpose. Click the link, and you're there. You can also keep track of your auctions by using the My eBay page.

All listing pages come with this friendly warning: Seller assumes all responsibility for listing this item.

Some eBay veterans just gloss over this warning after they've been wheeling and dealing for a while, but it's an important rule to remember. Whether you're buying or selling, you're always responsible for your actions.

For the first 24 hours after your sale is underway, eBay stamps the Item page with a funky sunrise icon next to the listing in the category listing page or search results page. This is just a little reminder for buyers to come take a look at the latest items up for sale.

Making Midcourse Corrections

If you made a mistake filling out the Sell an Item page but didn't notice it until after the listing is up and running, don't worry. Pencils have erasers, and eBay allows revisions. You can make changes at two stages of the game: before the first bid is placed and after the bidding war is underway. This section explains what you can (and can't) correct — and when you have to accept the little imperfections of your Sell an Item page.

Making changes before bidding begins

Here's what you can change about your auction before bids have been placed, as long as your auction does not end within 12 hours:

✦ The title, subtitle, or description

✦ The item category

✦ The item's Minimum Bid price

✦ The item's Buy It Now price (or adding a Buy It Now price)

✦ The reserve price (you can add, change, or remove it)

✦ The duration of your listing

✦ The URL of the picture you're including with your auction

✦ A private-auction designation (you can add or remove it)

✦ Accepted payment methods, the item location, and shipping terms

When you revise a listing, eBay puts a little notation on your page that reads: Description (revised).

To revise an auction before bids have been received, follow these steps:

1. **Go to the item page and click the Revise Your Item link.**

This link will appear only if you've signed in on eBay. If the item hasn't received any bids, a message appears on your screen to indicate that you may update the item.

You're taken to the Revise Your Item page, which outlines the rules for revising your item. At the bottom, the item number is filled in.

2. **Click Revise Item.**

You arrive at the Revise Your Item page which looks suspiciously like the Sell an Item form.

3. **Click the link that corresponds to the area you'd like to change.**

4. **Make changes to the item information.**

5. **When you've finished making changes, click the Save Changes button at the bottom of the page.**

A summary of your newly revised auction page appears on your screen. If you've incurred any additional fees, the amount is listed at the bottom of the page. If you want to make more changes, click the Back button of your browser and redo the Update Your Information page.

6. **When you're happy with your revisions, click Submit Revisions.**

You're taken to your newly revised auction item page, where you see a disclaimer from eBay that says you've revised the auction before the first bid.

Making changes after bidding begins

If your auction is up and running and already receiving bids, you can still make some slight modifications to it. Newly added information is clearly separated from the original text and pictures. In addition, eBay puts a time stamp on the additional info in case questions from early bidders crop up later.

After your item receives bids, eBay allows you to add to your item's description. If you feel you were at a loss for words in writing your item's description or if a lot of potential bidders are asking the same questions, go ahead and make all the additions you want. But whatever you put there the first time around stays in the description as well.

Follow the same procedure for making changes before bidding begins. When you arrive at the Revise Your Item page, you can *only* add to your description, add features, or add additional payment information. Your initial listing will not be changed — only appended.

Don't let an oversight grow into a failure to communicate — and don't ignore iffy communication until the listing is over. Correct any inaccuracies in your listing information *now* to avoid problems later on.

Always check your e-mail (or your My eBay page) to see whether bidders have questions about your item. If a bidder wants to know about flaws, be truthful and courteous when returning e-mails. As you get more familiar with eBay (and with writing auction descriptions), the number of e-mail questions will decrease. If you enjoy good customer service in your day-to-day shopping, here's your chance to give some back.

Chapter 4: Using eBay's Turbo Lister

In This Chapter

✔ **Knowing the requirements**

✔ **Downloading the software**

✔ **Preparing your listing**

Not much in this world is free, but for now, eBay offers you a free, convenient tool you can use to list your items for sale: Turbo Lister. This powerful software helps you organize your items for sale, design your ads, and list them. It organizes your items for future relisting as well by saving your initial item input and allowing you to create folders for storage. Your items disappear from the program only if you delete them.

I like Turbo Lister because it's simple and easy to use, with a built in WYSIWYG (what you see is what you get) HTML editor that makes preparing your eBay listings offline a breeze. You can also copy and paste in your pre-made templates made in SeaMonkey (see Book V Chapter 3). After you've input your items and are ready to list, you can just click a button and they're all listed at once. You can also stagger listings and schedule them for a later date for a fee. In this chapter, you get an inside look at how Turbo Lister works.

Although using Turbo Lister is free, you're still responsible for any fees you incur when listing an item on the site.

Features and Minimum Requirements

Turbo Lister is robust software with the following features:

✦ **Self-updates:** Turbo Lister automatically updates itself regularly from the eBay site and includes any new eBay enhancements so your listings always take advantage of eBay's latest features. Whenever you invoke the program, it loads and then immediately checks with the eBay server for updates. This can be a bit laborious (especially if the servers are busy or you have a slow Internet connection), so if you plan on listing items at a particular time, be sure to open Turbo Lister earlier, giving it a few minutes to work its updating magic.

+ **Templates:** Predesigned templates are built into the program's Listing Designer. If you use one of eBay's multitude of colorful themes or layouts, you will be charged an additional $.10 on top of your listing fees. You can use a template of your own design to jump-start your ad design without incurring extra charges by pasting the template into the HTML view. You can even use templates from other sources (such as those in Book V), as long as they are in HTML format.

+ **WYSIWYG interface:** If you choose to design your own ads from scratch, you can do it with Turbo Lister's easy-to-use WYSIWYG (what you see is what you get) layout design.

+ **Bulk listing tool:** Prepare your listings whenever you have the time. When you're ready to launch a group of them, just transfer them to the upload area, and, well, upload them.

+ **Item preview:** You can preview your listings to be sure they look just as you want them to.

+ **All item listing capabilities are available offline:** By using Turbo Lister (and its constant auto-upgrading), you don't sacrifice any of the features available to you when you list on the site using the Sell an Item form.

Although this software is definitely useful, you have to decide whether it's really for you. The first thing to check is whether your computer meets Turbo Lister's minimum requirements.

+ Your computer must be a PC, not a Mac (sorry, Mac users). You have to have the Windows 2000, XP, or Vista operating system.

+ The processor must be at least a Pentium II. The faster your processor, the better.

+ You must have at least 128 MB of RAM (and that's a bare minimum).

The more RAM you have, the better things work.

+ You should have at least 250 MB of free space on your hard drive to run the installation.

+ A monitor setting of at least 800 x 600 resolution, 256 colors (8-bit). Keep in mind the software interface looks a lot better with 16-bit color and 1024 x 768 resolution. All monitors today have this capability, so you should be just fine here.

+ Microsoft Internet Explorer version 5.5 or later.

To check your version of Internet Explorer with the browser open, click the Help menu and then choose About Internet Explorer. On the top line, your Internet Explorer version number is listed.

Downloading and Starting Turbo Lister

To use Turbo Lister, you must first download it at

`pages.ebay.com/turbo_lister`

After you install Turbo Lister on your computer, you can list your sales on the easy-to-use form. What could be simpler?

From any eBay page, click the eBay site map from the link above the navigation bar. (Most everything on eBay is on the site map.) Scroll down to Selling Tools, and then click Turbo Lister.

After you get to the Seller Tools page, download Turbo Lister. Follow these steps:

1. **Click the Download Now link.**

   The requirements for using Turbo Lister appear at the bottom of the page.

2. **Click the Turbo Lister Web Setup link.**

   The Windows Security warning appears, cautioning that you're about to download something foreign to your computer.

3. **Click Yes.**

   Clicking Yes downloads Turbo Lister. Clicking No doesn't. Just trust me (and eBay) and click Yes.

From this point on, installation is automatic. Voilà! Turbo Lister is on your computer!

Note that this procedure first downloads a small setup version of the program that checks your computer for preinstalled files. When that task is finished, Turbo Lister checks back with mothership eBay and automatically downloads any files it needs.

After you've installed the program, you'll see a new icon on your desktop; a little green man juggling magic pixie dust over his head. This is the icon for Turbo Lister. Double-click it and you'll see the Turbo Lister splash screen with eBay's tips of the day. This will pop up every time you open the program, which can get annoying. It doesn't do anything for you and wastes precious seconds of your time. If you want to avoid it, select the check box labeled *Do not show me this screen again*, and then click Start Here. The splash screen will be forever banished.

**Book III
Chapter 4**

**Using eBay's
Turbo Lister**

When the program is open, the first thing you do is to set up a new Turbo Lister file:

1. **Select the Start option from the opening screen, and click Next.**

2. **Fill in your eBay user ID and password, and then click Next.**

   Turbo Lister now wants to connect back to eBay to retrieve your eBay account information.

3. **Make sure your Internet connection is live, and then click the Connect Now button.**

   In a minute or so, a small window opens asking you to give eBay permission to access your eBay data, as shown in Figure 4-1.

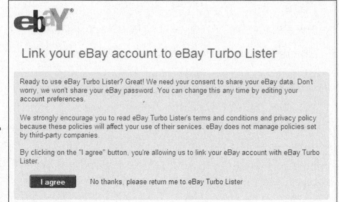

Figure 4-1:
Linking your
account to
Turbo Lister.

4. **Click I Agree, if you do; otherwise click the No Thanks, Please Return Me to eBay Turbo Lister link.**

5. **Click Finish.**

   The program fires up and is ready to list.

Preparing an eBay Listing

Now that you have Turbo Lister at hand, you can prepare hundreds of eBay listings in advance — and launch them with a single mouse click. Or, if you want to start your auctions at a particular date and time, you can select a scheduled item launching format. (More on that later.)

Follow these steps to list an item for sale:

1. **Click the New button (the one with the sunburst symbol) in the upper-left corner.**

   This is where you decide what you wish to create. Most of the information requested is identical to the eBay Sell an Item form.

2. **Select the Create New Item from the drop down menu.**

   A page appears, as shown in Figure 4-2, ready for you to enter your title, subtitle, and lots of other information.

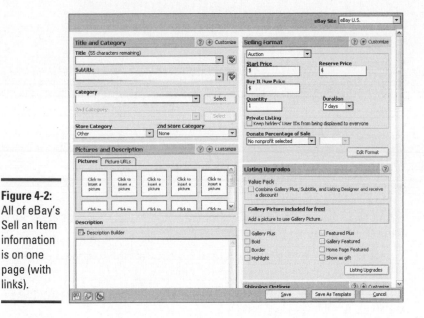

Figure 4-2:
All of eBay's Sell an Item information is on one page (with links).

**Book III
Chapter 4**

**Using eBay's
Turbo Lister**

You can save bunches of time if you write your titles and descriptions in Notepad or Word, at your leisure, before you go into Turbo Lister. You can use your own templates or use the Design View to doll up your text.

3. **In the Title box, enter the title.**

   If you want to use a subtitle, type that as well. Subtitles are handy for adding selling points that accompany your title in search results. (Entering a subtitle for your auction costs an additional $.50.)

4. **Select your category from the Category drop-down list and then click Select.**

You are presented with a screen that lists all eBay categories in a hierarchal format. The main categories are listed with a plus sign next to them. When you find your main category, click the plus sign, and subcategories are displayed, as shown in Figure 4-3. To drop even lower into the world of nether-categories, keep clicking plus signs next to subtopics. You know you've hit the bottom rung of the category ladder when you see only a minus sign.

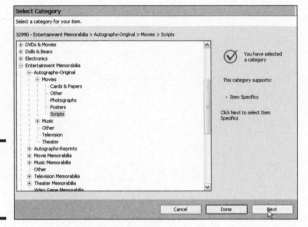

Figure 4-3:
Select the final category.

5. **If you have an eBay Store, select a category for the item in your store from the drop-down list.**

   This area is automatically populated from your eBay Store when eBay updates your Turbo Lister installation.

6. **Continue filling in the blanks and choosing from lists. When you're finished, click Save.**

Importing your existing eBay listings

If you have items listed on eBay (that you've listed through the Sell an Item page or with eBay's relisting feature), you can import those listings into Turbo Lister for future use and relisting. Just click the Synchronize button on the toolbar. In a moment or two, you're presented with a complete tally of everything you have listed for sale on the site. You'll also see (if you've indicated you want this information) sold and unsold items. All these listings automatically import into Turbo Lister, and you can then save your listings as templates or for uploading at a later date.

Designing Your Listing

When it comes to designing your listing, you have several options. eBay's Turbo Lister makes it a snap to design your item listing with a few easy features:

+ **WYSIWYG HTML design form:** When in the Create new item form, this feature is somewhat hidden. By clicking on the words Description Builder, a new window will pop up to reveal the form. You can base your ad on this very easy-to-use design tool. In Design View, it has a toolbar similar to the formatting toolbar in Microsoft Word (see Figure 4-4), so the buttons should be familiar.

Figure 4-4:
The design toolbar.

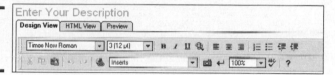

+ **Templates and themes:** I'm sure you've seen eBay listings with nice graphics in the borders. These come from eBay's easy-to-use theme templates, which are listed on the left side of the screen. You may select any of these colorful templates to doll up your listing. Themes make the listing look pretty, but they may draw attention away from the selling strength of your pictures. Remember that your good description and a quality photo will sell your item. Also keep in mind that eBay charges an additional $.10 to use these themes in your listing. You don't have to use any of the themes; just be sure *not* to select the box next to Use Designer (shown in Figure 4-5).

+ **Layout:** These options are available only if you are going to pay for using Designer. You may select from Standard, Photos Left, Photos Right, One Photo Top, Photos Bottom, or Slide Show.

When you use eBay Picture Services, the first picture is free. By using your first free picture, you can have a great-looking header picture at the top of your listing page. Additional pictures are $.15 and a slide show will cost you the princely sum of $.75.

eBay has graciously included a photo-icon tool that allows you to include your own images from the Web without paying eBay their requisite $.15 a picture. Figure 4-5 shows me adding a URL to tell Turbo Lister where my pictures are. There's also a command to insert a hyperlink into your description (see Figure 4-6) so you can have the prospective buyer e-mail you with a click of the mouse.

Book III
Chapter 4

Using eBay's
Turbo Lister

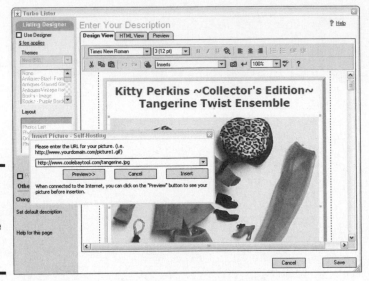

Figure 4-5:
Inserting
photo URL
insert in the
description
area.

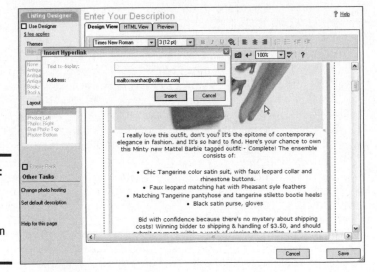

Figure 4-6:
Inserting
an e-mail
link in the
description
area.

✦ **HTML view:** If you have a smattering of HTML knowledge, you may want to edit your listing design in HTML view. You can also insert your hosted images by entering supplementary coding into the HTML view. (See Book V for additional information about coding and inserting your pictures in the description area.) Also, if you have your own predesigned template, you can copy and paste the HTML for the template into the HTML view box.

At any time during the design process, click the Preview tab to see what your listing looks like in an Internet browser.

Be sure to add at least one more picture using eBay's Picture Services so you can use the free header picture. Just click one of the boxes labeled Click Here to Insert Picture, and select any picture on your computer's hard drive. When your picture appears in the Turbo Lister box, click Next.

At the end of the Create New Item form is a Save as Template button. Suppose you've finally designed a simple template that you'd like to use over and over for your auctions. (I have two pet templates — one with a vertical picture and one with a horizontal picture. They may be simple, but I use them again and again.) You can save any listing you've created as a template — and then merely substitute the new text the next time you want to use that template format.

Filling In Item Specifics

Now it's time to get all the little details into your listing, such as the number of days to run the listing and your shipping and payment information. You do all this in the Selling Format side of the page, as shown in Figure 4-7

eBay fills in much of this information for you. To edit the information pertaining to an option, such as Payment Methods or Item Location, click the Edit button in the appropriate area. Clicking the Change button displays a small menu for adding text or changing defaults. After you've made your changes, click OK.

Save time by saving repetitive text as the default. For example, when you want all your listings to have the same information in Payment Instructions or Payment Methods, select the Save for Future Listings check box in the detail area that appears when you click Edit. This saves the information as the default. You can always change the information on a case-by-case basis when listing another item.

After you've filled out all the information in the areas, click Save.

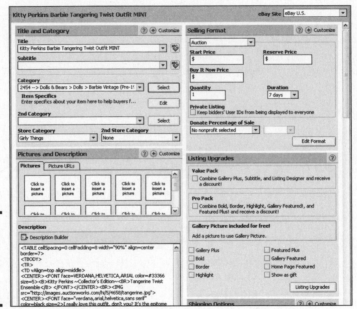

Figure 4-7: Finishing up your listing with the final details.

Organizing Your Listings

After you've put together a few listings, your Turbo Lister item Inventory will look something like Figure 4-8. Just click the link on the left to get there. Note that you can add folders to the folder list to save inventories for different categories of items.

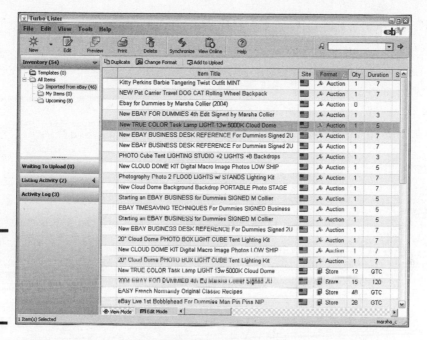

Figure 4-8:
My Turbo
Lister item
Inventory
view.

To create a folder and move items into it, follow these steps:

1. **Open the Turbo Lister program.**

2. **Near the top of the screen, click the arrow just to the right of the *New* button and select the command to create a new folder.**

3. **Give your new folder a name, and then click OK.**

   The folder appears in the folder list on the left side of the screen.

4. **To move a listing to a different folder, highlight the listing and drag it to the folder.**

   To move multiple listings at once, press the Control key or the Shift key and then click the listings.

You can look at all your items, including those in folders, by clicking the Inventory link. To see the contents of a particular folder, just click the folder name.

Uploading Listings to eBay

After you've input a few listings, you may want to upload them so they will become active on eBay. Turbo Lister makes it easy to upload items from your items Inventory on your computer to eBay.

1. **Highlight the listing you want to upload.**

2. **If you want to schedule the listing to upload at a later date or time, select the *Schedule* option (at the top of the screen) and choose a date and time.**

   You're charged an additional $.10 fee for any item you choose to schedule for a Scheduled listing.

3. **Click the Add to Upload button, which is at the top of the item list.**

   Your listing is copied to the listings Waiting to Upload tab, as shown in Figure 4-9.

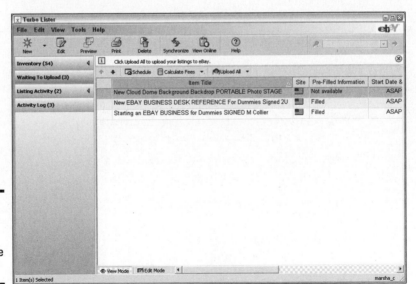

Figure 4-9:
Just waitin'
around is
what they're
doing.

4. **Repeat Steps 1 through 3 to upload additional listings.**

You can define the order in which your listings upload to eBay by high-lighting the item you want to move on the listings Waiting to Upload page and then clicking the up or down arrow at the top of the list.

5. **To send items to eBay to be listed immediately, click Upload All to eBay.**

eBay calculates your fees before posting the listings; you can approve or cancel the upload before the listing goes live on the site.

6. **Approve the upload and your items will be live on the site!**

Chapter 5: Managing Your Sales on My eBay

In This Chapter

✔ **Understanding the All Selling area in My eBay**

✔ **Sending out notices and invoices**

✔ **Keeping track of payments**

✔ **Relisting items**

✔ **Working with bidder-management tools**

For the beginning seller, the My eBay page will ease your way into selling by giving you complete control of your auctions. When you start running more listings than you can handle comfortably with My eBay, you may want to consider upgrading your My eBay page to Selling Manager.

This chapter explains how you can get the most out of the My eBay: All Selling page, and how it can benefit your business.

Managing Your All Selling Area

eBay provides some smooth management tools on your My eBay, All Selling summary page. You can track items you currently have up for sale and items you've sold. The All Selling page is a quick way to get a snapshot of the dollar value of your auctions as they proceed. Although this page isn't as good for marketing information (detailed counters are best — see Book VIII), it is a pretty good way to tell at a glance how your items are faring.

The All Selling home page, which is shown in Figure 5-1, has several areas:

✦ **Scheduled:** If you've scheduled listings to begin at a later time, they're listed here.

✦ **Active Selling:** In the middle of the page, these give you a clear idea of what is going on with your eBay sales.

✦ **Sold:** Further down, you'll see the list of items you've (thankfully) sold.

✦ **Unsold:** Here is the netherworld of unsold items. It's time to relist, sell similar, or put them in your store. (Find out how in the section "Relisting Items without Extra Work," later in this chapter.) If you continue to scroll waaaay down the page, you'll see far too much information. To avoid all that scrolling, click the links on the left side of the page to go to each individual area on its own page.

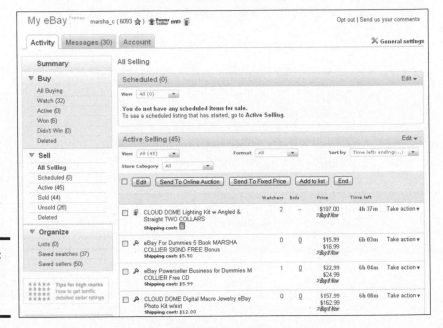

Figure 5-1: All Selling hub at My eBay.

---

eBay's Handy Icons

On the My eBay page, eBay uses a very colorful and handy group of icons to signify tasks to be accomplished or to indicate certain actions. Take a look at the icons and what they stand for:

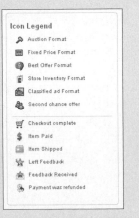

eBay's All Selling area allows you to customize various pages. Also, hidden features allow you to perform "paperwork" tasks. These features are available in different areas, so before I tell you what each page can do, you should be familiar with the pages.

Dealing with the My eBay: Active Selling Page

With Active selling page, shown in Figure 5-2, you can keep an eye on your store's item listings, your fixed-price sales, and the progress of your auctions.

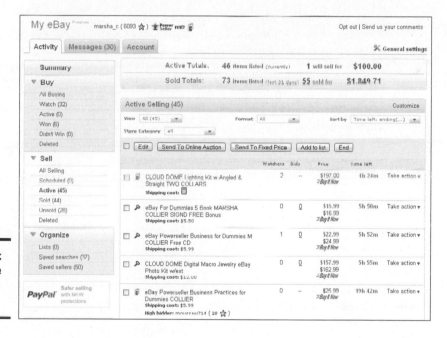

Figure 5-2: The Active Selling page.

The general layout

At the top of the page, you'll see a tote board that gives you an idea of your sales during the past 31 days. eBay also shows the total items currently up for sale. The total dollar amount of the items that have been bid on appears with these totals. At the left side of each listing, eBay has a column for icons.

Depending on how you customize the view (which I describe in the next section), you can see how many bids your auctions have, whether your reserves have been met, and how much time remains before the auction closes. By clicking an auction title, you can visit the auction to make sure your pictures are appearing or to check your counter.

Don't be frustrated if you don't have a ton of bids. Many, many people watch auctions and don't bid until the last minute, so you may not see a lot of bidding activity on your page. Be sure to customize your page and select the # of Watchers option so you can get a grip on how many people are interested in your item.

Customizing your display

To customize what you see when you go to your My eBay Page, just click the *General Settings* link. Some of us prefer the Summary page to show up first, and others prefer to see the Active Selling page. It's up to you. Click the link in the upper right to set your options. After you click it, you see the screen shown in Figure 5-3.

Optionally, you can select whether or not you want the item ID, listed-on date, picture, and so on to appear alongside the item on the page. Also, if you scroll to the bottom of the listing page, you'll see a tool that will allow you to indicate the number of items you would like to view per page. You can choose from 10 (default), 25, 50, 75, 100 (and if you love to scroll) 200 items per page. Otherwise you'll click the links that can take you to the next page of your listings.

Figure 5-3:
Customizing
your Active
Selling
page.

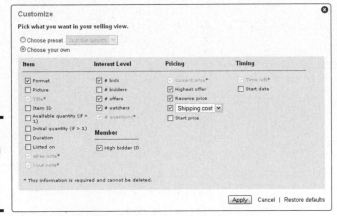

Filtering your view

By clicking on the Format drop-down box (as in Figure 5-4) you can segregate the display. Rather than seeing a listing of All (which is the default), you can sort your items to get a shorter page to view. You can choose

✦ Auction Only

✦ Fixed Price Only

 ✦ Store Inventory Only

 ✦ Classified Ads Only

 ✦ Best Offer Only

Figure 5-4:
Selecting
the format
of items
shown on
the Active
Selling
page.

Aside from selecting the format of the items you'd like to see you can
perform several actions via the drop-down menus at the top of the Active
Selling page:

 ✦ **View:** You can further filter the listings you see. To select only items
   with bids, open offers (on the Best Offer format), items without bids, or
   Reserve not met.

 ✦ **Store Category:** If you have an eBay Store, you can view the listings by
   your own named store categories.

 ✦ **Sort By:** As in any easy Search, you can choose to see those listings with
   Time left: Ending Soonest, Newly Listed, or sort by Price; lowest first or
   highest first.

If you have an eBay Store, you're entitled to use Selling Manager — for *free*
— which is quantum leaps better than using the All Selling page. The only
caveat is that eBay expects you to request to use it. To do so, choose
Sell⇨Seller Tools in the eBay navigation bar. On the resulting page, you can
sign up for Selling Manager, and the sign-up page will reflect your no-charge
status.

Taking action when necessary

Make sure you pay attention to the Action drop-down list that appears at
the end of each listing (refer to Figure 5-2). This menu has powerful menu
options that allow you to do the following:

 ✦ **Sell Similar:** List an item similar to the one on your page.

 ✦ **Search in Want It Now:** Clicking here takes you to the Want It Now area
   that relates to the category your item is listed in. I'm not sure why you
   would ever want to do this.

✦ **Revise:** Change a listing that has no bids.

✦ **Add to Description:** Add text to your listing's description *after* the listing has bids.

✦ **End Item:** When the dog plays tug-of-war with your item, you can end the listing.

✦ **Add note:** If you want to add a notation (which only you can see and only on this page), select the check box to the left of the item and then click the Add Note button at the top of the listings. Just type your comment on the page that appears and click Save.

Auctions that appear in green have received one or more bids (and met any reserves you've set). Auctions in red haven't received any bids or the reserve price hasn't been met. Dutch auctions aren't color-coded and appear in black.

Getting Excited About the My eBay: Sold Page

Clicking the *Sold* link (on the left side of the page in the Summary box under the *Sell* header) takes you to a list of all the items you've sold.

The Sold page keeps your sales in a concise place, as shown in Figure 5-5. I use it in lieu of fancy auction management software. If you're selling hundreds of items, your list will probably be too long to monitor individual auctions — but you can view the total current price of the items that will sell.

Figure 5-5:
The Sold
Items page
in My eBay.

The Sold items page has the following features, which I'm sure you'll find helpful in completing your transactions:

✦ **Check box:** Select a check box to perform a task on one or more of the items, such as remove from the list, add a note, or print a shipping label.

✦ **Buyer's user ID and feedback rating:** The eBay ID of the winner of the sale. Click it to go to the user's Member Profile, where you can use eBay's e-mail sever to contact the buyer (or just use the drop-down menu to Contact Buyer). (You can also customize this area to display the buyer's e-mail address instead of his or her user ID for identification.)

✦ **Quantity:** If the sale was for multiple items, the number of items is displayed here.

✦ **Item title:** A direct link to the auction. You can click this link to check on your auction and see the other bidders, should you want to make a second chance offer.

✦ **Item ID number:** An optional setting that I don't use, it's the listing number for your records.

✦ **Sale price:** The final selling price for your item.

✦ **Total price:** The final selling price plus the shipping amount.

✦ **Sale date:** Keep an eye on the end date so you can be sure you get your payment as agreed.

✦ **Action:** Here's where you find a hidden drop-down list that works with the icons to the right, offering links to various actions you can take:

 • **Mark as paid:** If the customer hasn't paid using PayPal, you can indicate the method of payment (after you receive it).

 • **View payment status:** See a copy of the payment receipt (if the buyer paid using PayPal) or see a notation you inserted regarding other payment methods.

 • **Print shipping label:** You can print a shipping label from here. See Book VII for more professional options.

 • **Leave feedback:** Leave feedback with a single click once you've heard that the item arrived safely and your customer is happy.

 • **Mark shipped:** After you've shipped the item, click here to indicate that it's on the way.

 • **Second chance offer:** Click here to make a second chance offer to one of your underbidders if you have multiple items for sale.

 • **Sell similar:** When you want to list a similar item (or relist a sold one) you can do it quickly here.

 • **Relist:** Here you can relist your item on the site.

TIP

Not all the action links appear on every item; they appear based on the progress of the item in the sales process.

✦ **Icons:** My eBay has several icons that appear dimmed until you perform an action with the Action command. You may also click the icons at the top of the list to sort your listings by auctions completed, although most sellers prefer to keep the listings in the default chronological order.

  • **Shopping cart:** The buyer has completed checkout (supplying a shipping address and a planned payment method).

  • **Dollar sign:** The buyer has paid using PayPal, or you've noted that the buyer has paid with a different form of payment (such as a money order or a personal check) on the drop-down list within the sale record.

  • **Shipping box:** You've indicated that the item has shipped.

  • **Star with Pen:** You've left feedback for the buyer.

  • **Star in an envelope:** The buyer has left you feedback. A plus sign (+) indicates a positive comment, and a minus sign (−) indicates a negative comment.

Trying Again with the My eBay: Unsold Page

The Unsold page, shown in Figure 5-6 indicates the items that didn't sell. To get to that area, you can scroll way down the page or click the Unsold link in the Summary sidebar under the Sell header (on the left side of the page).

Figure 5-6:
Why not give your item another chance to sell?

The Take Action drop-down list beside each item allows you to

✦ **Relist,** so that you can get a listing credit for the first run of the item if it sells the second time.

+ **Sell Similar,** if the item hasn't sold after two listings. This option starts the cycle in eBay's computer fresh as new.

+ **Relist as Store Inventory,** if you have an eBay store.

+ **Add to List,** for items that you for some unknown reason would like to add to a list. You can use eBay's suggestions for Wish List, Research, or Gift List. You can also make up your own.

Notifying Winners and Sending Invoices

Thank goodness — somebody submitted a winning bid on one of your items in an auction. It's a good feeling. When I get those end-of-transaction e-mails from eBay, I whisper a silent *yeah!* Then I hold my breath to see whether the buyer will go directly to PayPal and make the payment. Usually, that's what happens. More and more buyers are getting savvy and understand about paying immediately after winning an item.

New buyers and those who buy or win multiple items from you (my favorite kind of buyer!) usually wait to hear from you regarding payment and shipping. Many newbies feel more comfortable hearing from you and knowing who they're doing business with. Also, in the case of multiple purchases, you have to recalculate the postage. The sooner you contact the buyer, the sooner you'll get your payment.

Notifying winners

eBay sends out an end-of-transaction e-mail to both the buyer and the seller. The e-mail is informative to the seller and a welcome e-mail for the buyer.

Figure 5-7 shows you a typical, "yippee, you won" e-mail. It's brightly colored and joyful, probably designed to evoke some strong level of excitement in the buyer.

Both e-mails have similar information; the e-mail to the buyer has a Pay Now button, as shown in the figure. The seller's e-mail has a link to create an invoice to send the buyer. Either of these linked forms includes:

+ Item title and number.

+ The final bid or Buy It Now price.

+ Quantity.

+ Seller or buyer's user ID and e-mail address.

+ Ship-to ZIP code.

+ A link to update your ZIP code.

+ A link for viewing the item. This link is good for up to 90 days. Note that this is the only place you get this link, and unless you subscribe to eBay's Selling Manager, you'd better keep hold of it. Sold items remain on your My eBay page for 60 days, but the items disappear from the eBay search engine within 2 weeks.

+ A buyer's link to complete checkout to let the seller know how the buyer intends to pay.

+ Links to e-Bay help and feedback.

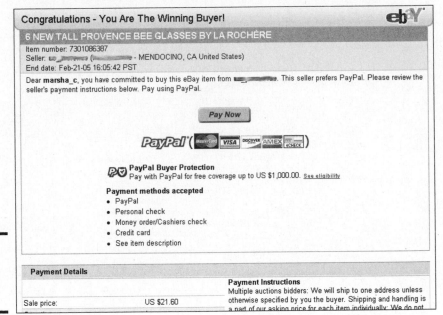

Figure 5-7:
Lucky you!
You're a
winner!

That's a lot of information, and I'll bet the average user just glances over it and either deletes it (bad idea) or files it in a special folder in his or her e-mail program.

If you think eBay's notification is good enough, it's time to rethink your customer service policy. An e-mail to the buyer at this point is important. Customer contact is the key to a good transaction. If the buyer sprints directly to PayPal and sends you some money to pay for a purchase, a special e-mail from you is required. Thank the buyer for the payment and mention when the item will ship, as detailed in the next section, "Thanking them kindly."

Thanking them kindly

Now's the time to let the customer know just how darned tickled you are that this person spent hard-earned money with you. Your thank-you e-mail is a quasi invoice and informational note. What should go in it? Well, try to keep in mind what your mother said — always say "please" and "thank you." After thanking the buyer for purchasing your goods, be sure to cover the following points (this is where the "please" part comes in):

✦ **Item name:** You don't want the buyer to forget what was purchased.

✦ **Payment terms:** Let the buyer know what forms of payment you accept and how long you intend to wait for your money.

✦ **Payment address:** Be sure to tell the buyer where you want the payment sent (should the item be from a category that permits alternate forms of payment).

✦ **PayPal button:** Inserting a PayPal button in your e-mail is a snap and may pay off in some rapid payments; see Book II, Chapter 4 for instructions.

✦ **Return policy:** Will you accept returns? Under what circumstances? It's okay if you don't accept returns, but be sure that you had that information in your item description *before* the purchase was made.

✦ **Reminder to print the e-mail and enclose it with payment:** Veteran eBay sellers can tell you stories about the money order that arrived with no item number, no return address, and no e-mail address — basically no clue as to what the payment was for.

✦ **Store pitch:** If you have an eBay store, mention it here. If not, just be sure to tell buyers that you're happy to have them as customers and you look forward to serving them again.

✦ **Feedback pitch:** Most PowerSellers that I know include a small pitch at the closing of the e-mail for leaving feedback about you on eBay. Remind the customers to e-mail you immediately if there's a problem when the order arrives. Stress how you want them to be happy with their purchases. That may stave off a knee-jerk negative that beginners tend to leave when an item arrives cracked. (They shoulda bought insurance — it helps to require it on fragile items.)

That ought to do it. Including this information will make your newbie buyer or old-time veteran feel at home doing business with you.

Thanks for the money!

Sometimes you have to beg for payment. On the other hand, when some blessed buyer pays immediately through PayPal, it's time to show your gratitude by sending a "thanks for the money" e-mail. The e-mail can be short and sweet and to the point. Be sure to

✦ Thank the customer for the purchase and swift payment.

✦ Let the customer know when the item will ship.

✦ Let the customer know when feedback will be left. I leave feedback only when the buyer has received the item and is happy with the transaction.

Tracking Payments in All Selling

You've created a winning ad, run a successful auction or sale, notified the winner, and sent off an invoice. Now it's time for the big payoff: getting the money in hand for your item. eBay and PayPal work in concert to offer several tools to notify you when a payment is made.

Once again, the Sold items area of My eBay comes to the rescue. As if by magic, every time one of your buyers makes a payment through the PayPal service, your My eBay page indicates that the item has been paid by changing the dollar-sign icon from dimmed to solid. Take a look back at Figure 5-5, and note the items that have been paid using PayPal.

PayPal also sends you a payment received e-mail — but I have a few caveats about using this form of notification.

If you do not receive any form of notification of a payment received from a buyer, check your PayPal account before going through the trouble of sending a nonpaying bidder notice. A new eBay buyer may have misspelled your e-mail address or applied the payment to an incorrect item number. If this is the case, you'll have to e-mail the buyer and ask the person to cancel any payment made and pay for the item with the correct item number and your correct e-mail address.

To confirm the information about a payment shown on the Sold page of My eBay, follow these steps:

1. **Click the drop-down list next to the item's listing, and select the View Order Details option.**

   The Order Details page appears, as shown in Figure 5-8.

2. **For further information, click the View PayPal payment link, at the top of the page.**

3. **Sign into PayPal with your password and click Continue.**

   The PayPal Web site's payment-details screen appears, giving you complete information on the purchase.

After you've finished viewing this page, you may click the Return to Log button at the bottom of the page to go to your account history page. From here, you can transfer the money to your bank account.

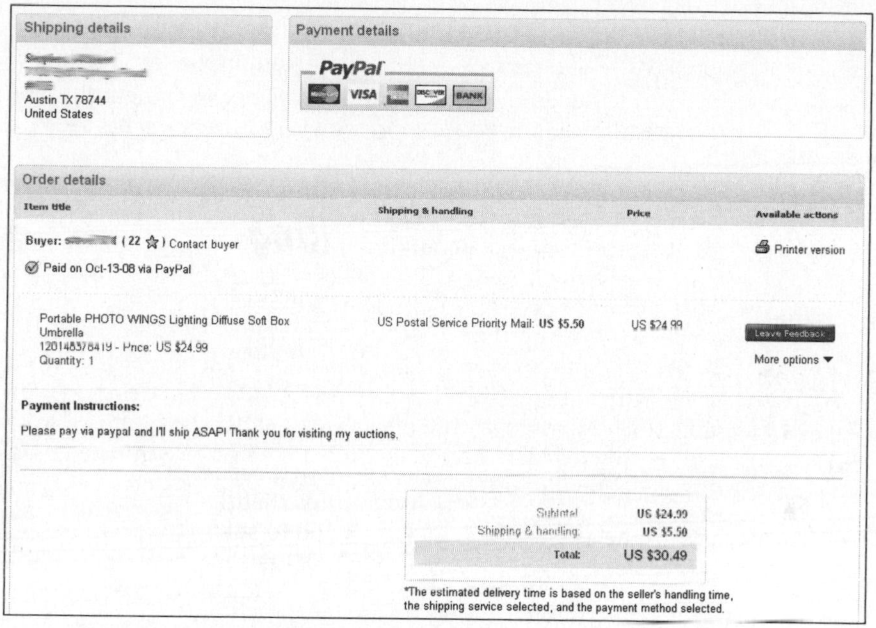

Shipping details

Austin TX 78744
United States

Payment details

PayPal

VISA BANK

Order details

Item title	Shipping & handling	Price	Available actions
Buyer: ▓▓▓▓▓ (22 ☆) Contact buyer			🖨 Printer version
☑ Paid on Oct-13-08 via PayPal			
Portable PHOTO WINGS Lighting Diffuse Soft Box Umbrella 120148378419 - Price: US $24.99 Quantity: 1	US Postal Service Priority Mail: US $5.50	US $24.99	Leave Feedback More options ▼

Payment Instructions:

Please pay via paypal and I'll ship ASAP! Thank you for visiting my auctions.

Subtotal	US $24.99
Shipping & handling:	US $5.50
Total:	**US $30.49**

*The estimated delivery time is based on the seller's handling time, the shipping service selected, and the payment method selected.

Figure 5-8:
The eBay Order Details page.

If you don't want to do any other business using your PayPal account, click the Back to eBay link.

Relisting Items without Extra Work

One of the most efficient ways to run an eBay business is to stock the same item in quantity. After getting some eBay experience under your belt, you're bound to find several items that you're comfortable selling. And if you follow my suggestions in Book IV, you'll buy multiples (dozens? cases? pallets?) of the items at a seriously discounted price. When you have all these items lying around the garage, your goal is to get them into buyers' hands at a profit.

In Book VIII, I talk about opening an eBay store. But in addition to your own store, you must be running auctions on the eBay site. Why? Auctions are the key to drawing buyers into your store. Stores are not only added potential sales but a distinct marketing tool for your personal eBay brand.

I know several sellers who bought items in such bulk that they're stocked with the item to sell once a week for the next few years! That's a good thing only if the product is a staple item that will always have a market on eBay.

Relisting after a sale

Yeah! Your space-age can opener with a built-in DVD player sold! Since you have three dozen more to sell, the quicker you can get that item back up on the site, the sooner you'll connect with the next customer.

When bidders lose an auction on eBay, one of the first things they do is search for somebody offering the same item. The sooner you get an item relisted, the sooner a disappointed underbidder will find your listing. Of course, relisting the item also makes it available to other interested bidders who may not have bid on the item before.

When you offer an item for bidding and it reaches well beyond your target price, why not offer another one with a Buy It Now option? True, this may slow (or possibly end) further bidding on the first item, but if you've exceeded your target price and folks are hot for your item, sell it to them now! That kind of initiative is what eBay is all about.

If at first you don't succeed

Boo! Your Dansk Maribo dinner plate didn't sell. Don't take it personally. It's not that someone out there doesn't love you. It doesn't mean your merchandise is trash. It's just that this particular week, no one was looking for Maribo plates (go figure).

Often eBay shoppers shop with no discernable pattern. No one may want your item at a certain price one week, and then you may sell five or six the next week. It happens to me all the time.

When relisting, you often need to make adjustments. Perhaps the keywords in your title aren't drawing people to your listing. To help you figure out whether the problem is you or the market, search for other, similar items to see whether anyone is buying. If there's just no bidding activity (perhaps you're selling bikinis in January?), perhaps that item needs to be retired from eBay for a while.

Consider some other variables. Are other items selling on the site with a lower starting price? If you can comfortably lower your price, do so. If not, wait until other sellers run out of the item. Then put yours up for auction — you may just get more bidding action if you're one of the few sellers offering the same item.

I have quite a few items that I purchased by the case — right along with a bunch of other eBay sellers. They desperately dumped theirs on the site, without paying any attention to the competition. I waited and got my target price for the item the following season.

eBay is a supply and demand marketplace. If the supply exceeds the demand, prices go down. If you have an item that sells as fast as you can list it, prices go up.

Okay, time to relist (rather Sell Similar)

eBay gives you many ways to relist an item. Because this chapter features My eBay, I'll cover that method here. When you upgrade to Selling Manager, the procedure is a bit different; visit Book VIII, Chapter 1 for details.

Figure 5-9 shows the seller's version of a sold item (only the seller sees this when he or she is signed in), which (at the very bottom of the page) includes Sell One Like This link. Rather than go to each item's page to relist, however, get off the auction page by clicking the Track Your Items in My eBay link and go to your My eBay page. The relisting process will be much faster.

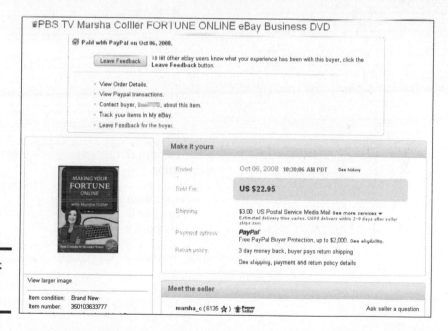

Figure 5-9: Yeah! My item sold!

Book III Chapter 5

Managing Your Sales on My eBay

Relist is best used for unsold items, so you might benefit from a listing fee refund if your item sells a second time. The Sell Similar process is used for sold items because it starts a new item cycle with eBay — if the item doesn't sell, you can relist it for the unsold-item refund.

To sell a similar item, from the Sold page on My eBay, click the drop-down list next to the listing and select the Sell Similar option. Now the review step of the Sell an Item form appears. You can make any changes you want — or not!

You can go to the All Selling: Unsold items page of My eBay to relist unsold items for a possible listing fee credit (in the case of auctions) in the same fashion (see Figure 5-10).

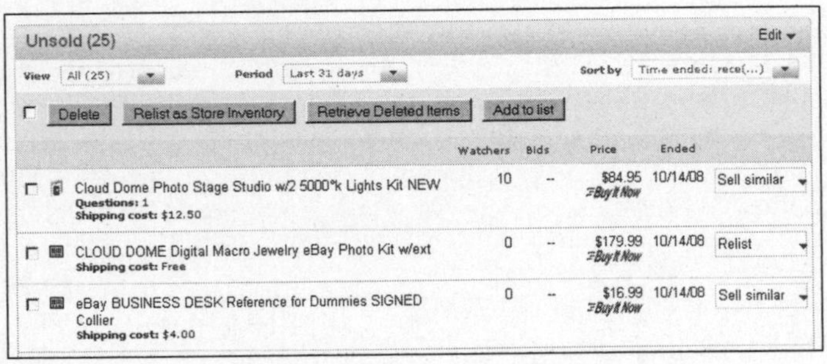

Figure 5-10:
Selling
similar from
Unsold
Items.

eBay Bidder-Management Tools

Most eBay users don't know the extent of eBay's seller-specific services. And sometimes sellers are so involved with their auctions that they don't take the time to find out about new helper tools. So I've gone deep into the eBay pond to dig up a few excellent tools to help you with your online business. Even if you've used some of these before, it might be time to revisit them because eBay has implemented quite a few changes during the past year.

Canceling bids

Did you know that you don't have to accept bids from just anyone? Although many people include notices in their auction descriptions attempting to qualify bidders ahead of time, this doesn't always prevent them from bidding on your auction. Alas, part of the business is watching your bidders. With bidder-management tools, you can save yourself a good deal of grief.

You could have any number of reasons for wanting to cancel someone's bid. Here are a few more legitimate reasons for canceling a bid:

✦ The bidder contacts you to back out of the bid; choosing to be a nice guy, you let him or her out of the deal.

✦ Your bidder has several negative feedbacks and hasn't gone through with other transactions that he or she has won.

✦ You're unable to verify the bidder's identity through e-mail or the phone.

✦ You need to cancel the auction.

eBay preferences settings

Many eBay sellers bemoan the fact that international buyers bid on their items, when the items clearly state that they do not ship internationally. Also, they get upset when a bidder with minus-level feedback wins an item.

Quit whining and do something about it! On your My eBay➪My Account➪Site Preferences page, you can set defaults that will affect your bidders. On this page, scroll to Site Preferences: Buyer Requirements.

Click the Edit link to change your preferences. On the Buyer Requirements page (see the figure), you may indicate whom you do not want to be permitted to bid on your items. If any of your bidders fall into that category and attempt to bid, they will see a notice saying they are unable to bid.

In the case of international buyers, I have found that they e-mail me to ask me to ship to them. I check their feedback, and if it's clear to me that they know the ropes, I can put their user ID on my Blocked Bidder Exception list and they're free to win my item.

Buyer Requirements

Buyer requirements can help you reduce your exposure to buyers who might make transactions more difficult or expensive.

To allow specific eBay members to bid on or purchase your items regardless of any requirement(s) you select, add them to your buyer requirements exemption list

Select requirements

⚐ **Important:** Select buyer requirements carefully - they may reduce your selling success. The requirement(s) you select will be applied to your current and future listings, except as noted. eBay encourages you to learn more by visiting the Buyer Requirements Help page.

Buyers without a PayPal account
☐ Block buyers who don't have a PayPal account. (Note: This block **only** applies to future listings and can be disabled per item on the Sell Your Item form.)
This requirement can help you avoid Unpaid Items, as PayPal account holders have up to an 80% lower Unpaid Item rate.

Buyers with Unpaid Item strikes
☑ Block bidders and buyers who have received [2 ▼] Unpaid Item strike(s) within [1 ▼] month(s)
This requirement can help you avoid bidders and buyers with a history of not paying for the items they have agreed to purchase.

Buyers in countries to which I don't ship
☑ Block buyers who are registered in countries to which I don't ship.
This requirement can help you avoid buyers who agree to purchase your items without realizing you don't ship to their location.

Buyers with policy violation reports
☑ Block buyers who have [4 ▼] Policy violation report(s) within [1 ▼] month(s)
This requirement can help you block buyers who have been reported to have violated eBay policies.

Buyers with a negative feedback score
☑ Block buyers who have a feedback score of [-1 ▼] or lower.
This requirement can help you avoid buyers who have received more negative than positive feedback from other eBay members bidding on your item.

Buyers who may bid on several of my items and not pay for them
☑ Block buyers who are currently winning or have bought [2 ▼] of my items in the last 10 days.
  ☑ Only apply this block to buyers who have a feedback score of [5 ▼] or lower.
Consider selecting this requirement if you are selling expensive items and don't want to sell over a certain number to any single buyer. Learn more about how this requirement works.

Book III Chapter 5

Managing Your Sales on My eBay

When you plan to cancel someone's bid, you should first e-mail that person and clearly explain why you're doing so. Your bid cancelation appears in the auction's bidding history and becomes part of the auction's official record. For that reason, I recommend that you leave a concise, unemotional, one-line explanation on the cancelation form as to why you've canceled the bid.

To get to the bid cancelation form, start on the eBay Site Map (the link at the right hand side of the page – just below the navigation bar, Under the Selling activities head, find the link to Cancel Bids on your listing. You'll now be able to access the bid-cancelation form. You can get to the cancelation form directly by typing the following in your browser:

```
http://offer.ebay.com/ws/eBayISAPI.dll?CancelBidShow
```

Ending your listing early

You may decide to end a listing early for any number of reasons. If any bids are on your auction before ending it, you are duty-bound to sell to the highest bidder. So before ending an auction early, it's polite to e-mail everyone in your bidder list, explaining why you're canceling bids and closing the auction. If an egregious error in the item's description is forcing you to take this action, let your bidders know whether you're planning to relist the item with the correct information.

After you've e-mailed all the bidders, you must then cancel their bids by using the bid cancelation form; for the link to this form, see the preceding section "Canceling bids."

When ending a listing that has bids, the seller has the option of canceling all bids or leaving the bids, thus making the high bidder the winner of the closed listing.

To end a listing, use the drop-down list next to the listing on the Active Selling page. Select the drop-down menu next to the item and click the *End Item* link to end your listing. You can also go directly to

```
http://cgi3.ebay.com/aw-cgi/eBayISAPI.dll?EndingMyAuction
```

Following are some legitimate reasons for ending your sale:

✦ **You no longer want to sell the item.** Your account may be subject to a nonselling seller warning unless you have a good reason.

✦ **An error occurred in the minimum bid or reserve amount.** Perhaps your spouse really loves that lamp and said you'd better get some good money for it, but you started the auction at $1.00 with no reserve.

✦ **The listing has a major error in it.** Maybe you misspelled a critical keyword in the title.

✦ **The item was somehow lost or broken.** Your dog ate it?

I don't recommend canceling an auction unless you absolutely have to because it's just bad business. People rely on your auctions being up for the stated amount of time. They may be planning to bid at the last minute, or they may just want to watch the action for a while. Also, if you have bids on the item, you may be in violation of one of eBay's policies and be branded as a nonselling seller.

Blocking buyers

If you don't want certain buyers bidding on your auctions, you can remove their capability to do so. Setting up a list of bidders that you don't want to do business with is legal on eBay. If someone that you've blocked tries to bid on your auction, the bid won't go through. A message will be displayed notifying the bidder that he or she can't bid on the listing and should contact the seller for more information.

You can block as many as 1000 users from bidding on your auctions. However, I recommend that you use this option only when absolutely necessary. Situations — and people — change, and it's best to try to clear up problems with particular bidders.

You can Block Buyers from the Managing Bidders and Buyers page, located at

`http://pages.ebay.com/help/sell/manage_bidders_ov.html`

You can reinstate a bidder at any time by going to the Buyer Blocking box at

`http://cgi1.ebay.com/ws/eBayISAPI.dll?bidderblocklogin`

and deleting the bidder's user ID.

Chapter 6: Using PayPal to Organize Your Sales

In This Chapter

✓ Getting the PayPal overview

✓ Registering as a seller

✓ Introducing the auction and merchant tools

✓ Downloading reports

✓ Using the Outlook Payment Request Wizard tools

PayPal is the largest of the online person-to-person payment services. Thankfully, eBay had the presence of mind to acquire this previously independent service, so it is now the *de facto* standard for making payments on eBay.

PayPal Particulars

PayPal (see Figure 6-1) is a reliable payment service that allows buyers to safely click and pay with a credit card, eCheck, or PayPal balance, directly from eBay, after they've won an auction or made a purchase. It's conveniently integrated into all eBay transactions, and if your auction uses the Buy It Now or Smart Logo feature, you can have buyers immediately pay for their purchases with PayPal payments.

You must register a special account to accept PayPal payments and you must have a premier- or business-level account to accept credit-card payments. Buyers may join when they win their first auctions and want to pay with PayPal, or they can go to www.PayPal.com and sign up. The story is slightly different for the seller. For convenience, you should set up your PayPal account before you choose to accept PayPal in your auctions or sales.

Figure 6-1:
The PayPal
home page,
money
central for
eBay buyers
and sellers.

Here are more than a few particulars about PayPal accounts:

✦ **eBay sales payments are deposited into your PayPal account.** Choose
one of several ways to get your money:

• Have the money electronically transferred directly into your registered checking account.

• Receive payment by check (PayPal charges $1.50 for the check).

• Keep the money in your PayPal account for making payments to
other sellers.

• Withdraw the cash from an ATM with a PayPal debit card.

• Use the PayPal debit card and get 1.5% cash back on purchases
made with the card.

• Shop online with a virtual MasterCard debit card that carries your
balance to any Web site that accepts MasterCard.

✦ **PayPal has its own feedback system, the Seller Reputation number.**
The number after a user's name reflects the number of unique PayPal-
verified users with which the user has conducted business. The higher
the number, the more likely the user is experienced and trustworthy.
Clicking the number displays a report like the one shown in Figure 6-2.

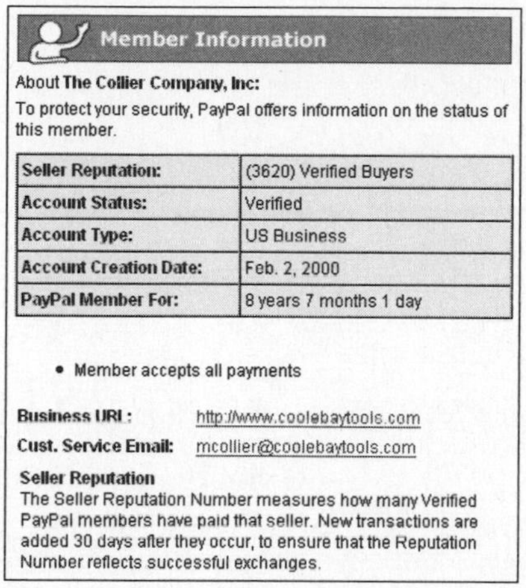

Member Information

About **The Collier Company, Inc:**

To protect your security, PayPal offers information on the status of this member.

Seller Reputation:	(3620) Verified Buyers
Account Status:	Verified
Account Type:	US Business
Account Creation Date:	Feb. 2, 2000
PayPal Member For:	8 years 7 months 1 day

• Member accepts all payments

Business URL :	http://www.coolebaytools.com
Cust. Service Email:	mcollier@coolebaytools.com

Seller Reputation
The Seller Reputation Number measures how many Verified PayPal members have paid that seller. New transactions are added 30 days after they occur, to ensure that the Reputation Number reflects successful exchanges.

Figure 6-2:
My PayPal Member Information box.

✦ **As a seller with a premier or business account, you can choose to accept or deny a payment without a confirmed address.** A confirmed address means that the ship-to address indicated by the buyer is the same as the billing address on the credit card the buyer chose to register with PayPal. On the Accept or Deny page, information about the buyer is shown — including verification status, account-creation date, and participation number.

✦ **PayPal assesses your account $10 for any chargeback.** The fee is waived if you've fulfilled the requirements in the PayPal seller-protection policy.

To specify whether you want to accept a credit card payment from a buyer without a confirmed address, log on, go to your account, and then click the Profile tab. Next, scroll down the Selling Preferences area and click Payment Receiving Preferences. At the top of the page that's displayed, you have the option of choosing to accept, not accept, or decide on a case-by-case basis payments from users without confirmed addresses.

✦ **The PayPal seller protection policy protects you against chargebacks, unauthorized card use, and nonshipments.** To comply with this policy, you must do the following:

• **Have a verified business or premier account:** Allow PayPal to confirm with your bank that your checking account and address are your own.

• **Keep proof of shipping that can be tracked online:** Here's where those delivery confirmation things really come in handy. You can also input your tracking or delivery confirmation numbers on the PayPal site, and they will send an e-mail to the buyer with that number.

- Require signature receipt on items valued at more than $250.00.

- **Ship tangible goods:** PayPal doesn't cover goods transmitted electronically.

- **Accept only single payments from a single account:** Don't let a buyer try to pay portions of a purchase from different e-mail address accounts. Someone who's trying to pay using several accounts may be attempting to defraud you.

One of the truly brilliant features of PayPal is that you can download your sales history and your deposit history to your computer. Although they also offer files that integrate with QuickBooks (more on QuickBooks in Book IX), the standard downloads are feature-rich. Rather than importing just sales figures, you see each and every detail of your transaction — dates, names, addresses, phone numbers, amounts, and more. Even fees and taxes (if you charge sales tax) are broken down separately, making your bookkeeping a breeze. The download imports into Microsoft Works (which comes on almost every new computer) and Excel. Downloading your history will help you calculate income taxes and sales taxes, reconcile your accounts, predict sales trends, calculate total revenues, and perform other financial reporting tasks. It will also give you an excellent customer database.

The Deposits download will give you detailed information for all the deposits that you receive: payments, transaction and deposit fees, refunds, rebates, and any adjustments made to your account. To find out more about downloading, check out Book II, Chapter 4.

Registering with PayPal

If you aren't registered with PayPal yet (what's holding you up?), you'll find a convenient link on your My eBay: All Selling page in the Selling links area. To register, just click the PayPal link. The PayPal Seller Overview page appears, as shown in Figure 6-3. Click the Sign Up button, and you arrive at the beginning of the PayPal registration process. Tell them what country you're from, fill in the basic required information, and you're in.

The convenience of PayPal's integration with eBay shines when you put the Smart Logo option in your auctions. Winners just click a link that pops up on your auction page immediately after the auction closes. When you list auctions, you preset the shipping and handling charges that appear in the shipping box at the bottom of the page. When winners click the Pay Now button (see Figure 6-4), they're taken directly to a payment page set up with your information. It's just as easy as when they purchase something through Buy It Now (as shown in Figure 6-5).

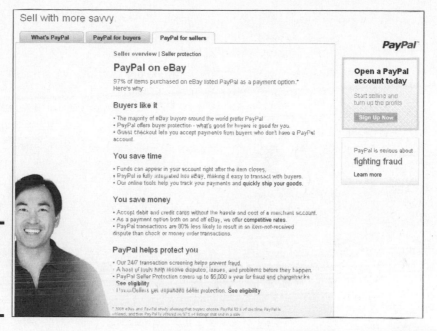

Figure 6-3:
Begin your
PayPal
registration
here.

Figure 6-4:
The Pay
Now button
appears
after an
auction is
won.

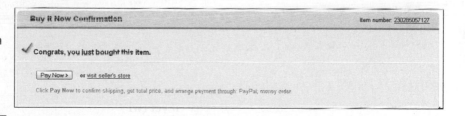

If the buyer doesn't pay immediately, then he or she will see a Pay Now button on the listing's page when returning to the listing to pay. It will be there until the buyer pays.

The buyer can add optional insurance or combine other items, as shown in Figure 6-6. When the final total amount is correct, the buyer is brought to PayPal to pay for the item. The payment is deposited in your PayPal account and held until you choose how you want to withdraw it.

Figure 6-5:
The listing page with the Pay Now button.

Figure 6-6:
Item consolidation when paying.

PayPal accepts payments from more than 45 countries. For a current list of countries from which PayPal accepts payments, sign on to your PayPal account and go to the following:

```
www.paypal.com/us/cgi-bin/webscr?cmd=_display-approved-
    signup-countries
```

It's a lovely Web page, and you get to see all the country's flags.

Because credit-card and identity theft is so prevalent on the Internet — and such an expensive burden to e-commerce — PayPal uses the extra security measure provided by Visa and MasterCard called CVV2. This system requires you to input the 3 additional numbers (immediately following the regular 16-digit number) from the back of your credit card. Because merchants aren't allowed to store these numbers, but merely use them for security and verification purposes, the numbers are presumably protected from hackers. However, in the unlikely event that your credit card doesn't have these numbers yet, PayPal still allows you to use your card by verifying it through a procedure known as *random charge*. PayPal charges about $1 to your card and asks you to disclose the PIN number printed on your statement. Then PayPal knows that you control the card and didn't steal it.

Withdraw your funds from the PayPal account on a regular basis; you need that money to operate your business. Don't let it become a temporary savings account — unless you choose the PayPal Money Market fund account (check out www.PayPal.com for more details). Realize that any money you have in your account can be extricated for a chargeback, and chargebacks can be applied as many as 60 days after the transaction. For more about chargebacks, see Chapter 7.

The Auction and Merchant Tools

When you're logged into your PayPal account, you'll see two tabs at the top of the screen labeled Merchant Tools and Auction Tools. The merchant tools are mostly for use on your business Web site (discussed in Book VIII). One that you might find handy is the e-mail invoice tool, discussed later in this chapter. What you need for your eBay sales are the auction tools. Click the Auction Tools tab, and the screen shown in Figure 6-7 appears.

Figure 6-7:
The PayPal
Auction
Tools page.

It seems PayPal acknowledges that their merchants are more than likely also sellers on eBay. (Ya think?) In the Auction Tools page, you'll find lots of links to all the information you'd ever care to know for example, Add PayPal to Your Listings. This link goes to your PayPal preference settings for your auction accounts. Here you may insert PayPal logos manually or automatically in your eBay sales pages.

On this page you see a list of your PayPal registered eBay user IDs. By clicking the on/off links, you can turn on and off Automatic Logo Insertion, Winning Buyer Notification, and PayPal Preferred.

You may also add another eBay user ID (if you have more than one). To add another user ID, click the Add button. To change any of your eBay passwords, click the Edit Password button.

Payment Tracking Information

PayPal is the premier tool for verifying that a payment has been made. Although PayPal has numerous methods for confirming payment, you need to make the final confirmation.

Payment notification through e-mail

When you receive a payment through PayPal, they send you a payment confirmation e-mail. The e-mail is a good tip-off that you've received a payment. Notice I said good, but not infallible.

In these days of spoofed e-mail sent by scammers to remove money from hard-working people's wallets, I rarely rely solely on e-mail confirmation. When I receive one of these e-mails, I open my Internet browser and go right to PayPal's secure server at

```
https://www.PayPal.com
```

When I get to the PayPal Web site, I can confirm with certainty that the payment has been made by looking at my PayPal Account Overview.

The Outlook Payment Request Wizard

Have you ever done business with someone who asks you, "How do I pay by PayPal?" Or how about when someone wants to purchase multiple items from your Web site and you need to send a combined invoice?

The Outlook Payment Request Wizard enables you to give an e-mail a more professional look by including a custom icon link to a PayPal payment page. If you're using Outlook or Outlook Express (2000, 2002, and 2003 on) and Windows 2000 or XP, you can get this great tool.

To download the wizard (it's a 3.8MB file for Outlook and 1.9MB for Outlook Express), follow these steps:

1. **Go to the Merchant Services tab, and scroll down to locate *Request Money with Outlook* (under the Manage Payments heading). You can also go directly to `https://www.paypal.com/us/cgi-bin/webscr?cmd=p/sell/payment_wizard_intro`.**

   That will take you to a page as in Figure 6-8.

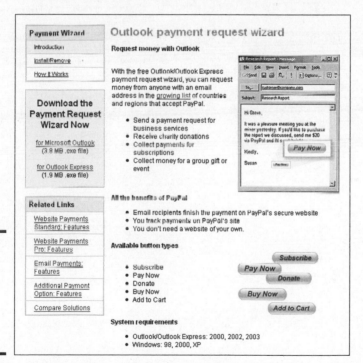

Figure 6-8: The super-tool — the Outlook Payment Request Wizard.

**Book III
Chapter 6**

Using PayPal to
Organize Your Sales

2. **Click the Download the Payment Request Wizard Now link.**

   A window appears, asking what you'd like to do with the file you're about to download.

3. **Click Save.**

A new Window appears, showing the contents of the hard drive of your computer.

4. **Select the directory where you want to save the file, and then click Save.**

The file is downloaded and saved to your hard drive.

5. **Open the directory you saved the file to and double-click the file name.**

The file opens and is installed on your computer.

Now that the wizard is installed, you'll see a new option at the top of Microsoft Outlook, as shown in Figure 6-9.

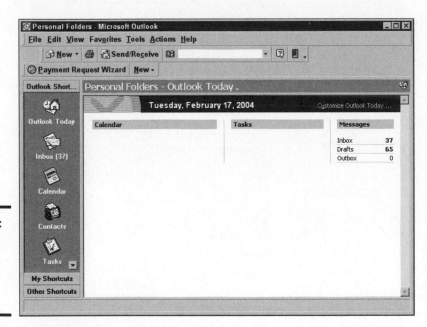

Figure 6-9:
The newly installed Payment Request Wizard.

Now, to send a PayPal payment request in an e-mail, follow these steps:

1. **Open your Outlook program and click the Payment Request Wizard tab.**

2. **Click Next when the introductory window appears.**

3. **Select the type of payment button you want in your e-mail.**

   Your button choices are Basic payment, Product, Service, Auction payment, and Donate. To include a button that allows buyers to pay for an item bought at auction, select the Auction payment button.

   If you select any button option other than Auction, you'll be asked for specific information about the item, including price and shipping amount.

4. **Click Next.**

   A window like the one shown in Figure 6-10 appears.

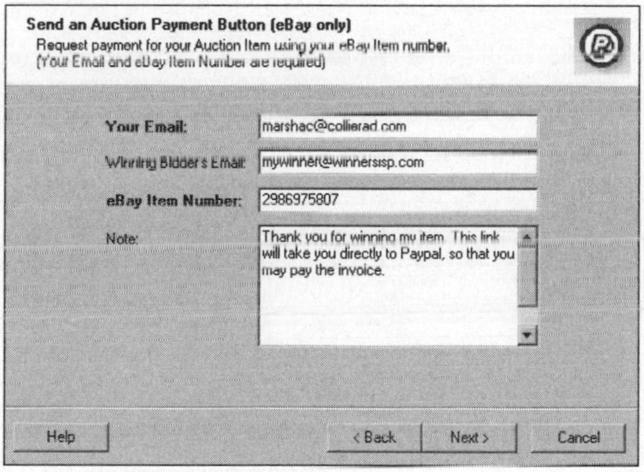

Send an Auction Payment Button (eBay only)
Request payment for your Auction Item using your eBay Item number.
(Your Email and eBay Item Number are required)

Your Email: marshac@collierad.com

Winning Bidder's Email: mywinner@winnersisp.com

eBay Item Number: 2986975807

Note: Thank you for winning my item. This link will take you directly to Paypal, so that you may pay the invoice.

Help   < Back   Next >   Cancel

Figure 6-10: Filling out the wizard's form.

Book III
Chapter 6

Using PayPal to Organize Your Sales

5. **Fill in your e-mail address, the winning bidder's e-mail address, and the eBay item number.**

   You may also include a note, if you'd like.

6. **Click Next.**

7. **Select which style of PayPal button you'd like to include in your e-mail.**

8. **Click Next.**

   The next screen is where you confirm your work, as shown in Figure 6-11. Double-check everything before previewing the button.

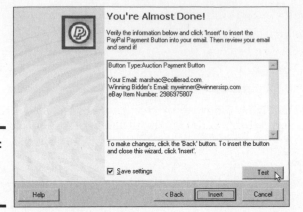

Figure 6-11:
You're
almost
finished!

9. **Click Test (at the bottom of the confirmation window).**

A preview of the PayPal payment window appears, as shown in Figure 6-12, so you can see what your buyer will see when he or she clicks the button to make a payment.

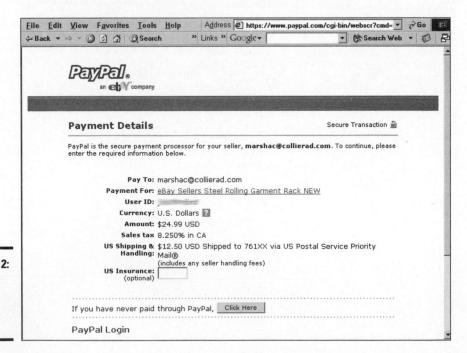

Figure 6-12:
PayPal
payment
window
preview.

10. **If you aren't happy with the results, click the Back button to make changes.**

11. **When you're satisfied with the way the payment window looks, click Insert.**

    The payment button appears in your e-mail.

12. **Enter any additional information in your e-mail (a thank-you would be nice), and then click Send to send the e-mail on its merry way to your buyer.**

Book III
Chapter 6

Using PayPal to
Organize Your Sales

Chapter 7: Checking Out Payment Alternatives

In This Chapter

✔ **Getting paid by money order**

✔ **Receiving cash on delivery**

✔ **Accepting checks**

✔ **Discovering the ins and outs of escrow services**

✔ **Setting up a merchant account for credit-card payments**

Your hard work finally pays off. The hours spent in selecting your items, photographing them, and writing brilliant auction copy all come down to one thing: getting paid. At first thought, you might be happy to take any form of negotiable paper, bonds, and stocks (okay, no dot-com stock). However, receiving and processing payments takes time and patience. The more payment methods that you accept, the more you have to keep track of. Narrow the payment choices you offer and you'll have less bookkeeping hassle. Throughout this chapter, I detail the various payment options (including how to handle payments from international buyers) and how each affects your business.

Watching for Changes in Policy

In early 2009, eBay plans policy changes regarding how sellers may accept payments for their items. All sellers must accept some sort of paperless payment and may accept checks or money orders for items listed in only certain categories.

If you're selling in the following areas of eBay, you can still accept old fashioned, paper payments:

✦ eBay Motors

- Cars & Trucks
- Motorcycles
- Powersports

- Boats
- Other Vehicles & Trailers

✦ Business & Industrial

- Agriculture & Forestry ⇨ Tractors & Farm Machinery
- Construction ⇨ Heavy Equipment, Trailers
- Restaurant & Catering ⇨ Concession Trailers & Carts ⇨ Concession Trailers
- Healthcare, Lab & Life Science ⇨ Imaging & Aesthetics Equipment
- Industrial Supply, MRO ⇨ Fork Lifts & Other Lifts
- Manufacturing & Metalworking ⇨ Manufacturing Equipment
- Office, Printing & Shipping⇨ Commercial Printing Presses

✦ Real Estate

✦ Everything Else⇨ Mature Audiences

I highly recommend that you watch eBay's announcements pages for any changes in policy. If you violate this new payment policy, eBay may end your listing, and you'll have a ding on your eBay permanent record (kinda like getting detention in high school — but dangerous to your income).

Accepting the Simple Money Order

I begin my discussion of payments with money orders and cashier's checks because I think they're just the greatest way to receive payment. Money orders and cashier's checks are fast, cheap, and negotiable (just like cash). Cashier's checks are purchased at a bank and are generally debited immediately from the winner's checking account at purchase. For some unknown reason, banks take it upon themselves to charge a minimum of $5 to issue a cashier's check. This is a pretty steep charge to the winner, which is why I suggest money orders.

Money orders cost less than a dollar and are available almost anywhere. After a quick survey of my neighborhood, I found money order dealers galore. All the stores I spoke to charge 99 cents for a money order in amounts up to $500. In this section, I detail just four vendors (both online and off) that offer money order services. Table 7-1 shows a cost comparison of these vendors.

Table 7-1	Money Order Cost Comparison	
Vendor	*$25 Money Order*	*$110 Money Order*
7-Eleven	$0.99	$0.99
United States Post Office (Domestic)	$0.90	$0.90
United States Post Office (International)	$3.25	$3.25
Canada Post (in U.S. currency)	$4.00 CDN	$4.00 CDN

If you want money orders, you should familiarize yourself with the various charges so that you can recommend the most reasonable amount to your auction winners. Asking buyers to pay a large fee to pay you is unfair — unless they're international. In that case, paying by money order through an issuer such as American Express (with offices in most countries) is the best way for them to pay you. International buyers deal in the currency of their own countries; when they purchase a money order and send it in dollars, you're paid with cash in good old American greenbacks.

TIP

Many sellers bring their money orders to the post office when they ship their packages and cash them for their petty cash funds or to pay for outgoing postage.

Pay Me When You Get This

I can't say enough about COD — to *discourage* you from using this payment method. But I'm gonna try! Even though soliciting a C.O.D. payment is a violation of eBay policy, sometimes a buyer will want an item quickly and ask for the item to be shipped in this fashion (for any number of creative reasons).

You give your package to the post office, UPS, or FedEx, who collects the payment after delivering the package. Sound straightforward and easy? What happens when the carrier tries to deliver the package and the recipient isn't home? Your item can sit with the shipper for a week or two, during which time the buyer may decide that he or she doesn't want to pick up the item from the shipper. If you're lucky, you'll get the item back in two to three weeks. The cash-on-delivery service is also expensive. In addition to postage, the post office charges $5.50 for COD service.

Another bad part of COD? You might wait a month to receive payment, even when the addressee is home the first time and accepts delivery. Do yourself a favor and don't offer COD as a payment option. You're only asking for trouble. You're not a bank, and you're not in the finance business. Even if you are, *get your money up front.*

The Check Is in the Mail

Personal checks are the easiest way for buyers to make payments: They just dash off a check and put it in the mail. It doesn't always work out so easily for the seller. You have to deposit the check into your bank account first and then wait for the check to clear. Believe it or not, in these days of electronic transfers, wiring funds, and international money transfers, you still might wait more than two weeks for a check to clear.

Paper checks

After you deposit a check, your bank sends it to a central clearinghouse, which sends it to the signatory's bank clearinghouse. Then the individual bank decides whether the check can be paid. You may think that a way around the system is to call the bank and see whether the account currently has sufficient money in it. The account may have sufficient funds when you call, but the check will bounce if the depositor withdraws money before the check gets through the system.

Don't forget the 24-hour turnaround rule: Even if the bank has the money and you're standing there with the check, the bank can deny payment within 24 hours after telling you the money is in the account, leaving you with a bad check.

Even though everything seems to be electronic these days, the paper routing of old-fashioned checks can take two weeks or longer. The only bad check I've ever received as an eBay payment was deposited. After waiting ten business days, I shipped the item. On the eleventh business day, I got the bounced check back from the bank. The buyer clearly knew that the check had bounced but didn't notify me. Luckily the buyer made good on the check.

If you find yourself with a check bouncing higher than a superball and an uncooperative buyer, remember that it's against the law to pass bad checks. To see a list of penalties, state by state, visit the National Check Fraud Center at

www.ckfraud.org/penalties.html#civil

WARNING!

Accepting cash payments

In concordance with eBay's new policies, the only way you are allowed to accept cash for an item is for an in-person transaction. I'm sure you've received cash from some of your winners. I don't like cash. If the buyer doesn't send the exact amount due, you have to call the buyer, who may claim that the correct amount should be there. And mail can be stolen. We had a rash of mail thievery where I live; people were stealing envelopes right out of mailboxes.

All of a sudden, *you* must have lost the difference — and you have no recourse with cash.

Postal inspectors are constantly battling this problem, but you won't know your mail is being stolen until you've missed enough mail — usually bills and outgoing checks. Explaining to a buyer that the money never arrived is difficult. You can e-mail, phone, talk, and discuss, but the bottom line is that you haven't received your money and the buyer insists that you have.

For example, if a California or Indiana resident passes a bad check, you are legally able to collect three times the amount of the bad check!

Bottom line? Warn your winners that you may hold the check for more than two weeks before you ship. I make exceptions for buyers I've successfully done business with before or those with an impeccable feedback rating.

Dealing with personal checks isn't worth the potential grief they can cause. Try to get an eCheck or an instant transfer through PayPal (as described in the next section), or have your winners pay with credit cards through a payment service (as described in the "I Take Plastic" section, later in this chapter).

eChecks and instant transfers

Despite the attached fees and a short waiting period, accepting a PayPal eCheck or an instant transfer is a nice, clean transaction. After indicating that they want to pay with an eCheck, buyers must register their bank accounts with PayPal and give PayPal the information required.

When a buyer pays with an electronic check, it takes as many as four days to clear. An instant transfer, on the other hand, credits your account immediately — as long as the buyer has a credit card or bank debit card as a backup funding source. PayPal allows you to accept eChecks for up to $10,000 but will charge you up to $5 fee per transaction.

Hold This for Me — in Escrow

Escrow.com, eBay's official escrow service, makes it more comfortable for the buyer to proceed with transactions over $2000, which is the upper limit for PayPal buyer protection. Buyers gain peace of mind by using escrow because they know the transaction will be completed securely and easily. (A less expensive way to reassure your buyer when you're participating in high-dollar transactions is called a *bonded auction*. See Book VIII, Chapter 2 for the details.)

As a new user, you or your buyer must register to use the service. When you want to offer escrow as a payment option in one of your listings, be sure to indicate such on the Sell an Item form so that it appears on the listing page. After the sale closes, the seller should initiate the escrow by going to the Escrow.com site or to eBay.

To initiate escrow go to www.escrow.com. On the home page, shown in Figure 7-1, register or sign in under the Start an Escrow Now heading. On the following page, you start the process by typing the eBay item number.

Figure 7-1: Start an escrow through Escrow.com's home page.

To proceed with escrow, the process goes something like this:

1. **The buyer sends payment to Escrow.com.**

   Escrow.com accepts most credit cards (including American Express and Discover), cashier's checks, money orders, wire transfers, and personal or business checks. A check is subject to a ten-day delay.

2. **After the buyer makes the payment, Escrow.com asks the seller to ship the item to the buyer.**

   When the buyer receives the merchandise, the inspection period begins promptly at 12:01 a.m. the next weekday and continues for a time previously set by the buyer and seller.

3. **If the merchandise passes inspection, the buyer notifies Escrow.com that the merchandise is approved, and then Escrow.com releases payment to the seller.**

4. **If the buyer doesn't feel that the merchandise is what was represented in the listing, the buyer must return the item to the seller in its original condition, adhering to the Escrow.com shipping requirements.**

   The buyer also must log on to the Escrow.com Web site to input return shipping information. In the event of a return, the seller has the same inspection period to ensure that the item was returned in its original condition.

5. **After the successful return of the merchandise is confirmed, Escrow.com refunds the buyer (less the escrow fee and, if agreed upon ahead of time, the shipping fee).**

Either the buyer or the seller can pay the escrow fee; the two can even split the cost. But you need to decide who will pay the fee up front and indicate this in your listing. The buyer is responsible for paying the escrow fee for all returns, no matter who had initially agreed to pay the fees. In Table 7-2, I include a listing of escrow fees. (Credit cards are not accepted for payment for amounts over $5,000.00.)

Table 7-2	Escrow.com Escrow Fees	
Transaction Amount	*Check or Money Order*	*Wire Transfer*
Up to $5000.00	3.25% ($25 minimum)	same
$5,000.01-$25,000	$162.50 + 0.26% of amount over $5000	same
$25,000.01 and up	0.89%	same

Sadly, escrow service has *also* become one of the most highly publicized scams on the Internet. Unscrupulous sellers set up fake escrow sites, sell a bunch of high-dollar items to unsuspecting buyers, and then direct the buyers to the faux-escrow Web site to set up what they think will be an escrow account. The buyers send their money (thinking the transaction is safe), and after the fraudulent sellers collect a bunch of money, they shut down the Web site and abscond with the money! Small wonder that many buyers are gun-shy of using escrow to pay for expensive items. Consider bonding your transactions to lure higher bids and confer a guarantee to the buyer. (Read the details of bonding in Book VIII, Chapter 2.)

I Take Plastic

As people become more comfortable using credit cards on the Internet, credit cards become more popular for eBay payments. Plus, major credit-card payment services have made insured eBay payments available to their registered users — making credit cards safe for the buyer and easy for you. And credit-card transactions are instantaneous; you don't have to wait for a piece of paper to travel cross-country.

For all this instantaneous money transfer, however, you have to pay a price. Whether you have your own *merchant account* (a credit-card acceptance account in your business's name) or take credit cards through a payment service (more on this in a minute), you pay a fee. Your fees can range from 2 to 7 percent, depending on how you plan to accept cards and which ones you accept. Unfortunately, many states have made it illegal to charge a credit-card surcharge to make up this difference. You have to write off the expense of accepting credit cards as part of your business budget.

The fees to the seller for accepting credit cards for brick-and-mortar stores are much less than those for online, mail, or phone orders. In most promotional material, the vendor usually quotes the "swiped card" rates. Since you won't have the buyer's card in hand to swipe, be sure to inquire with your provider for the proper rate before signing any papers.

I have to explain the downside of accepting credit cards for your online sales. To protect yourself, please be sure to check the bidders' feedback — both the feedback they've received and feedback they've left — before accepting any form of credit-card payment for a high-ticket item. Some buyers are chronic complainers and are rarely pleased with their purchases. If someone like that isn't satisfied with your item after it ships, he or she can simply call the credit-card company and get credit for the payment; you'll be *charged back* (that is, your account will be debited) the amount of the sale. For more info, see the "Forget the buyer: Seller beware!" sidebar.

Credit-card payment services

Person-to-person payment systems, such as eBay's PayPal, allow buyers to authorize payments from their credit cards or checking accounts directly to the seller. These services make money by charging percentages and fees for each transaction. It's all done electronically through an automated clearing-house — no fuss, no muss. The payment service releases only the buyer's shipping information to the seller; all personal credit-card information is kept private. This speeds up the time it takes for the buyer to get merchandise because sellers are free to ship as soon as the service lets them know that the buyer has made payment and the payment has been processed.

From the seller's point of view, person-to-person payment service transaction fees are lower than the 2.5 to 3.5% (per transaction) that traditional credit-card companies charge for merchant accounts. (Get the details in the "Your very own merchant account" section, coming up.) So even traditional retailers may switch their online business to these services to save money. Throughout this section, I discuss the top payment services and how each works.

Before you decide which credit-card payment service to use, get out your calculator and check out Web sites for current rates. Calculate your own estimates; don't rely on a site's advertised samples. Charts on the Web sites tend to leave out certain minor fees. I've also found that for promotional purposes (I assume), comparison charts quoting the competition's prices tend to include optional fees.

When you pay the fee to your payment service, the total amount of your transaction — including shipping fees, handling charges, and any sales tax that you charge — incurs a fee. The payment service charges a percentage based on the total dollar amount that's run through its system.

ProPay payments

There's a new eBay Certified Provider that's a payment provider; ProPay. Before you get too excited, recognize that ProPay services are offered to eBay PowerSellers in the silver, gold, platinum, and titanium levels. ProPay's eAuction Account is integrated with the eBay checkout process so that sellers can receive payments as easily as with PayPal.

Of course, there's nothing free in this world, and so the eAuction Account has an annual fee of $24.00. ProPay will reimburse this fee (as a credit to their processing charges) after a seller processes over $3,000 with ProPay during the first six months following account activation.

Book III
Chapter 7

Checking
Out Payment
Alternatives

Transaction fees are determined by the seller's PowerSeller tier. For Visa, MasterCard, and Discover processing, the fees are as follows:

+ **Silver:** 2.7 percent and $0.30 USD per transaction.

+ **Gold:** 2.4 percent and $0.30 USD per transaction.

+ **Platinum:** 2.4 percent and $0.30 USD per transaction.

+ **Titanium:** Possibly negotiable.

(Transaction fees for processing American Express are higher.)

Your very own merchant account

If your eBay business is bringing in more than $10,000 a month, a credit card merchant account may be for you. However, I recommend that you look at the costs carefully. I get at least one e-mail a week soliciting me to set up my own merchant account, and each one offers lower fees than the last. But fees are often hard to calculate and even harder to compare. Charges are buried in the small print. Even those who advertise low fees often don't deliver. Be sure to look at the entire picture before you sign a contract.

The best place to begin looking for a merchant account may be your own bank. Your bank knows you, your credit history, and your business reputation — and has a vested interest in the success of your business. If, for whatever reason, your credit isn't up to snuff, I recommend building good credit *before* pursuing a merchant account; as your business grows, your credit rating is your feedback to the offline world.

If your bank doesn't offer merchant accounts for Internet-based businesses, find a broker to evaluate your credit history and hook you up with a bank that fits your needs and business style. (As a last resort, join Costco, as detailed in the following section.) These brokers make their money from your application fee, from a finder's fee at the bank that you finally choose, or from both.

After you find a bank, you're connected to a *processor* (or transaction clearinghouse). Your bank merely handles the banking; the clearinghouse is on the other end of your Internet connection when you're processing transactions, checking whether the credit card you're taking is valid and not stolen or maxed out.

The next step is setting up your *gateway,* the software (ICVerify or PCAuthorize, for example) with which you transmit charges to the clearinghouse. Some gateways use HTML Web sites and take the transactions directly on Web-based forms (Cybercash or VeriFone, among others). Web-based gateways connect your Web forms to real-time credit-card processing.

Forget the buyer: Seller beware!

When a buyer disputes a sale, he or she can simply call PayPal or the credit-card company and refuse to pay for the item; you lose the sale and possibly won't be able to retrieve your merchandise. A payment service or merchant account will then charge back your account without contacting you and without negotiating. Technically, the buyer has made the purchase from the payment service — not from you — and the payment service won't defend you. I've heard of chargebacks occurring as long as two months after the transaction. And no one is standing at your side, forcing the buyer to ship the merchandise back to you. Just like eBay fraud protection — see Book I, Chapter 5 — the credit card companies skew the rules to defend the consumer. As the seller, you have to fend for yourself; see the same chapter on how to report fraudulent buyers. You usually have no way to verify that the shipping address is actually the one the credit card bills to. So, to add to your problems, the card may actually be stolen.

PayPal confirms through AVS (address verification service) that the buyer's credit-card billing address matches the shipping address; PayPal gives you the option to not accept payments from buyers whose addresses don't match. PayPal offers seller protection against spurious chargebacks under certain circumstances:

- Credit-card chargebacks from fraudulent card use
- Credit-card chargebacks for false claims of nondelivery
- Buyer complaints for false claims of nondelivery

If the issuing bank resolves a chargeback in the buyer's favor, PayPal charges you $10 if you are determined to be the one at fault, but waives the fee if you meet all the requirements of the PayPal seller protection policy.

Here's some good news: Major credit-card companies are trying to curb online fraud for their merchant accounts. Visa has the new Verified by Visa acceptance, which takes buyers to a Visa screen (through software installed on the merchant's server) and verifies their identity through a Visa-only password. MasterCard uses SET (Secure Electronic Transactions), a similar encrypted transaction verification scheme. These systems are expected to substantially reduce fraud and chargebacks.

In Table 7-3, I highlight various possible costs associated with setting up and maintaining a merchant account. Remember that not all merchant accounts pass these charges along. Some may charge just a few; others may take a bunch of little snipes at your wallet.

In the following list, I define some of the fees listed in Table 7-3:

✦ **Setup fee:** A one-time cost that you pay to your bank or your broker.

✦ **Discount rate:** A percentage of the transaction amount (a discount from your earnings that goes to the bank) taken off the top, along with the transaction fee, before the money is deposited into your account.

✦ **Transaction fee:** A fee per transaction, paid to the bank or to your gateway; the fee pays for the network.

✦ **Gateway or processing fee:** Your fee for processing credit cards in real time, paid to the Internet gateway.

✦ **Application fee:** A one-time fee that goes to the broker (or perhaps to the bank).

✦ **Monthly minimum processing fee:** If your bank's cut of your purchases doesn't add up to this amount, the bank takes it anyway. For example, if your bank charges a minimum monthly fee of $20, and you don't hit $20 in fees because your sales aren't high enough, the bank charges you the difference.

Table 7-3	Possible Internet Merchant-Account Fees
Fee	*Average Amount*
Setup fee	$25.00–$250.00
Monthly processing fee to bank	2.5% (1.5%–5%)
Fee per transaction	$0.20–$0.50
Processor's fee per transaction	$0.35–$0.50
Internet discount rate	2%–4%
Monthly statement fees	$9.00–$15.00
Monthly minimum processing fee	$15.00–$30.00
Gateway processing monthly fee	$20.00–$40.00
Application fees	$50.00–$500.00
Software purchase	$350.00–$1000.00
Software lease	$25.00 per month
Chargeback fee	$15.00

If you're comfortable with all the information in the preceding list and in Table 7-3, and you're looking for a broker, heed my advice and read everything a broker offers — carefully. Be sure you aren't missing any hidden costs.

If you run your business solely on the Internet, you'll have to be approved for an *Internet commerce account*. In this case, you *should* already have the following:

✦ Products and pricing

✦ A return and refund policy in place

✦ An active customer-service phone number

✦ Posted delivery methods and shipment time

✦ A privacy policy stating that you will not share your customers' information with another entity

✦ A registered domain in your name or your business name

✦ A secure order page with `https` (secure HTTP) and the lock icon

If you haven't set up all of the above, you are *not* ready to sign up for a merchant account. No matter what any well-meaning salesperson may tell you. To invest in a business, you need to have some history, some success. Biting off more than you can chew at the beginning of an enterprise leaves things open for disaster. Always start with the basics, like PayPal. As you grow, you can add the merchant account. Trust me on this.

All-in-One Plastic Processing

A far more economical way to process credit cards is with an all-in-one solution. When you want to accept credit cards from customers, you can also sign up for the various offerings that keep the costs down and yet give you all of the expensive services I talk about in the prior sections of this chapter.

In this section, I give you a sample of a couple all-in-one solutions that I found on the Web. I'm sure there are more, but checking out these Web sites will give you an idea of what to look for. Be sure to get the bottom line on what costs are involved before you sign up for any service!

Costco member's credit-card processing

Here's some true discount credit-card processing: a one-stop merchant account and gateway in one! Now you can not only buy a case of giant-sized cans of tuna with a Costco membership, but also obtain a reasonably priced way to handle a merchant account through Elavon.

Costco has gotten together with Elavon (née Nova Information Systems), one of the nation's largest processors of credit-card transactions, to offer Costco executive members a discounted Internet credit-card processing service. See Table 7-4 for a list of fees. Costco executive membership brings the cost of a Costco membership up from $45 to $100, but you get the benefit of receiving 2 percent back for most purchases (not including tobacco, gas, food, and some other purchases).

Table 7-4	Fees for Costco Internet Credit-Card Processing*
Fee	**Amount**
Discount rate per Internet transaction	1.99%
Per-transaction fee	$0.27
Monthly fees minimum	$20.00

You will also need a gateway to use their service. This can be in the form of software (available for a one-time fee) such as PC Transact It or a relationship with a gateway service.

To begin the application process, go to www.costco.com and click the Services link at the top of the home page. Scroll to the Services for your Business area and click the Credit Card Processing link. The page shown in Figure 7-2 appears.

Read the information and click the online link under the Apply Now heading. On the application page, enter your Executive Membership number and fill out a secure form. Filling out the form speeds up the application process. After sending your form, you'll receive a full application package via two-day air. A Costco representative will also contact you by telephone.

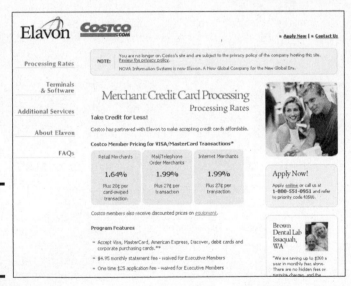

Figure 7-2:
Costco offers credit-card processing.

PayPal's Virtual Terminal

PayPal has a very simple service that will allow you to accept credit cards from a phone, fax, mail, or Internet. You process the payments directly on your own computer. Anyone who has a United States PayPal business account can apply. To get current pricing and information, go to www.PayPal.com and click Merchant Services. You'll see the Virtual Terminal hub, as shown in Figure 7-3.

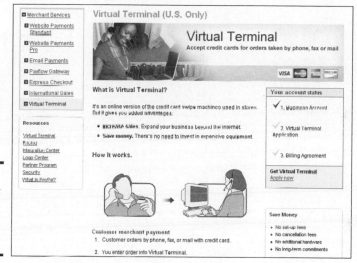

Figure 7-3:
PayPal's
Virtual
Terminal
home page.

With Virtual Terminal, when you get a credit-card order, you simply enter the order into a form online (as in Figure 7-4), and your packing slip will print out for your order. It's just that easy.

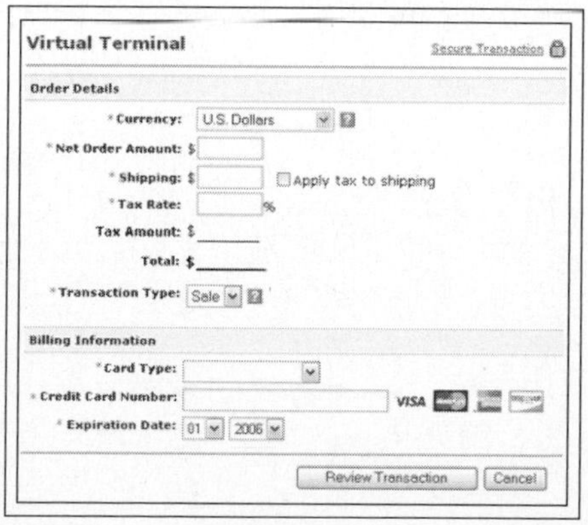

Figure 7-4:
The
on-screen
form you fill
out when
processing
payments.

Book IV
Sourcing Merchandise

Contents at a Glance

Chapter 1: Understanding Online Retailing

In This Chapter

✔ Evaluating your six-month merchandising plan

✔ Using demographics to market your business

✔ Knowing your market — right now

✔ Catching trends

✔ Knowing what's hot on eBay

✔ Finding what's hot on Yahoo!

'll bet it's no surprise to you that most eBay sellers lack a solid retail education. Most of us come from different walks of life, and all we know about retailing is shopping — that's probably how we first found eBay. Now that game is about to change. The more we choose to sell, the more our businesses grow, and the more we need to know about the business of retail.

eBay sellers use many types of business models. Some sellers are constantly on the prowl for new products and stock their merchandise as soon as they find a deal. Others follow the trends and try to get stock of the latest and greatest gizmo that they hope will sweep the country (and eBay). And sellers who run their businesses by selling for others are constantly beating the pavement for new customers to serve. Then there's the new eBay e-tailer. Just like a brick-and-mortar retailer, today's eBay e-tailers have to keep up on the trends so they can stock up on the most popular items for the coming seasons.

Taking Aim with a Six-Month Marketing Plan

The eBay e-tailer buys merchandise to sell on eBay. E-tailers are always looking for new wholesalers, but the e-tailers usually specialize in a particular type of stock item, such as dolls, sports cards, lighting fixtures, or apparel. Their eBay business is organized; they sell their merchandise and then buy more to replenish their stock. But is this the best way to handle things? It definitely works for most sellers, but those who studied retailing know that there's a better way.

One of the first things one learns when studying retail buying is the use of a six-month merchandise plan. It's the ultimate tool in the arsenal of a successful retail buyer. Although it was originally designed for brick-and-mortar retailers, I've adapted it here for eBay e-tailers.

Here's what establishing a six-month merchandising plan gives you:

+ **A clear, concise look at your business activity:** After you fill out the plan, you'll be able to combine it with the reports generated by your bookkeeping program to get a clear, concise picture of your eBay business. (I explain proper bookkeeping in Book IX.) This is a business and not a guessing game, and handling your business in a professional manner will save you a great deal of time and money.

I admit that running by the seat of your pants is fun and exciting, but it's not a solid business practice. One of the reasons I started my own business is that an unorganized business format appealed to me. To my dismay, I soon learned that organization and planning really *did* make a difference in my bottom line.

+ **A basis for growth plans:** Anyone who has participated in management in a corporation knows about the annual plan. Every year, management gets together (with Ouija and dart boards) to projects sales, expenses, and profits for the coming year. From this annual exercise, the budget for the coming year arises. These are the magic numbers that form everyone's annual raises — along with the company's plans for growth.

+ **A set of attainable and repeatable goals:** So, assuming that eBay sellers are online retailers, retail evaluation could help eBay sellers make sound business decisions. Making a merchandise plan is a good step in that direction. A merchandise plan covers six months at a time and sets sales goals. It also helps estimate how much money must be spent on merchandise (and when) so that a particular season's success can be replicated and magnified.

Pulling Together Your Inventory Data

You need a few numbers to get your merchandising plan on paper. If you aren't using bookkeeping software yet, you must put together a report that reflects the dollar value of your existing inventory. (Book IX, Chapters 2 and 3 will give you more insight.) If you are using bookkeeping software, you can get these numbers easily from the program's Inventory Valuation report:

+ **BOM:** The value, in dollars, of your beginning-of-month inventory
+ **EOM:** The value, in dollars, of your end-of-month inventory

The EOM figure for a specific month is the same as the BOM figure for the following month. For example, the end-of-month figure for April is the same as the beginning-of-month figure for May.

✦ **Gross sales:** Total revenue from sales (not including shipping and handling)

✦ **Markdowns:** Total revenue of merchandise you have sold on eBay below your target price

To put together your six-month plan, you need to have sales history for a six-month period. To get a good historical picture of your sales, however, it's preferable to have at least an entire year's worth of figures.

Your six-month plan can be based on your total eBay sales or only one segment of your business. For example, if you sell musical instruments along with many other sundry items, but you want to evaluate your musical-instrument sales, you can use just those figures for a six-month plan for your music department.

What you're going to establish is your *inventory turnover* — that is, measure how much inventory sells out in a specified period of time. The faster you turn over merchandise, the sooner you can bring in new merchandise and increase your bottom line. You can also evaluate whether you need to lower your starting price to move out stale inventory to get cash to buy new inventory.

When you prepare your six-month plan, set out the months not by the regular calendar but by a *retail calendar,* which divides the year into the seasons of fall/winter (August 1 through January 31) and spring/summer (February 1 through July 31). This way, if you want to refer to top national performance figures in trade publications or on the Internet, you can base your figures on the same standardized retail seasons.

Using the Formulas That Calculate Your Data

Okay, I can admit that bigger minds than mine came up with standard formulas for calculating business success. These formulas are used by retailers around the world. If you're not pulling the figures from a bookkeeping program, you can make the calculations as follows:

✦ EOM stock = BOM stock + Purchases – Sales

✦ BOM stock = EOM stock from the previous month

✦ Sales + EOM – BOM = monthly planned purchases

You can make your calculations in dollar amounts or number of units of the item. To figure out how much of an item to buy, you must know how much you have left in stock.

Prepare a chart for your own business, similar to the one shown in Table 1-1. Study your results and find out which months are your strongest. Let the table tell you when you might have to boost your merchandise selection in lagging months. It will help bring your planning from Ouija board to reality.

Table 1-1	Sample Six-Month eBay Merchandise Plan						
Fall/Winter	*Aug*	*Sept*	*Oct*	*Nov*	*Dec*	*Jan*	*Total*
Total sales	$2875	$3320	$3775	$4150	$3950	$4350	$22,420
+ Retail EOM	$1750	$3870	$4250	$3985	$4795	$4240	$22,890
+ Reductions	$575	$275	$250	$175	$425	$275	$1975
− Retail BOM	$3150	$1750	$3870	$4250	$3985	$4795	$21,800
= Retail purchases	$2050	$5715	$4405	$4060	$5185	$4070	$25,485
Cost purchases	$3310	$3540	$4725	$5150	$2775	$3450	$22,950
% of season's sales	12.82%	14.81%	16.84%	18.51%	17.62%	19.40%	
% of season's reductions	29.11%	13.92%	12.66%	8.86%	21.52%	13.92%	
Average stock	$3815						
Average sales	$3735						
Basic stock	$1000						

Marketing to Your Customers

When you're in business, you can't just consider yourself a retailer; you have to be a marketer too. eBay enables sellers in the United States to market across a massive geographic area. I'm sure you know how large the area is, but what about the *people* you sell to? You've heard of advertising being targeted to the lucrative 18-to-49 age demographic, but what about all the other age groups? Who are *they?* If you learn about your customer, you'll know how to sell to them. It's all about targeting.

Decide who buys what you want to sell — or, better yet, decide with whom you want to deal. If you don't want to deal with e-mails from teenage gamers, for example, perhaps you shouldn't be selling items that Gen N (defined in a moment) is gonna want.

Marketers often provide blanket definitions about the population based on their stages in life, what they're expected to buy, and which activities they participate in. The marketing generations are formed less by biological dates than by life experiences and influences. We all know that outside influences make a big difference in how we look at things; they also affect how and why we buy things.

Table 1-2 gives you the population figures of the United States. With the knowledge from this table, you can better decide just how many people will be shoppers for your products in the future. The 2000 census pegged the country at a total population of 281,421,906: 49.1% male and 50.9% female.

Table 1-2	U. S. Census 2000*	
Age Range	*Population*	*Percent*
20–24	18,964,001	6.7
25–34	39,891,724	14.2
35–44	45,148,527	16.0
45–54	37,677,952	13.4
55–59	13,469,237	4.8
60–64	10,805,447	3.8
65–74	18,390,986	6.5
75–84	12,361,180	4.4
85 and over	4,239,587	1.5

* The United States Census is taken every ten years. The next census will occur in 2010.

Knowing the Current Market

Just as successful stockbrokers know about individual companies, they also need to know about the marketplace as a whole. Sure, I know about the 90 Webkinz out there, and so does nearly everyone else. To get a leg up on your competition, you need to know the big picture as well. Here are some questions you should ask yourself as you contemplate making buckets of money by selling items at eBay:

✦ **What items are currently hot?** If you see everyone around you rushing to the store to buy a particular item, chances are good that the item will become more valuable as stocks of it diminish. The simple rule of supply and demand says that whoever has something everyone else wants stands to gain major profits.

✦ **Do I see a growing interest in a specific item that might make it a big seller?** If you're starting to hear talk about a particular item, or even an era ('70s nostalgia? '60s aluminum Christmas trees? Who knew?), listen carefully and think of what you own — or can get your hands on — that can help you catch a piece of the trend's action.

✦ **Should I hold on to this item and wait for its value to increase, or should I sell now?** Knowing when to sell an item that you think people may want is a tricky business. Sometimes you catch the trend too early — and find out that you could have commanded a better price if you'd waited. Other times you may catch a fad that's already passé. It's best to test the market with a small quantity of your hoard, dribbling items individually into the market until you've made back the money you spent to acquire them. When you have your cash back, the rest will be gravy.

✦ **Is a company discontinuing an item I should stockpile now and sell later?** Pay attention to discontinued items, especially toys and novelty items. If you find an item that a manufacturer has a limited supply of, you could make a tidy profit. If the manufacturer ends up reissuing the item, don't forget that the original run is still the most coveted and valuable.

✦ **Was there a recall (due to non-safety issues), an error, or a legal proceeding associated with my item?** If so, how will it affect the value of the item? For example, a toy recalled for reasons other than safety may no longer be appropriate, but it could be rare and collectible if sealed and intact.

Some people like to go with their gut feeling about when and what to buy for resale at eBay. By all means, if instinct has worked for you in the past, factor instinct in here, too. If your research looks optimistic but your gut says, "I'm not sure," listen to it; don't assume you're just hearing that lunchtime taco talking. Test the waters by purchasing one of the prospective items for resale at eBay. If that sale doesn't work out, you won't have a lot of money invested, and you can credit your gut with saving you some bucks.

Exploiting your talent

If you're talented in any way, you can sell your services on eBay. Home artisans, chefs, and even stay-at-home psychics are transacting business daily on the site. What a great way to make money on eBay — make your own product!

Many custom items do well on eBay. People go to trendy places (when they have the time) such as Soho, the Grove, or the Village to find unique custom jewelry. They also go to eBay. There's a demand for personalized invitations, cards, and announcements — and even return address labels. Calligraphic work or computer-designed items are in big demand today, but no one seems to have the time to make them. Savvy sellers with talent can fill this market niche.

Catching Trends in the Media

Catching trends is all about listening and looking. You can find all kinds of inside information from newspapers, magazines, television, and, of course, the Internet. Believe it or not, you can even find out what people are interested in these days by bribing a kid. Keep your eyes and ears open. When people say, "That Taco Bell Chihuahua is *everywhere* these days," instead of nodding your head vacantly, start getting ideas.

In newspapers

Newspapers are bombarded by press releases and inside information from companies the world over. Look for stories about celebrities and upcoming movies and see whether any old fads are making a resurgence (you can sell items as retro chic).

Read the accounts from trade conventions, such as the New York Toy Fair or the Consumer Electronics show. New products are introduced and given the thumbs up or down by journalists. Use the information to help determine the direction of your area of expertise.

On television

No matter what you think of television, it has an enormous effect on which trends come and go and which ones stick. Why else would advertisers sink billions of dollars into TV commercials? For example, one Oprah appearance for an author can turn a book into an overnight bestseller. Tune in to morning news shows and afternoon talk shows. The producers of these shows are on top of pop culture and move fast to be the first to bring you the next big thing. Take what they feature and think of a marketing angle. If you don't, you can be sure somebody else will.

Catch up with youth culture . . .

. . . or at least keep good tabs on it. If you remember cranking up The Beatles, James Brown, or The Partridge Family (say what?) until your parents screamed, "Shut that awful noise off," you may be at that awkward time of life when you hardly see the appeal of what young people are doing or listening to. But if you want tips for hot auction items, tolerate the awful noise and listen to the kids around you. Children, especially preteens and teens, may be the best trend-spotters on the planet.

Check out magazines

Magazines geared to the 18-to-34 age group (and sometimes to younger teens) can help you stay on top of what's hot. See what the big companies are pitching to this target audience (and whether they're succeeding). If a celebrity is suddenly visible in every other headline or magazine, be on the lookout for merchandise relating to that person. (Are we talking hysteria-plus-cash-flow here or just hysteria?)

Visit social Web sites

So, you say you haven't been to My Space or Facebook, and you haven't started to Twitter? Wow, you're living in the days of black-and-white television! This is the place to be. The "social Web" as it's called is branded with the top of the top; the most happening things and products. Visit these sites and you'll soon have a clue to what the "cool kids" are doing now.

Finding eBay's Soon-to-Be-Hot Sellers

Everyone wants to know what the hot ticket is on the eBay site. They want to know what's selling best so that they can run out, buy it, and *make big money* on eBay. Whoa, there, big fella.

As you may know, I'm not a believer in the notion that eBay is a get-rich-quick program. Nobody has or can give you secret information that magically transforms you from a garage seller to a warehouse tycoon overnight. You get there by studying the market and finding out what works and what doesn't. There are no shortcuts. That said, here's where you can find information on what's hot or what's going to be hot on the site.

Hot on the home page

New shoppers to the site generally enter from the home page. In case you haven't noticed, eBay runs promotions smack dab in the center of the home page — immediately drawing the attention of anyone who drops in to browse the site, as shown in Figure 1-1. Featured items link to an eBay search for such items.

Figure 1-1.
The eBay home-page feature promotion.

Now wouldn't you be the smart one if you were to list items that coincided with the hot items on the site? Oh yeah — and I'll tell you where you can find out what eBay will be listing on the home page ahead of time.

You can click the Sell drop-down menu on the navigation bar and find the link to eBay's *What's Hot* area. Or you can go directly to the following:

```
pulse.ebay.com/
```

You'll find a current list of items that account for the most popular searches on the site. Use the drop-down category menu (see Figure 1-2) to select the leaders within the particular category you plan to list.

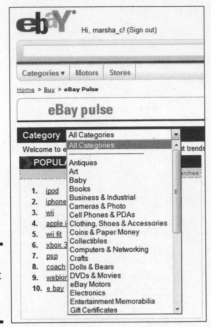

Figure 1-2:
eBay's most
popular
searches.

eBay Marketplace Research

eBay maintains an area that evaluates item sales on an ongoing basis. Click the Sell drop-down menu and choose Seller Tools & eBay Stores. On the resulting page, click eBay Marketplace Research from the Choose a Topic list on the left; the page you land on is shown in Figure 1-3. Or visit the page directly by going to

```
pages.ebay.com/marketplace_research/
```

Here eBay sellers (and buyers, if they so wish) can access up to 90 days of eBay data on completed items. By doing so, you'll get a firm grip on the demand for items you're planning to sell — with charts trending the average bids per item, number of completed items, and more. You'll also have access to the top searches within a category — or the entire site — to see what buyers are searching for.

There's much more available these days since eBay smartly partnered with Terapeak, a service I have used for ages. This company developed an eBay toolset that can really dig deep and do research for you. You'll be amazed at the data you'll see — especially once you've narrowed down the items you're interested in selling to just a few. Too much research can cause your eyes to glaze over and make you see funny spots in front of your face. That doesn't happen to you? OK, perhaps it's just me.

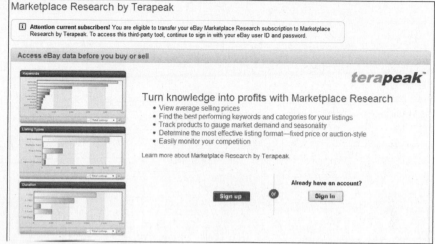

Figure 1-3:
The eBay
Marketplace
Research
home page.

All this excellent data isn't free

For $24.99 (or $197.95 for a yearly subscription), you can really go to town and access huge amounts of historic data. Because you may cancel your subscription at any time, why not at least give it a try for a month? Research a bunch of items, and think about what you will sell now. You can always sign up again later to check out how things are trending in the future. This way, you can dip your toe in first and save some of your hard-to-come-by cash for actually *buying* the merchandise you're going to sell.

Checking Out the Buzz on Yahoo!

The eBay site is the world's host for popular culture. If it's hot, people come to eBay to look for it. You should also look on the Internet to find the buzz. By *buzz* I mean the latest gossip, rumor, or thing that's talked about at the water cooler at work. Something that's the buzz can become a trend — and *trends* are those periodic waves of people buying the latest gotta-have items. They're what you look for to follow into the world of eBay.

You can find the beginnings of buzz in any news report or on your Internet provider's home page. Yahoo!, for example, has Yahoo!'s Buzz Index, at buzz.yahoo.com. It's a compilation of items that have received the largest number of searches on their system. You can see what's new on the list, what's going up, and what's going down. Figure 1-4 is the buzz list from May 24, 2008 at 2:21 p.m. Pacific Time.

Figure 1-4:
What's hot
on Yahoo!,
an hourly
snapshot of
the week's
pop culture.

Top Searches - Updated Hourly

1	Ufc 84
2	American Idol
3	Karen Allen
4	David Cook
5	Obama
6	Gas Prices
7	Iran
8	David Archuleta
9	Big 12 Baseball Tournament
10	Cougars For Cook

Chapter 2: Buying Merchandise Like the Pros

In This Chapter

✔ Taking the mystery out of finding merchandise

✔ Getting the best wholesale deals

✔ Finding unusual (and cheap) deals

I'm often asked, "Where do I find merchandise to sell on eBay?" This, of course, is followed by "What can I sell to make the most money on eBay?" Good questions. But what successful sellers have an answer they want to give to the competition?

When eBay PowerSellers have a good, solid source of merchandise, they're not likely to share the name of that source with anyone — nor would any brick-and-mortar retailer. (Think about it for a minute.) When I was teaching a class for advanced sellers at eBay Live (eBay's user convention), I was asked *the* question in an auditorium-size room filled with PowerSellers. I answered a question with a question: Were there any PowerSellers in the audience who would like to share their sources with the rest of the group? You could have heard a pin drop. So I upped the ante — "I'll pay anyone $10 for one solid source" — still silence. Business is business.

The bottom line here is that all successful sellers tweak out their own sources. What works for one may not work for another. Methods for finding goods that I include in this chapter are gleaned from my own research, as well as from interviews with successful online retailers.

Tips for the Modest Investor

If you're interested in making money in your eBay ventures but you're starting with limited cash, follow this list of eBay inventory dos and don'ts:

✦ **Don't** spend more than you can afford to lose. If you shop at boutiques and expensive department stores, buy things that you like to wear yourself (or give as gifts) in case they don't sell.

✦ **Do** try to find something local that's unavailable in a wider area. For example, if you live in an out-of-the-way place that has a local specialty, try selling that at eBay.

✦ **Don't** go overboard and buy something really cheap just because it's cheap. Figure out who would want the item first.

✦ **Do** consider buying in bulk, especially if you know the item sells well on eBay or is inexpensive. Chances are good that if you buy one and it sells well on eBay, the item will be sold out by the time you try to buy more. If an item is inexpensive (say $.99), I always buy at least five. If no one bids on the item when you hold your auction, you're only out $5. (Anyone out there need any Bicentennial commemorative coffee mugs?)

As an eBay seller, no doubt you'll receive tons of spam (unsolicited e-mails) guaranteeing that the sender has the hottest-selling items for you to sell on eBay. Think about this for a second. If you had the hot ticket, wouldn't you be selling it on eBay and making the fortune yourself? These people make money by preying on those who think there's a magic way to make money on eBay. There isn't. It takes old-fashioned elbow grease and research.

Buying for Retail: The Basic Course

If you're not sure what you want to sell for profit at eBay — but you're a shop-till-you-drop person by nature — incorporate your advanced shopping techniques into your daily routine. If you find a bargain that interests you, chances are you have a knack for spotting stuff that other shoppers would love to get their hands on.

When you're new at eBay selling, you probably want to get your feet wet first, before shelling out large sums for wholesale merchandise. Some great deals are available in the open market for resale!

Joining the hunt for e-Bay inventory

Check your favorite eBay category and see what the hot-selling item is. Better yet, go to your favorite store and make friends with the manager. Store managers will often tell you what's going to be the new hot item next month. After you're armed with the information you need, search out that item for the lowest price you can, and then give it a shot on eBay.

Keep these shopping locales in mind when you go on the eBay hunt:

✦ **Upscale department stores, trendy boutiques, outlet stores, or flagship designer stores** are good places to do some market research. Check out the newest items and then head to the clearance area or outlet store and scrutinize the bargain racks for brand-name items.

Figuring out who's who in the industry

It would be simple if you just bought merchandise from a manufacturer. But that's rarely the case. A full team of players participates in the wholesale game, and each player performs a different task, as follows:

- **Manufacturers:** Buying directly from a manufacturer may get you great prices, but it may not be the place for a beginner to start. Manufacturers usually require large minimum orders from retailers. Unless you have a group of other sellers (perhaps a friend who owns a retail store?) to split your order with, you may have to make your purchase from a middleman.

  An exception to the large-quantity requirement may be in the apparel industry. Because apparel has distinct, rapidly changing fashion seasons, a quick turnover in merchandise is a must. Apparel manufacturers may allow you to make small purchases towards the end of the season to outfit your eBay Store. It never hurts to ask.

- **Wholesalers:** Here's your first step to finding your middleman. Wholesalers purchase direct from the manufacturer in large quantities. They sell the merchandise to smaller retailers who can't take advantage of the discounts from manufacturers for large orders.

Find a wholesaler who is familiar with (or better yet, specializes in) the type of merchandise you want to sell. Obviously, someone who specializes in prerecorded DVDs and videos will not have a clue about the fashion market — and vice versa.

Don't forget to check local wholesalers, as described in the "Finding merchandise locally" section.

- **Manufacturer's reps:** These are generally the type of people you'll meet at trade shows or marts. They represent one or many noncompeting manufacturers and selling their merchandise to retailers for a commission.

- **Jobbers or brokers:** These independent businesspeople buy merchandise anywhere they can at distressed prices. They deal mostly in liquidation or salvage merchandise. To find out more about this source, see Chapter 3.

Don't forget to negotiate. Almost everything in the wholesale merchandise world is negotiable. Although merchandise may have a set price, you may be able to get a discount if you offer to pay on delivery or within ten days. Ask whether they can help you out with shipping costs and perhaps promotions. They just may give you a discount if you promote their product through banner ads. Ask, ask, ask. The worst they can say is no.

- ✦ **Discount club stores** such as Sam's Club and Costco made their mark by selling items in bulk to large families, clubs, and small businesses. In case you haven't noticed, these stores have recently upscaled and sell just about anything you could want. And both Sam's Club and Costco have Web sites: `auctions.samsclub.com` and `www.costco.com`.

In another book, I talked about a special on the Costco Web site, www. costco.com, for a new *Snow White & the Seven Dwarfs* DVD. For $18.49, you could pre-order the Snow White DVD and get a second Disney DVD for *free*. When there's an offer like this, you can sell two items on eBay for the price of one. If I had followed my own advice — bought a case of this deal and held some for future sales — I'd be in the money today. It seems that Disney movies are released for a limited time only. That original DVD set now sells on eBay for around $40.

If you were smart enough to get on the Costco site on the date of the Wii Fit game launch, you could have bought the item for its retail price of $89.99. Due to the rarity of the item, it's price soared as high as $475 on eBay. (Now, *that's* a tidy profit.) They're still selling steadily at $125. Even if you make $40 a sale, you're in the money, so always be on top of what's gonna sell big!

When an item is new but has some collectability, I suggest you buy in bulk, sell some of the item to repay your investment, and save the balance for later. This has paid off for me a good many times with Disney films, Barbies, and Andy Warhol dinnerware.

✦ **Dollar stores** in your area. Many of the items these places carry are *over-runs* (too many of something that didn't sell), *small runs* (too little of something that the big guys weren't interested in stocking), or out-of-date fad items that need a good home at eBay. I've found profitable books, Olympics memorabilia, and pop-culture items at this type of store.

It's not unusual for dollar-store warehouses to sell direct to a retailer (that's you). Find out where the distribution warehouse is for your local dollar store chain and make contact. The 99¢ Only stores, for example, have a wholesale unit called Bargain Wholesale that runs out of their City of Commerce, California offices. They sell directly to retailers, distributors, and exporters.

✦ **Thrift stores** are packed with used — but usually good-quality — items. And you can feel good knowing that the money you spend in a nonprofit thrift shop is going to a good cause. Some branches of Goodwill and the Salvation Army receive merchandise from a central warehouse. Ask the manager (whom you've befriended) when the truck regularly comes in.

Goodwill Industries is definitely gearing up for the 21st century. You can shop at its online auctions and get super values on the best of their merchandise. Don't forget to check the going prices on eBay before you buy. Have fun at www.shopgoodwill.com.

✦ **Garage, tag, moving, and estate sales** offer some of the biggest bargains you'll ever come across. The stuff you find at estate sales is often of a higher quality. Keep an eye out for "moving to a smaller house" sales. These are usually people who have raised children, accumulated a houseful of stuff (collectibles? old toys? designer vintage clothes?), and want to shed it all so that they can move to a condo in Palm Springs.

✦ **Liquidation and estate auctions** are two types of auctions where you can pick up bargains. Before you go to any auction, double-check payment terms and find out whether you must bring cash or can pay by credit card. Also, before you bid on anything, find out the *hammer fee,* or *buyer's premium.* These fees are a percentage that auction houses add to the winner's bid; the buyer has the responsibility for paying these fees.

When a company gets into serious financial trouble, its debtors (the people to whom the company owes money) obtain a court order to liquidate the company to pay the bills. The liquidated company then sells its stock, fixtures, and even real estate in a liquidation auction. Items sell for just cents on the dollar, and you can easily resell many of these items on eBay. Look in the phone book under Auctioneers: Liquidators and call local auctioneers' offices to get on mailing lists.

Estate auctions are the higher level of estate garage sales. Here you can find fine art, antiques, paper ephemera, rare books, and collectibles of all kinds. These auctions are attended mostly by dealers, who know the local going prices for the items they bid on. But because they're buying to sell in a retail environment, their high bids will generally be the wholesale price for your area. And local dealers are buying what's hot to resell in your city — not what's going to sell across the country. That entire market will be yours.

✦ **Newspaper auction listings** are an excellent source of merchandise for resale, particularly the listings of liquidations and estate auctions (usually appear on Saturday) and the daily classified section, which often has ads that announce local business liquidations. Do not confuse any of these with garage sales or flea-market sales (run by individuals and a great source for one-of-a kind items). Liquidation and estate sales are professionally run, usually by licensed liquidators or auctioneers, and involve merchandise that may be new but is always sold in *lots* (in a quantity).

If your local newspaper has a Web site, use its online search to view the classifieds for major liquidations, estate auctions, or other similar deals. Right there online, you can often find just what you are looking for locally. To find the paper's Web site, run a search on Google like the one shown in Figure 2-1.

✦ **Going-out-of-business sales,** some of which run week by week, with bigger discounts as time goes by. Don't be shy about making an offer on a quantity of items.

Going-out-of-business sales can be a bonanza, but be careful and don't be misled. Many states require businesses that are putting on a going-out-of business sale to purchase a special license that identifies the business as *really* going out of business. Some store ads may read "Going Out for Business" or some similar play on words, so you need to be sure that you're going to the real thing.

Figure 2-1:
A Google search for *newspaper classified los angeles* brings up plenty of hits to peruse online.

✦ **Flea markets or swap meets** in your area may have some bargains you can take advantage of.

✦ **Gift shops at museums, monuments, national parks, and theme parks** can provide eBay inventory — but think about where to sell the items. Part of your selling success on eBay is *access*. People who can't get to Graceland may pay handsomely for an Elvis mini-guitar with the official logo on the box.

✦ **Freebies** are usually samples or promotion pieces that companies give away to introduce a new product, service, or, best of all, a media event. Hang on to these! If you receive handouts (lapel pins, pencils, pamphlets, books, interesting napkins, flashlights, towels, stuffed toys) from a sporting event, premiere, or historic event — or even a collectible freebie from a fast-food restaurant — they could be your ticket to some eBay sales. For example, when *Return of the Jedi* was re-released in 1997, the first 100 people to enter each theater got a Special Edition Luke Skywalker figure. These figures are still highly prized by collectors and when the next part of the *Star Wars* saga was released, the prices on this figure went up yet again.

When you go to the cosmetic counter and buy a way-too-expensive item, ask for tester-sized samples. Name brand cosmetic and perfume samples of high-priced items sell well on eBay. Also, look for *gift with purchase* deals. If it's a specialty item, you can usually sell it on its own to someone who'd like to try a sample, rather than plunge headlong into a large purchase. Less-special items can be grouped together as lots. Be sure to put the brand names in the title.

One of my mottoes is "Buy off-season, sell on-season." You can get great bargains on winter merchandise in the heat of summer. January's a great time to stock up on Christmas decorations, and the value of those trendy vintage aluminum trees doubles in November and December. Cashmere sweaters, too! In the winter, you can get great deals on closeout summer sports merchandise. It's all in the timing.

Looking for resale items on eBay

Another place to find items to sell is on eBay itself. Look only for good-quality merchandise to resell. Remember that the only way to make a living on eBay is to sell quality items to happy customers so that they'll come back and buy from you again.

Be sure to search eBay auction titles for the following keywords: *resale, resell, "case of"* (see Figure 2-2), *"case quantity", "lot of", "pallet of", closeout,* and *surplus*. Use the quotation marks anywhere I've included them here because this forces the search engine to find the words in the exact order.

2664 items found for: "case of" (Save this search)

① Want to organize your search results below? Try "Sort by Category" now
Get it new. Buy it now: 662 *"case of"* items on eBay Express!

List View | Picture Gallery   Sort by: Time: ending soonest ▾ | Customize Display

	Item Title	Price*	Bids	Time Left ▲	Shipping to 91325, USA	Item #	Distance to 91325, USA
	O'Cedar Twist N Mop, Cotton Mop Refill; Case of 5	₽ $28.95	-	9m	$6.50	370052778748	2360 mi New York
	Square D Circuit Breakers 20A Tandem Case of 10 NEW	₽ $81.00	14	11m	$5.00	250250709568	2330 mi Pennsylvania
	Tyvek Breathable Painter's Suit (Case of 25) Size XXXL	₽ $20.25	4	21m	$16.00	190223623017	1380 mi Missouri
	CASE OF 6 SUPRE 18 oz HEMPZ HERBAL MOISTURIZER LOTION	₽ $53.50 $64.95 ⇒Buy It Now		26m	$12.90	390000006013	1925 mi Tennessee
	Case of 6 PAINT MIXERS Mud Mixing Wholesale NEW Lot	₽ $5.49 $9.49 ⇒Buy It Now		36m	$14.94	230253611429	1575 mi Arkansas
	PIZZA DOUGH STORAGE BOX NEW CASE OF 6	₽ $61.95 ⇒Buy It Now or Best Offer		36m	$45.98	280228042747	2480 mi New York

Figure 2-2: Results of a "case of" search on eBay.

Tuesday Morning

One of my editors is going to kill me for mentioning one of her favorite eBay merchandise sources, but here it is: Tuesday Morning, which has more than 500 stores scattered over the United States. They sell first-quality designer and brand-name closeout merchandise at deep, deep discounts — 50% to 80% below retail. The key here is that the store sells recognizable brand names, the kind of items that eBay shoppers look for. I've seem items at their store from Samsonite, Thomas Kinkade, Limoges, Wedgwood, Royal Doulton, Madame Alexander, and even Barbie! Find your local store at their Web site, `www.tuesday morning.com`. If you sign up for their eTreasures newsletter, you get advance notice of when the really good stuff arrives at the store.

Also be sure you check out the wholesale categories on eBay. After noticing how many sellers were buying from other sellers, eBay set up wholesale subcategories for almost every type of item. You can find the wholesale items in the category list on the left side of the page after performing a search, or just go to the eBay home page, scroll down the list of categories, and select your favorite category to sell. You'll be brought to the Category hub page; scroll down to find the links to Wholesale Lots, as shown in Figure 2-3. Then click the category of your choice to find some great deals.

Figure 2-3: eBay's Wholesale lots in the Clothing Shoes and Accessories category.

Wholesale, Large & Small Lots
Boys
Girls
Infants
Men's Accessories
Men's Clothing
Men's Shoes
Uniforms
Vintage
Women's Accessories, Handbags
Women's Clothing
Women's Shoes
Mixed Lots
Other

Buying Wholesale

After you get the hang of finding items in stores to resell on eBay, it's time to move to the wholesale source. As a side note, I want you to know that although my eBay business is based on wholesale merchandise, I still love going to the sources mentioned in the last section and finding great deals to resell. It's become a fun hobby! Don't we all love to find a piece of merchandise that we *know* we can sell for a profit?

Okay, you want to set up shop on eBay. You kind of know what type of merchandise you want to sell, but you don't know where to turn. Anyone in the brick-and-mortar world who plans to open a new store faces the same quandary: finding merchandise that will sell quickly at a profit.

Merchandise that sits around doesn't give you cash flow, which is the name of the game in *any* business. (*Cash flow* = profit = money to buy better, or more, merchandise.) I spoke to several successful retailers and they all gave me the same answers about where they began their quest. The upcoming sections give you a look at the answers these retailers shared.

Setting up to buy

Purchasing wholesale merchandise may require that you have your state's *resale license,* which identifies you as being in the business. Be sure that you have one before you try to purchase merchandise directly from another business. Also, when you have a resale number and purchase merchandise from another business — known as a *business-to-business* (B2B) transaction — you probably won't be charged sales tax when you purchase your stock because you'll be *paying* sales tax when you sell the items. Go to Book IX, Chapter 1 to find out how to get that magic resale number.

When you have your resale number, you can go anywhere you want to buy merchandise. If you want to buy direct from a manufacturer, you can. Unfortunately, many manufacturers have a minimum order amount, which may be more than you want to spend (and you'd get more of a particular item than you'd ever want at once). To remedy that, see whether you can find independent retailers who buy in quantity — and who will (perhaps) let you in on some quantity buys with manufacturers. I often buy in with a couple of local shops when they purchase their orders.

To gain access to legitimate wholesale sources, you must be a licensed business in your city or county. You also usually have to have a resale permit and tax ID number from your state. (See Book IX, Chapter 1 for details.)

Finding merchandise locally

Always remember that the cost of shipping the merchandise to you adds a great deal of expense. The higher your expense, the lower your return may be. The more you buy locally to resell, the more profit you can make.

The first place most potential retailers go is to their local wholesale district. You can find yours in your yellow pages (remember that giant brick of a book they drop in your driveway once a year?) under the name of your item. For example, suppose you want to sell women's apparel. Look up *Women's Apparel* in the yellow pages and find the *Wholesale* subcategory. Bingo! Immediate merchandise sources, within driving distance of your home! Also be sure to check the directories in neighboring communities as well. The value of this printed (and usually overlooked) resource is immeasurable when you're starting up a business.

Regional merchandise marts

Your next stop — should you be lucky enough to live in a major metropolitan area — is to find out whether there's a merchandise or fashion mart near you. These are giant complexes that hold as many as several thousand lines of merchandise in one area.

Merchandise marts are hubs for wholesale buyers, distributors, manufacturers, and independent sales representatives. They have showrooms within the property for manufacturers or their representatives to display their current merchandise. Under one roof, you may find both fashion and gift merchandise for your eBay business.

See Table 2-1 for a representative sprinkling of the many marts across the country. This is not a comprehensive list, just one to get your mind moving. You can contact the individual marts for tenant lists and more information. If you're a legitimate business, the marts will be more than happy to teach you the ropes and get you started.

Table 2-1		Wholesale Merchandise Marts	
Name	*Location*	*Web Site Address*	*Trade Shows*
Americas Mart	Atlanta, GA	www.americas mart.com	Apparel, jewelry, shoes, fashion accessories, gifts, home furnishings
California Market Center	Los Angeles, CA	www.california marketcenter. com	Apparel, accessories, textiles, toys, gifts, furniture & décor, garden accessories, stationery, personal-care products
The Merchandise Mart	Chicago, IL	www.mmart.com	Apparel, office, home, decorative accessories, textiles, gifts
The Chicago Market	Chicago, IL	www.giftand home.com	Apparel, home furnishings, antiques, gifts, bridal

Name	Location	Web Site Address	Trade Shows
Columbus Marketplace	Columbus, OH	www.the columbusmarket place.com	Gifts, garden, home furnishings, décor
Dallas Market Center	Dallas, TX	www.dallas marketcenter. com	Apparel, gift products, decorative accessories, home furnishings, lighting, garden accessories, floral, and gourmet
Denver Merchandise Mart	Denver, CO	www.denver mart.com	Apparel, gifts, souvenirs, gourmet, collectibles, home décor
International Home Furnishings	High Point, NC	www.ihfc.com	Home furnishings and décor of all types
Kansas City Gift Mart	Kansas City, MO	www.kcgift mart.com	Gifts, gourmet, design, home décor
The L.A. Mart	Los Angeles, CA	www.lamart.com	Gifts, home décor, furnishings
Miami Merchandise Mart	Miami, FL	www.miamimart. net	Apparel, gifts, accessories, home décor
Minneapolis Gift Mart	Minneapolis, MN	www.mplsgift mart.com	Gifts, home décor, accessories
New York Merchandise Mart	New York, NY	www.41madison. com	Gifts, home décor, accessories
7W	New York, NY	www.225-fifth. com	Gifts, home décor, accessories, stationery
San Francisco Gift Center	San Francisco, CA	www.gcjm.com	Apparel, jewelry, home furnishings, gifts, jewelry, stationery
The New Mart	Los Angeles, CA	www.newmart. net	Contemporary clothing and accessories

My favorite, the California Market Center (whose Web site is shown in Figure 2-4), even has a special program for new buyers, offering tons of useful information to help newbies get going.

Figure 2-4:
The
California
Market
Center page
featuring
its Fashion
week.

When you go to each mart's Web site, you'll find hundreds of links to wholesale sources. Many marts also send you a directory of the manufacturers represented in the mart.

Wholesale trade shows

By checking out the links to the marts listed in Table 2-1, you'll also end up with links to the thousands of wholesale trade shows that go on across the country each year. Trade shows are commonly held in convention centers, hotels, and local merchandise marts.

A super source for finding gift shows is the `greatrep.com` Web site, shown in Figure 2-5. Here you find a list of all the major gift shows — with clickable links to contact information for the show coordinators. For more on `great rep.com`, see the "Buying Online for Resale" section later in this section.

When visiting a show or a mart, view all merchandise before you place an order. Bring a notebook with you to make copious notes of items you find interesting and where you find them.

Necessary ID for trade shows and marts

Professional trade shows and marts are not open to the general public, and they want to keep it that way. When you attend these venues, they want to be sure that you represent a business. Following is a list of items that you may be asked to provide, as proof that you are a retailer:

✔ Business cards

✔ A copy of your current resale-tax certificate or state tax permit

✔ Current occupational or business tax license

✔ Proof of a business checking account or a letter of credit from your bank (if you're applying for credit)

✔ Financial statement

✔ Cash and checks

Be sure to check with the organization sponsoring the trade show or mart before attending so that you'll have everything you need. Don't let this list scare you — wholesale marts are fun, and the organizers and vendors will do everything they can to help you make your retailing venture a success!

Figure 2-5: Check the greatrep.com Web site for an updated trade show schedule.

greatrep.com — The premier Internet directory for the wholesale giftware, home furnishing and furniture industries

Show Name	Location	Start Date	End Date	Year
Kansas City Gift Show	Overland Park, KS	Jun 6	Jun 10	2008
Dallas Total Home & Gift Market	Dallas, TX	Jun 18	Jun 24	2008
Columbus MarketPlace Show	Columbus, OH	Jun 20	Jun 24	2008
Summer Holiday Show - Northeast Market Center	Billerica, MA	Jun 21	Jun 25	2008
Market Square Valley Forge	Valley Forge, PA	Jun 26	Jun 29	2008
Biloxi Gift Show	Biloxi, MS	Jun 28	Jun 30	2008
Charlotte Gift & Jewelry Show	Charlotte, NC	Jun 28	Jun 30	2008
NASFT Summer Fancy Food Show	New York, NY	Jun 29	Jul 1	2008
Messe Frankfurt Tendence	Frankfurt, Germany	Jul 4	Jul 8	2008
Atlanta International Gift and Home Furnishings Market	Atlanta, GA	Jul 8	Jul 16	2008
GIFTEX	Tokyo, Japan	Jul 9	Jul 11	2008
L.A. Mart Gift Show	Los Angeles, CA	Jul 15	Jul 21	2008
Chicago Market: Living and Giving	Chicago, IL	Jul 17	Jul 23	2008
California Gift Show	Los Angeles, CA	Jul 18	Jul 21	2008
Philadelphia Gift Show	Reading, PA	Jul 20	Jul 23	2008
Oasis Gift Show	Glendale, AZ	Jul 24	Jul 26	2008

Book IV Chapter 2

Buying Merchandise Like the Pros

These trade shows are gargantuan bourses of hundreds of wholesale vendors all lined up and ready to take your orders. The vendors have samples of the merchandise in the lines they carry and are delighted to answer all your questions about their products, credit applications, and minimum orders. These shows are designed to move products to retailers like you!

Few trade shows are more exciting than the Consumer Electronics Show (CES), sponsored by the Consumer Electronics Association. If you buy breakthrough technologies to sell online, this show is a must! You'll find the latest in everything high-tech, including digital imaging, electronic gaming, home electronics, car audio, home theater, and satellite systems. You'll see what's new — but more importantly, you'll see what will be passé in a hurry — great merchandise to sell (in a timely way, of course) on eBay!

CES draws more than 100,000 buyers each year, and the vendors are there to sell their goods to *you*. Visit the CES Web site at `www.cesweb.org` to get an idea of the excitement that the show generates.

See whether the item is selling on eBay before you make your purchase. Bring a laptop and conduct research either on the spot or later in the day for next-day purchases. *Getting* a good deal is one thing — selling it on eBay is another.

Buying Online for Resale

I've come across many legitimate sources of goods on the Internet. But the Internet is loaded with scam artists; it's up to you to check vendors out for yourself before spending your hard-earned money. Even if I mention sellers here, I want you to check them out as if you know nothing about them. I can't guarantee a thing; all I know is that at the time of this writing, they were reliable sources for eBay merchandise.

Kijiji and Craigslist

If you haven't visited either of these site, you're missing quite a bit! Both sites feature free local classifieds. You'll find anything and everything listed here, and you never know when there will be something worthwhile to resell. These sites are always worth at least a once-a-week visit. Much of the stuff on these two sites is listed by people who are either too lazy or too afraid to sell on eBay.

Craigslist has been well known to the Internet cognoscenti for years, and Kijiji (shown in Figure 2-6) is eBay's new offering in the "free classifieds" arena. You can find the sites at

`www.kijiji.com`
`www.craigslist.org`

Tips for buying wholesale online

Because the online world can be fraught with problems, keep in mind the following:

✔ **Protect your e-mail address.** Check every site you sign up with for a privacy policy. Watch out for wording like this in the Privacy Policy: "Our Privacy Policy does not extend to our affiliated sellers or advertisers. They are free to maintain their own privacy policy independent of us." Again, get an anonymous e-mail address to spare yourself spam.

✔ **Look for the *About Us* page.** Be sure the site has an address and a phone number. Call the number to see whether it is a "real" business, not a fly-by-night. While you're at it, see how you're treated on the phone.

✔ **Look for safety seals.** Seeing the Better Business Bureau Online, TrustE, or SquareTrade logo on the Web site can bolster trust in the company.

✔ **Check out the shipping costs.** Sometimes the shipping can cost more than the item. Before placing your order, make sure you know all the shipping costs and terms.

You must have a Federal tax ID number (that's your identification to do business) to even register on most legitimate wholesale sites. Finding wholesale Web sites with this restriction is a good thing. It's another way to verify that you're dealing with a true wholesale supplier.

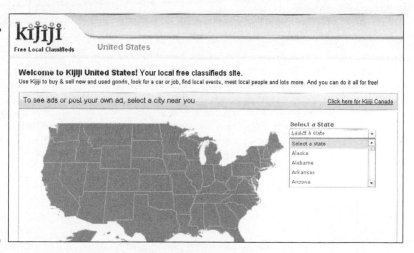

Figure 2-6: After you arrive at Kijiji, click the drop-down menu to select your state (then the city), and you're off and shopping.

B2B wholesale clearinghouses

Legitimate online sites for retailers are rare. Many of the business to business (B2B) merchants and wholesale directories reflect nothing but flea market goods and highly marked-up drop-shipping items. Don't be disappointed! That doesn't mean you can't find a deal on some great merchandise. The benefit of the Internet is that you have access to many sources. The challenge is to find the good, solid, reliable sources of information, like the following:

✦ **MadeInUSA.com:** One of the best ways to find an item to sell is to find that item in your everyday life. If you have the manufacturer's name but no contact information, go to the MadeInUSA Web site (see Figure 2-7), which has a huge database of manufacturer contact info.

Figure 2-7: Search more than 400,000 manufacturers at this Web site.

✦ **Greatrep.com:** Here's a Web site directory where buyers (that's you) can hook up with manufacturer's representatives that carry lines of merchandise in the wholesale giftware, home furnishings, and furniture industries. It's fantastic! After you register (and provide your state resale license), you have access to their listings of thousands of manufacturers. In the listings you may find out how much they require for a minimum order and you can request a catalog.

Buying directly from online wholesalers

Following are a few sources that have some unusual merchandise. I've bought from almost all of them.

Liquidation.com

If you like auctions (and I *know* you do) check out `Liquidation.com`. This is a massive all-auction Web site that has incredible deals on all types of merchandise, as shown in Figure 2-8.

Figure 2-8:
The
Liquidation.
com Web
site.

One of the things that I love about this site is that most individual auctions provide a link to the *manifest* — a list of every piece of merchandise in the lot. If you click the View Manifest link at the top of the auction page, you see a piece-by-piece list of the items included in the lot you're bidding on.

It's best to buy from vendors closer to your geographic area because after you add the shipping fee, you might be paying too much for your lot. Liquidation.com has a shipping calculator to help you know ahead of time how much your shipping may be.

Oriental Trading Company

The Oriental Trading Company has been in business for a long time. I used to buy from their catalog for school and charity affairs. This site offers everything from crafts to costumes to party goods — and all priced perfectly for resale on eBay. Use your practiced eye (and completed search) to ferret out the unique items that will sell. Visit them at www.orientaltrading.com.

**Book IV
Chapter 2**

Buying
Merchandise Like
the Pros

Big Lots Wholesale

If you're familiar with the Big Lots stores scattered around the country, you have an idea of what you can buy at `biglotswholesale.com`. A quick click to their Web site showed me that they were loaded with great deals on everything from health and beauty items to toys to lawn and garden tools. A seller's tax ID number is required to get pricing on this site.

Chapter 3: Selling Other People's Stuff

In This Chapter

✔ Organizing your consignment business

✔ Competing with consignment store chains

✔ Becoming a Trading Assistant

✔ Promoting your consignment business

✔ Writing an effective contract

Consignment sales are the up-and-coming way for you to help non-techie types by selling their items on eBay. Lots of sellers do it, and several retail locations base their business on it. You take property of the item from the owner and sell it on eBay. You're responsible for taking photos and marketing the auction on eBay — for a fee. In addition to the money you earn selling on consignment, you also get excellent experience for future auctions of your own merchandise.

Getting Organized to Sell for Others

To set up your business for consignment sales, you should follow a few guidelines:

1. Design a consignment agreement (a contract), and send it to the owners of the merchandise before they send you their items. Doing so ensures that all policies are set up in advance and that no questions will arise after the transaction has begun.

2. Have the owners sign and give the agreement to you (the consignor) along with the item.

3. Research the item based on past sales so you can give the owners an estimated range of what the item might sell for on eBay.

4. Photograph the item carefully (see Book V for some hints) and write a thoughtful, selling description.

5. Handle all e-mail inquiries as though the item were your own; after all, your fee is generally based on a percentage of the final sale.

Traditional auction houses handle consignment sales in a similar fashion.

Compete with the Trading Posts

Several chains have opened up across the country with retail locations accepting merchandise from the general public. By becoming an official Trading Assistant, you can compete with the big boys in your own area.

The best part is that if you're running your eBay business out of your home, from a garage, or from a low-rent industrial office, you're a step ahead of the big guys who have to pay high rents in fancy neighborhoods to get their drop-in business. They also have to hire people who are familiar with running auctions on eBay — and aren't you *already* set up for that?

Don't worry about the competition! You may hear about the many brick-and-mortar eBay consignment stores that are opening up. (As a matter of fact, one company is selling franchises for this business for up to $15,000!) You already know how to sell on eBay, why would you need a franchise? Use your good sense (and positive feedback) to build your own eBay consignment store.

Following are some of the chains that sell goods on eBay for consumers:

- ✦ AuctionDrop, www.auctiondrop.com
- ✦ iSold It, www.i-soldit.com
- ✦ Instant Auctions, www.InstantAuctions.net
- ✦ eSavz.com, www.eSavz.com

Retail locations have a much higher cost of business than you do. They need to be open for set hours a day and have several employees on duty at all times. Many of these stores won't accept an item worth less than $75. There's still a lot of profit left for you in the realm of under-$75 items.

Table 3-1 shows the fees charged by various consignment chain stores, as of this writing.

Table 3-1	Consignment Chain Fees	
Chain	*Sold Price*	*Fee Percentage*
Auction Drop	up to $200	38
	$201 to $500	30
	over $500	20
iSoldIt	up to $500	35
	over $500	20

In addition to the fees shown in Table 3-1, these chain stores also charge for all eBay and PayPal fees (of course). There's also a $5.00 minimum commission per item. Check out these sites regularly so you can keep up with the competition in your own area.

What do you charge for all your work? I can't give you a stock answer for that one. Many sellers charge a flat fee for photographing, listing, and shipping that ranges from $5 to $10 plus as much as a 30 percent commission on the final auction total (to absorb eBay fees). Other sellers base their fees solely on the final sale amount and charge on a sliding scale, beginning at 50 percent of the total sale, less eBay and payment-service fees. You must decide how much you think you can make on an item.

Table 3-2 gives you some ideas based on the input I've received from some successful eBay consignment sellers. (These percentages may be in addition to the listing fee and gallery charges.)

Table 3-2	Sample Progressive Commission Schedule
Final Value ($)	**Your Commission**
Under 50	40%
50.01–150.00	35% of the amount over $50
150.01–250.00	30% of the amount over $150
251.00–500.00	25% of the amount over $500
501.00–1000.00	20% of the amount over $500
Over 1000	15%

Remember that you can always choose to charge a flat commission, if that works best in your area. Check out the eBay Trading Assistants in your area to see what they charge.

Becoming an eBay Trading Assistant

What is an eBay Trading Assistant? Simply put, an eBay Trading Assistant sells merchandise for people on eBay. A more complex definition is that a Trading Assistant sells items on consignment for those who are not familiar with the eBay site or simply don't want to bother to learn the ropes.

The first thing to take into consideration before becoming a Trading Assistant is to be sure you are familiar with the eBay site and its rules and regulations and — most of all — are experienced in selling items at a profit. To be a successful Trading Assistant, you need to know how to research items on eBay and how to parlay keywords into winning auction titles.

The Trading Assistants hub appears on the eBay site at

`www.eBay.com/tahub`

To find a Trading Assistant in your area, click the link on the hub page and you'll be taken to a search page (see Figure 3-1). Potential customers can search for a Trading Assistant to sell their items by city and state, postal ZIP code, eBay ID, or name.

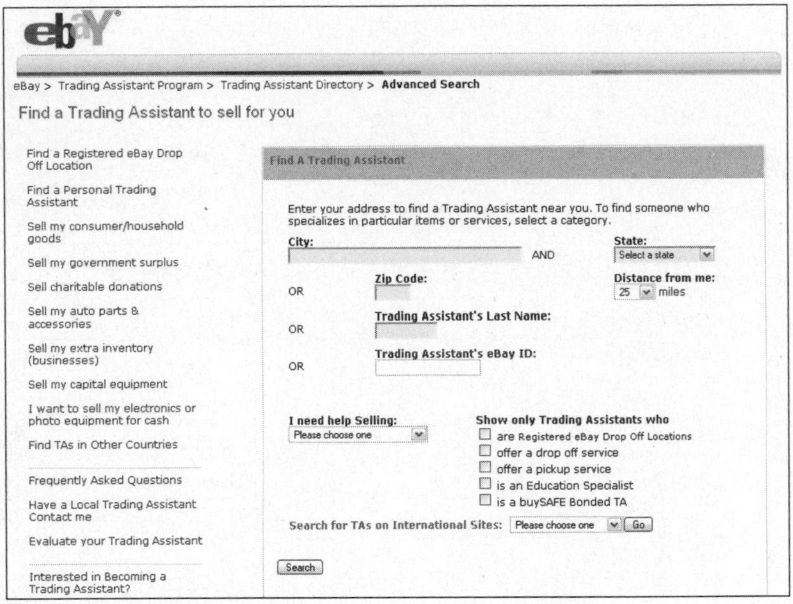

Figure 3-1: The Find a Trading Assistant page.

This page is promoted on the eBay site to new users and in eBay promotions. Being listed on this page will help your customers find you.

eBay makes it very clear that whether you fulfill the requirements for Trading Assistant or not, being a Trading Assistant is a privilege. If eBay receives complaints about your services, they have the right to remove you from the Trading Assistant directory. Following are eBay's requirements:

✦ **Listings:** You must have sold at least ten items in the last three months.

✦ **Feedback rating:** You must maintain a minimum rating of 100 or higher, with a minimum of 98-percent positive comments.

✦ **Activity:** You must have continued to sell (at least ten items in the previous three months).

✦ **Follow Terms.** eBay offers a style guide that outlines the use of the eBay brand. eBay takes the use of its name and graphics seriously, so if you intend to become a Trading Assistant, you must hold them in high honor. You can see the details at

```
ebaytradingassistant.com/index.php?page=userAgreements&type=
    taSG
```

You may notice on the directory-search screen that there's an option to search for buySAFE bonded sellers. This is a real selling point when it comes to doing business with strangers. A seller who's *bonded* is basically backed by insurance. (See Book VIII Chapter 2 for more on joining buySAFE.) Note that in Figure 3-2, buySAFE bonded sellers are listed first (here, in a search of Los Angeles, California).

Figure 3-2:
buySAFE
bonded
sellers
receive
choice
positions
in search
results.

As a Trading Assistant, you acquire merchandise and sell it on eBay on consignment. You are also responsible for the following:

✦ **Consulting with consignors about their items.**

✦ **Researching the value of the item.** Many non-eBay users may have unreasonable expectations of the price their items will sell for. It's your duty to check this out beforehand and explain the realities to them.

✦ **Coordinating the listing.** Take digital photos and write a complete and accurate description of the item.

✦ **Keeping a close accounting of fees and money collection.**

That's not much in the way of requirements, so get ready to become a TA.

Becoming a Trading Assistant does *not* make you an employee, agent, or independent contractor of eBay. Make sure you refer to yourself as an independent business.

When you sign up as a Trading Assistant, you have to fill out a form describing your business to prospective customers. Think through the things you want to say before posting them. Your information here works like an ad for you. Following are the items to put on your Trading Assistant listing page:

✦ **Personal information:** This includes your eBay user ID, your real name and address, and the languages spoken. Your personal information appears in the listing, such as the one from a professional Trading Assistant, borntodeal, shown in Figure 3-3.

Figure 3-3:
Trading
Assistant
Contact
Information
box.

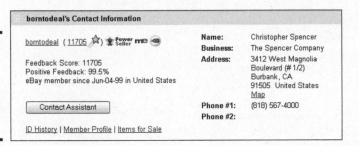

✦ **Category specialty:** If you specialize in a particular category, be sure to mention it. You may indicate eBay home page categories.

✦ **Service description:** In this area you can say as little or as much as you like about your eBay experience and the services you provide. Remember that the more you communicate in advance, the more successful you'll be.

Here is a sample service description (also look at the Specialties and Services in Figure 3-4):

> I've been active on the site since 1996 and am an eBay PowerSeller. I specialize in selling all types of eBay items and am particularly familiar with the fashion category. I can handle large numbers of listings. Please contact me so that we can discuss your particular needs and time availability.

> I can visit your home within 15 miles from my place of business to inventory the items. I will list, ship, and provide you with an itemized list of all items sold with the sale price and my fees.

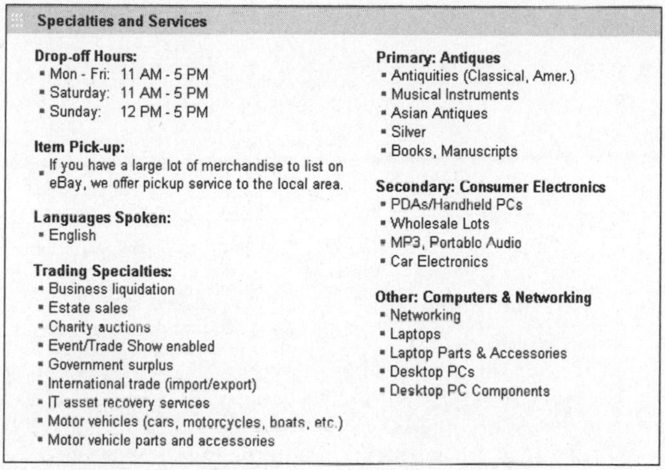

Specialties and Services

Drop-off Hours:
- Mon - Fri: 11 AM - 5 PM
- Saturday: 11 AM - 5 PM
- Sunday: 12 PM - 5 PM

Item Pick-up:
- If you have a large lot of merchandise to list on eBay, we offer pickup service to the local area.

Languages Spoken:
- English

Trading Specialties:
- Business liquidation
- Estate sales
- Charity auctions
- Event/Trade Show enabled
- Government surplus
- International trade (import/export)
- IT asset recovery services
- Motor vehicles (cars, motorcycles, boats, etc.)
- Motor vehicle parts and accessories

Primary: Antiques
- Antiquities (Classical, Amer.)
- Musical Instruments
- Asian Antiques
- Silver
- Books, Manuscripts

Secondary: Consumer Electronics
- PDAs/Handheld PCs
- Wholesale Lots
- MP3, Portable Audio
- Car Electronics

Other: Computers & Networking
- Networking
- Laptops
- Laptop Parts & Accessories
- Desktop PCs
- Desktop PC Components

Figure 3-4:
The Specialties and Services area.

✦ **Policy description:** Ensure that consignees understand your policies. A sample description follows:

> I will list your items for two listing cycles, spread up to 30 days. If items do not sell, they will be returned to you. Items must be in my possession to be submitted to eBay unless contractual arrangements are made in advance. I handle all correspondence and shipping. A consignment contract is required. I also do independent consulting specializing in Internet auctions and their application to your business.

✦ **Fee description:** This is where you need to do some research. Search your ZIP code on the Trading Assistants Directory page and see what other fees are being charged in your area. After you have an idea of what you want to charge, you can put that information here.

Take a look at the descriptions for the Trading Assistant shown in Figure 3-5. There's no question about how this seller handles his business once you read this text. See if you can come up with text that will sell your services without being overbearing.

You can provide incentives for higher-value items by charging lower commissions (such as "40 percent if the item sells for less than $50, but 30 percent if the item sells for more"). Also, charging a higher percentage and including fees allows an easier fee discussion with the client (for example, "40 percent and all fees included versus 30 percent and you pay all the fees, which include . . .").

Service description

The Spencer Company is a full-service Trading Assistance firm that provides consultation, photography, listing, fulfillment and all other services related to the selling of goods on eBay's Trading Community. We can help you liquidate your merchandise easily and quickly without a lot of hassle.

Fees

Bring your item to our location for a free consultation and rate quote for providing our services. Our commission covers all eBay Insertion Fees, Final Value Fees, payment processing fees, such as PayPal fees and any other costs plus our fee. We never charge anything extra for our excellent service.

Terms and Conditions

We provide services that are customized to the individual companies with whom we work. Please feel free to contact us for a consultation. We are Power Sellers and we are SquareTrade Seal members. Please feel confident in dealing with our company as we have well over seven years of experience with the eBay Trading Community and we work within the eBay Tradeshows and eBay University programs as a contractor.

Figure 3-5:
Company description portion of a Trading Assistant listing.

Many Trading Assistants also quote transaction fees for listing with a reserve (knowing it probably won't sell because the consignor doesn't have a fair guess at the market valuation).

When you've decided everything you need to list, click the Trading Assistant Requirements and Sign-up link on the Trading Assistant home page (mentioned at the beginning of this chapter). Fill out the forms and, just like magic, you've become a Trading Assistant!

Promoting Your Business

When I was working in the newspaper advertising business, we had a saying about someone who opened a new store: If all the advertising they do is their Grand Opening ad and nothing after, it won't be long before you'll be seeing the Going-Out-of-Business sale ad. The same is true with your Trading Assistant business.

Adding the Trading Assistant logo to your listings

Your best customers may come from people who see your existing items when browsing eBay. Why not show all viewers that you're a Trading Assistant by including the Trading Assistant logo in your listings. When prospective customers click the link, as shown in Figure 3-6, they'll be sent to your Trading Assistant Information page (just as if they searched for you in the directory).

Figure 3-6:
The eBay Trading Assistant link.

I am a Trading Assistant - I can sell your stuff on eBay!

Add the Trading Assistant logo when your regular eBay business is slow, and take it out when you're overly busy. That way, you can control the amount of work you have.

To add the link to your listings, you have to use a little HTML. Don't panic. It's easy. You can easily download the code from the Trading Assistant's secure area, or just use the following code. Add this HTML code at the end of your listing description, replacing *marsha_c* with your eBay User ID:

```
<p align="center"><img src="http://pics.ebaystatic.com/aw/pics/logos/logoUS_R_
    TA_RGB_141x106.jpg" alt="I am a Trading Assistant on eBay" width="141"
    height="106" border="0" longdesc="TA Logo" /></a></p>
<p align="center" class="style3"><a href="http://ebaytradingassistant.com/
    directory/index.php?page=profile&ebayID=
    marsha_c" target="_blank">I am a Trading Assistant - I can sell your stuff
    on eBay!</a></p>
```

That's all. Now the link and button shown in Figure 3-6 appear in your eBay listings.

Posting flyers

Why not design a flyer that you print on your own printer. Put it up at the supermarket, the car wash, the cleaner — anywhere and everywhere flyers are allowed.

Even if you don't see flyers in a retail location, ask the owner of the business if you can put one up — maybe even offer a discount to the business owner for selling their items on eBay in exchange!

To get to the eBay Trading Assistant logos and Toolkit, sign into your eBay Trading Assistant account and go to

```
ebaytradingassistant.com/tahome/index.php?page=resource
```

On this page, you can find the current graphical offerings from eBay.

You might want to make a flyer like the one shown in Figure 3-7, and include small tear-off strips where you can place your contact information. When people see your promotion, they can just snip off your phone number (or e-mail address) and contact you when they get home.

Figure 3-7: Excellent Trading Assistant promotional flyer.

Handling Your Business Professionally

How you conduct your business can demonstrate to your customers that you're a responsible person. You need to present a professional appearance when you meet your client, and you should have a professional attitude in your dealings.

Being professional also means anticipating possible problems. In addition to being very clear about financial issues with your clients (especially fees and the realistic selling value of your clients' merchandise), you may want to consider getting additional insurance to cover the merchandise you're holding in your home.

You may also want to consider designing a few forms to reinforce your clients' awareness that this is your business and that you know it well. For example:

✦ **Inventory form:** This form lists the entire inventory you receive from the client and should include as detailed a description of the item as your client can supply. Also, include the minimum amount (if any) the client will accept for the item — this will be your reserve price if necessary.

✦ **Sales agreement:** Professional Trading Assistants have their clients sign a sales contract. Read on for some good suggestions about what to put in your contract. You may want to have a lawyer look at your contract before you use it.

The following information was graciously supplied by eBay's successful Trading Assistants, Kate and Phil Bowyer. It includes quotes from their own Trading Assistant contract that cover many things you might overlook when you put together your own contract. This, of course, is not a full agreement, but it provides some of the salient points.

Be sure to include an explanation of the consignment process:

✦ The Consignor will bring item(s) to the Seller, who, upon both parties signing this contract, will take possession of the items for the duration of the auction.

✦ Acceptance of any item consigned will be at the Seller's sole discretion.

✦ The Seller will inspect the item(s) for quality and clean if necessary (a fee may apply).

✦ The Seller will take quality photographs and write an accurate description of item(s).

✦ The Seller will research eBay for similar items to assure proper pricing.

✦ The Seller will start the auction(s) and handle all aspects of the sale including correspondence with bidders.

✦ The Seller will collect payment from the winning bidder ("Buyer") at the end of the auction and will ship the item(s) in a timely manner, once funds have cleared.

✦ The Seller will follow up the sale by contacting the Buyer to make sure the Buyer is satisfied with the transaction.

✦ Once the Seller and Buyer are satisfied with the transaction, payment will be made to the Consignor.

✦ The Seller will keep the Consignor aware of the auction progress by telephone or e-mail and by supplying the Consignor the auction number(s) to track the item(s) themselves.

✦ The Seller will return unsold item(s) to the Consignor upon payment of outstanding fees.

It's also a good idea to provide the consignor with a statement of items sold, summarizing the total purchase price, all fees, and the amount the consignor receives.

✦ **Outline your fees:** "The Consignor will be billed the actual rates and fees as incurred for all services, to include the Seller's *00%* Commission. Any services or upgrades requested by the Consignor will carry the exact fee and will be deducted from payment, or after three (3) failed auction listings, will be due to the Seller payable in cash. If the auction sells, these fees will be subtracted from the winning bid before the Consignor receives payment."

Be sure to include a copy of current eBay fees: listing, options, reserves, PayPal, and final value fees.

✦ **Outline the terms of your commission:** "The Seller's commission for this service is a percentage based on the auction's winning bid. If the auction does not sell, the Consignor is only responsible to pay the applicable insertion and reserve price auction fees. An Unsold Reserve fee of *$0.00 [fill in your amount]* will be due to The Seller for a reserve price auction that does not sell."

✦ **Be sure you don't guarantee the item will sell.** "If an item does not sell, the Seller will re-list it two additional times. The Seller may contact the Consignor to discuss combining individual items into lots to attract buyers. The Consignor's verbal consent, or e-mail consent, will be documented in the Consignor's file and will serve as a revision to this contract. After a third unsuccessful listing, the Consignor will be billed for the fees associated with all three auctions, plus a $5.00 surcharge. Items will be returned to the Consignor upon payment of those fees. Items not claimed within 14 days from the end of the final listing will become the property of the Seller."

✦ **Protect yourself and your eBay reputation:** "The Consignor of said item(s) consents to the sale of said item(s) based on the terms described in this agreement. The Consignor also attests that said item(s) are fully owned by the Consignor and are not stolen, borrowed, misrepresented, bogus, etc."

You might also mention that you will only sell the item if eBay policies allow the item to be sold.

"The Seller will do everything possible to secure the safety of the Consignor's item(s), however, the Seller is not responsible for any damage to the item, including fire, theft, flood, accidental damage or breakage, and acts of God. The Consignor releases the Seller of any such responsibility for any unforeseen or accidental damage."

I choose to protect myself additionally, because reputation on eBay is paramount. I have a small business rider on my homeowner's insurance that covers merchandise in my home up to $5,000. It's an inexpensive addition to your policy — *definitely* worth looking into.

✦ **Ending a sale prematurely:** "If such an instance arises that the Consignor demands the item(s) to be pulled, the Consignor will pay a cancellation fee of $75. Items will not be surrendered to the Consignor until this fee is paid in cash."

✦ **Protect yourself from possible shill bidding:** An important line you should add protects you from possible shill bidding. How about: "The Consignor also agrees not to place a bid on an auction that the Seller has listed for the Consignor (hereafter "Shill Bid") on eBay, nor to arrange for a Shill Bid to be made on the behalf of the Consignor by a third party. If the Consignor or an agent of the Consignor submits a Shill Bid on an auction listed by the Seller, the Consignor agrees to pay all fees, commissions, and penalties associated with that auction, plus a $75.00 fine, and the Seller may refuse to grant auction services to the Consignor in the future."

Again, I strongly suggest that you get professional advice before putting together your own contract or agreement.

Chapter 4: Liquidation and Drop-Shipping

In This Chapter

✓ **Speaking like a merchandiser**

✓ **Understanding the different types of salvage**

✓ **Practicing safe shopping**

✓ **Drop-shipping without drop-kicking your customers**

You're likely to find various levels of quality when you look for merchandise to resell on eBay. Receiving a box of ripped or stained goods when you expected first-quality merchandise can be disheartening. If you take the time to evaluate the condition of the merchandise you're interested in buying, you save time (and money) in the long run. But to make that evaluation, you need to know what the industry language tells you about the quality of the merchandise.

In addition to qualifying the goods you buy, take the time to qualify the processes and partners you use. For example, *drop-shipping* (shipping goods straight from the stockpile to the consumer) has become a popular method for moving merchandise sold on eBay, but it comes with many caveats. For example, eBay has a policy about preselling items, so be sure to check it out — and make sure your drop-shipper has the merchandise ready to go when you place your order. Use this chapter to become a savvy buyer of goods to resell *and* an effective mover of those same goods.

Know the Lingo of Merchandisers

To help ensure that industry jargon won't trip you up, this section describes the lingo you need to know and offers pointers on making the right decisions about your merchandise and methods. Here are some terms you're likely to come across:

✦ **Job lots:** A *job lot* simply refers to a bunch of merchandise sold at once. The goods may consist of unusual sizes, odd colors, or even some hideous stuff that won't blow out of your eBay store if a hurricane comes in. Some of the merchandise (usually no more than 15 percent) may be damaged. Super discounts can be had on job lots — and if the lot contains brand names from major stores, you may be able to make an excellent profit.

A good way to find a *jobber* (someone who wants to sell you job lots) on the Internet is to run a Google search on *wholesale jobber*. Another great place to find a jobber is in the phone book or industry newsletter classifieds.

✦ **Off-price lots:** If you can get hold of top-quality, brand-name items in off-price lots, you can do very well on eBay. These items are end-of-season *overruns* (more items were made than could be sold through normal retailers). You can generally find this merchandise toward the end of the buying season.

Many eBay sellers, without having the thousands of dollars to buy merchandise, make friends with the salespeople at manufacturers' outlet stores (where the merchandise may land first). Others haunt places like TJ Maxx, Marshall's, and Burlington Coat Factory for first-rate deals.

Search the classified ads of genuine trade publications for items to buy in bulk. Publications such as *California Apparel News* have classifieds that are accessible online. Visit its Web site at www.apparelnews.net and click Classifieds (see Figure 4-1). Subscribing to the online publication will no doubt get you quicker access to the choice sample and merchandise sales.

Figure 4-1: Access industry classifieds on the California Apparel News Web site.

Getting the 411 on refurbished goods

You can find great deals on refurbished electronic merchandise on eBay. Unfortunately, refurbished merchandise gets an unnecessarily bad rap. Very smart people may tell you to be wary of refurbished merchandise. Great advice . . . I guess. I tell people to be wary of *all* merchandise.

The way I figure it, refurbished merchandise has been gone over by the manufacturer twice — new merchandise has been gone over only once! I buy refurbished merchandise all the time. Let me explain what refurbished merchandise is and why it can be such a bargain. Refurbished merchandise can fall into one of these categories:

✔ **Canceled orders:** This is merchandise in perfectly good shape. Say a customer makes a special order and then changes his or her mind, or the order is somehow mucked up ("I ordered a PC. You sent me a Mac!"). Something has to be done with the merchandise. Enter you, the savvy shopper.

✔ **Evaluation units:** An evaluation unit is a piece of equipment that is sent to a member of the media or to a corporation for testing or review. Evaluation units must be returned to the manufacturer, and the manufacturer may decide to unload them.

✔ **Store returns:** This is probably pretty obvious to you, right? Joe Customer buys something in a store, takes it home and opens it, only to decide that he doesn't really want it. By law, as soon as the box is opened, a piece of merchandise can never be sold as new again, even if the merchandise was never used.

✔ **Defective units:** This is a piece of merchandise deemed defective by either the store or by the user and returned to the manufacturer.

✔ **Overstocks:** When manufacturers come out with a new model, they may take back the older models from retailers in an effort to encourage them to stock more of the newer, faster, cooler model.

Whenever an item is returned to the manufacturer for any reason and the original box has been opened, the item (whether it's a television, a computer, a camera, or some other technical device), must be reconditioned to the manufacturer's original quality standards. Any nonfunctioning parts are replaced with functioning components and the item is repackaged. The manufacturer usually gives refurbished items a 90-day warranty.

When buying refurbished goods, be sure the original manufacturer was the one doing the reconditioning. I'm sure that some technical geeks can fix things just fine in their garage, but you don't have the same level of protection (as in, you don't have a warranty from a reliable source) if you buy a piece of equipment that wasn't fixed by the manufacturer.

✦ **Liquidations:** All eBay sellers think of liquidations as the mother lode of deals. And, yes, they may be the mother lode of deals if you can afford to buy and store an entire 18-wheeler truckload of merchandise. That takes a great deal of money and a great deal of square footage, plus the staff to go through each and every item.

The merchandise can be an assortment of liquidations, store returns, salvage, closeouts, shelf pulls, overstocks, and surplus goods. Some items may be damaged but repairable; others may be perfectly salable. As much as 30% or more of a truckload may be useless. Buying liquidation merchandise is a gamble but can have advantages. By buying a full truckload, you have a wide breadth of merchandise, you pay the lowest amount for it, and some of it may be good for spare parts. Just make sure beforehand that you have a place to put it all.

Save yourself some money. Don't go on eBay and buy some wholesale list for $5. You can get the same names by running a Google search on the term *wholesale*. Every true wholesaler Web site has a dealer login page, so try searching for *dealer login* along with a category name, such as *dealer login jewelry*.

Salvage: Liquidation Items, Unclaimed Freight, and Returns

The easiest to buy for resale, *salvage merchandise* is retail merchandise that has been returned, exchanged, or shelf-pulled for some reason. Salvage can also encompass liquidation merchandise and unclaimed freight. Generally, this merchandise is sold as-is and where-is and may be in new condition. To buy this merchandise directly from the liquidator in large lots, you must have your resale (sales tax number) permit and be prepared to pay the shipping to your location.

Several types of salvage merchandise are available:

✦ **Unclaimed freight:** When a trucking company delivers merchandise, a manifest accompanies the freight. If, for some reason, a portion of the shipment arrives incomplete, contains the wrong items, or is damaged, the entire shipment may be refused by the merchant. The trucking company is now stuck with as much as a truckload of freight. The original seller may not want to pay the freight charges to return the merchandise to his or her warehouse (or accept blame for an incorrect shipment), so the freight becomes the trucker's problem. The trucking companies arrive at agreements with liquidators to buy this freight in the various areas that the liquidators serve. This way, truckers are never far from a location where they can dump, er, drop off merchandise.

✦ **Returns:** Did you know that when you return something to a store or mail-order house, it can never be sold as new again (in most states anyway)? The merchandise is generally sent to a liquidator who agrees in advance to pay a flat percentage for goods. The liquidator must move the merchandise to someone else. All major retailers liquidate returns, and much of this merchandise ends up on eBay or in closeout stores.

If you're handy at repairing electronics or computers, you'd probably do very well with a specialized lot. You may easily be able to revitalize damaged merchandise, often using parts from two unsalable items to come up with one that you can sell in like-new working condition.

✦ **Liquidations:** Liquidators buy liquidation merchandise by truckloads and sell it in smaller lots. The merchandise comes from financially stressed or bankrupt companies that need to raise cash quickly.

The liquidation business has been thriving as a well-kept secret for years. As long as you have space to store salvage merchandise and a way to sell it, you can acquire it for as low as ten cents on the dollar. When I say you need storage space, I mean lots of space. To buy this type of merchandise at bottom-of-the-barrel prices, you must be willing to accept truckloads — full 18-wheelers, loaded with more than 20 pallets (4 feet x 4 feet x 6 or 7 feet) — of merchandise at a time. Often these truckloads have *manifests* (a document containing the contents of the shipment) listing the retail and wholesale price of each item on the truck. If you have access to the more-than-10,000-square-feet of warehouse that you'll need to unpack and process this amount of merchandise, you're in business.

I'm a fan of Liquidatation.com and often find myself scrolling their home page to see the current offerings (see Figure 4-2). Buying from them at a good price can mean healthy profits.

see Figure 4-2

Closing Soon			
Title	Qty/Lot	Price/Lot	Closing
HIGHEND JUNIORS APPAREL: BUFFALO- GUE...	101	$552.00	10:00AM
NEW DESIGNER SUNGLASSES: HOT NEW STYLES	50	$125.00	10:00AM
LOT OF DESIGNER GLASSES EYEWEAR SUNGL...	50	$100.00	10:00AM
Portable Photo Printers (no cameras) ...	10	$150.00	10:00AM
Insignia Receivers and CD Changers	18	$128.00	10:05AM
ROSE RING FOR WOMEN - MANY COLORS	100	$100.00	10:05AM
PC Power Adapters & Batteries From Ke...	12	$252.00	10:05AM
South Shore Full/Queen Platform Stora...	7	$100.00	10:10AM
Western Digital Hard Drives	24	$1,025.00	10:10AM
1248PC LOT OF FASHION JEWELRY! SHELLS...	1248	$325.00	10:10AM
Appliances & Housewares From AeroBed,...	20	$350.00	10:10AM
Disk Recorders & Turntables From Pion...	11	$125.00	10:10AM
GLASS PEARL BRACELETS HUGE LOT BRAND ...	500	$100.00	10:10AM
VICTORIAN CHOKER NECKLACE SETS WITH A...	40	$100.00	10:15AM
Digital Cameras by Disney, Spectra	21	$150.00	10:15AM
MASSIVE LOT OF NECKLACE SETS MANY STYLES	1120	$159.00	10:20AM
10 Portable DVD Players - Various Brands	10	$205.00	10:25AM
DESIGNER GLASSES W/ RHINESTONES BRAND...	100	$175.00	10:25AM
CURRENCY CONVERTER AND 6 LANGUAGE TRA...	50	$150.00	10:25AM

Figure 4-2: Liquidation.com's current closing liquidation auctions.

Buying liquidation merchandise on eBay

Liquidation merchandise can be new, used, or trashed. Searching through a liquidator's eBay auctions is like digging through the "Final Sale" bin at a store, where prices are marked down to absurd levels.

Liquidators buy merchandise from companies that are in financial distress and need to raise cash quickly. The kinds of issues companies face can vary — the why isn't important. All you need to know is that you can get access to some astonishing deals because some of it is sold in lots on eBay.

Merchandise arrives by the truckload. From there the merchandise is unloaded, inspected, and sorted — and then the fun begins. Some of the merchandise can be put together in wholesale *lots* (the goods are grouped by the pallet or by the case and sold to wholesalers or retailers), and some of the merchandise may be put aside to be sold to sellers for resale on eBay.

Buying items from liquidators can be a risky enterprise. There's no warranty, and no one you can complain to if something is wrong with the item. All items are always sold *as is* and *where is*. Essentially, what you see is what you get; if it works, it's a bonus.

Here are some tips for buying this type of item:

✔ **Look for "sealed in the box":** Look at the picture and read the description carefully. If the description states that the item is sealed in the manufacturers packaging, you have a pretty good chance that the item is in new condition.

✔ **Don't spend a bundle:** This kind of goes without saying, right? It's supposed to be a bargain.

✦ **Seasonal overstocks:** My motto is "Buy off-season, sell on-season." At the end of the season, a store may find its shelves overloaded with seasonal merchandise (such as swimsuits in August) that it must get rid of to make room for the next season's stock. These brand-new items become salvage merchandise because they're seasonal overstocks.

✦ **Shelf-pulls:** Have you ever passed up one item in the store for the one behind it in the display because its box was in better condition? Sometimes the plastic bubble or the package is dented, and you'd rather have a pristine one. That box you just passed up may be destined to become a *shelf-pull*. The item inside may be in perfect condition, but it's cosmetically unsalable in the retail-store environment.

Some liquidation items, unclaimed freight, and returns may be unsalable. Although you'll acquire many gems that stand to bring you profit, you'll also be left with a varying percentage of useless items.

Some liquidation sellers sell their merchandise in the same condition that it ships in to their location, so what you get is a crapshoot. You may lose money on some items while making back your money on others. Other sellers who charge a bit more will remove less desirable merchandise from the pallets. Some may even make up deluxe pallets with better-quality merchandise. These loads cost more, but if they're filled with the type of merchandise that you're interested in selling, you'll probably write better descriptions and subsequently do a better job selling them.

Before you glaze over and get dazzled by a low, low price on a lot, check the shipping cost to you *before* you buy. Many so-called wholesalers will lure you in with bargain-basement prices, only to charge you three times the normal shipping costs. Do your homework before you buy!

Staying Safe When Buying Online

Nobody offers a quality or fitness guarantee when you buy liquidation merchandise. You could end up with pallets of unsalable merchandise, and you must steer quickly away from anyone who guarantees that you'll make money. Remember that liquidation merchandise is always sold as-is.

Unfortunately, this market is rife with unscrupulous sellers who are middlemen. They buy the truckloads, go through everything with a fine-tooth comb, and pull out all the saleable merchandise. Then they repack the pallets and sell them to unsuspecting newbies who think that they *may* get a good deal.

When buying online, it's hard to know about the company you're dealing with because you've probably just found them after performing a Web search. When you find a source from which you want to buy merchandise by the pallet, check out a few things before spending your hard-earned cash:

✦ **Get an anonymous free e-mail address from Yahoo! before signing up for any mailing lists or newsletters.** Some Web sites that offer these publications make most of their money by selling your e-mail address to spammers. If you give them an anonymous e-mail address, the buckets of spam will never end up in your *real* mailbox. (I learned about that the hard way.)

✦ **Raise your shields if the wholesalers also link their Web sites to miscellaneous make-big-profits-on-eBay Web sites.** They may be making most of their money from commissions when the e-book of "road-to-riches secret tips" is sold to you.

+ **Be sure the site has a phone number.** Give them a call and see how you're treated. It's no guarantee of how they'll treat you if you're unhappy with a purchase, but you may get a human being on the phone (rare and precious these days).

+ **Look for a physical address.** Do they have a place of business or is the company running out of some guy's pocket cell phone? (Often it's not a good sign if there's no place to *hang* a sign.)

+ **Ask for references.** Seeing the Better Business Bureau Online, TrustE, or SquareTrade logo on the Web site can bolster trust in the company. (They have to qualify for those seals.)

+ **Before you purchase anything, go to eBay and see whether that item will sell — and for how much.** Often you find hundreds of listings for an item with no bids. Check completed auctions and be sure that the item is selling for a solid profit over what you expect to pay for it (including shipping).

+ **Never buy anything just because it's cheap.** That was true in Thomas Jefferson's day and is still true today. Be sure you can actually *sell* the merchandise. (I also learned *this* the hard way.)

+ **Guarantee:** Does the source guarantee that you *will* make money or that you *can* make money by buying the right merchandise? Remember that no one can guarantee that you'll make money.

+ **References:** Does the supplier offer on its Web site references that you can contact to find out some usable information on this seller's items and the percentage of unsalable goods in a box or pallet?

+ **Look for *FOB*.** That means *freight on board.* You will be charged freight from the location of the merchandise to your door. The shorter the distance, the cheaper your freight costs.

Before doing business on any Web site, be sure its owners have a privacy policy that protects your personal information. Also check for an About Us page and make sure the page talks about the business and the people behind it. I hate to be repetitive, but be sure you can reach a human being on a phone or in person (with a street address) if need be.

Dealing with Drop-Shippers

A *drop-shipper* is a business that stocks merchandise, sells the merchandise to you (the reseller), but ships it directly to your customer. By using a drop-shipper, you transfer the risks of buying, storing, and shipping merchandise to another party. You become a *stockless* retailer with no inventory hanging around — often an economical, cost-effective way to do business.

The following steps outline the standard way to work with most drop-shippers on eBay:

1. Sign up on the drop-shipper's Web site to sell their merchandise on eBay or in your Web store. Check out their terms before you sign up to be sure there's no minimum purchase.

2. Select the items from their inventory that you want to sell. The supplier gives you descriptive copy and photographs to help make your sales job easier.

3. Post the item online and wait (fidgeting with anticipation) for someone to buy it.

4. As soon as your buyer pays you for the item, e-mail the drop-shipper (or fill out a special secure form on their Web site) and pay for the item with your credit card or PayPal.

5. Relax while the drop-shipper ships the item to your customer for you.

6. If all goes well, the item arrives quickly and safely.

You make a profit and get some positive feedback.

The drop-shipper's Web site provides you with descriptions and images. Fine. But you and everybody else who sells that item on eBay will have the same photos and descriptive copy. Do yourself a favor and get a sample of your item, take your own pictures, and write your own description. Then at least you have a chance at beating the competitive sameness on eBay.

Drop-shipping works especially well for Web-based retail operations. Web stores can link directly to the drop-shipper to transmit shipping and payment information. When you're selling on eBay, it's another thing. There's more competition and you can't list hundreds of items at no additional cost.

Listing items on eBay costs money and may build up your expenses before you make a profit. You can't just select an item from a drop-shipper and throw hundreds of auctions on eBay without losing money. That is, unless your item is selling like gangbusters at an enormous profit. If that were the case, believe me, there would be another eBay seller buying directly from the manufacturer and undercutting your price.

I must interject that I bought (for research) several drop-shipper lists from eBay sellers. I am saddened to report that I couldn't find *any* that fulfilled my security requirements for doing business with an unknown business online. The drop-shippers whose merchandise I could track had a penchant for flooding the eBay market by selling the same item to too many sellers — thereby driving down the price. I also found little brand-name merchandise available. If any of my readers find a reputable drop-shipper who allows room for profit on eBay, please e-mail me through my Web site. I think this is a business that *could* work, but only if the right businesses were involved.

Drop-shipping to your customers

Some middlemen, wholesalers, and liquidators specialize in selling to online auctioneers through a drop-ship service. Some crafty eBay sellers make lots of money selling lists of drop-shipping sources to eBay sellers — I hope not to you. Dealing with a drop-shipper means that you don't ever have to take possession of (or pay for) the merchandise. You're given a photo and, after you sell the item, you give the vendor the address of the buyer. They charge your credit card for the item plus shipping, and then ship the item to your customer for you.

This way of doing business costs *you* more and lowers your profits. Your goal as a business owner is to make as much money as you can. Because the drop-shipper is in business too,

they'll mark up the merchandise (and the shipping cost) so they can make their profit.

Be careful when using a drop-shipper. Ask for references. See whether a zillion sellers are selling the same merchandise on eBay — and not getting any bites. Also, what happens if a drop-shipper runs out of an item that you've just sold? You can't just say "oops" to your buyer without getting some nasty feedback. It's your online reputation at stake. If you find a solid source and believe in the product, order a quantity and have it shipped to your door. Don't pay for someone else's mark-up just for the convenience of having them ship to your customers.

It's one thing to sign up for a free newsletter — or even to register with a particular site — but it's something else to have to pay to see what the drop-shipper intends to offer you. *You should not pay anything in advance for the opportunity to check out a drop-shipper's merchandise.*

Finding a good drop-shipper

Thousands of Web companies are aching to help you set up your online business. Some of them are good solid companies with legitimate backgrounds, but others are just trying to get your money. These guys hope you don't know what you're doing; they're betting you'll be desperate enough to send them some cash to help you get your share of the (har, har) "millions to be made online."

Consider the following when you're choosing drop-shippers to work with:

✦ **Skepticism is healthy.** When you come across Web sites that proclaim that they can drop-ship thousands of different products for you, think twice. *Thousands?* I don't know many stores that *carry* thousands of items — if they do, they have vast square footage for storage and hundreds of thousands of dollars to invest in merchandise. Most drop-shipping services don't. A much smaller offering of merchandise may indicate that the drop-shipper has the merchandise ready to ship and isn't relying on ordering it from someone for you.

✦ **Look out for long lines of distribution.** Drop-shippers are often middle-men who broker merchandise from several sources — for example, from other middlemen who buy from brokers (who in turn buy from manufac-turers). The line of distribution can get even longer — which means that a slew of people are making a profit from your item before you even buy it "wholesale." If even one other reseller gets the product directly from the distributor or (heaven forbid) the manufacturer, that competitor can easily beat your target selling price. Verify with the drop-shipper that they stock the merchandise they sell.

Coping with the inevitable out-of-stock

What happens when you sell an item and you go to the distributor's site and find that it's sold out? Before your heart stops, call the drop-shipper. Perhaps they still have one or two of your items around their warehouse and took the item off the Web site because they're running too low to guarantee delivery.

If that isn't the case, you're going to have to contact your buyer and 'fess up that the item is currently out of stock at your supplier. I suggest calling your customers in this situation; they may not be *as* angry as they might be if you just e-mail them. Offer to refund the money immediately. Somebody else's foul-up may net you bad feedback, but that risk goes along with using drop-shipping as a business practice.

Book V
Presenting Your Items

The 5th Wave   By Rich Tennant

"Try putting a person in the photo with the
product you're trying to sell. We generated
a lot of interest in our eBay Listing once Leo
started modeling my hats and scarves."

Contents at a Glance

Chapter 1: Your eBay Photo Studio

In This Chapter

✔ Setting up a photo studio

✔ Looking into digital camera features

✔ Scanning your items

✔ Buying other tools for your photo studio

*W*elcome to the cyberworld of *imaging,* where pictures aren't called pictures, but *images.* With a digital camera or a scanner and software, you can manipulate your images — crop, color-correct, and add special effects — so they grab viewers by the lapels.

Sellers, take heed and read why you should use well-made digital images in your auction pages:

✦ If you don't have a picture, potential bidders may wonder whether you're deliberately hiding the item from view because you know something is wrong with it. Paranoid? Maybe. Practical? You bet.

✦ Fickle bidders don't even bother reading an item description if they can't see the item.

✦ Taking your own pictures shows that you have the item in your possession. Many scam artists take images from a manufacturer's Web site to illustrate their bogus sales on eBay. Why risk being suspect? Snap a quick picture!

✦ Everyone's doing it. I hate to pressure you, but digital images are the custom on eBay, so if you're not using them, you're not reaching the widest possible number of people who would bid on your item. From that point of view, you're not doing the most you can to serve your potential customers' needs. Hey, fads are *driven* by conformity. You may as well use them to your advantage.

So which is better for capturing images: a digital camera or a digital scanner? As with all gadgets, here's the classic answer: It depends. For my money, it's hard to beat a digital camera. But before you go snag one, decide what kind of investment (and how big) you plan to make in your eBay auctions. If you're already comfortable with 35mm camera equipment, don't scrap it — scan (or find a digital SLR — single lens reflex). The scoop on both alternatives is coming right up.

Setting Up Your Studio

Taking pictures for eBay? No problem! You have a digital camera, and you know how to use it. Just snap away and upload that picture, right? Sorry, but no. There's a good way and a bad way to take photos for eBay and, believe it or not, the professional way taught by many instructors isn't necessarily the best way.

I recommend that you set up a mini photo studio for your eBay auction pictures. That way, you won't have to clean off your kitchen counter every time you want to take pictures.

If you must use the kitchen counter or a desktop, be sure to use an inexpensive photo stage, which you can find on — where else? — eBay.

You need several basic things in your photo studio; the extras you should have are based on the type of merchandise you're selling. An eBay *generalist,* someone who sells almost anything online — like me! — should have quite a few extras for taking quality photos. Check out a portion of my home photo studio in Figure 1-1. This setup works well for small as well as large items.

Figure 1-1:
One of my
eBay photo
setups.

Alternatively, in Figure 1-2, I use a photo cube combined with either small clamp lights (shown), true color lamps, or tall floodlights. A photo cube works well for finely detailed and collectible objects — as well as any object that will fit in them. By using a translucent fabric cube, you can fully illuminate your item and have no glare, harsh shadows, or detail burnout!

Figure 1-2: Using a photo cube on my dining room table to photograph antiques.

Hands down, the equipment for photographing jewelry and teeny, tiny items is the Cloud Dome (see "Other Studio Equipment" later in this chapter). It not only helps with lighting, but also holds your camera steady for difficult super-magnified (*macro*) shots.

What you find in this section might be more than you thought you'd need to produce good pictures. But your photographs can help sell your merchandise, so you need to consider this part of your business seriously. Of course, if you sell only one type of item, you won't need such a varied selection of stuff, but you should have the basic photo setup. Check my Web site (www. coolebaytools.com) for more ideas.

Your #1 Tool: A Digital Camera

Digital cameras are mysterious things. You may read about *megapixels* (a million pixels) and think that more is supposed to be better, but that doesn't apply to eBay applications or to Web images. Megapixels measure the image resolution that the camera is capable of recording. For online use, all you need from a camera is 640 x 480 pixels (or, at the most, 800 x 600 pixels) because computer monitors are incapable of taking advantage of more pixels. If you use a higher-resolution picture, you'll have a pixel-bloated picture that takes a looooong time to load online.

The camera you use for eBay is a personal choice. Would-be big-time sellers starting out in an eBay business (with no experience on the Internet) usually go out and buy the most expensive digital camera they can find. Maybe having lots of megapixels is a macho thing, but a camera with a bunch of megapixels is the last thing you need for eBay images.

You don't need a million pixels, but you do need the following:

✦ **Quality lens:** I'm sure anyone who has worn glasses can tell the difference between a good lens and a cheap one. Really cheap cameras have plastic lenses, and the quality of the resulting pictures is accordingly lousy. Your camera will be your workhorse, so be sure to buy one from a company known for making quality products.

✦ **Removable media:** Most cameras can connect to your PC with a USB cable, and many sellers are happy with that type of connection. Others find that taking their camera to the computer and using cables and extra software to download pictures to the hard drive is annoying. Removable media eliminate this annoyance. Here's a starter list of removable storage media:

 • **CompactFlash memory card:** This is a small medium, slightly smaller than a matchbook. You insert it into a media reader to transfer the data to your computer. CompactFlash cards come in different sizes, and hold from 16 MB to 16 GB.

 • **Secure digital card:** The fairly new incarnation in mini storage is the secure digital card. This amazing little piece of technology (the size of a postage stamp) is one of the most durable of the small media. It's encased in plastic, as is the CompactFlash card and the Memory Stick. It also uses metal connector contacts (rather than pins and plugs like other cards), making it less prone to damage. These cards can be set to hold up to 32 GB.

 • **Mini and micro secure digital cards:** If the matchbook-size SD card wasn't small enough, manufacturers decided to miniaturize them further — and increase the amount of data they can carry. The mini version is about the size of a postage stamp and the micro? When I first saw this card, I was afraid to touch it. It's about the size of my pinky nail and can hold up to an astounding 12 GB (check out Figure 1-3). The micro card can often be purchased with an adapter that will allow it to be inserted into a carrier so it can be used in any standard SD card slot.

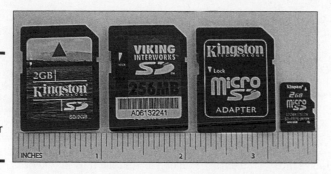

Figure 1-3:
You'll find
many
sizes and
adapters for
SD cards.

- **SmartMedia cards:** A SmartMedia card is slightly smaller than a CompactFlash card, is very thin, and has no plastic outer case. It's used in only a few brands of digital cameras (such as Olympus). SmartMedia cards come in different data sizes, from 8MB to 128MB.

- **Memory Stick:** A tiny media card (about the size of a piece of chewing gum and as long as a AA battery), the Memory Stick is a Sony device used in most Sony products. Memory Sticks now hold as much as 2 GB. One of the great things about a Memory Stick is that it can be used in numerous devices besides cameras, including PCs and video recorders.

- **Mini CD, CD/RW, or DVD:** These optical discs hold tons of pics for eBay. You can read them right in your computer's CD or DVD reader. Check out your disc platter, and you'll notice a smaller round indentation; that's what holds the mini disc.

You insert any of these media directly into your computer, if your computer has ports for them. Or get an adapter that connects to your computer through a USB or parallel port. You can get appropriate readers on eBay for about $20.

You may find that you use more than one type of medium with your digital camera. And because you can record any type of digital data on these types of removable media, you may find other uses for them. For example, sometimes when I want to back up files (or move larger files) and don't have access to my flash drive, I copy them onto one of my camera memory cards in the reader on my desktop computer and then transfer the files by plugging the card into the adapter on my laptop.

✦ **Optical zoom versus digital zoom:** Two characteristics to keep in mind when looking for a camera are convenience and *optical* zoom. Choose a camera that is easy to use and has the accessories you want. Also, make sure that the optical-zoom capabilities will help you capture the level of detail that your merchandise requires.

When shopping for your camera, find one with the highest-power optical zoom that you can afford. *Optical zoom* is magnified by the camera's lens (using the camera's internal optics), producing a vivid picture.

Digital zoom is valuable with a camcorder when you're shooting moving pictures, because the eye can't focus as easily as the camera on moving results. When your camera uses digital zoom, it does the same thing as enlarging a picture in photo-editing software. The camera centers the focus over half the focal plane, and uses software interpolation to enlarge the picture. This makes your image slightly fuzzy.

✦ **Tripod mount:** Have you ever had a camera hanging around your neck while you're trying to repackage some eBay merchandise that you've just photographed? Or perhaps you've set down the camera for a minute and then can't find it? Avoid this hassle by using a tripod to hold your camera. Tripods also help you avoid blurring your pictures if your hands are a bit shaky. To use a tripod, you need a *tripod mount*, the little screw-hole that you see at the bottom of some cameras. Later in this chapter, I give you some tips on finding the right tripod.

✦ **Macro setting capability or threading for a lens adapter:** These features will come in handy if you plan to photograph coins, jewelry, or small detailed items. A camera's macro setting enables you to get in really close to items while keeping them in focus. Usually the macro mode can focus as close as 1 inch and as far away as 10 inches. A small flower icon in the camera's menu normally signifies the macro setting. A threaded lens mount is an alternative that enables you to add different types of lenses to the camera for macro focus or other uses.

The average camera's *focal length* (focus range) is from 3 feet to infinity. If you have a camera that says the macro focus range is set at 5.1 inches, it means you can't focus it clearly on an object any closer than 5.1 inches. Macro pictures require a steady hand (or affix your camera to a Cloud Dome or at the very least to a tripod); any vibration can blur your image.

✦ **Battery life:** When you're choosing your camera, be sure to check into the length of time the camera's battery will hold a charge. The last thing you want to do is run out of juice at the wrong moment. Consider the following:

• Look for a camera battery with at least three hours of photo-taking time.

• Keep a spare battery on hand. I keep a Lithium CR-V3 battery (which replaces two AA batteries) in my purse so I'll be prepared if my camera battery runs low while I'm on the road.

• Invest in a charger and rechargeable batteries. I have a rechargeable backup battery for my camera in the office. These batteries last a long time and are worth the investment.

Cameras have presets for different focal ranges, and they're usually set in meters. (There's an *m* following the focus range number.) Just so you won't forget, a meter is approximately 3 feet in distance.

✦ **White-balance setting:** This is a tricky feature. Most eBay digital photographers set the camera to Auto (if there is a setting) and hope for the best. If you can adjust the white balance, do so. Manufacturers use different presets. The list of options can include settings for incandescent lights, twilight, fluorescent lights, outdoor, indoor, or shade. All these lighting situations have different color temperatures, as I discuss in the "Lighting" section later in this chapter.

It's worthwhile to take the time to play with the various white-balance settings of your camera in the different places where you normally photograph eBay merchandise. Make notes on settings that give you the truest colors in your digital images.

✦ **Autofocus and zoom:** These options just make life easier when you want to take pictures, and should be standard features.

The bottom line is that you should buy a brand-name camera. I often still use an antique Sony Mavica FD92 for eBay pictures. (I use a Nikon CoolPix for shooting around as well.) The Mavica is way outdated, but it's also loaded with all the bells and whistles I need for eBay photos. It stores images on a floppy disk (remember those?) or on a Sony Memory Stick, which I just pop out and insert in my computer. The camera's storage convenience makes the Mavica FD series a favorite of eBay sellers.

I bet you could find a camera that fits your needs right now on eBay for considerably less than $150. (The old Mavica FD series can be had dirt-cheap, and they're still big sellers on eBay). Remember that many digital camera users buy the newest camera available and sell their older, low-megapixel cameras on eBay for a pittance. Many professional camera stores also sell used equipment.

Scanning Your Wares

Scanners have come a long way in the past few years. A once-expensive item can now be purchased new for a little more than a $100. If you sell books, autographs, stamps, or documents, a scanner may be all you need to shoot your images for eBay.

When shopping for a scanner, don't pay too much attention to the resolution. Some scanners can provide resolutions as high as 12,800 dpi, which looks awesome when you print the image. But to dress up your eBay auctions, all you need is (are you ready?) 72 dpi! That's it. Your images will look great, won't take up much storage space on your computer's hard drive, and won't take forever to load when a buyer looks at them. Basic scanners can scan images up to 1200 dpi, so even they are more powerful than you need for your eBay images. As with digital cameras, you should stick with a brand-name scanner.

You should use a *flatbed* scanner, on which you lay out your items and scan away. I replaced my old scanner with an HP All-in-One, which is not only a scanner but also a printer, a fax machine, and a color copier! These nifty flat-bed units are available new on eBay. I've seen HP models, new in box, sell for as low as $100.

A few tips on scanning images for eBay:

✦ If you're taking traditionally processed photographs and scanning them, print them on glossy paper because they'll scan much better than those with a matte finish.

✦ You can scan 3-D items, such as a doll, on your flatbed scanner and get some respectable-looking images. To eliminate harsh shadows, lay a black or white T-shirt over the doll or her box so that it completely covers the glass. This way, you will have a clean background and get good light reflection from the scanner's light.

✦ If you want to scan an item that's too big for your scanner's glass, simply scan the item in pieces, and then reassemble it to a single image in your photo-editing program. The instructions that come with your software should explain how to do this.

✦ Boxed items are a natural for a flatbed scanner. Just set them on top of the glass, and scan away. You can crop the shadowed background with your photo-editing software.

Don't ignore your video camera!

The majority of eBay sellers use a digital camera or a scanner to dress up their auctions with images, but some just use what they already own — their digital video cameras! Yup, after filming your day at the beach, point your lens at that Victorian doll and shoot. Most new (and inexpensive) video cameras have a single-frame setting so you can create your digital image right from the camera. Then just hook up the USB cable and download a stream of images quickly!

I am totally enamored with my Flip Video camera and my wonderful Sanyo Xacti. I use them often to take eBay pictures. Check online for the lowest prices — the Flip Video is often under $100. Of course, then search eBay for the best prices and see where you get the best deal.

Other Studio Equipment

What you find in this section might be more than you thought you'd need for photographing your items. But photographs can help sell your merchandise, so you need to take this part of your business seriously. Of course, if you sell only one type of item, you won't need such a varied selection of stuff, but you should have the basic photo setup.

Tripod

A *tripod* is an extendable, three-legged aluminum stand that holds your camera. You should look for one that has a quick release so if you want to take the camera off the tripod for a close-up, you don't have to unscrew it from the base and then screw it back on for the next picture.

The legs should extend to your desired height, lock in place with clamp-type locks, and have a crank-style geared center column so you can move your camera smoothly up and down for different shots. Most tripods also have a *panning head* for shooting from different angles. You can purchase a tripod from a camera store or on eBay for as low as $25.

Power supplies

If you've ever used digital cameras, you know that they can blast through batteries faster than sugar through a 5-year-old. A reliable power supply is a must. You can accomplish this in a couple of ways:

✦ **Rechargeable batteries:** Many specialists on eBay sell rechargeable batteries and chargers. Choose quality Ni-MH (nickel metal hydride) batteries because this kind, unlike Ni-Cad (nickel-cadmium) batteries, has no "memory effect." That means you don't have to totally discharge them before recharging.

✦ **Lithium-ion batteries:** The CR-V3 is a new kind of battery that takes the place of two standard AA batteries. Lithium batteries (also available in other sizes) are the longest lasting and lightest batteries available, but they're also expensive. Then some smart guy figured out a way to put two batteries into one unit; considerably cutting the price. This new battery can average 650 photos before you have to change it. The CR-V3 is available also in a rechargeable form, thereby extending the life even farther (and reducing your battery budget significantly).

If your eBay photo studio includes a camera on a tripod (and it should), you can charge your camera directly with the good old-fashioned AC adapter (you know, it's the one that plugs into the wall).

Lighting

Trying to take good pictures of your merchandise can be frustrating. If you don't have enough light and use the camera's flash, the image might be washed out. If you take the item outside, the sun might cast a shadow.

The autofocus feature on most digital cameras doesn't work well in low light. I've seen some eBay sellers use a flash and instruct their children to shine a flashlight on the item as they photograph it from different angles — all the while hoping that the color isn't wiped out.

After consulting specialists in the photo business to solve the problem of proper lighting for digital cameras, I put together an inexpensive studio lighting set for online auction photography. Please check my Web site (www. coolebaytools.com) for information on how to obtain this package. It's the same one that I successfully use in my home photo studio (refer to Figures 1-1 and 1-2).

Professional studio lights can be expensive, but you might be able to find a set for around $150. (You need at least two lights, one for either side of the item, to eliminate shadows.) Search eBay for used studio lighting; I'm sure you'll find a good deal.

If you're photographing small items, you can successfully use an Ott-Lite or a less expensive, generic true-color version, as shown in Figure 1-4. The lamp's bulb is a full-spectrum, daylight 5000K florescent tube, good enough for jewelry photography. This same light is used for grading diamonds.

The color temperature of a light, which ranges from 2500°K to 7800°K, is a number given to a lighting condition. The K after the number signifies the Kelvin temperature range. Actual daylight color temperature is about 5500°K, and it's best to get your lighting as close to that as you can. Using a bulb with a daylight number is important because it's a *pure neutral*, which means that it throws no blue or yellow cast on your images.

Photo cube

How much do I love my photo cube? I could write a poem! It allows me to take the most detailed photos of antiques and specialty items at night in my home. It works incredibly well wherever I use it because my kit includes two floodlights (and it all packs up into a neat bag). The nylon cube diffuses the light so that there are no harsh shadows and I don't burn out minute details with too much light. Take a look at the details in Figure 1-5.

Figure 1-4:
True-color
and folding
diamond-
grading
lights.

Figure 1-5:
The fine
details in
this antique
ivory
carving
really
show up
due to the
spectacular
lighting
diffused by
the photo
cube.

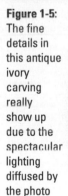

Photo background and stage

Backgrounds come in many shapes and sizes. You can get paper, fabric, or
use one of the portable photo stages for smallish items:

✦ **Seamless:** In professional photo-talk, *seamless* is a large roll of 3-foot (and wider) paper that comes in various colors and is suspended and draped behind the model and over the floor. (Ever wonder why you never see the floor and wall come together in professional photos?) Photographers also drape the seamless over tabletop shots. Some people use fabrics such as muslin instead of seamless.

✦ **Fabrics:** I recommend using neutral fabrics (such as white, light gray, natural, and black) for photographing your merchandise so the color of the fabric doesn't clash with or distract from your items. Some of the photo cubes on eBay come with great low-wrinkle fabric backgrounds as well.

✦ **Photo Stage:** A photo stage is another valuable tool for taking pictures indoors or out. Textured ABS plastic is manufactured so you can set it in a curve shape (see Figure 1-6); the stage can be set on any surface and will permit you to take a clean picture without any extraneous backgrounds. You can store it flat on a bookshelf till you need it next.

Figure 1-6:
Easy kitchen-counter eBay photography (just crop out the back-ground).

Cloud Dome

If you're going to photograph a lot of jewelry, collectible coins, or other metallic items, you'll become frustrated at the quality of your pictures. Metallic objects seem to pick up random color from any kind of light you shine on them for picture-taking. Bad results: Gold jewelry will photograph with a silver tone and silver will look gold-ish!

After conferring with lots of eBay photo gurus, I was told the secret of getting crisp, clear, close-up pictures: use a Cloud Dome. It stabilizes your camera (just as if you were using a tripod) and filters all unwanted color tones, resulting in image colors that look like your item.

The Cloud Dome is a large plastic bowl on which you mount your camera. You take your pictures through the dome. The translucent white plastic diffuses the light so your item is lit evenly from all sides, eliminating glare and bad shadows. Check out the manufacturer's Web site at www.clouddome.com to see some amazing before and after pictures.

The Cloud Dome also manages to get the best images from gems. You can actually capture the light in the facets! Pearls, too, will show their luster. Several eBay members (including yours truly) sell the Cloud Dome; I highly recommend it! In Chapter 2 of this minibook, I show you how to use it.

Props

To take good photos, you need some props. Although you may think it strange that a line item in your accounting program will read *props,* they do qualify as a business expense. (Okay, you can put it under "photography expenses" — *props* just sounds so Hollywood!)

How often have you seen some clothing on eBay from a quality manufacturer, but you just couldn't bring yourself to bid more than $10 because it looked like it had been dragged behind a car and then hung on a hanger before it was photographed? Could you see how the fabric would hang on a body? Of course not.

Mannequin

If you're selling clothing, you'd better photograph it on a mannequin. If you don't want to dive right in and buy a mannequin, at least get a body form to wear the outfit. Just search eBay for *mannequin* to find hundreds of hollow forms selling for less than $20. If you sell children's clothing, get a child's mannequin form as well. The same goes for men's clothes. If worst comes to worst, find a friend to model the clothes. There's just no excuse for hanger-displayed merchandise in your auctions.

I got my mannequin (Midge) at a department store liquidation sale here in Los Angeles. I paid $25 for her. Her face is a little creepy, so I often crop her head out of the photos. She has a great body and everything she wears sells at a profit. Many stores upgrade their mannequins every few years or so. If you know people who work at a retail store, ask when they plan to sell their old mannequins; you may be able to pick one up at a reasonable price.

Display stands, risers, and more

Jewelry doesn't photograph well on a person's hand and looks a lot better when you display it on a stand (see Figure 1-7) or a velvet pad. If you're selling a necklace, display it on a necklace stand, not on a person. I bought my display stands from a manufacturer but had to wait several months to receive them. Apparently, this type of quality display stand is made to order, so I recommend searching for them on eBay (you'll get them sooner).

Ralph Lauren Signed Silver 16' Necklace

This stunning, brand new designer necklace is just the right length, 16" - and adjustable for smaller necks. Signed on reverse of stirrup goldtone plate *(see photo below)*, also signed on the silver toggle. Your chance to get this retail $48 necklace for a fraction of the cost! The perfect gift for you or a friend.

Bid with confidence and bid whatever you feel this item is worth to you, as it is selling with *NO RESERVE*! I pack all my items carefully. Winning bidder to pay shipping & handling of $3, and must submit payment within a week of winning the auction. I will accept credit cards through BillPoint and PayPal - Good Luck, Happy Bidding!

Figure 1-7: eBay listing featuring a professional jewelry display.

Risers can be almost anything that you use to prop up your item to make it more attractive in a picture. Put riser pieces that aren't attractive under the cloth that you use as a background. Keep a collection of risers and propping materials in your photo area so they're always close at hand.

You wouldn't believe what the back of some professional photo setups look like. Photographers and photo stylists think resourcefully when it comes to making the merchandise look good — from the front of the picture, anyway! Throughout my years of working with professional photographers, I've seen the most creative things used to prop up items for photography:

✦ **Bottles of heavy stuff:** A photographer I once worked with used little bottles of mercury to prop up small boxes and other items in a picture. Mercury is a heavy liquid metal — but also a poison, so I suggest you do the same with small bottles (prescription bottles work well) filled with other weighty stuff (how about sand?).

✦ **Beeswax and clay:** To set up photos for catalogs, I've seen photographers prop up fine jewelry and collectible porcelain with beeswax (the kind you can get from the orthodontist works great) or clay. Beeswax is a neutral color and doesn't usually show up in the photo. However, you must dispose of beeswax afterward, often because it picks up dirt from your hands and fuzz from fabric.

✦ **Museum Gel or Quake Hold:** These two products are invaluable when you want to hold a small object at an unnatural angle for a photograph. (They're like beeswax and clay, but cleaner.) Museums use this putty-like product to securely keep breakables in one place — even during an earthquake! Museum Gel can sometimes be difficult to remove from items (and can leave a residue), so that's why I use Quake Hold putty for my eBay items.

✦ **Metal clamps and duct tape:** These multipurpose items are used in many photo shoots in some of the strangest places. For example, if your mannequin is a few sizes too small for the dress you want to photograph, how do you fix that? Don't pad the mannequin; simply fold over the dress in the back and clamp the excess material with a metal clamp, or use a clothespin or a small piece of duct tape to hold the fabric taut.

Chapter 2: Mastering eBay Photography

In This Chapter

✓ Discovering photo tips and tricks

✓ Photographing jewelry and coins

✓ Taking great clothing shots

✓ Viewing common photo mistakes

Photography has always been a passion for me. The hobby led me (at the age of 10) from developing film in a tiny storage-closet darkroom through my first side-advertising job for a camera store (yes, I was always a moonlighter) to a great professional gig taking photographs of NASCAR auto racing for magazines and newspapers. I worked also with professional catalog photographers and picked up some tricks for setting up pictures, buffing up the merchandise, and making everything look picture-perfect. In this chapter, I pass on the tips and shortcuts to you. Use these ideas to take great pictures that flatter your merchandise and help you sell!

Photo Guidelines

The idea behind using images in your auctions is to attract tons of potential buyers. With that goal in mind, you should try to create the best-looking images possible, no matter what kind of technology you're using to capture them.

Point-and-shoot may be okay for a group shot at a historical monument, but illustrating your auction is a whole different idea. Whether you're using a traditional film camera (so you can scan your developed photographs later) or a digital camera to capture your item, some basic photographic guidelines can give you better results:

✦ **Do** take the picture of your item outside, in filtered daylight, whenever possible. That way the camera can catch all possible details and color. If you can't take your images during the day, use a good set of true-color lights, either on clamps or stands.

✦ **Do** forget about fancy backgrounds; they distract viewers from your item. Put small items on a neutral-colored, nonreflective towel or cloth; put larger items in front of a neutral-colored wall or curtain. You'll crop out almost all the background when you prepare the picture on your computer before uploading the image.

✦ **Do** avoid getting yourself in the photo by shooting your pictures from an angle. If you see your reflection in the item, move and try again.

One of my favorite eBay pictures featured a piece of fine silver taken by the husband of the lady selling the piece on eBay. Silver and reflective items are hard to photograph because they pick up everything in the room in their reflection. In her description, the lady explained that the man reflected in the silver coffeepot was her husband and not part of the final deal. She handled that very well! To solve this reflective problem, take pictures of silvery objects in a photo cube.

✦ **Do** use extra lighting. You can do this with your camera's flash mode or (even better) with extra photo lighting. Use extra lighting, even when you're taking the picture outside. The extra lighting acts as *fill light* — it adds more light to the item, filling in some of the shadowed spots.

✦ **Don't** get so close to the item that the flash washes out (overexposes) the image. The easiest way to figure out the best distance is by trial and error. Start close and keep moving farther away until you get the results you want.

✦ **Do** take two or three acceptable versions of your image. You can choose the best one later on your computer.

✦ **Do** take a close-up or two of detailed areas that you want buyers to see (in addition to a wide shot of the entire item), if your item relies on detail.

✦ **Do** make sure that the items are clean. Cellophane on boxes can get nasty-looking, clothing can get linty, and all merchandise can get dirt smudges. Not only will your items photograph better if they're clean, they'll sell better, too. Further in this chapter I give you some tips on cleaning specific items.

If you're selling coins, don't clean them! If your coin is of any value at all, the price will plummet (and your selling reputation be ruined) once the savvy coin collector discovers your efforts.

✦ **Do** make sure that you focus the camera; nothing is worse than a blurry picture. If your camera is a fixed-focus model (it can't be adjusted), get only as close as the manufacturer recommends. Automatic-focus cameras measure the distance and change the lens setting as needed. But just because a camera has an autofocus feature doesn't mean that pictures automatically come out crisp and clear. Low light, high moisture, and other things can contribute to a blurred image. Double-check the picture before you use it.

Some eBay creeps, whether out of laziness or deceit, steal images from other eBay members. (They simply make a digital copy of the image and use it in their own auctions. This is so uncool because the copied image doesn't actually represent their item.) This pilfering has happened to me on several occasions. To prevent picture-snatching, you can add your user ID to all your photos. The next time somebody lifts one of your pictures, it has your name on it. If you're familiar with adding HTML code to your auctions, check out the simple Java code on my Web site (`www.coolebaytools.com`) that you can insert in your auction descriptions to prevent unscrupulous users from stealing your images.

Lifting another seller's photos is against eBay's rules, so be sure to report any photo-thieving sellers you find to eBay's Security Center at

```
http://pages.ebay.com/securitycenter/
```

Avoid using incandescent or fluorescent lighting to illuminate the photos you take. Incandescent lighting tends to make items look yellowish, and fluorescent lights lend a bluish tone to your photos. One exception is *GE Reveal* incandescent bulbs, which throw a good natural light. Halogen lights give a nice bright white, but they have a tendency to get very hot!

Photographing the Tuff Stuff: Coins and Jewelry

I've been selling on eBay since 1997 and thought I was pretty good at showing off and selling my wares. But then I purchased a small lot of Morgan silver dollars to resell. I figured, no problem, I'd take my standard digital picture and sell away. Oops, my mistake. The digital pictures made my beautiful silver coins look gold!

Then came my next challenge: photographing some silvertone and goldtone costume jewelry. My setup — with its perfect positioning, beautiful lighting, and black velvet jewelry pads — looked stunning. The pictures should have been perfect. But the silvertone looked gold, and the goldtone looked silver. What's the deal?

The deal is lighting — specifically, the need for ambient lighting. *Ambient* light (light that occurs naturally) is the best light for photographing many types of items, especially shiny items. I thought back to when I worked with catalog photographers who took pictures of jewelry — and I remembered the elaborate setup they used to produce the sparkling images you see in the ads. And although I can closely recreate the experts' silk tents with photo cubes, the minimalist lighting and multiple light flashes per exposure of the professional photographer's setup can't be duplicated easily at home.

Enter the Cloud Dome, a giant bowl that you place upside-down over the object you want to photograph. This bowl evenly diffuses ambient room light over the surface area of the object. This way, you can produce quality digital images in average room lighting. The Cloud Dome also helps with the following:

✦ **Eliminating camera shake:** When taking close-focus, highly zoomed-in pictures, holding your camera steady is of utmost importance. Using a tripod is difficult with close-up pictures, so using a Cloud Dome is the best option because your camera mounts directly to the Dome and is held as still as if you were using a tripod.

✦ **Consistent lighting:** When you use flash or flood lighting alone (without a Cloud Dome) for pictures of metallic objects, your photographs can include shiny hotspots from reflections (off walls and ceilings), washed-out areas from the glare of the lights, shadows, and loss of proper color.

Shooting with the Cloud Dome

The Cloud Dome looks like a giant Tupperware bowl with a camera mount attached. Figure 2-1 shows a Cloud Dome being set up to photograph jewelry.

Figure 2-1:
Taking a picture with the Cloud Dome.

Follow these steps to take a picture with the Cloud Dome:

1. **Attach your camera to the Cloud Dome's mount with the lens positioned so that it peers into the hole at the top of the dome.**

2. **Place your item on top of a contrasting background.**

See the following section, "Tips for taking Cloud Dome pictures," for ideas on choosing a background.

3. **Place the dome with camera attached over your item.**

4. **Check the item's position through your camera's viewfinder or LCD screen.**

   If the item is not in the center, center it. If you feel you need additional lighting to bring out a highlight, use a lamp outside the dome.

5. **Focus your camera and shoot the picture.**

Many items benefit from being photographed through a Cloud Dome, especially the following:

✦ **Jewelry:** I've found that taking pictures with the Dome keeps the gold color gold and the silver color silver. Also, using the Cloud Dome helps your camera pick up details such as engraving and the metal surrounding cloisonné work. It also gives pearls and gold their unique luster and soft reflection, as shown in Figure 2-2.

Figure 2-2:
A quartz stone with gold inclusions and diamonds, photographed with the Cloud Dome.

✦ **Gems and stones:** I've seen some beautiful pictures taken of gems and stones with the Cloud Dome. To achieve a special look, you can use a Cloud Dome accessory, a reversible gold-and-silver reflector. Especially when you use the silver side, facets of diamonds glisten as if they were in the pinpoint lights at the jeweler's. You may also want to focus a floodlight or lamp on the outside of the dome for extra sparkle.

✦ **Coins and stamps:** The Cloud Dome allows you to hold the camera steady for extreme close-ups. It also allows you to photograph coins without getting any coloration that is not on the coin. For both coins and stamps, the Cloud Dome helps you achieve sharp focus and true color.

✦ **Holographic or metallic accented items:** If you've ever tried to photograph collector cards, you know that the metal accents glare and holograms are impossible to capture. Also, the glossy coatings confuse the camera's light sensors, causing overexposed highlights.

✦ **Reflective objects:** Items such as silverware or even computer chips reflect a lot of light when lit properly for photos. The Cloud Dome diffuses the light so that the pictures become clear. Check out the before and after photos in Figure 2-3.

Figure 2-3: Computer chips, before and after shooting with the Cloud Dome.

Tips for taking Cloud Dome pictures

Surprisingly, there's little learning curve to using a Cloud Dome. The simple steps in the preceding section attest to this fact. What may take you more time is discovering the tips and tricks that help you achieve professional-looking results. This section should kick-start your discovery process:

✦ **Focus, focus:** Due to the focus limitations of many of today's digital cameras, I found it best to use the Cloud Dome with the extension collar (often sold along with the dome), which allows you to have your camera 17 inches away from the item if you're photographing on a flat surface.

✦ **Get in close to your item:** When attempting *macro* (extreme close-up) photography, the Cloud Dome holds your camera still while you shoot the picture. If you prefer, after you've centered your item, stand away and take the picture using your camera's self-timer.

✦ **Find upstanding items:** If your item is vertical and doesn't lend itself to being photographed flat, use the Cloud Dome's angled collar, which allows you to shoot the item from an angle instead of from the top.

✦ **Keep background where it belongs:** When selecting a background for your item, choose a contrasting background that reflects the light properly for your item. Make it a solid color; white is always safe and black can add dramatic highlights.

Prepping and Photographing Clothing

When photographing apparel for eBay, the one rule is: Take the *best picture* you can and move on to the next item so that you can hurry up and list all the items for sale. Period.

And even though I've just said there's only one rule, I also know that taking the *best picture* involves a bit of preparation on your part. Figure 2-4 shows the results of an eBay search for the keyword *dress*. Which of these items looks better — the ones laid out on the floor or those on a mannequin or model? A designer dress in this search probably would have sold for twice the amount if it had been on a mannequin!

Figure 2-4: Random search for *Dress* on eBay.

One of the worst ways to photograph clothing is on a tabletop or folded on the floor. The camera misses essential details in the folded items, and you miss the opportunity to show off the clothing in all its glory — as worn on a body. To get the highest bids, give your clothing an authentic, lifelike appearance.

Scanning photographs from a catalog is just as much of a copyright violation as stealing a picture from the manufacturer's Web site. eBay may end your listing if such a violation is reported.

Apparel photography can be tricky by all measures, especially when you don't have a model. Using a model is a great idea if you have plenty of time to spare. When you work with a model (even if it's a son or daughter or a friend), you'll have to take many shots of them wearing the same item, because you want the model to look as good as the clothing, and vice versa. Not a timesaver.

What's the best way to shoot fashion for eBay? Assembly-line-style. Henry Ford had it right. Have everything assembled in one area and the process can go smoothly and quickly. In this section, I tell you about how to prepare your studio, your props, and your clothing to get the best picture for the least effort. And best of all, the time you spend preparing the clothes to photograph also makes them customer-ready. Now, *there's* a timesaver!

Cleaning and pressing essentials

Before you photograph your clothing, make sure the clothing itself imparts the image you want your buyers to see. For example, remove any loose threads and lint that has accumulated on the fabric.

Have the following items handy to help you with the cleaning and pressing chores:

✦ **Garment rack:** When you unpack your merchandise from the carton it was shipped to you in, it can look pretty ragged. And if you've purchased some hanging merchandise and it's in tip-top shape, you'll want to keep it that way. Hanging the merchandise on a garment rack (see Figure 2-5) keeps it fresh-looking so it looks great when you get ready to ship.

✦ **Steamer:** Retail stores, clothing manufacturers, and drycleaners all use steamers. Why? Because steaming the garment with a steam wand is kinder to the fabric and takes wrinkles out in a hurry. Steam penetrates the fabric (not crushing it, as does ironing) and seems to make the fabric look better than before.

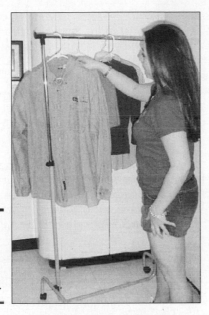

Figure 2-5:
Garment rack, with clothes to list on eBay.

TIP

Steaming is also five times *faster* than ironing (and not as backbreaking), so that's why it's truly the professional's choice. Steaming garments is a breeze; see for yourself in Figure 2-6.

Figure 2-6:
Kristy helping with my steaming for eBay!

A handheld travel steamer will work for beginners who sell one or two apparel items a month. While you can steam a garment with a professional-style steamer in a minute or two, you might have to work on a garment with a travel steamer for 15 minutes. If you're thinking about selling a quantity of clothes on eBay, a professional-style, roll-base steamer is what you should look for.

I use a Jiffy Steamer that I've had for quite a while. (I even bought it on eBay and got a great deal.) It's the same kind they use in retail stores, only slightly smaller.

✦ **Dryel:** A popular, reasonably priced, home dry-cleaning product you use in your dryer, Dryel can be used with almost any type of garment (be sure to double-check the packaging before you use it). After going through a Dryel treatment, clothes come out of the dryer sweet and clean. The starter kit even comes with a spot remover. You can buy Dryel at your local supermarket.

According to eBay rules, all used clothing must be cleaned before it is sold on the site. Even if the vintage garment you have up for sale is clean, it can always benefit by a roll in the dryer with Dryel. New garments, too, benefit; Dryel removes any smells that have clung to the garment during its travels.

✦ **Spot cleaners:** I recommend that you use spot cleaners only if you know what you're doing. Some really great ones out there will remove a small spot, but you'd best practice on items that you're *not* selling first.

Steaming hot tips

Keep these tips in mind when steaming the clothes you sell on eBay:

✔ Always keep the steam head in an upright position so that the condensation inside the hose drains back into the steamer.

✔ Run the steam head lightly down the fabric.

✔ Hang pants by the cuff when steaming.

✔ Don't let the steam head come directly in contact with velvet or silk; otherwise you may spot the fabric.

✔ Steam velvet (or any fabric with a pile) from the reverse side.

✔ Heavy fabrics may do better by steaming from the underside of the fabric.

✔ When you're through steaming your clothes for eBay, try steaming your mattresses and furniture. Steaming has been proven to kill a majority of dust mites and their accompanying nastiness.

Assembling your fashion photo studio

Photographing fashion right takes a little time, but the right tools make the project easier. Here's a list of some of the items you'll need when photographing clothing:

✦ **Mannequin body double:** You don't want to deal with supermodels and their requirements for nonfat vanilla lattes, so you have to find someone who will model the garments and not give you any grief. Figure 2-7 pictures my mannequin, Midge, who has sold lots of dresses on eBay for me.

Figure 2-7: Midge modeling a vintage fur (photo was cropped before listing).

Full-body mannequins can be purchased on eBay for about $100. (Dress forms for around $50). I bought Midge from a local store that was updating their mannequins. Major department stores often liquidate their display merchandise in auctions, so keep your eyes peeled in your local newspaper for auctions of store fixtures.

Keep in mind that you needn't spend a mint on a brand-new model. If your mannequin is used and has a few paint chips — so what?

Following are some less expensive alternatives to a mannequin:

• **Molded body form:** Before you decide to jump in with both feet, you might want to try using a hanging *body form* — a molded torso that has a hanger at the top. You can find molded styrene forms on eBay for as little as $20. If you decide to stay in the apparel-vending business, you can always upgrade to a full-size mannequin.

- **Dressmaker's adjustable form:** You can also use a dressmaker's form to model your eBay clothing. The best part about using these is that you can adjust the size of the body to fit your clothing. You can often find new or good-condition used ones on eBay for under $60.

✦ **Vertical photo lights on stands:** To light your merchandise, you'll do best to invest in some floodlights. You don't have to spend a mint, but as you'll see when you start taking pictures, the little flash on your camera can't accentuate the good parts of your apparel. You may want to stop the flash on your camera from going off altogether when you take pictures of clothes, because too much light coming from the front will wash out the detail in the fabric.

Place the mannequin in the middle of your studio area. Situate a floodlight on either side, closer to the camera than to the mannequin. Your setup will be a V-shape, with your mannequin at the point, your floodlights at the top of each V-side, and you (or a tripod) holding the camera in the middle at the top of the V. Adjust the distance that you place your lights as needed. Be sure to tilt the light heads to pick up extra detail in the clothing.

✦ **Clothespins:** To fit your clothing on the mannequin, use clothespins to take up any slack in the garment (be sure to place the clothespins where the camera won't see them). Before you think I'm crazy, I'll have you know that clothespins were used in almost every apparel photo-shoot that I've participated in. Think about it: The clothing you're selling will come in different sizes and may not always hang right on your mannequin.

eBay Gallery of Horrors

This section shows you a bunch of big-time don'ts. We've seen images like these all over eBay at one time or another.

Mistake #1

Figure 2-8 shows a nice item, but the picture suffers from two major flaws:

✦ **A glare from the camera's flash shows in the cellophane on the item.** This can be avoided by turning the item slightly at an angle so that the flash doesn't give off such a bright glare.

✦ **The price sticker is smack on the front of the item.** Often you'll buy things for resale that have stickers. Be a pro — use a commercial product (see Chapter 1) to remove stickers.

Figure 2-8:
Glaring
errors here!

Mistake #2

Don't dress your picture with props to decorate the scene. Your photo
should be a crisp, clean image of the product you're selling, and only that.
Figure 2-9 shows a common eBay seller mistake. What a cute teddy — but
what are you selling here?

Figure 2-9:
You're
selling
what?

Mistake #3

I never knew how much colorful upholstery people had in their homes. I've seen items photographed on plaid, floral, and striped fabrics (see Figure 2-10). It distracts from your item. Don't do it.

Figure 2-10:
Nice sofa!

Mistake #4

I'm sure the item in the box shown in Figure 2-11 is desirable, but who can make that judgment without seeing the item? Take the item out of the box. If the box is a crucial part of the deal (as in collectibles), be sure to mention that the box is included in the sale.

If you can't open the box without ruining the value of the item, pull in for a macro close-up. When you have a quantity of the item, bite the bullet and open one up. A good picture gets you higher bids, and perhaps that loss of one item will be made up by the higher bids on the sales with good pictures.

Figure 2-11:
Peek-a-boo.

Mistake #5

Can you say *close-up?* Use the zoom on your camera to fill the frame with a full picture of your item. Draw your camera close to the item so the prospective customer can see some detail. Don't take a wide picture of the area around the item, like the shot shown in Figure 2-12. Don't just rely on cropping the picture in an image-editing program; that only makes the image smaller.

Figure 2-12:
Pay no
attention to
the object
on the
carpet.

Chapter 3: Sprucing Up Your Listings with HTML

In This Chapter

✔ Writing a good description

✔ Using eBay's HTML tool

✔ Buffing up your auctions with basic HTML

✔ Making friends with tables

✔ Generating auction descriptions and Templates with SeaMonkey

✔ Creating an ad — fast

I must admit, the very thought of using HTML in my auctions used to terrify me (pinky-swear you won't tell the people at eBay). HTML. Doesn't it sound so high-tech and geeklike? But HTML isn't all that scary after you realize that it's just a fancy name for HyperText Markup Language, an easy-to-use language for creating online content. All you need to know is the markup part.

HTML uses tags to mark pages to include elements such as text and graphics in a way that Web browsers understand. A Web browser sees the tags, and knows how to display the document (that is, the Web page). HTML also makes possible the whole work of links. When you click a link, you jump to another place: another Web page, document, or file, for example.

Luckily, you don't have to know a lot of code to produce eBay auctions. My small grasp of HTML gets me only so far, so I usually use SeaMonkey to produce code for my Web site or eBay listings. I've developed my own templates so that all I have to do is replace the text with each new listing. This chapter shows you how to do that, too.

In addition, the Sell an Item form has an excellent (but basic) HTML generator that you use like a word processor to format text. I show you how to make this convenient tool do magic with your listings.

Writing Good Descriptions

Many eBay sellers somehow think that putting dancing bears, flaming graphics, and background music in their auctions will bring in more bids. Unfortunately, that's pretty far from the truth. People go to your auctions to find information and a great deal on something they want, not to be entertained. They need to see the facts, placed cleanly and neatly on the page.

The addition of music to your auction may cause another problem: An extremely s-l-o-o-o-o-w page load for those with dial-up connections. If loading your page takes too long, believe me, most people will go to another listing.

So what should you do to attract buyers? I spent most of my career in the advertising business, and the byword of good advertising is, "Keep it simple!" An organized and well-written selling description will outsell dancing bears and pictures of your children every time.

When you write the descriptions for your auctions, be sure that you describe your items clearly and completely. Mention everything about the item; be honest and even mention flaws or damage. When you're honest up front, you'll have a happy bidder. Remember to include your terms of sale and specify what type of payments and credit cards you accept. Be sure to include your shipping charges, too.

After you list all the facts, get excited and add a little flowery text in your description. Think infomercial! Think Shopping Channel! Whoopee! They make things sound so good that you feel that you *must* have whatever item they're selling. You can do the same, if you just take the time. In Book III, Chapter 3, I give you basic pointers on writing the best auction descriptions possible.

HTML the Easy eBay Way

Luckily, you don't have to know a lot of code to produce eBay auctions. The Sell an Item form has an excellent (but basic) HTML generator that has features similar to a word processor, as shown at the top of Figure 3-1 (where you see 'em just below the Standard and HTML tabs).

To apply any of these features (such as bold or italic) to your text, you simply highlight the text and click one of the buttons.

When inputting text, you may notice that eBay's tool inserts a line space after text when you start a new paragraph. If you want the text to wrap (as in the headline of Figure 3-1) and not have a blank space between text lines, hold down the Shift key while you press the Enter (or Return) key. That forces an HTML line break instead of a paragraph break.

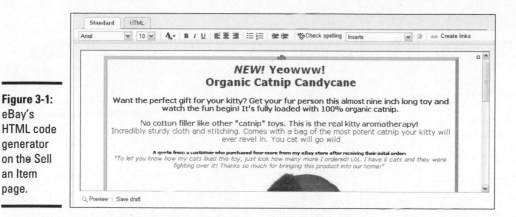

Figure 3-1:
eBay's
HTML code
generator
on the Sell
an Item
page.

Starting at the top left in Figure 3-1, you see three drop-down lists. Click to the right of each box and the following options appear:

✦ **Font name:** Apply different fonts to your text. Play around with the different fonts to see which ones you prefer. Figure 3-2 shows you the fonts from which you can choose.

Figure 3-2:
The different
fonts that
eBay
currently
offers.

Arial · **Arial Black** · Comic Sans · Courier · Georgia · **Impact** · Times · Trebuchet · Verdana

✦ **Size:** You can increase or decrease the size of the type. It reads in numbers, or point size. The smallest is 8-point and the largest is 36-point.

✦ **Color:** Want to add some color to your text? Just highlight the text and select black, blue, red, green, yellow, or brown from the plethora of colors available.

After these three drop-down lists, you see a row of buttons:

 ✦ **Boldface** text

 ✦ *Italicize* text

 ✦ <u>Underline</u> text

- ✦ Align text to the left

- ✦ Center text

- ✦ Align text to the right

- ✦ Create a numbered list

- ✦ Create a bulleted list

- ✦ "Outdent," or move indented text back to the left

- ✦ Indent text to the right

- ✦ Check the spelling in your description

Next you'll come to an amazing and powerful tool. Do you have text (or HTML) that you'd like to have in all your listings? Most of your listings? Click the Inserts box, shown in Figure 3-3, and you'll see some basic inserts for your text that eBay created based on your seller's profile.

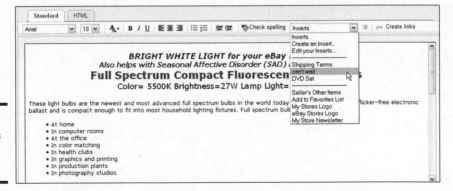

Figure 3-3:
The Inserts
drop-down
list.

To add an insert to your description, simply place your cursor where you'd like the insert to appear, and click that selection from the menu.

You can even create custom inserts up to 4000 characters! Create inserts for frequently used text, such as promotional messages, custom policies, or warranty information. Just follow these steps:

1. **Choose Insert⇨Create an Insert.**

   The screen shown in Figure 3-4 appears.

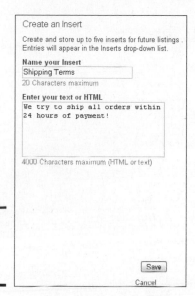

Create an Insert

Create and store up to five inserts for future listings.
Entries will appear in the Inserts drop-down list.

Name your Insert

Shipping Terms

20 Characters maximum

Enter your text or HTML

We try to ship all orders within
24 hours of payment!

4000 Characters maximum (HTML or text)

Save

Cancel

Figure 3-4:
Creating
a custom
insert.

2. **In the first box, type a name for your insert.**

3. **In the second box, type your text or HTML coding (up to 4000 characters).**

4. **When you're through, click the Save button.**

After you create your custom insert, you can add it to any of your descriptions with a click of your mouse. How convenient!

Getting Friendly with HTML

When you want to dress up your auctions, you *could* use one of eBay's graphic themes. (That would add an additional $.10 to your listing fee.) Or you could insert your own graphics into your listing, and it wouldn't cost you any extra fees. But even if you use one of eBay's lovely graphic designs, you still need to format your text. That's where HTML coding comes in.

You can also use HTML to insert multiple pictures into your descriptions to better promote your item. This won't cost you extra, and you can still use the one free photo from eBay's Picture Services for your top-of-listing picture. For information on how to upload your images to a server, see Chapter 5.

What HTML can do

Take a look at Figure 3-5. It contains an auction description I typed in the Notepad program (which you can find under Windows Accessories).

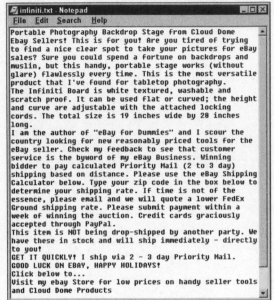

Figure 3-5: Raw auction text in Notepad.

If I add some appropriate HTML coding to the file, the auction page looks a whole lot different, as you can see in Figure 3-6. Pretty cool, huh?

How HTML works

HTML uses a series of codes to indicate display information to a browser, such as when text should be bold or italic or when text is actually a link. Brackets are used to indicate commands. What's within the brackets is an instruction rather than actual text; only the text of your description will appear on your page.

In the example that follows, the *b* and *i* in brackets indicate that text between them should be formatted bold and italic, respectively. Notice that there is both a start formatting and end formatting indication (<b> starts bold formatting and </b> ends it.) Here's one example:

HTML start and end tags: <b><i></i></b>

Tags with text between them: <b><i>eBay tools</i></b>

The resulting text on your page: ***eBay tools***

**Portable Photography Backdrop Stage
from Cloud Dome**

Ebay Sellers! This is for you! Are you tired of trying to find a nice
clear spot to take your pictures for eBay sales? Sure you could spend
a fortune on backdrops and muslin, but this handy, portable stage
works (without glare) flawlessly every time. This is the most versatile
product that I've found for tabletop photography.

The Infiniti Board is white textured, washable and scratch proof. It can be used flat or curved;
the height and curve are adjustable with the attached locking cords. The total size is 19
inches wide by 28 inches long.

I scour the country looking for new reasonably priced tools for the eBay seller. Check my
feedback to see that customer service is the byword of my eBay Business. Winning bidder to
pay calculated Priority Mail (2 to 3 day) shipping based on distance. Please use the eBay
Shipping Calculator below. Type your zip code in the box below to determine your shipping
rate. If time is not of the essence, please email and we will quote a lower FedEx Ground
shipping rate. Please submit payment within a week of winning the auction. Credit cards
graciously accepted through PayPal.

**This item is NOT being drop-shipped by another party. We have these in stock and will
ship immediately - directly to you!**
GET IT QUICKLY! I ship via 2 - 3 day Priority Mail.

Click below to...
<u>Visit my ebay Store **for low prices** on handy seller tools and Cloud Dome
Products</u>

Figure 3-6:
Auction
description
dolled up
with HTML.

Table 3-1 lists many common HTML tags to get you started. Keep in mind
that HTML is not case-sensitive, so feel free to leave your Caps Lock on if it
makes you happy. But if you want to stay compatible with XHTML (the new
standard for all kinds of devices), start getting in the habit of using lowercase for your tags.

Table 3-1   **Basic HTML Codes**

Text Codes	How to Use Them	What They Do
`<b></b>`	`<b>eBay tools</b>`	**eBay tools** (bold type)
`<i></i>`	`<i>eBay tools</i>`	*eBay tools* (italic type)
`<b><i></i></b>`	`<b><i>eBay tools</b></i>`	***eBay tools*** (bold and italic type)

(continued)

Table 3-1 *(continued)*

Text Codes	How to Use Them	What They Do
`<font color=red> </font>`	`<font color=red>eBay tools</font>`	Selected text appears in red. (This book is in black and white so you can't see it.)
`<font size=+1> </font>`	`<font size=+3> eBay tools</font>`	**eBay tools** (font size normal +1 through 4, increases size *x* times)
` `	`eBay tools`	eBay tools (inserts line break)
`<p>`	`eBay<p>tools`	eBay tools (inserts paragraph space)
`<hr>`	`cool eBay<hr>tools`	cool eBay ――――――― tools (inserts horizontal rule)
`<h1><h1>`	`<h1>eBay tools</h1>`	**eBay tools** (converts text to headline size)

List Codes	How to Use Them	What They Do
`<ul><li></ul>`	`<ul><li>I accept <li>PayPal <li>Money Orders <li>Checks</ul>`	I accept • PayPal • Money Orders • Checks
`<ol><li></ol>`	`<ol><li>I accept <li>PayPal <li>Money Orders <li>Checks</ol>`	I accept 1. PayPal 2. Money Orders 3. Checks

Linking (Hyperlink) Codes	How to Use Them	What They Do
`<img src>`	`<img src="http:// www.yourwebsite. com/imagename. jpg">`	Inserts an image from your server into the description text

Text Codes	How to Use Them	What They Do
`<A HREF= >`	`<A HREF= http:// www.yourwebsite. com/shipping info.htm>Click here for shipping info</A>`	When selected text is clicked (in this instance, *Click here for shipping info*), the user's browser goes to the page you indicate in the URL
`TARGET=_BLANK`	`<A HREF= http:// www.yourwebsite. com/shippinginfo. htmTARGET=_BLANK>`	When inserted at the end of a hyperlink, it opens the page in a separate browser window

Table Codes	How to Use Them	What They Do
`<table border>`	`<table border=4>`	Puts a border around your table at a width of 4 pixels
`<table></table>`	`<table> sample text sample text</table>`	The table command must surround *every* table
`<tr></tr><td> </td>`	`<tr><td>text</td> <td>text</td></ tr><tr><td>text</ td><td>text</ td></tr>`	Table row `<tr>` must be used with `<td>`. Table data to end and open new boxes text text text text

A few things to keep in mind about HTML:

✦ Don't worry about pressing Enter at the end of a line. You must use a command to go to the next line, so pressing Enter on your keyboard has no effect on what the page looks like.

✦ Most HTML coding has a beginning and an end. The beginning code is in angle brackets. To end the formatting, you repeat the code in brackets, only this time with a slash to end the command `</>`.

✦ It's not necessary to put the paragraph command at the beginning and at the end of the paragraph. This is one command that doesn't need a close. Just put the command, `<p>`, where you want the breaking space. This applies also for a horizontal rule, `<hr>`. Just place the command where you want the line and it will appear.

✦ People have different fonts set up on their computers, so they may not have the funky font you want to display. Be sure to list alternate fonts for your text. If you don't, different browsers may substitute other fonts that might look *really* funky on some readers' pages!

Following is an auction description with the HTML code in bold so it's easier to spot:

```
<center><font face='VERDANA,HELVETICA,ARIAL' color='crimson'
    size=5>
<B>Portable Photography Backdrop Stage<BR>from Cloud Dome</B>
</font></center>
<center><font face='verdana,arial,helvetica,sans serif'
    color='Black' size=4>
Ebay Sellers! This is for you! Are you tired of trying to
    find a nice clear spot to take your pictures for eBay
    sales? Sure you could spend a fortune on backdrops and
    muslin, but this handy, portable stage works (without
    glare) flawlessly every time. This is the most versatile
    product that Iíve found for tabletop photography. </font>

<BR><center><font face='verdana,arial,helvetica,sans serif'
    color='Black' size=2>
The Infiniti Board is white-textured, washable, and
    scratchproof. It can be used flat or curved; the height
    and curve are adjustable with the attached locking cords.
    The total size is 19 inches wide by 28 inches long. <P>
<img src="http://www.collierad.com/whiteboard.jpg">
<font face='verdana,arial,helvetica,sans serif' color='Black'
    size=2><center>
I scour the country looking for new reasonably priced tools
    for the eBay seller. Check my feedback to see that
    customer service is the byword of my eBay Business.
    Winning bidder to pay calculated Priority Mail (2- to
    3-day) shipping based on distance. Please use the eBay
    Shipping Calculator below. Type your zip code in the box
    below to determine your shipping rate. If time is not of
    the essence, please e-mail and we will quote a lower FedEx
    Ground shipping rate. Please submit payment within a week
    of winning the auction. Credit cards graciously accepted
    through PayPal.<br>
<b>This item is NOT being drop-shipped by another party. We
    have these in stock and will ship immediately - directly
    to you!<BR></font>
<font face="verdana,arial,helvetica,sans serif"
    color="crimson" size=2><I>
GET IT QUICKLY! I ship via 2 - 3 day Priority Mail.</b> </
    I></font><P>
```

```
<I><font face='verdana,arial,helvetica,sans
    serif'color='Black' size=3><p>
Click below to... <BR>
<A HREF= http://cgi6.ebay.com/ws/eBayISAPI.dll?ViewSellersOt
    herItems&include=0&userid=marsha_c&sort=3&rows=50&since=-
    1&rd=1 TARGET=_BLANK>
Visit my eBay Store <B><I>for low prices </I></B>on handy
    seller tools and Cloud Dome Products</A></B></FONT></
    CENTER>
```

Note that the HTML code shown here is boldfaced to help you spot it, but it's not necessary to bold your HTML code when you *use* it.

Add Pictures to Your Listing for Free

"How do I put pictures in my auction description?" Here's the answer to the question I'm asked most when I teach a class on eBay. Many sellers have more than one picture within the auction description area. By putting extra images in the description, they don't have to pay extra for eBay's hosting services. This isn't magic, you can do it too. Just add a tiny bit of HTML code in your auction description. Don't freak out on me now, you can do this. Here is the HTML code to insert one picture in your auction:

```
<img src=http://www.yourserver.com/imagename.jpg>
```

Be sure to use the angle brackets (they're located above the comma and the period on your keyboard) to open and close your code.

When you want to insert two pictures, just insert code for each picture, one after the other. If you want one picture to appear below the other, use the HTML code for line break, <BR>. Here's how to write that:

```
<img src=http://www.yourserver.com/imagename1.jpg> <BR>
<img src=http://www.yourserver.com/imagename2.jpg>
```

Using HTML Table Codes to Make Templates

Have you ever noticed how some people manage to have a photo on both the right or the left sides of their descriptions? It's not that difficult to do. You add a little HTML code to the listing using a feature called *tables*.

For example, Figure 3-7 shows a picture contained in a table on the left side of the description. (By the way, when the full version of this auction ran on eBay, with the kind cooperation of the people on *The View*, we raised more than $1000 for UNICEF!)

Figure 3-7:
An auction using tables with the picture on the left.

The HTML code for this description goes like this. (The `<tr>` and `<td>` codes create the table format.)

```
<table align=center cellpadding=8 width='80%' border=7
    cellspacing=0 bgcolor='White'>
<tr><td>
<center><font face='VERDANA,HELVETICA,ARIAL' color='crimson'
    size=5>
<B>"The View"<br>Cast Autographed<br>Coffee Mug</B></font><P>
<img width=250 src='http://images.auctionworks.com/viewmug.
    jpg'>
</td>
<td>
<center><font face='VERDANA,HELVETICA,ARIAL' color='crimson'
    size=3>
<b><i>Signed by</i><br><b>Joy Behar<br>Star Jones<br>Barbara
    Walters<br>Meredith Vieira</b>
</font><p>
<font face='verdana,arial,helvetica,sans serif' color='Black'
    size=2>
<B>All you fans of <i>The View </i>, this is your chance to
    own a coffee cup autographed by all four stars of the
    show. The proceeds from this auction will be donated
    to UNICEF. The winner will be announced on ABCís <i>The
    View</i> TV show on Monday. Weíll be checking this auction
    live on the show on Wednesday, April 23rd, 2003 with
    Marsha Collier, the author of <i>îeBay for Dummiesî</i></
    B>.</font><P>
<font face='verdana,arial,helvetica,sans serif' color='Black'
    size=1>
```

```
Shipping will be via Priority Mail. Credit cards are accepted
     through PayPal. </font>
</CENTER></td></tr></table>
```

After you get the hang of it, tables aren't so scary. As a matter of fact, if you want to use my templates for your listings, be my guest!

Creating Your Own HTML Template

Once you're ready to take on eBay in earnest, it really helps to have a few auction-description templates all set up and ready to go. This is what the big guys, those top sellers on eBay, do (granted, some do a better job than others). Although it's fun to play around with using different graphics as you sell on eBay — and I must admit, I've seen some cute ones — having a standard look to your ads establishes you as a serious, professional seller. After all, how often does eBay change its look? The answer is, not too often. The colors and the basic look remain the same because this is eBay's (very valuable) brand.

What might go into a template? Well, you can insert your logo within your description, or put links to your About Me page or your store, for example. Your template can become your brand. Many auction-management services offer predesigned templates for your descriptions, but they often charge a lot of money for their services. Alternately, you can put together your own template, and update it occasionally.

Keeping your look simple and showing off your product will bring in high bids. Getting carried away with graphics that have nothing to do with your item is distracting (unless you have a cute picture of your dog or cat — everyone likes a fluffy mascot).

In this section, I show you how to design simple templates using SeaMonkey. It's a great free software suite that grows with you. I use it for the Composer module (a WYSIWYG — What You See Is What You Get — HTML editor). The more HTML you understand, the more you can do with Composer. In the next section, you use an HTML generator on my Web site to create a template that you can customize with a little extra knowledge of HTML.

Downloading SeaMonkey

Few things in this life are absolute necessities, but photos in your eBay listings definitely are! It's a good idea to begin developing templates by building a simple one that includes a space for a photo.

Because I like to use what the Internet offers for free . . . I use a Mozilla program called SeaMonkey Composer to do just that.

SeaMonkey is a free, fully functional Windows or MAC Internet suite from Mozilla (the same folks who brought to you Firefox). It consists of a Web browser, an e-mail and news-client program, and an HTML editor. In other words, you can get all these programs in one. Many people enjoy replacing their Internet Explorer or Firefox with the feature-rich, faster, less-memory-hogging SeaMonkey. I use it because I like HTML Composer.

You can download the free suite at

`www.seamonkey-project.org`

Since SeaMonkey is a *suite* (meaning it has several programs all in one), you decide which program you want to run when you click the SeaMonkey icon. If you just want to use the HTML Composer (as I do), take the following steps:

1. **After downloading the software, open it by double-clicking the SeaMonkey icon.**

   You might just want to play with its superfast Web browser and maybe get a feel for its other features... but right now? I'm using the Composer.

2. **Click the Edit link in the toolbar.**

3. **Select Preferences and then Appearance.**

   On the Appearance page, you can indicate which program you would like to see when you open the suite.

4. **Put a check mark next to Composer and click OK.**

   The next time you click the SeaMonkey icon, the Composer will open.

Adding text and graphics

After you open SeaMonkey Composer, you'll see that it looks like an eBay or Word page layout, but it has far more features.

The most important for you to see are the four tabs at the bottom of the screen. These tabs enable you to view your template in several ways:

✦ **Normal.** This is your standard design mode, where you can highlight text — change it or color it — and add pictures or tables, as shown in Figure 3-8.

✦ **HTML Tags.** This view shows you your template with the symbols of the tags you have created. Check out Figure 3-9.

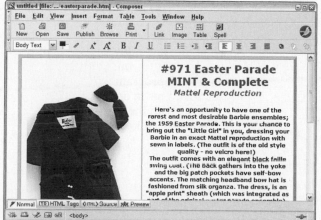

Figure 3-8:
It took
just a few
seconds to
put together
this simple
template.

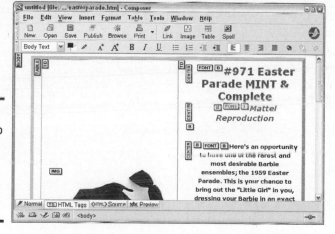

Figure 3-9:
How easy to
learn HTML
when the
tags are
spelled out
for you.

✦ **HTML Source.** Figure 3-10 shows the raw HTML code that you see when you click the Source tab. From this view, you can save the template to your hard drive and change the text at will through the Normal tab.

✦ **Preview.** This tab displays your work pretty much the same as the Normal setting, but it's good to double check that everything is perfect before you save it.

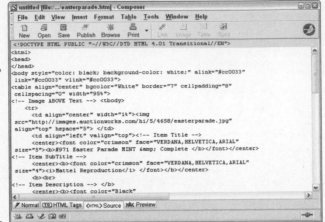

Figure 3-10:
Just copy
and paste
this source
code into
the eBay
Sell an Item
form and
voila!

In the following steps, you create a table that contains a photo on the left and text on the right:

1. **Click the Table button on the toolbar or choose Tools⇨Insert Table.**

    An Insert Table screen appears..

2. **If you want a photo next to your text, indicate 1 row with 2 columns, as in Figure 3-11.**

    This creates a table with two cells side-by-side.

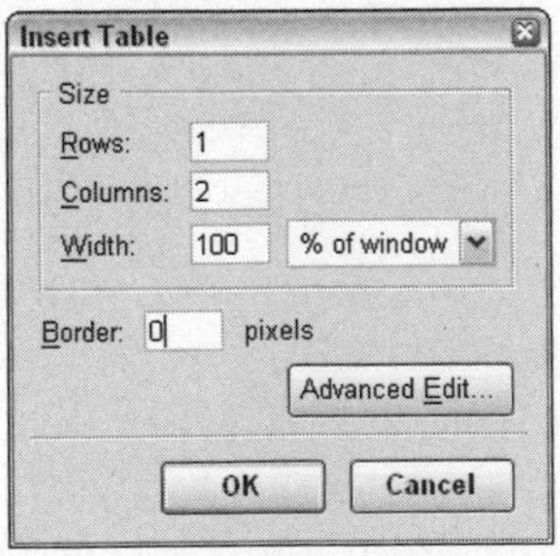

Figure 3-11:
Creating a
table with
two cells.

3. **Click OK.**

    The table palette disappears, and you see the table or the HTML coding (as shown in Figure 3-12) for two cells on the screen.

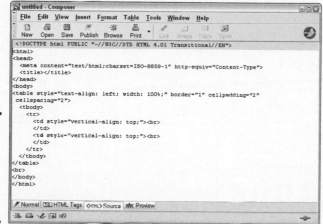

Figure 3-12:
Coding
for a 2 x 1
table in the
SeaMonkey
screen.

4. **Click the** `Row 1 Cell 1` **on the screen, (in Source mode this would be between the HTML opening and closing codes (**`<td>` **and** `</td>`**), and then click the Image button on the toolbar.**

   (The Image button looks like a little picture.) The Image Tag dialog box appears.

5. **In the Image Properties box, type the Internet address (URL) where your image is stored.**

   You can get the URL from your image hosting service, website or by locating the image on the Internet and copying the URL from the top of your browser. If you want to alter the size of your image, you can also type the width or height (or both), in pixels, in the Dimensions boxes.

6. **Click OK.**

   The HTML code for the image appears inside the text area.

7. **Click the** `Row 1 Cell 2` **on your screen, and enter the description text you want to appear next to the picture.**

   For convenience, you can also open an auction description you've already written in Windows Notepad, and copy and paste it into the space.

Adding HTML formatting

If you have prewritten your description text you can paste it into the open window. But as shown in Figure 3-13, all the sentences run together in one mammoth paragraph.

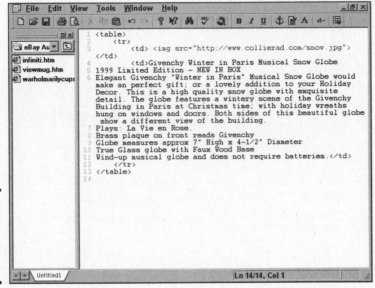

Figure 3-13: Shows the screen filled in with straight text.

To distinguish and emphasize parts of your description — and to simply make it look better — you can add HTML text attributes as follows:

1. **Highlight the text you want to change.**

2. **Click the button on the toolbar for the text formatting style you want to apply.**

   The B button is for bold, I is for italic, and U is for underline. The formatting is applied automatically.

After some final tweaking, the final auction description looks like Figure 3-14.

Choose File⇨Save to save your HTML when you're happy with the results. When you're ready to use that auction description, just open the file, copy the code, and paste it into the eBay auction description area (be sure you're typing in the area under the HTML tab) for the appropriate item.

**Givenchy Winter in Paris
Musical Snow Globe**
1999 Limited Edition - NEW IN BOX

Elegant Givenchy "Winter in Paris" Musical Snow Globe
would make an perfect gift; or a lovely addition to your Holiday
Decor. This is a high quality snow globe with exquisite detail.
The globe features a wintery scene of the Givenchy Building in
Paris at Christmas time; with holiday wreaths hung on
windows and doors. Both sides of this beautiful globe show a
different view of the building.

- Plays: La Vie en Rose.
- Brass plaque on front reads Givenchy
- Globe measures approx 7" High x 4-1/2" Diameter
- True Glass globe with Faux Wood Base
- Wind-up musical globe and does not require batteries.

Figure 3-14:
A beautiful,
quickly
created
listing!

When inserting HTML code into your listings, be sure you have the HTML
tab selected,, or your listing will look like a bunch of code (which isn't very
attractive).

SeaMonkey has many other features, including custom colors, anchors, and
spell check. After you've created a template or two, poke around and see
how fancy you can get with this small (but powerful) program.

Getting a Quick, Basic Template

Because there are times you're in too much of a hurry to fool with *anything*,
I've put a free ad tool on my Web site:

```
www.coolebaytools.com
```

When you land on my home page, click the link in the navigation bar labeled
Tools. On the resulting page, click the Cool Free Ad Tool link and you jump
to the instant template page, shown in Figure 3-15.

To set up a quick eBay template using this tool, follow these steps:

1. **In the Title box, type the headline for your description.**

2. **In the Description box, enter a description.**

   You can copy and paste prewritten text from Notepad or a word-
   processing program, or just write your copy text as you go along.

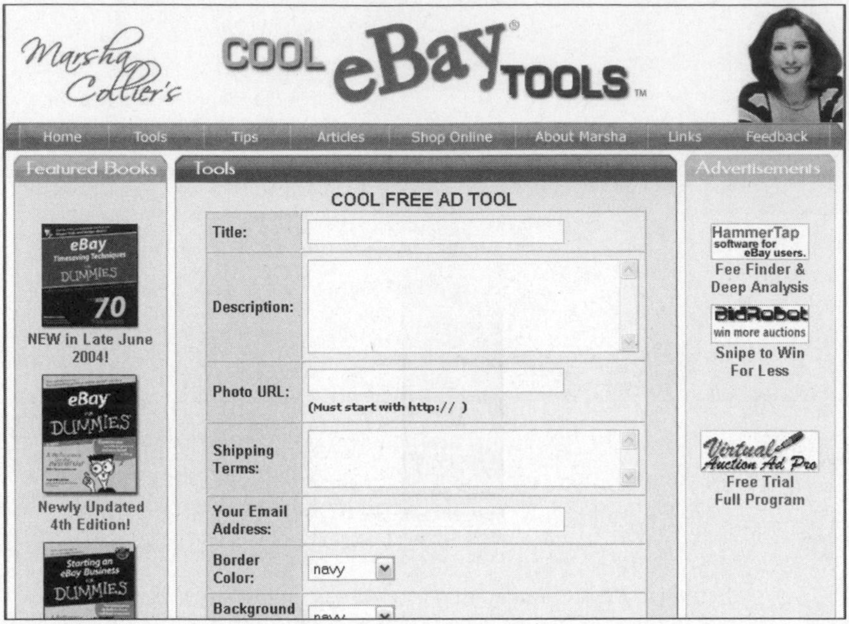

Figure 3-15:
The Cool
Free Ad Tool
page on my
site.

3. **In the Photo URL box, enter the URL of your image.**

4. **In the Shipping Terms box, type the pertinent information (optional).**

5. **Enter the e-mail address that you use for eBay.**

   The address is used to put code in your description for an E-mail for Questions link. I do not keep your e-mail information.

6. **Select the border and background colors from the drop-down lists.**

7. **Click View Ad.**

   You see how your new auction description looks. Mine is shown in Figure 3-16.

Scroll down until you see a box containing the auction description's HTML code, as shown in Figure 3-17.

You can copy and paste this code directly into the eBay description area of the Sell an Item form (or any eBay listing tool). You can also add HTML codes and even another picture to your auction description.

Givenchy Winter in Paris Musical Snow Globe

Description

Elegant Givenchy "Winter in Paris" Musical Snow Globe would make an perfect gift; or a lovely addition to your Holiday Decor. This is a high quality snow globe with exquisite detail. The globe features a wintery scene of the Givenchy Building in Paris at Christmas time; with holiday wreaths hung on windows and doors. Both sides of this beautiful globe show a different view of the building. Plays: La Vie en Rose. Brass plaque on front reads Givenchy Globe measures approx 7" High x 4-1/2" Diameter True Glass globe with Wooden Base Wind-up musical globe and does not require batteries.

Shipping & Payment Terms

Winning bidder to pay calculated Priority Mail (2 to 3 day) shipping based on distance. Please use the eBay Shipping Calculator below. Type your zip code in the box below to determine your shipping rate. If time is not of the essence, please email and we will quote a lower FedEx Ground shipping rate. Please submit payment within a week of winning the auction. Credit cards graciously accepted through PayPal.

HAVE A
QUESTION?

Figure 3-16:
Your instant
eBay ad.

Copy & Paste the following code into the auction's description box:

```
<CENTER><table border="3" bordercolor="navy"
cellspacing="0" cellpadding="0" width="500"
bgcolor="#ffffff"><tr><td colspan="3"
bgcolor="#ffffff"><center><font face="arial black"
color="navy" size="+2">Givenchy Winter in Paris
Musical Snow Globe </font><br><br><table border="0"
width="500" bordercolor="#000000" cellspacing="0"
cellpadding="5"><tr><td width=500 align="center"><img
src="http://www.collierad.com/snowglobe.jpg"
hspace="0" vspace="0" border="0"></td></tr> <tr><td
align=center bgcolor="navy"><font color="white"
size="+1"
face="arial"><b>Description</b></font></td></tr><tr><td
 align=center><font face="arial">Elegant
```

Figure 3-17:
HTML
coding
for your
auction.

Chapter 4: Getting Your Photos Ready for eBay

In This Chapter

✔ **Getting the photo's file size right**

✔ **Considering edits to your photo**

✔ **Touching up your photo**

I n this chapter, I show you how fast you can get the photos you take — or the scans you make — spruced up for eBay. No eBay seller should spend hours playing with and perfecting images for eBay listings (although some do). One pass through a simple image-editing software program gets any reasonable picture Internet-ready.

Then, after your pictures are, well, picture-perfect, look to Chapter 5 for some easy ways to upload your images to the Web.

Size Matters

The prime concern to have about the pictures you put on eBay is size — that's right, in this case, size *does* matter. You need to limit the picture file size so you don't bog down the prospective buyer's viewing of your item page (especially if you're using multiple pictures in the item description). Why? That's easy. The larger your item's picture files, the longer the browser takes to load the item page. And four out of five eBay users will click back out of a listing to avoid a long page load. (I'm guessing that you don't want your listings to elicit that behavior.)

To get a better idea of the size for the images you use online, remember that no matter which camera setting you choose, your image should be designed to be viewed on a monitor. Low resolution is just fine because the average computer monitor isn't an HDTV.

The average monitor resolution settings (in pixels) are

+ 640 x 480 (VGA)

+ 800 x 600 (Super VGA)

+ 1024 x 768 (XVGA)

These settings determine the number of pixels that can be viewed on the screen. No matter how large your monitor is (whether 15, 17, or even 21 inches), it shows only as many pixels as you determine in its settings. On larger screens, the pixels just get larger — and make your pictures fuzzy. That's why most people with larger screens set their monitors for a higher resolution.

Remember that scanned images are measured in dpi (dots per inch). The average monitor displays scanned images at 72 dpi. Do not confuse this with pixel size.

Lots of people are checking eBay on their cell phones, and although they have higher resolution, the high-end iPhone is only 480-by-320-pixel resolution at 163 pixels per inch. Because higher resolutions make the screen images smaller, many users prefer their screens at the 800 x 600 size for eye comfort. They don't want to squint!

If you use eBay's Picture Services for your all eBay items, setting your image size is not a big issue. eBay Picture Services applies a compression algorithm that forces your pictures into eBay's prescribed size.

The more compression put into computer images, the less sharp they appear. So you might as well use your camera or image-editing program to set your images to a monitor-friendly size *before* uploading them.

Here's a checklist of tried-and-true techniques for preparing elegantly slender, fast-loading images to display on eBay:

+ **Set your image resolution at 72 pixels per inch.** You can do this with the settings for your scanner. Although 72 ppi may seem like a super-low resolution, it only nibbles computer memory, shows up fast on a buyer's screen, and looks great on eBay.

+ **When using a digital camera, set the camera to no higher than the 640 x 480 format.** That's custom made for a VGA monitor. You can always crop the picture if it's too large. You can even save the image at 320 x 240. It will display well on eBay but take up less space, so you can add more pictures!

+ **Make the finished image no larger than 480 pixels wide.** When you size your picture in your image software, it's best to keep it no larger than 300 x 300 pixels or 4 inches square. These dimensions are big enough for people to see the image without squinting, and the details of your item show up nicely.

✦ **Crop any unnecessary areas of the photo.** You need to show only your item; everything else is a waste.

✦ **Use your software to darken or change the photo's contrast.** When the image looks good on your computer screen, the image looks good on your eBay auction page.

✦ **Save your image as a JPG file.** When you finish editing your picture, save it as a JPG file. (To do this, follow the instructions that come with your software.) JPG is the best format for eBay; it compresses information into a small file that builds fast and reproduces nicely on the Internet.

✦ **Check the total size of your image.** After you save the image, check its total size. If the size hovers around 40K or smaller, eBay users won't have a hard time seeing the image in a reasonable amount of time.

✦ **If your image is larger than 50K, reduce it.** Small is fast, efficient, and beautiful. Big is slow, sluggish, and dangerous to your sales. Impatient eBay users will move on to the next listing if they have to wait to see your image — or (worse) it will lose quality during eBay's image conversion.

Adding the Artist's Touch

Pictures don't always come out of the camera in perfect form. However, you can do a few tweaks to bring them into perfection range:

✦ **Alter the size:** Reduce or increase the size or shape of the image.

✦ **Change the orientation:** Rotate the image left or right; flip it horizontally or vertically.

✦ **Crop the background:** Sometimes there's a little too much background and not enough product. Don't waste precious bandwidth on extraneous pixels. To *crop* your image means to cut away the unnecessary part of the picture.

✦ **Adjust the brightness and contrast:** These two functions usually work together in most photo programs. By giving your picture more brightness, the picture looks brighter (duh). Raising contrast brings out the detail, and lowering it dulls the difference between light and dark.

✦ **Sharpen:** If your camera was not perfectly in focus when you took the picture, applying a photo-editing program's sharpening feature can help. If you sharpen too much, however, you can destroy the smoothness of the image.

If your image needs any more help than these alterations, it's probably easier and faster to just retake the picture.

Image-Editing Software

eBay sellers use a wide array of image-editing software. As a matter of fact, some listing software has built-in mini-editing capabilities. (See Book VIII for more on third-party software for eBay.) Choosing software for your images is like choosing an office chair. What's right for some people is dreadful for others. You might want to ask some of your friends what they use — and take a look at it.

When you buy a camera, it will no doubt arrive with a CD that includes some type of image-editing software. Give the software a try. If it works well for you, keep it. If not, check out the two options I mention later.

Every image-editing software program has its own system requirements and capabilities. Study the software that comes with your camera or scanner. If you feel that the program is too complicated (or doesn't give you the editing tools you need), investigate some of the other popular programs. You can get some excellent shareware (software that you can try before you buy) at www.tucows.com and www.shareware.com.

I used to be happy using Photoshop, but it's a large and expensive program. It's also a bit of overkill for eBay images. Two other new tools have caught my eye: LunaPic and Fast Photos.

Perfecting your picture in LunaPic

You need to know that I am lazy. When it comes to editing my images for eBay, I'm still looking for a magic wand. Sometimes I'm too lazy to open a program. So in my laziness, I browsed the Internet and found a *free* online photo-editing Web site, www.lunapic.com.

Although I prefer to use a program on my computer, LunaPic works great for quick, on-the-fly editing that I often need. You can even edit pictures on someone else's computer because there's no need to install software. Take a look at Figure 4-1. Here's LunaPic, a Web site that makes photo editing as easy as getting a burger at the drive through window.

Register on the site, and you have full photo-editing capabilities. Upload photos from your computer (or webcam) to the site, perform your touch-up, and then save and download! LunaPic has a full-featured toolset on the site; in it, you find tools to adjust brightness, contrast, and color, and to sharpen your images — and many more.

Figure 4-1:
Upload your
picture and
use the
online tools
to improve
the image.

Quick touchup and FTP in Fast Photos

If PhotoShop is too expensive and complex (it really is for eBay purposes),
you might be happy giving Fast Photos by Pixby Software a try. It's a simple,
all-in-one photo-editing program designed especially for e-commerce and
eBay sellers. The developer of the software knew exactly what processes
online sellers need for their images and included just those — and nothing
else. There are tools for cropping, JPEG compression, sharpening, resizing,
enhancing, rotating, and adding watermark text and borders.

The software is a PC application that runs on Windows XP, 2000, ME, and 98
SE. For a 21-day free trial, visit their Web site at

www.pixby.com/marshacollier

I said that Fast Photos is *all-in-one* because it not only allows you to touch up
your images quickly, but also has a built-in FTP program so that you can
upload your images immediately after editing them.

Using Microsoft's simple photo editor

Microsoft Office Picture Manager is a software program included with Microsoft Office suite starting with the 2003 edition. (It replaced Microsoft Photo Editor, which had been included with the Microsoft Office suite since Office 97). Picture Manager offers basic picture-editing features, and it may be a good place to start. If you have Microsoft Office, you find Picture Manager on your Start menu under Microsoft Office Tools.

Microsoft Office Picture Manager gives you some basic tools: You can auto-correct, fix "red eye," compress, resize, crop, and rotate. It's all pretty basic, but if all you want to do is fix the colors and reduce the photo size before uploading the image to eBay, it may be all you need. Clicking the Auto Correct command works well to correct the quality of an image. Select the Export task pane, and you can choose the exact size for the final image.

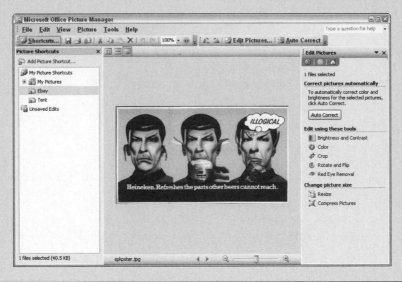

Editing an image for eBay in Fast Photos is simple:

1. **Open the program.**

2. **Click Browse and find the directory containing your image.**

3. **Find the photo, click it (see Figure 4-2), and then click the Add to Tray button (near the top of the screen).**

4. **Choose Edit.**

5. **Click to perform any of the following tasks, as shown in Figure 4-3:**

Figure 4-2:
Selecting
a photo for
editing in
Fast Photos.

Figure 4-3:
Editing your
image.

- **Rotate:** If you've shot your picture sideways or upside-down, you can rotate it here.

- **Crop:** In Crop mode, a gray rectangle appears with corner dots. Click a corner dot, drag the rectangle until it closes in on your item, and then click Apply.

- **Enhance:** Brighten, darken, increase, or decrease the contrast and work with image gamma and color. Don't worry — everything you do is visible on-screen and can be undone if you mess things up.

- **Resize:** You can resize your image to the standard eBay sizes or make the image a custom size.

- **Sharpen:** Is your image a little fuzzy? Click here to bring out the details.

- **Add border:** If you want a border or a drop shadow on your image, you can apply it here.

- **Add text:** Type your user ID so you can watermark your images (which helps dissuade those who try to use your images as their own).

- **JPEG compress:** By moving a sliding bar, you can compress the image as much as you dare. The more you compress, the less detailed the image will be.

6. **To save the changes you've made to your image, click Save As and give your file a name.**

Now you can upload your newly edited image to the Web. Just choose Publish (on the toolbar).

To set up an FTP account for uploading, click the Add button on the Publish screen. The screen shown in Figure 4-4 appears. Input the data required for your FTP server, click OK, and then upload your image with a mouse click.

As I write this, the developer is adding a batch mode to the program so you can edit and upload entire groups of images at once. Check out Chapter 5 for more information on uploading your images.

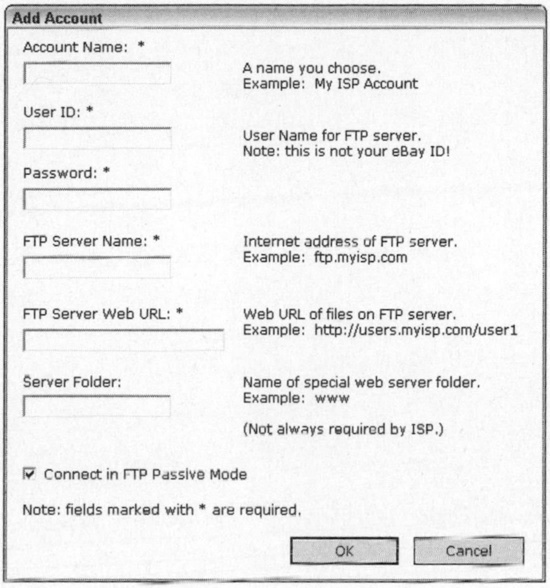

Add Account

Account Name: *

[   ]   A name you choose.
                         Example: My ISP Account

User ID: *

[   ]   User Name for FTP server.
                         Note: this is not your eBay ID!

Password: *

[   ]

FTP Server Name: *

[   ]   Internet address of FTP server.
                         Example: ftp.myisp.com

FTP Server Web URL: *

[   ]   Web URL of files on FTP server.
                               Example: http://users.myisp.com/user1

Server Folder:

[   ]   Name of special web server folder.
                         Example: www

                         (Not always required by ISP.)

☑ Connect in FTP Passive Mode

Note: fields marked with * are required.

[OK   ]   [Cancel   ]

Figure 4-4:
Fill in the
form with
your FTP
information.

Chapter 5: Getting Your Photos on the Web

In This Chapter

✔ Finding an online home

✔ Taking advantage of Picture Services

✔ Using your ISP space — for free

✔ Sending images to AOL

✔ Subscribing to Picture Manager

After you get your image perfect (following the suggestions in Chapter 4), it's time to emblazon it on your auction for all the world to see. When most people first get the urge to dazzle prospective buyers with a picture, they poke around the eBay site looking for a place to put it. Trade secret: You're not actually putting pictures on eBay; you're telling eBay's servers where to *find* your picture so that, like a good hunting dog, your auction points the buyers' browsers to the exact corner of the virtual universe where your picture is. That's why the picture has to load fast — it's coming in from a different location. (Yeah, it confused me in the beginning too, but now it makes perfect sense. Uh-huh. Sure.)

Finding a Home for Your Pictures

Because your image needs an address, you have to find it a good home online. You have several options:

✦ **Your ISP (Internet service provider):** All the big ISPs — AOL, AT&T, Road Runner, and Earthlink — give you space to store your Internet stuff. You're already paying for an ISP, so you can park pictures there at no extra charge.

✦ **An image-hosting Web site:** Web sites that specialize in hosting pictures are popping up all over the Internet. Some charge a small fee; others are free. The upside here is that they're easy to use.

✦ **Your server:** If you have your own server (those of you who do, well, you know who you are), you can store those images in your own home.

✦ **eBay Picture Services and Picture Manager:** These are eBay-based tools that host your photo on eBay's servers for a fee. (You may upload one image per listing at no charge.)

To most users, uploading pictures to their own Web spaces at their ISP remains a mystery. Many users are still convinced that they have to pay for an image-hosting service — but that's rarely the case these days.

Using eBay's Picture Services

I highly recommend that your first move be to take advantage of the one free picture per listing from eBay's Picture Services. First, it's available at no charge; second, Picture Services offers many other benefits.

At this point, I'll go back to my basic assumptions about you. I assume you know how to list an item on eBay — or at the very least, you can make your way through the Sell an Item form and get to the Add Pictures step.

Once you arrive there, you need to upload a picture to eBay, whether or not you have pictures in your description. Why? Because the first picture is free (and why turn down anything free?), and because your uploaded picture becomes part of the ultra-important top area of the item page, as shown in Figure 5-1. This picture will also be the default for use as your all-important gallery image.

Figure 5-1:
The item image is often where the prospective buyer looks first.

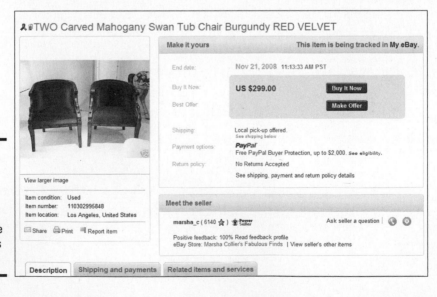

Have you ever noticed that some items that you browse on eBay do not have this crucial picture at the top? That's a shame, because these sellers are not availing themselves of eBay's Picture Services and they're losing sales as a result. Having that picture at the top of the page is a first-rate way to pull a buyer into your listing. (And did I mention that it's *free?*)

I suggest that you use eBay Picture Services for your primary image but host other images of the item elsewhere. Why? Because the quality of your photos is better if you host them directly from a site. Really clear pictures on Picture Services are few and far between. Picture Services reformats your photo to fit in a layout 400 pixels wide by 300 pixels tall, and then compresses the file for quick viewing. This process can destroy the quality of your carefully photographed images if you haven't saved them in a compatible size. You're running a business, so be businesslike and use the method that presents your photos in their best light.

Uploading your picture

In this section, I assume that you've already taken a picture, uploaded or scanned it, and saved it somewhere on your computer's hard drive.

For organization's sake, you might consider making a subfolder in your My Pictures directory called eBay Photos. That way you can always find your eBay pictures quickly, without searching through photos of your family reunion.

eBay offers two versions of Picture Services. The basic version, which is shown in Figure 5-2, allows you to upload eBay-ready images as they appear on your computer. If you want to rotate or crop the picture, you need Enhanced Picture Services. You'll be using the advanced version in the steps that follow.

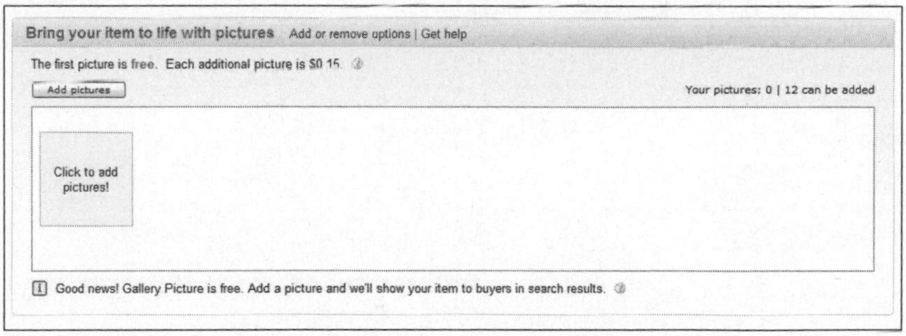

Figure 5-2:
The basic
Picture
Services
photo-
hosting
page.

> **Bring your item to life with pictures**   Add or remove options | Get help
>
> The first picture is free. Each additional picture is $0.15
>
> [Add pictures]   Your pictures: 0 | 12 can be added
>
> Click to add
> pictures!
>
> ⓘ Good news! Gallery Picture is free. Add a picture and we'll show your item to buyers in search results.

When you reach the part of the Sell an Item form that allows you to add pictures, does the screen look like Figure 5-2? If you're using Microsoft's Internet Explorer browser (the only one supported now), scroll down and click the Add or Remove Options link.

Clicking the Add or Remove Options link causes a window to pop up, as in Figure 5-3. Click the box next to Show eBay Enhanced Picture Services Options. (Also, why not click the Host Pictures on Your Server Instead of eBay Servers option in case you want to use that in the future?) Click Save.

Figure 5-3: eBay adds (or removes) your photo options here.

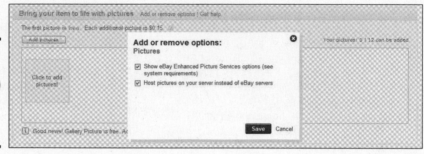

If you've never used eBay's Enhanced Picture Services before, a Windows security warning pops up, asking your permission to install a small program on your computer, as shown in Figure 5-4. This is safe (and the only way you can use eBay's Enhanced Picture Services features), so click Install.

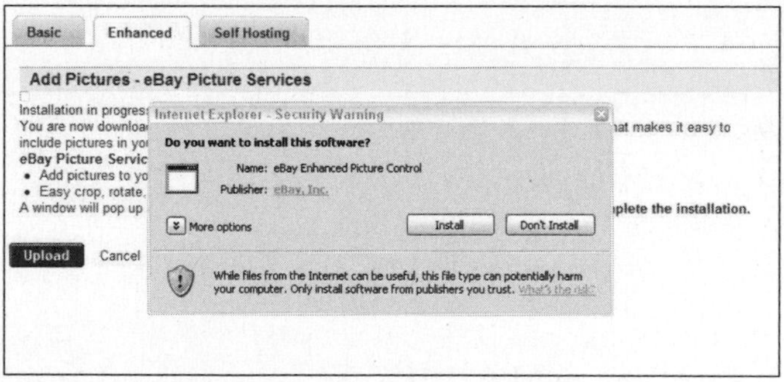

Figure 5-4: Windows security warning — it's okay to install.

Once your computer whirs a bit you'll be sent to eBay's Enhanced Picture Services screen, which is shown in Figure 5-5.

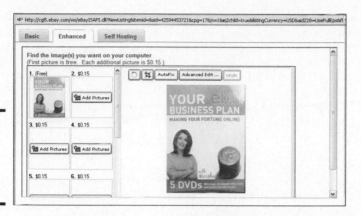

Figure 5-5:
eBay's
Enhanced
Picture
Services.

Then, to upload your picture, follow these steps:

1. **In the Enhanced Picture Services screen (refer to Figure 5-3), click the Add Pictures button.**

   A window pops up, prompting you to open an image file on your computer.

2. **Navigate to the directory that holds your eBay images on your computer.**

3. **Click the image in the browsing window.**

   The image name appears in the filename box.

4. **Click the Open box.**

   The selected image appears in the picture frame.

5. **To rotate the image, click the circular arrow (at the upper right of the main image box).**

6. **To crop the image:**

   a. *Click the crop box in the right corner of the larger image.*

      Two squares appear at opposite corners of your main image.

   b. *Click the frame on the outside of your image, and move the bar until the offensive area is cropped out.*

      You can do this from the sides, top, and bottom of the picture.

7. **When you're finished, click Continue.**

   A pop-up window notifies you that your picture is being uploaded to eBay's picture server.

Sometimes Picture Services will shrink your image to a too-small size, but you can't do much about it. Just be sure to reload the image any time you relist the item; otherwise the gallery image may just get smaller and smaller. eBay continues to improve Picture Services, so don't give up on it. Use it for the free image, and be sure to upload secondary images from an outside site.

If you accidentally select the wrong picture, click the X in the lower-left corner to make the picture disappear so you can select a different one.

Understanding the costs

You may notice that you have the option to upload more pictures. eBay charges for the additional images (see Table 5-1). You can include more images at no extra cost by uploading them from a server (more on that later).

Table 5-1	eBay Picture Services Fees		
Feature	eBay.com Fee ($)	eBay Stores Fee	Fixed-Price (3-, 5-, 7-, 10-Day) Fee / (30-Day, Good Till Cancelled)
First picture	Free	Free	Free
Gallery	Free	Free	Free
Gallery Plus	0.35	0.35 per 30 days	0.35 / 1.00
Picture Pack (gallery and up to six pictures)	0.75		0.75
Picture Pack (gallery and up to twelve pictures)	1.00	0.50	1.00

The Gallery option is no longer an option. The small photo of your item that appears next to your listing *is* the Gallery picture — and it's free.

Using Your Free ISP Space

In this section, I show you some easy ways to upload your pictures to your Web site or to your ISP's Web space. Doing so means you don't incur extra fees from eBay for including multiple pictures in your listings.

Everyone who connects to the Internet from his or her computer has an Internet service provider, or ISP. You pay this company a monthly fee for the privilege of hooking up to the Internet using their servers. AT&T Worldnet, Earthlink, Road Runner, AOL, or a local provider in your area are examples of ISPs.

Many ISPs give you a minimum of 5 MB of space to put a personal home page on the Internet. You can usually store your images for your eBay sales there — unless your provider has some strict rules about not doing that (it's a good idea to check first).

Internet providers may supply you with an image upload area, but they may require you to use File Transfer Protocol (FTP) to upload your images. You may be able to find a free or shareware (requiring a small fee) FTP program on sites such as the following:

+ www.tucows.com

+ www.download.com (formerly cNet)

+ www.shareware.com

If you use the Fast Photos image-editing program (described in Chapter 4), you get an FTP program as part of the software at no extra charge!

I've been using the Firefox browser and I really like it. It has a free FTP program, FireFTP, that's reliable and easy to use. FireFTP has never given me a whit of a problem, and I highly recommend it.

You can add FireFTP to your Firefox browser (MAC or PD) by visiting

fireftp.mozdev.org/

After you install the program, open it and follow these steps to upload a file to your ISP server:

1. **Click Manage Accounts ➪New.**

The Account Manager appears.

2. **Type in the name of your ISP in the Account Name box.**

3. **Where prompted, type the FTP address for your ISP account and then click Next.**

4. **Type the user name and password that you use to log in to your Internet account. Then click OK.**

5. **Click the Browse button (shown in Figure 5-6) to locate the directory on your computer where you store your eBay images.**

6. **Click OK, and you're good to go.**

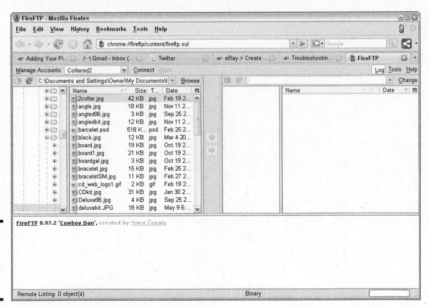

Figure 5-6:
Selecting your default directory.

From this point on, every time you click the Connect button, FireFTP logs on to your Web space and displays the screen shown in Figure 5-7. Note that the left side of the program is open to the directory you selected as the default for your eBay images. The right side of the screen shows what is currently on your ISP-provided home page.

To upload an image, highlight it and click the transfer arrow in the center. Faster than I could take a screen shot (okay, I took it anyway, and it's Figure 5-8), the image is uploaded to my Web space!

Figure 5-7:
Signing onto
your FTP
space.

Figure 5-8:
Instant
image
upload!

Uploading Images to AOL

AOL handles image uploads a bit differently from other ISPs. (But those of you on AOL knew that already.) Many people love AOL because it provides an easy, step-by-step interface. As you probably imagine, uploading pictures is handled in that same AOL style.

To upload pictures to AOL, follow these steps:

1. **Sign on to your AOL account.**

2. **Display the FTP area of AOL.**

   Search keywords for `ftp-click go` by typing it in the text line. On the next page, click `members ftp space`. Then double-click `members.aol.com`.

3. **Click See My FTP Space.**

   You're sent to your AOL storage area.

4. **Click Upload.**

   A screen appears so you can name the file you want to upload, called the remote file.

5. **In the Remote Filename box (see Figure 5-9), enter a name for your picture.**

   Use all lowercase letters and no more than eight characters.

6. **Click Continue.**

   A window opens so that you can locate the file on your computer, as shown in Figure 5-10.

7. **Locate the file, click its filename, and then click Open.**

   Your file will whiz through the wires to the server at AOL, as shown in Figure 5-11.

You can now double-check that your file arrived safely by typing its URL in your browser as follows, and pressing Enter:

`http://members.aol.com/yourscreenname/picturename.jpg`

You use the URL when you insert the picture into your eBay item description, as follows:

`<img src= http://members.aol.com/yourscreenname/picturename.jpg>`

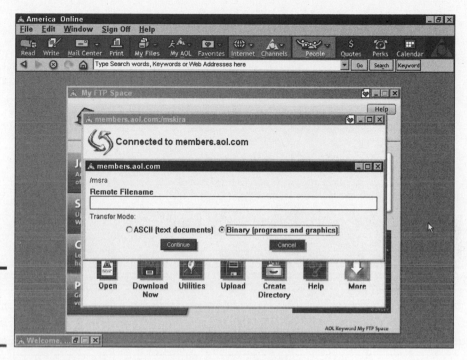

Figure 5-9:
Giving your
file a name
for AOL.

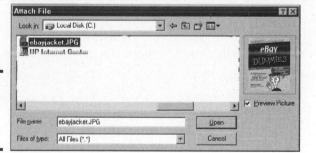

Figure 5-10:
Finding the
file on your
computer.

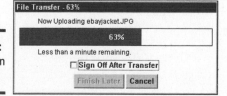

Figure 5-11:
The file is on
its way!

Using eBay's Picture Manager

If you really can't find a place to host your own pictures, you can store them with eBay's Picture Manager. Go to your My eBay page, and click the Picture Manager link. The screen shown in Figure 5-12 appears.

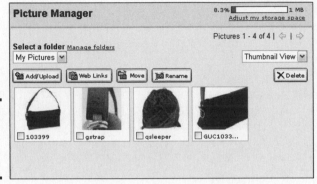

Figure 5-12: eBay's Picture Manager.

In the Picture Manager, you see any pictures you have uploaded, plus four buttons:

✦ **Add/Upload:** Click this button to display the basic uploader. (More on the basic and full-featured uploaders in a minute.)

✦ **Web Links:** When you put a check mark in the corner of one of the images and click the Web Links button, you are presented with the HTML code to copy and paste into your auction description. Should eBay decide to give you only the URL of the picture, be sure to write it in HTML code, as shown in Figure 5-13.

    Standard: 400 x 300 (bottom of the page size)

    Header: 200 x 150 (header image size)

    Thumbnail: 96 x 72 (gallery size)

✦ **Move:** Move a picture into another folder.

✦ **Rename:** If you don't like the name your camera gave the picture, you can rename the image here.

Two upload screens are available: basic and full-featured. The basic uploader screen appears when you click the Add/Upload button on the Picture Manager screen. The basic screen uploads your pictures one at a time, as in the basic Picture Services.

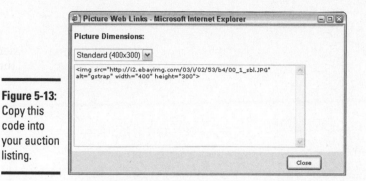

Figure 5-13:
Copy this
code into
your auction
listing.

To see the full-featured uploader, click the Try the Faster Full-Featured
Uploader for Free! link on the basic uploader screen. The full-featured version works the same way as the advanced version of Picture Services.

In the Upload window, you have a few additional options:

- **Optimal picture size:** Remember that eBay optimizes your pictures
  for faster display, which may affect the quality of the image. You can
  have eBay upload a copy of your original picture along with the opti-
  mized version.

- **Picture watermark:** You can add a watermark with your user ID (up
  to 24 characters) or the eBay Picture Services logo. The watermark
  makes it more difficult for someone to lift your auction images.

- **Upload to:** If you set up separate folders in Picture Manager, you may
  select the folder you want to upload your images to.

If you have an eBay store, you get 1 MB of storage space for free. That's
enough for about 40 pictures! If you don't have a store, you have to pay a fee
to use this service. See Table 5-2 for eBay's current charges for this service.

Table 5-2	eBay Picture Manager Fees
Storage Space	*Monthly Fee ($)*
1 MB	Free to eBay store owners
Up to 50 MB	9.99
Up to 250 MB	14.99
Up to 1 GB	24.99

Please keep in mind that for the same amount of money (and possibly even
less), you can use a third-party management and listing tool with more features. See Book VIII for more details on management services.

Book VI
Promoting Your Goods

Contents at a Glance

Chapter 1: Developing Your Web Site

In This Chapter

- Finding free Web space
- Choosing a host
- Deciding on the perfect name
- Registering the perfect name

Your eBay store is important to your business, but it doesn't replace an e-commerce Web site. You should establish your own presence on the Web. And although you should link your site to eBay, don't miss out on the rest of the Internet population.

You don't have a Web site yet? The Web has so many sites with pictures of people's dogs and kids that I just assumed you had your own site, too. The space for a Web site comes *free* from your ISP (I even have an embarrassing one with family pictures). One of these sites can be the practice site for your business. Take down pictures of the baby, and have a page to post pictures (and links) to items you're selling.

You do have a Web site? Have you taken a good look at it lately to see whether it's up to date? (I just looked at mine — ugh.) Does it link to your eBay auctions, eBay store, and your gallery?

Whether or not you have a Web site, this chapter has something for you. I provide a lot of detail about Web sites, from thinking up a name to choosing a host. If you don't have a site, I get you started launching one. If you already have a site, read the pointers about finding the best host. For the serious-minded Web-based entrepreneur (that's you), I also include some important marketing tips.

Free Web Space — a Good Place to Start

Although I love the word *free,* in real life it seems like nothing is *really* free. *Free* generally means something won't cost you too much money — but may cost you a bit more in time. When your site is free, you can't have your own direct URL (Universal Resource Locator) or domain name. Most likely, a free Web site has an address such as one of the following:

```
www.netcom.com/~marshac
home.socal.rr.com/marshac
members.aol.com/membername
```

Having some kind of site at least gives you experience in setting one up. When you're ready to jump in for real, you can always use your free site as an extension of your main business site.

When you signed up for Internet access, you had to sign on with an Internet service provider (ISP), which means you probably have your own Web space. Take a look at Table 1-1, where I compare some popular ISPs.

Table 1-1	ISPs That Provide Free Web Space	
ISP	*Number of E-Mail Addresses*	*Total Space per Account*
America Online (AOL)	7	2 MB per e-mail address (14MB)
Earthlink	8	10 MB
AT&T	10	60 MB
RoadRunner	5	25 MB
Comcast	7	175 MB
Yahoo! GeoCities*	1	15 MB (Unlimited $11.95 / month)
msnTV 2 (Internet on your television)	11	2 GB

*Yahoo! GeoCities isn't an ISP, but it is a reliable online community that gives each member online Web space. Membership is free. Extra megabyte space is available for purchase.

Most ISPs allow you to have more than one e-mail address per account. Each e-mail address is entitled to a certain amount of free Web space. Through the use of *hyperlinks* (small pieces of HTML code that, when clicked, route the clicker from one place to another on the page or on another Web site), you can combine all the free Web space from each e-mail address into one giant Web site.

If America Online (AOL) is your Internet provider, you may already know that AOL often has serious issues regarding its users getting e-mail from the rest of the Internet. You can't afford to run a business in an area that has e-mail issues. Your AOL account gives each of your seven screen names 2 MB of online storage space. You can best utilize this space by using it to store images for eBay, not to run a business site. Each screen name, at 2 MB, can store fifty 40K images. (For more information on how to use this space for your extra images, see Book V.)

Many ISPs have their own page-builder (HTML-generating) program that's free to their users. Poke around your ISP's home page for a Community or Your Web Space link.

**Book VI
Chapter 1**

Developing Your
Web Site

For example, after poking around the RoadRunner ISP's home page (www.rr.com), I found and clicked the Member Services link, which led me to a page offering various options. I finally found a Personal Home Page link, which took me to a page that would walk me through setting up my own home page. After agreeing to the terms of service, I can simply log on and set up my home page. You can also use software that you keep on your own computer to build Web pages. Microsoft's new Expression Web is an amazing program that allows you to build cohesive Web sites quickly.

Keep in mind, that most of the free ISP Web space is backed up with free page builder software — so be sure to check there first. In lieu of getting involved in a huge (and expensive) program such as Microsoft Expression Web, you might want to consider using a quick and easy HTML generator such as the one in Mozilla's free SeaMonkey. You can use this with the Firefox FireFTP upload extension for a complete Web hookup. See Book V Chapter 3 for more information on the SeaMonkey program.

Your first Web pages may be simple, and that's okay. You have to get used to having a Web site before you can really use it for commerce. Put up a home page that links to a few product-related pages and your eBay auctions, and, voilá, you're in business. If you're feeling more adventurous about your Web site, check out the next section, where I describe a handful of Web-site hosts.

Paying for Your Web Space

If you've been on the Internet for any length of time, you've been bombarded by hosting offers through your daily spam. A Web-hosting company houses your Web-site code and electronically doles out your pages and images to your Web page's visitors.

If you take advantage of PayPal's free Pay Now buttons or shopping cart, you can turn a basic-level hosted site into a full-on e-commerce store without paying additional fees to your hosting company. The PayPal tools are easily inserted into your pages with a snippet of code provided by PayPal.

Before deciding to spend good money on a Web-hosting company, check it out thoroughly. Go to that company's site to find a list of features offered. If you still have questions after perusing the Web site, look for a toll-free number to call. You won't find any feedback ratings like you find on eBay, but the following are a few questions to ask (don't hang up until you're satisfied with the answers):

✦ **How long has the company been in business?** You don't want a Web host that has been in business only a few months and operates out of the founder's basement. Deal with someone who's been around the Internet for a while (hence knows what he or she is doing). Is the company's Web site professional-looking? Does the company look like it has enough money to stay in business?

✦ **Who are some of the company's other clients?** Poke around to see whether you can find links to sites of other clients. Take a look at who else is doing business with the hosting company and analyze the sites. Do the pages and links come up quickly? Do all the images appear in a timely manner? Web sites that load quickly are a good sign.

✦ **What is the downtime-to-uptime ratio?** Does the Web host guarantee *uptime* (the span of time its servers stay operational without going down and denying access to your site)? Expecting a 99-percent-uptime guarantee is not unreasonable; you're open for business — and your Web host needs to keep it that way.

✦ **How much Web space do you get for my money?** MSN (Microsoft Network Internet-access service) gives you 30 MB for free; you'd better be getting a whole lot more if you're paying for it!

✦ **What's the host's data transfer limit?** *Data transfer* is a measurement of the amount of bytes transferred from your site on the server to the Internet. In July 2001, my site had 93,000 hits; in July 2004, it had more than 500,000. Each hit transfers a certain amount of bytes from your host's servers to the viewer's computer.

✦ **Does the Web host offer toll-free technical support?** When something goes wrong with your Web site, you need it corrected immediately. You must be able to reach tech support quickly without hanging around on the phone for hours. Does the Web host have a technical support area on its Web site where you can troubleshoot your own problems (in the middle of the night)?

Whenever you're deciding on any kind of provider for your business, take a moment to call its tech-support team with a question about their services. Take note of how long you had to hold and how courteous the techs were. Before plunking down your hard-earned money, you should be sure that the provider's customer service claims aren't merely that — just claims.

✦ **What's the policy on shopping carts?** In time, you're probably going to need a shopping cart interface on your site. Does your provider charge extra for that? If so, how much? In the beginning, a convenient and professional-looking way to sell items on your site is to set up a PayPal shopping cart or PayPal Pay Now buttons. When you're running your business full-time, however, a shopping cart or a way to accept credit cards is a must.

✦ **What kind of statistics will you get?** Visitors who go to your Web site leave a bread-crumb trail. Your host collects these statistics, so you'll be able to know which are your most and least popular pages. You can know how long people linger on each page, where they come from, and what browsers they're using. How your host supplies these stats to you is important.

✦ **Are there any hidden fees?** Does the Web host charge exorbitant fees for setup? Charge extra for statistics? Impose high charges if your bandwidth suddenly increases?

✦ **How often will the Web host back up your site?** No matter how redundant a host's servers are, a disaster may strike, and you need to know that your Web site won't vaporize. *Redundancy* is the safety net for your site. Ask how many power backups a company has for the main system. Perhaps it has generators (more than one is good) and more.

**Book VI
Chapter 1**

Developing Your
Web Site

If you have a Web site and you're like me, you're always looking for other hosts that offer more bang for your buck. It takes time to look behind the glitzy promotional statements and find out the facts behind each company. Go to www.tophosts.com and click the link to their current top Web hosts. Table 1-2 provides a comparison of some host service costs. In the rest of this section, I fill you in on the details about the four Web-hosting companies listed in the table. Make sure you check out their Web sites since the features offered change almost as often as eBay does to get the most current information.

Keep in mind that 200 MB of disk storage space can host as many as 6000 HTML pages.

Table 1-2	Comparing Entry-Level Hosting Costs			
Feature	*ReadyHosting.com*	*Web.com*	*Microsoft Office Live Small Business*	*Yahoo! Web Hosting*
Monthly plan cost	yearly only	$11.95	Free	$11.95
Yearly discount rate	$99.00	N/A	N/A	N/A
Disk space storage	100 GB	10 GB	500 MB	Unlimited
Data transfer/ month	1000 GB	Unlimited	10 GB	Unlimited
24/7 toll-free tech	No	Yes	No (Basic Plan)	Yes
E-mail aliases	Unlimited	50	100	1000

ReadyHosting

ReadyHosting is a little guy who's worked hard. The company has been hosting Web space since June 2000 and is a C-net Certified Award Winner. More than 150 new sites sign up with the service each day. Sites are hosted on servers running state-of-the-art software, and each site comes with a Cart32 e-commerce shopping cart. Cart32 integrates directly into Microsoft Expression Web (if you've got it), holds inventory, validates credit cards, and more. For details, check out

www.readyhosting.com

Web.com

Web.com is a big company with big sophisticated equipment, and it hosts a bunch of the big guys on their own private servers. Web.com has been in the hosting business since 1995 and hosts sites for millions of small and medium-sized businesses.

For little guys, Web.com offers shared hosting, and that's probably what you'll be using for quite a while. With shared hosting, your site resides with others on a single server, sharing all resources. Web.com even offers an eBay Store integrator at no extra cost in the basic package.

$10 private domain registration

In the never-ending battle of the giants, Google is now offering free Web space and $10 Domain registration (per year). Private registration is important these days because it prevents anyone from looking up who owns your Web site — and then deluging you with spam and other "offers."

New domains are instantly configured with a complete array of Google applications: personalized Gmail, Google Calendar, instant messaging, online document editing, and more. It's also loaded (at no charge) with other features.

✔ Full DNS control and management so you can move your domain settings to another Web host

✔ Private registration at no additional cost to protect your personal information

✔ Free domain locking to protect you from unauthorized domain transfers

You can find this hidden Google feature at

www.google.com/a

If your Internet sales gross more than $100,000 a year, you might have to look into *dedicated hosting,* in which your site is on a server of its own and is managed by the technical experts at your hosting company.

One of the best features of the company is its 24/7 toll-free technical support: Its online support gives extensive advice on how to solve problems on your own. Check out this site at the following address:

www.web.com

Microsoft Office Live Small Business

If Web.com is big, Microsoft is gargantuan; it's the leader in everything related to personal computing (as if you didn't know that). To grab a piece of the e-commerce market, Microsoft is making a strong push with its improved Office Live Small Business Center (formerly bCentral) site — which has always been a home for business Internet utilities — and has now come full circle to hosting Web sites and promoting e-commerce. Figure 1-1 shows the Office Live Small Business site.

Figure 1-1: Free Web Sites from Microsoft's Office Live.

Office Live's goal is to get all small businesses on the Web — for *FREE*. Yes, *free*. Trust me, the free Web site is a good deal — but realize that down the line, when you want to add the e-commerce tools you're offered, it's going to cost you. Availing yourself of the Web hosting is an easy procedure. You can find out the details of Microsoft's current offerings at

```
http://smallbusiness.officelive.com/
```

Office Live Small Business handles everything you need — free templates, design, and Domain setup. Your domain name is free for the first year; after that, you will be charged $14.95 annually. Your domain name will automatically renew each year unless you cancel prior to the renewal date.

You even get integrated e-mail and free registration. You can get up to 100 e-mail accounts for free for the first year, and you pay $14.95 per additional year.

For an additional $39.95 per month, you can add e-commerce tools to your Office Live Small Business Web.

Yahoo! Web-site services

Yahoo! is trying to do a little bit of everything these days. I'm never sure which direction it's going. When Yahoo! took over GeoCities (one of the original free Web site hosts) a few years back, my family Web site became a free Yahoo! site. Considering that I have a free site, I must admit that the services that Yahoo! offers have been top-drawer, disproving the notion that you get *only* what you pay for. But then again, I'm not running a business from the site; it's just a bunch of family pictures.

When you subscribe to one of Yahoo!'s Web-hosting plans, you can access their free design software, which allows you to be up and running with the basic site quickly. Thank goodness you don't have to know any HTML to use it. The download includes access to more than 300 stock templates that you can customize any way you want. If you don't want to the online tool, you can use Microsoft Web Expression (or any other HTML composer) to design your site. Figure 1-2 shows the Yahoo! Small Business Web site.

**Book VI
Chapter 1**

Developing Your
Web Site

Figure 1-2:
Yahoo's award-winning Web-hosting services.

Check out their award-winning offerings at

`smallbusiness.yahoo.com`

Naming Your Baby

What to name the baby, er, Web site? It's almost as much of a dilemma as deciding on your eBay user ID or eBay store name. If you don't have an existing company name that you want to use, why not use the same name as your eBay store? Register and lock it up now so that you can keep your brand forever.

Name your site with a word that identifies what you do, what you sell, or who you are. And be sure you like it — because once it's yours and you begin operating under it and establishing a reputation, it'll be with you 20 years from now when you're still selling online! (I know, it should only happen!)

A few Web sites offer wizards to help you decide your domain name. A particularly intuitive one can be found at the following:

`http://snapitnow.com/`

In a small, Web-based form, you input your primary business type and keywords that describe your business. The wizard then displays a large number of options and also lets you know whether the options are available. Very convenient.

Before you attempt to register a name, you should check to be sure it isn't anyone else's trademark. To search an updated list of registered United States trademarks, go to the following and use the electronic trademark search system:

`www.trademarksearchforfree.com`

After a search, you may want to trademark your site name. `www.legalzoom.com` is an online service that can help you with that. It offers online trademark applications and also refers you to an attorney if you'd like to use one; just go to their site for further information.

Domain parking

Suppose you've come up with a brilliant name for your site and your business gets really big and famous. Then someone else uses your Web site's name but registers it as a `.net` — while yours is a `.com`. To avoid this situation, make sure you register both domains (`.com` and `.net`) and park them with your registrar. That way any permutations of your domain will point to your active Web site. For example, `www.ebay.net` and `www.ebay.org` are registered to (guess who?) `ebay.com`. You can check the owner of any domain name at any of the Web-hosting or registrar sites.

Registering Your Domain Name

Talk about your junk e-mail. I get daily e-mails advising me to Lose 40 pounds in 40 days, accept credit cards now, and of course REGISTER MY NAME NOW! The last scam seems to be geared to obtaining my e-mail address for other junk mail lists rather than trying to help me register my Web site. Choosing a select *registrar* (the company that handles the registering of your site name) is as important as choosing the right Web host. You must remember that the Internet is still a little like the Wild West — and that the cyber-equivalent of the James Gang might be waiting to relieve you of your hard-earned cash. One of the ways to protect yourself is to understand how the registry works (knowledge *is* power), so read on.

Before you decide on a registrar for your domain name, take a minute to see whether the registrar is accredited by ICANN (Internet Corporation for Assigned Names and Numbers — the international governing body for domain names) or is reselling for an official ICANN-accredited registrar. (You'll have to ask who they register with.) The Accredited Registrar Directory is updated constantly, so check the following for the most recent list:

www.internic.com/regist.html.

For a comparison of registration fees, see Table 1-3.

Table 1-3	Yearly Domain Name Registration Fees	
Registrar	*Registration Fee ($) per year*	*URL Forwarding ($)*
Google	10.00 (Private Registration)	Free
yahoo.com	9.95 (free with web hosting package)	Included
namesarecheap.com	14.00	Included
networksolutions.com	24.99 (free with hosting package)	12.00

You'll usually get a substantial discount from the more expensive registrars when you register your domain name for multiple years — a good idea if you plan on staying in business. Also, if you register your name through your hosting service, you might be able to cut the prices in Table 1-3 in half! The only drawback is that your prepaid registration might go out the window if you choose to change hosting companies.

If you're registering a new domain name but already have a site set up with your ISP, you need a feature called URL forwarding, or Web address forwarding. This feature directs any hits to your new domain name from your existing long URL address. Some registrars offer this service, but watch out for hidden surprises — such as a free offer of the service, which means they'll probably smack a big fat banner at the bottom of your home page. Your registrar should also have some available tech support. Trying to troubleshoot DNS issues is a job for those who know what they're doing! Remember, sometimes you *do* get what you pay for.

Making your personal information private

ICANN requires every registrar to maintain a publicly accessible whois database that displays all contact information for all domain names registered. Interested parties (or, for that matter, fraudsters) can find out the name, street address, e-mail address, and phone number of the owner of the site by running a whois search on the domain name. You can run a whois search by going to www.whois.net and typing the domain name in question.

Unfortunately, this information can be useful to spammers who spoof your e-mail address as their fake return address to cloak their identity;

identity thieves, stalkers, and just about anyone up to no good may also take an interest. To see the difference between private and public registrations, run a whois search on my Web site, www.coolebaytools.com — which is private — and www.ebay.com, which is public.

Registrars such as Network Solutions offer private registration for an additional $9 a year (Google for FREE). Check to see whether your registrar offers this service. For updated information on private registration, visit my Web site.

Chapter 2: Marketing Your Web Site and eBay Store

In This Chapter

✔ Using banner-ad exchanges

✔ Becoming an affiliate

✔ Advertising via Web CPC

✔ Getting listed in a search engine

✔ Installing eBay Marketplace

After you set up your Web site and eBay store, it's time to let the world know about it. Having spent many years in the advertising business, I can spot businesses that *want* to fail. They open their doors and expect the world to beat a path to them and make them rich. This doesn't happen — ever.

You must take a proactive approach to letting the world in on the goodies you have for sale. This means spending a good deal of time promoting your site by running banner ads, buying keywords on Google, and getting your URL into a search engine. There are no shortcuts.

About a trillion (at least!) people out there want to take your money for advertising your Web site. There are affiliate programs, link exchanges, banner exchanges — the list just goes on! As with all transactions regarding your Web site, knowing who you're dealing with is the key to success. If you want to run your banner on someone else's site, don't spend money; ask to do an exchange. The more advertising that you can get for free, the better. If you decide that you want to pay for advertising, I recommend that you wait until after you've made a profit selling merchandise from your site.

A simple link to your Web site from your eBay About Me page will draw people to your site initially. You'll be pleasantly surprised.

Engaging Banner-Ad Exchanges and Services

The way banner ad exchange services work is simple. First, to design a full-size banner ad in your graphics program, you need to design to a designated size — according to the following standards:

- ✦ 468 pixels wide by 60 pixels high
- ✦ GIF format (no JPEGs)
- ✦ Nontransparent
- ✦ File size less than 10 KB (10,240 bytes)
- ✦ If animated, the animation stops at seven seconds and doesn't include loops

Aside from the "standard" banner size, many sites will offer options for ads in different sizes. Once you decide on a service for your banner, check which of these standard sizes are accepted. See Table 2-1 for the standard sizes.

Table 2-1:	Current Standard Ad Sizes on the Web
Rectangular and pop-up ads	*Width by height in pixels*
Large rectangle	336 by 280
Medium rectangle	300 by 250
Square pop-up	250 by 250
Vertical rectangle	240 by 400
Rectangle	180 by 150
Banner and button ads	
Leaderboard	728 by 90
Full banner	468 by 60
Half banner	234 by 60
Button 1	120 by 90
Button 2	120 by 60
Micro bar	88 by 31
Micro button	80 by 15
Vertical banner	120 by 240
Square button	125 by 125
"Skyscraper" ads	
Thin Skyscraper	120 by 600
Standard skyscraper	160 by 600
Half-page	300 by 600

The exchange service displays your banner on other sites. When Web-surfers click your banner, they're taken to your site, where they'll see all the great stuff you have for sale. You can even target what type of sites you want your banner to appear on as well. Remember that this is an *exchange*. Someone else's banner will appear on your pages in exchange for showing yours on other sites.

You can also purchase space for your banner on a cost-per-click basis. When you pay, your Web banner is displayed whenever a Web page that refer-ences the banner is loaded into a Web browser. This practice is what the technorati call an *impression*. When viewers click the banner, they're sent to your Web site. The act of a viewer clicking the ad is called a *click-through*, and you pay per click-through. (Get it? Cost per click?)

Banner design

If you think that designing an eye-catching banner ad is beyond your graphic talents, you'll be happy to know that many excellent graphic artists on the Internet can produce one for you at a reasonable price. Type *banner design* into any search engine, and you'll come up with a ton of listings (also use the *animated banner* search on eBay as described in Chapter 1). To find a designer who matches your needs, look at samples (and pricing) on their Web sites. Figure 2-1 shows the banner ad that I bought it on eBay for one of my books.

Book VI
Chapter 2

Marketing Your
Web Site and eBay
Store

Figure 2-1:
One of my
animated
banner ads.

When planning your banner, keep a few points in mind:

✦ **Go online and study the banner ads.** Visit the major search engines and portals and see how the pros do it.

✦ **Decide on what you want to say.** A banner ad is like a mini-billboard. There's no room for a lot of text and graphics; to get attention you have to keep it simple.

✦ **Write down key phrases that describe your business.** Then write and rewrite them again, shortening the verbiage. The shorter the message, the better — as long as it gets your point across.

✦ **If you must use an image or graphic, settle on one.** Having more than one picture in your banner can be distracting. Remember: You only have a couple of seconds to get the customer's attention.

Finding banner advertising networks

Go to your favorite Web search engine and do a search for *banner ad*, or *banner ad exchange*. I ran these searches on Google and found tons of offerings. Take a look at the various companies that show up and find the one that fits your needs. Be sure the company you select gives you stats on your banner views, your page visits, and your *click-through ratio* (the number of times people click your banner and visit your site compared to the number of times your banner is displayed).

Trying Affiliate Programs

An *affiliate program* is a partnership between your Web site and an online merchant (a company that sells goods or services). It allows you to earn money when visitors from your site click through to the merchant's Web site or when a visitor clicks through to the other party's site and makes a purchase.

An affiliate program can represent a value-added service to your Web site's visitors or, when carried to an extreme, can dilute your own site's message by cluttering your pages with banner ads many find more annoying than useful. I'm certain you've been to Web sites that had more ads than their own message. Those sites aren't giving their customers anything to visit.

Carefully consider the companies with whom you want to affiliate. Be sure their core product ties into the theme of your Web site. Also be sure that they're not in competition with you. Wouldn't it be a bummer if your customer found that an item you're selling was available on the affiliate's site for less?

Companies can arrange affiliate links between you and other sites. The Cadillac (Rolls-Royce? Mercedes?) of these is LinkShare.

LinkShare

LinkShare hosts a password-protected Web site that offers affiliates a choice of hundreds of top-quality merchant programs. On this site, affiliates can join new programs, get links to put on their sites, and then see reports about how their links are performing and how much they've earned.

Here's what LinkShare offers its affiliates:

✦ **Commission potential:** When a visitor clicks a link or banner that you've inserted on your site and goes to a merchant's site (say, American Express), LinkShare keeps track of all the transactions that the visitor makes. If that visitor buys something on the merchant's site, you get a commission. In some cases, you can be compensated even if your visitor doesn't buy anything; you're paid just for having driven traffic to the merchant's site.

✦ **Program help and updates:** LinkShare also provides affiliates with customer service, notifies affiliates about new programs and new opportunities, and offers resources for affiliates to learn about how to get the most out of their programs.

✦ **Name-recognition clout:** You can also include text links to affiliates in your e-mails and newsletters. Gussying up your site with some top-name vendors (you must be approved by each vendor) can give your site some clout.

Sign up with LinkShare at `www.linkshare.com`. When your site is approved, you can start making some extra money!

eBay's affiliate program

I've heard that Web site owners have made tens of thousands of dollars a year with the eBay affiliate program, the eBay Partner Network. The affiliate program pays like this:

✦ **For new active eBay registrations:** For every person who goes to eBay from your Web site (using the specified link or banner), registers with eBay for the first time, and places a bid on an item, you can get up to $30. Not a bad return.

Tables 2-1 and 2-2 show the current payment schedules. For a registration to be considered active, the user must place a bid on an item or use Buy It Now to buy within 30 days of their initial registration. The rates in both tables are effective as of this writing.

✦ **For winning bidders:** You also get paid when someone bids on an item after clicking through from your link. This payment is based on monthly winning bids. You can actually get a percentage of eBay's fees (insertion fee and the Final Value Fee) based on purchases made through your click-through. Nice!

Table 2-1	Monthly Active Confirmed Users
Quality Tier	*Payment per Active Registration ($)*
Very Low	$1.00
Low	$10.00
Medium	$28.00
High	$40.00
Very High	$50.00

Table 2-2	Monthly Winning-Bid Revenue Tiers	
Total winning bid revenue generated	Percentage of Revenue
$0.00 – $99.99	50
$100.00 – $4,999.99	55
$5,000.00 – $199,999.99	60
$200,000.00 – $699,999.99	65
$700,000.00 – $2,999,999.99	70
$3,000,000.00+	75
$0.00 – $99.99	50

The eBay affiliate program pays for one bid or Buy It Now per click from your Web site. Your site links must be used as a navigation point from which the buyer comes to the eBay site before every bid or Buy It Now.

To check the current information and sign up for the program, visit

ebaypartnernetwork.com

Some eBay affiliates have issues with the program. To educate yourself *before* you sign up, I suggest you read the public-affiliate message board at

forums.ebay.com/db1/forum.jsp?forum=118

so you'll be familiar with any issues that may affect you or your site. Remember, there's *no free lunch.*

An alternate idea is to put links on your site to your eBay store (read further in this chapter). Any purchases made from the special links on your Web site in your eBay store net you a 75 percent Final Value Fee credit. Read all about this little-known discount in Book VIII.

Cost-per-Click Advertising with Google

Wouldn't it be cool if you could run ads all over the Internet at a low price? You can!

One excellent example is Google's cost-per-click (CPC) offering, AdWords. Being a regular user of the Google index, I began to notice small ads on the right side of my searches under a headline called Sponsored Links. I thought they were expensive links from high-dollar operations — until I found out the truth. If you take a look at the results of a Google search in Figure 2-2, you'll see the ads that companies bought to show up on searches for my name on the right. (By the way — notice that my eBay Store shows up in the Google search on my name.)

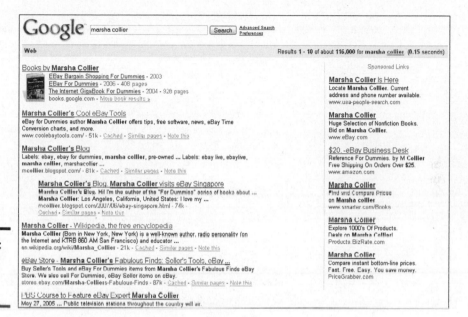

Figure 2-2:
Okay, I
Googled
myself.

People use Google more than 300 million times a day. Google AdWords allow you to create these profitable little ads. You choose keywords to let Google know where to place your ads. Certainly you can come up with some relevant keywords to promote your Web site or eBay Store! (If you're stumped, try the 30-day free trial of Sellathon mentioned in Book VIII.)

The coolest part of the deal is that you pay for the ad only when someone clicks it (similar to eBay banners, which are described in Chapter 1). Want to know more? Go over to `www.adwords.com`. Once you're there, you can go over the details and set up your own campaign.

For your campaign, keep the following in mind:

✦ **Keywords and keyword phrases:** Come up with a list of keywords that would best describe your merchandise. Google allows you to estimate, based on current search data, how often your selected keyword will come up every day. Google will also estimate your daily cost based on the current amount of clicks on that word. That can be a shocking number. Don't worry — not everyone who sees your ad will click it — but if they did, eeyow!

✦ **CPC (cost-per-click):** You determine how much you'll pay for each click on your keywords. You can pay as little as $.05 or as much as $50.00 a click. The dollar amount you place on your clicks makes the basis for how often your ad appears.

✦ **CTR (click-through rate):** This statistic reflects how many people click your ad when they see it. If your CTR falls below .5% after 1000 impressions, AdWords may slow or even discontinue your ad views. When one of your keywords isn't passing muster, it will be indicated on your reports.

Without showing my keywords, Figure 2-3 shows you a month's worth of keyword analysis for my account. You can see clearly that some keywords are doing their jobs and others aren't. To keep my account current, I evaluate my CTR every month and delete the laggers.

Status	Clicks	Impr.	CTR ▼	Avg. CPC	Cost	Avg. Pos
	657	37,770	1.7%	$0.08	$46.21	3.7
	272	726,644	0.0%	$0.08	$19.10	3.1
Strong	34	111	30.6%	$0.05	$1.70	1.0
Strong	13	256	5.0%	$0.09	$1.10	1.2
Strong	22	434	5.0%	$0.09	$1.89	5.1
Strong	221	9,712	2.2%	$0.08	$17.61	4.2
Strong	40	1,853	2.1%	$0.06	$2.12	1.2
Strong	106	6,138	1.7%	$0.06	$5.79	1.3
Strong	156	10,423	1.4%	$0.07	$10.87	1.5
Strong	28	3,199	0.8%	$0.08	$2.13	3.4
Strong	5	649	0.7%	$0.06	$0.28	1.9
Moderate	9	1,191	0.7%	$0.10	$0.84	14.2
Strong	23	3,247	0.7%	$0.09	$1.88	7.1
Moderate	0	161	0.0%	-	-	6.4
Moderate	0	158	0.0%	-	-	33.9
Moderate	0	99	0.0%	-	-	103.1

Figure 2-3: AdWords keyword statistics.

✦ **Daily budget:** You can set the cap in dollars on how much you'll spend a day. Otherwise, if you had some really hot keywords, you could spend thousands on clicks!

Setting up an AdWords account takes a while and some thinking. So wait until your mind is clear (Saturday morning?) and sit down at the AdWords site with a cup of coffee.

Google gives you excellent step-by-step instructions after you're signed in at www.adwords.com. This is the general process:

1. **Decide whether you want to target your ads geographically.**

   You can pinpoint your market if you'd like, or you can blast the entire world. Choose from a list of 14 languages, 250 countries, or as far down as 200 United States regions.

2. **Create your ad.**

   This is not as easy as I thought! You can create only three lines of ad text with a total of 95 characters. Be as concise as possible. Don't throw in useless adjectives. Figure out the perfect 95 characters that will sell your site to the world. You must also supply the URL for your Web site or eBay Store.

3. **Select your keywords.**

   Type your keywords and key phrases in the box provided. You can use Google's Keyword Suggestion tool to help you out. Because this is your initial pass and won't be etched in granite, take some wild stabs and see what happens.

4. **Choose you maximum CPC (cost per click) and then click Calculate Estimates.**

   Here's where the sticker shock gets you. The displayed data lets you know which keywords you can afford to keep and which ones must be discarded. If you want to change your CPC amount, do so and click Recalculate Estimates. The Traffic Estimator calculates how much, on average, you'll end up spending in a day.

5. **Specify your daily budget.**

   There will be a prefilled amount that would ensure that your ad stays on top and gets full exposure every day. (No, Mr. Google, I do not want to spend $50 a day on my keywords.) Set a cap on your budget and Google will never exceed it. You may make it as low as you want; there's no minimum spending amount.

6. **Enter your e-mail address and agree to the terms.**

7. **Enter your billing information.**

   You're minutes away from your ads going live on the Google index.

Interestingly, your ads may also appear on other places on the Internet through Google's Webmaster's program. Take a look at Figure 2-4. My ad ended up on my book's listing page on Amazon because one of my key phrases is *eBay For Dummies* (and my targeting is considered relevant).

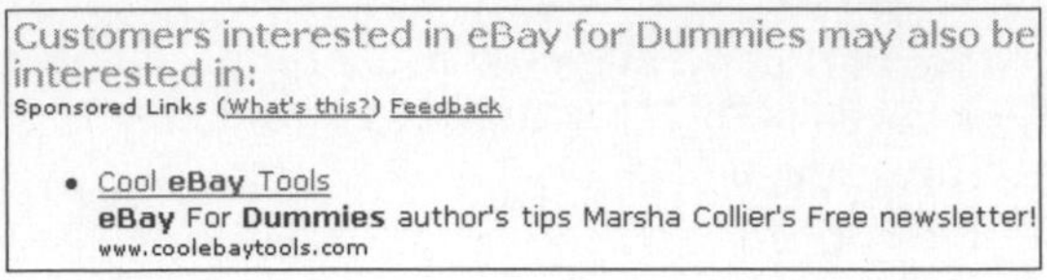

Figure 2-4:
My
AdWords
campaign
on Amazon.

Customers interested in eBay for Dummies may also be
interested in:
Sponsored Links (What's this?) Feedback

- Cool **eBay** Tools
  eBay For **Dummies** author's tips Marsha Collier's Free newsletter!
  www.coolebaytools.com

To find out more about the Google AdWords program, check out *AdWords For Dummies* (also from Wiley Publishing).

Getting Your Site into a Search Engine

For people to find your site (and what you're selling), they must be able to locate you. A popular way people do this is by searching with a search engine, so you should submit your site to search engines. Go to the search engines that interest you and look for a link or a help area that will enable you to submit your site. Be sure to follow any specific instructions on the site; some may limit the amount of keywords and the characters in your description.

To submit your URL to search engines, you need to do a little work (nothing's easy, is it?). Write down 25 to 50 words or phrases that describe your Web site; these are your *keywords.* Now, using as many of the words you came up with, write a description of your site. With the remaining words, create a list of keywords, separating each word or short phrase with a comma. You can use these keywords to add meta tags to the header in your HTML document for your home page. *Meta tags* are identifiers used by search-engine *spiders,* robots that troll the Internet looking for new sites to classify on search engines. Specifying a meta tag in HTML looks like this:

```
<META NAME = ìinsert your keywords here separated by commasî
    CONTENT = ìshort description of your siteî>
```

If you have a problem coming up with keywords, check out Yahoo! GeoCities handy meta tag generator, which you can use for free:

```
http://geocities.yahoo.com/v/res/meg.html
```

Not to be outdone, Google also have a free generator as part of the AdWords program:

```
https://adwords.google.com/select/KeywordToolExternal
```

Have Yahoo! Search Submit do the work

Search Submit Basic is part of Yahoo's search-marketing services. It handles your site submissions in non-sponsored search results on Yahoo! (as well as on other portals such as AltaVista and AllTheWeb), saving you the trouble of going from site to site. For $49 a year, the service will submit and resubmit as many as five URLs as often as you'd like. You even get access to a page online where you can check the status of your site's performance.

Visit `http://searchmarketing.yahoo.com/srchsb/ssb.php` for more information and to sign up.

Most Web-hosting companies provide this service (of submitting URLs) to their clients. Double-check to be sure that your Web-hosting company doesn't offer a similar service free or, at the very least, at a discount.

Get listed on Yahoo!

Yahoo! is one of the more difficult sites to list with, although you *can* get a free listing if you fill out all the forms correctly and wait six to eight weeks (see Figure 2-5). You can find instructions for the free listing at

`https://siteexplorer.search.yahoo.com/submit`

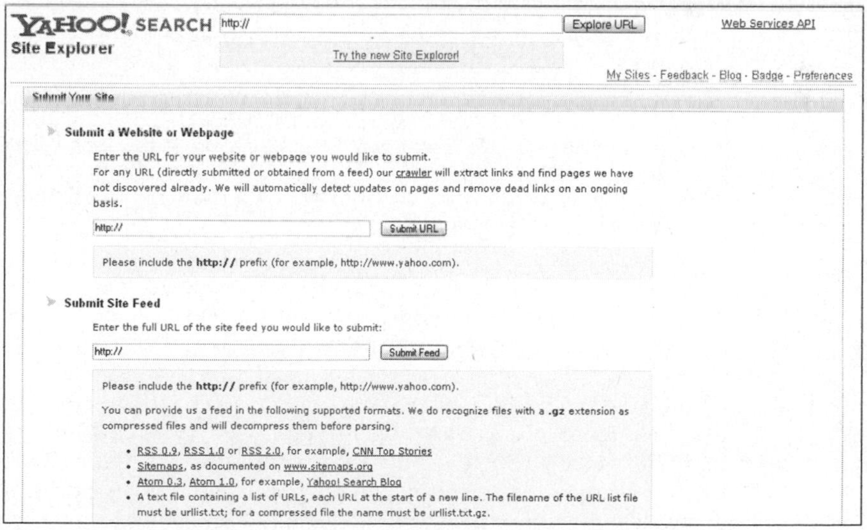

**Book VI
Chapter 2**

**Marketing Your
Web Site and eBay
Store**

Figure 2-5:
Get seen on
Yahoo!.

YAHOO! SEARCH   http://   [Explore URL]   Web Services API
Site Explorer   Try the new Site Explorer!
My Sites · Feedback · Blog · Badge · Preferences

Submit Your Site

▸ **Submit a Website or Webpage**

Enter the URL for your website or webpage you would like to submit.
For any URL (directly submitted or obtained from a feed) our crawler will extract links and find pages we have not discovered already. We will automatically detect updates on pages and remove dead links on an ongoing basis.

http://   [Submit URL]

Please include the **http://** prefix (for example, http://www.yahoo.com).

▸ **Submit Site Feed**

Enter the full URL of the site feed you would like to submit:

http://   [Submit Feed]

Please include the **http://** prefix (for example, http://www.yahoo.com).

You can provide us a feed in the following supported formats. We do recognize files with a **.gz** extension as compressed files and will decompress them before parsing.

- RSS 0.9, RSS 1.0 or RSS 2.0, for example, CNN Top Stories
- Sitemaps, as documented on www.sitemaps.org
- Atom 0.3, Atom 1.0, for example, Yahoo! Search Blog
- A text file containing a list of URLs, each URL at the start of a new line. The filename of the URL list file must be urllist.txt; for a compressed file the name must be urllist.txt.gz.

Catch attention on Google

Have you ever Googled your eBay Store? I did, by searching for the name of my eBay Store and including the word *eBay* in the search parameters. Figure 2-6 shows you the results.

Figure 2-6:
Wow! My eBay store is listed (even on the Canada and UK eBay sites)!

You, too, should Google your Web site and eBay store to see whether it's listed. If it isn't, you're missing out on a huge opportunity for free promotion. Google runs spiders (just picture the way a spider runs — swiftly and all over the place) that scour the Internet on a monthly basis looking for data to become part of the Google index.

Thousands of sites (and you do know that since your eBay store has a unique URL, it's considered to be a Web site) are added to the Google index every time their spiders crawl the Web.

If your eBay store *isn't* listed, go to www.google.com/addurl/, as pictured in Figure 2-7. When you get to this page, type your eBay store URL. To find your store's URL, click the red *store* tag next to your eBay user ID to go to your store, and then copy and paste the URL (in the address line of your browser) into the URL line on the form. When I went to my eBay store, I got this URL:

```
http://stores.ebay.com/Marsha-Colliers-Fabulous-Finds
```

(That's the URL I use in my e-mail and printed propaganda to promote my store.)

**Book VI
Chapter 2**

Marketing Your
Web Site and eBay
Store

Share your place on the net with us.

We add and update new sites to our index each time we crawl the web, and we invite you to submit your URL here. We do not add all submitted URLs to our index, and we cannot make any predictions or guarantees about when or if they will appear.

Please enter your full URL, including the `http://` prefix. For example: `http://www.google.com/`. You may also add comments or keywords that describe the content of your page. These are used only for our information and do not affect how your page is indexed or used by Google.

Please note: Only the top-level page from a host is necessary; you do not need to submit each individual page. Our crawler, Googlebot, will be able to find the rest. Google updates its index on a regular basis, so updated or outdated link submissions are not necessary. Dead links will 'fade out' of our index on our next crawl when we update our entire index.

URL:

Comments:

Optional: To help us distinguish between sites submitted by individuals and those automatically entered by software robots, please type the squiggly letters shown here into the box below.

tingl

Add URL

Figure 2-7:
Get your
free shot at
the big time.

In the second line, add a comment if you want, describing your store merchandise. Then click Submit. There are no guarantees here, but odds are you'll find your little shop on Google within a few weeks.

What's the zeitgeist?

It's all about the zeitgeist. And what the heck, you may wonder, is a zeitgeist? *Zeitgeist* comes from the German (originally *geist der zeit*) words *zeit* meaning time and *geist* meaning spirit. It's the all-embracing intellectual atmosphere of a distinct time period. In today's terms? It's the buzz.

Similar to the Yahoo! Buzz, the Google *zeitgeist* keeps current and historic data on the site. The *zeitgeist* is based on the total number of queries on a particular subject in a certain period of time. It's updated on a weekly, monthly, and, when called for, daily basis, and can be found at

(continued)

(continued)

`www.google.com/press/zeitgeist.html`.

From that page, you can also see the zeitgeist (what's hot and what's not) in other countries (invaluable information if you're selling on eBay internationally) including the United Kingdom, Canada, Germany, Spain, France, Italy, the Netherlands, Australia, and Japan. This page also links to historical zeitgeist data.

The zeitgeist page is where you can get the nuggets of thought for your marketing and selling plans. The zeitgeist also has information for previous periods. If you take a look at the figure, you'll find some obvious data (hindsight *is* 20/20). If you were selling items based on any of the popular queries or brands in 2007, it's fair to say you did very well. Check out the zeitgeist. It could be your crystal ball into stocking your store.

If you'd like a smile, the people at Google like to put up harmless spoof sites. One of my favorites "explains" how Google ranks things. Check out

`http://www.google.com/technology/pigeonrank.html`

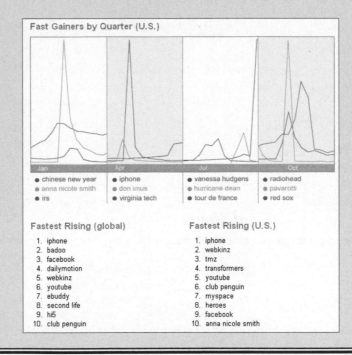

Fast Gainers by Quarter (U.S.)

Jan	Apr	Jul	Oct
● chinese new year	● iphone	● vanessa hudgens	● radiohead
● anna nicole smith	● don imus	● hurricane dean	● pavarotti
● irs	● virginia tech	● tour de france	● red sox

Fastest Rising (global)

1. iphone
2. badoo
3. facebook
4. dailymotion
5. webkinz
6. youtube
7. ebuddy
8. second life
9. hi5
10. club penguin

Fastest Rising (U.S.)

1. iphone
2. webkinz
3. tmz
4. transformers
5. youtube
6. club penguin
7. myspace
8. heroes
9. facebook
10. anna nicole smith

Chapter 3: Using PayPal to Increase Your Sales

When you think of PayPal, you might think of it as just a payment service on eBay, but it's much, much more. Did you know that PayPal has shops? Yes! It's another place to sell your wares online. PayPal also has some great tools for your Web site. In this chapter, I give you the information you need to be fully PayPal-enabled!

Setting Up Shop at PayPal

Before PayPal joined eBay, it was pulling out every trick in the book to get members. The company was founded with a desire to give its customers plenty of extras for their loyalty — and it offers tons of tools to enhance the seller's online selling experience. The tools and the prices charged by PayPal are unmatched by any other online payment service.

Joining PayPal shops

The best part of joining PayPal shops is that there's no cost to you. A PayPal shop is not a separate online store but a link from the PayPal mall (so to speak) to a unique group of shops. More than 40 million PayPal members may browse this area at any time, so why not avail yourself of this free marketing opportunity?

The shop can link to your eBay store, or you can link to your PayPal-enabled business Web site. Think of it as a way to double your store's visibility on the Web without spending more in fees. Your store will be listed in the PayPal Shops directory, as shown in Figure 3-1.

Figure 3-1:
The PayPal
Shops hub
page.

Notice that the PayPal hub has categories (on the left side of the page) and a shop search. The categories whittle down into subcategories; they work just like those on eBay (minus the sub-subcategories).

I used the search box to find some pretty things and came up with the search results shown in Figure 3-2. Notice the number next to each store name. No, it's not the seller's feedback rating; it's the PayPal *seller reputation number.*

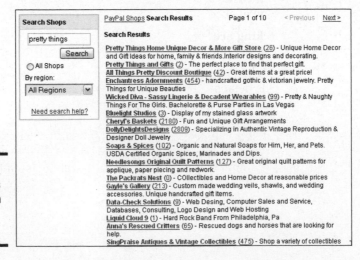

Figure 3-2:
The results
of a search
in PayPal
Shops.

PayPal shopping invitations

As a PayPal shop owner, you have an additional benefit. When a customer sends you payment from an area other than your Web site (hmm, sound like your sales on eBay?), PayPal displays an invitation to shop at your store! A sample invitation is shown in Figure 3-3.

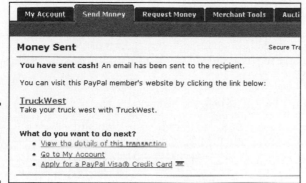

Figure 3-3: An invitation from PayPal Shops.

That's a cool deal, don't you think? Who would have figured you'd get help for your outside Web site from an eBay company? But, as with any cool deal, you must meet a few requirements before you can set up your shop at PayPal:

✦ **Verified premier or business account:** You must maintain one of the higher-level PayPal accounts.

✦ **Registered credit card:** You must maintain a current credit card registered to your PayPal account.

✦ **Confirmed checking account:** You must have at least one confirmed checking account tied into your PayPal account.

✦ **Money market fund:** You are required to sign up for the PayPal money market fund. This means you must supply PayPal with your Social Security number or the Federal ID number for your business.

PayPal does not send out Federal 1099 forms on your PayPal sales. That income is coming from your buyers, and because you're not paid by PayPal, they won't issue a 1099 for your PayPal sales.

PayPal offers you FDIC pass-through insurance. PayPal deposits your money as part of pooled accounts in several banks: Wells Fargo Bank, N.A., Comerica Bank — California, USA, and Bank of America, N.A. In the very unlikely event that any of these major banks should fail, your money would be covered under the FDIC pass-through deposit insurance, along with any other deposits you have at that bank, up to $100,000. FDIC pass-through deposit insurance protects you only against the failure of the bank in which PayPal places your funds; it does *not* protect you against PayPal's (very unlikely) insolvency.

After you're committed to the idea that you'd like a PayPal shop (and assuming that you're qualified), the application process is easy. Just follow these steps:

1. **Give your PayPal shop a name.**

   The name doesn't have to match your Web site. Give your shop a smart marketing name, something that will catch a person's eye while browsing the stores.

2. **Give PayPal the URL that you want to link your PayPal shop to.**

   This can be your eBay store or your own e-commerce, PayPal-enabled Web site.

3. **Type a short description of your Web site.**

   Be as descriptive as possible and make it interesting!

4. **Select the two categories from the PayPal Shops category list that best describe your store.**

5. **List up to ten keywords to describe your store to search engines.**

   Be smart! Find out which are your best keywords with the Google keyword tool at

   ```
   https://adwords.google.com/select/
       main?cmd=KeywordSandbox
   ```

Featured Shop consideration

After you set up your PayPal shop, you can apply to be selected as a featured shop — with your logo — on the PayPal logout page (the page that appears when you sign off from PayPal).

To apply, you must include another brief Web-site description, along with all the reasons you'd make a great selection as the featured shop.

PayPal then selects their shops from the applications, basing their choice on the quality of the site and how well and prominently PayPal is integrated into it. Not a bad deal!

Just think: If only a few of the 150 million PayPal members click through to your Web site when they're exiting their transactions, you *could* be rolling in orders!

Site statistics

Every month, PayPal sends statistics on hits to PayPal shopkeepers. Don't worry; these statistics aren't a bunch of useless information — they're all about your Web-site hits! Take a look at a sample in Figure 3-4. Remember that this report only counts hits as placed through links from the PayPal Shops area, not any independent hits you get from the Internet.

Figure 3-4:
Monthly
PayPal hit
statistics.

```
Sent: Tuesday, February 24, 2004 5:51 PM
Subject: Your PayPal Shops Weekly Traffic Report

Dear Pretty Girlie Things TM,
Here are the current PayPal Shops traffic statistics for your website:

This week's visitors to your site:  1649
Total visitors to your site, ever:  3534
Total websites in PayPal Shops:  46664
```

Cashing In on the PayPal Merchant Referral Program

And you thought the days of getting money for referring people to PayPal were over? Hah! PayPal has set its sights a little higher. Now they want business-account referrals rather than personal users.

You can send invitations to use PayPal in your e-mails using a custom link, or you can place a banner on your Web site. You receive $10 if a merchant you refer uses any of PayPal's Web-site tools. You can earn more after your referral sells $1000 worth of products or services.

It's kind of like multilevel marketing. After the referral posts the initial $200 in sales, you receive a percentage of your referral's revenue, up to a maximum of $1000, for the first twelve months of the referral's PayPal account. The residual payout equals .5% of the merchant's net (non-eBay) sales.

No spamming!!!

To get in on this good deal, go to the little navigation bar at the bottom of the page and click Referrals. After you arrive at the target page, you're presented with two links, as shown in Figure 3-5. One is a referral link for e-mail, and the other is a big honking PayPal banner that you can put on your Web site. (HTML custom coding is generated for you — just copy and paste it into your Web page.)

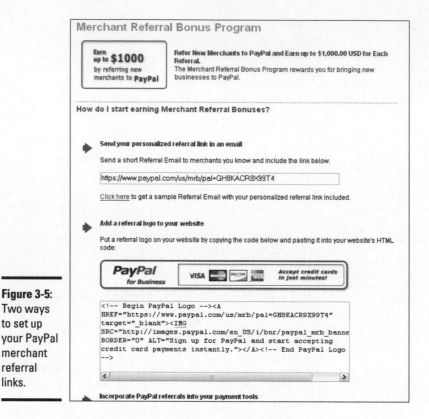

Figure 3-5:
Two ways
to set up
your PayPal
merchant
referral
links.

Generating Sales Using PayPal

If you think that PayPal is only for your eBay business, think again! Before eBay purchased PayPal, approximately 15 percent of PayPal's revenues came from online gaming. When eBay took over in late 2002, PayPal no longer received revenue from this arena. And there's good news for us: Today they offer the same tools to process PayPal payments on your own personal or business Web sites.

Aside from your eBay Store, you can sell directly from your Web site or your AOL HomeTown page. In time, as your eBay business grows into your own Web site, you'll find that using PayPal as your payment provider is a great deal. You pay the same transaction fees — to PayPal only — for processing your credit-card sales.

Build business by including your Web site URL in your e-mail signature, letting the world know you're open for business 24/7. Your About Me page can also include links to your e-commerce-enabled Web site — it's fully in line with the eBay rules!

In this section, you discover how to make your own Web site an extra revenue builder. I'm going to use my Web site as the example. It's a basic Web site, but people can (and do) shop there from time to time. Remember: Any sale you make from your own Web site involves no eBay fees and means extra income for you.

Making the PayPal payment option available on your site

After you get a few items in your garage or business location that you stock in quantity, you've got the makings of your own Web store. Don't let the thought of this spook you. You *can* do this!

The first step is to create a Web site. When you have the site up and running, Buy Now buttons are the most basic way to enable sales through PayPal from your site. These buttons are easy to insert — you don't have to be a computer whiz to create the links because PayPal makes this almost automatic.

There's no fee to use this service (other than the processing fee when someone buys an item). All you need is a verified PayPal Premier or Business account.

When someone buys something from your Web site, the procedure is the same as when someone pays for an eBay item. You receive an e-mail from PayPal telling you that a Web payment (versus an eBay payment) has been received. The e-mail subject includes the item number you've assigned in your code (it can also be an item name, as shown in Figure 3-6).

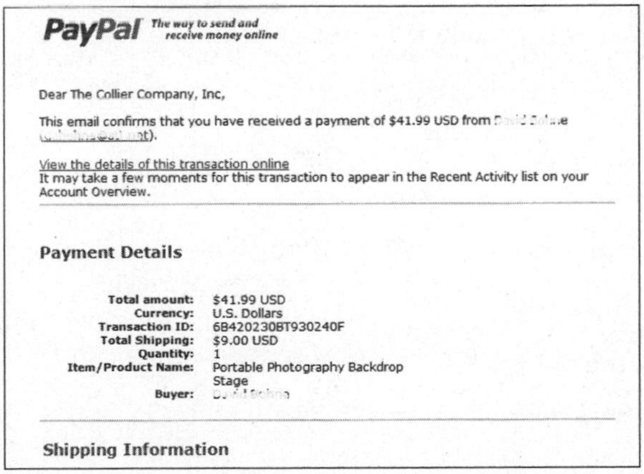

Figure 3-6: The PayPal e-mail when someone makes a purchase.

Creating a button on the PayPal Web site

TIP

If you want to save a bunch of time, try to use the sample coding in the "Coding for do-it-yourselfers" section. Just customize the HTML coding (with your Web site details) and put it into your Web page. If it doesn't work (or you're too nervous to do real coding), follow the next set of instructions for placing the PayPal button on your site.

To create a payment button on your Web site, first log on to the PayPal Web site. From there, follow these steps:

1. **Click the Merchant Services tab, at the top of the page, as shown in Figure 3-7.**

Figure 3-7:
The first step in creating a button.

2. **Click the Buy Now Button link.**

   The Buy Now Buttons page for selling items on your site, as shown in Figure 3-8, appears.

3. **Indicate the type of item you want to Accept payments for. Your choices are**

   • **Products:** If you're selling physical merchandise.

   • **Services:** If your customer is buying a psychic reading, bookkeeping, or some other service from you.

   • **Subscription and recurring billing:** If you're selling subscriptions to a newsletter or collecting dues for a membership.

   • **Donations:** If you have a Web site and you'd like to get donations — here's the right button. (Asking ain't getting.)

   • **Gift Certificates:** If you're selling gift certificates to your store.

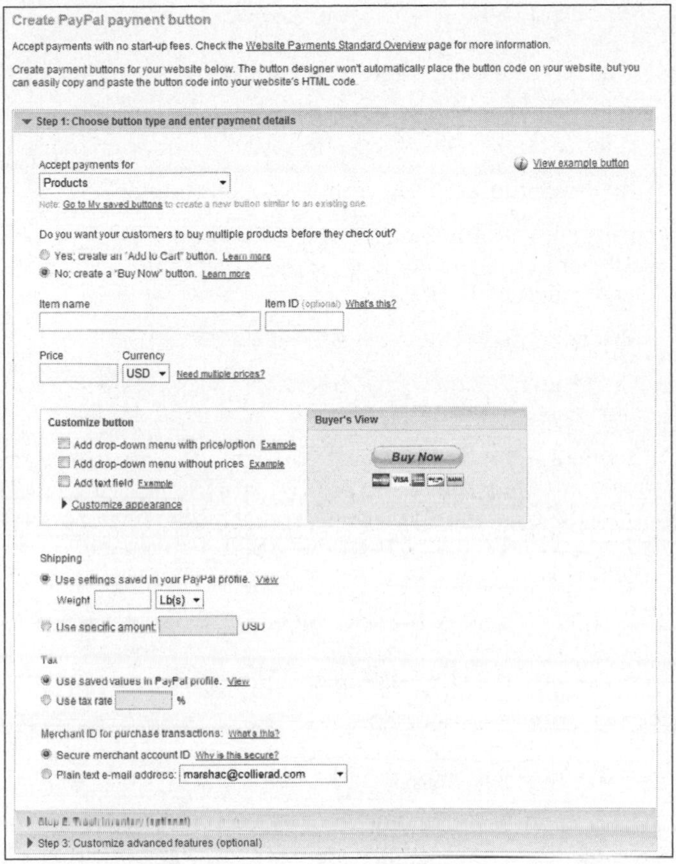

**Book VI
Chapter 3**

**Using PayPal to
Increase Your Sales**

Figure 3-8:
Creating a
Buy Now
button.

4. **Decide what kind of button you want. For this, you have two choices**

    • **Add to Cart:** If you're selling lots of item and you'd like to encourage your buyers to make multiple purchases.

    • **Buy Now:** When your customers will pick only one item from a number of choices.

    In this example, I choose the Buy Now button.

5. **Enter your item information, including the item name, ID, price, currency, default buyer's country, and weight.**

Here's a list of all the items you're asked to enter in the Create Buy Now Button section. Refer to this list when you examine the full sample code shown later in this chapter. It will help explain what goes into each `input type` field. Some of this information is optional:

- **Item name/service:** Input your item (or service) name.
- **Item ID/number:** Give your item an ID number or name.

I recommend that you use a number and abbreviated name, which appear in the subject line of the e-mail that PayPal sends when someone makes a purchase.

- **Price:** Enter the item price here.
- **Currency:** Decide what currency you're willing to accept for your purchases. (If you're in the U.S., go for the dollars.)
- **Buyer's Default Country:** If you accept international orders, specify here whether you want your buyer's payment page to default to a specific country. If you don't specify, buyers can choose for themselves. But I selected the United States to make it faster for most purchasers.
- **Weight:** Weight of the packaged item when it's ready to mail.

6. **Select a button in the Customize Button section.**

Choose a Buy Now button to insert on your page. If you don't like the ones pictured, click the *Customize Appearance* link to see more options, as shown in Figure 3-9.

I like using the buttons that include the different credit card icons so that folks who aren't familiar with PayPal will know that they can use any credit card. You also have the opportunity to design your own button, but hey, why make extra work for yourself right now? Just set up a standard button and get fancy later.

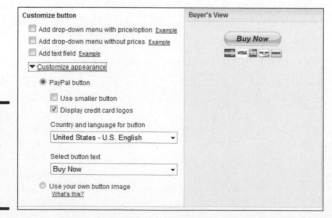

Figure 3-9: Your options for additional button choices.

7. Continue to scroll down the page and make choices or fill in information as prompted.

You see the following prompts and options:

- **Button Encryption:** Decide whether you want your button to be encrypted (increasing security by ensuring that the item's details cannot be changed by a third party).

Encrypting your button may seem like a simple "yes" answer, but keep this in mind: If you want to be able to customize your button (adding more options) by changing the HTML code, you won't be able to do that if you encrypt. I don't encrypt my buttons. If someone sends the incorrect amount for an item — by some nefarious behavior — I can just send it right back to them through PayPal.

In the future, PayPal plans to allow users to encrypt buttons *and* add dynamic options. Watch for that!

- **Shipping Method Option:** From this area, select a flat shipping and handling charge or one based on a percentage of the item's price.

Unfortunately, PayPal doesn't supply a cool shipping calculator. You can put a postal shipping chart on your item page and let your buyers insert the proper shipping amount, or you can enter a shipping amount on this page that lands somewhere in the middle of the highest (farthest away) and lowest (closest) zone to your shipping location. You'll lose a little on some but make it up on others.

- **Sales Tax Options:** Select your state and enter the appropriate sales tax to be applied to your in-state purchases. If you already have a sales-tax provision in your PayPal profile, it will be listed here automatically. PayPal will apply the sales tax for sales shipped within your state.

8. After you make your selections and choose a button to insert, click Create Button Now.

9. If you want to add options, click Add More Options.

On the next page, you can add extended options for your button. Included (definitely use these!) are the following:

- **Item options:** If your item has options (if, for example, it comes in different sizes or colors), you can create a custom drop-down list for your payment page so the customer can choose; just type the offered options in this box.

- **Insert your logo:** To add a logo to your payment page, type the URL where the file is stored. PayPal will place the logo on your payment page.

The logo you use must be sized at 150 x 50 pixels or PayPal won't accept it.

- **Payment landing page:** If you want your customers to land on a specific page after they've made a payment — setting up a thank-you page on your Web site is a nice idea, for example — enter that URL here. Figure 3-10 shows a portion of my Web site's basic thank-you page. The page also has links to take the buyer back to my Web site.

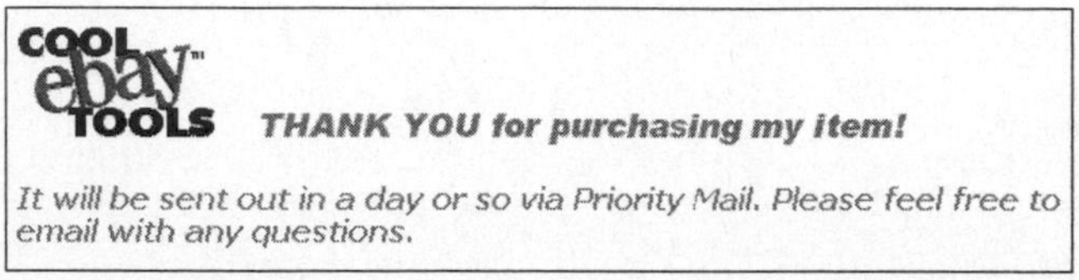

Figure 3-10:
Thanks for
buying my
item!

THANK YOU *for purchasing my item!*

It will be sent out in a day or so via Priority Mail. Please feel free to email with any questions.

- **Cancel Transaction page:** If you want to include a page where people are taken if they cancel the transaction before completing it, you can insert that address here. If you don't specify a page, they will land at a PayPal Web page that allows cancellation of the transaction.

- **Quantity:** If you'd like your customers to be able to purchase more than one of your item at a time, you may indicate that here. The buyers will then be able to fill in a number in a quantity field.

- **Shipping address:** Click Yes if you'd like the customer's shipping address. I guess it would be kind of useless not to ask for a shipping address when you're expected to ship the item somewhere, huh? It *does* kind of take the guesswork out of things to include this field!

- **Optional instructions:** If you'd like your buyers to be able to write you a note, click Yes in this field.

10. **Click Preview.**

   You see a sample of the page your customer will see after making a Web payment to you.

11. **If the page is okay, click the Create Button Now button.**

12. **If you want to go back and edit, click the Edit button.**

That's all there is to creating your first Buy Now button and the payment page that appears when it's clicked. When you get the hang of it, I'm sure you'd rather code your own. It's really easy (even I can do it) and considerably faster. Read on.

Coding for do-it-yourselfers

Yes, there's an easy way *and* a formal way to do everything. Because I am unreasonably busy, I did my Web site PayPal buttons the easy way — without a bunch of options.

The items I sell on my Web site can't be combined in one box. Each has to be shipped in an individual box, and postage must be charged for each item. I therefore don't use the shopping cart method.

Figure 3-11 shows a payment button on one of the pages on my site. When the mouse "rolls over" the payment button, a PayPal message appears.

Figure 3-11: My PayPal payment button.

When you click the payment button, you land on my Cool eBay Tools PayPal payment page (shown in Figure 3-12, complete with custom logo). The PayPal payment page is a secure page (as indicated by the lock icon) directly from PayPal. The URL for the page begins with `https`; the s at the end indicates that the site is secure.

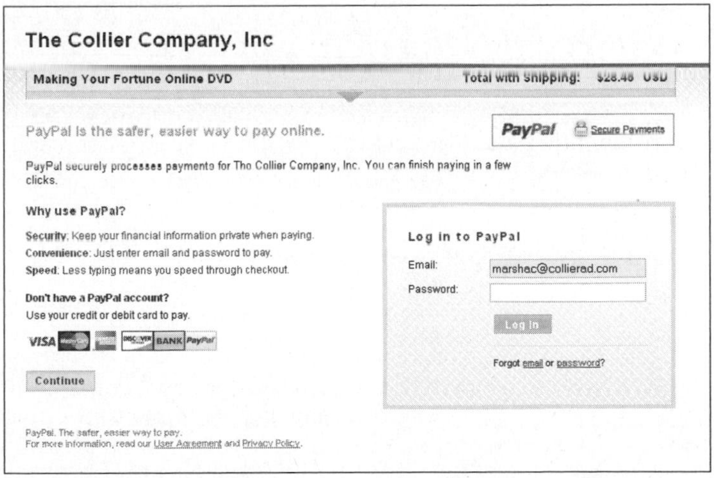

Figure 3-12: The resulting PayPal payment page.

Here's the code I used to create that payment button and link to the resulting page:

```
<form action="https://www.paypal.com/cgi-bin/webscr"
    method="post">
<input type="hidden" name="cmd" value="_xclick">
<input type="hidden" name="business" value="marshac@
    collierad.com">
<input type="hidden" name="undefined_quantity" value="1">
<input type="hidden" name="item_name" value="INFINITI Board">
<input type="hidden" name="item_number" value="INFINITI
    Board">
<input type="hidden" name="amount" value="38.50">
<input type="hidden" name="shipping" value="8.00">
<input type="hidden" name="image_url" value="http://
    coolebaytools/images/coolT.gif">
<input type="hidden" name="return" value="http://
    coolebaytools/thankyou.htm">
<input type="hidden" name="cancel_return" value="http://
    coolebaytools">
<input type="hidden" name="no_note" value="1">
<input type="hidden" name="currency_code" value="USD">
<input type="image" src="https://www.paypal.com/en_US/i/btn/
    btn_buynowCC_LG.gif" border="0" name="submit" alt="PayPal
    - The safer, easier way to pay online!">
<img alt="" border="0" src="https://www.paypal.com/en_US/i/
    scr/pixel.gif" width="1" height="1"> </form>
```

My coding doesn't contain all the possible options that PayPal offers, but it does get the job done.

PayPal coding with all the bells and whistles

Listed next is the full-octane version of the code for a PayPal button, with sample values filled in. All you have to do is fill in your own values (see Step 4 in the "Creating a button on the PayPal Web site" for the definitions of corresponding items on the Selling Single Items page), and then copy and paste the code into your own Web page:

```
<form action="https://www.paypal.com/cgi-bin/webscr"
    method="post">
<input type="hidden" name="cmd" value="_xclick">
<input type="hidden" name="business" value="me@
    myemailaddress.com">
<input type="hidden" name="return"
value="http://www.mysite.com/thankyou.htm">
<input type="hidden" name="undefined_quantity" value="1">
<input type="hidden" name="item_name" value="TShirt">
<input type="hidden" name="item_number" value="Tshirt01">
<input type="hidden" name="amount" value="9.95">
<input type="hidden" name="shipping" value="3.00">
<input type="hidden" name="image_url"
value="https://www.yoursite.com/logo.gif">
<input type="hidden" name="cancel_return"
```

```
value="http://www.mysite.com/cancel.htm">
<input type="hidden" name=" no_note" value="0">
<table><tr><td><input type="hidden" name="on0"
    value="Color?">Color?
<select name="os0">
<option value="Blue">Blue
<option value="Green">Green
<option value="Red">Red</select></td></tr></table>
<input type="hidden" name="cn" value="How Did You Hear About
    Us?">
<input type="image" src="http://images.paypal.com/images/x-
    clickbut01.
gif" name="submit" alt="Make payments with PayPal - it's
    fast,
free and secure!">
</form>
```

Adding a PayPal Buy Now button to your AOL HomeTown page

The procedure for adding a payment button for AOL users is easy. And what's better than making money from your own free Web page!

Here's how to insert your button:

1. **Sign in to your AOL Hometown account.**

2. **Click the Edit My Pages link.**

3. **Select the page to which you want to add the PayPal Buy Now button.**

4. **Click the Insert button on the toolbar.**

5. **Select Advanced HTML.**

   A dialog box where you type your HTML appears.

6. **Copy the HTML code generated by the Button Factory (or your own homemade coding, as shown in the preceding section), and paste it in the text box.**

7. **Click Save.**

You can type the resulting URL in the browser to test your page.

Book VII
Storing and Shipping

The 5th Wave   By Rich Tennant

Serch Injin
Optamazashun
Kee Werd
Stratageez
1. Top

"How long has he been writing the item titles for your eBay listings?"

Contents at a Glance

Chapter 1: Organizing Your Merchandise and Shipping Department

In This Chapter

✔ **Organizing your stock**

✔ **Keeping inventory**

✔ **Packing up**

✔ **Buying stamps without a trip to the post office**

The more items you sell, the more confusing things can get. As you build your eBay business, the little side table you use for storing eBay merchandise isn't going to work anymore. You must think industrial. Even part-time sellers can benefit by adding a few professional touches to their business areas.

In this chapter, I emphasize the importance of setting up and organizing your back office. I cover everything from stacking your stock to keeping inventory to getting those indispensable packing materials and saving time by buying postage online. Organization will be your byword. Dive right in. The sooner you read this chapter, the sooner you can build your eBay back office and get down to business.

The Warehouse: Organizing Your Space

Whether you plan to sell large items or small items, you need space for storing them. As you make savvy purchases, maintaining an item's mint condition will be one of your greatest challenges. In this section, I cover the details of what you'll need to safeguard your precious stock.

Shelving your profits

Before you stock the shelves, it helps to have some! You also need a place to put the shelves: your garage, a spare room, or somewhere else. For the home-based business, you have a choice between two basic kinds of shelves:

✦ **Plastic:** If you're just starting out, you can always go to the local closet-and-linen-supply store to buy inexpensive plastic shelves. They're light and cheap but they'll buckle in time.

✦ **Steel:** If you want to do it right the first time, buy steel shelving. The most versatile steel shelving is the wire kind (versus solid steel shelves), which is light and allows air to circulate around your items. Steel wire shelving assembles easily; I put mine together without help. You can combine steel-wire shelving units to create a full wall of shelves. Each shelf safely holds as much as 600 pounds of merchandise.

To save you time, dear reader, I researched the subject and found some readily available, reasonably priced shelves. Just go to Target or Costco and look for Seville Classics four-shelf commercial shelving, sold in 36- and 48-inch-wide units. Believe it or not, Seville Classics also has an eBay store (but you have to pay for shipping). Look for them at

```
stores.ebay.com/Seville-Classics
```

You can easily convert a garage or a spare room to a professional and functional stock room. Figure 1-1 shows a portion of my stock area.

Figure 1-1:
A portion of my merchandise storage area.

Box 'em or bag 'em?

Packing your items for storage can be a challenge. For smaller items, pick up some plastic bags in sandwich, quart, and gallon sizes. When items are stored in plastic, they can't pick up any smells or become musty before you sell them. The plastic also protects the items from rubbing against each other and causing possible damage. If you package them one item to a bag, you can then just lift one off the shelf and put it directly into a shipping box when the listing is over.

Your bags of items will have to go into boxes for storage on the shelves. Clear plastic storage boxes, the kind you often find at superstores, are great for bulky items. They're usually 26 inches long, so before you buy these big plastic containers, make sure that they'll fit on your shelving comfortably and that you'll have easy access to your items. Using cardboard office-type file storage boxes from an office supply store is another option. These cardboard boxes are 10 x 12 x 16 inches, which is a nice size for storing medium-size products. At around $1 each, they're the most economical choice. The downside is that you can't see through cardboard boxes, so if your label falls off, you have to take the box off the shelf and open it to check its contents. Smaller see-through plastic boxes with various compartments (such as the type home-improvement stores carry for storing tools) work great for storing very small items.

When using these large plastic bins, it's always a good idea to tape a pad of Post-it notes on the end of the box so you can quickly identify the contents. You *can* use regular sticky labels, but changing them will leave large amounts of paper residue over time, and that makes your storage look sloppy and icky.

Speaking of bins, Figure 1-2 shows you the bins in the small parts area of the warehouse of eBay seller banderson-at-fuse. His setup isn't exactly what the home seller will need, but it sometimes helps to see how the big guys do it.

Figure 1-2:
Nice,
organized
little bins
of products
at Barry
Anderson's
eBay
business.

Keeping Track of What You Have

Savvy eBay sellers have different methods of handling inventory. They use everything from spiral-bound notebooks to sophisticated software programs. Although computerized inventory tracking can simplify this task, starting with a plain ol' handwritten ledger is fine, too. Choose whichever works best for you, but keep in mind that as your eBay business grows, a software program that tracks inventory for you may become necessary.

Most of these systems wouldn't work for a company with a warehouse full of stock — but will work nicely in an eBay sales environment. Many sellers tape sheets of paper to their boxes to identify them by number, and use that as a reference to a simple Excel spreadsheet for selling purposes. Excel spreadsheets are perfect for keeping track of your auctions as well, but if you're using a management service or software, you don't need both for physical inventory.

When you're running a full-time business, however, you have to keep Uncle Sam happy with a dollars and cents accounting of your inventory, so keep your inventory records in a standardized program such as QuickBooks (discussed in Book IX). I describe a variety of auction management software and Web sites, many of which include physical inventory tracking features.

TIP

Planning: The key to good organization

When I had to put my eBay merchandise in order, I was busy with my regular business, so I hired a friend to organize my eBay area. This decision turned out to be one massive mistake. My friend organized everything and put all my items in boxes — but didn't label the boxes to indicate what was stored in each. To this day I still haven't recovered and don't know where a bunch of my stuff is!

A bit of advice: Think things out and plan where you'll put everything. Organize your items by theme, type, or size. If you organize before planning, you might end up with organized disorganization.

Figure 1-3 shows some of the merchandise stocked at an eBay seller's warehouse.

You may also want to use Excel spreadsheets for your downloaded PayPal statements, to hold information waiting to transfer to your bookkeeping program. I post my sales each time I make a PayPal withdrawal (a couple of times a week). I keep the PayPal downloads only for archival purposes.

Book VII
Chapter 1

Organizing Your Merchandise and Shipping Department

Figure 1-3: Part of the many aisles of eBay items ready to be sold.

In my eBay business, I keep my inventory record in QuickBooks. Each time I purchase merchandise for my business, I post it in the program. When I post my sales each week, QuickBooks automatically deducts the sold items from my inventory. I then do a physical inventory as product stock runs low.

The Shipping Department: Packin' It Up

In this section, I review some of the things you must have for a complete, smooth-running shipping department, such as cleaning supplies and packing materials. The *handling fee* portion of your shipping charges pays for these kinds of items. Don't run low on them — and pay attention to how you store them. They must be kept in a clean environment.

Pre-packaging clean up

Be sure the items you send out are in tip-top shape. Here are a few everyday chemicals that can gild the lily:

✦ **WD-40:** This decades-old lubricant works very well at getting price stickers off plastic and glass without damaging the product. And if the plastic on a toy box begins to look nasty — even when stored in a clean environment — a quick wipe with a paper towel and a dash of WD-40 will make it shine like new. It also works well for untangling jewelry chains and shining up metallic objects.

✦ **Goo Gone:** Goo Gone works miracles in cleaning up gooey sticker residue from nonporous items.

✦ **Vamoose.** Is there a smoker in your house? Cigar or cigarette smoke can permeate most items. Even if you're an occasional smoker, this product is worth its weight in gold. It's a chemical miracle that totally removes these stale, smoky smells. Read up about it on the Web at www.vamooseproducts.com.

✦ **un-du:** This amazing liquid easily removes stickers off cardboard, plastic, fabrics, and more without causing damage. It comes packaged with a patented miniscraper top that you can use in any of your sticker-cleaning projects.

Packing materials

The most important area where sellers drop the time-and-money ball is in shipping. I buy hundreds of items from eBay and have seen it all when it comes to packing, padding, and shipping. I've seen money thrown out the window by e-tailers that have used incorrect packing materials, which are expensive for the seller and often increase the shipping cost of the package for the buyer due to the final weight.

Removing musty smell from apparel items

Clothing can often pick up odors that you just don't notice. I recently bought a designer dress on eBay from a seller who had the typical disclaimer in her description: "No stains, holes, repairs, or odors. Comes from a smoke-free, pet-free home."

Unfortunately, the minute I opened the box I could smell the musty odor of an item that had been stored for a long time.

To prevent that stale storage odor, keep a package of Dryel Fabric Care System around. This is a safe, do-it-yourself dry cleaning product. Just toss your better eBay clothing items in the patented Dryel bag with the special sheet and toss it in the dryer as per the instructions on the box. Your garment will come out smelling clean — and wrinkle free. For more information, visit their Web site at www.Dryel.com.

The packing materials that you use for your shipments can either make or break your bottom line in the shipping income/expense column of your business reports.

Many sellers remark, "The buyer pays shipping, so what do I care what it costs? I pass on all those expenses to my buyers." Well, yes and no. Prudent packing can be a boon to your business because having lower shipping costs can often make the difference between a sale and no sale (and your shipping charges affect your position in eBay's search). This is especially true when several people have the same item up for sale, with a minuscule difference in the item's selling price. Reasonable shipping charges can make the difference.

Pay attention to packing. It's only expensive if you don't know what you're doing. You can ship your items in quality packing, keep buyers happy, and still make a dollar or so on each item for your handling fees.

Buying your shipping materials online is *très* economical. eBay shipping supply e-tailers make their living selling online. Their overhead is much lower than any retail outlet. Even after paying shipping to get the bubble wrap to your door, you save money and time. Most of these sellers ship the same day they get your order.

Only use as much packing material as necessary to get the item where it's going intact. This saves time, money, and space.

Using void fill

Nope! Void fill is not a new drug to prevent hunger pangs when dieting. Void fill is the industry term for the stuff you use to fill up space in shipping boxes to keep items from rolling in transit. (It's really the modern term for the old-fashioned word *dunnage*.)

There are many forms of void fill, and the best kind depends on the item you're shipping. Here are the most popular types, and a description of their plusses and minuses.

So that you can always be sure that your items will arrive at their destinations in one piece, you'll want to keep the following on hand at all times:

✦ **Air packing pillows**: I found out about these nifty little pillows when I received books from a major online bookseller. Buying air packing pillows from sellers on eBay is economical, mainly because the manufacturing and shipping costs are low. What these folks are essentially shipping you is 99 percent air (something the post office hasn't yet figured out how to charge for). You can find *air pillows* in the Business and Industrial category.

   Air packing pillows are perfect for filling in the area around smaller boxed items that you want to double box. They are also handy if you have breakables that you've prewrapped in bubble wrap; just use the pillows to fill out the box. They're crushproof and can support plus or minus 150 pounds without a blowout.

✦ **Bubble wrap:** Made up of air-filled cushions of polyethylene, bubble wrap is supplied in rolls of different widths and lengths (see Figure 1-4). It shines for those who wrap delicate, breakable items. When wrapping an item with bubble wrap, wrap it one way and then the other, and then affix some packing tape to make your item an impenetrable ball. Depending on your product, you may have to carry two sizes of bubble wrap to properly protect the goods. Bubble wrap is reasonably priced (check out the many vendors on eBay) and adds next to no weight to your packages.

Figure 1-4: Different sizes of bubble wrap.

When you purchase bubble wrap, be sure you buy the perforated, or tear-off, kind. Cutting a giant roll of bubble wrap with a box cutter can be a dangerous proposition.

✦ **Plain old white newsprint:** In the right shipping situation, plain white newsprint is fantastic. eBay sellers dealing in glass, china, and breakable knick-knacks often use white newsprint to wrap each piece before placing it in a box full of packing peanuts.

White newsprint is cheap and easy to store. The bad news? It's heavy and sellers often use too many sheets to wrap the items they pack. If you feel you must use newsprint, I suggest you buy it by the roll and use a table-mounted roll cutter to cut the exact size you need. (This is the kind of thing you may have seen in old-style butcher shops and delis.) This setup helps you to avoid using too much paper.

✦ **Styrofoam packing peanuts:** Every serious eBay seller has to have a stock of packing peanuts. When properly placed in a box, peanuts fill every nook and cranny and cushion your shipment to make it virtually indestructible. They're handy for padding Tyvek envelopes and filling boxes so that items don't shift around. A bonus: They're cheap and if you recycle them, they don't hurt the environment.

When packing with peanuts, the key is to not go short in the land of plenty. Use enough peanuts to fill the box completely; leaving any airspace defeats the point of using the peanuts in the first place.

More packing supplies

Your shipping department needs just a few more items. Don't forget to include the following at the outset of your packing career:

✦ **Plastic bags:** Buy plastic bags in bulk to save money. Make sure you buy various sizes and use them for both shipping and storing. Even large kitchen or trash bags are good for wrapping up posters and large items; the plastic protects the item from inclement weather by waterproofing the item.

✦ **Two- or three-inch-wide shipping tape:** You'll need clear tape for securing packages and to place over address labels to protect them from scrapes and rain. I once received a package with an address label soaked with rain and barely legible. Don't risk a lost package for want of a few inches of tape.

✦ **Hand-held tape dispenser:** You need a way to get the tape off the roll and onto the box. Using a tape dispenser can be a bit tricky to the uninitiated, but once you get than hang of it, you'll be sealing up boxes in no time flat!

Storing pesky packing products

Storing shipping supplies is the tricky part. I store peanuts in the bags they were shipped in (note the ones in the figure) or in 33-gallon plastic trash bags, and then hang the bags on cup hooks around the garage ceiling. (By the way, bags of peanuts make great bumpers in the garage.) To store my bubble wrap from Bubblefast, I hung a broomstick with wire from the rafters. I made the broomstick into a dispenser (of sorts).

Shipping in mailing envelopes

You'll be shipping your stuff in an envelope or a box. Don't be quick to discount shipping in envelopes. Any item under 13 ounces can be shipped via First Class mail — and that can represent quite a savings.

Mailing envelopes come in many types of materials. Some are sturdier than others. Here's what many eBay sellers use:

✦ **Polyvinyl envelopes:** If you've ever ordered clothing or bedding from any of the television-shopping clubs, this is what they came in. Polyvinyl envelopes are lightweight and puncture- and tear-resistant. They are the most durable envelopes available. Who says you *have* to ship in boxes?

✦ **Tyvek envelopes:** You know those really cool, indestructible white envelopes you get from the post office or FedEx? They're made of DuPont Tyvek, a spun-bonded olefin fiber. Tyvek has all the benefits of vinyl envelopes, plus it breathes (allows air to reach your product) and has a higher strength-to-weight ratio than other envelope materials. (That "ratio" business means it's very strong, yet feather-light.)

✦ **Bubble-padded mailers:** These envelopes are lined with small bubbles, similar to bubble wrap. They're great for shipping a variety of items and are the most popular with eBay sellers (see Figure 1-5).

Mechanizing your labeling

Printing labels on your printer is convenient until you start sending out a dozen packages at a time — then cutting the paper and taping the label gets too time-consuming. Plus, those cut-out labels are not professional. I highly recommend you do yourself a favor and get a label printer. Yes, they can be expensive, but you can find some great deals on eBay. I bought my heavy-duty, professional Eltron Zebra 2844 thermal label printer on eBay for one-fourth the retail price. (Search eBay for *zebra 2844*.) It's saved me countless hours. Another good label printer for beginners is the Dymo LabelWriter.

**Book VII
Chapter 1**

Organizing Your Merchandise and Shipping Department

Figure 1-5:
Bubble-wrap-lined envelopes for sale from eBay PowerSeller Bubblefast.

Box of 25 10-1/2" x 16"
(Industry Size #5)
SELF SEALING BUBBLE MAILERS(Internal Dimensions 9-1/2" x 14-1/2")

bubble*FAST!'s* Bubble Lined mailers are lightweight, yet hold up under the toughest mailing conditions. Air cushioning offers maximum protection. These Mailers are Self-Seal with a 1" Peel and Seal Strip.

And by the way, did you see the price from that national **Office** store? It sure is **MAX!**

Bubble-lined mailers come in different materials:

- Plain-paper bubble mailers are the cheapest way to go, but they can be damaged in the mail if you use them to ship heavy items. The way around that problem is to wrap cheap, clear packing tape once around the envelope in each direction.

- Vinyl bubble mailers aren't expensive and are a super protective way to ship. They're 15 percent lighter than paper bubble mailers and are water-resistant.

If you send items that can fit nicely into bubble-padded envelopes, use them. This type of envelope is perfect for mailing small items or clothing using First Class mail. The envelopes are available in quantity (an economical choice) and don't take up much storage space. Table 1-1 shows you the industry-standard sizes of bubble envelopes and their suggested use.

Table 1-1	Standard Bubble-Padded Mailer Sizes	
Size	*Measurements (in Inches)*	*Suggested Items*
#000	4 x 8	Collector trading cards, jewelry, coins
#00	5 x 10	Postcards, paper ephemera
#0	6 x 10	Doll clothes, CDs, DVDs, Xbox or PS2 games
#1	7¼ x 12	Cardboard-sleeve VHS tapes, jewel-cased CDs and DVDs
#2	8½ x 12	Clamshell VHS tapes, books
#3	8½ x 14	Toys, clothing, stuffed animals
#4	9½ x 14	Small books, trade paperbacks
#5	10½ x 16	Hardcover books, dolls
#6	12½ x 19	Clothing, soft boxed items
#7	14½ x 20	Much larger packaged items, framed items, plaques

Another of my favorite sources (with reasonable prices and free shipping) is RoyalMailers.com. They carry every size imaginable, and if you use my Web site's name as your discount code, you *get an additional 10 percent off your order*. Just go to

www.royalmailers.com/coolebaytools

Boxing your items

Depending on the size of the items you sell, you can purchase boxes in bulk at reliable sources. Because you have a resale number, look in your local yellow pages for wholesale boxes (you still have to pay tax, but the resale number identifies you as a business and often can result in lower prices). Try to purchase from a manufacturer that specializes in B2B (business-to-business) sales. Some box companies specialize in selling to the occasional box user.

You also need to know a little about what it takes to make a sturdy box. The *de facto* standard for quality in general-use shipping boxes is 200-pound double-wall corrugated.

You can save big money if your items fit into boxes that the post office supplies and you plan on using Priority Mail. The USPS will give you all the boxes and mailing envelopes you need free, and it offers plenty of sizes. See Table 1-2 for available sizes.

Table 1-2	Free Priority Mail Packaging
Size (in Inches)	*Description*
$8\frac{5}{8}$ x $53\frac{3}{8}$ x $1\frac{5}{8}$	Small video box (#1096S)
$9\frac{1}{4}$ x $6\frac{1}{4}$ x 2	Large video box (#1096L)
$7\frac{9}{16}$ x $5\frac{7}{16}$ x $1\frac{3}{8}$	Electronic Media Box
$11\frac{1}{2}$ x $13\frac{1}{8}$ x $2\frac{3}{8}$	Medium (#1097)
$11\frac{7}{8}$ x $3\frac{3}{8}$ x $13\frac{5}{8}$	Flat-rate Priority box (FBR2)
$12\frac{1}{2}$ x $15\frac{1}{2}$ x 3	Large (#1095)
12.125 x 13.375 x 2.75	Medium (#1092)
6 x 38	Large triangle tube
6 x 25	Small triangle tube
7 x 7 x 6	Small square (BOX4)
12 x 12 x 8	Medium square (BOX7)
11 x $8\frac{1}{2}$ x $5\frac{1}{2}$	Flat-rate Priority box (FBR1)
12 x 12x $5\frac{1}{2}$	Large Flat-rate Priority Mail Box
7.5 X 5.125 X 14.375	Priority Mail Shoe Box
11.625 X 15.125	Tyvek envelope
6 x 10	Cardboard envelope
$12\frac{1}{2}$ x $9\frac{1}{2}$	Flat-rate cardboard envelope
5 x 10	Cardboard window envelope

Book VII
Chapter 1

Organizing Your
Merchandise and
Shipping Department

You can get six sizes of Priority Mail boxes imprinted with the eBay logo from the United States Postal Service Zone on eBay at `ebaysupplies.usps.com`. However, think twice before you do this. What would look more inviting to a postal thief? A plain package? Or one that is clearly an eBay purchase? I polled some major PowerSellers on this subject and they recommend against using them.

To order your boxes, labels, forms, and just about anything else that you'll need to ship Priority Mail, go to the Postal Store (see Figure 1-6) at `http://shop.usps.com/`. Orders can take a month or so to arrive, so be sure to order early.

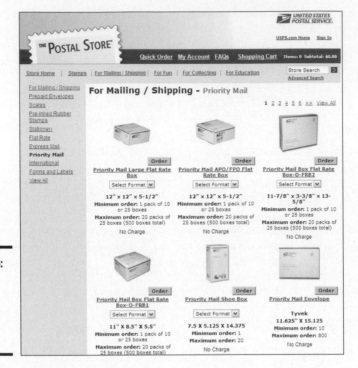

Figure 1-6:
Order shipping supplies from the USPS.

Buying Postage Online

In 1999, the United States Postal Service announced a new service: information-based indicia (IBI), postage that you can print on envelopes and labels right from your PC. In this section, I give you the lowdown on the main Internet postage vendors: Endicia.com, Stamps.com, and the post office's own Click-N-Ship.

I'm a savvy enough consumer and businesswoman that I don't believe in paying for extras — nor do I believe in being a victim of hidden charges. The online postage arena — while providing helpful tools that make running your eBay business easier — is fraught with bargains, deals, and introductory offers. I urge you to read these offers carefully so you know what you're getting yourself into: Evaluate how much it will cost you to start *and to maintain* an ongoing relationship with the company. Although you may initially get some free hardware and pay a low introductory rate, the fine print might tell you that you have agreed to pay unreasonably high monthly prices six months down the line. I always double-check pricing before getting into anything, and I urge you to do the same.

Free USPS package pick up

Yes! Some things *are* free! If you print electronic postage for just one Priority Mail or Express Mail package through one of the vendors mentioned in this section, you can request a free pickup for all your packages. Go the post office Web site at www.usps.com and type *carrier pickup* in the search box or go directly to http://carrierpickup.usps.com. You can request a next-day pickup as late as 2:00 a.m.

Click-N-Ship from the USPS

Your old pal the United States Postal Service has Web tools that enable you to print your postage and get Priority Mail delivery confirmation free of charge (that's right — no more $.65 each). You can't print postage for Media Mail, Parcel Post, or First Class mail through this service. One caveat: This is a no-frills online service, and you often get what you pay for. You have to download software to your computer to use this service, and you can't print the labels on a label printer. (You can print two or more labels on 8½ x 11 label sheets. You may also print on regular 8½ x 11 paper.)

Click-N-Ship has the following benefits:

✦ **Online address book:** The address book stores up to 1000 addresses.

✦ **E-mail ship notification:** You can send recipients an e-mail notifying them that a package is on its way.

✦ **Shipping cart:** You can print up to ten domestic labels with a single credit card transaction.

✦ **Shipping history section:** Your shipping history for the past six months is stored online for easy access.

For more details, go to

www.usps.com/clicknship

Endicia.com

At the beginning of PC graphics in the early '90s, I attended a cutting-edge industry trade show. I had a successful graphics-and-advertising business, so I was interested in the latest and greatest innovations to bring my business off the light table and onto my computer. In a smallish booth were a couple of guys peddling new software that enabled artists to design direct-mail pieces from the desktop. Wow! What an innovation! Their inexpensive software even let you produce your own bar-coding for the post office. I fell in love with that software and used it throughout my graphics career.

Getting the "commercial" discount

Printing your postage electronically (online) gives a new benefit; the new Commercial Base Price reduction, which is available for Priority Mail and Express Mail. For Priority Mail, commercial base prices are 1 to 11 percent lower than retail prices, and are based on zone and weight. For Express Mail, the commercial base prices are 3percent lower than the retail prices.

For international shipping, you'll get 5- and 8-percent discounts on Priority Mail International and Express Mail International.

That program, DAZzle, combined with their patented Dial-A-Zip became the basis for today's software (see Figure 1-7) that is distributed to all Endicia. com customers. There isn't a more robust mailing program on the market.

Figure 1-7: DAZzle, the label and design software that comes with Endicia. com.

Endicia.com has all the features of PayPal.com shipping and more:

✦ **Buy your postage online:** With a click of your mouse, you can purchase your postage instantly using your credit card or by direct debit from your checking account. You can register your preferences when you sign up with Endicia.com.

✦ **Print postage for all classes of mail, including international:** From Anniston, Alabama, to Bulawayo, Zimbabwe, the DAZzle software not only prints postage but also lists all your shipping options and applicable rates. For international mailing, it also advises you as to any prohibitions (for example, no prison-made goods can be mailed to Botswana), restrictions, necessary customs forms, and areas served within the country.

✦ **Print customs forms:** You no longer have to go to the post office with your international packages. Just print the customs form from the DAZzle software and give the package to your letter carrier.

✦ **Free delivery confirmations on Priority mail:** Delivery confirmations may be printed also for First Class, Parcel Post, and Media Mail for only $.16 each (a savings of $.57 from post-office retail purchases).

✦ **Mailpiece design:** Endicia Internet postage is based on DAZzle, an award-winning mailpiece design tool that lets you design envelopes, postcards, and labels with color graphics, logos, pictures, text messages, and rubber stamps. You can print your mailing label with postage and delivery confirmation on anything from plain paper (tape it on with clear tape) to fancy 4 x 6 labels in a label printer from their extensive list of label templates.

✦ **Integration with insurance:** If you've saving time and money using U-PIC (a private package insurer — see Chapter 3) or Endicia's own insurance, you can send your monthly insurance logs electronically at the end of the month — a service integrated into the DAZzle software. There's no need to print a hard copy and mail in this information.

✦ **No cut-and-paste necessary:** Endicia integrates with most common software programs. With their DAZzle software open on your computer, highlight the buyer's address from an e-mail or the PayPal site and press Ctrl+C. The address automatically appears in the DAZzle postage software. No pasting needed.

Endicia.com offers two levels of service. All the features just listed come with the standard plan. Their premium plan adds customizable e-mail, enhanced online transaction reports and statistics, business reply mail, return shipping labels (prepaid so your customer won't have to pay for the return), and stealth indicias.

The *stealth indicia* (also known as the *postage-paid indicia*) is an awesome tool for the eBay seller. By using this feature, your customer will not see the exact amount of postage you paid. This allows you to add reasonable shipping and handling costs and not inflame the buyer when they see the final label.

With all these features, you'd think that endicia's service would be expensive, but it's not. The standard plan is $9.95 a month, and the premium plan is $15.95 a month. For a free 60-day trial just for my readers, go to my "friends" page at endicia (as shown in Figure 1-8) at

www.endicia.com/coolebaytools

Figure 1-8: My friends get a 60-day free trial. Be my friend and save $20!

PayPal shipping services

PayPal continues to add great features for sellers. Now you cannot only buy postage and ship with UPS through PayPal but also print labels on your own printer. If you ship lots of items and use a different service for printing your postage, PayPal allows you to input the tracking information on the site. Just click the Details link for the transaction, and then click the Add button that appears, as shown in Figure 1-9. Input the USPS, UPS, or other shipping company's tracking or delivery-confirmation information, and PayPal sends an e-mail to your buyer with that information.

The information you added appears in both the record of your PayPal transaction and the buyer's record in their account, as shown in Figure 1-10. (You can check the information by clicking the Details link again.)

PayPal shipping services work great when you're just starting out in your eBay business — but after you get rolling, you need a mailing service that includes e-mail and recordkeeping, such as Endicia.com or Stamps.com. The issue connected with using PayPal for shipping is important: When you process your shipping (UPS or USPS) on PayPal, the shipping amount is deducted from your PayPal (sales revenue) balance.

Figure 1-9:
Add the shipper's tracking information.

Figure 1-10:
Tracking information becomes part of the sales record on PayPal.

If you're starting a business in earnest, you need to keep track of your online expenses separately. Allowing PayPal to deduct your shipping costs from your incoming revenue creates a bookkeeping nightmare. You need to have exact figures for expenses and income — and it helps keep confusion to a minimum when your deposits (withdrawals from your PayPal account to your bank) match your sales receipts. If you want to ship through PayPal, be sure you withdraw your sales amount to your checking account *before* you process your shipping. That way your shipping can be charged to your business credit card for easier tracking.

To purchase postage and print your label for a specific purchase, click the Print Shipping Label button next to the payment record in your PayPal account overview, as shown in Figure 1-11. You'll be taken through a step-by-step process for paying for your shipping and printing the appropriate label on your printer.

My Account Overview

Last log in marshac@_____ on May 18, 2008 11:53 AM PDT

Welcome, **Marsha Collier** (_____) Edit profile
Business Name: The Collier Company, Inc
Account holder since 2000
Account type: Business
Status: Verified (3496)

Get a **30-second** credit decision
Apply Now

PayPal balance

Currency	Balance
U.S. Dollar:	$396.56 USD

Account history: All account activity | Payments sent | Payments received

Recent activity - Last updated 5/18/2008 12:18 PDT

File	Type	To/From	Name/Email/Phone	Date	Status	Details	Action	Amount	Fee
☐	Payment	From	T_____	May 16, 2008	Completed	Details	Check Shipment	$30.98 USD	-$1.20 USD
☐	Payment	From	A_____	May 15, 2008	Completed	Details	Check Shipment	$21.49 USD	-$0.92 USD
☐	Refund	From	F__	May 14, 2008	Completed	Details		$12.00 USD	$0.00 USD
☐	Payment	From	C_____	May 14, 2008	Completed	Details	Print shipping label	$252.00 USD	-$7.61 USD
☐	Payment	From	____	May 13, 2008	Completed	Details	Check Shipment	$30.49 USD	-$1.49 USD

Figure 1-11: Click the Print Shipping Label button to ship your item through UPS or the USPS.

Stamps.com

Stamps.com purchased 31 Internet postage patents from e-stamp, making its services a combination of the best of both sites. (e-stamp discontinued its online postage service late in 2000; I was a big fan.) Many eBay sellers moved their postage business over to Stamps.com.

Stamps.com works with software that you probably use every day, such as Microsoft Word, Outlook, and Office; Corel WordPerfect; Palm Desktop; and Quicken. Here are some features you might enjoy:

✦ **Use your printer to print postage:** If your printer allows it, you can even print your envelopes along with bar-coded addresses, your return address, and postage. This saves quite a bit in label costs.

TIP

The Stamps.com Envelope Wizard permits you to design your own envelopes, including a logo or graphics. You can purchase a box of 500 #10 envelopes for as little as $4.99 at an office-supply store. (Endicia.com provides a more robust envelope-graphics wizard.)

✦ **Have Stamps.com check that your addresses are valid:** Before printing any postage, the Stamps.com software contacts the USPS database of every valid mailing address in the United States. This Address Matching System (AMS) is updated monthly.

✦ **Have Stamps.com add the extra four digits to your addressee's ZIP code:** This nifty feature helps ensure swift delivery while freeing you of the hassle of having to look up the information.

Purchasing postage is as easy as going to www.stamps.com and clicking your mouse. Your credit-card information is kept secure on its site. With Stamps.com, you don't *need* any extra fancy equipment, although most introductory deals come with a free 5-pound-maximum scale. The scale also functions on its own. Serious users should get a better-quality postage scale from a seller on eBay or through Office Depot.

Because Office Depot delivers any order more than $50 free the next day, it's a great place to get paper and labels. Better buys on scales, though, can be found on eBay, especially if you search *postage scale*. I use a super-small, 13-pound-maximum scale manufactured by Escali that I bought on eBay for only $29.95, complete with a five-year warranty.

Stamps.com charges a flat rate of $15.99 per month. The site regularly offers sign-up bonuses that include as much as $20.00 free postage or a free 5-pound-maximum digital postage scale. To find the Stamps.com deal of the month, visit its Web site.

Book VII
Chapter 1

Organizing Your
Merchandise and
Shipping Department

Chapter 2: Shipping without Going Postal

In This Chapter

✐ **Understanding the overall shipping process**

✐ **Checking out different shippers**

✐ **Signing up with Federal Express**

✐ **Shipping with the United States Postal Service**

✐ **Using UPS**

✐ **Shipping directly from PayPal**

I think the best part of eBay is making the sale and receiving payment. After that comes the depressing and tedious process of fulfilling your orders. You shouldn't feel bad if this is the point that makes you pause and sigh. Order fulfillment is one of the biggest problems (and yuckiest chores) that face any mail-order or online enterprise.

But as an eBay businessperson, you *must* attend to these tasks, however much you'd rather not. In this chapter, you explore your shipping options. I give you the lowdown on the three major carriers — FedEx, UPS, and the U.S. Postal Service — so you can see who fits your requirements. (For the scoop on insurance coverage, see Chapter 3.)

Shipping: The Heart of Your Business

Shipping can be the most time-consuming (and dreaded) task for eBay sellers. Even if the selling portion of your transaction goes flawlessly, the item has to get to the buyer in one piece. If it doesn't, the deal could be ruined — and so could your reputation.

The best way to avoid shipping problems is to do your homework beforehand, determine which method is likely to work best, and spell out in your item description exactly how you intend to ship the item. I always say "Buyer pays shipping, handling, and optional insurance" in my item description, and that's what I charge, although I can make allowances if the buyer wants a specific method of shipment within reason.

U.S. postage at a big discount!

I just had to share this with you! The figure shows a picture of an envelope I received on an eBay purchase. I had to e-mail the seller to find out how and why she used so many stamps.

The seller is a collector of U.S. postage. She checks out eBay auctions and buys deals on old sheets of mint state stamps. United States stamps, no matter how old, are always good, so she buys these stamps at discount and uses them on her eBay packages. However, she did mention that when she brings her packages to the post office, all the clerks scatter to take a break!

As a footnote, I just checked eBay and found a whole lot of United States postage stamps selling for under face value! Like a *1997 NM Mars Rover (Pathfinder) $3.00 Sheetlet* that went for $1.80. The hint to finding these deals is to search for the type of stamp — but don't include the word *stamp* in your keyword search — and then select the Stamps category. I guess some sellers will never learn.

Shipping is the heart of a mail-order business like yours and can make or break a successful transaction. Don't even think of selling an item without evaluating your shipping options:

1. **After the sale, get the package ready to ship.**

You don't have to seal the package right away, but you should have it ready to seal because the two critical factors in shipping are weight and time. The more a package weighs and the faster it has to be delivered, the higher the charge. The time to think about packing and shipping is *before* you put the item up for auction.

2. **Know your carrier options.**

   In the United States, the three main shipping options for most eBay transactions are the U.S. Postal Service, FedEx, and UPS. See the section "Shopping for a Shipper" (try saying *that* five times fast) for information on how you can get rate options from each service, painlessly and online.

3. **Before quoting the shipping fees, make sure that you include all appropriate costs.**

   I recommend that you charge a nominal handling fee (up to $1.50 isn't out of line — even more under special circumstances) to cover your packing materials, which can add up quickly as you start making multiple transactions. You should also include any insurance costs and delivery-confirmation costs. (For more on insurance and delivery confirmation, see Chapter 3.)

   eBay's policy reads:

   "Sellers may charge a reasonable shipping and handling fee to the final price of their item, provided that this fee is disclosed up front in the listing. A shipping and handling fee can cover the seller's reasonable costs for mailing, packaging and handling the item. Shipping and handling fees cannot be listed as a percentage of the final sale price."

   It's best to post a flat shipping amount (or use the eBay online shipping calculator) to give buyers an idea of how much shipping will be. This way, buyers can include this cost when they consider their bidding strategies. Figure out what the packed item will weigh and then estimate shipping costs; the online calculators can help

   Keep in mind, though, that if your idea of a reasonable handling fee doesn't gel with your buyers, you may end up with a ding in your DSR feedback rating for shipping fees.

   If the item is particularly heavy and you need to use a specialized shipping service, be sure to say in your listing description that you're just giving an estimate and that the final cost will be determined prior to shipping. Optionally, you could tell the bidder how much the item weighs, where you're shipping from, and what your handling charges are (a few bidders don't mind doing the math).

   Occasionally, shipping calculations can be off target, and you may not know that until after you take the buyer's money. If the mistake is in your favor and is a biggie, notify the buyer and offer a refund. But if shipping ends up costing you a bit more, take your lumps and pay it. You can always let the buyer know what happened and that you paid the extra cost. Who knows, it may show up on your feedback from the buyer! (Even if it doesn't, spreading goodwill never hurts.)

4. **E-mail the buyer and congratulate him or her on winning; reiterate your shipping choice and how long you expect shipping will take.**

Make sure you're both talking about the same timetable. If the buyer balks at either the price or the shipping time, try working out an option that will make the buyer happy.

5. **Send the package.**

When should you ship the package? Common courtesy says it should go out as soon as the item and shipping charges are paid. If the buyer has followed through with his or her side of the bargain, you should do the same. Ship that package no more than a day or so after payment (or after the E-check clears). If you can't, immediately e-mail the buyer and explain the delay.

Send a prompt follow-up e-mail to let the buyer know the item's on the way. In this e-mail, include when the item was sent, how long it should take to arrive, any special tracking number (if you have one), and a request for a return e-mail confirming arrival after the item gets there. I also include a thank-you note (a receipt would be a businesslike addition) in each package I send out. I appreciate when I get one in an eBay package, and it always brings a smile to the recipient's face. It never hurts to take every opportunity to promote goodwill (and future business and positive feedback).

More often than not, you do get an e-mail back from the buyer to let you know the item arrived safely. If you don't, it doesn't hurt to send another e-mail (in about a week) to ask whether the item arrived in good condition. It jogs the buyer's memory and demonstrates your professionalism as a seller. Use this opportunity to gently remind buyers that you'll be leaving positive feedback for them. Ask whether they're satisfied, and don't be bashful about suggesting they do the same for you. Leave positive feedback right away so you don't forget.

Shopping for a Shipper

When you're considering shipping options, you must first determine what types of packages you'll generally be sending (small packages that weigh less than two pounds or large and bulky packages) and then decide how you'll send your items. Planning this before listing the item is a good idea.

Deciding on your carrier can be the most important decision in your eBay business. You need to decide which one is more convenient for you (located close to your home base, provides pick up service, gives better customer service) and which is the most economical. Settling on one main shipper to meet most of your needs is important because all your records will be on one statement or in one area. However, you might also need a secondary shipper for special types of packages.

Shipping can make or break your customer service. Whoever delivers the package to the buyer is an extension of your company. Professional labels, clean boxes, nifty packing peanuts — those are the things you control. Safe and timely delivery falls into the hands of complete strangers, but the buyer will blame you for the tardiness or sloppiness of the shipping. Your bottom line isn't the shipper's, and no matter how many refunds they offer when they don't meet their promised schedules, it won't help when you have irate customers. Simple equation: Irate customers = lousy feedback.

So, what's a seller to do? Do you use the shipper that other sellers rave about? Perhaps opt for convenience or low price? Once you decide on a shipper, how often do you re-evaluate its services?

The rest of the chapter will help you with this decision.

Meeting your front line

Who constitutes the front line of your eBay business? My shipping front line is Scott, the UPS man; Tim, the Post Office carrier; and Jorge, who picks up for FedEx Ground. I know the front-line guys because they help my eBay business run smoothly. They don't leave deliveries outside under a bush, and they always deliver packages to my neighbor if I'm not home. They pick up my sundry packages with a smile and a lighthearted "They're sure buying things on eBay, aren't they?" I respond with a smile and a bit of friendly chitchat.

Wait, are you telling me that you don't get the same service? Have you ever taken a moment to chat with your delivery person? When you personalize a business relationship (such as addressing them by name), you become more than a street address, you become . . . well . . . a *person*. When you're no longer a number, you become a fellow human being with needs and wants. Believe it or not, people *want* to make other people happy.

I leave a signal when there are packages to be picked up, and every one is picked up. When somebody delivers a big box, it goes to the back door near my studio, so I don't have to drag it through the front door and across the house.

Try building a relationship with your shipping front line. I've invited them to company holiday parties and offered them a cool drink on a hot summer day. The result? My shipping is the easiest part of my business.

Location, location, location

What happens if you have to drop off your packages for shipment? It's important to consider the closest local drop-off point for your carrier. Each of the major carriers has a search feature on its Web site to find the nearest drop-off location. You input your address or zip code, and the feature tells you the locations closest to you.

To get the location lowdown quickly, go to the following sites:

✦ **FedEx:** www.fedex.com/us/dropoff

✦ **USPS:** www.usps.com/locator/welcome.htm/

✦ **UPS:** www.ups.com/dropoff

Be sure to read the details about each location online. Different fees may be involved in dropping off packages. Some locations may accept certain types of packages and not others. Read the fine print.

Comparing prices

The consensus is that a particular method of shipping is cheaper for large items and another is cheaper for small packages. Each method has its own peculiarities.

Take a look at Table 2-1 and compare the pricing for certain types of packages. Know that there are extras for some services, so become familiar with the variations and hidden costs. For example, FedEx and UPS include tracking numbers for delivery confirmation, but USPS charges extra (delivery confirmation is $.45 for Priority Mail and $.55 for Media Mail, First Class, and Parcel Post).

Table 2-1			Shipping Times and Costs (NY to LA)			
Weight (lbs)	*USPS Priority*: 2–3 Days ($)*	*UPS Select: 3 Days ($)*	*FedEx Ground 4–5 Days ($)*	*UPS Ground: 5–6 Days ($)*	*USPS Parcel Post: 7–9 Days ($)*	*USPS Media Mail: 7–10 Days ($)*
1	4.80	20.78	6.95	10.32	4.55	2.23
2	8.25	23.81	7.99	11.55	6.67	2.58
3	11.50	26.83	8.89	12.60	8.12	2.93
4	14.25	29.52	9.46	13.27	9.38	3.28
5	16.80	32.15	10.03	13.96	10.58	3.63
6	17.65	35.17	10.37	14.35	11.72	3.98
7	20.15	38.27	10.87	14.94	12.81	4.33
8	22.60	41.49	11.55	15.74	13.85	4.68
9	25.15	44.45	12.30	16.63	14.86	5.03
10	27.55	47.55	13.14	17.61	15.83	5.38

*USPS Priority Mail also has flat-rate envelopes for $4.80 and two sizes of flat-rate boxes that can be stuffed and shipped for $9.80 and $12.95.

Shipping the BIG stuff!

When it comes to shipping heavy or big stuff, you have a few options. Because I like using FedEx, I check with FedEx Freight first. My husband once purchased four large heavy-equipment tires on eBay, and there was no way they could go with a regular carrier. We told the seller to place the tires on a pallet and secure them. They were picked up by FedEx Freight. Shipping was reasonable, but the caveat was that the shipment had to be delivered to a place of business, not a residential location.

The www.freightquote.com Web site negotiates rates with several major freight-forwarders. Before attempting to sell a heavy item, sign on to their Web site with the weight and dimensions of your shipment, and they'll give you a free quote on the spot.

There are further discounts when printing your USPS postage electronically. Priority Mail will save an average of 3.5 percent for customers who use electronic postage.

Table 2-1 should get you thinking about your carrier, especially when you realize that USPS charges only a tad more money for 2- to 3-day Priority Mail service over Parcel Post.

You, Too, Can Use Federal Express

Federal Express (or FedEx, as it's known to everyone) is world-famous for its reliable service. It's the number-one choice for all major companies who "Absolutely, positively have to get it there on time." FedEx also has a reputation for some of the highest costs in the business — but only to the untrained eye. FedEx acquired Roadway Package Service (RPS) and formed FedEx Ground, which has a separate division called FedEx Home Delivery that delivers to residences. For the services they provide, you'll be happy to pay what you do. Read on.

FedEx Ground and Home Delivery

When FedEx's Home Delivery began, their slogan was "The neighborhood friendly service that fits the way we live, work, and shop today." Although I rarely get warm fuzzies from my package delivery, this slogan brought meaning to the philosophy behind their service: to bring professional shipping to your home residence. Now FedEx Home Delivery is part of FedEx Ground, and offers low rates and high-quality service. They're the only shipper that offers a money-back guarantee on home service. They deliver until 8:00 p.m. *and* on Saturdays, but not on Mondays.

To open an account, visit the FedEx Ground Web site, shown in Figure 2-1, at

`www.fedex.com/us/ground/main`

Figure 2-1:
The FedEx
Ground
home page.

Even if you have a current Federal Express account, you need to sign on to add the Ground service (which includes Home Delivery). Registering for Ground service is even easier than registering on eBay, so give it a shot. (Check the next section to see how easy it is.)

I opened my FedEx Ground account through a link on the FedEx home page, and got the skinny on how to use the service. FedEx Home Delivery gives you a service schedule to let you know how long it will take your package to arrive at its destination (see Figure 2-2). The online calculator allows you to choose the option of home delivery, so you don't even have to look up alternative rates and charts.

Here are a few fast facts about FedEx Ground services:

✦ You print your own labels and barcodes for your packages and track them online.

✦ FedEx Home Delivery works on a zone system based on your ZIP code and how far the package is going. Refer to the FedEx Home Delivery zone chart or get the cost online through the online calculator.

✦ Each shipment is covered for $100.00 in declared value. Additional insurance is $.60 per $100.00 or a fraction thereof.

✦ Residential deliveries are limited to 70-pound packages.

✦ Daily pick-up service adds an additional weekly charge of $8.00 to $12.00 to your account.

✦ Dropping off packages at Federal Express counters (this includes all those handy FedEx Kinko's locations) incurs no additional charge.

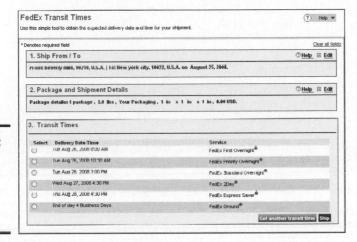

Figure 2-2: Home Delivery schedule from LA to NY.

To find the closest drop-off location for your FedEx packages, go to `www.fedex.com/us/dropoff` and type your ZIP code. Check that the location accepts Ground, and check the cutoff times.

Signing up with FedEx

You sign up for a FedEx account only once, but it's a two-step process. First you sign up for a Web site login, and then you sign up for an actual, for-real FedEx account. After you have a fedex.com login and account, you'll be able to ship your items quickly from your own private FedEx Web space.

To get a FedEx account and be able to ship right away, follow these steps:

1. **Go to** `www.fedex.com/us`.

2. **On the left side of the screen, click the FedEx Ground link.**

The FedEx Ground page appears.

3. **From the FedEx Ground page, click the Ship tab, at the top.**

You'll land at the login page. If you've previously signed up for an account with a password and user ID, you can log in immediately here.

4. **If you're signing up for a new account, click the Sign Up Now! link.**

5. **On the resulting registration page, type the following information:**

   • **User ID:** Make up an ID you'll remember. (I tried my eBay user ID and it was already taken — I guess they have lots of customers.)

   • **Password:** Come up with a password you'll remember. For tips on selecting safe passwords, see Book IX, Chapter 4.

   • **Password reminder:** Input your password reminder question and answer. This way, if you ever forget your password or have to prove your identity to FedEx, you'll have a mind jogger.

   • **Contact information:** Type your name, company name (optional), address, city, state, e-mail address, and phone number.

   • **Agree to the terms of use:** If you want to ship via FedEx, you must agree to their terms. Click the link provided if you want some boring legalese to read. When you decide to play by their rules, click I Accept.

6. **Read the FedEx License Agreement (I'm sure you'll read every word) and then click Yes, indicating that you accept the Agreement.**

   Next you're asked whether you have a FedEx account number.

7. **Click the Open a FedEx Account link.**

8. **Follow the prompts and input your credit-card information.**

   Finally, you're presented with your very own nine-digit FedEx account number!

If you want to ship something now, click Start Using FedEx Ship Manager. Otherwise, log in later when you're ready to ship.

FedEx online

FedEx has one of the most intuitive online applications for shipping. The FedEx Ship Manager interface will turn your computer into a one-person shipping shop. You can search for rate quotes, track packages, and use the shipping notification option to send tracking information e-mails to your recipients.

To ship your item from the FedEx Web site, just go to the online Ship Manager by clicking the Ship tab. You'll be presented with a simple, all-in-one online waybill, similar to the one you fill out by hand. Figure 2-3 shows you what it looks like.

You can copy and paste addresses from your PayPal account into the online form. Just highlight the text you want to copy and press Ctrl+C. To paste the text, place your cursor in the area you want to fill and press Ctrl+V.

**Book VII
Chapter 2**

Shipping without Going Postal

Figure 2-3:
FedEx Ship Manager online shipping.

When you're filling out the form, note some important entries:

✦ **Service type:** If you're shipping to a residence, use the FedEx Home Delivery option from the drop-down list.

✦ **Dimensions:** Be sure that you know the proper dimensions for the package you're sending.

If you sell repeat items in your eBay business, why not measure the boxes ahead of time and keep a list near your computer so you'll know the size? (For example: *Light kit 14 x 12 x 26.*)

✦ **FedEx Ship Alert:** Select the e-mail option to send the buyer (and yourself) a notice that the package was shipped. Add a personal message so that the e-mail won't have a cold automated feel to it.

After you fill out the form, you can click the Courtesy Rate button at the bottom to get a shipping-cost estimate (not including any special discounts).

When shipping with FedEx online, if your package is valued over $100.00 and you use U-PIC for your insurance (see Chapter 3), put $0 in the Declared Value box. Make note of the package on an insurance log and submit it to U-PIC. (FedEx charges $.60 cents per $100.00 in value but U-PIC charges only $.15 per $100.00.)

Saving more by paying with American Express

If you have an American Express Business credit card (which also allows you access to the American Express Open Network), you can save even more on your FedEx shipments!

✔ **Save 5%** of all FedEx Ground shipments when you fill out your forms online.

✔ **Save 10% to 20%** on your FedEx Express shipments.

To be sure your American Express card is officially linked so you get the discount, call the FedEx/Open Network desk at 1-800-231-8636. As a member of the Open Network, you can also save money on other business needs.

Shipping with USPS

I'm a big fan of the U.S. Postal Service. Just ask my wonderful letter (er, multiple parcel) carrier, Tim. I use the post office for the bulk of my eBay sales because it's convenient. In my eight years selling items on eBay, they've never lost a package.

The USPS is open to everyone. You don't have to set up an account to use its services. To get a basic idea of what you'll pay to send a package, you can access a rate calculator on the USPS Web site (www.usps.com), shown in Figure 2-4.

Figure 2-4: The United States Postal Service Web site.

Convenient and fast

The post office has worked hard to keep up with the competition in the parcel business by offering many online features and custom pickup. They also offer many classes of service, with a weight maximum of 70 pounds. Table 2-2 shows the services that are most popular with eBay sellers.

Table 2-2		Most Popular USPS Services
Service	*Time to Cross the Country (Days)*	*What You Can Ship*
First Class	3–5	First Class mail can be used to mail anything, as long as it weighs 13 ounces or less. You can send a letter, a large envelope, or a small package.
Priority Mail	2–3	Priority Mail is just First Class mail on steroids (for heavier items).
Parcel Post	8	Parcel Post is cheaper (and slower) than Priority Mail.
Media Mail	8	Media Mail is the least expensive way to mail heavy items. The only caveat is that you can use Media Mail to ship only books, film, manuscripts, printed music, printed test materials, sound recordings, scripts, and computer-recorded media such as CD-ROMs and diskettes.

Read on for details on the most popular forms of mail used by eBay sellers.

First Class

Good old regular mail — in particular, First Class — is the way we send bills and letters. It works also as an economical alternative for eBay items up to 13 ounces. When you print your postage online with some services, you can get a delivery confirmation for First Class mail for only $.18.

Too many sellers make the jump to Priority Mail because they don't take the time to think about the weight of their items. It doesn't have to ship in an envelope to go via First Class mail.

Priority Mail

The 2- to 3-day Priority Mail service is the most popular form of shipping for eBay packages. You can get free cartons, mailing tape, and labels from the post office. (See Chapter 1 for a complete list of what the USPS supplies for your mailing needs.) You can also print postage online through endicia.com or stamps.com (see Chapter 1 again).

The Priority Mail rates are perfect for 1-pound packages ($4.80 flat-rate cross-country) and 2-pound packages (from $4.80, based on distance). They also have a flat-rate Priority envelope in which you can jam in as much as possible (regardless of the package's final weight) for $4.80.

Because USPS rates are based on distance and weight, you can save money by using their new flat-rate Priority Mail boxes. I've been able to jam quite a bit into them and it's a deal at a flat rate of $9.80 (and $12.95 for an even larger Flat Rate box) anywhere in the United States.

The Priority Mail rates (including free shipping materials) are attractive until you get into heavier packages. Also, if you don't print your postage online, delivery confirmation costs you an additional $.65 for Priority Mail ($.75 for Parcel Post and Media Mail). Delivery confirmation tells you only *if* the package was delivered; it doesn't trace the package along its route.

Parcel Post

If you want to use the USPS and have a heavy package (up to 70 pounds) that doesn't fit the requirements for Media Mail, use Parcel Post. Since the 2008 rate changes, USPS Parcel Post rates can be highly competitive when you compare them to the UPS or FedEx Ground rates.

Media Mail

To stay new and hip, the post office has renamed its old Book Rate to Media Mail, causing many eBay sellers to mistakenly miss out on this valuable mailing tool. The savings are immense. The drawback is that you must mail only books, cassettes, videos, or computer-readable media. Transit time on Media Mail is at least 7 to 10 days, but the cost savings on heavy packages may be worth it — as long as your customers realize how long transit time can be.

Understanding the costs

The Postal Service levies additional charges for some often-used services but also gives free services to online postage customers:

+ **Pickup:** If you have a postal license and print your own postage from an online service (see Chapter 1) or print direct from eBay or the PayPal site, the post office offers free pickup, as shown in Figure 2-5. You have to give your packages to your carrier at the time of your regular delivery or schedule a pickup on the USPS site at

     http://www.usps.com/shipping/carrierpickup/welcome.htm

Figure 2-5:
Put in your
request for
pickup the
day before
your pickup
day.

✦ **Insurance:** This guarantees that you're covered if your package doesn't arrive safely and will reimburse you up to the value you declare when purchasing the insurance, up to a maximum of $5000.00. If your package gets lost or severely mangled in shipping, the Postal Service will, after a thorough investigation (see Chapter 3), pay your claim. Fees start at $1.70 for packages up to $50.00. For discounted insurance, read Chapter 3.

✦ **Delivery confirmation:** Delivery confirmation provides you with proof of delivery or attempted delivery. You can purchase delivery confirmation for $.65 (for Priority Mail) or $.75 (Parcel Post) at the post office when you mail a package. They provide you with a tracking number that you can check online at

        www.usps.com/shipping/trackandconfirm.htm

You can also verify a package's delivery by calling a toll-free number, 800-222-1811.

The post office now charges for your Parcel Post and Priority Mail package shipping based on miles sent as well as weight. To estimate postage charges for your packages, go to

    http://postcalc.usps.gov/Zonecharts

DHL SmartMail

The United States Postal Service is the nation's largest transportation entity, delivering to close to 130 million addresses per day. The USPS sought partners who could help with long-haul transportation of the mail; the USPS would handle the local delivery. In 1996, DHL SmartMail signed on as a forwarder of mail. They ship mail — envelopes or parcels — from high-volume shippers.

Many high-level PowerSellers take advantage of the DHL SmartMail service. When you're sending out hundreds of small items a day, you can save big time using this service for your shipping. For more information, visit their Web site at

```
http://www.smartmail.com/
service_services.asp
```

Just type your ZIP code and the site will generate a custom zone chart for your mailing location.

Getting on the UPS Bandwagon

Today's UPS is a $30 billion company focusing on enabling commerce around the world. Every day UPS delivers more than 13.3 million packages and documents — I'm sure much of which represents eBay transactions.

UPS considers neither Saturday nor Sunday to be delivery days. So when your package is quoted for a 5-day delivery and the 5 days cross over a weekend, add 2 days to the delivery schedule. (The USPS and FedEx Ground deliver on Saturday.)

Here are some quick facts about UPS:

✦ Shipping with UPS requires that you pay a different rate for different zones in the country (zones 1–8). The cost of your package is based on its weight, your zip code (where there package ships from), and the addressee's ZIP code (where the package is going). To figure out your cost, use the handy UPS cost calculator shown in Figure 2-6.

✦ UPS offers a chart that defines the shipping time for your ground shipments.

✦ Each package has a tracking number that you can input online to verify location and time of delivery.

✦ Delivery to a residence costs over $1.00 per pound more than delivery to a commercial location.

✦ UPS delivers packages Monday through Friday.

Figure 2-6:
The UPS cost (and transit time) calculator.

Comparing costs

Although we always complain when the U.S. Postal Service raises their rates, you should know that all other shipping carriers raise their rates every year.

Annual rate increases are why being lulled into complacency can be dangerous. Evaluate your shipping charges and your shipper's fees every year to keep up with the increases and possible cuts into your bottom line.

UPS charges a different rate for home delivery than they do for deliveries to a business. In their last rate increase, residential delivery took the biggest hit. The premium for Home Delivery rose 22 percent; the previous year it was 4.5 percent. That's a raise from $1.10 to $1.95 in just two years.

While we all *think* that UPS Ground is cheaper than the post office, it's not true in every case. Check out Table 2-3 for a summary of FedEx and UPS rate increases.

**Book VII
Chapter 2**

Shipping without
Going Postal

Table 2-3	FedEx and UPS Percentage Rate Increases for 2008						
Weight (in lbs.)	Zone 2	Zone 3	Zone 4	Zone 5	Zone 6	Zone 7	Zone 8
1 – 5	3.8% to 5.7%	5.6% to 5.8%	4.9% to 5.7%	5.8% to 5.9%	5.7% to 5.8%	5.5% to 5.7%	4.7% to 5.6%
10 – 50	4.4% to 5.1%	4.9% to 5.0%	4.9% to 5.0%	4.9 to 5.8%	4.9% to 5.0%	2.6% to 5.0%	0.4% to 5.0%
60 – 100	2.9% to 5.8%	3.0% to 5.8%	3.1% to 5.7%	3.2% to 5.8%	3.3% to 6.0%	4.4% to 5.8%	4.3% to 5.0%

Every UPS package is automatically insured for up to $100 assuming you declare a value. Insurance up to the first $300 is $1.80. After the first $300, it runs $.60 per $100. The post office charges extra for the service, but you can save money either way by using a private insurance policy for your packages (see Chapter 3).

The de-facto standard for eBay shipping is Priority Mail. Compared to UPS 3-Day Select, Priority Mail is the clear cost-saving winner if you must ship packages for swift delivery.

For heavier packages, UPS is considerably cheaper than Parcel Post for packages over 6 pounds. After your packages pass that point, and if time is *not* of the essence, UPS may be the best way to go.

Variable UPS rates

When you ship via UPS and are trying to figure out how to get the best rates, you have quite a conundrum. UPS basically has three rates for small-time shippers:

✦ **Retail rate:** This is the rate you pay when you go to the UPS Customer Center and they create the label for you. It's the most expensive. With the eBay/PayPal solution, you can save yourself some bucks by printing your own bar-coded labels and dropping the packages at the Customer Center or giving the packages to a UPS driver.

✦ **On demand rate:** Use UPS for the rare large box or heavy shipment. An on demand, or occasional, shipper can call UPS for a next-day pickup. You have to pay an additional $4 per package for the driver to pick up from you if you don't feel like bringing the package to the UPS local counter.

✦ **Pickup account:** When you hit the big time, you're able to get the lowest UPS rates and have a driver make daily stops to pick up your packages. Fees for a pickup account run from $7 to $16 per week (based on the amount of packages you ship each week) over the cost of your package shipping.

Saving by getting heavier packages picked up

Are you suffering from the delusion that it costs a bundle to have regular UPS package pickup service? (I was, too.) Surprise, it doesn't, as you'll see.

As shown in Table 2-4, fees for UPS pickup service are on a sliding scale from $7.00 to $16.00, based on the amount of postage that you use in a week. Shipping seven 10-pound packages coast-to-coast or eight 5-pound packages would easily meet the weekly minimum of $60.00 in postage. If you're selling heavier items on eBay, UPS service with package pickup wins over the post office, hands down!

Table 2-4	UPS Pickup Charges
Postage per Week ($)	*UPS Charges for Pickup ($)*
0–14.99	17.00
15.000–59.99	12.00
60.00 and up	8.00

If you have daily pickup service, you'd net a savings of close to $2 per package, as shown in Table 2-5. You must print your labels directly from the UPS Web site and have a preprinted manifest ready for the driver.

Table 2-5		UPS Residential Rate Comparison (NY to LA)		
Service	*Weight (lbs)*	*UPS Retail Rate ($)*	*eBay/ PayPal On Demand Rate ($)*	*eBay/PayPal UPS Daily Pickup ($) (plus applicable fuel surcharges)*
Residential Ground	2	10.48	11.55	7.65
	5	12.66	13.96	9.29
	10	15.97	17.81	11.56
3-Day Select	2	17.70	23.81	14.25

(continued)

Book VII
Chapter 2

Shipping without Going Postal

Table 2-5 *(continued)*

Service	Weight (lbs)	UPS Retail Rate ($)	eBay/ PayPal On Demand Rate ($)	eBay/PayPal UPS Daily Pickup ($) (plus applicable fuel surcharges)
	5	23.90	32.15	19.05
	10	35.35	47.55	27.90
2-Day Air	2	33.85	30.40	29.35
	5	39.65	43.65	33.30
	10	54.30	66.85	43.60

Shipping Directly from PayPal

I consider PayPal to be *de rigueur* (a *must have,* to all you non-French speakers) for all eBay sellers. By using PayPal, a seller can streamline the buyer's shopping experience, making it simple to buy, click, and pay. Those out in the eBay world who haven't used PayPal find using the service to be a life-changing experience. Along with all the timesaving tools PayPal supplies for the seller, they now offer online shipping services for items through the United States Postal Service or UPS at no extra charge. This is a convenient system for those who don't ship many packages each week because there's no need to use additional software or sign up with an additional service.

But (I hate the *buts* — don't you?) the PayPal postage system can make bookkeeping a nightmare for large-scale shippers. That's because PayPal withdraws the postage amounts directly from your PayPal account balance. This is problematic because your books won't balance: Your final deposits won't match your posted eBay or Web sales.

You can make this work more efficiently by posting your PayPal sales to your bookkeeping program and then withdrawing your money before processing your shipping. Then simply charge your shipping to a credit card, which will help you balance your books at month's end.

When you're ready to deal with shipping, you simply sign on to your PayPal account and handle it right on the site. To begin the shipping process, follow these steps:

1. **Log in to your PayPal account page.**

2. **Click the Ship button next to the item in the row.**

   You arrive at the page shown in Figure 2-7.

3. **Choose which method of shipping you'd like to use: U.S. Postal Service or UPS.**

Figure 2-7:
Choose your
shipper!

PayPal shipping with the USPS

If you plan to use the ever-popular United States Postal Service, printing your postage and label through PayPal gives you a free delivery confirmation with Priority Mail. A delivery confirmation is available also for Media Mail, Parcel Post, and First Class mail for a minimal charge.

After you've chosen USPS as your shipper, you'll see a confirmation page similar to the one shown in Figure 2-8. At the top of the page (not pictured) your mailing address and the ship-to address are listed. After you've confirmed that this information is correct, fill out the details of the form, including

✦ **Service type:** Choose the level of mailing service you want for your package from this drop-down list. Priority Mail is usually the standard.

✦ **Package size:** From this drop-down list, select the type of package you're sending. Keep the following in mind:

- **Package/thick envelope:** Your package or envelope qualifies for this status if the length and girth (all the way around) is no more than 84 inches.

- **Large package:** Your package is larger than the preceding category, but doesn't exceed 108 inches in combined length and girth.

- **USPS flat-rate envelope:** These are handy Express and Priority Mail envelopes (available free from the USPS; see Chapter 1 for information on how to get them delivered to your door). They allow you to ship whatever fits into the envelopes at a flat rate, no matter how much the package weighs. (If you really stuff them, you can always reinforce your envelope with clear shipping tape — I do!)

✦ **Weight:** Here you enter the weight of your package.

✦ **Delivery confirmation:** Confirmation is free with Priority Mail.

✦ **Signature confirmation:** Signature confirmation provides you a signature and date of delivery and is available for many levels of service. If you'd like a signature confirmation for your package, it will add $1.30 to the postage cost. You can request proof of delivery from the USPS online or on the phone.

Don't forget that — if you ship an item with a value over $250 — PayPal requires signature confirmation for the item to be covered under the PayPal Seller Protection program.

✦ **Display value of postage on label:** If you'd prefer not to show the amount of the postage on the label, do not check this box. That way, whatever handling fees you charge your customer are transparent.

On the other side of the coin, if you're trying to be a good seller (so you can receive great DSR ratings), you might not want to hide how much you actually pay for shipping. That way, the customer can see that you haven't padded the shipping fees to pad your wallet.

✦ **E-mail message to buyer:** Customer service to the fore! Type a nice note letting customers know you appreciate their business. This might also be a good place to ask them to e-mail you immediately if there are any problems with the item when it arrives (a good defense against knee-jerk negative feedback).

✦ **Item(s) being shipped to your buyer:** In this area you see the item number and name of the item you're shipping.

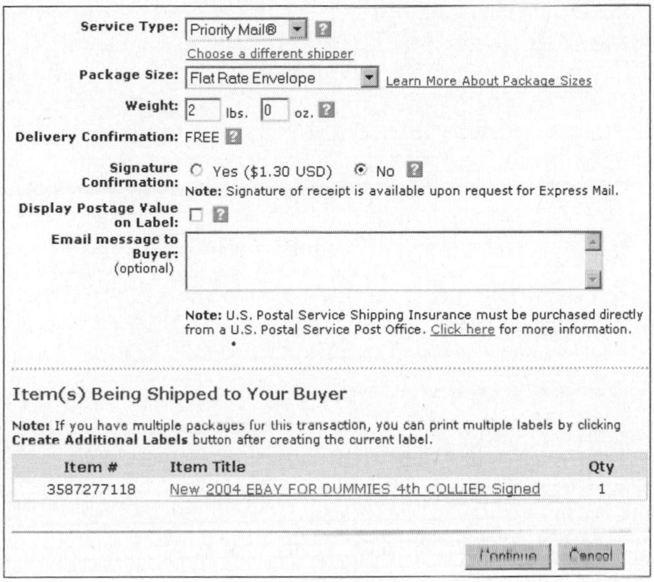

Figure 2-8:
Confirming
the details
of your
shipment.

When you've finished filling in the form and everything looks okay, complete
your USPS shipping with these steps:

1. **Click Continue.**

   The USPS Shipping Confirmation page appears. All the information from
   the previous page is listed. If you've made a mistake at any entry, click
   Edit Shipment Details, or cancel the transaction by clicking Cancel.

2. **If everything looks okay, click Pay.**

3. **Click Continue.**

   Your PayPal account is charged for the postage amount, and a new
   window opens to allow you to print postage on your printer.

4. **Print the sample label.**

   The option to print a sample label is a good idea because it ensures that
   your printer and all the connections are working properly.

5. **Print the label by clicking Print Label.**

   The label will look like the one in Figure 2-9.

Figure 2-9:
The printed
PayPal
Priority Mail
label.

You can now request a pickup from the post office by clicking the Request Pickup link, which takes you directly to the USPS site.

PayPal shipping with UPS

Shippers such as UPS charge different rates based on how often you use their services. If you're shipping many packages a week, it might be best if you print your labels directly from the UPS site. All PayPal UPS shipments are charged the Occasional Shipper rate. If you only use UPS once in a while, the PayPal method will work perfectly for you.

If you've selected UPS as your shipper on the PayPal Shipping page, you will be brought to a page with these choices:

✦ **UPS account:** You can open a new UPS account immediately online or, if you have an existing UPS account number, you may type it in this field.

To open a new account you'll have to verify your company data (it's already entered here from your PayPal account information) and let UPS know approximately how many packages you ship a week.

✦ **Shipping payment information:** You also have to indicate whether you'd like to pay for your shipping with your PayPal account, or if you'd like the shipping billed to your existing UPS account.

When you've finished filling in the form, finish by following these steps:

1. **Click Continue.**

   You'll see a confirmation page.

2. **If the information is correct, click Continue.**

   If any information is wrong, click Edit and go back and make your corrections.

3. **If the shipping agreement appears, read it and, if you agree, click I Agree.**

   Now you're ready to print a label.

4. **Fill out the requested information.**

5. **Print the sample label.**

   By printing a sample label, you make sure that your printer is working properly.

6. **Print the label by clicking Print Label.**

When your label has printed, you may elect to go back to your PayPal Overview page to track the package by clicking Check Shipment, as shown in Figure 2-10.

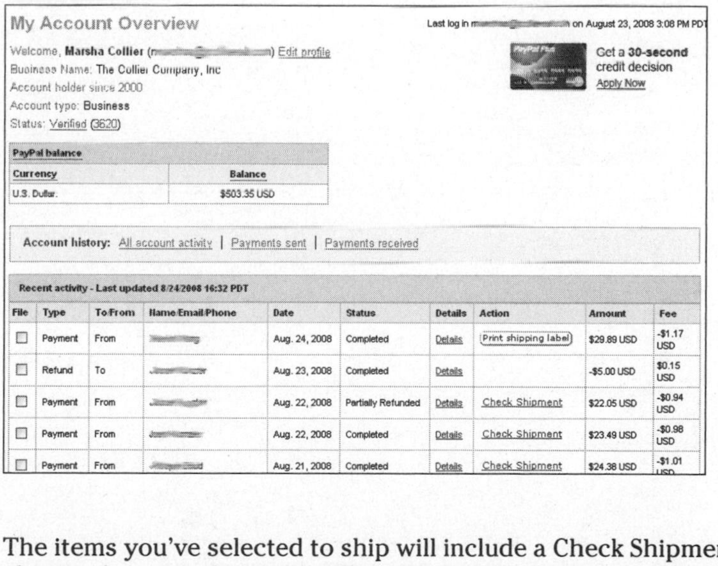

Figure 2-10: Your PayPal Overview page after shipping.

The items you've selected to ship will include a Check Shipment link, and the charges for your shipment will appear in your history log. You may click the Check Shipment button at any time after you've shipped your item to track the package's progress and confirm delivery.

Chapter 3: Insuring Your Item's Delivery

In This Chapter

✔ Knowing your insurance options

✔ Addressing your packages correctly

✔ Filing a claim with the major carriers

*W*hen someone buys an item from you, the buyer assumes that the item will be shipped in 24 to 48 hours. A little-known rule of the online world is the Federal Trade Commission's 30-day mail-order rule. This rule applies to all online sales, as well as mail-order businesses. It states that unless you state a specific shipping time, all items must be shipped within 30 days.

Adopted in 1975, the FTC rule proclaims

✦ You must receive the merchandise when the seller says you will.

✦ If you are not promised delivery within a certain time period, the seller must ship the merchandise to you no later than 30 days after your order.

✦ If you don't receive the merchandise within that 30-day period, you can cancel your order and get your money back.

This rule must be part of the reason why eBay won't allow items on the site for presale (or drop-shipping) unless you can guarantee that the item will be shipped within 30 days. In each of those cases, you must indicate in your description that the item is a presale or drop-ship.

Another thing comes to light here. Note that the rule states that the merchandise must be delivered in 30 days. The rule doesn't say "unless the item gets lost in the mail." This means that *you,* the seller, are responsible for your packages arriving at their destinations. This makes insurance more important than ever, especially on expensive items.

Insurance Options

When you're shipping a large amount of merchandise on a regular basis, you're going to have to deal with the issue of whether you offer buyers insurance against damage or loss. Either way, you (the seller) are responsible for getting the product to the buyer. The lost-in-the-mail excuse doesn't cut the mustard, and having a delivery-confirmation number doesn't guarantee anything, either.

You may *think* that it's the buyers' responsibility to pay for insurance. If they don't, you say, it's their hard luck if the package doesn't arrive. This is far from the truth; buyers who don't receive an item that they've paid for can file a fraud report against you. Buyers can also have the payment removed from your PayPal account, and you have no defense against this.

Again, you'd best realize that the responsibility for delivering the goods is in the seller's hands. So offering insurance to your buyers is good business, and including insurance with every shipment is *excellent* business.

Self-insuring your items

Some sellers on eBay self-insure their packages. In other words, they take the risk and use money out of their own pockets if they have to pay a claim. In this sense, *self-insuring* is considered seller's jargon, not an official legal status (only licensed insurance agents can offer insurance).

These sellers are usually careful about packing their items to prevent damage. (Check out Chapter 1 to find out about choosing and finding packing materials.) They also purchase delivery confirmation when using the Postal Service.

Savvy self-insurers usually do *not* self-insure items of high value. If you sell mostly lower-priced items (under $100) and decide to self-insure, consider making an exception when you do occasionally sell an expensive item. Bite the bullet and pay for the shipping insurance; doing so could save you money and hassle in the long run.

How do you afford to self-insure? Well, tack an additional $1.00 onto every item's postage amount as part of your handling fee. The more items you sell and ship, the more that little dollar-per-item profit builds up and gives you a fund that you can use to cover the rare instance of a damaged or missing item.

Insuring your peace of mind (and your shipment)

Sure, "lost in the mail" is an excuse we've all heard hundreds of times, but despite everyone's best efforts, sometimes things do get damaged or misplaced during shipment. The universe is a dangerous place; that's why we have insurance. I usually offer to get insurance from the shipper if the buyer wants to pay for it, and I always get it on expensive, one-of-a-kind, or very fragile items. In my item description, I spell out that the buyer pays for insurance.

The major shippers offer insurance that's fairly reasonably priced, so check out their rates at their Web sites. But don't forget to read the details. For example, many items on eBay are sold MIMB (mint in mint box). True, the condition of the original box often has a bearing on the final value of the item inside, but the U.S.

Postal Service insures only what is *in* the box. So, if you sold a Malibu Barbie mint in a mint box, USPS insures only the doll and not the original box. Pack carefully so your buyer gets what's been paid for. Be mindful that shippers won't make good on insurance claims if they suspect that you caused the damage by doing a lousy job of packing.

Alternatively, when you're selling on eBay in earnest, you can purchase your own parcel-protection policy from a private insurer. When you use this type of insurance, combined with preprinted electronic postage, you no longer have to stand in line at the post office to have your insured packaged logged in by the clerk at the counter.

WARNING!

This method of building your self-insurance fund may be a risky proposition — especially if you get hit with two expensive lost items in a row! But if you sell a lot of items for under $100, you might find that this works for you.

Insuring through the major carriers

All the major shippers are in the shipping business (duh), not in the insurance business. Insuring is an annoying — but necessary — sideline to their package transit businesses.

Most carriers, other than the United States Postal Service, cover all shipments automatically (and at no extra charge) for the first $100 of package value. By the way, the *package value* of an item sold on eBay is the final bid (or Buy It Now) amount. Of course, you can always buy additional package insurance for your shipped items. Should a package get lost or damaged, making a claim opens an entirely new can of worms.

Table 3-1 shows you what the major carriers charge for their additional insurance.

Table 3-1	Insurance Rates for Commercial Carriers
Shipper	*Shipper Rate*
DHL	$0.70 per $100 (after first $100 of value)
FedEx	$0.60 per $100 (after first $100 of value)
UPS "Declared Value Charge"	$1.80 minimum for $100.01 to $300.00 (after first $100.00 of value) plus $.60 per each $100.00 (or part of $100.00) up to $50,000.00
USPS	$1.70 for $0.01– $50.00 value
	$2.2`15 for $50.01–$100.00 value
	$2.60 for $100.01–$200.00 value
	$4.60 for $200.01–$300.00 value
	$5.55 for $300.01–$400.00 value
	$6.50 for $400.01–$500.00 value
	$7.45 for $500.01–$600.00 value
	$7.45 for $600.01–$5000.00 value plus $.95 for each additional $100 of value over $600.00

Getting private shipping insurance

If you think that printing your own postage is slick, you're gonna love Universal Parcel Insurance Coverage (U-PIC), a service that automates the post-office-insurance hassle because you can handle your insurance electronically. You can insure packages that you send through USPS, UPS, FedEx, and other major carriers. If you use its insurance on USPS-shipped packages, you can save as much as 80 percent on insurance rates.

U-PIC caters to individual eBay sellers amidst its many big-business clients. Here are some great features of the U-PIC service:

✦ **No time wasted standing in line at the post office:** The U-PIC service is integrated into online postage solutions such as endicia.com (described in Chapter 1).

✦ **Quick payments on claims:** If you have a claim, U-PIC pays it within 7 days of receiving all required documents from the carrier.

As with any insurance policy, assume that if you have many claims against your packages, you can be dropped from the service. (This thought only gives me more impetus to package my items properly — I never want to be banished to the counter lines again!)

✦ **Blanket approval:** U-PIC is approved by all major carriers. And turnabout is fair play: All carriers covered must be on the U-PIC approved carrier listing.

+ **Savings:** Again, depending on the quantity and type of items you ship, using U-PIC may save you between 65 and 90% on your insurance costs.

Table 3-2 outlines the U-PIC standard rates that apply when you ship with major carriers, and Table 3-3 compares U-PIC and USPS insurance rates. UPS charges $.60 per $100.00 package value (after the initial $100.00) with a $1.80 minimum, but U-PIC charges only $.20 per $100.00 of package value. FedEx charges $.60 per $100.00 of package value with a $1.80 minimum. By using U-PIC, you can insure your FedEx packages for $.20 per $100.00 value.

Table 3-2	U-PIC Standard Rates
Shipper	*U-PIC Rate*
DHL	$0.20 per $100
FedEx	$0.20 per $100
LTL Freight	$0.50 per $100
UPS	$0.20 per $100
USPS	$0.55 per $100 with delivery confirmation

Table 3-3	USPS and U-PIC Domestic Insurance Coverage Rate Comparison		
Coverage	*USPS*	*U-PIC Standard*	*U-PIC with USPS Delivery Confirmation*
$.01 to $50.00	$1.10	$.75	$.50
$50.01 to $100	$2.00	$.75	$.50
$100.01 to $200.00	$3.00	$1.50	$1.00
$200.01 to $300.00	$4.00	$2.25	$1.50
$300.01 to $400.00	$5.00	$3.00	$2.00

Visit the U-PIC Web site (see Figure 3-1) and poke around. However, to get the best information, give them a phone call at their toll-free number. Your U-PIC sales representative will explain to you exactly how to declare value based on your present system. At the end of each shipping month, you fax, e-mail, or snail-mail your shipping reports to U-PIC.

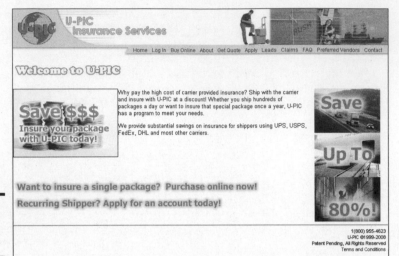

1(800) 955-4623
U-PIC ©1999-2008
Patent Pending, All Rights Reserved
Terms and Conditions

Figure 3-1:
The U-PIC
home page.

To apply for your own U-PIC policy — with no charge to apply and no minimum premium — go directly to the application on their Web site at

    http://delta.u-pic.com/Apply/rtp.aspx

They're a great bunch of people — tell 'em Marsha sent ya!

To apply for the U-PIC service, you must fill out a Request to Provide (RTP) form. You must answer questions about who you are, how many packages you send, how many insurance claims you've filed in the past two years, and your average value per package.

After you fill out the online form and agree to the policy (Evidence of Insurance), a U-PIC representative will contact you within 48 hours. The representative will answer your questions and help you decide which of their programs will work best for your eBay business:

✦ The occasional shipper program is for the person who ships one to five packages per month. You can pay for your insurance online using a credit card, but the rates are not as attractive as those for the standard program.

✦ The offline standard program is the service for eBay businesspeople who ship a large number of packages per month. At the end of each shipping month, you generate an insurance report and use it to calculate your premium. You can pay the premium by check or through PayPal.

To place a claim with U-PIC on a USPS shipment, you must do so no sooner than 21 days on a lost shipment and no later than 90 days after the date of mailing. You must supply the following:

✦ A signed letter, stating the loss or damage from the consignee

✦ A copy of the monthly insurance report you turned in to U-PIC reflecting the insured value

✦ A completed U-PIC claim form (one claim form per claim)

✦ A copy of the original invoice or the end-of-auction form

Because you're paying for private insurance, U-PIC suggests that you include in the package a copy of your insurance policy (or at the very least a note explaining that you have an insurance policy covering your shipments) so that your buyer doesn't think you're overcharging (which makes some folks a bit cranky).

U-PIC will also insure international shipments. The cost to insure international USPS parcels is only $1.00 per $100.00, with no deductible.

If you're a high-volume shipper, you can negotiate an even lower rate with U-PIC. To reach U-PIC, call them toll-free at 800-955-4623.

Avoiding Mistyped Addresses

Lost packages are the bane of all carriers. The post office has been dealing with this problem since they opened the Dead Letter Office in 1825.

The Postal Service's Dead Letter Office employees (I'll call them DLOs) are the only people legally permitted to open lost mail. When an address label gets smooshed, torn, wet, or otherwise illegible — which means the box can't be delivered — it finds its way into the hands of the DLOs, who open the package with the hope of finding enough information to get it to the rightful owner.

Make sure that you always include a packing slip — like the kind you print from Selling Manager or My eBay — inside your packages. The packing slip should have both your address and the buyer's address so that if the label is illegible, the packing slip will identify the owner and the package can be delivered.

Of course, having the buyer's address correct on the label is critical to begin with. The following ideas and practices will help you create accurate shipping labels:

**Book VII
Chapter 3**

Insuring Your
Item's Delivery

✦ **Cut and paste the buyer's address:** The safest way to correct addressing is to cut and paste the buyer's address information from an e-mail or the PayPal payment confirmation or download. If your buyer's address shows as unconfirmed through PayPal, send a quick e-mail to your buyer to verify. People do make mistakes, even when writing their own addresses.

✦ **Don't depend on the carrier to correct an address:** No carrier is going to tell you whether the address you have is incorrect. The only time I've had inaccurate addresses corrected is when I used the DAZzle software.

✦ **Use software or online services to check your buyer's address:** It's good business practice to confirm the viability of an address before you send your item. Software such as DAZzle (from endicia.com, which I discuss in Chapter 1) corrects most common addressing errors such as misspelled city or street names. If you have a question about a ZIP code, you can check it at the post office Web site at www.usps.com/zip4. See how it corrected the city (and questions the address) in Figure 3-2?

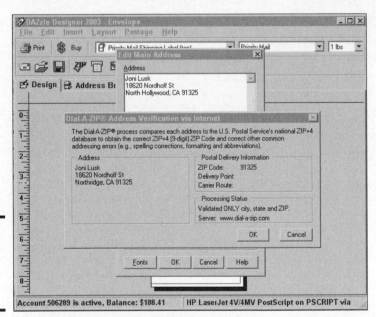

Figure 3-2: Address verification in DAZzle's Dial-A-ZIP.

If you have the Google toolbar (which I highly recommend in Book VIII), or go to www.google.com, you can type any UPS, post office, or FedEx tracking number and find the current tracking information from the carrier's Web site. Just copy and paste the tracking number into the Google search box and start your search. You'll come to a page that presents a link to track packages — with your number and carrier showing. Click the link and you end up at the carrier's site with all the current tracking information! Nice!

A couple of claim stories

Several years ago, I purchased an original-wardrobe uniform tunic from the *Star Trek* series that was framed and autographed by Leonard Nimoy. When it came, in an appropriate large box surrounded with lots of Styrofoam peanuts and bubble wrap, it also sported a 4" x 4" hole in the side, and it looked like someone had taken a sword to the box! Not only that, but there was a sad sound of glass tinkling when I shook the box. Oh, yes — the delivery man had dumped the box, rung the bell, and run.

The carrier couldn't argue about the damage. The claim department tried to give me the line that the item was packed incorrectly. (Does that mean it was sent with a big hole already in the side of the box?) Then they offered me a partial payment. Gee, I really wanted the glass-particle-infested, ripped tunic now. It took a while, but the damages were so obvious that the carrier had to give in and agreed to send a check to the seller. Upon hearing this decision, the seller refunded my payment. (I wonder how long the seller had to wait for *his* payment?)

There was also a dress that I sold and shipped Priority Mail. It never arrived. I had a boiling-hot buyer on the other end, but luckily, I had proof of mailing in the form of a delivery confirmation to show her. I nagged the post office about the package, but as you'll read in the section, "Filing a claim with the post office," you have to wait 30 days for a package to be *officially* declared lost. On the 29th day, the box was returned to me with no explanation or fanfare, and just a return-to-sender stamp on the front.

Making a Claim When Shipping Goes Bad

If you've been selling or buying on eBay for awhile, odds are you've made a claim for lost or damaged packages. The process is often grueling — with all the paperwork that's involved — and the decision of the carrier is final. If you don't agree with the carrier, you could try small claims court. But realize that you'll lose a day of work — and when you're in court, you'll face all the legalese you find in the teeny-tiny print on the carrier's terms of service.

I understand the hassles because I've had to make several claims myself. I'd like to help you avoid similar unpleasant experiences, or at least make them less unpleasant. I present information about the U.S. Postal Service first because their claim process is more stringent than that of the other carriers. With any carrier, however, you need to gather the same type of backup information before making a claim.

Filing a claim with the post office

Making a claim with the post office: Oh man, talk about a hassle. But making a claim with any carrier isn't a bowl of cherries on any day! Before making a claim with the USPS, check to make sure your package was covered by postal insurance, purchased at the time of mailing. If you use private insurance instead, you make a claim with your insurance carrier, not the post office.

When a package is lost in transit, you must wait a minimum of 30 days after the mailing date before you make the claim. If an item arrives at the buyer's door damaged, you may make a claim with the post office immediately.

There's always a question as to who makes the claim:

✦ **Damaged or lost contents:** Either the seller or the buyer can file the claim.

✦ **Complete loss:** When a package has not turned up within 30 days, the seller files the claim.

First, you must get a copy of *PS Form 1000, Domestic Claim or Registered Mail Inquiry*. Go to the post office or download it at

`http://www.usps.com/forms/_pdf/ps1000.pdf`

Fill out the form with all the details required and bring your backup information.

To make a damage claim, you must produce evidence of insurance. This can be either of the following documents:

✦ **Original mailing receipt:** The receipt that was stamped at the post office counter when the item was mailed.

✦ **Original box or wrapper:** This must show the addresses of both the sender and the recipient along with whatever tags or stamps the post office put on the package to say it's insured.

If only the box or wrapper is presented as proof of insurance, the post office will likely limit the claim to $100.

You must also produce evidence showing the value of the item *when it was mailed*. The following list shows some of the documents accepted by the post office for damage claims (however, they may ask for more thorough proof):

✦ Sales receipt or descriptive invoice

✦ Copy of your canceled check or money order receipt

✦ Picture and description of a similar item from a catalog if your receipt isn't available

✦ A letter from the seller stating the value of the item

✦ Your own description of the item, including date and time the item was purchased and whether it is new or vintage

For missing packages, you (the seller) need a letter from the buyer (dated 30 days after the package was mailed) stating that the buyer never received the package.

If your buyer is too cranky to cooperate, go to the post office where you mailed the package. Ask for a written statement that there is no record of the delivery being made. Postal employees can look up the insurance or delivery confirmation numbers to find whether the delivery took place, but the post office will charge you $6.60 for their efforts. That amount will be reimbursed if the post office pays your claim and doesn't locate your package under a bale of hay in Indiana.

If all goes well and your claim is deemed legit, you should get your payment within 30 days. If you don't hear from the post office within 45 days (maybe the payment got lost in the mail?), you have to submit a duplicate claim using the original claim number.

Note to self (and to you): Always make a copy of any form you give to the government.

Filing a claim with UPS

Whoa! The stories of filing claims with UPS are legendary. Almost any eBay seller can tell you quite a story. I must admit that making a claim with UPS is a good deal easier than making a claim with the post office. After they file and accept your damage claim, you get a check within five days.

For damaged packages, UPS recently streamlined the process, although the buyer must make the claim. You *can* (if you really want to) call 1-800-PICK-UPS (cute, eh?) to file your claim. The better idea is to go directly to the online reporting instructions at

```
www.ups.com/content/us/en/resources/service/tracking/claims.
   html
```

Be sure you make your report to UPS within 48 hours of delivery.

On the online claim form, you'll be asked to input all information about the package and the damage. UPS seems to be familiar with its own handiwork because you get to select your particular type of damage from a menu.

**Book VII
Chapter 3**

Insuring Your
Item's Delivery

Buying lost packages

When the post office pays your claim, it will usually ask to keep your item. Your item and thousands of others will end up at one of the Mail Recovery Centers across the country. Here it joins the other lost and salvage mail to be sold, usually at auction. The post office used to run these auctions on eBay under the user ID `usps-mrc-everythingelse`. I used to buy some great case lots from them and turn around and resell them on eBay!

Now the post office sells the stuff at live auctions. If you'd like to attend one, check their Web site at `www.usps.com/auctions` for dates and times. The post office always has good stuff for sale and usually in good quantity. If you're interested in buying post-office surplus (such as an old truck or supplies), check out eBay sellers `usps-ne-spring field` and `usps-al-pmsc`.

After you've filled out and submitted the form, just sit on your haunches and wait for the UPS claims department to contact you.

I recommend that you print your form after filling it out so you can keep all claim reference information in one place.

After the buyer makes the claim, UPS sends a Damage/Loss Notification Letter form to the seller. The seller must fill out the form to state the item's value and attach supporting documentation. The form can then be faxed back to UPS for final verification.

Save the damaged item and all the packaging that it came in. UPS may send an inspector out to look at the package before they approve a claim.

If a UPS shipment appears to be lost, the seller must call UPS to request a package tracer. If UPS is unable to prove delivery, the claim is paid.

Filing a claim with FedEx

Filing a claim with FedEx is similar to the UPS procedure, except FedEx gives you a little more leeway as to time. Instead of the 48-hours-after-delivery deadline, you have 15 business days to make your claim. (This extra time sure helps out when a package is delivered to your house and you're out of town.) FedEx processes all Concealed Loss and Damage claims within five to seven days after receiving all the paperwork and information.

As with UPS, keep all packaging, along with the item, in case FedEx wants to come and inspect the damage.

You can make your FedEx claim in a couple of ways:

✦ **By fax:** You can download a PDF claim form with instructions at

    `www.fedex.com/us/customer/claims/Claims.pdf`

Fill out the form and fax it to the number on the form.

✦ **Online:** Fill out the online claim form on a secure server at

    `https://www.fedex.com/us/claimsonline`

You must have a FedEx login to begin your claim. (See Chapter 2 on how to get this.) You still have to mail or fax your supporting documentation. When you file online, you can also choose to receive e-mail updates from FedEx regarding your claim (good idea).

The claim payment will be sent to the seller, so it's up to the seller to make restitution with the buyer. As the seller, you should refund the money as soon as the claim is approved.

Book VIII
Power Selling

Contents at a Glance

Chapter 1: Upgrading to eBay's Selling Manager

In This Chapter

✔ Signing up for a free trial

✔ Understanding Selling Manager features

✔ Sending invoices

✔ Tracking your payments

✔ Relisting the easy way

✔ Downloading reports

*O*nce the selling bug has bitten you, it's a natural transition to go from listing a few items a month to 50 or more. And that, dear reader, means you are officially running an eBay business. Congratulations!

There's a good and a bad side to this. The good is that you're making considerably more cash than you did before hooking up with eBay. The bad? It's time to start investing in some tools to keep your business professional.

The first tool that can help smooth your transition makes the process of running eBay auctions and sales consistent — Selling Manager.

Book III gets into eBay's free Turbo Lister program (it gets your items on the site without putting you through the slow, sometimes-torturous Sell an Item form). As with Turbo Lister, Selling Manager is a suite of tools for managing your selling business from any computer (as long as it has an Internet connection). eBay gives you 30 days to try out the service for free, thereafter charging you $4.99 per month. Believe me, the time that Selling Manager will save you is well worth the fee.

I've run well over 60 listings at a time, successfully managing them with Selling Manager Pro. I use it along with PayPal and QuickBooks (see Book IX for more about this method). This approach provides a one-stop, professional solution for my medium-size eBay business.

Trying Out Selling Manager

To download your free Selling Manager trial program, follow these steps:

1. **Click the Site map link on the eBay navigation bar, which is at the top of every eBay page.**

2. **In the middle column of the Site Map, under the Selling Tools heading, click the eBay Selling Manager link.**

3. **Read the information on the Selling Manager hub page.**

4. **Click the Subscribe Now link.**

You're now subscribed to your 30-day free trial. eBay automatically populates Selling Manager for you with your information from the My eBay Selling link. The Selling link is changed to Selling Manager.

Later in the chapter, I tell you about Selling Manager Pro. But for now, just know that there are a few differences. Selling Manager Pro gives you everything you get with Selling Manager, plus automatic listing and relisting of items, automated payment, shipping status, and feedback to buyers.

You can click the Selling Manager link to view a summary of your auction activities. Figure 1-1 shows my current Selling Manager Pro Summary page. (The Selling Manager and Selling Manager Pro pages look the same).

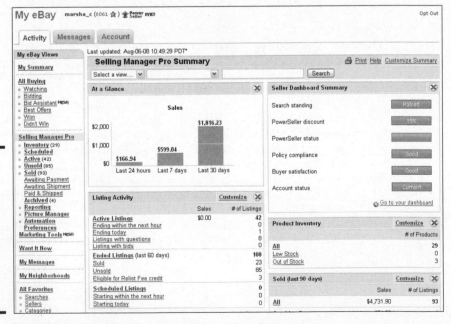

Figure 1-1: The heartbeat of my eBay business: My Selling Manager Pro Summary page.

The Summary page lists at-a-glance statistics so I can see what's going on with my sales quickly, at any time — from any computer. Links to other pages in the Selling Manager tool are also included.

TIP

If you plan to exceed 75 transactions at a time, consider using Selling Manager Pro; it has bulk feedback and bulk invoice-printing features. You can also go off-eBay to a third-party solution.

Selling Manager Features

A versatile program, the standard version of Selling Manager allows you to monitor or automate many of the more tedious eBay tasks. The My eBay Views section on the left has nine main headings.

At a Glance

We all like to know how we're doing, and the *At A Glance* area allows you to do just that. A bar chart (see Figure 1-2) that shows sales for the last 24 hours, last 7 days, and last 30 days is integrated with eBay so there's no lag time from selling to viewing.

Figure 1-2: You can see your sales figures on the fly in this area.

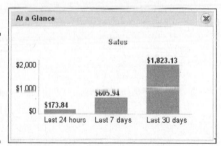

Seller Dashboard summary

The Seller Dashboard gives you a good way to check your status on eBay. As shown in Figure 1-3, the dashboard covers the all important results of the DSR ratings you get from your buyers. It also keeps you apprised of whether you're following eBay's policies or, instead, have violated any in the recent past.

If you're a PowerSeller, you also see your DSR-based Final Value Fee discount (more on that in Book VIII, Chapter 4) as well as your PowerSeller standing. If you're not a PowerSeller, these areas will indicate just that.

At the bottom of the Seller Dashboard Summary is a link that takes you to the official dashboard. Click it, and you see a page like the one in Figure 1-4. Here you can find out the details of what makes you a good seller in eBay's eyes — and your customers' eyes, too.

Figure 1-3: My current Seller Dashboard Summary.

Figure 1-4: My Seller Dashboard page, showing details of my eBay reputation.

Don't obsess about your dashboard. Okay, I did (and still do sometimes). Check it once a week. Bottom line: If you're doing the best job you can, there's not much more you can do to change things. If your dashboard indicates a problem with your sales; once a week is good enough to evaluate and make the necessary changes to your system.

Listing Activity

An important box on the Selling Manager page is Listing Activity. You'll get some valuable information there. It references what you did — or didn't — sell, along with even more stats on your sales. The next sections describe the activities you can view.

Scheduled listings

The Scheduled Listings link on the Summary page takes you to any auction, fixed-price, or store listing you've sent to eBay through Turbo Lister (or listed on the Sell an Item page) and scheduled for a later starting date or time. You can also view these pending (scheduled) listings through links that narrow them to listings that start within the next hour — or start today.

When you enter the Scheduled Listings area (by clicking the Scheduled Listings link), you can go directly to any of your listings If you want to promote your listing-to-be in a banner ad (or create a link to it from elsewhere on the Internet), you can do so using the URL of the pending listing. (See Book VI for more information on promoting your eBay business.)

From the Scheduled Listings page, you can confirm all information about the sale, as well as make any changes to the listing or to the scheduling time.

Active listings

Click the Active Listings link on the Summary page, and you can observe the bidding action just as you can from the My eBay Selling page. The color-coding that indicates bidding activity is the same as on the My eBay Selling page. (If the current price is in green and bolded, your item has a bid and the number reflects the high bid. The current price is in red if there are no bids in an auction.) Your listings are accessible with a click of your mouse.

You have the option to show only auctions, store listings, or fixed-price items on the Active Listings page. You can also search your own listings by keyword or item number.

For more about active listings, visit the Summary page, which includes links to items ending within the hour and within the next 24 hours.

Ended listings

You can really access your Ended listings from the links on the left side of the page. But the important link here is the link to *Eligible for Relist Fee credit*. This link will conveniently take you to the listings that you can relist, and if they sell the second time, eBay will refund you initial listings fees.

**Book VIII
Chapter 1**

Upgrading to eBay's
Selling Manager

You need to know that to be eligible for relisting credit, the item gets only one shot at reselling. If it's been relisted twice, you need to start the listing again by using the *Sell Similar* link. The Sell Similar link (versus the Relist link) starts the transaction in a new cycle for the eBay servers, thereby making it eligible for the relisting credit if it doesn't sell.

Sold

The Sold Listings feature (which you get to by clicking the Sold Listings link on the Summary page), is where Selling Manager really shines. You'll find quite a few links here, including these:

✦ **Awaiting payment:** This is where items that have been won or bought are shown before a payment is made.

✦ **Buyers Eligible for combined purchases:** Here you'll see when a buyer buys more than one item from you (yay!) and you need to combine the items into a single invoice. Otherwise the buyer may pay you once for each transaction — and then you'll incur extra transaction fees from PayPal. Also, combined purchases help if you want to give your good customers a break on shipping.

✦ **Awaiting Shipment:** Once a buyer has sent payment through PayPal, the transaction automatically moves to this category.

✦ **Paid and Shipped:** After an item is paid for, a reference to it appears here so you can keep track of the feedback you need to leave.

✦ **Dispute Console:** This is where you turn in non-paying buyers and start an Unpaid Item Dispute.

My eBay Views links

On the left side of the My eBay page, you see more links for Selling Manager: Unsold items (for relisting), Archived items, and eBay's Picture Manager photo-hosting solution. From the Archived link, you can access completed items that closed within the last four months. You can also download this information to your computer. There are good records here, so you should download and keep them. For more on what you can do with these records, see Book IX.

Seller tools links

Scroll down the page and you'll see the Seller Tools box on the left side of the Summary page. It's a powerful group of links that allow you to download and export your sales history to your computer. You also have quick links to PayPal, Picture Manager, Accounting Assistant (see Book IX for more on Accounting Assistant), My eBay Store, and the good old My eBay Selling page — in case you get nostalgic for the old, pre-Selling Manager days.

Working your Dispute Console

I hate to see items in the Sold Listings Past Due area of the Summary page, because it means there's a good chance I'm not going to get paid for an item. I always keep an eye on my Sold, Awaiting Payment items and send out a payment reminder when three days has passed. If seven days pass without payment, the item drops into Sold Listings Past Due: Unpaid and becomes eligible for an unpaid item reminder.

✔ **Eligible for unpaid item dispute:** This is where the items awaiting payment fall when they become eligible for you to file a Non-Paying Bidder alert. This happens when 7 days have passed without a payment being received.

✔ **Disputes awaiting your response:** After you've filed an unpaid-item reminder, the item goes into this area. It links to a dispute page that lists all outstanding disputes. The buyer has the right to answer your dispute here — and you can answer that answer.

✔ **Eligible for Final Value fee credit:** This is the sad category where buyers from the Non-Paying Bidder column go if, after all your attempts to get action, they haven't responded and haven't sent payment. (If they don't cough up within 10 days after you file a Non-Paying Bidder Alert, the listing moves to this category automatically.)

✔ **Items not received or not as described.** Here's where you can see if a buyer has ratted you out to eBay for an item that hasn't shown up when expected. (Surprisingly, some buyers think their items should arrive within 48 hours of winning.) Or it could be lost in the mail. This is the area where you can see the disputes against you.

Manage My Store

If you have an eBay store, you'll see a box with all the links you need to manage your store, as shown in Figure 1-5. You can access reports, e-mail marketing tools, Markdown Manager, and more. (See Book VIII Chapter 6 for more on the eBay Store tools.)

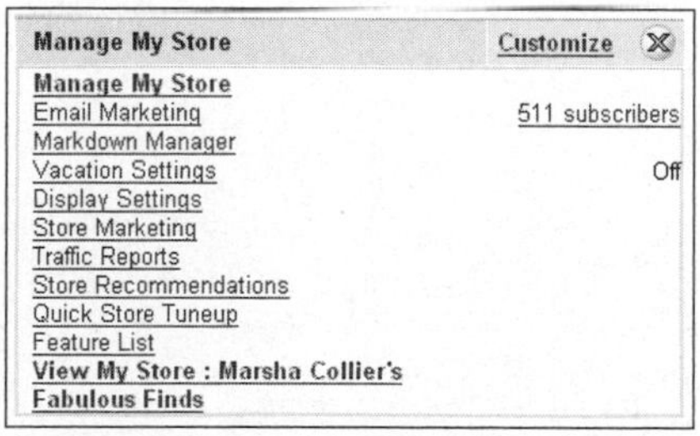

Figure 1-5: The Manage My Store links box.

Auto-Sending Invoices

One of my favorite features of Selling Manager is that I can follow the progress of my sales from the Summary page. When an item has been won or paid for using PayPal, I can click the appropriate link to see the list of items ready for an action (such as shipping!). Figure 1-6 shows my Sold Items: Paid & Waiting to Ship area in Selling Manager.

Selling Manager's customizable e-mail templates

Selling Manager has seven e-mail templates that you can quickly and easily customize. These templates allow you to add *auto text*, information that eBay's server fills in for that particular transaction. Note in the figure the drop-down list, which provides shortcuts to edit the eBay-supplied templates. When a winner buys an item, I have a preformatted winning buyer-notification letter I created from one of these templates. When a winner pays immediately using PayPal, I also have a payment-received e-mail.

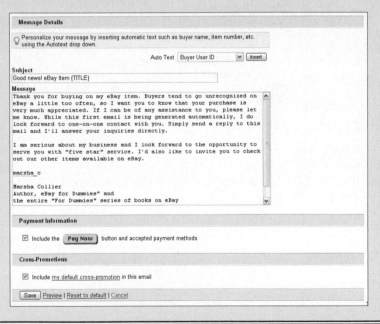

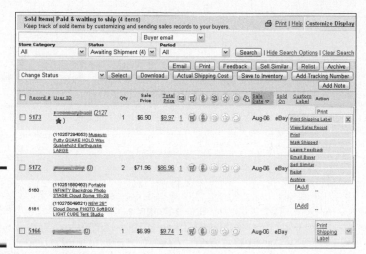

Figure 1-6:
Sold and
ready to
ship.

Notice the record number next to the winner's e-mail address. To send an e-mail or invoice, follow these steps:

1. **Click the record number to the left of the buyer's e-mail address.**

The sales record for that transaction appears. You see the items sold to that buyer, as shown in Figure 1-7. If the buyer has made more than one purchase, you'll see a notation stating as much. You then have the option to click the link to combine purchases in the sales record.

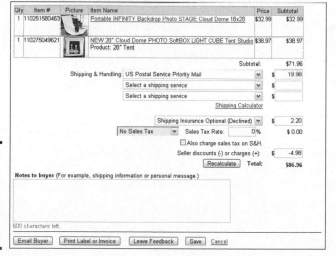

Figure 1-7:
Item
summary
and the
Email Buyer
button.

2. **Click the E-Mail button.**

3. **Select the appropriate e-mail template to send.**

   If you want, you can personalize the e-mail by altering one of the templates that Selling Manager supplies. (See the "Selling Manager's customizable e-mail templates" sidebar for details.)

4. **When you're ready to send the e-mail, click Send.**

Tracking Payments

Selling Manager makes many selling processes considerably easier. Take a look your Selling Manager Summary page. From here, you can see how many buyers have paid for their purchases — and, sadly, how many haven't.

If you're expecting payments, be sure to check the Summary page several times a day. When a buyer makes his or her payment using PayPal, eBay will update your records. (PayPal also sends you a payment received e-mail, but this type of notification is often late.)

After you ship the item, you can indicate that on the Sales Status & Notes screen, shown in Figure 1-8. The transaction information in Figure 1-8 is available when you click the record number next to the item that's been shipped. If you ship the item, input that info, and click Save, the record will move from the Sold Listings, Paid and Ready to Ship page to the Paid and Shipped page. This change will also be reflected on the Summary page.

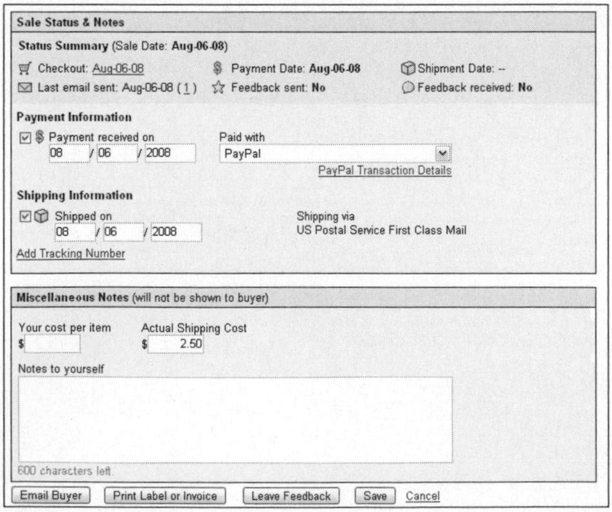

Figure 1-8: You can edit sales-record information.

Relisting

Wouldn't it be better if you could select a whole bunch of items and relist them all together? Step up to Selling Manager for a one-click option.

You can access items that have not sold, logically enough, from the Unsold Items area (as shown in Figure 1-9). Relisting is accomplished with a click of the mouse!

Let me stress the difference between Relisting and Sell Similar. You need to *relist* an item that hasn't sold so you can get a refund on your listing fees if it sells the second time. (This doesn't work on the third try.) When an item has been sold, you use the Sell Similar link to start the listing in a new cycle in eBay's master computers. That way, if it doesn't sell, you'll be able to relist and take advantage of the possible refund.

To relist an item (or Sell Similar) through Selling Manager, follow these steps:

1. **Go to the Unsold Items listings.**

   To do so, click the links in the Selling Manager box on the left of the page (or just link through the summary).

2. **Select the items to relist (or Sell Similar) by selecting the check box next to each item's Title.**

   You may select any or all of the items listed on the page.

3. **Click the Relist button (or the Sell Similar button).**

   The Relist Multiple Items page appears.

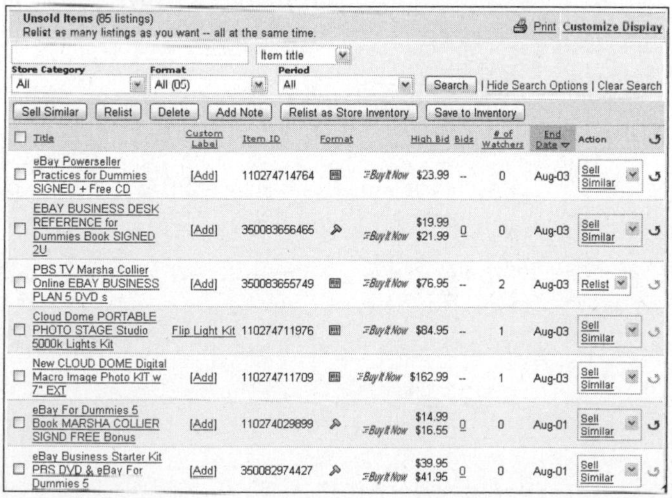

**Book VIII
Chapter 1**

**Upgrading to eBay's
Selling Manager**

Figure 1-9:
Relisting
from the
Unsold
Items page.

Unsold Items (85 listings)									

Relist as many listings as you want -- all at the same time.   🖨 Print Customize Display

Store Category	Format	Period							
All	All (85)	All	Search	Hide Search Options	Clear Search				

[Sell Similar] [Relist] [Delete] [Add Note] [Relist as Store Inventory] [Save to Inventory]

☐ Title	Custom Label	Item ID	Format	High Bid	Bids	# of Watchers	End Date ▽	Action	↻
☐ eBay Powerseller Practices for Dummies SIGNED + Free CD	[Add]	110274714764	🖩 =BuyItNow	$23.99	--	0	Aug-03	Sell Similar ▾	↻
☐ EBAY BUSINESS DESK REFERENCE for Dummies Book SIGNED 2U	[Add]	350083656465	🔨 =BuyItNow	$19.99 $21.99	0	0	Aug-03	Sell Similar ▾	↻
☐ PBS TV Marsha Collier Online EBAY BUSINESS PLAN 5 DVD s	[Add]	350083655749	🔨 =BuyItNow	$76.95	--	2	Aug-03	Relist ▾	↻
☐ Cloud Dome PORTABLE PHOTO STAGE Studio 5000k Lights Kit	Flip Light Kit	110274711976	🖩 =BuyItNow	$84.95	--	1	Aug-03	Sell Similar ▾	↻
☐ New CLOUD DOME Digital Macro Image Photo KIT w 7" EXT	[Add]	110274711709	🖩 =BuyItNow	$162.99	--	1	Aug-03	Sell Similar ▾	↻
☐ eBay For Dummies 5 Book MARSHA COLLIER SIGND FREE Bonus	[Add]	110274029899	🔨 =BuyItNow	$14.99 $16.55	0	0	Aug-01	Sell Similar ▾	↻
☐ eBay Business Starter Kit PBS DVD & eBay For Dummies 5	[Add]	350082974427	🔨 =BuyItNow	$39.95 $41.95	0	0	Aug-01	Sell Similar ▾	↻

4. **Review all the items listed (along with the fees).**

5. **Submit the items by clicking the Submit Listing button.**

Figure 1-10 shows a portion of the Relist Multiple Items page that includes a complete review of the details of each item. If you proceed at this point, the items will be relisted exactly as you had them listed before. At the bottom of the list, eBay recaps all relisting fees.

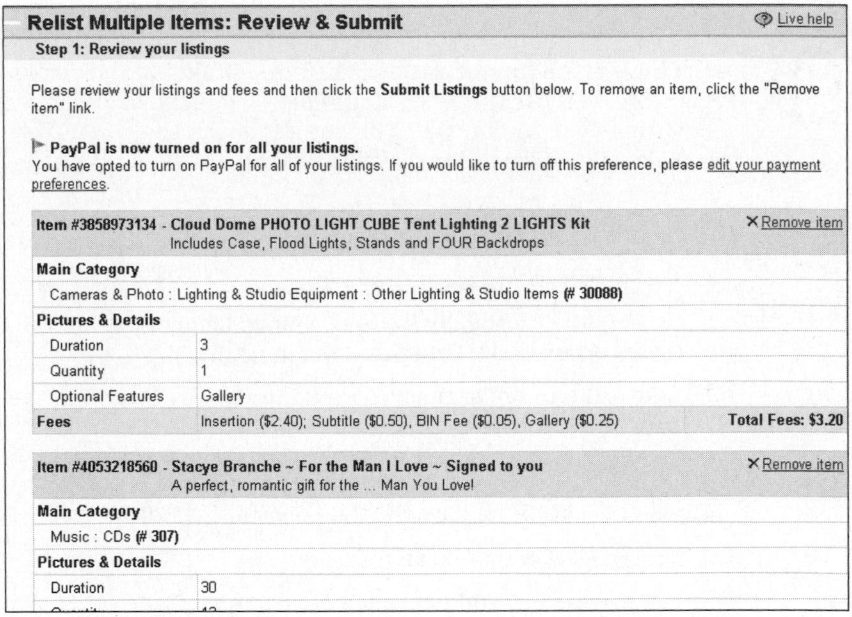

Figure 1-10: Relisting several items at once.

Selling Manager Reports

I like Selling Manager because it gives you the opportunity to keep all your selling information in one place. It also provides a downloadable report in a spreadsheet format that you can archive for your business records. Here is the information you can expect to find in the report:

✦ **Sales record number:** The number assigned to the transaction by Selling Manager for identification purposes.

✦ **User ID:** The eBay user ID of the person who purchased the item from you.

✦ **Buyer zip:** The buyer's ZIP code.

- ✦ **State:** The state the buyer resides in.

- ✦ **Buyer country:** The country your buyer lives in.

- ✦ **Item number:** The eBay number assigned to the item when you listed it for sale on the site.

- ✦ **Item title:** The title of the listing as it appeared on eBay.

- ✦ **Quantity:** The number of items purchased in the transaction.

- ✦ **Sale price:** The final selling price of the item.

- ✦ **Shipping amount:** The amount you charged for shipping the item.

- ✦ **Shipping insurance:** If the buyer paid insurance, it's listed next to his or her sales record.

- ✦ **State sales tax:** If you've set up Selling Manager to calculate sales tax for your in-state sales, and sales tax was applied to the item when it was sold, that amount is listed here.

- ✦ **Total price:** The GSA (gross sales amount) for the transaction.

- ✦ **Payment method:** The method of payment used by the buyer. This is inserted automatically if the item is paid through PayPal, or manually inserted by you into the sales record if paid by another method.

- ✦ **Sale date:** The date the transaction occurred on eBay.

- ✦ **Checkout:** The date of checkout. This is usually the same as the transaction date.

- ✦ **Paid on date:** The date the buyer paid for the item.

- ✦ **Shipped on date:** The ship date you entered in Selling Manager.

- ✦ **Feedback left:** Whether you left feedback for the buyer is indicated by a Yes or No in this column.

- ✦ **Feedback received:** The feedback rating left for you by the buyer (positive, negative, or neutral).

- ✦ **Notes to yourself:** If you input any personal notes regarding the transaction in the sales record, they appear here.

Keep in mind that Selling Manager reports are available on the site for only four months, so be sure to download your information regularly.

Notice that there is no column reflecting the eBay fees you paid for listing and selling the item. If you have plenty of time on your hands, you can create another column and input the fees from your eBay invoice for each item. Save time by posting the monthly total once a month in your bookkeeping program.

**Book VIII
Chapter 1**

Upgrading to eBay's
Selling Manager

To get the file from eBay to your computer, follow these steps:

1. **From your My eBay page, click the Selling Manager link.**

The opening page of Selling Manager is your Summary page.

2. **Under Seller Tools, click the File Management Center link.**

This takes you to the File Management Center.

3. **Click the Create a Download Request link.**

A Create a Download Request page appears, as shown in Figure 1-11.

Create a Download Request

Select active listings and sales history records that you want to download.
Note: Your sales records are available for the current month and the past three calendar months.

Listings and records
Sold

Date Range
○ All records
○ All new records since last download only (Last downloaded: May-01-08 00:00:00 PDT)
○ From Yesterday

⊙   August   1   2008   at 12:00 AM   US Time (PST)
From
    To August   6   2008   at 12:00 AM   US Time (PST)

Email address
mcollier@coolebaytools.com
Your downloads will be sent to this email address. Separate multiple email addresses with commas.

Save Cancel
Note: Downloads may take a day past your scheduled time to become available.

4. **Select the listings and records you want from the drop-down menu.**

Your e-mail address is already filled in, but you may add another if you want duplicate notifications.

5. **Select the time period you want to include in your report.**

It's best to generate monthly or quarterly reports, so that your reports coincide with specific tax periods. You can always combine more than one report in your spreadsheet program to show different periods of time.

6. **Click the Save button.**

You then see a confirmation page and a confirmation number for your request. eBay will send you an e-mail when your report is ready.

7. **You will receive an e-mail (almost immediately).**

   Click the link in the e-mail, and you're taken to the View Completed Downloads page.

8. **Click the link to download the file.**

   The Save As dialog box appears, as shown in Figure 1-12.

9. **Rename the file to reflect the sales month and year, and then click Save.**

   After the file is downloaded, you'll see a confirmation with your new filename.

It's a good idea to create a directory on your computer with a name such as eBay Sales. In this directory, you can store all the reports you download from eBay, PayPal, or any other online service. Be sure to include this directory when you perform regular data backups.

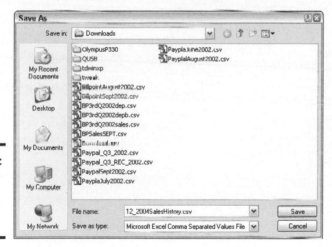

Figure 1-12: Downloading my eBay Sales report.

Now you can open the new file in Microsoft Excel or Microsoft Works. It will look similar to Figure 1-13.

	A	B	C	D	E	F	G	H	I	J	K
2	Sales	User Id	Buyer Zip	State	Buyer Country	Item Number	Item Title	Quar	Sale Price	Shipping a	US Ta:
3											
4	724		40380	KY	United States	3576574627	Author SIGNED 2U eBay	1	$19.99	$4.95	$0.
5	725		92169	CA	United States	2975999491	NEW YEAR Keychain A	1	$12.09	$3.00	$1.
6	726		53706	WI	United States	2974745375	Cloud Dome Background	1	$36.99	$9.35	$0.
7	727		75025	TX	United States	2975999490	FREE SHIP Cloud Dome	1	$165.99	$0.00	$0.
8	728		12033	NY	United States	2975260136	2 Photography Photo Lig	1	$150.00	$23.90	$0.
9	729		22801	VA	United States	2931822191	un-du Adhesive Remover	3	$4.99	$4.75	$0.
10	730		83702	ID	United States	2976544136	2 Photography Photo Lig	1	$120.99	$16.75	$0.
11	731		19462	PA	United States	2966720670	eBay TIPS for Dummies	1	$4.50	$2.00	$0.
12	732		47203	IN	United States	2976544136	2 Photography Photo Lig	1	$120.99	$23.90	$0.
13	733		53593	WI	United States	2964392864	CLOUD DOME Complete	1	$232.99	$15.00	$0.
14	734		66801	KS	United States	2964392864	CLOUD DOME Complete	1	$232.99	$15.00	$0.
15	735		40383	ky	United States	2966720670	eBay TIPS for Dummies	1	$4.50	$2.00	$0.
16	736		85210	AZ	United States	2979287892	Cloud Dome Background	1	$36.99	$7.55	$0.
17	737		11944	NY	United States	2966720670	eBay TIPS for Dummies	1	$4.50	$2.00	$0.
18	738		94022	CA	United States	2964392864	CLOUD DOME Complete	1	$232.99	$15.00	$19.
19	739		1089	MA	United States	2976009854	eBay Sellers Steel Rollir	1	$21.99	$15.55	$0.
20	740		29033	SC	United States	3578659417	Starting an Ebay Busine	1	$21.99	$4.95	$0.
21	741		92064	CA	United States	3578660928	eBay TIPS for Dummies	1	$5.50	$2.00	$0.
22	742		20003	DC	United States	3580553691	eBay TIPS for Dummies	1	$5.00	$2.00	$0.
23	743		76904	TX	United States	2964392864	CLOUD DOME Complete	1	$232.99	$15.00	$0.
24	744		75650-611	TX	United States	2977621063	FREE SHIP Cloud Dome	1	$159.99	$0.00	$0.
25	745		98023	WA	United States	2966720670	eBay TIPS for Dummies	1	$4.50	$2.00	$0.
26	746		95460	CA	United States	2978127410	eBay Sellers Steel Rollir	1	$22.99	$11.30	$1.
27	747		98290	WA	United States	2980166675	FREE SHIP Cloud Dome	1	$170.99	$0.00	$0.
28	748		45601	OH	United States	2966720670	eBay TIPS for Dummies	1	$4.50	$2.00	$0.

Figure 1-13:
My imported
eBay sales
report.

With simple spreadsheet commands, you can customize the look of your report. For example, if the column for Buyer Country is unnecessary for your records (you ship only within the United States, so the information is not useful), you can delete the column in to quick steps:

1. **Highlight the column by clicking the column letter.**

2. **Choose Edit⇨Delete.**

   Voilá! The offending column is no more.

All spreadsheet tasks mentioned here can be performed in similar fashion in Microsoft Works or Excel.

The spreadsheet generated by Selling Manger is much more useful if you total the columns. That way, you can see your total sales at a glance. To total a spreadsheet column:

1. **Click in the blank box at the bottom of the column you want to total.**

2. **Click the AutoSum button.**

3. **Click and drag over the cells you want to sum.**

4. **Press Enter, and the total appears.**

If you want to total the columns next to the one you just totaled, you don't have to re-input the formula. Just highlight the results cell from your last formula, and highlight cells in the same row that you want to contain totals of the columns. Then choose Edit⇨Fill⇨Right, as shown in Figure 1-14. This copies the formula to the connecting cells and all the columns are totaled.

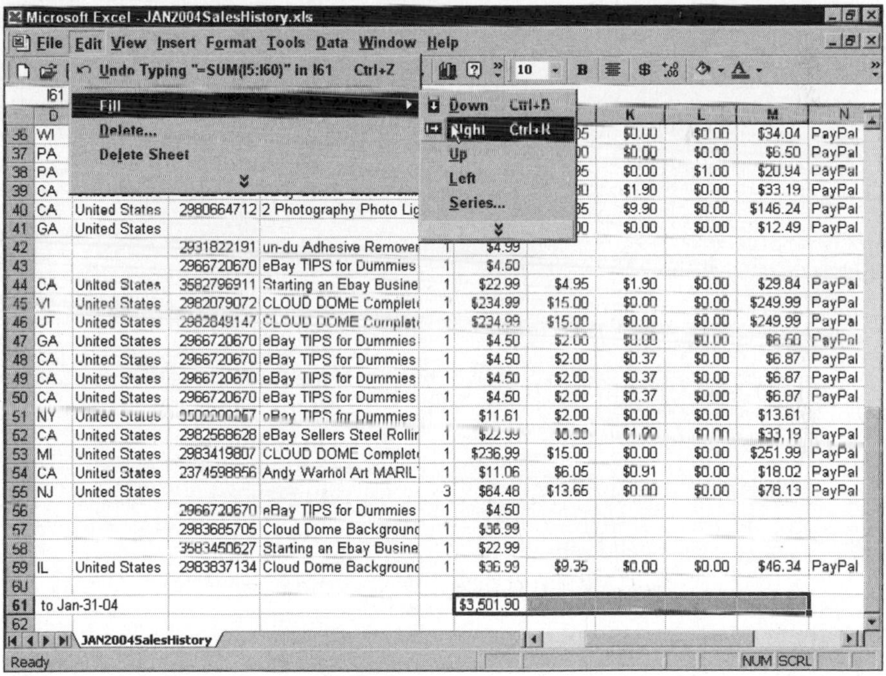

Figure 1-14:
Totaling the
columns.

Chapter 2: Managing Your Business with Third-Party Tools

In This Chapter

✔ Deciding among the available tools

✔ Checking out auction management services

✔ Figuring out what tasks you can automate

✔ Getting bonded for good measure

When you get to the point of running up to 20 auctions at a time, I highly recommend that you begin to use a management tool. At this level of activity, using eBay's Selling Manager will suit you nicely, and I go over how Selling Manager works in Chapter 1. But when your eBay business begins to push 100 listings a week, I recommend that you get additional help in the form of an auction-management service or software.

Whether you use an online service or software residing on your own computer is a personal decision. You may find it easier to use an online system because you can log on to your selling information at any time from any computer. But if you have a slow Internet connection or pay usage fees by the hour, managing your eBay business online can become impractical.

Most desktop-based software packages have features that enable you to do your work on your computer and then upload (or download) your data when you go online. If having multiple locations to work from is not important, and you run your eBay business from a single computer in your office, you may feel more comfortable with a desktop-based software product.

In either case, if your business has reached the level where you need an auction-management tool, congratulations! In this chapter, I want to save you some time finding the service or software that's right for you. I outline some of the tasks that an auction-management product should provide, and compare prices of several services.

Choosing Your Auction-Management Tools

If you searched the Internet for auction-management services and software, you'd come up with a bunch. For simplicity's sake, I've chosen to examine just a few of these services in this chapter. After speaking to many sellers, I've found online services that offer two important features:

✦ Uptime reliability (uptime is vital here; you don't want the server that holds your photos going down or mislaunching your auctions)

✦ Software that's continually updated to match changes to eBay

Using a site or software to run your auctions takes practice, so I suggest that you try any that appeal to you and offer free preview trials. As I describe these different applications, I include a link so you can check them out further.

Some software and services work on a monthly fee; others work on a one-time purchase fee. For a one-time-purchase software application to truly benefit you, it *must* have the reputation for updating its software each time eBay makes a change in its system. The programs I discuss in this chapter have been upgraded continually to date.

Most services have a free trial period. Be sure that you don't spend a bunch of your precious time inputting your entire inventory, only to discover you don't like the way the service works. Instead, input a few items to give the service a whirl.

There's a huge difference between auction-*listing* software and sites and auction-*management* products. For many a seller, listing software like eBay's Turbo Lister (see Book III, Chapter 4) may just do the trick. Combine that with eBay's Selling Manager (a *management* program) and your eBay business will be humming along just fine.

When your business activity level increases and you turn to an auction-management solution for your eBay business, you should look for certain standard features (described next). Also consider what information management features you currently have through your bookkeeping program (see Book IX). You have the data there, regardless of whether you use it in a management solution.

Many of the products listed have several pricing tiers, so Table 2-1 provides the link to the product's pricing page. I've also listed the minimum price for each company's *management* products. Some offer less expensive options for listing your auctions (with templates and all kinds of swell bells and whistles), but the price shown in the table is for the minimum management product.

Third-party checkout phases out?

Have you ever purchased anything on eBay only to be directed off the eBay site to checkout? I've always hated this — and the checkout didn't work for me about 50% of the time. I felt more secure with my purchases when the checkout and payment was performed all on eBay and PayPal.

Sellers used this third-party checkout to mechanize their e-mail lists and to upsell you to more items — which would not be covered by the Fraud Protection because they were bought off the eBay site.

eBay's Trust and Safety department took the buyers' woes to heart, and to give the site a better buyer experience, announced they may discontinue third-party checkout in mid-2009.

Some of the official reasons for the phase-out are as follows:

- Lack of trust by buyers in "off-eBay" checkout
- Lack of consistency in the checkout process among eBay providers
- Higher-than-anticipated failures during the checkout process

At one time, third-party checkout was a highly touted and well used "feature" of auction-management providers. It also easily enables the buyer to use a credit card for payment rather than using PayPal. PayPal/eBay checkout currently provides for all of this while keeping the buyer in a trusted environment.

Table 2-1	Desktop Auction-Management Software		
Name	*URL*	*Prices Start At*	*Image Hosting Included*
AAA Seller	www.aaaseller.com	$9.95/month	Yes
AuctionHawk	http://www.auction hawk.com/html/ pricing.html	$12.99/month	Yes
AuctionTamer	http://www.auction tamer.com/auction/ purchase.asp	$22.95/year	No
Auction Wizard 2000	www.auctionwizard 2000.com	$100 first year, $50 renewal	No
Auctiva	www.auctiva.com	Free	Yes
Shooting Star	www.foodogsoft ware.com	$120.00 first year $60.00 renewal	

Certifying a Certified Provider

eBay endorsement is something I've wanted to talk about for a long time. I get e-mails upon e-mails from people asking me about one company or another, telling me a particular company is

✔ Recommended by eBay

✔ Endorsed by eBay

✔ Owned by eBay (because the eBay logo appears in the Web site)

None of the above is ever true. There is a Certified Provider program from eBay where eBay qualifies businesses who want to do business with the eBay community. Note that I used the word *qualify*. That does not mean *endorse*.

By having the Certified Provider program, eBay manages to keep the very worst of the worst from aligning themselves with eBay. The initial requirement (as stated by eBay) is "Participants *(in the program)* must have extensive experience with eBay, pass a strict certification exam and provide a number of proven customer references that are checked by eBay."

That description (again) does not say *endorsed*, *approved*, or any other title implying formal authorization by eBay. It only says that participants have passed an eBay exam, proved references, and paid their fee. The best way to check out one of eBay's providers is to find other sellers who've done business with them and get their feedback (not necessarily the ones the provider supplies to you). Whenever I do business with someone who gives eBay advice, I run a Google search on the company's name (or their eBay User ID) and the word *fraud* to see whether they've been involved in any fraudulent activities that haven't been made widely public.

Never choose auction-management tools on the sole basis of price. Go to the various Web sites and take a look at everything they offer for the price stated. You may find out that a service charging a bit more may just be worth it because of all the extra tools offered.

Looking for Essential Features

Here are some must-have features to look for when you evaluate the offerings of auction-management services and products:

✦ **Image hosting:** Some Web sites dazzle you with high-megabyte storage numbers. Keep one thing in mind: If your average eBay image is around 40 K, you could store 128 pictures in a 5MB storage space and about 2500 images in a 100MB storage space. Unless you're a big-time seller, you really don't need that much space. Your eBay images should be archived on your computer (how about in a folder called eBay Images?). Images for current listings should be on the hosted site — only while the transaction is in progress. After the buyer has the item and all is well, you can remove the images from the remote server.

You probably already have free image hosting on your ISP's Web site, as noted in Book V.

✦ **Designing listings:** The basis of most of these products is a good listing function. You'll be able to select from supplied templates or design your own and store them for future use. An important feature now coming into use is a spell checker. There's nothing worse than a misspelling in a listing!

✦ **Uploading listings:** Most products have a feature that launches a group of listings to eBay all at once. They may also allow you to schedule auctions to get underway at a prescribed time.

You can also expect to be able to put together your listings at your leisure offline and upload them to your service. Most products archive your past listings so that you can relist at any time. Many services also offer bulk relisting.

✦ **E-mail management:** You can expect to be provided with sample e-mail letters (templates) that you can customize with your own look and feel. The services should also offer auto-generated e-mails for end-of-auction, payment received, and shipping.

✦ **Feedback automation:** Post feedback in bulk to a number of your completed listings, or leave predesigned feedback for each, one by one. Some products support automatic positive feedback that kicks in when a buyer leaves you positive feedback.

✦ **Sales reports:** Some services (even the least expensive) offer you some sort of sales analysis. Be sure to take into account how much you really need this feature, basing your estimate on data that you may already receive from QuickBooks, PayPal, eBay Stores, or SquareTrade.

Exploring Advanced Features

Depending on the type of business you run, you may need some of the more advanced features offered by management products:

✦ **Inventory tools:** Management products may allow you to create inventory records for your different products, such that you can click a bunch of them to list them automatically. When an item is sold, the tool deducts the item from your inventory automatically.

✦ **Sales-tax tracking and invoicing:** With full management, you can expect your sales tax to be calculated into your invoices and complete line-item invoices to be sent automatically. Multiple items, when purchased by the same buyer, will be combined.

✦ **Consignment tracking:** If you're a Trading Assistant, be sure to look for a product that enables you to separately track the products you sell for different clients. You should also be able to produce reports of consignment sales by customer.

✦ **Shipping:** Most of the services will give you the option of printing your packing lists and shipping labels directly from the product. Some of the larger services integrate with the major shippers, allowing you to go directly to particular shippers' sites and ship your items using their software.

Table 2-2 gives you the dollars and cents of subscribing to the various online and offline services. To put together this table, I disregarded lower subscription levels, where companies offered only listing products. These are the lowest prices for products that are truly management tools.

Table 2-2	Third-Party Auction Management Solutions		
Name	*URL*	*Prices Start At*	*Image Hosting*
ChannelAdvisor MarketplaceAdvisor	`www.channel advisor.com/ marketplaces/ mpa.htm`	$29.95/month	Yes
InkFrog	`www1.inkfrog. com`	$9.95/month	Yes
Meridian	`http://www. noblespirit. com/products- pricing.html`	$9.95/month	Yes
Vendio	`http://www. vendio.com/ pricing.html`	$14.95 $0.06/listing Final Value Fee: 1%	No

Opting for Online Auction Management

You may want to run your business from any computer, anywhere in the world. If that's the case, you might do best with an online service. Auction-management Web sites handle almost everything, from inventory management to label printing. Some sellers prefer online (or hosted) management sites because you can access your information from any computer. You might use every feature a site offers, or you might choose a bit from column A and a bit from column B and perform the more personalized tasks manually. Read on to determine what service might best suit your needs.

Although quite a few excellent online services for automating sales are available, I have room here to show you only a few. Many services are similar in format, so in the following sections I point out some of the highlights of a few representative systems.

When you use an online service, your information resides on a server out there in cyberspace; if you're a control freak, that may be a bit much to bear.

When selecting a service, look for a logo or text indicating that the service is an eBay Certified Developer, Preferred Solution Provider, or API licensee. These people have first access to eBay's system changes and can implement them immediately. Others may have a day or so lag time to update their software.

ChannelAdvisor Marketplaces

ChannelAdvisor's founder Scot Wingo got into the auction business around the turn of the century. His first foray into the eBay world was AuctionRover (founded in July 1999), a site that had tools to perform an extensive eBay search, list auctions, and check pricing trends. The company's cute Rover logo was fashioned after Wingo's Border Collie, Mack.

Fast forward to today. ChannelAdvisor is a highly popular management service for all levels of eBay sellers. They supply listing and management services to everyone from Fortune 1000 companies to the little old lady next door. How? They offer two levels of software: MarketplaceAdvisor Premium for midsized to large businesses and higher-level PowerSellers, and MarketplaceAdvisor for small businesses and individuals. These powerful software suites help eBay sellers successfully manage and automate the sale of their merchandise.

Starting at the entry level, you can get the MarketplaceAdvisor for $29.95 a month. Here's what they offer the beginning-level seller:

+ **Listing design and launching:** Create your listings with their standard templates or use your own HTML to design auction descriptions. List your items immediately or schedule a listing. ChannelAdvisor will launch the auction when you tell it to.

+ **Item and inventory management:** If you want to keep your inventory online, you can create it on the MarketplaceAdvisor system. If you want to input your inventory offline, you can import it from their Excel template. You can also import open auctions or store listings to your ChannelAdvisor account for relisting or servicing.

+ **Image hosting:** You get 250 MB of space to host your images. You can upload images to the site four at a time, or use FTP to upload a large quantity.

+ **Post-auction management:** This function merges your winning auction information and generates customized e-mail and invoices to your buyers. You can print mailing labels too.

Book VIII Chapter 2

Managing Your Business with Third-Party Tools

TIP

To tour the various offerings of ChannelAdvisor and find out about their free trial period, visit their Web site (as in Figure 2-1):

www.channeladvisor.com

Figure 2-1:
Channel
Advisor's
home page
gets you
started
quickly.

Vendio

I have fond memories of the early days on AuctionWeb (the forerunner of eBay). Some are especially about the other folks I met when we were all beginning. The site (originally AuctionWatch), was founded in summer of 1998 as a message board for online sellers. In 1999, when I was struggling to get out the first edition of *eBay for Dummies,* Mark Dodd and Rodrigo Salas were laying hands on multiple millions from venture capitalists to begin a new auction-service site.

Hard work pays off, because today that site is Vendio — and it has served more than a million sellers over the years to improve their bottom line. One of the things that make Vendio (shown in Figure 2-2) unique is their range of offerings. In addition to auction management, Vendio has a full complement of research tools and other offerings. Each tool, should you choose to use it, is offered *a la carte.*

Here are just a few features of their auction-management suite:

✦ **Item and inventory management:** Keep track of your items and launch with a click from their site.

✦ **Image hosting:** For eBay auctions, image hosting is based on how much you need at a time. For $2.95 a month, you can store up to 3 MB of pictures.

✦ **Auction reporting:** Generates accounts receivable, item history, and post-sales reports from the Reports area. Reports include customizable views of your sales data, item and auction data, accounts receivable, and sales tax.

✦ **Templates and listing:** Over 160 very professional templates. You can use their predefined color templates or use your own home made templates.

✦ **Post-auction management included in Basic Sales Manager:** Sends out automated e-mail to your winners, linking them to your own branded checkout page. If customers want to pay with PayPal or your own merchant account, they have to link from there. Vendio combines multiple wins for shipping and invoicing. You have the option to set six different feedback comments, which you choose at the time of posting.

Vendio offers a fully customizable Store you can place in your own Web space — at no additional charge. When you set up yours, all your items are seamlessly integrated. To get current information and sign up for a free trial, go to www.Vendio.com.

Figure 2-2:
Vendio "Smart Services for Smart Sellers."

**Book VIII
Chapter 2**

Managing Your
Business with
Third-Party Tools

Meridian

Meridian Software was developed by eBay Shooting Star PowerSeller Joe Cortese. Through his own experience on eBay, he developed this service to fulfill all the needs of an eBay seller, at a very reasonable price of $9.95 a month.

As a high-volume eBay seller, he was looking for an easier way to handle his 3000 unique auctions a month. You can apply the same technology to your auctions. Meridian features enterprise-level listing and more:

✦ **Item and inventory management:** Includes calendar- and time-based scheduling (that is, dates and times for launching auctions), automated auction launching and relisting, the capability to import past or current auctions, and the capability to import auction data from a spreadsheet or database.

✦ **Image hosting:** Offers space for storing pictures. You can upload bulk images to its Web site or FTP your images directly.

✦ **Auction reporting:** Generates current running auction statistics — the total number and dollars of current and past auctions — and an itemized report of each auction.

✦ **Post-auction management:** Allows you to send (manually or automatically) a variety of customized e-mails to winners and nonpaying bidders. Your invoices can link directly to PayPal.

✦ **Consignment tools:** For sellers who sell for others (see information on eBay's Trading Assistants program in Book IV, Chapter 3), Meridian offers complete tracking and inventory by consignor.

The post-auction management features also include the ability to send automatic feedback and to create mailing labels for each sale. So that feedback isn't posted until you're sure the transaction is successfully completed, you have the option of disabling the automatic feedback feature. Visit their Web site (pictured in Figure 2-3) at

www.noblespirit.com

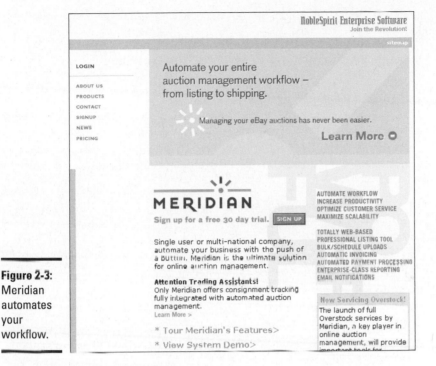

Figure 2-3:
Meridian
automates
your
workflow.

Offline Auction-Management Software

You may be like many sellers and prefer to run your business from a fixed location. In this case, you probably feel more comfortable with downloadable software that will handle most of your auction business chores on your own computer. I happen to like the option of being able to reference my old auctions on my backups. Luckily, some valuable auction software programs are available to perform all the tasks you get from the online services. To those who would rather have the software at home, there are some solid choices other than the ones I examine in this section. You might also want to visit these other sites to check out their quality auction-management software.

**Book VIII
Chapter 2**

**Managing Your
Business with
Third-Party Tools**

You can accomplish almost all the same tasks on your own computer as you can with online services.

Following is a description of a few of the leading products.

Auction Wizard 2000

Way back in 1999, Standing Wave Software developed a product that would handle large inventories and meet the needs of the growing eBay population. Enter Auction Wizard. In 2000, the company introduced a more robust version, Auction Wizard 2000, to meet the challenges presented by changes on eBay.

This software is a tour-de-force of auction management whose pieces are integrated into one program. Some of its special features enable you to

✦ Handle consignment sales. Keep track of consignment sales by consignees, including all fees.

✦ Edit your images before uploading. The software allows you to import your images, and crop, rotate, or resize images for your auctions.

✦ Upload your pictures with built-in FTP software while you're working on your auctions, eliminating the need for another piece of auction-business software.

The program interface is straightforward. I always plunge into new programs without reading the instructions, and I was able to use the program right off the bat. I'm still not a whiz at it, but that's probably because Auction Wizard 2000 has so many features that I haven't had the time to study them all.

To begin using the software, simply download your current eBay auctions directly into the program. When your auctions close, send customized e-mails (the program fills in the auction information) and manage all your end-of-auction business. Some sellers launch their auctions using Turbo Lister, and then retrieve them and handle the end-of-auction management with Auction Wizard 2000 (see Figure 2-4).

For a 60-day free trial, go to their site at

www.auctionwizard2000.com

Selling Manager and Selling Manager Pro

If you would prefer to manage your listings directly on eBay, you might just want to give eBay's Selling Manager and Selling Manager Pro a look. Figure 2-5 below shows you my Selling Manager Pro page for today (it changes by the minute). If you haven't read Chapter 1 in this book, take a moment to back up and give it a read.

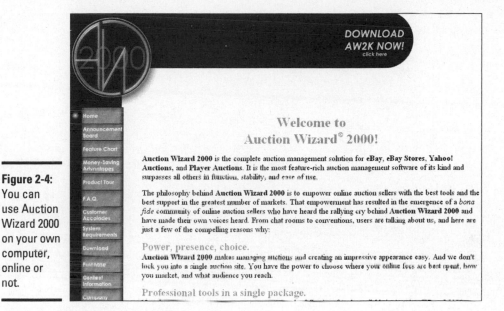

Figure 2-4:
You can
use Auction
Wizard 2000
on your own
computer,
online or
not.

I like using Selling Manager because my eBay business is in one location. I confuse easily and having everything laid out for me makes my business a whole lot easier.

To check out the latest changes and upgrades, and to compare the two program versions, visit

```
http://pages.ebay.com/selling_manager/comparison.html
```

Turbo Lister

I like Turbo Lister because it's simple and easy to use. It has a built-in WYSIWYG (what-you-see-is-what-you-get) HTML editor, and makes preparing my listings offline easy. Then, when I'm ready, I just click a button and they're all listed at once. You can also stagger listings and schedule them for a later date (for a fee).

For all the details on Turbo Lister, see Book III, Chapter 4.

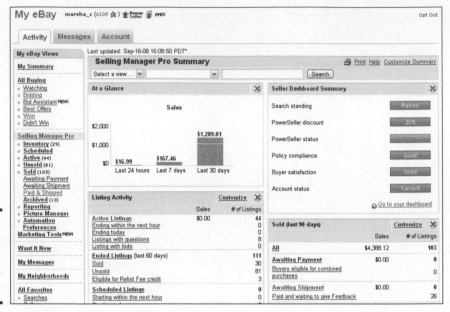

Figure 2-5:
My Selling
Manager
Pro page . . .
for now.

Finding More to Automate

Now that eBay has become a world marketplace, a single-page auction or item listing is becoming an increasingly valuable piece of real estate. Millions view your sale, and the more auctions and fixed-price items that you can list, the better your chance to make a good living. Time is money: You need to post your auctions quickly and accurately.

Posting auctions, keeping records, cataloging inventory, managing photos, and gathering statistics are all tasks that you can automate. The more your business grows, the more confusing things can become. Automated tools can help you keep it all straight. But remember: The more paid tools you use, the more expense you may be adding to your business. Always keep your bottom line in mind when evaluating whether to use fee-based software and services.

You'll have to perform certain office tasks, no matter how few (or how many) auctions you're running. Depending on your personal business style, you may want to automate any or all of the following tasks. You may choose to use a single program, a manual method, or use some features from one program and some from others. For those who aren't ready for the automated plunge, I offer alternatives here. Where appropriate, I insert references that guide you to places in this book (or on the Web) where you can find more information about the automated services I discuss.

Setting up an auction photo gallery

Until you get your own eBay store, setting up a photo gallery is a great alternative. That way, if your customers have a high-speed connection, they can browse your auctions through photographs. Some auction-management sites can host your gallery. Some charge for this service; others do not. The best part is that you can produce your own gallery without any fancy programs or auction-management software, and at no additional cost to you.

To make your own gallery on eBay without installing fancy scripts in your listings, you need to do three things:

1. **Include eBay gallery photos with all the listings you want to appear in your gallery.**

   Be sure to put your user name in the text of your item's descriptions.

2. **Test the following URL in your browser, substituting your own user ID in place of the bold italics:**

   `http://shop.ebay.com/merchant/`*yourUserID*

   Figure 2-6 shows a sample of what you'll see.

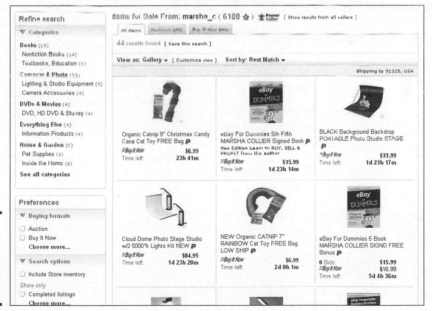

**Book VIII
Chapter 2**

Managing Your Business with Third-Party Tools

Figure 2-6: My home-made gallery-linked page.

3. **After you've checking your gallery, insert the following HTML into your auction to include a link to your gallery:**

```
<a href="http://shop.ebay.com/merchant/yourUserID">
   <B>Click <I>here</I> to view YourUserID Gallery</B>
   </a >
```

You can also use this in your e-mails to customers to show them just what's for sale at that very moment.

Sorting auction e-mail

A vital function of any auction software or system is the ability to customize and send e-mails to your winners. Many sellers use the default letters, which tend to be a bit — no, incredibly — impersonal and uncaring. You must decide whether you want the program to receive e-mail as well.

Most *computer-resident* auction-management programs (programs installed on your own computer versus going online to do your business) have their own built-in e-mail software. When you download your winner information from eBay, the program automatically generates invoices and congratulatory e-mails.

How to handle your auction-related e-mail is a personal choice. Although I currently use eBay's Selling Manager to send auction-related e-mails, I *receive* auction e-mail through Outlook, using a separate folder titled "Auctions" that contains subfolders for eBay Buy and eBay Sell.

Automating end-of-auction e-mail

If you want to set up e-mails to be sent automatically after an auction ends, you must use a software application. The software should download your final auction results, generate the e-mail, and let you preview the e-mail before sending it out. Many of the online sites discussed previously in this chapter send out winner confirmation e-mails automatically when an auction is over.

If you want to use this option, be sure that you set your preferences to preview the e-mail before sending.

Keeping inventory

Many eBay PowerSellers depend on the old clipboard or notebook method — crossing off items as they're sold. If that works for you, great. Others prefer to use an Excel spreadsheet to keep track of inventory.

Most of the auction-management packages detailed in this chapter handle inventory for you. Some automatically deduct an item from inventory when you launch an auction. You have your choice of handling inventory directly on your computer or keeping your inventory online with a service that's accessible from any computer, wherever you are.

I handle my inventory on my desktop through QuickBooks. When I buy merchandise to sell, and I post the bill to QuickBooks, it automatically puts the merchandise into inventory. When I input my sale, it deducts the items sold from standing inventory. I can print a status report whenever I want to see how much I have left — or have to order.

Composing HTML

Fancy auctions are nice, but fancy doesn't make the item sell any better. Competitive pricing and low shipping rates work in your favor — especially with eBay's Compare Items feature in Search. Also, a clean listing with as many photos as necessary goes a long way to sell your product. Some software and services offer a large selection of templates to gussy up your auctions. But you must think of your customers; many of them are still logging on with dial-up connections, which are notoriously slow. The use of simple HTML doesn't slow the loading of your page, but the addition of miscellaneous images (decorative backgrounds and animations) definitely makes viewing your auction a chore for those dialing up. And forget background music — it *really* slows things down!

Don't fret; you can make do by repeatedly incorporating two or three simple HTML templates, cutting and pasting new text as necessary. Most auction-management programs offer you several template choices. I recommend that you stick with a few that are similar, giving a standardized look to your listings, which is just the way major companies give a standardized look to their advertising and identity. Your customers will get used to the look of your auctions and feel comfortable each time they open one.

I use SeaMonkey (a free program from the people who brought us Firefox) to generate much of my code for auction descriptions. Visit Book 5 Chapter 3 for more information on this handy program).An important line of code that everyone seems to forget is the one that inserts a picture into your auction description. On the Sell an Item page, click the tab to view in HTML mode, and insert the following line below where you'd like your image to appear in your description:

```
<img src="http://www.yourserver.com/imagename.jpg">
```

Be sure to substitute your own server and image name. If you want to put one picture above another, type <P> and then repeat the HTML line with a different image name.

If you're in a rush and need a quick and easy HTML generator, go to my Web site at www.coolebaytools.com and click Tools. In addition, Book V has sample HTML code for auction descriptions, as well as a chart of all the code you'll ever need for an eBay auction.

One-click relisting or selling similar

Using auction software or an auction service speeds up the process of posting or relisting items. After you input your inventory into the software, posting or relisting your auctions is a mouse click away. All the auction management software packages that I detailed previously in this chapter include this feature.

If you buy your items in bulk, you might want to take advantage of eBay's free relisting tool. By clicking the Sell Similar link (see Figure 2-7) on any successful listing on your My eBay Sold area, you can automatically relist your items. Sell Similar starts the listing as new, so if it doesn't sell you can avail yourself of the Relist feature. This way, if the item sells the second time, your listing (insertion fees) for the first listing will be credited.

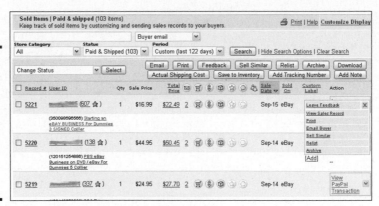

Figure 2-7: The Relist and Sell Similar buttons live near the top of the My eBay Sold Items page.

Although eBay says that Sell Similar is for relisting items, it works also when listing a duplicate of an item that has sold successfully. The only difference is that you aren't credited for the unsold auction listing fee.

One savvy seller I know uses the eBay Sell Similar feature to post new listings. She merely clicks the Sell Similar link, and then cuts and pastes her new information into the existing HTML format. That's why her items all have the same feel and flavor.

Scheduling listings for bulk upload

If you want to schedule the unattended launch of your auctions without incurring eBay's $.10 fee, you must use an online management service (check out the "Online auction-management sites" section). If you can be at your computer to send your auctions to eBay singly or in bulk, you can use the Turbo Lister application, which eBay offers at no charge.

Hosting photos

If all you need is photo hosting, and you've checked out your ISP but they don't give you any free Web space to use (please check Book V for a list of ISPs and the amount of Web storage space they give to their customers), you can always use eBay's Picture Services to host an additional picture in each auction at $.15 an image.

Checking out

When someone wins or buys an item, eBay's checkout integrates directly with PayPal. If you're closing less than 100 auctions a day, that's all you need. eBay and PayPal will also send an e-mail to you and the buyer so that you can arrange for payment.

A personalized winner's notification e-mail can easily contain a link to your PayPal payment area, making a checkout service unnecessary.

Printing shipping labels

Printing shipping labels without printing postage can be the beginning of a laborious two-step process. I recommend two companies, Endicia.com and Paypal.com; they can print your labels and postage all in one step. Check out Book VII, Chapter 1 for information on how this works.

Some sites, as well as eBay's Selling Manager, print your winner's address label without postage. That works well if you don't mind carrying your packages to the post office for postage. (Why would you do that? A burning need to stand in line, I guess!)

Tracking buyer information

Keeping track of your winners isn't rocket science. You can do it in an Excel spreadsheet or a Word document, both of which are exportable to almost any program for follow-up mailings promoting future sales. If you choose to have an online management service do this for you, be sure that you can download the information to your computer (in case you and the online service part ways someday).

Generating customized reports

Sales reports, ledgers, and tax information are all important reports that you should have in your business. Online services and software supply different flavors of these reports.

PayPal allows you to download your sales data into a format compatible with QuickBooks, a highly respected and popular bookkeeping program. You can also choose to download your data in Excel spreadsheet format (the downloads also work in Microsoft Works). PayPal reports are chock full of intensely detailed information about your sales and deposits. Putting this information in a standard accounting software program on a regular basis makes your year-end calculations easier to bear.

Submitting feedback

If you're running a lot of listings, leaving feedback can be a chore. One solution is to automate the submission of feedback through an online service eBay's Selling Manager Pro. But timing the automation of this task can be tricky.

Don't leave feedback for an eBay transaction until after you've heard from the buyer that the purchase is satisfactory. Leaving positive feedback immediately after you've received payment from the buyer is too soon. After you receive an e-mail assuring you that the customer is satisfied, manually leaving feedback by going to the feedback forum (or the item page) can be just as easy — if not easier — as bulk-loading feedback.

Bonding

Competition for the buyer's dollars is fierce on eBay. New users arrive at the site with three predetermined concepts about eBay:

- ✦ They're going to find fun and unique items.
- ✦ They're going to get a deal.
- ✦ There's a good chance they'll get ripped off.

For those of us selling on eBay, that last comment hits us right in the gut. Most of us work hard to make each customer's experience a good one on the site, and hate it when the 1/100 of 1 percent of bad sellers get all the publicity.

You can counter the public's misconception that eBay sellers are dishonest in two ways: by getting a SquareTrade seal and (ultimately) by getting your listings bonded through BuySAFE. In this chapter, I explain both programs and show you how they can boost your bottom line — and help you avoid getting negative feedback.

Bonding your sales with buySAFE

When it comes to high-dollar transactions on eBay, in the past the only thing a seller could throw into the sale was escrow. Escrow is a great way to protect the buyer, but it ties up the seller's money for considerably longer than necessary. The only approved escrow company currently on eBay is `escrow.com`.

Lately there have been many scandals in the online escrow arena. Fraudsters put up bogus Web sites, offer expensive items for sale online, and then run the escrow through their bogus site. The buyer, thinking everything is legit, sends his or her money. After the money arrives, however, the Web site is taken down, the bad guys disappear with the money. Escrow has gotten a bad reputation with buyers. The issue is so serious that if you go to the escrow.com Web site area at `https://escrow.com/fic`, you'll find helpful information on how to recognize escrow fraud.

There's finally a viable alternative to escrow. Something that will make the customer feel good about spending buckets of money on your site. Bonding. It's all about potato chips, beer, and Monday Night Football. (No, wait, that's male bonding.) The bonding we're talking about here refers to guaranteeing that a seller will perform *as advertised*.

All about bonding

A bond warrants that the person (or business) performing the task will complete his or her part of the deal as contracted.

A bond is *not* insurance. Insurance assumes that a loss is a possibility. A bond *guarantees* that a buyer will not suffer a financial loss.

The buySAFE company (an eBay certified developer) has come up with a traditional bonding plan exclusively for eBay sellers. buySAFE procures surety bonds through companies such as Liberty Mutual (one of America's largest financial services provider) to bond eBay sellers' transactions. The bond provides that Liberty Mutual will refund the item sale price or replace the item if the seller does not perform as promised in the item listing.

The bond can protect buyers when

✦ The bonded seller fails to deliver the item

✦ The seller delivers an item different from the one described and pictured in the item listing

✦ The seller offers a return or refund policy but refuses to honor it

✦ The seller fails to use the shipping method as described in the item listing and the item arrives damaged (as when the buyer pays for insurance, but the seller fails to insure the package)

- ✦ The seller refuses to follow the payment policy described in the item listing

- ✦ The seller experiences financial setbacks and does not fulfill the conditions of the sale

A bond basically guarantees that the seller will perform, period. Bonding your auctions tells your prospective bidders that you care about the buyer, and that you're a professional seller. This assurance easily can translate into more bids and higher final selling prices.

The best part? The seller receives his or her money through regular channels and doesn't have to ship the item until paid. No waiting around for weeks to get your money because, as is the case with an escrow, you're at the mercy of the system.

I thought bonding was just for high-dollar transactions, but not so! I've heard from small-time sellers that their total number of bids and their final selling price increased by one-third after bonding *all* their items (even the $5 sales!) with the buySAFE seal.

When one of your items is bonded, a seal is displayed, like the one shown in Figure 2-8. If prospective buyers click it, they see the details of what the seal represents.

Figure 2-8:
This item is bonded!

BONDED
Trustworthy, Reliable Seller
Financial Protection to $25,000
Verify Now

Seller bonding on eBay

You may be wondering whether getting your items bonded on eBay is a big deal. It's not really. Here's how it works.

Your auctions can get bonded up to a total prescribed dollar amount. The total amount of bonded auctions cannot exceed this figure. Think of the maximum like a line of credit. You can draw against it until you've maxed out your line. (The maximum bond coverage per item is $25,000!)

To become bonded, you must meet some minimum requirements:

- ✦ $1000 a month in eBay sales
- ✦ An eBay feedback rating of 100
- ✦ eBay feedback that's 98-percent positive
- ✦ An eBay business based in the United States (but not in the state of Hawaii)

If you fulfill those requirements, you then fill out a form on the buySAFE Web site, which asks you information about yourself and your business. After applying, you undergo a thorough qualification process that evaluates your online sales experience and reputation; verifies your identity; and analyzes your financial stability. Then you must also legally commit to either honoring their terms of sale or repaying any losses that you may inflict.

Yes, you may have great feedback, but bonding is not about the people who are already buying from you — the point is to attract new buyers with a signal that *proves* you're professional and rock-solid.

Bonding items

After you receive approval and know your total bonding amount (based on how you were qualified), you may choose which of your auctions to bond and which not to bond.

The auctions you choose to bond cost you 1% of the final selling price. If the bonded item sells for, say, $3.00 (shipping, handling fees, and taxes are not included in the bonded total), your fee is $.03. You pay nothing in advance, there are no hidden fees or commitments, and there is *no* minimum fee. You don't pay a fee if a bonded item doesn't sell.

A sample Bonded Seller's Log In page at buySAFE is shown in Figure 2-9. At a glance, you can see any of your items that aren't bonded, as well as check your total bonding limit, bonds outstanding (bonds on a sold item are kept open for 30 days), and the total of your bonded transactions. Note that live help is also available, should you have a question during business hours.

To take a look at your bonded transactions, click the Bonded Transactions tab, as shown in Figure 2-10. Here you can see any open items with bonds and view any problems that may have arisen.

If you click the item title, you can see the details of an open auction, as shown in Figure 2-11.

**Book VIII
Chapter 2**

Managing Your Business with Third-Party Tools

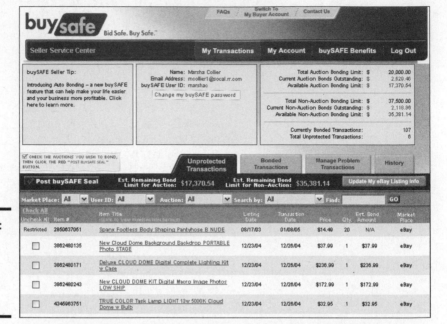

Figure 2-9:
The
buySAFE
seller-
services
area.

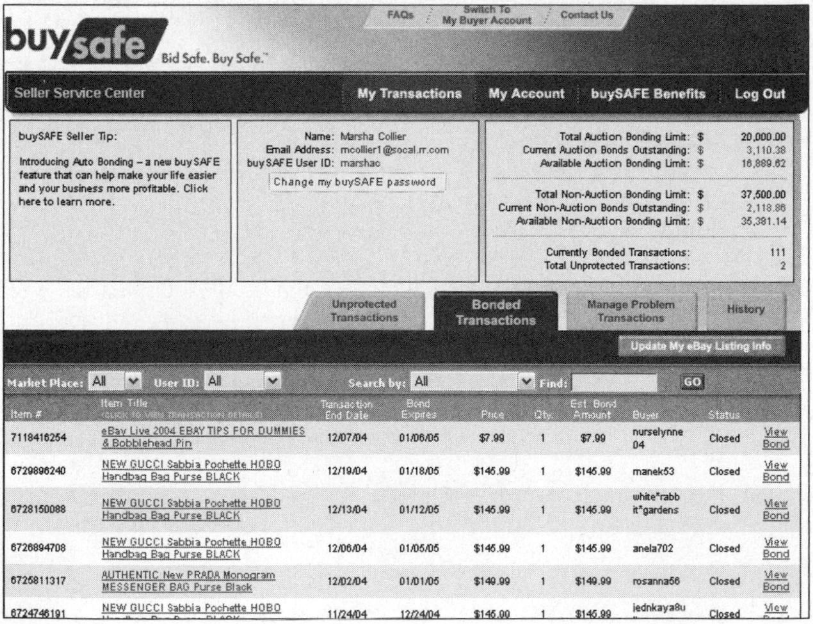

Figure 2-10:
Your bonded
trans-
actions.

Figure 2-11:
Details of
an open
auction.

What happens when something goes wrong?

When a buyer feels slighted in a transaction, that customer is still yours to solve the problem with. If the customer contacts buySAFE, he or she is sent directly back to you.

If, for some reason, the customer still insists on help resolving the issue, he or she may fill out a problem transaction report on the buySAFE Web site, stating the problem and what the seller can do to resolve the issue. On your Seller Services page, you'll see a red View Problem button. Click it to display the Problem Summary page, and then click the Problem button to see the buyer's comments.

An e-mail is sent to you, and your response is recorded. If nothing has been solved after two e-mail exchanges, a professional mediator (a claims representative) joins in to solve the problem.

There is no charge for the mediation. The mediator may contact both the buyer and seller by phone to get both sides of the story. A bond from a surety company, such as Liberty Mutual, is a legal obligation to protect both parties. The bond *protects the seller from false allegations* and the buyer from losing his or her money. If no compromise happens, the mediator will make a binding decision, based on the evidence provided, in favor of one party or the other.

Liberty Mutual is regulated by each state's insurance department and is held accountable by them for adequately investigating each claim.

Bonding is the only licensed and regulated form of seller guarantee.

Although bonding is new to eBay, it has proven to be successful with many sellers. If you'd like to give it a whirl, go to

```
http://coolebaytools.buysafe.com/index.php?adid=cet1004
```

for a special offer just for my readers.

Chapter 3: Studying Your Statistics

In This Chapter

✔ Using a quality tool to increase sales

✔ Finding out when people visit your auctions

From my background in advertising, I know that good-quality research can make the difference in whether a business endeavor is a success or a failure. In my books and lectures, I always advocate the necessity of doing at least the minimal research on any item's eBay availability and current selling pricing.

I also recommend using certain advanced counters (those that break down Web-page visits to hours and days, rather than showing only totals), because just the number of people who click your page doesn't tell you much. Wouldn't it be nice to know not only how many people visited your listing, but also which page sent them there and what city they come from?

The problem with gathering this kind of information is that the coding and programming involved is probably beyond the skill set of even top-level eBay sellers. After all, they're merchants, not computer programmers. In this chapter, I tell you about eBay's Store Traffic Reports, eBay Sales Reports Plus, and an online service called ViewTracker that gives you all the research you can use. eBay Traffic Reports and Sales Reports Plus are automatic (and free) for every eBay Store owner. (If you don't have an eBay Store, Sales Reports Plus can be purchased separately by subscription for $4.99 a month.

Best of all, this information, while important for your sales efforts, remains noninvasive for your potential customers. For example, in ViewTracker, you may find out the timeslots and keywords used by your listing visitors, but you find out nothing that compromises their identities.

The information service presented in this chapter doesn't turn your computer into a data-mining robot. It merely gives you the information available to every Web site on the Internet. That is, it gives you information such as geographic location, which follows the IP address of all eBay users who visit your listings. This service is not an invasion of privacy like the data-mining cookies explained in the sidebar "Flushing out the moles."

Flushing out the moles

There's no place to hide on the Internet: Every one of your keystrokes and visits to Web sites can be traced back to you. There's big money in this data as well. If you've ever used a program like Spybot Search & Destroy (a program that finds data-mining programs that have been placed on your computer when you visit certain Web sites), you know how much more data sites want about their visitors. My daughter downloaded the free version of Spybot and found 632 data-mining cookies slowing down her computer! Spybot can be downloaded for free from many sites; just Google *Spybot* to find it.

Companies such as Mediaplex and DoubleClick make a living by placing cookies on your computer as you browse the Internet. These cookies follow your browsing trail and report your comings and goings to their motherships. Mediaplex and DoubleClick sell that information to the big guys so they can better figure out who their customers are. If you never want Mediaplex to track your Internet browsing, go to `www.mediaplex.com/mojo_privacy_statement.shtml,` scroll down the page to the Click Here to Install Mediaplex Opt-Out Cookies link. Click it and you will automatically be opted out on the computer you're using. To disengage DoubleClick from your Web roaming, visit `http://optout.doubleclick.net/cgi-bin/dclk/optout.pl` to opt out. I've found that page working only intermittently, so you can also go to `www.doubleclick.com/privacy/` and scroll down to the many opt-out links.

eBay Sales Reports Plus

eBay offers a useful tool to track your sales in one place. No longer do you need to download sales files, place them on a spreadsheet, and start to cipher — its all done for you. You can view the report at any time from your My eBay page, and see an instant graphic chart of your sales progress. Take a look at my current Sales Reports Plus report in Figure 3-1.

You'll get the following sales information:

✦ **Total sales:** The total revenue generated by sales of your items by month.

✦ **Month-to-month sales growth:** The percentage of increase (or decrease) of your gross revenue from month to month. It may also be viewed from week to week.

✦ **Ended listings:** The total number of listings completed during the month.

✦ **Ended items:** The number of items represented in your ended listings. (Store and fixed-price listings usually represent multiple quantities.)

✦ **Successful items #:** The total number of listings that ended with a buyer.

✦ **Successful items %:** The percent of items that sold in your successful listings.

✦ **Average sale price per item:** The average of the final value of your sold items.

✦ **Total buyers:** The total number of winning buyers that purchased items from you.

✦ **Unique buyers:** The total of unique (one user ID) buyers that purchased from you. If a buyer purchased several items from you over the month, they are counted only once in this figure.

✦ **Repeat buyers %:** The percentage of buyers who shopped with you more then once within the time period.

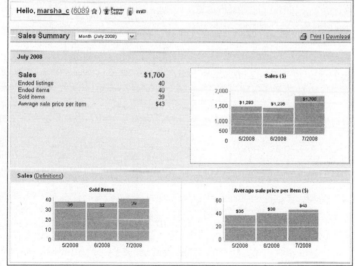

Figure 3-1:
Sales Reports Plus graphic data for my part time eBay business.

Book VIII
Chapter 3

Studying Your Statistics

Thank goodness eBay also supplies data on fees. eBay fees (for listing, options, and Final Value) can often get out of control and cause a seller's profits to spiral downward quickly. Here you can see your total eBay fees (less any credits) as well as your total PayPal fees. Sadly, you'll have to work out the fees as a percentage of your sales yourself:

Fee percentage = (net eBay and PayPal fees / total sales) * 100

You'll also get to see how many unpaid item reminders you filed, how many final value fee refunds you claimed, and the percentage of unpaid items as a percentage of your total sales. You will not see the actual dollar figure.

eBay store traffic reports

When you have an eBay store, you will also have access to traffic reports supplied by Omniture. These reports give you data on the number of hits to various pages in your store.

You'll also be able to compare present data with previous periods. The reports are an incredibly useful tool for historical data.

You can also access this data segregated by auctions, fixed-price sales, and store items.

Lastly, you can see which days of the week were most successful for you and your average price per item. You get this data in chart format, as shown in Figure 3-2, and in text. Although nothing can replace using a quality book-keeping program such as QuickBooks, these reports can give you good sales data at a glance.

Figure 3-2: My successful days of the week (during the slow month of July) and average sales price per item by day of the week.

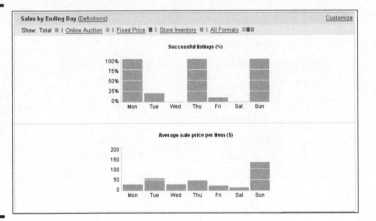

When looking at the graphics in this chapter, note that most of them were taken during the slowest part of the summer for online sales!

Using Sellathon ViewTracker

ViewTracker from Sellathon answers the most popular questions I'm asked by eBay sellers. Before ViewTracker, when trying to figure out the exact time and day to end an auction, you had to do a considerable amount of research by running test auctions on the eBay site. Now you can follow the body clocks of your buyers and find out when they search for your type of item.

You will also find out (I just love this!) which keywords the visitor's browser was using when he or she came to your listing. This information is crucial when writing titles — and planning keyword campaigns.

Here's a partial list of the type of data you can get by using the ViewTracker system:

✦ Sequential number of the visitor. Is this the 19th visitor or the 104th — and did this person come back again?

✦ Date and time the visitor arrived at your auction.

✦ Visitor's IP address. (By clicking the IP address in the Sellathon screen, you can see only those visits originating from this IP address.)

✦ What city, state, and country your visitor is from.

✦ Whether the reserve price was met when the visitor arrived.

✦ When the item receives a bid (and how many have been placed to that moment).

✦ Whether the current visitor is the high bidder, a bidder who has been outbid, or not a bidder.

✦ Whether the visitor has chosen to watch this listing in his or her My eBay page.

✦ Whether your visitors browsed a category, searched a category, searched all of eBay, used eBay's Product Finder utility, or came from See Seller's Other Items page or some other page.

  • If they were browsing, which category were they browsing when they clicked your listing?

  • If searching, what search terms did they use to find your item?

  • If they were searching when they came upon your item, did the visitors search titles only, or titles *and* descriptions?

✦ Whether the user elected to view Auctions Only, Buy It Now, or both.

✦ Whether the user refined his or her searches using specific parameters, including these: Show/Hide pictures, Sellers that accept PayPal, Price Range, International Availability, Regional Searching, Gallery View, and Show Gift Items.

✦ Was there a preference in the way the visitor sorted his or her search results? Did the search sort items from high price to low price?

Amazing stuff, eh? By applying the information from ViewTracker, you can change tactics to help your little business become a big one. You'll be able to customize your items to match your very own eBay market.

Setting up your account is painless. After you give your contact information to Sellathon (and make up a new user ID and password for the site), you are presented with a small amount of code to add to your listing's description. It's that easy.

Checking out your data

In this section, I show you a portion of the data screens from my ViewTracker account. But keep one thing in mind: I've been busy writing this book, so I haven't had much time to list tons of items on eBay. The few I have listed (I have to keep up my status as a PowerSeller!) will give you a good idea of what you'll see.

When you first log on to ViewTracker, you'll be presented with your General (Combined items) page. Here you'll see a couple of statistics. Keep in mind that ViewTracker constantly tracks your items in real time, so the data may change by the minute as you're changing screens within the program!

After you log on to your account, you see a snapshot of your current sales activity and a graph showing your views (hits) over the past 24 hours, as shown in Figure 3-3.

On the initial home page, you'll see some other very interesting data:

✦ The total value of all bids placed on your auctions, the number of people watching your items, the average visits per auction, and the total hits on all your items.

✦ A listing of your live and expired auctions. You can click links here to get general information on all your auctions, or click the folder to view information on individual items.

Although I don't really want to give away any of my deep dark secrets, I can show you a few screens of data from my expired (closed items) so you know what to look for. The first, in Figure 3-4, shows the most active time of the day for my auctions by hits.

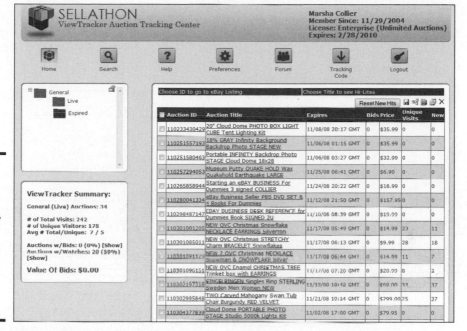

Figure 3-3:
My
Sellathon
home page,
with links
to check
out how
my sales
are being
viewed.

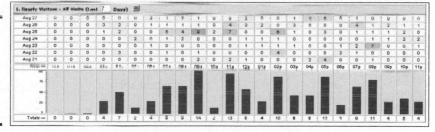

Figure 3-4:
My most
active hits,
by the hour,
for a seven-
day period.

The next graph you access is the most active day of the week. Figure 3-5 is a portion of the composite report for all my auctions. Think how valuable this data would be when you analyze data from auctions from a similar category. For example, golf equipment, DVD, women's apparel — you get the picture. Remember, this data covers all my listings; this isn't for one particular item (although you can get that data as well).

Figure 3-4 was captured mid-day on the last days of August 2008. Compare that to Figure 3-6, which was taken in Spring 2004. Note the differences in the hit pattern. The comparison clearly demonstrates how important it is to stay on top of these statistics.

**Book VIII
Chapter 3**

**Studying Your
Statistics**

Most Active Day of the Week

AuctionID: 110233430429, 110251557193, 110251580463, 110257294053, 110265858944, 110280041334, 110298487147, 110301081205, 110301085011, 110301091129, 110301096151, 110302197318, 110302995848, 110304377839, 110304385585, 120148378419, 120149874336, 120150290304, 120151254886, 120161701759, 120175501727, 120175847853, 120175848594, 120175859657, 350056042715

Most Active Day of the Week (Last 7 Days ▶)

Figure 3-5:
Most active days in the past week.

Date	Visits	AE	Ratio
Sunday	7	0	0
Monday	36	23	1.5652173913043478260869565217
Tuesday	8	0	0
Wednesday	35	25	1.4
Thursday	22	0	0
Friday	13	6	2.1666666666666666666666666667
Saturday	17	0	0

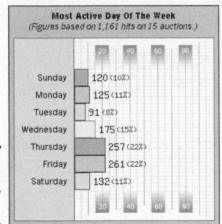

Figure 3-6:
Most active days in early spring.

There is also a chart that shows you the way people came to your auctions. This is the best way to see whether things you've been doing to boost sales are working. For example, are you taking the best advantage of targeting your cross-promotions? Does your Web site send people to your eBay listings?

Other data graphs are available, but the very best is the Top Search Terms Used to find your items. This chart will give you definitive data so you'll know which keywords to include in your titles. (Sorry, I'd *love* to show you my top keywords, but that's a secret! When you work up a list of your own, you'll know exactly where I'm coming from.)

Getting additional information from your listings

With ViewTracker, you can also view data for individual listings. Figure 3-7 shows you data from a quick auction that ended with a Buy It Now transaction.

The data collected and shown here is combined with data from other listings to make up the charts and statistics shown in the figures in this chapter.

Date/Time	Length	IP Address	R?	Method of Arrival	Search Term	Sort By	Pg	Ops
10/27/08 21:30 GMT		75.82.51 [?]	Yes	Searching All Of eBay	singelringen	Best Match	1	
10/27/08 03:52 GMT		66.207.254 [?]		Searching Category	singelringen	Best Match	1	
10/26/08 09:59 GMT	7	24.4.174 [?]		Searching Category	celebrity	Ending First	5	
10/25/08 16:17 GMT		75.82.51 [?]	Yes	Unknown		n/a	n/a	
10/25/08 14:56 GMT	12	80.31.92 [?]		Searching Category	singelringen	Best Match	1	
10/25/08 12:47 GMT	18	211.245.164 [?]		Search Engine		n/a	n/a	
10/25/08 06:05 GMT	72	71.91.32 [?]		Searching All Of eBay	singelringen	Best Match	1	
10/24/08 02:46 GMT	100	198.53.130 [?]		Searching All Of eBay	swed sterling	Best Match	1	
10/24/08 02:17 GMT	67	71.255.239 [?]		Searching Category	singelringen	Best Match	1	
10/23/08 21:15 GMT		71.34.20 [?]		Direct Link		n/a	n/a	
10/23/08 20:01 GMT		68.225.236 [?]	Yes	Visitor's My eBay Page		n/a	n/a	
10/23/08 05:24 GMT		75.82.51 [?]		Searching All Of eBay	singelringen	Best Match	1	
10/22/08 23:18 GMT	22	210.114.61 [?]		Searching All Of eBay	singelringen	Best Match	1	
10/22/08 22:52 GMT	69	68.225.236 [?]	Yes	Unknown		n/a	n/a	
10/22/08 21:14 GMT		68.225.236 [?]	Yes	Unknown		n/a	n/a	
10/22/08 21:14 GMT		68.225.236 [?]	Yes	Unknown		n/a	n/a	
10/22/08 20:59 GMT	215	72.134.26 [?]	Yes	Direct Link		n/a	n/a	
10/22/08 20:45 GMT	16	72.134.26 [?]	Yes	Direct Link		n/a	n/a	
10/22/08 13:38 GMT	53	24.240.52 [?]		Direct Link		n/a	n/a	

Figure 3-7: The first few of 77 ViewTracker hit details for a single listing.

Note a few things:

+ **IP address:** You don't get the complete IP address of the visitor, but you do see how many times the same person has visited your listing.

+ **Question mark:** If you click the question mark, you get a pop-up window with the city and state of your visitor.

+ **Search Terms:** What did the prospective buyer search for when they found your item?

+ **Method of arrival:** Here's where you can tell whether your individual promotions are working.

There's a whole lot more to this amazing program. The cost starts at $49.00 a year for a small-time eBay seller (like me). For a 30-day free trial, go to

```
http://www.sellathon.com/?af=0-186
```

Chapter 4: Becoming a PowerSeller

In This Chapter

- ✔ Qualifying for PowerSeller status
- ✔ Moving up the tiers
- ✔ Understanding the benefits

*W*hen you browse through the items on eBay, you're bound to notice a PowerSeller icon next to a member's user ID. To the uninitiated, this may look like an award given to a used car salesman for bullying hundreds of people into expensive car leases — but it's not. The eBay PowerSeller status is given only to those sellers who uphold the highest levels of professionalism on the site. Take a look at mine in Figure 4-1.

Figure 4-1:
My proudly displayed PowerSeller icon.

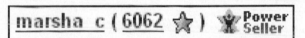

eBay refers to PowerSellers as "pillars of the community." I say they're smart businesspeople. PowerSellers have to maintain certain monthly levels of gross merchandise sales (total dollar amount of eBay sales — GMS in eBay-speak), and they get there by providing good items for sale and excellent customer service.

You may notice that many sellers on the site with feedback ratings in the tens of thousands do not have the PowerSeller embellishment on their auctions. That's not because they're not good people; it's just that some of their transactions may have gone awry and resulted in negative feedback. In this case, be sure to check the seller's feedback and thoughtfully evaluate it. Many times buyers do not read the seller's policies before they buy — and then give negative feedback (as in the case of buyers not reading the seller's warnings when buying liquidation merchandise).

First Steps to PowerSeller Status

To become a PowerSeller on eBay, you must fulfill the following requirements:

✦ Be an active eBay member for at least 90 days

✦ Sell a minimum of $1,000 in sales or 100 items per month, for three consecutive months

Or

a minimum average of items sold on the site per month for the past three months

✦ Sell a minimum of $12,000 or 1,200 items for the prior twelve months

✦ Have a minimum overall feedback rating of 100

✦ Maintain at least a 98 feedback percentage

✦ Keep your eBay account current

✦ Comply with all eBay policies

✦ Maintain a maintain a rating of 4.5 or higher for the past 12 months in all four Detailed Seller Ratings (DSRs)

✦ Run your business by upholding eBay's community values (see sidebar).

eBay sends you a notification when you qualify. If you feel you have qualified and may have accidentally deleted the e-mail, find the PowerSeller's page from the Site Map link and attempt to log in.

PowerSeller Tiers

Being a PowerSeller gives you membership in an exclusive club. That club has five levels of membership, depending on your monthly sales, as shown in Table 4-1. Each PowerSeller tier gives the seller more privileges from eBay. One of the most valuable benefits is that when an issue needs to be addressed with eBay, PowerSellers can access priority customer-service support.

eBay community values

The eBay community values aren't taken lightly by the eBay community and eBay employees. The values were set out early on by the company's founder, Pierre Omidyar.

✔ We believe people are basically good.

✔ We believe everyone has something to contribute.

✔ We believe that an honest, open environment can bring out the best in people.

✔ We recognize and respect everyone as a unique individual.

✔ We encourage you to treat others the way that you want to be treated.

All eBay sellers are expected to uphold these tenets in all their dealings on the site. Okay, no snickering from the peanut gallery; we all know that quite a few sellers don't follow these precepts. But then, they're not PowerSellers, are they?

Table 4-1	PowerSeller Tiers			
Tier	*Monthly GMS ($) or Items sold*	*Priority E-Mail Support*	*Toll-Free Phone*	*Manager Support*
Bronze*	$1000 or 100 items	Yes	No	No
Silver	$3000 or 300 items	Yes	Yes	No
Gold	$10, 000 or 1,000 items	Yes	Yes	Yes
Platinum	$25,000 or 2,500 items	Yes	Yes	Yes
Titanium	$150,000 or 15,000 items	Yes	Yes	Yes
Diamond	$500,000 or 50,000 items	Yes	Yes	Yes

Bronze Tier PowerSellers get phone support if they meet the annual requirement of a minimum of $12,000 or 1,200 items for the prior twelve months

There's no official indication of it, but I'll bet if you're a Diamond level PowerSeller that John Donahoe (eBay's CEO) will arrange babysitting for you when you're in a jam. Now I don't *know* it to be gospel . . . but I'm just sayin' . . .

It's a serious matter to comply with eBay policies, but PowerSellers get a little leeway. They also get to know exactly how much "leeway" they can get away with. Table 4-2 below shows how much eBay allows the various levels of PowerSellers to get away with.

Table 4-2	Policy Violations by Tier
PowerSeller Tier	*# of violations in 60 days*
Bronze	4
Silver	5
Gold	5
Platinum	6
Titanium	7

PowerSeller Program Benefits

As a PowerSeller, you have access to some super-secret places on the eBay site reserved for PowerSellers! There's a PowerSeller newsgroup, PowerSeller discussion board, and even special items at the eBay store. All this magic is accessed by the screen shown in Figure 4-2, at

```
pages.ebay.com/powerseller
```

You must log in to this area, and only PowerSellers are allowed to enter.

eBay has come to value that quality sellers give people the best buying experience on the site. So they've devised a plan (tied into those gnarly Detailed Seller Ratings) to reward PowerSellers who play by the rules. In addition to receiving premium support, eBay PowerSellers get other benefits:

✦ **Increased visibility in Best Match search:** Now eBay gives the advantage to the listings of the upper half of sellers in terms of buyer satisfaction. Sellers with detailed seller ratings above 4.7 in the last 30 days will receive 5 to 25 percent more exposure than the average seller.

✦ **Discounts on Final Value Fees:** Now, this is a reward I can appreciate. eBay discounts the Final Value Fees on the monthly bill to PowerSellers who maintain high standards. (Your DSR ratings must be 4.6 or higher in all four categories to get the discount). See Table 4-3 for the discount amounts.

Figure 4-2:
The
PowerSeller
portal on
eBay.

✦ **Health care:** PowerSellers, their employees and their immediate families have the opportunity to purchase exclusive health insurance.

✦ **Approved use of PowerSeller logo:** eBay supplies PowerSellers with special templates so that they may print custom business cards and stationery that includes the official PowerSeller logo.

✦ **Unpaid Item Protection:** PowerSellers not only get Final Value Fee and listing credits when faced with a non-paying buyer, they also get a credit for any Listing Upgrade Fees (for example, Buy It Now, Bold, or Subtitle) — you know, all that extra fluff.

✦ **Reseller Marketplace:** This is a super-secret benefit for PowerSellers — and certainly reason enough to become one. eBay runs a site (just for PowerSellers) that sells liquidations and wholesale merchandise to PowerSellers. The home page is pictured in Figure 4-3.

Table 4-3	eBay PowerSeller Final Value Fee Discounts
DSR Percentage for past 30 days	*Percentage Discount*
4.6	5
4.8	15
4.9	20

A 4.6-percent average DSR rating indicates that you are in the top 50 percent of sellers in terms of Buyer Satisfaction.

Becoming an eBay PowerSeller is an important step to eBay professionalism. It's something worth aspiring to!

Figure 4-3: Power Sellers have the ability to buy merchandise at wholesale through the Reseller Marketplace.

Chapter 5: Opening Your eBay Store

In This Chapter

✓ **Figuring out the lure of the online shop**

✓ **Understanding the costs**

✓ **Setting up an eBay Store**

✓ **Marketing and making a sale**

If you're doing well selling your items on eBay auctions, why open an eBay Store? Well, have you used the eBay Buy It Now feature in one of your listings? Did it work? In an eBay Store, all items are set at a fixed price and remain online until canceled (or listed for as few as 30 days), so it's kind of like a giant collection of Buy It Now featured items. Get the idea?

Opening an eBay Store can expand your business. eBay is stressing the fixed-price format on the site these days, and buyers are looking for that format. The more that savvy buyers learn about eBay Stores, the more popular they become. The more popular they become, the more people buy from them. Simple. An eBay Store provides you with your own little corner of eBay where you can leverage your good relationships with your customers and sell directly to them. But eBay Stores are not a total solution, and having an eBay Store isn't a one-way ticket to Easy Street.

I get e-mails all the time from people who open an eBay Store and are not successful in moving merchandise. Why? Because running an eBay Store takes an extra level of effort. Simple. No matter how many money-back guarantees you receive from online spammers promising magical success on eBay, the only magic is putting your shoulder, nose, and whatever else to the grindstone — and exerting the effort necessary to bring customers to your store.

If you're just beginning on eBay, the best advice I can give is to hold off on opening an eBay Store until your feedback rating is over 100. Participating in transactions on eBay is a natural teacher because you'll see mistakes that sellers make when they sell to you. Some sellers will send you e-mails that are plain unfriendly, and you'll have a true understanding of how quality customer service will help you build your business. You'll also learn from your own mistakes and be able to provide better service to your customers.

Locating Your Special Place Online

When you're opening a store, you have just three main rules to remember and apply: location, location, location. If you were going to open a brick-and-mortar store, you could open it, for example, in the corner strip mall, at a shopping center, or even somewhere downtown. You'd have to decide in what location your store would do best; that goes for an online store as well. You'll find tons of locations to open an online store, including online malls (when you can find them) and sites such as Amazon.com, Yahoo!, and (of course) eBay.

You have to pay rent for your online store, but opening and running an online store isn't nearly as expensive as a store in the real world (where you also have to pay electrical bills, maintenance bills, and more). Plus, the ratio of rent to sales makes an online store a much easier financial decision, and your store's exposure to the buying public can be huge.

eBay wants you to succeed as well. After all, the more you sell, the more eBay earns in Final Value Fees.

Checking Out Online Stores Galore

Amazon.com, WalMart, and eBay make up the big three of online stores. They're the top locations and get the most visitors. According to comScore Media Metrix, in July 2008 these sites garnered an astounding number of *unique* visitors (counting *all* of one person's visits to the sites just *once* a month):

- ✦ **WalMart:** 31,637,000 Think about this when you consider whether people are still shopping the Web looking for bargains.
- ✦ **eBay:** 120,173,000
- ✦ **Amazon.com:** 58,462,000 (it sells books, CDs, DVDs, and lots of other merchandise).

No doubt feeling competition from Yahoo! Small Business and Amazon.com, eBay decided to open its doors (in July 2001) to sellers who wanted their own stores. The fixed-price stores were a normal progression for eBay in its quest to continue as the world's marketplace. And eBay Stores make sense: They're a benefit to all current eBay sellers, and open doors to new shoppers who don't want to deal with auctions.

eBay itself is a kind of online store that specializes in selling *your* stuff, not *theirs.* It doesn't stock a stick of merchandise and it isn't in competition with you. In addition to its staggering number of visitors, eBay offers you the most reasonable store rent, as shown in Table 5-1.

Table 5-1	Monthly Costs for an Online Starter Store		
	eBay	*Yahoo! Merchant Solutions*	*Amazon MarketPlace*
Basic rent	$15.95	$39.95	$59.99
Listing fee	$0.03 to $0.10	0	0
Highest final value fee tier	12%	1.5%	7% (includes credit card processing fees)

Amazon ended their reasonably-priced zShops in October 2006, to move sellers to their more expensive Amazon WebStores. I don't think it's going to take a rocket scientist to convince you that having a space in eBay Stores (see Figure 5-1) is an excellent bargain. Keep in mind that eBay is based on merchandise sales, and the public actively shops eBay Stores. I know the stores aren't based on auctions, but Buy It Now items are as easy to handle as auctions. To review prices and rules before opening your store, go to

pages.ebay.com/storefronts/start.html

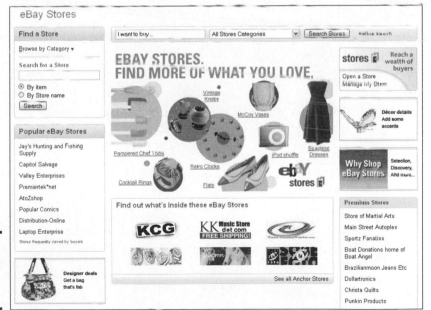

Figure 5-1: eBay Stores opening page.

Book VIII
Chapter 5

Opening Your eBay Store

Deciding to Open a Store

So you think it's time to open a store, eh? If you feel it in your gut and you're ready to take the leap, here's what you need to know. eBay has few requirements when it comes to opening an eBay Store:

✦ **Registered user:** You need to be a registered seller on the eBay site with a credit card on file.

✦ **Feedback rating:** You must have a feedback rating of 20 or higher, or be ID Verified, or have a PayPal account in good standing. .You can also qualify without the 20 feedback if you are ID Verified — but you really won't have enough experience to run your store.

It doesn't get much easier than that! Personally, I like to add these additional prerequisites to back you up for success:

✦ **PayPal account:** You need to have a business or premier (personal) PayPal account (and if you have that, you're PayPal Verified) to accept credit cards. Accepting credit cards is a necessity for building sales, and PayPal is integrated into the site, as well as being widely accepted by buyers.

  Be sure you understand how a PayPal account works so you can decide on the types of payments you will accept — and from which countries you intend to do business.

✦ **Sales experience:** Having selling (and buying) experience over and above the 20 transactions required by eBay is a big plus. The best teacher (aside from this book) is the school of hard knocks.

✦ **Merchandise:** Opening an eBay Store with only one each of ten items isn't a good idea. You need to have enough merchandise to support consistent sales in your store.

✦ **Devotion:** You need to have the time to check into your eBay business at *least* once a day, and the time to ship the purchased merchandise in a prompt manner.

The items listed as store inventory will not come up in an eBay search unless eBay can come up with thirty or less of the item searched for. The only way new buyers can find your store inventory is by clicking the Find Items in eBay Stores link in eBay Search, by searching items on the store hub page (as shown in Figure 5-2), or by clicking from one of your auction pages to see what else you have on sale.

Book VIII
Chapter 5

**Opening Your
eBay Store**

Figure 5-2:
The eBay
Stores hub.

Choosing Between Store Types

All eBay Stores are on a level playing field. They're all equally searchable for the eBay Stores hub page, so you can be right up there with the big guys and compete. The only cost differential is the type of store you want to open.

All eBay Stores have the following in common:

+ **Listings:** All your eBay listings, whether auction, fixed-price, or store inventory, will appear in your eBay Store.

+ **Custom URL:** Your eBay Store will have its own Internet address that you can use in links in promotional material — even to promote your store on the Internet.

+ **Store search:** When customers visit your eBay Store, they will be able to search within your listings for their desired item — with your own personal search engine.

+ **Cross-promotions:** You have the ability to insert thumbnail promotions for your store items within each of your items for sale on the regular eBay site.

+ **Seller reports:** You'll receive monthly reports on your store sales via e-mail.

How to save 75 percent on store Final Value Fees

Yes! The honchos at eBay are really smart. By promoting your eBay Store on your Web site and linking to your eBay Store, you can save 75 percent of your Final Value Fees on the items you sell through the referral link. It's a win-win situation. You draw people to your eBay Store, where you can have a more robust layout and features, and save on fees — and eBay gets more visitors coming to the site!

To get the referral bonus, you must set up a special link consisting of your eBay Store URL and some code. Here's my referral link, with the referral code in boldface text:

```
http://stores.ebay.com/marshac
    olliersfabulousfinds?refid
    =store
```

This code can also be used in promotional e-mails that you send out. The only bad thing is that customers have to purchase the item during the same browser session as when they enter your store from outside eBay.

It's definitely worth a try! Check out the figure to see a part of one of my eBay invoices; it shows how the savings can stack up!

120148373891	Final Value Fee - Fixed Price	-$2.39
110241603202	Insertion Fee	-$0.35
120149874336	Store Referral Credit	-$6.27

Although you will need to pay a small fee for each listing, eBay Store rental is available on three levels:

✦ **Basic store:** For $15.95 a month, you get your own eBay Store with all the benefits.

✦ **Featured store:** You get all the benefits of a basic store, plus there will be a link to your store from the store category page and randomly on the eBay Stores hub page. You also get more advanced sales reports. This type of store will set you back $49.95 per month.

✦ **Anchor store:** This is a top-of-the-line store on eBay. For $299.95 a month, your store logo rotates with others on the eBay Stores hub page. Your logo also randomly appears on eBay's home page. When prospective buyers are browsing eBay Store categories, you logo will show up at the top of the pages.

There is no limit to the number of items you put up for sale in the basic store. An anchor store can have as few or as many items as the basic store.

Many high-level PowerSellers find that the basic eBay Store fulfills their needs.

When people visit your eBay Store, they have no way of knowing whether you have a basic, featured, or anchor store. The design of your store is up to you — you can make it as fancy as you want.

Knowing the Fee Structure

When you have an eBay Store, other fees are involved (are you surprised?) in addition to the rental fee: listing fees, options fees, and final value fees. First up, the listing fees, which are shown in Table 5-2.

Table 5-2	Store Inventory Listing Fees
Item Price	*Listing ($) per 30 days*
$1.00 - $24.99	.03
$25.00 - $199.99	.025
$200.00 and above	.010

Listing your items for a l-o-o-o-n-g time may be tempting as a way to automate your listings — and it's a good strategy. However, after someone makes a purchase from an item listing, you can no longer make description changes; you can only update inventory. If you have a new picture or new ideas for a title or a description, you must close that listing and relist the item with the new information. Also, if you have an unpaid item, you must close the store listing to file for your Final Value Fee refund.

Items in an eBay Store carry a similar fee structure as items listed on the eBay site, but the actual numbers and percentages are different. The difference in cost helps you decide which items to put in your store, your auctions, or on your Web site. Knowing the prices in Tables 5-3 and 5-4 up front helps you to decide what you need to get for each item in the different sales formats.

Table 5-3	Store Inventory Listing Upgrades
Upgrade	*Cost per 30 Days of Listing Duration ($)*
Gallery Plus	0.35
Item subtitle	0.02
Listing Designer	0.10 (same as eBay core site)
Bold	1.00 (same as eBay core site)
Border	3.00 (same are eBay core site)
Highlight	5.00 (same as eBay core site)
Featured in search	9.95 to 24.95, based on starting price (same as eBay core site)

Mind your underscores and hyphens

If you want to use your eBay user ID for your store name, you can — unless it contains a hyphen (-) or an underscore (_). Remember how eBay recommends that you break up words in your user ID with a dash or an underscore? Uh oh, that's no good for an eBay Store name. I'm in that situation. My user ID is marsha_c — but without the underscore, it translates into a user ID that someone else has already taken!

Even though it hasn't been used since 1999, someone else has it, which means I can't use it. (marsha_c is probably a crummy name for a store anyway!) A favorite seller of mine — mrswarren — realized that mrswarren isn't a good name for a store, either. So she named her store *Pretty Girlie Things,* which suits her merchandise to a T.

Table 5-4	Store Final Value Fees
Final Item Price ($)	*Final Value Fee*
0.01 to 25.00	12% of the selling price
25.01 to 100.00	12% of the first $25.00 ($3), plus 8% of the remaining balance ($25.01 to $100.00)
100.01 to 1,000.00	12% of the first $25.00 ($3), plus 8% of $25.01 to $100.00 ($6), plus 4% of the remaining balance
1,000.01 and up	12% of the first $25.00 ($3), plus 8% of $25.01 to $100.00 ($6), plus 4% of $100.01 to $1,000 ($36) plus 2% the remaining balance

For a more detailed description on how to calculate fees, see Book III, Chapter 1.

The basic eBay Store gives you free use of Selling Manager. The only hook is, they don't just hand you the privilege; you have to go to the Selling Manager sign-up page and sign up. You'll see that as a store owner you won't be charged, but you must go through the Sign Up process to avail yourself of these great tools.

Selecting Your eBay Store Name

You've decided to take the plunge and open an eBay Store. Have you thought of a good name for your store? Your store name doesn't have to match your eBay user ID, but they're more recognizable if they relate to each other. You can use your company name, your business name, or a name that describes your business. I recommend that you use the same name for your eBay Store that you plan to use in all your online businesses. By doing so, you'll begin to create an identity (or as the pros call it, a *brand*) that customers will come to recognize and trust.

Your online eBay Store should not replace your Web site (see Book VI); it should be an extension of it. When people shop at your eBay Store, take the opportunity to make them customers of your Web site through your store's About the Seller page (which is also your About Me page on eBay). Good deal!

Setting Up Shop

It's time to get down to business. Go to the eBay Stores hub and click the Open a Store link, on the right side of the screen (refer to Figure 5-1). This takes you to the Seller's hub of eBay Stores. If you click all the links you see here, you get the eBay company line about how good an eBay Store can be for your business. You already know how good an eBay Store can be for your business, so skip the propaganda and get right down to business (but don't forget to check for any policy changes that may affect your store's operations).

Before you click that link to open your store, ask yourself two questions:

✦ **Can I make a serious commitment to my eBay Store?** A store is a commitment. It won't work for you unless you work for it. You have to have the merchandise to fill it and the discipline to continue listing store and auction items. Your store is a daily, monthly, and yearly obligation.

When you go on vacation, you need someone else to ship your items; otherwise your customers may go elsewhere. You can use the eBay Store's Vacation Feature and eBay will either close your items or put up a notification letting your customers know that you're on vacation until a specified date.

✦ **Will I work for my eBay Store even when I don't feel like it?** You have to be prepared for the times when you're sick or just don't feel like shipping, but orders are waiting to be shipped. You have to do the work anyway; it's all part of the commitment.

eBay gives you the venue, but it's in your own hands to make your mercantile efforts a success. If you can handle these two responsibilities, read on!

Subscribing to Stores and selecting a name

If you're serious and ready to move on, click the white Open a Store bar in the top center of the page (refer to Figure 5-2). Because you're always signed in on your home computer, you're escorted to Subscribe to eBay Stores and eventually a page reminding you that eBay Stores fall under the same User Agreement that you agreed to when you began selling on eBay.

eBay wants to ease you into this store thing. Make you feel comfortable, so you'll get the easy stuff first. Figure 5-3 below shows you the initial sign up screen, where you get to select the level of store you want. It's an easy choice, start small with the $15.95 version. Come to think of it, many sellers have been running the basic version for years and have been very happy with it.

You've decided on a store name, right? Because here's where you need to type it in. Your eBay Store name can't exceed 35 characters. Before you type it, double-check that you aren't infringing on anyone's copyrights or trademarks. You also can't use any permutation of eBay trademarks in your store's name.

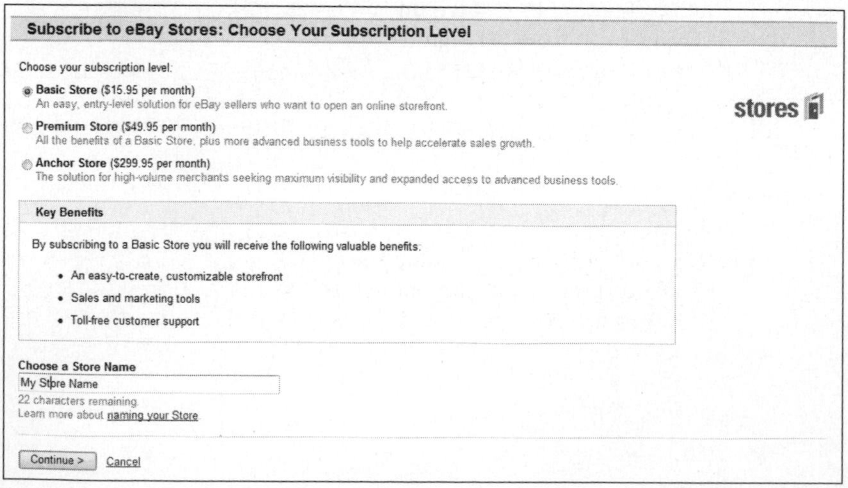

Figure 5-3: Taking the big step — go ahead and just do it.

After you've clicked the page's proverbial *Continue* button, eBay has a little page to show you a couple of benefits of opening your store. With the basic store you get Selling Manager and Sales Reports Plus for free. You don't have to do anything but click Continue because eBay already inserted the checkmarks in the selection boxes for you. If for some reason they don't appear, put a check by clicking each of the boxes and click, duh.... Continue.

The resulting page is where they start to get serious. It shows your monthly charges and the User Agreement (see Figure 5-4). Here eBay changes their friendly *Continue* button to *Subscribe*. That's to let you know that this is serious. Once you click Subscribe the clock starts to tick on your monthly fees.

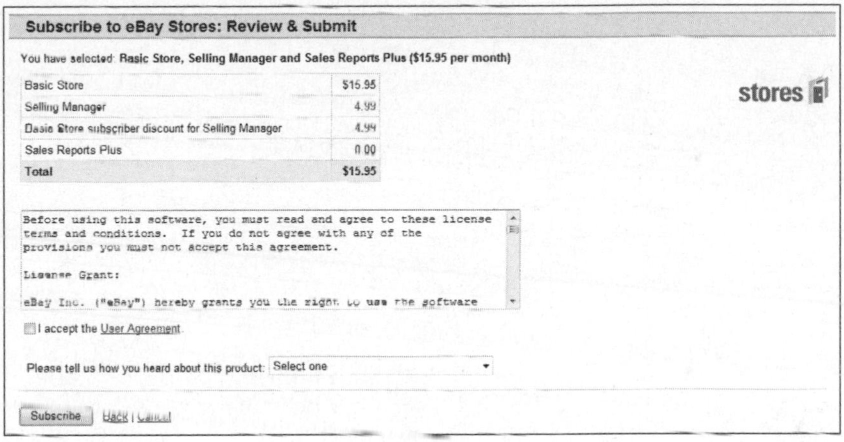

Subscribe to eBay Stores: Review & Submit

You have selected: Basic Store, Selling Manager and Sales Reports Plus ($15.95 per month)

Basic Store	$15.95
Selling Manager	4.99
Basic Store subscriber discount for Selling Manager	4.99
Sales Reports Plus	0.00
Total	$15.95

stores E

Before using this software, you must read and agree to these license terms and conditions. If you do not agree with any of the provisions you must not accept this agreement.

License Grant:

eBay Inc. ("eBay") hereby grants you the right to use the software

☐ I accept the User Agreement.

Please tell us how you heard about this product: Select one ▼

Subscribe | Back | Cancel

Figure 5-4: Why not give the User Agreement a read before checking the box?

Don't subscribe to a store unless you're ready to get started immediately. Fees start the day you sign up, so why not read this chapter first and get centered as to what you want to do.

Once you get to the Store Design pages, follow these steps:

1. **Choose a color theme.**

eBay provides some elegant color and graphics themes, as shown in Figure 5-5. Until you have the time to go hog-wild and design a custom masterpiece, you can choose one of the 14 clearly organized layouts, either predesigned or with easily customizable themes. You can always change the color scheme or layout for your eBay Store later. Don't select something overly bright and vibrant; you want something that's easy on the eyes, which is more conducive to a comfortable selling environment.

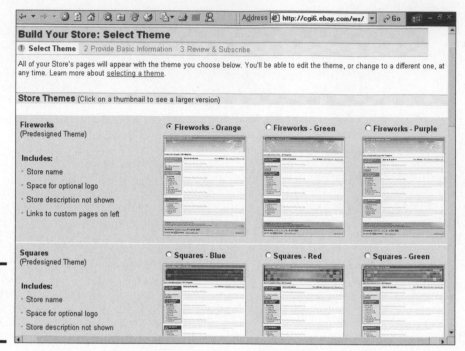

Figure 5-5:
Selecting a
theme for
your store.

You have the option of selecting a store theme that doesn't require you to insert a custom logo or banner. I vigorously recommend against skipping the logo. You need to establish a unifying brand for your online business.

2. **Click Continue.**

3. **Type a short description of your store.**

When I say short, I mean *short*. You have only 300 characters to give a whiz-bang, electric description of your store and merchandise. You can't use HTML coding to doll up the description, and you can't use links. Just the facts please, and a little bit of dazzle.

Write your copy ahead of time in Word. Then, still in Word, highlight the text and choose Tools➪Word Count. Word gives you the word count of the highlighted text. Check the character count with spaces, to be sure your text fits.

The description is hugely important. The keyword information you put here is referenced when someone searches eBay Stores and descriptions. Also, if the store header contains your description (as in the Classic style themes), search engines such as Google and Yahoo! look in this description for the keywords to classify your merchandise and list your store.

4. **Select a graphic to jazz up the look of your store.**

   You can use one of eBay's clip-art style banners or create a custom 310-by-90-pixel one. If you use one of eBay's graphics, you must promise (hand over heart) that you won't keep it there for long. (See the text after this set of steps for info on designing your own graphics — or hiring someone to do it.)

   Now you're getting somewhere. At this point, your eBay Store is just about ready to roll. You are about to open an eBay Storefront.

5. **Click Accept.**

   Your store is now live on the Internet with nothing up for sale — yet.

6. **Click the supplied link to get in the trenches and customize your store further.**

If you're wondering in which category your store will be listed on the eBay Stores home page, it's up to you. eBay checks the items as you list them in the standard eBay category format. For example, if you have six books listed in the Books: Fiction and Nonfiction category and five items in the Cameras & Photo category, you'll be in the listings for both categories. Your custom store categories (read on) are used to classify items only in your store.

Establishing a store logo

If you use one of eBay's prefab graphics, people shopping your eBay Store will know that you aren't serious enough about your business to design a simple and basic logo. I've had many years of experience in advertising and marketing, and I must tell you that a custom look will beat clip art any day. Your store is special — put forth the effort to make it shine.

If you have a graphics program, design a graphic with your store's name. Start with something simple; you can always change it later when you have more time. Save the image as a GIF or JPG file, and upload it to the site where you host your images (your own Web site, your ISP, or a hosting service).

To get a reasonably priced custom graphic for your eBay Store, search eBay for *eBay (banner, banners)*. (Don't add a space after the comma.) When I conducted that search, I found 86 Buy It Now listings for people who are willing to design a custom banner for under $20 — certainly worth the price in the time you'll save. Be sure you like the samples of the seller's designs and are comfortable with the terms before you buy.

Running Your Store

You can customize your store at any time by clicking the Manage Your Store link, which is at the bottom of your store's page and in the upper-right corner of the eBay Store's hub page. The page shown in Figure 5-6 appears, with headings describing important tasks for your store.

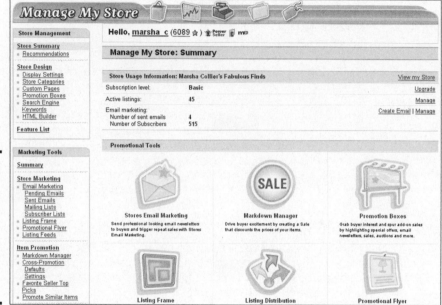

Figure 5-6: Here's where you can perform all the necessary tasks for running a store.

Store design and marketing

The Store Editing/Branding list of the Manage Your Store page (refer to Figure 5-6) has the following links for performing the major tasks required for your store:

✦ **Store Builder:** You can go back to the Store Builder (the original store setup area) to change the name of your store or the theme of your pages. You can also change the way your items are displayed: gallery view (as in Figure 5-7) or list view (as in Figure 5-8). Neither view is inherently better, but I like the gallery view because it shows larger thumbnails of your items.

Figure 5-7:
My eBay
Store in
gallery view.

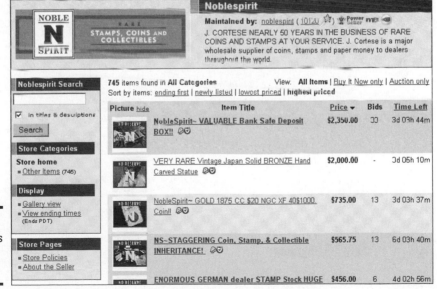

Figure 5-8:
Noblespirit's
eBay Store
in list view.

Create an About the Seller page

If you haven't already created an eBay About Me page, do it now! The About Me page becomes the About the Seller page in your store. This page is a primary tool for promoting sales. (See Book I, Chapter 8 for more on the About Me page.) You can put this page together in about ten minutes, max, with eBay's handy and easy-to-use templates!

You should also select the order in which your items will sort: highest-priced first, lowest-priced first, items ending first, or newly-listed first. I like "ending first" as my sort, so buyers can get the chance to swoop in on items closing soon.

✦ **Custom pages:** Most successful eBay sellers have a store policies page. Figure 5-9 shows you the one for my store. When you set up a policies page, eBay supplies you with a choice of layouts. Just click the Create New Page link to see the template that you want to use, as pictured in Figure 5-10. Don't freak out if you don't know HTML; eBay helps you out with an easy-to-use HTML generator as in the Sell Your Item form.

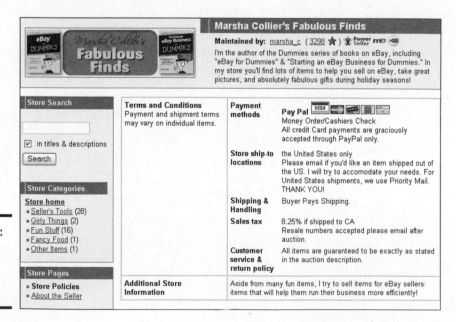

Figure 5-9: My eBay Store policies page.

Following are some important policies to include:

- **Indicate to what locations you'll ship.** If you won't ship items overseas, it's best to say so.

- **Specify the sales tax you plan to collect.** If your state doesn't require you to collect sales tax, leave the area blank. If it does, select your state and indicate the proper sales tax. Most states won't require you to collect sales tax unless the sale is shipped to your home state. Check the links in Book IX, Chapter 1, to verify your state's sales tax regulations.

- **State your customer service and return policy.** Fill in the information regarding how you handle refunds, exchanges, and so on. If you're a member of SquareTrade (see Chapter 4), mention here that you subscribe to its policies. Be sure to include whatever additional store information you think is pertinent.

You can also set up a custom home page for your store, but this isn't a popular option. It's best to let your visitors go right to the page that lists what you're selling, don't you think?

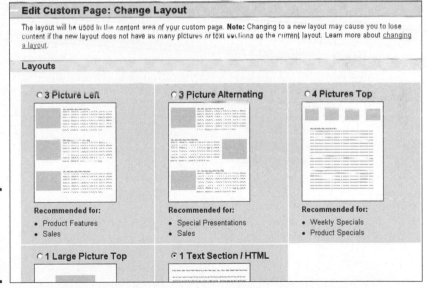

Figure 5-10: eBay Store page-customizing templates.

✦ **Custom categories:** Here's where you really make your store your own. You may name up to 300 custom categories that relate to the items you sell for your store.

✦ **Custom listing header:** Do this. Don't ask questions, just do it. The custom listing header display is one of the best tools you can use to bring people into your store. Click the link and select the option to show your custom listing header on all your eBay auctions and fixed-price sales. This will encourage shoppers to visit your eBay Store when they browse your eBay listings.

When customizing, be sure to include your store logo as well as a store search box. In Figure 5-11, you can see how the store header looks at the top of an eBay listing.

Figure 5-11: Add a link to your eBay Store and the capability to search the store.

Promotions

eBay has added some excellent ways to promote your store. As an eBay Store owner, you have access to promotional tools that other sellers can't use. The most valuable of these is the cross-promotions box — and there's no charge for using it! The cross-promotions box appears after a buyer places a bid on or purchases an item from an eBay seller.

The beauty of having a store is that the cross-promotions box appears *twice:* once within your regular listings and again, with a different assortment of items (if you want), after someone buys an item. Best of all? You get to select which items are shown with your individual auctions.

Figure 5-12 shows you a cross-promotions box that appears when someone views one of my auctions.

You can set up the promotions so they default to show other items from related store categories, or you can go in and set them up yourself for individual auctions. Again, every listing has two sets of options: one for when a user views your listings and the other for when someone bids or wins your item.

Figure 5-12: The cross-promotions box in one of my eBay auctions.

Making a sale

From the buyer's point of view, shopping at an eBay Store is much different than winning an auction. eBay Stores feature fixed-price sales; the buyer will get the merchandise as soon as you can ship it (instead of waiting for the auction to run its course). Even though your auctions show up on your store's home page, all regular listings in your eBay Store are Buy It Now items.

When a buyer makes a purchase from an eBay Store, here's what happens:

1. The buyer clicks the Buy It Now button on the listing page. The Review Payments page appears, where the buyer can review the purchase. This page contains the shipping amount that you specified when you listed the item.

2. The buyer provides shipping information (required). When eBay notifies you that a sale has been made, you have all the information you need.

3. The buyer reviews the transaction and then clicks the Confirm button. The information about the sale is e-mailed to you, and the buyer receives confirmation of the sale.

Your eBay Store is an essential backup to your auctions. It's a great place to put out-of-season items, accessories for the items you sell actively, and even consignment items between relistings. Considering the price of an eBay Store, you have to make only a few sales per month to pay for it. And when your sales start to build, your efforts will be greatly rewarded!

Book VIII Chapter 5

Opening Your eBay Store

Book IX
Office and Legal

The 5th Wave   By Rich Tennant

"Look—you can't just list an extraterrestrial embryo on eBay without using some catchy phrases or power words to make it seem interesting and unique."

Contents at a Glance

Chapter 1: Getting Legal with the State and the Feds

In This Chapter

✓ Filing a fictitious name statement (for real)

✓ Getting a business license and other regulatory details

✓ Choosing a legal business format

1 f you've played around on eBay, had some fun, and made a few dollars, good for you — enjoy yourself! Once you start making serious money, however, your business is no longer a hobby, It's time to consider some issues such as business structure, tax planning, and licenses.

When you're concentrating on fulfilling multiple orders and keeping your customers happy, the last thing you need is a G-man breathing down your neck. Worst case scenario: How about getting audited in December when you haven't been keeping good records all year? I know this sounds like stripping the fun out of doing business on eBay, but taking a bit of time and effort now can save you a ton of trouble later on (and will save you money in penalties).

Giving Your Business an Official Name

In most states in the U.S., you can find funny liner ads in the classified section of the local newspaper. They're called *fictitious name statements.* No, the statements aren't fictitious, but in effect, the names are — and as such, they need to be registered with your state before you can open a bank account in a business's name. They let the state know who owns and operates a business. In California, you must file a fictitious name statement within 40 days of the commencement of your business. (Other state laws vary, so check the Web sites listed later in this chapter for more information on your state's requirements.) Your statement must also include a physical address where the business is operated — not a post-office-box address.

Before you assume that registering a name isn't required in your state, check with your state's business code. (Links to all 50 states are presented later in the chapter.) Some states, such as Indiana, require that you register the assumed name of your business with the Secretary of State.

Don't waste your money!

All kinds of expensive services on the Internet are more than willing to handle the work for you for a fat fee. Don't spend too much of your money if you don't have to. If newspaper publication is required, look in the phone book for a small community newspaper (if they still exist in your part of the world) and call them to see whether they handle this type of legal ad. Most small newspapers are 90-percent supported by the money they make on filing legal ads. They're the experts on this type of filing. Plus, you get to help out another small business in your community. Every 5 years, it's a good thing to file your company's DBA (Doing Business As) with the nice gray-haired lady at the local newspaper office.

If there's no small-time newspaper near where you live, go to my Web site (`www.coolebay tools.com`) for a discount for the LegalZoom Web site (`www.legalzoom.com`). They will handle your DBA filing professionally and quickly (and you don't have to drive around).

In the states requiring publication, your fictitious name statement must be published in an adjudicated (officially approved) newspaper for a certain amount of time. Ostensibly, this is to let the community know that a business is starting and who owns it. The newspaper supplies you with a proof of publication, which you keep in your files as a record of your filing. You generally have to renew the statement after a prescribed number of years.

After you have your officially stamped proof of publication, you can bring that to the bank and open an account in your business name, which is an important step in separating your personal living expenses from the business.

Taking Care of Regulatory Details

Let me give you some important advice to make your life easier in the long run: Don't ignore city, county, state, and federal regulatory details. Doing so may seem to make life easier at the get-go, but if your business is successful, one day your casual attitude will catch up with you. The usual attitude of government is that "Ignorance of the law is no excuse." You must comply with all the rules and regulations that are set up for your protection and benefit.

Business license or city tax certificate

Business licenses are the official-looking pieces of paper you see behind the register at brick-and-mortar businesses. Every business must have one, and depending on your local laws, you may have to have a *city license* or a *city tax registration certificate*. Yes, even if you're running a business out of your home and have no one coming to do business at your home, you may still need this. If you don't have one, the authorities may charge you a bunch of penalties if they ever find out. Avoiding this step isn't worth that risk.

To save you hanging on the phone, listening to elevator music, and being transferred and disconnected ad nauseam, I supply you with the direct links to apply for your licenses in Table 1-1. These URLs are accurate at the time of this writing, but as everybody knows, URLs change frequently. Check the following for updates:

```
www.sba.gov/hotlist/license.html
```

Book IX
Chapter 1

Getting Legal
with the State
and the Feds

Table 1-1	Web Sites for Business License Information
State	**Link**
Alabama	www.ador.state.al.us/licenses/MunBusLic.htm
Alaska	www.dced.state.ak.us/occ/home.htm
Arizona	http://www.revenue.state.az.us/609/licensingguide.htm
Arkansas	asbdc.ualr.edu/business-information/1006-business-licenses taxes-permits.asp
California	www.calgold.ca.gov/
Colorado	http://www.sos.state.co.us/pubs/business/main.htm
Connecticut	www.ct-clic.com/Content/Smart_Start_for_Business.asp
Delaware	https://onestop.delaware.gov/osbrl public/Home.jsp
District of Columbia	http://mblr.dc.gov/main.shtm
Florida	www.myflorida.com/dbpr/
Georgia	www.sos.state.ga.us/firststop/
Hawaii	hawaii.gov/dcca/areas/breg
Idaho	http://commerce.idaho.gov/business/index.aspx
Illinois	business.illinois.gov/step_by_step_guides.cfm
Indiana	www.in.gov/business_guide.htm
Iowa	www.iowalifechanging.com/business/blic.html
Kansas	www.accesskansas.org/businesscenter/index.html?link=start

(continued)

Table 1-1 *(continued)*

State	Link
Kentucky	sos.ky.gov/business/
Louisiana	GeauxBiz.com\
Maine	www.maine.gov/portal/business/starting.html
Maryland	www.blis.state.md.us/BusinessStartup.aspx
Massachusetts	www.dor.state.ma.us/business/doingbus.htm
Michigan	www.michigan.gov/businessstartup
Minnesota	www.deed.state.mn.us/faq/business.htm
Mississippi	www.olemiss.edu/depts/mssbdc/going_into bus.html
Missouri	www.missouribusiness.net/docs/license_ registration_checklist.asp
Montana	/mt.gov/revenue/programsandservices/ onestop.asp
Nebraska	https://www.nebraska.gov/osbr/cgi/dome stic.cgi?/OSBRApplication/init/init/None
Nevada	www.nv.gov/new_DoingBusiness.htm
New Hampshire	www.nh.gov/revenue/business/dra_licenses. htm
New Jersey	www.state.nj.us/njbusiness/starting/
New Mexico	www.rld.state.nm.us/index.html
New York	www.gorr.state.ny.us/Main_GORR_Pages/ Business-Permit-Assistance.html
North Carolina	www.nccommerce.com/en/ BusinessServices/StartYourBusiness/ BusinessLicensesPermits/
North Dakota	www.nd.gov/businessreg/license/index.html
Ohio	www.odod.state.oh.us/onestop/index.cfm
Oklahoma	www.okcommerce.gov/licensing
Oregon	www.filinginoregon.com/business/ starting_a_business.htm
Pennsylvania	www.paopenforbusiness.state.pa.us/paofb/ site/default.asp
Rhode Island	http://www2.sec.state.ri.us/faststart/

**Book IX
Chapter 1**

**Getting Legal
with the State
and the Feds**

State	Link
South Carolina	www.scbos.com/Business+Information/License+-+Permits/Default.htm
South Dakota	www.state.sd.us/drr2/newbusiness.htm
Tennessee	www.state.tn.us/ecd/res_guide.htm
Texas	www.business.texasonline.com/?language=eng
Utah	www.utah.gov/business/starting.html
Vermont	http://www.thinkvermont.com/Grow/StartingaBusiness/tabid/280/Default.aspx
Virginia	http://virginiabos.sparkstudiosaas.com/onestop/VirtualLobby.jsp
Washington	www.dol.wa.gov/business/
West Virginia	http://www.business4wv.com
Wisconsin	www.wisconsin.gov/state/byb/
Wyoming	http://soswy.state.wy.us/Business/Business.aspx

State sales tax number

If your state has a sales tax, a *sales tax number* (the number you use when you file your sales tax statement with your state) is required before you officially sell anything. If sales tax applies, you may have to collect the appropriate sales tax for every sale that ships within the state that your business is in.

Some people also call this a *resale certificate* because when you want to purchase goods from a wholesaler within your state, you must produce this number (thereby certifying your legitimacy as a seller) so the dealer can sell you the merchandise without charging you sales tax.

To find the regulations for your state, try the following terrific site that supplies links to every state's tax board, which should have the answers to your questions:

www.taxadmin.org/fta/link/forms.html

Don't withhold the withholding forms

If you're going to be paying anyone a salary, you'll need an *employer identification number* (EIN), also known as a *Federal tax identification number*. Every business has one. It's like a Social Security Number for a business, identifying your business on all government forms: a nine-digit number assigned to all businesses for tax filing and reporting. You may also need one for your state.

If you have regular employees, you need to file *withholding forms* to collect the necessary taxes that you must send to the state and the IRS on behalf of your employees. You're also expected to deposit those tax dollars with the IRS and your state on the date required, which may vary from business to business. Many enterprises go down because the owners just can't seem to keep their fingers out of withheld taxes — which means the money isn't available to turn in when the taxes are due. (This is another reason you should have a separate bank account for your business.)

No need to dawdle. Why not get the number while you have the time:

✦ There's no charge to get your employer ID number (EIN).

✦ An employer ID number can be assigned by filing IRS form SS-4. Go to the IRS Web site to apply online:

> `www.irs.gov/businesses/small/article/0,,id=102767,00.`
> `html`

Or if you'd rather mail in the form, the details and downloadable form are available as a PDF file.

✦ State employer ID numbers for taxes may depend on your state's requirements. Visit the following for an overview of the requirements for every state in the country:

> `www.taxadmin.org/fta/forms.ssi`

Selecting a Business Format

After you've fulfilled all the regulatory details, you need to formally decide how you want to run your company. You need to set up a legal format and you need to make a merchandise plan. (For more on merchandise planning, visit Book IV, Chapter 2.)

When you have a business, any type of business, it has to have a legal format for licensing and tax purposes. Businesses come in several forms, from a sole proprietorship all the way to a corporation. A "corporation" designation isn't as scary as it sounds. Yes, Microsoft, IBM, and eBay are corporations, but so too are many individually run businesses.

Each form of business has its pluses and minuses — and costs. I go over some of the fees involved in incorporating later in this chapter. For now, I detail the most common types of businesses, which I encourage you to weigh carefully.

**Book IX
Chapter 1**

**Getting Legal
with the State
and the Feds**

I'm not a lawyer, so be sure to consult with a professional in the legal and financial fields to get the latest legal and tax ramifications of the various business formats.

Sole proprietorship

If you're running your business by yourself part-time or full-time, your business is a *sole proprietorship*. Yep, doesn't that sound official? A sole proprietorship is the simplest form of business; you don't need a lawyer to set it up. Nothing is easier or cheaper. Most people use this form of business when they're starting out. Many people often graduate to a more formal type of business as things get bigger.

If a husband and wife file a joint tax return, they *can* run a business as a sole proprietorship (but only one of you can be the proprietor). However, if both you and your spouse work equally in the business, then running it as a partnership — with a written partnership agreement — is a much better idea. (See the next section, "Partnership," for more information.) A partnership protects you in case of your partner's death. In a sole proprietorship, the business ends with the death of the proprietor. If the business has been a sole proprietorship in your late spouse's name, you may be left out in the cold.

Being in business adds a few expenses, but many things that you spend money on now (relating to your business) can be deducted from your state and federal taxes. A sole proprietorship *can* be run out of your personal checking account (although I don't advise it). The profits of your business are taxed directly as part of your own income tax, and the profits and expenses are reported on Schedule C of your 1040 tax package. As a sole proprietor, you're at risk for the business liabilities. All outstanding debts are yours, and you could lose personal assets if you default. Also, as your business becomes profitable, this business format forces you to pay an additional self-employment tax.

Also, you must consider the liability of the products you sell on eBay. If you sell foodstuffs, vitamins, or nutraceuticals (new-age food supplements) that make someone ill, you may be personally liable for any court-awarded damages. If someone is hurt by something you sell, you may also be personally liable as the seller of the product.

In a sole proprietorship, as with any form of home-based business, you may be able to get an insurance rider to your homeowner's insurance policy to cover you against some liabilities. Check with your insurance agent.

Partnership

When two or more people are involved in a business, it can be a *partnership*. A general partnership can be formed by an oral agreement. Each person in the partnership contributes capital or services and both share in the partnership's profits and losses. The income of a partnership is taxed to both partners, based on the percentage of the business that they own or upon the terms of a written agreement. Any losses are also split. The partnership must file its own tax return (Form 1065) reporting the business financials to the IRS.

You'd better be sure that you can have a good working relationship with your partner: This type of business relationship has broken up many a friendship. Writing up a formal agreement when forming your eBay business partnership is an excellent idea. This agreement is useful in solving any disputes that may occur over time.

In your agreement, be sure to outline things such as

+ How to divide the profits and losses

+ Compensation to each partner

+ Duties and responsibilities of each partner

+ Restrictions of authority and spending

+ How disputes should be settled

+ What happens if the partnership dissolves

+ What happens to the partnership in case of death or disability

One more important thing to remember: As a partner, you're jointly and severally responsible for the business liabilities and actions of the other person or people in your partnership — as well as your own. Again, this is a personal liability arrangement. You are both personally open to any lawsuits that come your way through the business.

The partnership has to file an informational return with the IRS and the state, but the profits of the partnership are taxed to the partners on their personal individual returns.

LLC (Limited Liability Company)

A *limited liability company,* or LLC, is similar to a partnership but also has many of the characteristics of a corporation. An LLC differs from a partnership mainly in that the liabilities of the company are not passed on to the members (owners). Unless you sign a personal guarantee for debt incurred, the members are responsible only to the total amount they have invested into the company. But all members *do* have liability for the company's taxes.

Book IX
Chapter 1

Getting Legal
with the State
and the Feds

Getting legal documents prepared online

You just *knew* legal services would go online eventually, didn't you? If you're thinking of setting up one of the business formats described in this chapter, you might be interested in putting things together online. Real lawyers are there to help you at www.legalzoom.com. They handle legal document preparation for business incorporation, partnerships, and more for low prices. This online venture was developed by a group of experienced attorneys, co-founded by Robert Shapiro (yes, *that* Robert Shapiro — of O.J. fame).

They feature an amazing online law library that can answer many of your questions and help you make informed decisions. Documents are prepared according to how you answer online questionnaires. LegalZoom checks your work, and e-mails your documents or mails them printed on quality acid-free paper for your signature.

LegalZoom handled the trademark for my name, and I couldn't believe how easy the process was. They had step-by-step instructions and FAQs to handle my silliest of questions. I got my paperwork quickly and the entire process was not only inexpensive but painless. You may want to also at least do a phone consultation with an attorney in your area, perhaps one who is a member of the local Chamber of Commerce.

You'll need to put together an operating agreement, similar to the partnership agreement. This also will help establish which members own what percentage of the company for tax purposes. Most states will require you to file Articles of Organization forms to start this type of business.

An LLC is taxed like a sole proprietorship, with the profits and losses passed on to the members' personal tax returns. An LLC may opt to pay taxes like a corporation and keep some of the profits in the company, thereby reducing the tax burden to individual members. Although members pay the LLC's taxes, the LLC must still file Form 1065 with the IRS at the end of the year. This gives the IRS extra data to be sure that the individual members properly report their income.

Some states levy additional special or minimum taxes on an LLC. Be sure to check with your state's business department.

C-corporation

A corporation has a life of its own: its own name, its own bank account, and its own tax return. A *corporation* is a legal entity created for the sole purpose of doing business. If you're a sole proprietor and you're incorporating, one of the main problems you face is realizing that you can't just help yourself to the assets of the business. Yes, a corporation can have only one owner — but that owner is the shareholder(s). If you can't accept that you can't write yourself a check from your corporation — unless it's for a specified salary or for the reimbursement of legitimate expenses — then you may not be cut out to face the responsibility of running your own corporation.

The state in which you run your business sets up the rules for the corporations operating within its borders. You must apply to the Secretary of State of the state in which you want to incorporate. Federal taxes for corporations presently range from 15 to 35 percent (see Table 1-2), and they're generally based on your net profits.

Table 1-2	Federal Tax Rates for Corporations
Taxable Income ($)	Tax Rate (%)
0 to 50,000	15
50,001 to 75,000	25
75,001 to 100,000	34
100,001 to 335,000	39
335,001 to 10,000,000	34
10,000,001 to 15,000,000	35
15,000,001 to 18,333,333	38
18,333,334 and more	35

Employee owners of corporations can use the company to shelter income from being taxed by dividing the income between their personal and corporate tax returns. This is frequently called *income splitting;* it involves setting salaries and bonuses so that any profits left in the company at the end of its tax year will be taxed at only the 15-percent rate.

It's kind of fun to compare what you pay and how much you'd pay in taxes if you left profits in a small corporation, so check out Table 1-2 for the rates.

Considering that the individual Federal tax-rate percentages for incomes up to $75,000 annually go as high as 30.5 percent, the trouble of keeping a corporation for your business may be a huge money-saver.

Most states also have their own taxes for corporations. In Table 1-3, you see the basic tax for C Corporations (assuming your corporation makes money after payroll and other expenses). Please check with your tax professional as many states have Franchise Taxes, Inventory taxes (and goodness knows what else) as well.

Book IX
Chapter 1

Getting Legal
with the State
and the Feds

Table 1-3	State Corporate Income Tax Rates as of January 1, 2008	
State	*Tax Rates and Brackets*	*Note This . . .*
Alabama	6.5%	
Alaska	1.0% > $0	
	2.0 > 10K	
	3.0 > 20K	
	4.0 > 30K	
	5.0 > 40K	
	6.0 > 50K	
	7.0 > 60K	
	8.0 > 70K	
	9.0 > 80K	
	9.4 > 90K	
Arizona	6.968%	Minimum tax of $50
Arkansas	1.0% > $0	
	2.0 > 3K	
	3.0 > 6K	
	5.0 > 11K	
	6.0 > 25K	
	6.5 > 100K	
California	8.84%	Minimum tax of $800
Colorado	4.63%	
Connecticut	7.5% or higher (income tax or tax on capital)	Minimum capital $250
Delaware	8.7% on the first $20 million	
District Of Columbia	9.975%	Minimum tax of $100
Florida	5.5%	
Georgia	6%	
Hawaii	4.4% > $0	
	5.4 > 25K	
	6.4 > 100K	

(continued)

Table 1-3 *(continued)*

State	Tax Rates and Brackets	Note This . . .
Idaho	7.6%	Minimum tax $20
Illinois	7.3%	
Indiana	8.5%	
Iowa	6.0% > $0	
	8.0 > 25K	
	10.0 > 100K	
	12.0 > 250K	
Kansas	4% > $0	
	7.35 > 50K	
Kentucky	4.% > $0	Plus the larger of a gross receipts tax equal to 0.095% of gross sales or 0.75% of gross profits, or a minimum tax of $175.
	5.0 > 50K	
	6.0 > 100K	
Louisiana	4.0% > $0	Federally Deductible
	5.0 > 25K	
	6.0 > 50K	
	7.0 > 100K	
	8.0 > 200K	
Maine	3.5% > $0	
	7.93 > 25K	
	8.33 > 75K	
	8.93 > 250K	
Maryland	8.25%	
Massachusetts	9.50%	Minimum tax of $456
Michigan	4.95%	
Minnesota	9.8%	
Mississippi	3.0% > $0	
	4.0 > 5K	
	5.0 > 10K	

**Book IX
Chapter 1**

*Getting Legal
with the State
and the Feds*

State	Tax Rates and Brackets	Note This . . .
Missouri	6.25%	
Montana	6.75%	Minimum tax of $50
Nebraska	5.58% > $0	
	7.81 > 50K	
Nevada	None	
New Hampshire	8.5% > $50K	
	9.25 > 150K	
New Jersey	6.5% > $0	
	7.5 > 50K	
	9.0 > 100K	
New Mexico	4.8% > $0	
	6.4 > 500K	
	7.6 > 1,000,000	
New York	7.1%	
North Carolina	6.9%	
North Dakota	2.6% > $0	
	4.1 > 3K	
	5.6 > 8K	
	6.4 > 20K	
	6.5 > 30K	
Ohio	5.1% > $0	
	8.5 > 50K	
Oklahoma	6.0%	
Oregon	6.6%	Minimum tax of $10
Pennsylvania	9.99%	
Rhode Island	9.0%	
South Carolina	5.0%	
South Dakota	None	
Tennessee	6.5%	
Texas	1.0%	
Utah	5.0%	Minimum tax of $100

(continued)

Table 1-3 *(continued)*

State	Tax Rates and Brackets	Note This . . .
Vermont	6.0% > $0	Minimum tax of $250
	7.0 > 10K	
	8.5 > 25K	
Virginia	6.0%	
Washington	Varies	
West Virginia	8.75%	
Wisconsin	7.9%	
Wyoming	None	

To get a clearer idea of the taxes in your state, check the following: (also call your tax person).

www.taxfoundation.org/news/show/230.html

Often, in small corporations, most of the profits are paid out in tax-deductible salaries and benefits. The most important benefit for a business is that any liabilities belong to the corporation. Your personal assets remain your own, because they have no part in the corporation.

Chapter 2: The Joys of Taxes and Business Reporting

In This Chapter

✔ Finding a tax professional

✔ Understanding first things first: Bookkeeping basics

✔ Saving your records to save your bacon

✔ Letting your reports talk to you

✔ Keeping your company records organized and safe

Bookkeeping, *bah!* You'll get no argument from me that bookkeeping can be the most boring and time-consuming part of your job. You may feel that you just need to add your product costs, add your gross sales, and bada-bing, you know where your business is. Sorry, not true. Did you add that roll of tape you picked up at the supermarket today? Although it cost only $1.29, it's a business expense. How about the mileage driving back and forth from garage sales and flea markets? Those are expenses, too. I suspect that you're not counting quite a few other "small" items just like these in your expense column.

I must confess that I enjoy posting my expenses and sales after I actually get into the task. It gives me the opportunity to know exactly where my business is at any given moment. Of course, I'm not using a pencil-entered ledger system; I use a software program that's easy and fun. In this chapter, I give you the lowdown on the basics of bookkeeping and emphasize the importance of keeping records in case Uncle Sam comes calling. Keep reading: This chapter is *required.*

Dealing with a Professional

Have you ever wondered why big businesses have CFOs (chief financial officers), vice presidents of finance, CPAs (certified public accountants), and bookkeepers? It's because keeping the books is the backbone of a company's business.

Do you have a professional going over your books at least once a year? You should. A paid professional experienced in business knows what to do when it comes to your taxes. Due to the complexity of the tax code, not just any paid preparer will suffice when it comes to preparing your business taxes. Here's a list of possible people who can prepare your tax returns.

✦ **Tax preparer (or consultant):** This is the person you visit at the local we-file-for-you tax office. Did you know that a tax preparer could be anybody? There is no licensing involved. H&R Block hires as many as 100,000 seasonal workers as tax preparers each year. Where do these people come from? I'm sure that some are experts on the tax code, but the sheer number of tax preparers and the lack of regulation can make using a we-file-for-you tax office a risky proposition for businesspeople who want to minimize their tax liability.

A United States General Accounting Office report estimated that, in 1998, American citizens overpaid their taxes by $945 million because they claimed the standard deduction when it would have been more beneficial to itemize. Half of those taxpayers used a paid preparer who clearly was not cognizant of the full tax law as it applied to these individuals. Scary, huh?

✦ **Volunteer IRS-certified preparers:** The AARP (American Association of Retired Persons) does an outstanding job of assembling nearly 32,000 tax preparers to serve the needs of low-to-middle-income taxpayers (special attention going to seniors). Their goal is to maximize legal deductions and credits, resulting in "tangible economic benefits" for their clients. These volunteers have to study, take a test, and become *certified by the IRS* before they can lend their services to the cause.

In recent years, AARP volunteers served a total of 1.85 million seniors in the United States. My mother was a retired corporate comptroller, and she volunteered in this program for many years. (She was disappointed when she made her lowest score on the IRS test — a 94%!) They staff more than 8500 sites around the United States. To find the one near you, call 1-888-AARP-NOW (1-888-227-7669) and select Tax-Aide Information or go to www.aarp.org/money/taxaide.

✦ **Public accountant:** A public accountant, or PA, must fulfill educational, testing, and experience requirements and obtain a state license. PAs must take an annual course to maintain their status.

✦ **Enrolled agent:** Often called one of the best-kept secrets in accounting, an enrolled agent is federally licensed by the IRS. (CPAs and attorneys are licensed by the state.) EAs must pass an extensive annual test on tax law and tax-return preparation every year to maintain their status. (They also have to pass annual background checks.) Enrolled agents are authorized to appear in place of a taxpayer before the IRS.

Many EAs are former IRS employees. To find an enrolled agent near you, go to the www.naea.org Web site and enter the Taxpayer's area.

✦ **Certified public accountant:** Certified public accountants (CPAs) must complete rigorous testing and fulfill experience requirements as pre-scribed by the state in which they practice. Most states require a CPA to obtain a state license.

CPAs are accountants. They specialize in recordkeeping and reporting financial matters. Their important position is as an advisor regarding financial decisions for both individuals and businesses. CPAs must take an annual course to maintain their status.

Keeping the Books: Basics to Get You Started

Although posting bookkeeping entries can be boring, clicking a button to generate your tax information is a lot easier than manually going over pages of sales information on a pad of paper. That's why I like to use a software program, particularly QuickBooks (more about that program later).

I suppose that you *could* use plain ol' paper and a pencil to keep your books; if that works for you, great. But even though that might work for you now, it definitely won't in the future. Entering all your information into a software program now — while your books may still be fairly simple to handle — can save you a lot of time and frustration in the future, when your eBay business has grown beyond your wildest dreams and no amount of paper can keep it all straight and organized. I discuss alternative methods of bookkeeping in Chapter 3 in this minibook. For now, I focus on the basics of bookkeeping.

Tracking everything in and out

To effectively manage your business, you must keep track of *all* your expenses — down to the last roll of tape. You need to keep track of your inventory, how much you paid for the items, how much you paid in shipping, and how much you profited from your sales. If you use a van or the family car to pick up or deliver merchandise to the post office (I can load eight of the light kits that I sell on eBay in our car), you should keep track of this mileage as well. When you're running a business, you should account for every penny that goes in and out.

Bookkeeping has irrefutable standards called GAAP (Generally Accepted Accounting Principles) that are set by the Financial Accounting Standards Advisory Board. (It sounds scary to me too.) *Assets, liabilities, owner's equity, income,* and *expenses* are standard terms used in all forms of accounting to define profit, loss, and the fiscal health of your business.

Accounting for everything — twice

Every time you process a transaction, two things happen: One account is credited while another receives a debit (kind of like yin and yang). To get more familiar with these terms (and those in the following list), see the definitions in the chart of accounts in Chapter 3 in this minibook. Depending on the type of account, the account's balance either increases or decreases. One account that increases while another decreases is called *double-entry accounting:*

✦ When you post an expense, the debit *increases* your expenses and *decreases* your bank account.

✦ When you purchase furniture or other assets, it *increases* your asset account and *decreases* your bank account.

✦ When you make a sale and make the deposit, it *increases* your bank account and *decreases* your accounts receivable.

✦ When you purchase inventory, it *increases* your inventory and *decreases* your bank account.

✦ When a portion of a sale includes sales tax, it *decreases* your sales and *increases* your sales tax account.

Manually performing double-entry accounting can be a bit taxing (no pun intended). A software program, however, will automatically adjust the accounts when you input a transaction.

Separating business and personal records

As a business owner, even if you're a sole proprietor (see Chapter 1 in this minibook for information on business types), you should keep your business books separate from your personal expenses. (I recommend using a program such as Quicken to keep track of your personal expenses for tax time.) By isolating your business records from your personal records, you can get a snapshot of which areas of your sales are doing well and which ones aren't carrying their weight. But that isn't the only reason keeping accurate records is smart; there's the IRS to think about, too. In the next section, I explain Uncle Sam's interest in your books.

Okay, posting bookkeeping can be boring. But at the end of the fiscal year, when you have a professional do your taxes, you'll be a lot happier — and your tax preparation will cost you less — if you've posted your information cleanly and in the proper order. That's why using a program such as QuickBooks (see Chapter 3 in this minibook) is essential to running your business.

Records Uncle Sam May Want to See

One of the reasons we can have a great business environment in the United States is because we all have a partner, Uncle Sam. Our government regulates business and sets the rules for us to transact our operations. To help you get started with your business, the IRS maintains a small-business Web site (shown in Figure 2-1) at the following address:

`www.irs.gov/businesses/small`

In this section, I highlight what information you need to keep and how long you should keep it (just in case you're chosen for an audit).

Figure 2-1:
IRS home
page for
small
businesses.

Supporting information

Aside from needing to know how your business is going (which is really important), the main reason to keep clear and concise records is because Uncle Sam may come knocking one day. You never know when the IRS will choose *your* number and want to examine your records. In the following list, I highlight some of the important pieces of supporting information (things that support your expenses on your end-of-year tax return):

✦ **Receipts:** Dear reader, heed this advice: *Save every receipt you get.* If you're out of town on a buying trip and have coffee at the airport, save that receipt — it's a deduction from your profits. Everything related to your business may be deductible, so you must save airport parking receipts, taxi receipts, receipts for a pen that you picked up on your way to a meeting, *everything.* If you don't have a receipt, you can't prove the write-off.

✦ **Merchandise invoices:** Saving all merchandise invoices is as important as saving all your receipts. If you want to prove that you paid $400 and not the $299 retail price for that PlayStation 2 that you sold on eBay for $500, you'd *better* have an invoice of some kind. The same idea applies to most collectibles, in which case a retail price can't be fixed. Save all invoices!

✦ **Outside contractor invoices:** If you use outside contractors — even if you pay the college kid next door to go to the post office and the bank for you — you should get an invoice from them to document exactly what service you paid for and how much you paid. This is supporting information that will save your bacon, should it ever need saving.

✦ **Business cards:** It may sound like I'm stretching things a bit, but if you use your car to look at some merchandise, pick up a business card from the vendor. If you're out of town and have a meeting with someone, take a card. Having these business cards can help substantiate your deductible comings and goings.

✦ **A daily calendar:** This is where your Palm or other handheld digital organizer comes in. Every time you leave your house or office on a business-related task, make note of it in your Palm. Keep as detailed a hoard of minutiae as you can stand. You can use your computer or Palm desktop to print a monthly calendar. At the end of the year, staple the pages together and include them in your files with your substantiating information.

✦ **Credit-card statements:** You're already collecting credit-card receipts (although mine always seem to slip through the holes in my purse). If you have your statements, you have a monthly proof of expenses. When you get your statement each month, post it into your bookkeeping program and itemize each and every charge, detailing where you spent the money and what for. (QuickBooks has a split feature that accommodates all your categories.) File these statements with your tax return at the end of the year in your year-end envelope (shoebox?).

I know that all this stuff will pile up, but that's when you go to the store and buy some plastic file-storage containers to organize it all. To check for new information and the lowdown on what you can and can't do, ask an accountant or a CPA. Also visit the IRS Tax Information for Businesses site, shown in Figure 2-2, at

www.irs.ustreas.gov/businesses

How long should you keep your records?

How long do you have to keep all this supporting information? I hate to tell you, but I think I've saved it all. I must have at least ten years of paperwork in big plastic boxes and old files in the garage. But you know, I'm not too extreme; the period in which you can amend a return or in which the IRS can assess more tax is never less than three years from the date of filing — and can be even longer.

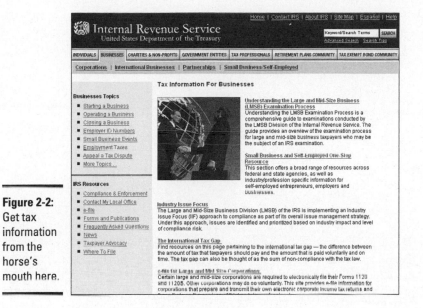

Figure 2-2:
Get tax information from the horse's mouth here.

The IRS wants you to save anything related to your tax return for three years. But if you take a look at Table 2-1, the IRS may want backup documentation for up to six years. So for safety's sake, keep things for six years, if only to prove you're innocent. (As an aside, because I'm paranoid, I still keep everything for the maximum mentioned by the IRS: seven years.)

Table 2-1	Keep Records for This Length of Time
Circumstance	*Keep Records This Long*
You owe additional tax (if the following three points don't apply)	3 years
You don't report all your income and what you don't report is more than 25% of the gross income shown on your return	6 years
You file a fraudulent tax return	Forever
You don't bother to file a return	Forever
You file a claim of refund or credit after you've filed	3 years or 2 years after the tax was paid (whichever is longer)
Your claim is due to a bad debt deduction	7 years
Your claim is from worthless securities	7 years
You have information on assets	Life of the asset

Even though I got the information in Table 2-1 directly from the IRS Web site and literature (Publication 583, "Starting a Business and Keeping Records"), it may change in the future. You can download a PDF copy of the booklet by going to the following address:

www.irs.gov/pub/irs-pdf/p583.pdf

If Adobe Acrobat Reader isn't installed on your computer, you can download the software (it's free) from the IRS Web site. It doesn't hurt to store your information for as long as you can stand it and stay on top of any changes the IRS may implement.

Getting the Most from Your Reports

After you're up and running with your eBay business, you can look forward to having lots of reports to evaluate. Of course, you get a plethora of reports from PayPal, eBay, and so on, but the most important reports are those you generate from your bookkeeping program (software such as QuickBooks). I use the QuickBooks software package to manage my business records, and it keeps several common reports (Balance Sheet, Accounts Payable, P&L, and so on) in an easily accessible area. If you check out the Reports tab in your bookkeeping program, I'll bet you find similar items. Before your eyes glaze over, though, check out this section for straightforward descriptions of these reports and the information they provide.

Similar sales and financial reports are common to all businesses, and reviewing them on a monthly basis can help you stay on top of yours.

To get your business reports when you need them, you must post your sales receipts regularly — and thereby update the "money in" and "inventory out" figures. Post your payments at least weekly (especially on your company credit card — post those transactions the minute you make purchases) — and reconcile your checkbook the moment your bank statement arrives.

What does posting and reconciling tasks get you? The opportunity to press a button and get a complete picture of your business. From the reports you generate, you find out whether your business is profitable, what products are selling, and if you're spending too much money in a particular area. Keeping your books up to date allows you to find problems before they become unmanageable.

If you run your sales and financial reports only quarterly rather than monthly, a problem — such as not pricing your items high enough — could be mushrooming out of control before you can detect and correct it.

Understanding the balance sheet

Your balance sheet provides the best information on your business. It pulls data from all the other reports and gives you a complete look at the financial condition of your business.

Your balance sheet shows all your assets:

✦ **Cash in bank:** The money in your business bank account.

✦ **Accounts receivable:** If you've invoiced anyone and not received payment as yet, that amount is reflected here.

✦ **Inventory assets:** This is the value of the merchandise you've purchased for resale but have not sold yet.

✦ **Other assets:** Things your business (not you) owns, such as furniture and vehicles. These are not considered in the current asset figure.

✦ **Accumulated depreciation:** This is deprecation on your assets, either produced by your accounting program or given to you by your accountant.

Your balance sheet also shows your liabilities:

✦ **Accounts payable:** Money you owe vendors and money due on unpaid credit cards show up here.

✦ **Sales tax:** The money you've collected on sales tax (that is due to your state) is a liability.

✦ **Payroll liabilities:** If you haven't made a bank deposit covering the money you've withdrawn from employees (withholding taxes, Social Security, Medicare, and so on), it shows up here.

Your equity shows up in the (literal and figurative) bottom line. It will include the initial investment in your business and the net income total from your profit-and-loss statement.

An important business ratio — the net working capital ratio — is drawn from your balance sheet. Subtracting your current liabilities from your current assets gets you the dollar amount of your net working capital. But to get the net working capital ratio, divide your current assets by your current liabilities. Any value over 1.1 means you have a positive net working capital. If you need a loan from a bank, this is the first figure the loan office will look for.

Tracking your accounts payable

When bills come in, post them in your accounting program. This will generate the *accounts payable* report. Accounts payable is the area that shows how much you owe and when it's due. This is crucial information for meeting your obligations on time.

When you pay an outstanding bill, the bookkeeping program deducts the money from your checking account and marks the bill as paid. It will no longer appear on this report.

Knowing your sales tax liability

One of the vendors you'll owe money to is your state. In California, it's the State Board of Equalization. Every time you post an invoice or sales receipt that charges sales tax, that amount shows up in the sales-tax liability report. You run this report on a timeframe determined by the state; you may be required to report monthly, quarterly, or yearly. Also, how often you report may depend on your total in-state sales. Just make sure you match your reporting with your state's requirements.

Analyzing your profit and loss statement

If your accountant asks for your income statement, he or she is asking for your *profit-and-loss statement*, or *P&L*. This report lays out clearly every penny you've spent and brought in. You can set these reports to generate by any period of time; usually eBay sellers produce them by calendar month.

A summary P&L itemizes all your income and expense accounts individually and totals them by category. This way, you'll be able to isolate individual areas where you may notice a problem, such as spending too much in shipping supplies.

Please use the following list of income and expense accounts as a guide, and not as gospel. I am not a tax professional, and I suggest that when you set up your own income and (especially) expense accounts, you go over them with a licensed tax expert. Here's a glimpse at the kinds of accounts and categories you see on a P&L statement:

✦ **Income:** Every dollar you bring in is itemized as income. For many sellers, this can break down into several individual accounts. These figures are automatically generated by your bookkeeping program from the sales receipts you input. The total of all these income areas is subtotaled at the bottom of this area as total income.

   • **Sales:** This totals eBay sales and shipping income in separate totals. These figures subtotal as total sales.

   • **Web site advertising:** If you're a member of any affiliate programs or have a newsletter that takes advertising, this income posts here.

   • **Consulting:** Income from consulting or teaching others.

✦ **Cost of goods sold (COGS):** This area itemizes by category all the costs involved in your eBay (and Web site) sales only. None of your business operating expenses, such as your telephone bill, show up here; they're farther down on the report. Your eBay COGS may subtotal in different accounts, such as

- **Merchandise:** The cost of merchandise that you bought to resell.

- **eBay fees:** Here's where you post your eBay fees from your credit-card statement.

- **PayPal fees:** This figure is automatically generated from your sales receipts.

- **Shipping postage:** The totals of the amounts you spend for shipping your eBay items.

- **Shipping supplies:** The costs of padded mailers, bubble wrap, tape, and boxes. When those items are paid for, the bookkeeping program inserts the totals here.

- **Outside service fees:** If you pay for photo hosting or third-party management tools, they appear here.

Cross-reference your cost of goods sold to your sales reports. You've expensed inventory bought, but your merchandise may be sitting idle in your storage area. The COGS report works with other reports, such as inventory reports (also generated by QuickBooks), sales reports, and P&Ls, to give you a solid picture of where your business is going.

Your cost of goods sold is subtotaled under the heading total COGS.

✦ **Gross profit:** Your bookkeeping program magically does all the calculations — and you'll be able to see in a snapshot whether your eBay business is in good, profitable health. This particular figure is the gross profit *before* you figure in your company expenses (often called G&A, for *general and administrative costs*).

Now come your expenses. Listed in individual accounts, you have subtotals for your various business operating expenses, as follows:

✦ **Payroll expenses:** The total amounts you pay your employees.

✦ **Taxes:** Broken out by state and federal, the taxes you've paid to the regulating agencies for running your business.

✦ **Supplies:** Computer and office supplies. How much paper goes through your printer? Not to mention those inkjet cartridges, pens, computers, telephones, copiers, and network equipment. All those expenses appear here.

✦ **Seminars and education:** Did you buy this book to educate yourself on your eBay business? It counts. Have you attended a seminar to educate yourself on eBay? Going to eBay Live? Those count too.

✦ **Contract labor:** This is the money you pay to anyone who is not an employee of your company, such as an off-site bookkeeper or a company that comes in to clean your office. The federal government has stringent rules as to who classifies as an independent contractor. Check this Web site for the official rules:

```
www.irs.gov/businesses/small/article/0,,id=115041,
   00.html
```

✦ **Automobile expenses:** This is where you post expenses, such as parking, gas, and repairs for an automobile used for your eBay business. If you have only one vehicle that you also use for personal transportation, your tax person may have you post a percentage of its use in this area.

✦ **Telephone:** Do you have a separate phone line for your business?

✦ **Advertising:** Expenses you incur when running advertising campaigns, such as in Google AdWords or in your eBay banner program.

Your expenses will come to a whopping total at the bottom. Then, at the very bottom of the page, will be your net income. This is your bottom-line profit. I wish you all a very positive bottom line!

Keeping Your Records and Data Safe

If the hazard of not backing up your computer isn't a tired subject, I don't know what is. Whenever you hear someone talking about their latest computer crash, all the person can do is stare blankly into the distance and say, "I lost everything!" I admit it's happened to me — and I'm sure that you've heard this cry from others (if you've not uttered it yourself): "If only I'd backed up my files!"

What about a natural disaster? It can happen, you know. When I went to sleep on January 16, 1994, I didn't know that the next day, when I attempted to enter my office, everything would be in shambles. My monitors had flown across the room, filing cabinets turned over, and oh, did I mention the ceiling had collapsed? The Northridge earthquake taught me some solid lessons about keeping duplicate records and backed-up data copies *in an offsite location.*

If a computer crash or natural disaster has happened to you, you have my deepest and most sincere sympathy. It's a horrible thing to go through.

What's another horrible thing? A tax audit: It can make you feel like jumping off a cliff if you've been filing your hard documentation with the shoebox method. (You know, one box for 2005, one for 2004, and so on.) Filing your receipts and backup documentation in an organized easy-to-find format can pay off in future savings of time (and nerves).

I want to tell you up front that I don't always practice what I preach. I don't always back up my stuff on time. I have a new box of backup software sitting on the floor next to me, and the box of receipts is getting fuller. But I'm gonna preach anyway about good practices for backing up your computer data and safeguarding the hardcopy documents that you inevitably will have. (I just really hope there are no disasters before I finish writing this book!)

Taking the time to organize and safeguard your data and records now may save you days, weeks, or months of work and frustration later.

Backing Up Your Data

I'm not specifically suggesting that you go out and buy backup software (though I think it's a good idea). I *am* suggesting that you back up the eBay transaction records and other data on your computer *somehow*. Consider the following points when choosing how to back up the data you can't afford to lose:

✦ Regularly back up at least your My Documents folder onto a CD or external hard drive. (You can find external 250GB hard drives for under $100 on eBay, so there's really no excuse not to make some sort of backup.)

✦ Backup software can make your backup chores less *chorelike*. Most packages enable you to run backups unattended and automatically, so you don't have to remember anything. (Western Digital external hard drives come with their own sync software to handle this for you.)

✦ Backup software doesn't have to be expensive. I just visited one of my favorite shareware sites, www.tucows.com, and searched the term *backup Windows*. This query returned more than 300 matching records!

There's no need for me to recommend a particular brand of backup software; almost any brand you buy will do a good job. When you search tucows or Amazon, read the customer comments and let these help direct you to the software that's right for you.

✦ Consider making monthly backups of the info from your PayPal account. You can download the data directly from the site and can archive several years' worth on one CD.

Saving Your Backup Paperwork

Business records are still mostly paper, and until such time as the entire world is electronic, you'll have some paperwork to store. You can buy manila file folders almost anywhere. A box of 100 costs less than $10, so expense is no excuse for lack of organization. If you don't have filing cabinets, office-supply stores sell collapsible cardboard boxes that are the perfect size to hold file folders. You can buy six of these for around $8.

And just what do you need to file in your new organized office? Here are a few important suggestions:

✦ **Equipment receipts and warranties:** You never know when some important piece of your office hardware will go on the fritz, and you'll need the receipt and warranty information so you can get it fixed. Also, the receipts are backup documentation for your bookkeeping program's data.

✦ **Automobile expenses:** Gasoline receipts, parking receipts, repairs — anything and everything to do with your car. You use your car in your eBay business (for example, to deliver packages to the post office for shipping), don't you?

✦ **Postal receipts:** Little slips of paper that you get from the post office. If you use an online postage service, print a postage report once a month and file it in your filing cabinets or boxes as well.

✦ **Credit-card bills:** Here in one location can be documentation on your purchases for your business. Make a folder for each credit card; file every month after you pay the bill and post the data.

✦ **Merchandise receipts:** Merchandise purchased for resale on eBay. Documentation of all the money you spend.

✦ **Licenses and legal stuff:** Important! Keep an active file of anything legal; you will no doubt have to lay hands on this information at the oddest moment. It's reassuring to know where it is!

✦ **Payroll paperwork:** Even if you print your checks and such on the computer, you should organize state and federal filing information in one place.

✦ **Canceled checks and bank statements:** The only ways to prove you've paid for something.

✦ **Insurance information:** Policies and insurance proposals should all be kept close by.

I'm sure you can think of some more things that can benefit from a little bit of organization. When you need the information quickly, and you can find it without breaking a sweat, you'll be glad you kept things organized.

Chapter 3: Using Bookkeeping Software

In This Chapter

✔ Taking care of bookkeeping with QuickBooks

✔ Using QuickBooks efficiently

When you meet with one of the professionals described in Chapter 2 in this minibook, you'll need to bring a complete and accurate set of books. To prepare accurate books, you can use a bookkeeper (who will use accounting software) or you can learn how to use professional accounting software yourself. Don't be a wussy; you *can* do this. Lots of people successfully using bookkeeping software today knew nothing about bookkeeping before they set up their own accounts. I'm one of them.

When your business gets so busy that you have no time to post your bookkeeping, you can always hire a part-time bookkeeper to come in and do your posting for you. I found mine on elance.com. We fax and e-mail data every month.

I researched various Web sites to find which software was the best selling and easiest to use. I had many discussions with CPAs, enrolled agents, and bookkeepers. The software that these professionals most recommend for business is Intuit's QuickBooks. (Thank goodness that's the one I use.) QuickBooks is considered the best, which is why I devote so much of this chapter to it. Some people begin with Quicken and later move to QuickBooks when their businesses get big or incorporate. My theory? Start with the best. It's not that much more expensive; on eBay, I've seen new, sealed QuickBooks Pro 2004 software for as low as $135 and QuickBooks for as low as $65.

QuickBooks: Making Bookkeeping Uncomplicated

QuickBooks offers several versions, from basic to enterprise (company-size) solutions tailored to different types of businesses. QuickBooks SimpleStart and QuickBooks Pro have a few significant differences. QuickBooks Pro adds job costing and expensing features and the capability to design your own forms. QuickBooks SimpleStart does a darn good job, too, so check out the comparison at quickbooks.intuit.com and see which version is best for you. I use (and highly recommend) QuickBooks Pro, so that's the version I describe in the rest of this section. If you're just purchasing QuickBooks Pro, you may have an updated version that works a bit differently. But the accounting basics that the software provides for your business don't change.

Stephen L. Nelson wrote *QuickBooks 2009 For Dummies* (published by Wiley). His book is amazingly easy to understand. I swear that neither Steve nor my publisher gave me a nickel for recommending his book. (Heck, I even had to pay for my copy.) I recommend it simply because it answers — in plain English — just about any question you'll have about using the program for your bookkeeping needs. Spend the money and get the book. Any money spent on increasing your knowledge is money well spent (and may be a tax write-off). And (oh yeah) be sure you file the receipt.

I update my QuickBooks software every few years, and the product improvements continue to save me time in performing my bookkeeping tasks. If you find that you don't have time to input your bookkeeping data, you may have to hire a bookkeeper. The bonus is that professional bookkeepers probably already know QuickBooks, and the best part is that they can print daily reports for you that keep you apprised of the condition your business is in. Also, at the end of each year, QuickBooks will supply you with all the official reports your enrolled agent (EA) or certified public accountant (CPA) will need to do your taxes. (Yes, you really *do* need an EA or a CPA.) You can even send them a backup on a Zip disk or a CD-ROM. See how simple bookkeeping can be?

QuickBooks Pro

When you first fire up QuickBooks Pro, you must answer a few questions to set up your account. Among the few things you need to have ready — before you even begin to mess with the software — are the following starting figures:

✦ **Cash balance:** This may be the amount in your checking account (no personal money, please!) or the amount of money deposited from your eBay profits. Put these profits into a separate checking account to use for your business.

✦ **Accounts receivable balance:** Does anyone owe you money for some auctions? Outstanding payments make up this total.

✦ **Account liability balance:** Do you owe some money? Are you being invoiced for some merchandise that you haven't paid for? Total it and enter it when QuickBooks prompts you.

Get Started with QuickBooks for FREE

I am such a fan of QuickBooks that the folks at Intuit allowed me to include a copy of their Simple Start beginning program on the CD for one of my books. My *eBay PowerSeller Business Practices For Dummies* has this software on a bound in CD, along with many other valuable tools.

If you're starting your business in the middle of the year, gather any previous profits and expenses that you want to include because you'll have to input this information for a complete annual set of diligently recorded books. I can guarantee that this is going to take a while. But you'll be thanking me for insisting that you get organized. It just makes everything work smoother in the long run.

QuickBooks EasyStep Interview

After you've organized your finances, you can proceed with the QuickBooks EasyStep Interview, which is shown in Figure 3-1. The EasyStep Interview is designed to provide a comfort level for those with accounting-phobia and those using a bookkeeping program for the first time. If you mess things up, you can always use the Back arrow and change what you've input. If you need help, simply click the Help button and the program will answer many of your questions. Hey, if worst comes to worst, you can always delete the file from the QuickBooks directory and start over.

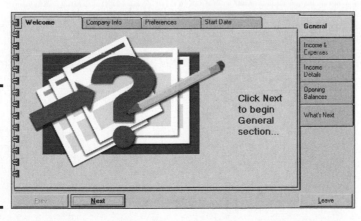

Figure 3-1:
The QuickBooks Pro EasyStep Interview start page.

QuickBooks integrates with PayPal

PayPal can provide your payment history in QuickBooks format. They even offer a settlement and reconciliation system download that breaks up your PayPal transactions into debits and credits. A handy feature! One warning, though: These are only financial transactions. When you use QuickBooks to its fullest, you will have your inventory in the program. When you purchase merchandise to sell, QuickBooks sets up the inventory — and deducts from it each time you input an invoice or sales receipt. This way your inventory receipts follow GAAP (more about GAAP in Book I). Later in the chapter, I show you the procedures for posting your weekly (or daily) sales in QuickBooks by using sales receipts.

For the whirlwind tour through the QuickBooks EasyStep Interview, just follow these steps (which are only a general guideline):

1. **Start QuickBooks, and choose the Create a New Company option.**

You're now at the EasyStep Interview.

2. **On the first page of the interactive portion of the interview, type your company name (this becomes the filename in your computer) and the legal name of your company.**

If you've filed a fictitious name statement (see Chapter 1 in this mini-book), the fictitious name is the legal name of your company.

3. **Continue to follow the steps, answering other questions about your business, such as the address and the type of tax form you use.**

4. **When QuickBooks asks what type of business you want to use, choose Retail: General.**

If you have a business other than your eBay sales — perhaps consulting or teaching others — you may want to just leave the company box blank in QuickBooks, specify no business option, and build your own chart of accounts from the one they give you — that's what I did.

QuickBooks doesn't offer an online sales business choice, so Retail:General is the closest to what you need (see Figure 3-2). With the chart of accounts that I feature in the following section, you can make the appropriate changes to your accounts to adapt to your eBay business.

5. **When QuickBooks asks whether you want to use its chosen chart of accounts, choose Yes.**

See Figure 3-3. You can always change the accounts later. If you want to spend the time, you can input your entire custom chart of accounts manually (but I *really, really* don't recommend it).

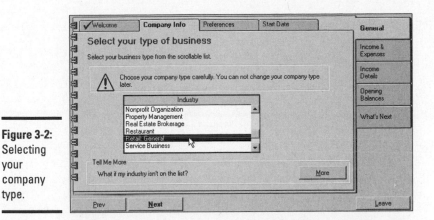

Figure 3-2:
Selecting
your
company
type.

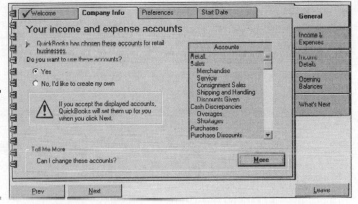

Figure 3-3:
Accepting
the
QuickBooks
chart of
accounts.

6. **Answer some more general questions, which I'm sure you can handle with the aid of the intuitive QuickBooks help feature.**

7. **When the preferences pages appear, I recommend that you select the "Enter the bills first and then enter the payments later" option.**

   That way, if you input your bills as they come in, you can get an exact idea of how much money you owe at any time by just starting the program.

8. **Click the box to indicate that you collect sales tax.**

9. **On the Sales Tax preferences page, indicate the agencies for which you collect sales tax, and then set up the tax-collecting information, as shown in Figure 3-4.**

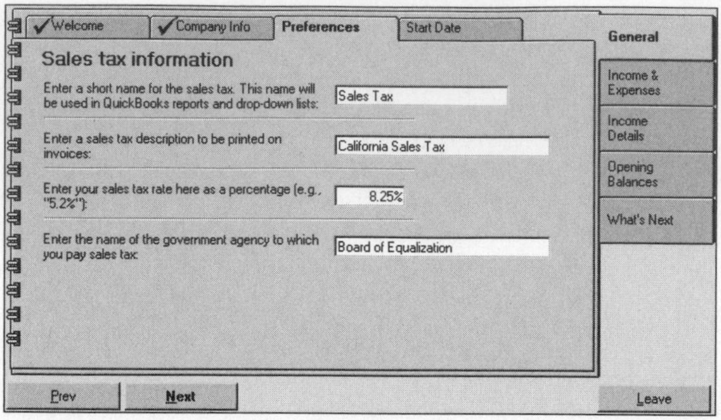

✓ Welcome	✓ Company Info	Preferences	Start Date	
				General

Sales tax information

Enter a short name for the sales tax. This name will be used in QuickBooks reports and drop-down lists: `Sales Tax`

Enter a sales tax description to be printed on invoices: `California Sales Tax`

Enter your sales tax rate here as a percentage (e.g., "5.2%"):   `8.25%`

Enter the name of the government agency to which you pay sales tax: `Board of Equalization`

Income & Expenses

Income Details

Opening Balances

What's Next

Prev   Next   Leave

Figure 3-4:
Inputting your sales tax information.

10. Decide whether you want to use QuickBooks to process your payroll.

Even if you're the only employee, using QuickBooks payroll information makes things much easier when it comes to filling out your payroll deposits. QuickBooks automatically fills in federal forms for your quarterly tax processing and prints the appropriate form — ready for your signature and mailing.

11. Answer a few more questions, including whether you want to use the cash basis or accrual basis of accounting.

The *accrual* basis posts sales the minute you write an invoice or post a sales receipt, and posts your expenses as soon as you post the bills into the computer. Accrual basis accounting gives you a clearer picture of where your company is financially than cash basis accounting does. The *cash* basis is when you record bills by writing checks — expenses are posted only when you write the checks. This way of doing business may be simpler, but the only way you'll know how much money you owe is by looking at the pile of bills on your desk.

12. If you're comfortable, just click Leave and then input the balance of your required information directly into the program without using the interview.

If you're new to bookkeeping, you may want to go through the interview step-by-step with a tutor at your side. For more details, remember to check out *QuickBooks 2009 For Dummies* — this book can teach you almost everything you need to know about QuickBooks.

Setting Up a QuickBooks Chart of Accounts

After you've finished the EasyStep Interview and have successfully set up your business in QuickBooks, the program presents a *chart of accounts* — essentially an organization system, rather like file folders, that keeps all related data in the proper area. When you write a check to pay a bill, it deducts the amount from your checking account, reduces your accounts payable, and increases your asset or expense account if that's appropriate.

You have a choice of giving each account a number. These numbers, a kind of bookkeeping shorthand, are standardized throughout bookkeeping. Believe it or not, everybody in the industry seems to know what number goes with what item. To keep things less confusing, I like to use titles as well as numbers.

To customize your chart of accounts, follow these steps:

1. **Choose Edit⇨Preferences.**

2. **Click the Accounting icon (on the left).**

3. **Click the Company preferences tab and indicate that you'd like to use account numbers.**

An editable chart of accounts appears, as shown in Figure 3-5. Because QuickBooks doesn't assign account numbers by default, you'll need to edit the chart to create them.

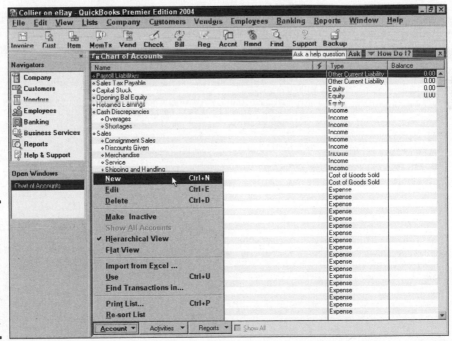

Figure 3-5:
Your chart of accounts now has numbers generated by QuickBooks.

4. **Go through your QuickBooks chart of accounts and add any missing categories.**

   You may not need all these categories and you can always add more later. In Table 3-1, I show you a chart of accounts that a CPA wrote for an eBay business. To get an idea of how you can customize the chart of accounts, also look at Figure 3-6, which shows you the chart of accounts from my own business.

Table 3-1		eBay Business Chart of Accounts
Account Number	Account Name	What It Represents
1001	Checking	All revenue deposited here and all checks drawn upon this account
1002	Money market account	Company savings account
1100	Accounts receivable	For customers to whom you extend credit
1201	Merchandise inventory	Charge to cost of sales as used, or take periodic inventories and adjust at that time
1202	Shipping supplies	Boxes, tape, labels, and so forth; charge these to cost as used, or take an inventory at the end of the period and adjust to cost of sales
1401	Office furniture and equipment	Desk, computer, telephone
1402	Shipping equipment	Scales, tape dispensers
1403	Vehicles	Your vehicle if it's owned by the company
1501	Accumulated depreciation	For your accountant's use
1601	Deposits	Security deposits on leases
2001	Accounts payable	Amounts owed for the stuff you sell, or charged expenses
2100	Payroll liabilities	Taxes deducted from employees' checks and taxes paid by company on employee earnings
2200	Sales tax payable	Sales tax collected at time of sale and owed to the state

Account Number	Account Name	What It Represents
2501	Equipment loans	Money borrowed to buy a computer or other equipment
2502	Auto loans	This is for when you get that hot new van for visiting your consignment clients
3000	Owner's capital	Your opening balance
3902	Owner's draw	Your withdrawals for the current year
4001	Merchandise sales	Revenue from sales of your products
4002	Shipping and handling	Paid by the customer
4009	Returns	Total dollar amount of returned merchandise
4101	Interest income	From your investments
4201	Other income	Income not otherwise classified
5001	Merchandise purchases	All the merchandise you buy for eBay; you'll probably use subaccounts for individual items
5002	Freight in	Freight and shipping charges you pay for your inventory, not for shipments to customers
5003	Shipping	Shipping to your customers: USPS, FedEx, UPS, and so on
5004	Shipping supplies	Boxes, labels, tape, bubble wrap, and so on
6110	Automobile expense	When you use your car for work
6111	Gas and oil	Filling up the tank
6112	Automobile repairs	When your business owns the car
6120	Bank service charges	Monthly service charges, NSF charges, and so forth
6140	Contributions	Charity
6142	Data services	Does an outside firm process your payroll?
6143	Internet service provider	What you pay to your Internet provider
6144	Web site hosting fees	Fees paid to your hosting company

(continued)

Table 3-1 *(continued)*

Account Number	Account Name	What It Represents
6150	Depreciation expense	For your accountant's use
6151	eBay fees	What you pay eBay every month to stay in business based on your sales
6152	Discounts	Fees you're charged for using eBay and accepting credit card payments; deducted from your revenue and reported to you on your eBay statement
6153	Other auction site fees	You may want to set up subcategories for each site where you do business, such as Yahoo! or Amazon
6156	PayPal fees	Processing fees paid to PayPal
6158	Credit-card or merchant-account fees	If you have a separate merchant account, post those fees here
6160	Dues	Membership fees you pay if you join an organization (relating to your business) that charges them
6161	Magazines and periodicals	Books and magazines that help you run and expand your business
6170	Equipment rental	Postage meter, occasional van
6180	Insurance	Policies that cover your merchandise or your office
6185	Liability insurance	Insurance that covers you if someone slips and falls at your place of business (can also be put under Insurance)
6190	Disability insurance	Insurance that will pay you if you become temporarily or permanently disabled and can't perform your work
6191	Health insurance	If provided for yourself, you may be required to provide it to employees
6200	Interest expense	Credit interest and interest on loans
6220	Loan interest	When you borrow from the bank

Account Number	Account Name	What It Represents
6230	Licenses	State, city licenses
6240	Miscellaneous	Whatever doesn't go anyplace else in these categories
6250	Postage and delivery	Stamps used in your regular business
6251	Endicia.com fees	Fees for your eBay business postage service
6260	Printing	Your business cards, correspondence stationery, and so on
6265	Filing fees	Fees paid to file legal documents
6270	Professional fees	Fees paid to consultants
6280	Legal fees	If you have to pay a lawyer
6650	Accounting and bookkeeping	Bookkeeper, CPA, or EA
6290	Rent	Office, warehouse, and so on
6300	Repairs	Can be the main category for the following subcategories
6310	Building repairs	Repair to the building you operate your business in
6320	Computer repairs	What you pay the person to set up your wireless network
6330	Equipment repairs	When the copier or the phone needs fixing
6340	Telephone	Regular telephone, fax lines
6350	Travel and	Business related travel, business meals
6360	Entertainment	When you take eBay's CEO out to dinner to benefit your eBay business (don't forget to invite me too)
6370	Meals	Meals while traveling for your business
6390	Utilities	Major heading for subcategories that follow
6391	Electricity and gas	Electricity and gas
6392	Water	Water

(continued)

Table 3-1 *(continued)*

Account Number	Account Name	What It Represents
6560	Payroll expenses	Wages paid to others
6770	Supplies	Office supplies
6772	Computer	Computer and supplies
6780	Marketing	Advertising or items you purchase to give out that promote your business
6790	Office	Miscellaneous office expense, such as bottled water delivery?
6820	Taxes	Major category for the following sub-categories below
6830	Federal	Federal taxes
6840	Local	Local (city, county) taxes
6850	Property	Property taxes
6860	State	State taxes

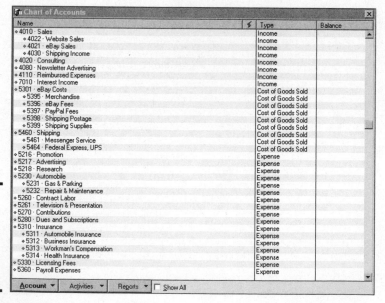

Figure 3-6: The chart of accounts from my eBay business.

Opting for QuickBooks on the Web

If you want to handle everything on the Web, use QuickBooks online service (they have a Basic and a Plus product), shown in Figure 3-7. The online QuickBooks program offers fewer features than the home version, but if your accounting needs are simple, it may be a solution for you. Before you decide, however, consider that while your accounting needs may be simple now, they may not be so simple later.

Intuit's charges start at $9.95 a month for the service, which is comparable to buying the QuickBooks Pro version. The online version also requires you to have a broadband connection to the Internet so that you're always online (dial-up connections need not apply). The online edition doesn't include integrated payroll, purchase orders, online banking, and bill payments.

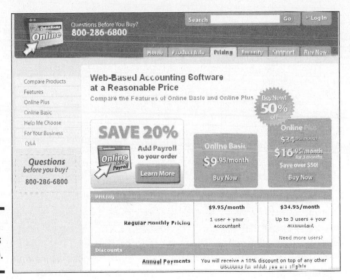

Figure 3-7:
QuickBooks
for the Web.

Having QuickBooks Report on Your eBay Business

QuickBooks can give you up-to-the-minute reports about the status of your eBay business and keep track of everything — including payroll and sales-tax liability — in the background. Here are a few things that I like about using QuickBooks to streamline an online business:

✦ **Inventory reports:** As you purchase inventory, aside from deducting the money from your checking account and expensing your merchandise account, QuickBooks adds the purchased merchandise to your inventory. Every time you sell an item, QuickBooks deducts the item from your inventory. QuickBooks has many other reporting features for your inventory and end-of-year reporting for taxes.

Figure 3-8 shows you a part of an inventory report that I pulled out of the program. You can see how valuable the data is. With a click of my mouse, I can see how much I have left in stock and the average number of items I've sold per week.

The Collier Company, Inc.
Inventory Stock Status by Item
January 1 through March 18, 2004

	Item Description	Pref Vendor	On Hand	Available	Sales/Week
Inventory					
Angled Collar	Cloud Dome Angled Collar		9	9	0.1
Book Sales					
4th Dummies	eBay For Dummies 4th Edition		7	7	1.2
Business Book Sales	Starting an eBay Business for Dummies		1	1	1.6
Shopping book	eBay Bargain Shopping for Dummies		22	22	0.4
Tips booklet	eBay Tips for Dummies Booklet		19	19	2
Book Sales - Other	eBay For Dummies 3rd edition		0	0	0.2
Total Book Sales			49	49	5.4
Cloud Dome Kit	Cloud Dome Kit		5	5	1
Deluxe Cloud Dome Kit	CLOUD DOME Complete Digital Kit		-5	-5	1.3
Flip Light	Flip Light		-1	-1	0.1
Garment Rack	Rolling Garment Rack		22	22	1.1
Infiniti Board	Infiniti Board		15	15	2.3
Light Set	eBay Seller's Pro Lighting Kit		-2	-2	2.8
Spanx B	Spanx Footless Pantyhose NUDE size B		4	4	0
un-du	un-du Adhesive Remover		72	72	2.2

Figure 3-8: A portion of my inventory-tracking report.

✦ **Sales-tax tracking:** Depending on how the program is set up (based on your own state sales tax laws), you can request a report that has all your taxable and nontaxable sales. The report calculates the amount of sales tax you owe. You can print this report for backup information of your sales-tax payments to the state.

✦ **Payroll:** Whether you use the online payroll service to prepare your payroll or input the deductions yourself, QuickBooks posts the appropriate withholdings to their own accounts. When it comes time to pay your employees' withholding taxes, QuickBooks can generate the federal reporting form (all filled in) for submitting with your payment.

✦ **Sales reports:** QuickBooks gives you a plethora of reports with which you can analyze your sales professionally. One of my favorite reports is the Sales by Item Summary. This report gives you the following information for every inventoried item you sell, in whatever time period you choose:

• Quantity sold

• Total dollar amount sold

• Percentage of sales represented by each item

• The average price the item sold for

• COGS (cost of goods sold) by item

- Average cost of goods sold by total sales per item
- Gross profit margin in dollar amounts
- Gross profit margin expressed as percentage

Depending on how you post your transactions, you can analyze your eBay sales, Web-site sales, and brick-and-mortar sales (individually or together). You can also select *any* date range for your reports.

Posting Sales in QuickBooks the Collier Way

Some online auction-management services integrate with QuickBooks. This integration means that your individual transactions can be downloaded into the QuickBooks program, setting up a new customer for each of your sales.

Although this process is quick and easy, inputting each sale as a new customer will make your database huge in no time. QuickBooks is a large program to begin with, and if you're going to use it (and update it) for several years, the database will become even larger.

If you've ever worked with large files, you know that the larger the data file, the more chance there is for the data to become corrupt. That's the last thing you want. Besides, QuickBooks will max out with over 14,000 customers — and you can easily get that many in several years on eBay.

To keep track of your customers, you can use an additional copy of your PayPal monthly report and combine the download with cash sales into an Excel (or Microsoft Works) spreadsheet to build your customer database.

Posting sales to match deposits

In this section, I show you a procedure I developed to process my PayPal sales. I've run it past several accountants and QuickBooks experts, and it's garnered rave reviews. I'm sharing it with you because I want you to be able to run your business smoothly. Lots of sellers use this method. It shortens your inputting time.

Rather than posting an invoice in my QuickBooks software for every customer (for those few customers who need formal invoices), I can print them on demand from eBay's Selling Manager or PayPal. I input my sales into a customer sales receipt as shown in Figure 3-9. Whenever I make a PayPal deposit into my business checking account — which is every few days, depending on how busy sales are — I post my sales into QuickBooks. This way, the total of my sales receipt equals the amount of my PayPal deposit. (If you've ever tried to reconcile your PayPal deposits with your sales *and* your checking account, you know how frustrating it can be.)

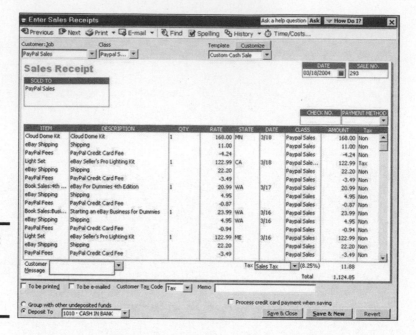

Figure 3-9:
My
customer
sales
receipt.

In my QuickBooks account, PayPal is the customer. It makes no difference who bought what; the only thing that matters is which item sold (to deduct from inventory) and for how much (to post to my financial data).

Customizing the sales data

The program gives you the flexibility to customize forms, and Figure 3-9 shows my customized sales receipt for PayPal sales. PayPal is a taxable customer when sales are made in the State of California, and the appropriate sales tax is applied automatically. I added the following when I customized the form:

✦ **PayPal fees:** I set up PayPal fees as a credit against sales. (In Figure 3-9, you can see they are applied as a negative.) This helps to match the total amount of the sales receipt to my PayPal deposit. It also gives me a discount line in my sales reports that tracks my total paid in PayPal fees. The PayPal fees line appears also in the cost of goods sold area of my financial statements.

In case you're wondering about eBay fees, they have their own line in my chart of accounts. I charge eBay fees to my company credit card. When the credit card expenses are posted, I post the eBay expense to the eBay fees account, which appears under "cost of goods sold" in my financial reports. (Earlier in the chapter, I show you how to set up QuickBooks for eBay and include a suggested chart of expense and income accounts.)

✦ **State:** I type the two-letter state abbreviation of the shipping location with each item. This serves as backup information for my State Board of Equalization (the California sales tax board) and also allows me to run reports on what has sold in which states.

✦ **Date:** The date at the top of the sales receipt is the posting date. The date in the product posting indicates the date the PayPal payment was posted.

✦ **Class:** Every item posted in QuickBooks can be part of a class to make it easier for you to isolate certain types of transactions. I set up two classes of PayPal sales: California sales and out-of-state sales. California sales are classified as taxable, and out-of-state sales are classified as nontaxable. QuickBooks calculates the tax liability automatically.

✦ **Tax classification:** When I type the first two letters into the class area (OU for out-of-state sales and CA for in-state sales), the tax line changes automatically to Tax or Non-Tax. QuickBooks would do this whether I show this field in the sales receipt or not, but by having it appear, I can use it as a secondary reminder to post the taxable class properly.

By inputting my eBay sales data in this way, I streamline the process in several ways. I post data to only one program once. From this sales receipt I get updated inventory reports, accurate sales tax data, and accurate expense and income tracking. It also eases the process of reconciling my checking account.

Using eBay's Accounting Assistant Software

I guess eBay figured out that sellers needed help with their accounting software. The company developed Accounting Assistant (see Figure 3-10) for use with QuickBooks software, which is available to eBay sellers who subscribe to Seller's Assistant or Selling Manager or who have an eBay store.

You can download the software from the following site:

```
http:// pages.ebay.com/accountingassistant/
```

As of this writing, Accounting Assistant is new to eBay and they haven't worked out all the kinks. But keep an eye on the software because it shows great promise for streamlining the posting of your sales.

Accounting Assistant will work with only the premium versions of QuickBooks: QuickBooks Pro, QuickBooks Premier, or QuickBooks Enterprise.

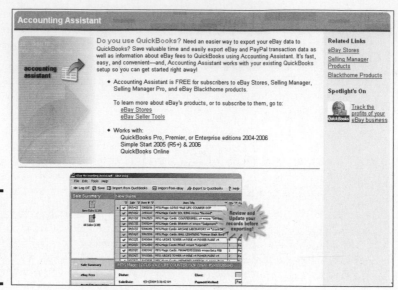

Figure 3-10:
The
Accounting
Assistant
home page.

Chapter 4: Keeping Your Business Secure Online

*O*nline security is something everybody worries about, but few people do anything about it. When people's accounts are hacked into, they whine and moan about online security, but they don't give a moment's thought to why using a user ID as a password *wasn't* the best choice.

Even if you avoid such classic blunders, you have to keep your wits about you online. Sad to say, some people out there *are* trying to dupe you; it's time to take charge of our own security and fight back in the best ways we can. Some scams pretend to be from eBay, PayPal, Citibank, and others — and try to bilk you out of your personal information. I show you a fairly foolproof way to recognize those. I also show you how spammers get your e-mail address. Even if you never give it out, they have ways of getting it from you. I hope to teach you how to be a little more savvy about which e-mails you open and how to fight back.

Staying Away from Spam

Every morning when I get to my computer, I have to allow about five minutes to clear the spam out of my e-mail. It used to take up to a half hour, considering that I flip on my computer and am greeted by close to 200 e-mails every day. Read on to see how I've cut my spam-scanning time!

Spam has become so sneaky. Everyone is scurrying to get the latest in antispam software, but I've found that antispam software was causing me to lose e-mail that I needed, because it seems that the word *eBay* is a favorite of spammers. I want *news* on eBay, but I don't want to get those make-a-fortune-on-eBay e-mails. Nor do I want to help out dear Mr. Felix Kamala, son of the late Mr. A.Y. Kamala. It seems his family lost millions in Zimbabwe to a scammer in the government, and he wants me to help him get his secret stash of "Fifteen million five hundred thousand united state dollars." He was going to give me 20% just for helping him — how thoughtful! (In case you didn't know, this e-mail is part of what the FBI calls the *Nigerian e-mail scam* — also called the 419 scam — named after the African penal code violated with this crime.)

A fine member of the Internet community collects these e-mails and posts them on his Web site, www.potifos.com/fraud. Check out the page when you have a minute — it's quite funny!

For the record, I'm also very comfortable with the size of my body parts; I don't want to buy drugs from some stranger over the Internet; and I don't need another mortgage from the Internet.

Keeping Your E-Mail Address Quiet

Have you ever signed up for anything on the Internet? Before you signed up, did you check to see whether the site had a posted privacy-policy page? You probably didn't. After you type your name in a box on the Internet on a site with no-spam or privacy policy, you're basically *giving your privacy away,* because you're considered an opt-in customer. *Opt in* means that you asked to be on a list, and the site that now has your e-mail address can sell it to spammers.

Take a look at Figure 4-1. It's a portion of an ad that should really scare you. It's an eBay auction for a CD containing 140,000,000 opt-in e-mail addresses. Yes, you can buy access to all those potential suckers for only $29.99.

Figure 4-1:
A tempting offer to violate people's privacy.

> **The possibilities with this HUGE email list are outragious!**
>
> If you send an email to 140 million customers with only a 10% response, that's 14 million people! If only 1% of them respond, that's 1.4 million people! If only .1% respond, that's 140,000 people! And even if only .01% respond, that sill 14,000 sales!

Just opening your e-mail can give you away as well. Spammers will often make up return e-mail addresses to mask their true location (as you can tell by some of the "From" addresses). If you open and view their e-mail, the e-mail sends a notice to the spammer's server, and then they know that the e-mail address is valid. This practice can also be masked in the HTML to occur when the e-mail consists of merely a picture — when it goes back to grab the picture for your e-mail, it reports that your e-mail address is good.

Recognizing Spam

Much of the spam you get can be recognized by the subject line. I used to check my e-mail once I downloaded it to my computer. That's a dangerous procedure, though, considering that some e-mails do their job even if you don't respond. Now I'm using a program called MailWasher Pro. The company also makes a free version, described next.

Finding spam before it finds you

When I flip on my computer in the morning, I open MailWasher and see a barrage of trash in my mailbox, as shown in Figure 4-2.

Delete	Bounce	Blackli	Status	Size	From	Subject	Sen	To	Attac
✔	✔	✔	Possible	2.7KB	dale halverson (astyllan@mail.bulgaria.com)	Cgllesiotv Re: Your H_y_d_r_0_c_0_d_0_	15 Mar	hans da	none
			Normal	4.3KB	Gordon Boucher (vipe23@tourspain.es)	Fw. Fw: Upt0 50% off on Prescr1pt1on DF	15 Mar	marshac	none
			Normal	3.0KB	Raphael Swanson (vgplqvj44@wanadoo.fr)	Re: crewel INdian generic Citratemorgen	15 Mar	marshac	none
			Normal	3.2KB	tiana peele (peela8384@proxad.net)	Fwd. Full Meds Here. Fwd: Xanlalx ™ Vali:	15 Mar	marshac	yes
			Normal	3.6KB	pqplylqvntzh@mail2rusty.com	Start saving now	15 Mar	marchar	none
			Normal	2.2KB	Alysha rosenberg (jp.rosenberg@umanheuminer)	Fwrt Have Pills x/ana/x < Valiu/m/ % yk	14 Mar	dummie:	yes
			Normal	2.2KB	Trina Garrison (umedriband@velnet.co.uk)	The NEW ISSUE STOCK I was telling you	14 Mar	marshac	none
			Normal	3.0KB	apjfbnh@attglobal.net	Re: ti Over Due wj Account	14 Mar	marshac	none
			Normal	3.3KB	Jeffery Haskins (jefferyhaskinshj@translate.ru	Spring time!	14 Mar	marshac	none
			Normal	8.0KB	velma_ewing@yahoo.com breeders	You Will Enjoy This	14 Mar	Marshac	none
			Normal	2.2KB	Lavonne N. Bingham (lbinghamcw@tvh.be)	06-Refinance as low as 2.90%	14 Mar	dummie:	none
			Normal	2.9KB	roniemvalofbo@baguda.com	dummies Boost Your Cable Modem Speec	14 Mar	Yvette L	none
			Normal	5.8KB	Viola Cantu (jsavcxy@yahoo.com)		14 Mar	marshac	none
			Normal	5.7KB	chun-she (carrie@t-online.de)	Tinaoeoa naietaa	14 Mar	marshac	none
			Normal	4.4KB	reports-headers (reports-response@habeas.cc	[habeas.com #240754] AutoReply: Spam	14 Mar	marshac	none
			Normal	7.6KB	apxbdnfp@germany.net	Be All You Can Be.d k o	14 Mar	dummie:	none
			Normal	4.3KB	Leigh Callahan (x505blli@150mail.com)	Re: Get it in the convenience of your hom	14 Mar	marshac	none
✔	✔	✔	Possible	4.2KB	Jarvis Sykes (sbyl9cz@aloha.net)	unhappy about the size of your love tool.	14 Mar	marshac	none
			Normal	2.7KB	rudy oato (gc7347@telesp.net.br)	Many On Stocks. Fwd: Vcod1n > X/A/NA	14 Mar	marshac	yes
			Normal	2.5KB	hourtnn.christian@yahoo.com	With this simple patch I became bigger an	10 Mar	marshac	none

Figure 4-2: The free version of Mail Washer.

MailWasher lists your e-mail directly from your ISP's server. It does not download the e-mail to your computer. By using MailWasher, you can delete the offending e-mails from your mailbox, and then bring only the ones you want into your e-mail program.

As you can see from Figure 4-2, I can find out the following:

✦ **Who sent the e-mail:** I'm not really acquainted with Lavonne N. Bingham (note that her e-mail address ends in `.be` — that's Belgium). I'm also not familiar with Viola Cantu, who strangely has `jsavcxy` as her e-mail ID at Yahoo. Not to mention my buddy, chun-she, otherwise known as `carrie@t-online.de`. (Hmmm, Germany? Don't know anyone there either.)

✦ **E-mail subject:** Just in case chun-she really does know me, he or she should know that I can't read the Cyrillic subject line (see the high-lighted row in Figure 4-2). I'm pretty sure I can delete that one. And although Velma sent me an e-mail letting me know how much I'd "enjoy" something, I'm really too busy to enjoy anything just now, so I guess I'll delete that e-mail too.

✦ **To:** The To line can be a definite tip-off that an e-mail is spam. If someone has e-mailed to a name other than my own or to an e-mail box at my Web site (with news about mortgages), I can assume that the e-mail wasn't sent by someone I know. For example, one e-mail was sent to Yvette. I have no Yvette at this e-mail address! There are no dummies here either.

✦ **Attachments:** If there's an attachment from someone I don't know, I delete the entire e-mail. As a matter of fact, I delete most e-mails with attach-ments. If a friend wants to send me something, they can always resend it.

MailWasher allows you to put check marks next to suspect e-mails. You can merely delete them, or you can bounce them back to whence they came and blacklist them (so they'll always be marked for deletion if they e-mail you again).

My e-mail program is set to get e-mail from the server only when I ask it to, so after I delete all the spam, I can click Send/Receive and feel considerably safer.

I use the Pro version of MailWasher (see my Web site for details), which can scan more than one e-mail account. However, I suggest that you download the free version for one e-mail account and see whether you like it before paying $39.95 for the Pro version. You can download the free version at `www.mailwasher.net`.

Checking out nefarious e-mail

What? It seems I've received an e-mail from PayPal. They say my account needs to be renewed. Oh my! I certainly don't want to lose my PayPal account.

Or how about an e-mail from PayPal that says:

> *We recently reviewed your account and suspect that your PayPal account may have been accessed by an unauthorized third party. Protecting the security of your account and of the PayPal network is our primary concern. Therefore, as a preventative measure, we have temporarily limited access to sensitive PayPal account features.*

> *Click below in order to regain access to your account:*

Uh-huh. Right. As in, STOP RIGHT THERE!

Take a good look at the e-mail. Who is it addressed to? When PayPal sends you an e-mail, the opening line says "Dear (*your registered name*)." In my case, a real e-mail from PayPal read, "Dear Marsha Collier." These spam e-mails are usually addressed to "Dear Valued User" or "Dear *youremail address*.com." PayPal will *never* address an e-mail to your e-mail address!

Responding to these e-mails is tantamount to giving away your information to a stranger. Let me give you a tip on another way to double-check these e-mails. Open the e-mail, as I have in Figure 4-3. Note: This trick works only with HTML e-mail. (An e-mail is in the HTML format if you can right-click it and see a View Source option.)

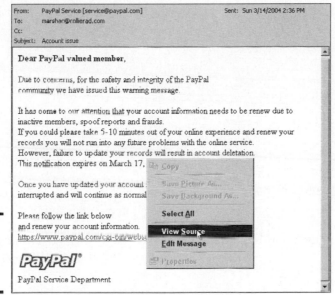

Figure 4-3:
Viewing the source on an e-mail.

Right-click your mouse and choose View Source. The Notepad program opens, and you see the e-mail in HTML text. Scroll to the bottom. In the example, I scrolled to the line that says *Please follow the link below* followed by a URL, as shown in Figure 4-4.

Figure 4-4:
The HTML coding for the link URL address.

```
<br>Please follow the link below <br>
<i></i> and
renew your account information.
<br><a
href="http://66.223.44.203/cgi/index.htm"onMouseOver="status
='https://www.paypal.com/cgi-bin/webscr?cmd=login-run';
return true"
onMouseOut="status='';return
true">https://www.paypal.com/cgi-bin/webscr?cmd=login-run</a
>
```

Take a good long look at the figure. You'll see the link to the URL in the e-mail. But look just before it in the source code and you can see that you're really being redirected to `http://66.223.44.203/cgi/index.htm` — not to the PayPal secure URL!

Okay, I investigated so I could show you what's going on (but don't try this at home, friends; it's risky). When I clicked the link, I came to a duplicate of the PayPal Log In page — or is it? A quick glance at the address bar of my browser confirmed I'd been misdirected, as shown in Figure 4-5. If I were really on PayPal, the URL address would have read like this:

`https://www.paypal.com/cgi-bin/webscr?cmd=_login-run.`

Note that the real PayPal URL begins with `https`, not `http`. The s in `https` stands for *secure*.

Figure 4-5:
My address bar with the misdirected URL.

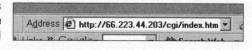

Even checking the URL may be misleading if you're using Internet Explorer as your browser. Bad-deed-doers can exploit a vulnerability in the browser to display a fake URL in the address and status bars. To avoid these Microsoft glitches, be sure to keep your Windows critical updates, er, up to date. Visit `http://windowsupdate.microsoft.com` regularly and install any critical security updates.

If you still question whether your PayPal or eBay account has a problem, close the e-mail and go directly to the site and log in at the *real* URL. If your account does have a problem, you'll know right away.

Fighting Back!

There's quite a bit that you can do to help stop spam. For openers, don't believe that link at the bottom of some spam you've received that says "Click here to have your name removed from the list." Have you ever clicked one of those? I have. Oops. I found out that those links are the gold standard for collecting valid e-mail addresses! If you respond to the spam in any way, shape, or form, they know they have a valid address — and watch the spam to your mailbox increase!

Never — I repeat, *never* — click one of those links again.

When signing up for some sort of newsletter with an organization you're new to or unsure of, use an anonymous Yahoo! or HotMail address. It's easy enough to sign up for one, and if spammers get hold of that address, they will not be privy to your private address.

Also, no matter how curious you are about enlarging certain parts of your anatomy, don't even open the e-mails you receive on those topics. And certainly don't respond.

Last, report spammers. Several legitimate sites take reports and forward them to the appropriate authorities. Don't bother trying to forward the spam to the sender's ISP. These days they're mostly forged with aliases, and all you'll do is succeed in clogging up the e-mail system. Here are a couple of places you can go to report spammers:

✦ **Federal Trade Commission:** Yes, your tax dollars are at work. The FTC would like you to forward the most annoying spam to uce@ftc.gov, where it will become available for law enforcement. (Especially in the case of e-mail trying to get your personal information.)

✦ **spamcop.net:** They've been around since 1988 and report spam e-mails to ISPs and mailers. They have a reporting link on their home page and work hard to get spammers out of the loop.

Keeping Your Password (and Accounts) Secure

When was the last time you changed your passwords? I mean the whole enchilada: eBay, PayPal, your online bank account? Hey, I'm not the keeper of the *shoulds,* but you *should* change your critical passwords every 60 days — rain or shine. That's not just me saying that. It's all the security experts who know this kind of stuff. The world is full of bad-deed-doers just waiting to get their hands on your precious personal information. Password theft can lead to your bank account being emptied, your credit cards being pushed to the max, and worst of all, someone unsavory out there posing as you.

You've seen the commercials on TV poking fun at the very real problem of identity theft. If you ask around your circle of friends, no doubt you'll find someone who knows someone who's been in this pickle. It can take years to undo the damage caused by identity theft, so a better plan is to stay vigilant and protect yourself from becoming a victim. It can also take a lot of money — a Utica College study found that it costs the average victim of identity theft an actual dollar loss of $31,356.

In this section, I give you some tips for selecting good passwords and other personal security information. I also show you the type of passwords to stay away from and what to do if (heaven forbid!) your personal information is compromised.

Reporting hacked accounts

If someone gets hold of your personal information, the most important thing to do is report it immediately. If you see any items that aren't yours on the Items I'm Bidding On or the Items I'm Selling area of your My eBay page, it's time to make a report — and *fast!*

Okay, you know that something hinky is going on with your eBay account because *you* never placed a bid on the Britney Spears stage-worn T-shirt (did you?). And you can't imagine that your spouse did either (but double-check just to be sure). Here's what to do immediately:

✦ **Change your personal e-mail account password with your ISP:** Go to your ISP's home page (for example `www.earthlink.net`) and look for an area called Member Center or something similar. In the Member Center, access your personal account information — probably through a link called something like My Account. You should be able to change your password there.

✦ **Change the e-mail account password on your home computer:** Don't forget to change the password on your computer's e-mail software as well (Outlook, Firefox, and the like), so you can continue to download your e-mail from the server.

Perhaps you discover that your private information has been compromised when you suddenly can't log in to your eBay or PayPal account. If this happens on eBay, follow these steps to request a new password:

1. **Go to the eBay Sign In page.**

Don't type your password. You just tried that and it doesn't work.

2. **Click the Forgot Your Password link, as shown in Figure 4-6.**

Doing this takes you to `http://cgi3.ebay.com/aw-cgi/eBay ISAPI.dll?ForgotYourPasswordShow`. Those silly security questions that you answered when you registered for eBay become very important now.

3. **Answer at least one of the questions you see on the page and provide your registered phone number and ZIP code.**

4. **Click Continue.**

eBay will e-mail you instructions for resetting your password.

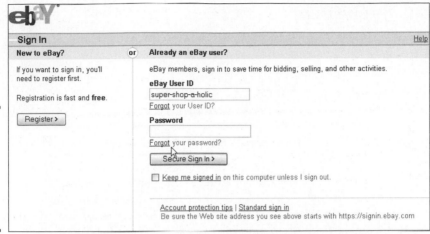

Figure 4-6:
The Forgot
Your
Password
link on the
Sign In
page.

5. **When the e-mail arrives, follow the steps and change your password.**

   If you *don't* get eBay's e-mail telling you how to change your password,
   that means some fraudster may have changed the contact information in
   your eBay account. See the sidebar "Freaking out is not a good thing" for
   instructions on what to do.

6. **If all goes well and you can change your password, go to the link pictured in Figure 4-7 to change your password hint (the secret question
   that lets the system know you're you).**

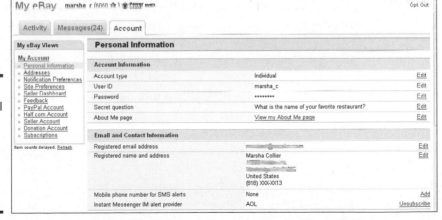

Figure 4-7:
My personal
account
information
with
important
change
links.

Choosing a good secret question

If you read the harrowing procedure in the "Freaking out is not a good thing" sidebar, you know that having someone sabotage your eBay account is something you never want to go through. But if your secret question is easy to figure out, a hacker can find it even easier to wreak havoc on your account.

Your password is only as secure as the secret question, so *don't relate your password and secret question to each other in any way.* For example, do not make your secret question a clue to your password — and *especially* don't make your password answer the secret question. Better yet, think of your secret question as a separate, auxiliary security device for your account.

Figure 4-8 shows eBay's Create a Secret Question and Answer page, which you can access from your My eBay Preferences page. It shows several suggested questions.

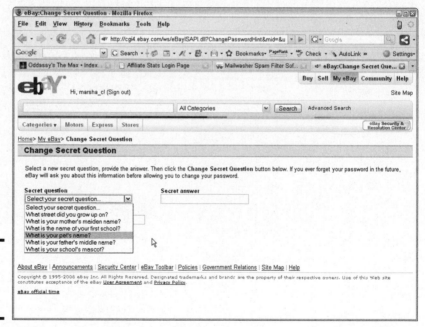

Figure 4-8:
Create
your secret
question.

Here are some tips for setting a secure secret question:

✦ **Never use your mother's maiden name.** That is most likely the *secret* that your bank uses as your challenge question. (They usually ask when you open the account.) So that is definitely out — you don't want to give *anybody* that word.

Freaking out is not a good thing

If you can't seem to get a new password for your eBay account, and you're unsuccessful at finding a Live Chat link, there's still hope. Remain calm, follow these steps, and take notes as you go:

1. **Go to any eBay page, scroll all the way to the bottom, and click the Security Center link (see the figure).**

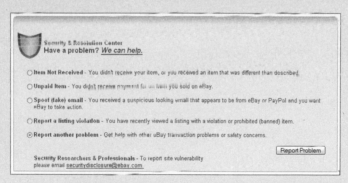

2. **When you get to the Security Center, click Report Problem.**

    The Contact Us form appears.

3. **Highlight the type of your problem, as pictured in the figure.**

4. **Click Report Problem.**

5. **On the following page, find the boldface headline that reads Contacting eBay. Click the E-mail us to report that you cannot sign in to your account link.**

    An e-mail form appears.

6. **Fill in the e-mail form and send it.**

    Be sure to tell eBay who you are (name, address, and phone number), your user ID and e-mail address, and a brief summary of the situation.

✦ **Select a question and provide a *creative* answer:**

- **What is your pet's name?** Give an answer like Ralph the Rhino or Graak the Pterodactyl or something creative. Don't give your actual pet's name (or species). Anyone who knows you is likely to know your pet's name.

- **What street did you grow up on?** Name an unusual landmark from your hometown. Don't use a street name.

- **What is the name of your first school?** Make up a good one — perhaps Elementary Penguin Academy? School of Hard Knox?

- **What is your father's middle name?** Make up a goodie or skip it.

- **What is your school's mascot?** There's a lot of creativity that can go on here. How about Red-and-white-striped zebra? Pink elephant?

Your bylaws for selecting answers to a secret question are two: be creative *and* be sure you remember the darned thing!

Avoiding easily-hacked passwords

Poorly chosen passwords are the number-one loophole for hackers. If you think that hackers are just a small group of hypercaffeinated teenagers, think again. It's now also the domain of small- and big-time crooks who hack into an account, spend a few thousand dollars that belong to someone else, and move on.

I searched Google for hacking software and came up with over 2 million matches. Many of these Web sites offer an arsenal of free hacking tools. They also provide step-by-step instructions for beginners on how to crack passwords. The Internet can be its own worst enemy.

Here are some industrial-strength tips for setting a secure password:

✦ **Number of characters:** Compose your password of more than 8 characters.

✦ **Case sensitivity:** Because passwords are case-sensitive, take advantage of the feature. Mix lowercase and uppercase in your passwords.

✦ **Letters and numbers:** Combine letters and numbers to make your passwords harder to crack.

✦ **Proper words:** Don't use proper words. Think of the title of your favorite book. Make your password the first two letters of each word with numbers in the middle (*not* sequential).

It should go without saying, but what the heck: Don't use any of the sample passwords shown here. It's safe to say that lots of people will be reading this book, and anything seen by lots of people isn't secret. (I know you know that, but still.)

Stay smart: Don't be a make-it-easy!

Any beginning hacker (or tech-smart teenager) can figure out your password if it falls into the following categories. Don't use 'em! They are pathetically easy!

✔ **The obvious:** The word *Password*. D'oh!

✔ **Birthdays:** Don't use your birthday, your friend's birthday, or John F. Kennedy's birthday. Not only are these dates common knowledge, but so is this truism: A series of numbers is easy to crack.

✔ **Names:** Don't use your first name, last name, your dog's name, or anyone's name. Again, it's common knowledge and easy to find out. (Most people know my husband's name; it's been in many of my books!)

✔ **Contact numbers:** Nix on *any* Social Security Number (if they get hold of *that* one — watch out!), phone numbers, your e-mail address, or street address. (Got the white pages? So do they . . . .)

✔ **Any of the lousy (easily cracked and most frequently used) passwords in the table:** The words in this table have been gleaned from password dictionaries available from hackers. Note that this is *not* a complete list by any means; there are thousands of common (lousy) passwords, and "unprintable" ones are a lot more common than you may think. If you really care to scare yourself, Google the phrase *common passwords*.

!@#$%	!@#$%^&	!@#$%^&*(	0	0000	00000000
0007	007	01234	123456	02468	24680
1	1101	111	11111	111111	1234
12345	1234qwer	123abc	123go	12	131313
212	310	2003	2004	54321	654321
888888	a	aaa	abc	abc123	action
absolut	access	admin	admin123	acocss	administrator
alpha	asdf	animal	biteme	computer	eBay
enable	foobar	home	internet	login	love
mypass	mypc	owner	pass	password	passwrd
papa	peace	penny	pepsi	qwerty	secret
superman	temp	temp123	test	test123	whatever
whatnot	winter	windows	xp	xxx	yoda
mypc123	powerseller	sexy			

Chapter 5: Networking Your Office

The first time I spoke to my editors about putting information in my books about networking, they scoffed at me. Bah! People who work at home don't need networks (as if networks were solely for big companies with lots of cubicles). The more I spoke to the eBay community, the more I saw the need for networks — and the more people asked me about them.

I started writing about eBay in 1999, and now it's almost 10 years later. A lot of technology has washed under the bridge, and many advances have been made. Setting up a network in 1999 meant spending hours (maybe days) changing settings, testing, checking computers, and cursing. That was if you were lucky enough to finally get it right. Otherwise — as was the case for most home users, including me — you'd give up, take the whole thing as a loss, and go on with your life.

Lucky for us non-techie types, Microsoft has made Windows considerably more home-network-friendly than in the old days. Also, more pleasant modes of networking (other than having miles of Ethernet cables snaking around the walls of your house) came to the fore of technology.

By networking your home (or eBay office) you'll save time by having the flexibility to work from different rooms or locations. You can also list auctions out by the pool (or in your backyard) in summer!

This chapter is a quick and dirty discussion of home networks installed on Windows-based PCs. I give you a lesson on what I know works for most people. (Hey, if it doesn't work, don't e-mail me — head back to the store and get your money back!)

At this point, I want to remind you that I'm not a super techno-whiz, even though I do host a Computer and Technology Radio show (just like I'm not a lawyer or an accountant). For more information about anything you'd think to ask about home networking, I defer to Danny Briere, Pat Hurley, and Edward Ferris, authors of *Wireless Home Networking For Dummies* (published by Wiley).

The What and Why of Networks

What is a network? A *network* is a way to connect computers so that they can communicate with each other — as if they were one giant computer with different terminals. The best part is that a network enables high-speed Internet connection-sharing, as well as the sharing of printers and other peripherals. By setting up a computer network, one computer might run bookkeeping, another might run a graphics server, and others might be used as personal PCs for different users. From each networked computer, it's possible to access programs and files on all other networked computers.

Today's technologies allow you to perform this same miracle on the home network. You can connect as many computers as you like, and run your business from anywhere in your home — you can even hook up your laptop from the bedroom if you don't feel like getting out of bed.

Now for the *whys* of a home network. A network is a convenient way to run a business. All big companies use them, and so should you. You can extend your DSL line or Internet cable connection so that you can use it anywhere in your home — as well as in your office.

In a network, you can set certain directories in each computer to be *shared*. That way, other computers on the network can access those directories. You can also password-protect certain files and directories to prevent others (your children or your employees) from accessing them.

Variations of a Home Network

You have a choice of four types of home networks: Ethernet, powerline, home phoneline, and wireless. See Table 5-1 for a quick rundown of some pros and cons of each.

Table 5-1	Network Pros and Cons	
Network Type	*Pros*	*Cons*
Traditional Ethernet*	Fast, cheap, and easy to set up	Computers and printers must be hardwired; cables run everywhere
Powerline	Fast; your home is prewired with outlets	Electrical interference may degrade the signal
Home phoneline	Fast; runs over your home phone lines	Old wiring or not enough phone jacks may be a drawback

Network Type	Pros	Cons
Wireless network**	Pretty fast; wireless (no ugly cords to deal with)	Expensive; may not be reliable because of interference from home electrical devices

*Connects computers over a maximum of 328 feet of cabling.

**Several flavors of wireless are available. See "Hooking up with wireless," later in this chapter.

The home phoneline network is growing because the new 3.1 version supports coax (you know, coaxial — like what your cable TV uses). In fact, a recently released report on home networking shows HomePNA, the latest version of phoneline networking, grew at its highest rate in 2007, and kept that up through 2008. Ya know why? It's the technology that cable companies use to get a telephone line to your home through a cable TV connection. But it's hardly used for home networking (see sidebar further on).

The wireless network is the hot ticket — and it's highly touted by the technorati. There may be interference with a wireless signal because it runs with the same 2.4GHz technology as some home wireless telephones. My primary network is a hybrid, combining Ethernet and wireless.

With broadband over powerline, you get high-speed Internet directly into your home electrical system. Just plug in your powerline boxes (more on that later) and you're up and running!

All networks need the following two devices:

✦ **Router:** A router allows you to share a single Internet IP address among multiple computers. A router does exactly what its name implies; it routes signals and data to and from the different computers on your network. If you have one computer, the router can act as a firewall or even a network device leading to a print server (a gizmo that attaches to your router and allows you to print directly to a printer without having another computer on).

✦ **Modem:** You need a modem for an Internet connection. You get one from your cable or phone company and plug it into an outlet with cable (just like your TV) or into a phone jack with the phone line for DSL. The modem connects to your router with an Ethernet cable.

If you have broadband, you don't even need to have a main computer turned on to access the connection anywhere in the house. If you keep a printer turned on (and have a print server), you can also connect that to your router and print from your laptop in another room — right through the network.

So many networks, so little time

The best part of networking today is that you can combine more than one type of network to form a fully functional, professional data-transfer medium with Internet access — throughout the house. In my house, I used to have an Ethernet/home phoneline/wireless combination. Home phoneline networks (10Mbps networks that operate over existing phone lines without the need for additional wiring, routers, or hubs) aren't popular with consumers. It's not that they didn't work flawlessly; they did. It just seems that I'm the only one in the United States with enough free phone jacks in my home and office to make it work.

After the downfall of phoneline networking, the geniuses began to think, "What does the average home have lots of outlets for?" Hmmmm, how about electricity? Duh, how about running the network through a home's electric outlets? And behold, the powerline network was born.

Now we have wireless networks too — and they're life-changing when they work. It's funny to see a whole new generation of people moving around tweaking antennas to try to get a good signal. It reminds me of television when I was a kid. (Maybe I should put some tin foil around the wireless antenna?)

Before touching your network card or opening your computer to install anything, touch a grounded metal object to free yourself of static electricity. (Otherwise a spark could go from your hand to the delicate components on the network card or other computer card — which renders the card useless.) Better yet, go to an electronics store and purchase a wrist grounding strap (a cord with a gator clip), which you clip to a metal part of the computer before touching anything inside it. The idea is to send the static electricity away from the components for safety.

Using a powerline network

An ingenious invention, a powerline network uses your existing home powerlines to carry your network and your high-speed Internet connection. You access the network by plugging a powerline adapter from your computer into an electrical outlet in the wall. Powerline networks have been around for a while and are in the second round of technological advances.

Hooking up a powerline network is so easy that it's a bit disappointing — you'll wonder why it isn't more complicated. Most installations work immediately right out of the box. Figure 5-1 shows you the base setup. Other rooms need only a powerline bridge adapter hooked up to the computer with an Ethernet cable to a network card.

To set up a powerline network, you'll need the following (in addition to a router and modem):

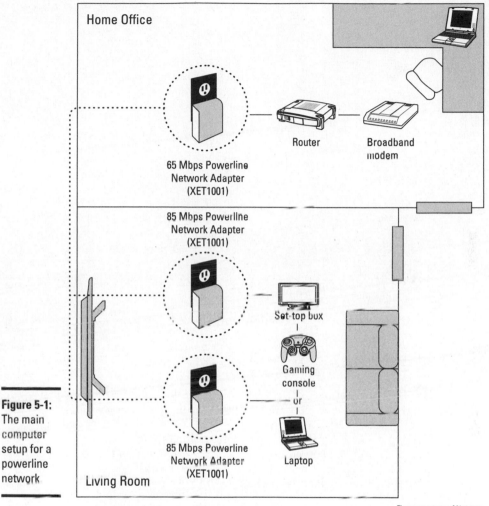

Figure 5-1:
The main
computer
setup for a
powerline
network

Home Office

65 Mbps Powerline
Network Adapter
(XET1001)

Router

Broadband
modem

85 Mbps Powerline
Network Adapter
(XET1001)

Set-top box

Gaming
console

or

Laptop

85 Mbps Powerline
Network Adapter
(XET1001)

Living Room

Figure courtesy of Netgear.

✦ **Electrical outlets:** I'll bet you have more than one in each room.

✦ **An Ethernet card for each computer:** Many new computers already
  have an Ethernet card. If yours doesn't, you can get inexpensive
  Ethernet cards for around $10 each.

✦ **Powerline Ethernet bridge for each computer:** You plug an Ethernet
  cable from your computer into the powerline *Ethernet bridge*, a small box
  (about the size of a pack of cigarettes) that plugs into any two- or three-
  prong electrical outlet. See Figure 5-2.

Figure 5-2:
Netgear's
wall-
plugged
Ethernet
bridge.

Photo courtesy of Netgear

The benefits of this nifty little system are as follows:

✦ **It's inexpensive.** The requisite powerline magic box costs around $40, but you'll need one for each computer.

✦ **It's fast — as fast as (or faster than) other network connections.** You could stream DVD movies from one room to another.

✦ **The networking connection is made through your existing electrical wiring.** It doesn't consume extra electricity.

✦ **Installation is easy.** Just plug a cable into your computer, and connect the cable to the powerline box. Plug in the powerline box.

✦ **If your computer has an Ethernet jack, you don't need to open up your computer.** Most new computers come with an Ethernet jack.

If you have a high-speed Internet connection, no doubt you received a modem when you signed up. Because it's not common to connect the modem directly to your computer (a router does the network routing for you), you may already have a router.

The integration works like this:

✦ The high-speed connection comes in through your DSL or cable line.

✦ The cable (or DSL) line plugs into your modem.

✦ An Ethernet cable goes from your modem into a router.

✦ One "out" Ethernet cable connection from the router goes to a local computer.

✦ Another "out" Ethernet cable goes to the powerline adapter.

✦ The powerline box plugs into a convenient wall outlet.

When you want to connect the computers in other rooms to the network, just plug in a magic powerline box.

Hooking up with wireless

Wireless networking (also known as WiFi or IEEE 802.11 networking) is the hot technology for all kinds of networks. It's an impressive system when it works, with no cables or connectors to bog you down.

As a matter of fact, I was in New York recently, staying on the 16th floor of a hotel. I turned on my travel laptop to check e-mail and my laptop found signals for *nine* wireless networks! I had to call the front desk to find out which one was the hotel connection. The whole world seems to be wireless.

Just so you know, I wouldn't have been able to connect to the other networks. Wireless networks are protected by their own brand of security. The original technology, called WEP (or *wired equivalent privacy*), led the way in home Wi-Fi security. WEP encrypted your wireless transmissions and prevents others from getting into your network. Sadly, it got so that a high school kid could crack this system, so now home users are using WPA (Wi-Fi Protected Access) and even WPA-2.

WPA utilizes a "pre-shared key" (PSK) mode, where every user on the network is given the same passphrase. In the PSK mode, security depends on the strength and secrecy of the passphrase. So, to link your laptop or desktop to a wireless network with WPA encryption, you need the pre-determined passphrase. Just enter it during setup — on every computer that uses the network — and you should be good to go.

Most Wi-Fi hotspots you may come across may not have any encryption, and some may be free for all to use.

The different flavors of wireless

If you've ever used a wireless telephone at home, you've used a technology similar to a wireless network. Most home wireless phones transmit on the radio frequency band of 2.4 GHz and have the option to choose from several channels automatically to give you the best connection.

The two prevalent forms of wireless networks also work on the 2.4GHz band, and you will need to preset the channel when you set up the system. But there are basically three types of wireless:

✦ **802.11a:** This is a wireless format that works really well — fast with good connectivity. It's used when you have to serve up a wireless connection to a large group of people, as in a convention center or a dormitory. It's fast, delivering data at speeds as high as 54 Mbps (megabits per second). It also runs at the 5GHz band (hence its nickname, WiFi5), so it doesn't compete with wireless phones or microwave ovens for bandwidth. It's also very expensive.

✦ **802.11b:** My laptop has a built-in 802.11b card, so I can connect to the ever popular hotspots in Starbucks and airports. It's the most common wireless type and is used on the most platforms right now. The *b* version is slower than the *a* version and can transfer data at only 11 Mbps. It's a solid, low-cost solution when you have no more than 32 users per access point.

The lower frequency of 2.4 GHz drains less power from laptops and other portable devices. Also, 2.4GHz signals travel farther, and can work through walls and floors more effectively than 5GHz signals.

✦ **802.11g:** This is the next incarnation of Wi-Fi-based on the 2.4GHz band. It speeds data to a possible 54 Mbps and is backward-compatible with 802.11b service.

✦ **802.11n:** The newest mode builds on the previous standards by adding multiple-input multiple-output (MIMO). MIMO is a technology that uses multiple antennas (usually built into the router) to carry more information than previously with a single antenna. It uses the 5GHz band (versus the 2.4 it used previously). It also increases speed through your TCP/IP connection to 100 Mbps.

For maximum speed, your entire network needs to be an 802.11n 5GHz network. In my house, an all-802.11n network doesn't work at full speed because I have existing laptops on 802.11b/g. I run a mixed 802.11b/g/n network until I replace all my laptops with 802.11n. Until I do that, my system runs at the old, pokey 54 Mbps.

Setting up your wireless network

With a wireless network, you have to hook your computer (a laptop works best) to a wireless access point to perform some beginning setup tasks such as choosing your channel and setting up your WPA passphrase.

When you complete the setup and turn on your wireless access point, you have a WiFi hotspot in your home or office. Typically, your new hotspot will provide coverage for at least 100 feet in all directions, although walls and floors cut down on the range. Even so, you should get good coverage throughout a typical home. For a large home, you can buy signal boosters to increase the range of your hotspot.

Simplified, this is how you configure your network:

1. **Run a cable from your DSL or cable line to your modem.**
2. **Connect an Ethernet cable from your modem to your router.**
3. **Type in the passphrase to all computers on the network.**

Take a look at this network diagram from Netgear in Figure 5-3.

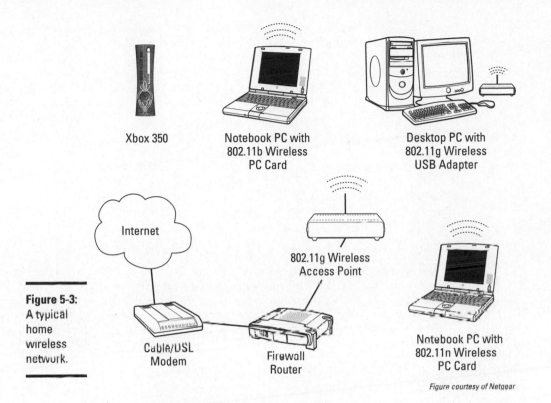

Xbox 350

Notebook PC with
802.11b Wireless
PC Card

Desktop PC with
802.11g Wireless
USB Adapter

Internet

802.11g Wireless
Access Point

Cable/DSL
Modem

Firewall
Router

Notebook PC with
802.11n Wireless
PC Card

Figure courtesy of Netgear

Figure 5-3:
A typical
home
wireless
network.

The home phoneline network

The technology that used to allow me (and millions of other users) to run
a network through my home phone line now drives much of the ability to
receive Internet, digital TV, and telephone on one line.

Obviously, this system is fast and reliable (320 Mbps), it carries tons of data
to homes each day. Unfortunately, the newest of this technology is not available for the home user — yet. Keep your eyes peeled for this, because a
high-speed wireless/HPNA 3.1 network will really rock.

Using a hybrid network

You may find that a wireless network may not work throughout your home.
That's easy to correct. You can combine different networks, allowing you to
have wireless connectivity in some rooms of your house and in your backyard, and a wired network inside your house.

I had an old-fashioned home-phoneline network coming from my router, along with a wireless access point. All the components were the same brand (Netgear), so there was no compatibility problem. I still go the single-brand route, so no matter where I go (or if my family wants to log on to the Internet), we can hook up with ease.

Internet Security and Your Home Network

A dial-up connection exposes your computer to the Internet only when you dial up and get connected. Most broadband Internet connections are always on — which means your computer is always exposed. You should shield your computer with a strong firewall and an antivirus program.

Exposing your computer's vulnerabilities

When you're connected to the Internet, you're exposed not only to hackers but also to threats such as *Trojan horses,* programs that can get into your computer when you innocently view an infected Web site. Once inside your computer, the Trojan horse, like ET, phones home. From there, an evil-deed-doer, who now has a direct line to your computer, may be able to wreak havoc with your precious data.

Visit the Web site for Gibson Research Corporation, at www.grc.com. Gibson Research is the brainchild of an early PC pioneer, Steve Gibson, who's renowned as a genius in the world of codes and programming. Steve is *the* expert when it comes to exposing the vulnerabilities of systems over the Internet. A few free diagnostic programs on this site will check your computer's vulnerability to Internet threats.

Shields Up and LeakTest test your computer and terrify you with results that expose the vulnerability of your Internet connection.

Adding antivirus and firewall software

You're going to need antivirus software to protect you from the idiots who think it's fun to send destructive code through e-mail. The most popular antivirus products (because they're bundled with new systems) are Norton and McAfee. I also like a product called Panda Security.

Index

security, 804
setting up, 796–804
types, combining, 798
wireless, 797, 801–803
neutral feedback. *See also* feedback
comments, 93
defined, 80
feedback number and, 81
guide, 88
seller response to, 98
when to leave, 140
newspapers
auction listings, 423
in finding trends, 413
Nigerian e-mail scam, 782
noise words, 166
nonpaying bidders, 52
notification
buyer, 201–202
PayPal payment, 382
winner, 363–364
NR (No Reserve Price), 316
NRFB (Never Removed from Box), 316
numbered lists, 500
Numismatic Guaranty Corporation of America (NGCA), 195
Numismatic News, 192
NWOT (New, but without tags), 316
NWT (New with Tags), 316

O

OEM (Original Equipment Manufacturer), 316
offline management software
Auction Wizard 2000, 682
Selling Manager, 682–683
Turbo Lister, 683–684
off-price lots, defined, 452
one-day auctions, 275–276
online appraisals, 194

online auction management. *See also* auction-management tools
ChannelAdvisor Marketplace Advisor, 676, 677–678
InkFrog, 676
Meridian, 676, 680–681
Vendio, 676, 678–679
Online Authentics, 196
online buying. *See also* buying merchandise
anonymous e-mail address, 457
B2B wholesale clearinghouses, 433–434
Craigslist, 432
direct from wholesalers, 434–436
freight on board, 458
Kijiji, 432–433
references, 458
safety, 457–458
seller physical address/phone number, 458
tips, 433
online checkout service, 130–131
online escrow, 329
online postage service, 271
online research, 192–196
online retailing
calculation formulas, 409–410
current market knowledge, 411–412
inventory data, 408–409
marketing, 410–411
retail calendar, 409
six-month marketing plan, 407–408
soon-to-be-hot sellers, 414–417
Yahoo! buzz, 417–418

OOAK (One of a Kind), 316
OOP (Out of Print), 316
operational abuses, 53
optical zoom, 469–470
Order Details page, 366
organization, this book, 2–4
Organize zone. *See also* My eBay
defined, 233
Saved Searches link, 233–235
Saved Sellers link, 235
Oriental Trading Company, 435
outage, mandatory, 326
Outlook Payment Request Wizard. *See also* PayPal
defined, 383
downloading, 383–384
illustrated, 384
payment buttons, 385
PayPal button types, 385
PayPal payment window preview, 386
Test button, 386
using, 384–387
overruns, 422, 452
overstocks, 453

P

P&L. *See* profit-and-loss statement
packing
attention to, 595
boxing, 600–602
pre-packing clean up, 594
prudent, 595
packing materials. *See also* shipping department
air packing pillows, 596
boxes, 600–602
bubble wrap, 596–597
mailing envelopes, 598–600
packing peanuts, 597